THE
PREACHER'S
OUTLINE & SERMON
BIBLE®

THE FIRST BOOK OF MOSES, CALLED

GENESIS

(Chapters 1-11)

THE
PREACHER'S
OUTLINE & SERMON
BIBLE®

OLD TESTAMENT

KING JAMES VERSION

Leadership Ministries Worldwide
Chattanooga, TN

Please address all requests for information or permission to:
Leadership Ministries Worldwide
PO Box 21310
Chattanooga, TN 37424-0310
Ph.# (423) 855-2181   FAX (423) 855-8616   E-Mail info@outlinebible.org
http://www.outlinebible.org

Library of Congress Catalog Card Number: 96-75921
ISBN Softbound Edition: 978-1-57407-015-6
ISBN Deluxe 3-Ring Edition: 978-1-57407-041-5

LEADERSHIP MINISTRIES WORLDWIDE
CHATTANOOGA, TN

Printed in the United States of America

14   15   16   17   18   14   15   16   17   18

DEDICATED

To all the men and women of the world who
preach and teach the Gospel of
our Lord Jesus Christ and
to the Mercy and Grace of God

- Demonstrated to us in Christ Jesus our Lord.

  "In whom we have redemption through His blood, the forgiveness of sins, according to the riches of His grace." (Ep.1:7)

- Out of the mercy and grace of God, His Word has flowed. Let every person know that God will have mercy upon him, forgiving and using him to fulfill His glorious plan of salvation.

  "For God so loved the world, that he gave His only begotten Son, that whosoever believeth in Him should not perish, but have everlasting life. For God sent not his son into the world to condemn the world, but that the world through him might be saved." (Jn.3:16-17)

  "For this is good and acceptable in the sight of God our Saviour; who will have all men to be saved, and to come unto the knowledge of the truth." (1 Ti.2:3-4)

6/07

The Preacher's Outline & Sermon Bible®

is written for God's servants to use in their study, teaching, and preaching of God's Holy Word…

- to share the Word of God with the world.
- to help believers, both ministers and laypersons, in their understanding, preaching, and teaching of God's Word.
- to do everything we possibly can to lead men, women, boys, and girls to give their hearts and lives to Jesus Christ and to secure the eternal life that He offers.
- to do all we can to minister to the needy of the world.
- to give Jesus Christ His proper place, the place the Word gives Him. Therefore, no work of Leadership Ministries Worldwide—no Outline Bible Resources—will ever be personalized.

ACKNOWLEDGMENTS AND BIBLIOGRAPHY

Every child of God is precious to the Lord and deeply loved. And every child as a servant of the Lord touches the lives of those who come in contact with him or his ministry. The writing ministries of the following servants have touched this work, and we are grateful that God brought their writings our way. We hereby acknowledge their ministry to us, being fully aware that there are many others down through the years whose writings have touched our lives and who deserve mention, but whose names have faded from our memory. May our wonderful Lord continue to bless the ministries of these dear servants—and the ministries of us all—as we diligently labor to reach the world for Christ and to meet the desperate needs of those who suffer so much.

THE REFERENCE WORKS

Archer, Gleason L. Jr. *A Survey of Old Testament Introduction*. Chicago, IL: Moody Bible Institute of Chicago, 1974.

Brown, Francis. *The New Brown-Driver-Briggs-Gesenius Hebrew-English Lexicon*. Peabody, MA: Hendrickson Publishers, 1979.

Cruden's Complete Concordance of the Old and New Testament. Philadelphia, PA: The John C. Winston Co., 1930.

Baker's Dictionary of Theology. Everett F. Harrison, Editor-in-Chief. Grand Rapids, MI: Baker Book House, 1960.

Encyclopedia of Biblical Prophecy. J. Barton Payne. New York, NY: Harper and Row, Publishers, 1973.

Funk and Wagnalls Standard Desk Dictionary. Lippincott and Crowell, Publishers, 1980, Vol.2.

Geisler, Norman. *A Popular Survey of the Old Testament*. Grand Rapids, MI: Baker Book House, 1977.

Good News Bible. Old Testament: © American Bible Society, 1976. New Testament: © American Bible Society, 1966, 1971, 1976. Collins World.

Harrison, Roland Kenneth. *Introduction to the Old Testament*. Grand Rapids, MI: Eerdmans Publishing Company, 1969.

Holy Bible, Pilgrim Edition. New York, NY: Oxford University Press, 1952.

Josephus, Flavius. *Complete Works*. Grand Rapids, MI: Kregel Publications, 1981.

Kohlenberger, John R. III. *The Interlinear NIV Hebrew-English Old Testament*. Grand Rapids, MI: Zondervan Publishing House, 1987.

Life Application® Bible. Wheaton, IL: Tyndale House Publishers, Inc., 1991.

Lindsell, Harold and Woodbridge, Charles J. *A Handbook of Christian Truth*. Westwood, NJ: Fleming H. Revell Company, A Division of Baker Book House, 1953.

Living Quotations For Christians. Edited by Sherwood Eliot Wirt and Kersten Beckstrom. New York, NY: Harper and Row, Publishers, 1974.

Lockyer, Herbert. *All the Books and Chapters of the Bible*. Grand Rapids, MI: Zondervan Publishing House, 1966.

_____. *All the Men of the Bible*. Grand Rapids, MI: Zondervan Publishing House, 1958.

_____. *All the Women of the Bible*. Grand Rapids, MI: Zondervan Publishing House, 1967.

Martin, Alfred. *Survey of the Scriptures*, Part I, II, III. Chicago, IL: Moody Bible Institute of Chicago, 1961.

McDowell, Josh. *Evidence That Demands A Verdict*, Vol.1. San Bernardino, CA: Here's Life Publishers, Inc., 1979.

Miller, Madeleine S. and J. Lane. *Harper's Bible Dictionary*. New York, NY: Harper and Row Publishers, 1961.

Nave's Topical Bible. Orville J. Nave. Nashville, TN: The Southwestern Company. Copyright © by J.B. Henderson, 1921.

New American Standard Bible, Reference Edition. La Habra, CA: The Lockman Foundation, 1975.

NIV Study Bible. Grand Rapids, MI: Zondervan Bible Publishers, 1985.

Orr, William. *How We May Know That God Is*. Wheaton, IL: Van Kampen Press, n.d.

Owens, John Joseph. *Analytical Key to the Old Testament*, Vols.1, 2, 3. Grand Rapids, MI: Baker Book House, 1989.

Roget's 21st Century Thesaurus, Edited by Barbara Ann Kipfer. New York, NY: Dell Publishing, 1992.

Stone, Nathan J. *Names of God*. Chicago, IL: Moody Press, 1944.

Strong's Exhaustive Concordance of the Bible. James Strong. Nashville, TN: Thomas Nelson, Inc., 1990.

The Amplified Bible. Scripture taken from THE AMPLIFIED BIBLE, Old Testament copyright © 1965, 1987 by the Zondervan Corporation. The Amplified New Testament copyright © 1958, 1987 by The Lockman Foundation. Used by permission.

The Holy Bible in Four Translations. Minneapolis, MN: Worldwide Publications. Copyright © The Iversen-Norman Associates: New York, NY, 1972.

The Interlinear Bible, Vol.1, 2, and 3, Translated by Jay P. Green, Sr. Grand Rapids, MI: Baker Book House Company, 1976.

The International Standard Bible Encyclopaedia, Edited by James Orr. Grand Rapids, MI: Eerdmans Publishing Company, 1939.

The New Compact Bible Dictionary, Edited by T. Alton Bryant. Grand Rapids, MI: Zondervan Publishing House, 1967. Used by permission of Zondervan Publishing House.

The New Scofield Reference Bible, Edited by C.I. Scofield. New York, NY: Oxford University Press, 1967.

The New Thompson Chain Reference Bible. Indianapolis, IN: B.B. Kirkbride Bible Co., Inc., 1964.

The Open Bible. Nashville, TN: Thomas Nelson Publishers, 1975.

The Zondervan Pictorial Encyclopedia of the Bible, Vol.1. Merrill C. Tenney, Editor. Grand Rapids, MI: Zondervan Publishing House, 1982.

Theological Wordbook of the Old Testament, Edited by R. Laird Harris. Chicago, IL: Moody Bible Institute of Chicago, 1980.

Unger, Merrill F. and White, William Jr. *Nelson's Expository Dictionary of the Old Testament*. Nashville, TN: Thomas Nelson Publishers, 1980.

Vine, Unger, White. *Vine's Complete Expository Dictionary of Old and New Testament Words*. Nashville, TN: Thomas Nelson Publishers, 1985.

Webster's Seventh New Collegiate Dictionary. Springfield, MA: G. and C. Merriam Company, Publishers, 1971.

Wilson, William. *Wilson's Old Testament Word Studies*. McLean, VA: MacDonald Publishing Company, n.d.

Wood, Leon. *A Survey of Israel's History*. Grand Rapids, MI: Zondervan Publishing House, 1982.

Young, Edward J. *An Introduction to the Old Testament*. Grand Rapids, MI: Eerdmans Publishing Company, 1964.

Young's Analytical Concordance to the Bible. Robert Young. Grand Rapids, MI: Eerdmans Publishing Company, n.d.

THE COMMENTARIES

Barnhouse, Donald Grey. *Genesis*, Vol.1. Grand Rapids, MI: Zondervan Publishing House, 1970.

Boice, James Montgomery. *Genesis, An Expositional Commentary*, Vol.1. Grand Rapids, MI: Zondervan Publishing House, 1938.

Criswell, W.A. *Expository Sermon on Revelation,* Vol.4. Grand Rapids, MI: Zondervan Publishing House, 1969.

Gill, John. *Gill's Commentary*, Vol.1. Grand Rapids, MI: Baker Book House, 1980.

Hamilton, Victor. *The Book of Genesis*, Chapters 1-17. "The New International Commentary on the Old Testament." Grand Rapids, MI: Eerdmans Publishing Co., 1990, Vol.1.

Henry, Matthew. *Matthew Henry's Commentary*. 6 Volumes. Old Tappan, NJ: Fleming H. Revell Co.

Keil-Delitzsch. *Commentary on the Old Testament*, Vol.1. Grand Rapids, MI: Eerdmans Publishing Co., no date listed.

Kidner, Derek. *Genesis*. "Tyndale Old Testament Commentaries." Downers Grove, IL: Inter-Varsity Press, 1979.

LaHaye, Tim and Morris, John. *The Ark on Ararat*. Nashville, TN and New York, NY: Thomas Nelson, Inc., 1976.

Leupold, H.C. *Genesis*, Vol.1. Grand Rapids, MI: Baker Book House, 1942.

McGee, J. Vernon. *Thru The Bible*, Vol.1. Nashville, TN: Thomas Nelson Publishers, 1981.

Morris, Henry M. *The Genesis Record*. Grand Rapids, MI: Baker Book House Company,

Pink, Arthur. *Gleanings in Genesis*. Chicago, IL: Moody Bible Institute of Chicago, Moody Press, 1922.

The Pulpit Commentary. 23 Volumes. Edited by H.D.M. Spence and Joseph S. Exell. Grand Rapids, MI: Eerdmans Publishing Co., 1950.

Thomas, W.H. Griffith. *Genesis, A Devotional Commentary*. Grand Rapids, MI: Eerdmans Publishing Co., 1946.

————. *Through the Pentateuch Chapter by Chapter*. Grand Rapids, MI: Eerdmans Publishing Company, 1957.

Whitcomb, John C., and Morris, Henry M. *The Genesis Flood*. Phillipsburg, NJ: Presbyterian and Reformed Publishing Co., 1961.

ABBREVIATIONS

&	=	and
Bc.	=	because
Concl.	=	conclusion
Cp.	=	compare
Ct.	=	contrast
e.g.	=	for example
f.	=	following
Illust.	=	illustration
K.	=	Kingdom, K. of God, K. of Heaven

O.T.	=	Old Testament
p./pp.	=	page/pages
Pt.	=	point
Quest.	=	question
Rel.	=	religion
Rgt.	=	righteousness
Thru	=	through
v./vv.	=	verse/verses
vs.	=	versus

THE BOOKS OF THE OLD TESTAMENT

Book	Abbreviation	Chapters	Book	Abbreviation	Chapters
GENESIS	Gen. or Ge.	50	Ecclesiastes	Eccl. or Ec.	12
Exodus	Ex.	40	The Song of Solomon	S. of Sol. or Song	8
Leviticus	Lev. or Le.	27	Isaiah	Is.	66
Numbers	Num. or Nu.	36	Jeremiah	Jer. or Je.	52
Deuteronomy	Dt. or De.	34	Lamentations	Lam.	5
Joshua	Josh. or Jos.	24	Ezekiel	Ezk. or Eze.	48
Judges	Judg. or Jud.	21	Daniel	Dan. or Da.	12
Ruth	Ruth or Ru.	4	Hosea	Hos. or Ho.	14
1 Samuel	1 Sam. or 1 S.	31	Joel	Joel	3
2 Samuel	2 Sam. or 2 S.	24	Amos	Amos or Am.	9
1 Kings	1 Ki. or 1 K.	22	Obadiah	Obad. or Ob.	1
2 Kings	2 Ki. or 2 K.	25	Jonah	Jon. or Jona.	4
1 Chronicles	1 Chron. or 1 Chr.	29	Micah	Mic. or Mi.	7
2 Chronicles	2 Chron. or 2 Chr.	36	Nahum	Nah. or Na.	3
Ezra	Ezra or Ezr.	10	Habakkuk	Hab.	3
Nehemiah	Neh. or Ne.	13	Zephaniah	Zeph. or Zep.	3
Esther	Est.	10	Haggai	Hag.	2
Job	Job or Jb.	42	Zechariah	Zech. or Zec.	14
Psalms	Ps.	150	Malachi	Mal.	4
Proverbs	Pr.	31			

THE BOOKS OF THE NEW TESTAMENT

Book	Abbreviation	Chapters	Book	Abbreviation	Chapters
MATTHEW	Mt.	28	1 Timothy	1 Tim. or 1 Ti.	6
Mark	Mk.	16	2 Timothy	2 Tim. or 2 Ti.	4
Luke	Lk. or Lu.	24	Titus	Tit.	3
John	Jn.	21	Philemon	Phile. or Phm.	1
The Acts	Acts or Ac.	28	Hebrews	Heb. or He.	13
Romans	Ro.	16	James	Jas. or Js.	5
1 Corinthians	1 Cor. or 1 Co.	16	1 Peter	1 Pt. or 1 Pe.	5
2 Corinthians	2 Cor. or 2 Co.	13	2 Peter	2 Pt. or 2 Pe.	3
Galatians	Gal. or Ga.	6	1 John	1 Jn.	5
Ephesians	Eph. or Ep.	6	2 John	2 Jn.	1
Philippians	Ph.	4	3 John	3 Jn.	1
Colossians	Col.	4	Jude	Jude	1
1 Thessalonians	1 Th.	5	Revelation	Rev. or Re.	22
2 Thessalonians	2 Th.	3			

HOW TO USE
The Preacher's Outline & Sermon Bible®

Follow these easy steps to gain maximum benefit from The POSB.

1 SUBJECT HEADING

2 MAJOR POINTS

3 SUBPOINTS
&
SCRIPTURE

4 COMMENTARY

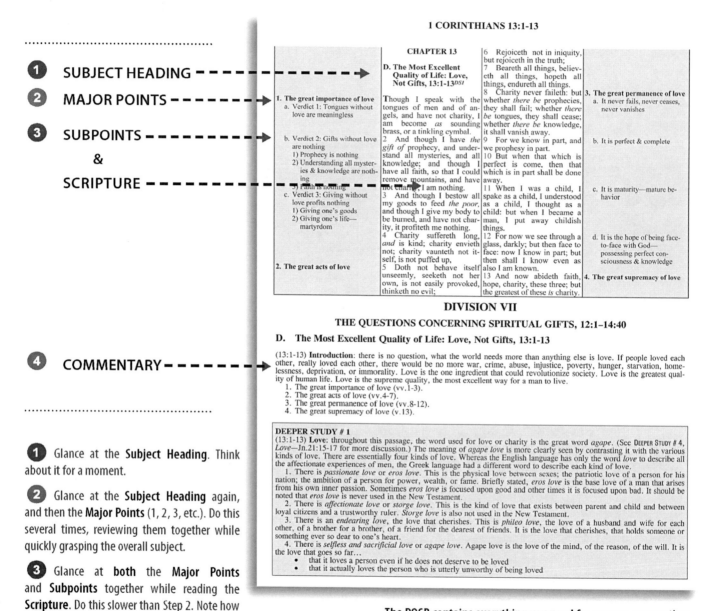

1 CORINTHIANS 13:1-13

CHAPTER 13

D. The Most Excellent Quality of Life: Love, Not Gifts, 13:1-13[DS1]

1. The great importance of love
a. Verdict 1: Tongues without love are meaningless
b. Verdict 2: Gifts without love are nothing
   1) Prophecy is nothing
   2) Understanding all mysteries & knowledge are nothing
   3) Faith is nothing
c. Verdict 3: Giving without love profits nothing
   1) Giving one's goods
   2) Giving one's life—martyrdom

2. The great acts of love

Though I speak with the tongues of men and of angels, and have not charity, I am become *as* sounding brass, or a tinkling cymbal. 2 And though I have *the gift of* prophecy, and understand all mysteries, and all knowledge; and though I have all faith, so that I could remove mountains, and have not charity, I am nothing. 3 And though I bestow all my goods to feed *the poor*, and though I give my body to be burned, and have not charity, it profiteth me nothing. 4 Charity suffereth long, *and* is kind; charity envieth not; charity vaunteth not itself, is not puffed up, 5 Doth not behave itself unseemly, seeketh not her own, is not easily provoked, thinketh no evil;

6 Rejoiceth not in iniquity, but rejoiceth in the truth; 7 Beareth all things, believeth all things, hopeth all things, endureth all things. 8 Charity never faileth: but whether *there be* prophecies, they shall fail; whether *there be* tongues, they shall cease; whether *there be* knowledge, it shall vanish away. 9 For we know in part, and we prophesy in part. 10 But when that which is perfect is come, then that which is in part shall be done away. 11 When I was a child, I spake as a child, I understood as a child, I thought as a child: but when I became a man, I put away childish things. 12 For now we see through a glass, darkly; but then face to face: now I know in part; but then shall I know even as also I am known. 13 And now abideth faith, hope, charity, these three; but the greatest of these *is* charity.

3. The great permanence of love
a. It never fails, never ceases, never vanishes

b. It is perfect & complete

c. It is maturity—mature behavior

d. It is the hope of being face-to-face with God—possessing perfect consciousness & knowledge

4. The great supremacy of love

DIVISION VII
THE QUESTIONS CONCERNING SPIRITUAL GIFTS, 12:1–14:40

D. The Most Excellent Quality of Life: Love, Not Gifts, 13:1-13

(13:1-13) **Introduction**: there is no question, what the world needs more than anything else is love. If people loved each other, really loved each other, there would be no more war, crime, abuse, injustice, poverty, hunger, starvation, homelessness, deprivation, or immorality. Love is the one ingredient that could revolutionize society. Love is the greatest quality of human life. Love is the supreme quality, the most excellent way for a man to live.
1. The great importance of love (vv.1-3).
2. The great acts of love (vv.4-7).
3. The great permanence of love (vv.8-12).
4. The great supremacy of love (v.13).

DEEPER STUDY # 1

(13:1-13) **Love**: throughout this passage, the word used for love or charity is the great word *agape*. (See DEEPER STUDY # 4, *Love*—Jn.21:15-17 for more discussion.) The meaning of *agape love* is more clearly seen by contrasting it with the various kinds of love. There are essentially four kinds of love. Whereas the English language has only the word *love* to describe all the affectionate experiences of men, the Greek language had a different word to describe each kind of love.
1. There is *passionate love* or *eros love*. This is the physical love between sexes; the patriotic love of a person for his nation; the ambition of a person for power, wealth, or fame. Briefly stated, *eros love* is the base love of a man that arises from his own inner passion. Sometimes *eros love* is focused upon good and other times it is focused upon bad. It should be noted that *eros love* is never used in the New Testament.
2. There is *affectionate love* or *storge love*. This is the kind of love that exists between parent and child and between loyal citizens and a trustworthy ruler. *Storge love* is also not used in the New Testament.
3. There is an *endearing love*, the love that cherishes. This is *phileo love*, the love of a husband and wife for each other, of a brother for a brother, of a friend for the dearest of friends. It is the love that cherishes, that holds someone or something ever so dear to one's heart.
4. There is *selfless and sacrificial love* or *agape love*. Agape love is the love of the mind, of the reason, of the will. It is the love that goes so far…
   • that it loves a person even if he does not deserve to be loved
   • that it actually loves the person who is utterly unworthy of being loved

1 Glance at the **Subject Heading**. Think about it for a moment.

2 Glance at the **Subject Heading** again, and then the **Major Points** (1, 2, 3, etc.). Do this several times, reviewing them together while quickly grasping the overall subject.

3 Glance at **both** the **Major Points** and **Subpoints** together while reading the **Scripture**. Do this slower than Step 2. Note how these points sit directly beside the related verse and simply restate what the Scripture is saying—in Outline form.

4 Next read the **Commentary**. Note that the *Major Point Numbers* in the Outline match those in the Commentary. A small raised number (**DS1, DS2, etc.**) at the end of a Subject Heading or Outline Point, directs you to a related **Deeper Study** in the Commentary.

Finally, read the **Thoughts** and **Support Scripture** (not shown).

As you read and re-read, pray that the Holy Spirit will bring to your attention exactly what you should preach and teach. May God bless you richly as you study and teach His Word.

The POSB contains everything you need for sermon preparation:

1. **The Subject Heading** describes the overall theme of the passage, and is located directly above the Scripture (keyed *alphabetically*).

2. **Major Points** are keyed with an outline *number* guiding you to related commentary. Note that the Commentary includes *"Thoughts"* (life application) and abundant Supporting Scriptures.

3. **Subpoints** explain and clarify the Scripture as needed.

4. **Commentary** is fully researched and developed for every point.

   • **Thoughts** (in bold) help apply the Scripture to real life.

   • **Deeper Studies** provide in-depth discussions of key words.

"Woe is unto me, if I preach not the gospel"
(1 Co.9:16)

TABLE OF CONTENTS
GENESIS 1

INTRODUCTION TO
THE HOLY BIBLE

The word *Bible* comes from the Greek word *biblos*, meaning a book. The Bible is also called...
* "The Holy Scriptures" (Ro.1:2; 2 Ti.3:15)
* "The Scriptures" (1 Co.15:3-4; Mt.21:42; 22:29; Lu.24:32; Jn.5:39; Ac.8:32; 18:24; Ga.3:22)
* "The Word of God" (He.4:12)

The Bible—"the Word of God"—did not originate in the mind of man, but in the mind of God. However, God used men as instruments and authors to communicate His message to the world. Over a period of some 1500 years, God chose people from all kinds of backgrounds—kings, soldiers, peasants, farmers, scholars, priests, statesmen, approximately forty authors from different nations, professions, and classes of society—to write the Holy Bible. The original manuscripts were written in three different languages: Hebrew, Aramaic, and Greek.

CONTENTS

The Bible is not a book, not in the technical sense. Rather, it is a collection of books, a great library of sixty-six books. However, the Bible naturally falls into two divisions that are separated by the birth of Jesus Christ. The two parts are...
* The *Old* Testament, which was written before Jesus Christ came to earth
* The *New* Testament, which was written after Jesus Christ came to earth

The word *testament* means a *covenant or an agreement*. Therefore, the Bible is God's covenant with man. The Old Testament is His covenant with man before Christ came, and the New Testament is His covenant with man after Christ came.

1. The Old Testament has thirty-nine books which were known by the Jews in Jesus' day as "the Law, the Prophets, and the Psalms" (Lu.24:44). Today, the thirty-nine books are usually divided as follows:
   a. Five Law Books:
⇒ Genesis	⇒ Numbers	
⇒ Exodus	⇒ Deuteronomy	
⇒ Leviticus		

   These five are known as the Pentateuch.

   b. Twelve History Books:
⇒ Joshua	⇒ I & II Chronicles
⇒ Judges	⇒ Ezra
⇒ Ruth	⇒ Nehemiah
⇒ I & II Samuel	⇒ Esther
⇒ I & II Kings	

   c. Five Poetic Books:
⇒ Job	⇒ Ecclesiastes
⇒ Psalms	⇒ The Song of Solomon
⇒ Proverbs	

   d. Seventeen Prophetic Books:
⇒ Isaiah	⇒ Joel	⇒ Habakkuk
⇒ Jeremiah	⇒ Amos	⇒ Zephaniah
⇒ Lamentations	⇒ Obadiah	⇒ Haggai
⇒ Ezekiel	⇒ Jonah	⇒ Zechariah
⇒ Daniel	⇒ Micah	⇒ Malachi
⇒ Hosea	⇒ Nahum	

2. The New Testament has 27 books which are divided as follows:
   a. Four Gospels:
* ⇒ Matthew
* ⇒ Mark
* ⇒ Luke
* ⇒ John

   b. One History Book: Acts
   c. Fourteen Pauline Epistles: Letters written by Paul the Apostle.
⇒ Romans	⇒ Philippians	⇒ Titus
⇒ I & II Corinthians	⇒ Colossians	⇒ Philemon
⇒ Galatians	⇒ I & II Thessalonians	⇒ Hebrews (probably)
⇒ Ephesians	⇒ I & II Timothy	

   d. Seven General Epistles: Letters written by several authors.
⇒ James	⇒ 2 John
⇒ 1 Peter	⇒ 3 John
⇒ 2 Peter	⇒ Jude
⇒ 1 John	

   e. One Prophetic Book: Revelation

INTRODUCTION TO THE BIBLE

ORIGIN

The Bible is the Word of God, but God Himself did not take a pen and write His Word down for man. God did what He has always done when He wished to speak to the human race: He chose certain persons to communicate His Word to the world. God inspired—"breathed His Word"—into the hearts of holy men and they proclaimed and wrote God's Word down for us all. In the words of the Bible itself, *holy men of God spoke as they were moved by the Holy Spirit* (2 Pe.1:21). It was these holy men who wrote and left us the heritage of the Word of God. Harold Lindsell and Charles J. Woodbridge state it well:

> *The Scriptures originated in the mind of God, but the manner in which He arranged for their human authorship and compilation is interesting.*
> *1. The Old Testament, according to the traditional view, was prepared somewhat as follows: Moses wrote the five books of the Law and placed them in the Tabernacle beside the Ark of the Covenant. Joshua added his record to the volume (see Joshua 24:26), and Samuel continued the story (cf 1 Sam.10:25). This entire library was subsequently lost. When rediscovered and publicly read, it produced a revival. (See 2 Kings 22:8.) The writings of the earlier prophets were then added to the series. The later prophets were familiar with these writings (e.g. Zech.7:12). Thus the collection gradually expanded.*
> *The assembling of the Old Testament books into an official canon began shortly after the captivity (586 B.C.). The word 'canon' means a 'rod,' or 'rule,' i.e. a standard of that which is to be believed. (See Gal.6:16.) When Haggai [the prophet] and others had completed their ministry, the need was felt for a formal collection of the documents which the people already regarded as of divine origin. According to the best tradition Ezra and Nehemiah, and after them a group of scribes, completed the canonization of the Old Testament.*
> *2. The New Testament canon came into being as follows. When the books appeared, addressed usually to particular churches, copies were made and sent to other congregations. Exchanges of books took place. (See Col.4:16.) Lists of these apostolic books were prepared. By the fourth century some fifteen such catalogues had been published. Gradually, not by the vote of any particular church council, but by the consent of the 'universal church consciousness' [it was recognized] that these books, and these alone were the inspired Word of God. The New Testament canon emerged as we have it today. We have here a magnificent example of the preserving and superintending power of the Holy Spirit."*[1]

TRANSLATIONS

The original manuscripts of the Bible were written in three different languages: Hebrew, Aramaic, and Greek. Great care—strict, meticulous, and painstaking care—was always taken in translating and copying the Bible. There were two professions of men among the Jews, called Mosoretes and Scribes, who dedicated their lives to the task of translating and copying the Scriptures. (See DEEPER STUDY # 1—Lu.6:2; DEEPER STUDY # 4—6:7 for more discussion.) In their translating and copying functions they were strict copiers, meticulously keeping count of every letter and syllable in every word and every word in every sentence and passage and book.[2] This exactness was necessary, for God Himself had given the written law to the Jewish nation. Therefore, the law was not only the very Word of God, it was the greatest thing in the life of the Jewish nation. It was considered the most precious possession in all the world; consequently, the Jewish nation was committed to the preservation of the law (the whole Word of God, Ne.8:1-8).

1. The Old Testament was translated into Greek some time between 250–150 B.C. It is called the *Septuagint* and is symbolized with the letters *LXX*. However, the oldest copies that we have today date back somewhere around 400–500 years after Christ.

2. "Other translations in Greek appeared soon after the beginning of the Christian era. Parts, at least, of the OT were rendered into Syriac as early as the first century; and a Coptic translation appeared probably in the third century. The NT was translated into Latin and Syriac c. 150 and into Coptic c. 200. In subsequent centuries versions appeared in the Armenian, Gothic, Ethiopic, Georgian, Arabic, Persian, and Slavonic languages."[3]

3. Around 400 A.D. Jerome translated the Latin version of the Bible known as the *Latin Vulgate*, which was used as the basic Bible for about 1000 years.

4. During the Reformation Period there were numerous versions of the Bible that flooded the scene. The most well known were...

- John Wycliff's version translated into English for the very first time in 1382
- William Tyndale's New Testament which was based upon the original Greek, published in 1525
- Martin Luther's German translation in the 16th century
- The King James version in 1603

There have been numerous versions of the Bible since the Reformation, and today the Bible has been translated in most of the languages and dialects of the world.

---

[1] Harold Lindsell and Charles J. Woodbridge. *A Handbook of Christian Truth*. (Westwood, NJ: Fleming H. Revell Company, A Division of Baker Book House, 1953), pp.20-21.

[2] Josh McDowell, "The Reliabilities of the Bible." *Evidence That Demands A Verdict*, Vol.1. (San Bernardino, CA: Here's Life Publishers, Inc., 1979), pp.39-65.

[3] *The New Compact Bible Dictionary*. Edited by T. Alton Bryant. (Grand Rapids, MI: Zondervan Publishing House, 1967), p.83.

INTRODUCTION TO THE BIBLE

INSPIRATION AND AUTHORITY

The Bible is the Word of God. How do we know this, know it for sure?

1. *Honest Reason and Logic*: God is a God of love, not of indifference and hate. A God of love would never leave man in the dark about the truth of life, feeling, searching, grasping, and stumbling about after the truth, ever seeking and never able to come to the truth. A God of love is bound to reveal the truth of life in the most perfect way possible. What is the most perfect way?

    a. The most perfect way is not nature (natural revelation). The hand of God can be seen in nature, but revealing Himself in nature is not the most perfect revelation that God can make.

    b. The most perfect way is not conscience (moral revelation). The righteousness of God can be sensed in conscience, but revealing Himself in conscience is not the most perfect revelation.

    c. The most perfect way to reveal Himself is by doing just what any person does when he wishes to communicate some truth:

      ⇒ He writes the truth down in a permanent form.

      ⇒ He presents the truth in person (if he is able).

    This God has done. He has given us both the *Written Word of God* and the *Living Word of God*.

    ⇒ The Bible is the Written Word of God.

    ⇒ Jesus Christ is the Living Word of God.

    ⇒ The Written Word testifies to the Living Word, and the Living Word (Christ Himself) testifies to the Written Word (see Mt.5:17-18).

Again, how do we know the Bible is the Word of God? By logic and reason, *honest logic and honest reason*. God is bound to reveal the truth to us in the most perfect way possible, both in writing and in person. (See Deeper Study # 1—Jn.1:1-5; 14:6; 14:7; 2 Ti.3:16.)

2. *Changed Lives*: millions of lives have been changed down through the centuries by the Bible. Some persons were changed when they were reading or else being confronted with its message; others were changed when they were hearing the Bible taught or preached. They had been living lives that were...

• worldly	• greedy	• secular	• indifferent
• immoral	• covetous	• lonely	• wasted
• drunken	• indulgent	• empty	• agnostic
• selfish	• materialistic	• meaningless	• atheistic

But the Bible—the Word of God—changed them. They were *born again*—spiritually converted, changed inwardly—by the Bible. The Bible does this for us: it *converts us spiritually*, makes a new creature and person out of us (2 Co.5:17; Ep.4:24).

> **"Being born again, not of corruptible seed, but of incorruptible, by the word of God, which liveth and abideth for ever" (1 Pe.1:23).**

The Bible stirs us to live for God, to live righteous and godly lives. But in return, the Bible gives us the perfect assurance that our sins are forgiven and that we are going to live eternally with God. The Bible stirs us to live moral and upright lives, unselfish and giving lives, the kind of lives that make a community and society strong in love and true justice, in joy and peace. As stated, millions of lives have been changed, and thousands are still being changed every day—spiritually converted—by the Bible. This is strong evidence that the Bible is truly the Word of God: it transforms lives.

3. *Unbelief and opposition*: the ungodly and worldly of this earth reject and deny the Bible, that it is the Word of God. Sometimes they have become vocal and oppressive, and they have ridiculed and persecuted those who profess and teach the Bible. The persecution has even become inflammatory:

    ⇒ Deliberate plots have been made to stamp out the Bible; even to the point of having community bonfires to burn them.

    ⇒ Governments have outlawed its presence within their lands, actually making it a crime for a citizen to own a Bible.

    ⇒ Worldly scholars attack the Bible, denying that it is the Word of God, attempting to water down its authority and meaningfulness in life.

    ⇒ The worldly and carnal neglect, reject, and deny the Bible and often ridicule those who hold its teachings dear to their hearts.

Why? Why do so many of this earth oppose the Bible? Because it tells us the truth about God and ourselves, demanding that we live righteous and godly lives. The Bible demands...

    • that we live lives that are moral, just, and good

    • that we accept, love, and live at peace with all people of all races and nations

    • that we sacrificially give to meet the needs of the poor and the spiritually lost

Very few people are willing to give their lives up to God and to accept and love people as brothers. And fewer still are willing to give to the point of sacrifice in meeting the needs of the poor and in carrying the gospel to the ends of the earth. This is why so many reject the Bible and its followers so much. Very simply, the Bible reminds people that they cannot live like they want.

But note: belief in the Bible has always grown when there has been a deliberate attempt made to stamp it out. Persecution stirs the flame of evangelism: it weeds out the weak and carnal—those who hold to a false profession—and it strengthens the true believers, making them more courageous and determined to stand true for the Word of God. How? How could the Bible, the Word of God, actually grow and be strengthened when it has been ridiculed and persecuted like it has? If any other book had been attacked, opposed, and burned as much as the Bible, that book would have disappeared long ago. How has the Bible endured so much denial and persecution?

There is only one answer: God. God has supernaturally protected His Word and kept it alive and working upon the earth. This is evidence—strong evidence—that the Bible is the Word of God.

> **"Heaven and earth shall pass away, but my words shall not pass away" (Mt.24:35).**
> **"For the word of God is quick, and powerful, and sharper than any twoedged sword, piercing even to the dividing asunder of soul and spirit, and of the joints and marrow, and is a discerner of the thoughts and intents of the heart" (He.4:12).**
> **"Is not my word like as a fire? saith the LORD; and like a hammer that breaketh the rock in pieces?" (Je.23:29; see Je.5:14).**

4. *The Unity of the Bible*: the unity of the Bible is a miracle of God. Think of the facts: approximately forty different authors from a number of diverse backgrounds wrote over a 1500 year period. Think of the number of diverse subjects that would be covered in detail within any book when written by so many different authors over so long a period of time. And think how much the subjects would change from generation to generation over a 1500 year period. Yet, when we study the Bible we find an amazing fact: the Bible follows one purpose and theme...

• God's eternal program for the ages, His eternal redemption and plan for the future of the universe and man

The glorious salvation of God—the great redemption that He has provided for man through His Son, the Lord Jesus Christ—is the great theme of the Bible. The whole Bible—all sixty-six books—focuses upon this one story, this one theme, and no writer ever conflicts or contradicts another writer. The harmony of purpose and theme in the Bible is astounding. There is only one explanation: God has spoken and has preserved an authoritative record of His message. *Holy men of God spoke as they were moved by the Holy Spirit* (1 Pe.1:21).

5. *The Writers of the Old Testament*: the very writers of the Old Testament claimed that the Bible is the Word of God, that it is revealed truth.

a. David claimed that the Spirit of God spoke through him:

> **"The spirit of the LORD spake by me, and his word was in my tongue. The God of Israel said, the Rock of Israel spake to me" (2 S.23:2-3).**

b. Scripture claims that it was God who spoke through all the prophets of God:

> **"And the LORD spake by his servants the prophets, saying" (2 K.21:10).**

c. Nehemiah claimed that it was God who spoke through Moses.

> **"Thou camest down also upon mount Sinai, and spakest with them from heaven, and gavest them right judgments, and true laws, good statutes and commandments: and madest known unto them thy holy sabbath, and commandedst them precepts, statutes, and laws, by the hand of Moses thy servant" (Ne.9:13-14).**

d. Isaiah claimed that his writings were what the Lord had given him:

> **"Moreover the LORD said unto me, Take thee a great roll, and write in it with a man's pen" (Is.8:1).**
> **"For the LORD spake thus to me with a strong hand" (Is.8:11).**

e. Jeremiah claimed to be speaking and writing the Word of God itself:

> **"Then the LORD put forth his hand, and touched my mouth. And the LORD said unto me, Behold, I have put my words in thy mouth" (Je.1:9, see 5:14; 7:27; 13:12).**

f. Ezekiel claimed that his writings were the very Word of God:

> **"And he said unto me, Son of man, go, get thee unto the house of Israel, and speak with my words unto them" (Eze.3:4, see Eze.3:10-11; Mic.3:8).**

g. Habakkuk claimed that his writings were the Word of God:

> **"And the LORD answered me, and said, Write the vision, and make it plain upon tables, that he may run that readeth it" (Hab.2:2).**

h. Zechariah claimed that God actually gave him His Word:

> **"Moreover the word of the LORD came unto me, saying" (Zec.4:8, see Zec.7:12).**

i. The writers of the Old Testament used the phrase "thus saith the Lord" or a similar expression over two thousand times.

j. The writers of the Old Testament referred to Scripture as "the Word," "the Statutes," "the Law," and "the Testimonies" claiming the authority of God for the Scriptures (see Ps.19:1f; 119:1f).

6. *The Writers of the New Testament*: these writers confirmed the claims of the Old Testament authors.

a. The New Testament writers declared that the word and prophecies spoken by the Old Testament prophets had to be fulfilled.

> "Now all this was done, that it might be fulfilled which was spoken of the Lord by the prophet, saying" (Mt.1:22).
> "That it might be fulfilled which was spoken of the Lord by the prophet" (Mt.2:15).
> "Men and brethren, this scripture must needs have been fulfilled, which the Holy Ghost by the mouth of David spake" (Ac.1:16).
> "And when they agreed not among themselves, they departed, after that Paul had spoken one word, Well spake the Holy Ghost by Esaias the prophet unto our fathers" (Ac.28:25).

b. Paul declared that the gospel itself was given to us by God through His prophets in the Holy Scriptures:

> "[The gospel] which he had promised afore by his prophets in the holy scriptures" (Ro.1:2).

c. The New Testament writers actually claimed this: that the Old Testament was not written by the will of man, but by the guidance and inspiration of God and of His Spirit.

> "For the prophecy came not in old time by the will of man: but holy men of God spake as they were moved by the Holy Ghost" (2 Pe.1:21).
> "Of which salvation the prophets have inquired and searched diligently, who prophesied of the grace that should come unto you: searching what, or what manner of time the Spirit of Christ which was in them did signify, when it testified beforehand the sufferings of Christ, and the glory that should follow" (1 Pe.1:10-11).
> "God, who at sundry times and in divers manners spake in time past unto the fathers by the prophets" (He.1:1).

7. *The Writers of the New Testament*: these writers also claimed that their own writings are the Word of God.

a. Paul claimed that his writings are the Word of God:

> "For I have received of the Lord that which also I delivered unto you" (1 Co.11:23).
> "What? came the word of God out from you? or came it unto you only: If any man think himself to be a prophet, or spiritual, let him acknowledge that the things that I write unto you are the commandments of the Lord" (1 Co.14:36-37).
> "But I certify you, brethren, that the gospel which was preached of me is not after man. For I neither received it of man, neither was I taught it, but by the revelation of Jesus Christ" (Ga.1:11-12).
> "In whom ye also trusted, after that ye heard the word of truth, the gospel of your salvation: in whom also after that ye believed, ye were sealed with that holy Spirit of promise" (Ep.1:13).
> "For this cause also thank we God without ceasing, because, when ye received the word of God which ye heard of us, ye received it not as the word of men, but as it is in truth, the word of God, which effectually worketh also in you that believe" (1 Th.2:13).

b. Paul and Peter both claimed that the writings of the New Testament writers are the Word of God.

> "Which things also we speak, not in the words which man's wisdom teacheth, but which the Holy Ghost teacheth; comparing spiritual things with spiritual" (1 Co.2:13. Note the word "we.")
> "That ye may be mindful of the words which were spoken before by the holy prophets, and of the commandment of us the apostles of the Lord and Saviour" (2 Pe.3:2. Note how Peter ascribes to the apostles the same authority as the prophets.)

c. Paul claimed that all Scripture, both the Old and New Testaments, is inspired by God.

> "All scripture is given by inspiration of God, and is profitable for doctrine, for reproof, for correction, for instruction in righteousness" (2 Ti.3:16). (Second Timothy was the last book Paul wrote; thus he was including the New as well as the Old Testament writings in the phrase "All Scripture." See all the verses in this point, pt.7.)

d. John claimed that what he wrote is the witness of God.

> "If we receive the witness of men, the witness of God is greater: for this is the witness of God which he hath testified of his Son" (1 Jn.5:9). (Note the word "this": what John is writing is the witness of God.)

8. *Jesus Christ*: the Lord Himself claimed that the Bible is the Word of God.
   a. Jesus Christ verified the Scripture time and again, and He actually verified most of the major events that are often questioned by scoffers. Jesus Christ said...
   - that "Scripture cannot be broken" (Jn.10:35)
   - that Scripture "must be fulfilled" (Lu.24:44)
   - "Till heaven and earth pass, one jot or one tittle, shall in no wise pass from the law [Scripture]" (Mt.5:18)
   - that not knowing the Scripture is a terrible mistake: "Ye do err, not knowing the scriptures, nor the power of God" (Mt.22:29)
   - that Adam and Eve actually existed and were created by God (Mt.19:4)
   - that Cain really did kill Abel (Mt.23:35)
   - that the Great Flood really happened in the days of Noah (Lk.17:27)
   - that God really did speak to Moses in the burning bush (Lu.20:37)
   - that Elijah did perform miracles (Lu.4:25)
   - that Jonah did survive in the belly of a large fish for 3 days (Mt.12:40)
   - that Daniel did make true predictions (Mt.24:15)

   b. Jesus Christ verified the writings of the New Testament. Before He left the earth and ascended into heaven, Christ promised these things:
   ⇒ that the Holy Spirit would supernaturally guide and teach the truth to the apostles and show them things to come.

   > **"But the comforter, which is the Holy Ghost, whom the Father will send in my name, he shall teach you all things, and bring all things to your remembrance, whatsoever I have said unto you" (Jn.14:26).**
   > **"Howbeit when he, the Spirit of truth, is come, he will guide you into all truth: for he shall not speak of himself; but whatsoever he shall hear, that shall he speak: and he will show you things to come" (Jn.16:13).**

   ⇒ that the Holy Spirit would supernaturally speak through them.

   > **"For it is not ye that speak, but the Spirit of your Father which speaketh in you" (Mt.10:20, see Mk.13:11).**

   ⇒ that they would have all the authority of heaven and earth in teaching men and that He (His presence and authority) would be with them until the end of the earth.

   > **"And Jesus came and spake unto them, saying, All power is given unto me in heaven and in earth. Go ye therefore, and teach all nations, baptizing them in the name of the Father, and of the Son, and of the Holy Ghost: teaching them to observe all things whatsoever I have commanded you: and, lo, I am with you alway, even unto the end of the world" (Mt.28:18-20).**

   ❖ (Please note: Norman Geisler has an excellent and thorough discussion on "Christ and the Inspiration of the Bible" for those who wish to research the subject more: *A Popular Survey of the Old Testament*. Grand Rapids, MI: Baker Book House, 1977, p.11-15.)

9. *The Holy Spirit*: the Holy Spirit of God Himself is the Author of the Bible. Scripture makes this clear. (Also see pt.7b immediately above.)
   a. Holy men of God spoke and wrote as they were moved upon by the Spirit of God.

   > **"For the prophecy came not in old time by the will of man: but holy men of God spake as they were moved by the Holy Ghost" (2 Pe.1:21).**

   The Holy Spirit is the Author of the Scriptures (2 Pe.1:19-21, esp.21). The *word of prophecy* is more accurately translated *prophetic word*. The origin of Scripture is found not in the will of man, that is, in his attempt to find truth and to interpret truth. But it is found in the Word of the Holy Spirit who reveals truth to man (see Jn.16:12-15; 1 Co.2:9-10).
   b. God inspired the Scripture by His Spirit.

   > **"All scripture is given by inspiration of God, and is profitable for doctrine, for reproof, for correction, for instruction in righteousness" (2 Ti.3:16).**

   Scripture is inspired of God. The phrase *inspired of God* (theopneustos) means *God-breathed*. What does this mean? What does it mean to say that *God breathed* the Holy Scriptures? No one can say for sure, but this much can be said.
   ⇒ The idea is that *God breathed out* the Scripture or *God produced* the Scripture somewhat like He did creation.

   > **"By the word of the LORD were the heavens made; and all the host of them by the breath of his mouth" (Ps.33:6).**

This must mean at least this: God supernaturally created His Word by the creative breath of God; that is, God's Word came from His mind and heart and His mind and heart alone. God Himself gave—supernaturally and creatively breathed—His Word to man.

Note: it is the Scripture that is inspired, not the man. The Bible does not claim to be written by inspired men. It does claim that the writing is supernaturally given or breathed by God. The Scripture is *breathed out by God, not breathed into by God*. The Bible claims to be given by the creative breath of God, by the power of His Holy Spirit. *Holy men of God spoke as they were moved by the Holy Spirit* (2 Pe.1:21).

10. *Fulfilled Prophecy*: there are over eight thousand prophecies in the Bible and over three hundred of these are Old Testament references to the Messiah. A prophecy is the prediction of some future event. Just imagine! The Bible has predicted over 8000 future events, and the astounding fact is this: thousands have been fulfilled exactly as they were predicted within the Holy Scripture. Just how accurate the prophecies of the Bible are fulfilled can be clearly seen by referring to the following notes in *The Preacher's Outline & Sermon Bible®* (see DEEPER STUDY # 1—Lu.3:23-38; notes—3:24-31; 3:32-38; DEEPER STUDY # 3—Jn.1:45; note—Mt.17:23; DEEPER STUDY # 1,2—Re.20:4-6). The accuracy and detailed fulfillment of Biblical prophecies is strong evidence for the inspiration and authority of the Bible. Fulfilled prophecy can mean only one thing: *holy men of God spoke as they were moved by the Holy Spirit* (2 Pe.1:21). (Note: the enormous number of prophecies that have been fulfilled tell us another fact as well: the events that the Bible has predicted for the future will come to pass; future prophecies of the Bible will be fulfilled even to the most minute detail. *The Encyclopedia of Biblical Prophecy* by the great scholar J. Barton Payne lists every prophecy in the Bible book by book and has several excellent charts to help the student of prophetic events. (Published by Harper & Row Publishers, Inc., New York, NY, 1973.)

11. *Archeology*: hundreds of archaeological discoveries have been made that verify various facts and events mentioned in the Bible. The accuracy of the Bible is being constantly supported by these discoveries, and although they do not prove the inspiration of the Bible, the findings do show how reliable the facts of the Bible are. Archeology definitely adds support to the inspiration and authority of the Bible. (The following two sources will give the interested reader specific examples of archaeological evidence for the Bible's authority: *The New Thompson Chain Reference Bible*, The Archaeological Supplement in the back of the Bible. Indianapolis, IN: B.B. Kirkbride Bible Co., Inc., 1964. Also Josh McDowell's *Evidence That Demands A Verdict*, Vol.1, pp.65-74.)

12. *The Trustworthiness of the Bible*: the Holy Scripture is absolutely trustworthy.

"For this cause also thank we God without ceasing, because, when ye received the word of God which ye heard of us, ye received it not as the word of men, but as it is in truth, the word of God, which effectually worketh also in you that believe" (1 Th.2:13).

"All scripture is given by inspiration of God, and is profitable for doctrine, for reproof, for correction, for instruction in righteousness" (2 Ti.3:16).

"For the prophecy came not in old time by the will of man: but holy men of God spake as they were moved by the Holy Ghost" (2 Pe.1:21).

THE STORY

The Bible has only one story: the story of God and man, of God's dealings and struggle with man. The Bible is a portrait of human history, a plot where man struggles to be his own master, ruling his own life and the lives of others, and doing his own thing, committing all kinds of evil ranging from murder, enslaving people, and cursing God over to just telling "little white lies" and deceiving people. The Bible reveals a true picture of man, where man is seen bungling and making a mess of things, but God in His love intervenes and saves man. How God intervenes time and again and saves man is the story of the Bible. God's supreme intervention and salvation in human affairs is seen in *the promised seed*—the Savior and Messiah of the world—Jesus Christ. The coming of Jesus Christ into the world is the great subject of the Bible. But there is another major subject seen in the Bible as well: the great struggle of Satan where he is seen fighting against God and His purposes for man.

In fact, the Bible reveals three great struggles operating in human history. The great story of the Bible can be seen by studying these three great struggles: one visible, one invisible, and one redemptive.
  ⇒ God and Man: The Visible Struggle
  ⇒ God and Satan: The Invisible Struggle
  ⇒ God and Man and Satan: The Redemptive Struggle

I. God and Man: The Visible Struggle

The struggle between God and man is a visible struggle, a conflict that every person experiences within his heart and mind every day of his life. Every temptation—whether thought or act—arouses the struggle within us, the struggle to follow God or self, to do right or wrong, to reject the temptation or to give in to it, to obey God or to disobey God. This struggle between God and man has existed from the beginning of human history. The *pivotal points* of the struggle are clearly seen in the Bible.

1. Adam and Eve: Man's perfect relationship with God was broken by man (Ge. Chapters 1-3).
   a. The Perfect Relationship (Ge.1-2). When God created man, God's purpose was to shower man with His love, goodness, and grace. Therefore, God put man in *the paradise of God, the Garden of Eden*, and established a perfect relationship with man. Man's responsibility was to keep the relationship alive. The way chosen to maintain the relationship with God was to obey God (Ge.2:15-17). If man disobeyed God, man would be showing distrust and unbelief in God, thereby rejecting God and severing the relationship. The consequences for such

disobedience was death, which meant both physical and eternal death, an eternal separation from God. For an unknown period of time, man walked as God willed, obeying and keeping the relationship alive. Man was unselfish, obeying God in all things. Man loved, worshipped, and served God; and he shared in God's love, goodness, and grace.

    b. The Broken Relationship (Ge.3:1-7). But the day came when man chose to disobey God. He chose to do as he willed and to walk as he wanted. Man became selfish: he rebelled against God and rejected God and His Word. He broke fellowship; he severed the perfect relationship with God. The penalty for disobedience had been pronounced (Ge.2:17). Now the penalty took effect: man's perfect relationship with God was severed; man was separated from God and doomed to die both physically and eternally (Ge.3:22-24; see Jn.5:24; Ro.5:12; 6:23; 1 Ti.5:6; Ep.2:1, 5; Col.2:13; He.9:27; Eze.18:4, 20).

    c. The Restored Relationship (Ge.3:8-24). However, God, who is love, intervened and sought man. When God found man, He promised to save man and to restore the perfect relationship through the *seed of the woman*, the Savior of the world, who was to be the Lord Jesus Christ.

2. Noah and the Flood (Ge. Chapters 6-10).
    a. Man continued to disobey God and became extremely immoral, lawless, and violent (Ge.6:1-7).
    b. But in love, God intervened and found one righteous man, Noah, and saved the human race through him (Ge.6:8 through Chapter 10, esp. 6:8-10).

3. The Tower of Babel (Ge.11:1-9).
    a. Man is seen attempting to build a worldwide empire and religion that were secular, that stood totally opposed to God (Ge.11:1-4).
    b. But again in love, God intervened and saved man from becoming totally secular, saved him by confusing the languages of the people and forcing them to scatter over all the earth (Ge.11:5-9).

4. Abraham and Israel (Ge.11:10 through Chapter 50).
    a. Man is seen doing nothing for God worthy of mentioning after the Tower of Babel, except bearing offspring and continuing the line of the human race (Ge.11:10-26).
    b. But God intervened in human history by choosing one man, Abraham, to father a new nation of people, Israel (Ge.11:27-32; 12:1-3). God chose and raised up a new nation of people for five basic purposes:
        1) To be a people who would love God supremely and give Him their first loyalty.
        2) To be a witness to the other nations of the earth, that God exists and that He is the only living and true God.
        3) To be *the chosen line* through whom God could send *the promised seed*, the Savior and Messiah, to the world (See Ge.3:15; 17:7; 22:18; Ga.3:16; Jn.4:22.)
        4) To be the recipient and channel of God's *written revelation* to the world, that is, His Word, the Holy Bible.
        5) To give Israel *the promised land* (Canaan) and to set before the world the goal of *the promised land* (a symbol of heaven).
    c. However, throughout the rest of Genesis, the immediate descendants of Abraham are seen failing God time and again. The Book of Genesis closes with Israel in bondage as slaves to Egypt (Ge. Chapters 12-50).

5. Moses and the Law (Exodus–Deuteronomy).
    a. God, in love, intervened by raising up another man, Moses, to lead Israel out of the Egyptian bondage. Through Moses God also gave His law to both Israel and the world. He gave man the law of God for three primary reasons:
      ⇒ to teach man that God is holy, just, and good (Ro.7:12).
      ⇒ to teach man's inability to save himself (Ro.3:20; Ga.3:10).
      ⇒ to teach man's need for *the promised seed*, the Savior of the world, the Lord Jesus Christ (Ga.3:24).

    b. But the people of Israel did not obey God's law nor follow God consistently. They deliberately chose to turn away from God and to go their own way all throughout their wilderness wanderings. Consequently, they constantly broke the heart of God and aroused His disapproval time and again (see Ex.16:2f; 17:1f; 32:1f).

6. The Establishment of a Kingdom: Joshua, the Judges, Saul, David, Solomon, and the other Kings of Israel (Joshua - Esther).
    a. Through the great courage of Joshua and the Judges, Israel was able to conquer enough of *the promised land* to gain a foothold and to move the whole nation into Canaan. But eventually the people began to look around and see how the worldly nations of the earth were ruled by kings. The result: they rejected the rule of God through His chosen prophets and law, and they demanded a king.
    b. God intervened and gave the people of Israel a line of kings; some turned out to be good and some bad. Over the generations of the kings, Israel became more and more like the kingdoms and nations of the world. The people became more and more worldly minded, immoral, covetous, prideful, and prejudicial. And, most tragic of all, they refused to be a witness to other nations; they failed to be the missionary force for which God had chosen them. In fact, they became so corrupted that they began to follow the religion of other nations, becoming idolaters themselves.
        The result: the kingdom of Israel fell just as all worldly kingdoms fall. The people were eventually conquered by a foreign power and led into captivity.

7. The Cry of the Poets and Prophets (Job–Malachi). God raised up poets and prophets throughout the history of Israel. His purpose: to plead with the people to return to Him. But the people continued to live like they wanted, rejecting God and turning further and further away from Him.

8. God's Supreme Intervention: Jesus Christ (Matthew–Jude).
    a. In the New Testament, God is seen intervening in the affairs and history of man in the greatest way possible: He sent *the promised seed*, His own Son, the Lord Jesus Christ, into the world to save man (Matthew - John).
    b. But man rejected God's Son and killed Him upon the cross.

   c. However, God still did not wipe man off the face of the earth. Despite man's terrible deed of killing God's Son, God intervened once again:
- ⇒ God laid the sins of the world upon Christ while He was dying upon the cross. Jesus Christ died for man's sins.
- ⇒ God raised His Son from the dead.

   d. The result was astounding: thousands and thousands of people trusted Jesus Christ as their Savior. They believed this glorious truth: that Jesus Christ had actually died for their sins upon the cross; and when they believed, they received the power of God's Spirit to live for God. Their belief in Christ gave them the power of God's Spirit, the power to follow God consistently day by day. Thereby the church was born, and began its triumphant march toward the glorious day of redemption (Acts - Jude).

  9. God's Climactic Intervention: Jesus Christ Shall Return Again (Revelation). God is going to intervene into history just one more time: to end human history. This climactic movement is yet to take place: it will happen when Jesus Christ returns to earth to bring all men into judgment (see Jn.5:28-29; 2 Pe.3:3-12).

II. God and Satan: The Invisible Struggle

The struggle between God and Satan is an invisible struggle, an invisible conflict that goes on behind the scenes of this world. If the curtain between this world and the spiritual world could be rolled back, it would show that Satan is behind all the evil and lawlessness, conflict and struggle of this world; it would show that a great spiritual warfare is being fought for the souls of men. Scripture says that Satan was probably the highest angel ever created by God, but he fell because of selfishness and pride (Is.14:12; see 1 Ti.3:6. See notes Re.12:3-4; Deeper Study #1—2 Co.4:4; 11:13-15; 1 Pe.5:8.)

Satan's purpose in making war against God is twofold:

   First, Satan's purpose is power and worship, to receive as much of the power and worship of the universe as possible (Is.14:12-17; Eze.28:11-17). He goes about this in three ways.
- ⇒ He opposes and disturbs God's work in the world (Is.14:12-17; Eze.28:11-17; Jb.1:6; 2:1-6; Mt.4:10; Mk.1:13; Lu.4:8; Re.12:7-9).
- ⇒ He discourages believers through various strategies (see notes—Lu.22:31; Ep.6:10-12).
- ⇒ He arouses God's justice against people by leading people to sin and to deny and rebel against God. And when they do, God's justice has to act and judge people to the fate of their choice: that of living apart from God and with Satan eternally (see notes—Mt.12:25-26; Jn.13:31-32).

   Second, Satan's purpose is to hurt and cut the heart of God. Why? Because God has judged and condemned him for rebelling against God. Therefore, Satan does all he can to get back at God. The best way he can do this is by trying to defeat the purposes of God, by turning the hearts of people away from God and leading them to sin and to follow the way of evil. (See notes, pt.3—Rev.12:3-4; pt.2—Rev.12:7-9; pt.2—Rev.12:10-11 for more discussion.)

However, God purposed from the beginning of human history that Satan's power would be broken by the *seed of the woman,* the Savior of the world, who was to be the Lord Jesus Christ. Since the *seed of the woman* was to be born of mankind, the devil has attempted from the beginning of history to corrupt and destroy man. If he could destroy man, in particular the promised line of God's people, he could prevent the birth of the Savior and defeat God's purposes. History flows with the traces of man's corruption and warring destruction. But it is the Bible that reveals the *invisible struggle* behind the scenes of history's corruption and destruction. It is the Bible that reveals the pivotal points of the *invisible struggle* waged by Satan against God, the *invisible struggle* of the devil to corrupt and destroy man and to defeat God's plan for man.

  1. The Creation of Man: Adam and Eve.
-    a. The devil is first seen attempting to frustrate the purposes of God in the creation of man. He tempted Adam and Eve to disobey God, knowing that the consequences of disobedience was to be death, that is, separation from God.
-    b. But God intervened and promised to give the woman *a seed*—a descendant—who would save man. This seed of the woman is *the promised seed*—the Savior, the Messiah—mentioned all throughout the Bible (Ge.3:15).

  2. Cain's False Worship and Murder.
-    a. The devil is seen prompting Cain, Adam's oldest son, to worship in self-will, rejecting the worship of God (Ge.4:1-7). Then knowing that Abel, Cain's brother, was faithful in worshipping God, the devil prompted Cain to attack *the faithful line* of God's people by killing Abel (Ge.4:8-9).
-    b. But God intervened again and gave Adam and Eve another son, Seth, whose name means *"the appointed one"* (Ge.4:25). Seth was appointed to carry on *the godly line* of God's people through whom *the promised seed* was to be born.

  3. The Terrible Corruption of the Whole Human Race.
-    a. Momentarily set back, the devil began to lead man into such vile corruption that eventually God was compelled to remove man from the face of the earth through the judgment of the flood.
-    b. But God in love intervened again and saved the godly line by raising up Noah (Ge., Chapters 6-10).

  4. The Tower of Babel: Man's Secularism and False Worship.
-    a. The devil instilled pride and selfishness in the heart of man and led man to reject God at the Tower of Babel, and the race had to be judged and scattered.
-    b. But God intervened and raised up a righteous man, Abraham, who was to father a righteous nation of people, Israel. Through that nation of people, God was to send *the promised seed*, the Savior, to the world (Ge.11:1-9, 31-32; 12:1-3; 17:1-8).

5. Abraham and Sarah: Their Being Childless.
   a. Sarah, Abraham's wife, bore no children, and *the promised line* was once again threatened (Ge.16:1).
   b. But God intervened and Isaac was miraculously born when Abraham was 100 years old. Thus the righteous line was continued (Ge.17:15-16; 21:1-8).
6. Esau and Jacob: Their Worldliness.
   a. Esau, Isaac's older son and inheritor of his father's estate by law, was a worldly man (Ge.25:27-34; He.12:16-17). Jacob, Isaac's other son, was "a cheat and deceiver" (Ge.27). Corruption of the "seed" seemed inevitable.
   b. But God intervened once more by confronting Jacob with his sin and leading him to repentance. Jacob became "a prince with God" and *the godly line* was saved. The hope of *the promised seed* was still alive (Ge.28:1-4; 32:24-30).
7. The History of Israel and of Man
   a. This history is recorded in the Bible from the Egyptian bondage to the coming of Christ. The history consists of threat after threat to *the godly line* of God's people. Time and again it looked as though Satan would be successful in his spiritual conflict against God, successful in his attempt to keep *the promised seed*, the Savior, from ever being born. (See note 5—Ge.3:15 for a chart on most of the attacks against *the promised seed* by Satan.)
   b. But God in love always intervened and saved the righteous line for *the promised seed*. The coming Savior was to provide permanent deliverance for man, deliverance from sin, death, and hell. The coming Savior was to bring the hope of eternal life to man, the hope of being restored to the original perfection known by Adam and Eve in the Garden of Eden.
8. Jesus Christ: The Attempts Upon His Life. The devil was frustrated throughout history in his attempt to destroy *the godly line*; consequently, when *the promised seed*, Jesus Christ, was born, he spared no effort in his attacks to destroy Christ.
   a. The events of Christ's life: the devil made unrestrained efforts to kill Christ...
      * through leading ungodly men to give Him no place in a crowded inn where He could be born (Lu.2:7)
      * through Herod's slaughter of the infants (Mt.2:13f)
      * through the flight into Nazareth from Archaleaus, Herod's son and successor to the throne (Mt.1-2)
      * through the devil's temptations in the wilderness (Mt.4)
      * through the persistent reaction of the Jews against His life (Jn.7:20-21, 25, 345-52)
      * through the betrayal by Judas (Mt.26:14f)
      * through the death upon the cross (Mt.27:33f)

   All this and much more seemed to indicate possible victory for the devil, and then the cross itself seemed to indicate that *the seed* had already perished. His "heel has been bruised" (Ge.3:15).
   b. But God intervened just as He had at every attempt upon the Saviour's life: He raised up Christ from the dead. Through the resurrection, the consequences of man's disobedience, death, and separation from God were conquered.

   Through the death and resurrection of Jesus Christ, the devil's "head has been bruised [the very seat of his faculties]" (He.2:14-15). The way back to a perfect relationship with God has been paved—all through *the promised seed,* the Lord Jesus Christ. Now man can approach God in Jesus Christ once again, face to face. The devil and his seed of unrighteousness—the ungodly—are defeated. The victory has been won. And the victory will become a living reality when God's desired number of the righteous have been converted and redeemed by *the promised seed* Himself, Jesus Christ (Re.21:1-8; 20:7-10; Ro.16:20).
9. The Church: The Attempts to Stamp Out God's People (Acts - Revelation; and Church History).
   a. Since Christ, Satan has continued his attempt to destroy *the godly line*, the followers of Christ. His attacks have taken two forms...
      * that of persecution. He leads the world—the ungodly, both individuals and governments—to oppress, threaten, attack, and martyr believers.
      * that of false teaching. He leads unbelievers to infiltrate the church and question the Word of God and the truth of Christ, and he leads carnal believers and ministers within the church to question the truth of Christ and the Scriptures and to teach false doctrine.

   These two forms of attack are seen all throughout the New Testament (Acts - Revelation), and they have been used to oppress the church down through the centuries of history. The history of the true church has been but a trail of persecution and blood down through the ages.
   b. But God has always intervened and preserved *the godly line*—His true church—through all the onslaught and persecution of the devil and his ungodly seed. And God will continue to preserve His church until the glorious day of redemption, the final triumph over the devil and those who have chosen to follow the ungodliness of his ways. The final triumph over Satan and all evil is assured—has already been secured—through *the promised Seed*, the Lord Jesus Christ (The Book of Revelation).

III. God and Man and Satan: The Struggle of Redemption and Salvation

There is a third struggle that runs throughout Scripture: the struggle of God to provide redemption and salvation for man. As seen in the first two struggles above, both man and Satan have fought against God and His plan of salvation from the beginning.
   ⇒ Satan seeks to hurt God, to cut His heart in order to get back at God for having judged and condemned him.
   ⇒ Man seeks to gain recognition and to exalt himself, to gain his independence and self-sufficiency; thus he ignores, rejects, and denies God. If he professes God at all, man claims to be religious and righteous, good

enough to be accepted by God and good enough never to be rejected by God. Man rejects the death of Christ for his sins, rejects any need for the cross. Man fights against God's plan of redemption.

Consequently, from the very beginning of history, God has had to struggle to provide redemption and salvation for man. This struggle is seen in the seed of the woman, who is the Savior of the world, the Lord Jesus Christ. God promised to send *the promised seed* to Adam and Eve in Genesis, and He has struggled throughout the centuries to send His Son so that He could provide redemption and salvation for man.

The struggle of redemption and salvation is seen by studying how Christ is the theme of the Bible, the underlying subject of every book of the Bible. Example after example can be found in each book: just one example is listed here to demonstrate the point. Christ is the focus of the Scripture, of every book of the Bible. The excellent commentator Norman Geisler has worded it well: Christ is within...

- Genesis: "The seed of the woman" (Ge.3:15)
- Exodus: "The Passover Lamb" (Ex.12:3f)
- Leviticus: "The Atoning Sacrifice" (Le.17:11)
- Numbers: "The Smitten Rock" (Nu.20:8, 11)
- Deuteronomy: "The Faithful Prophet" (De.18:18)
- Joshua: "The Captain of the Lord's Host" (Jos.5:15)
- Judges: "The Divine Deliverer" (Jud.2:18)
- Ruth: "The Kinsman Redeemer" (Ru.3:12)
- 1 Samuel: "The Anointed One" who is coming (1 S.2:10)
- 2 Samuel: "The Son of David" who is to sit upon the throne (2 S.7:13-14)
- 1 & 2 Kings: "The Coming King"
- 1 & 2 Chronicles: "The Builder of the Temple" (1 Chr.28:20)
- Ezra: "The Restorer of the Temple" (Ezr.6:14-15)
- Nehemiah: "The Restorer of the Nation" (Ne.6:15)
- Esther: "The Preserver of the Nation" (Est.4:14)
- Job: "The Living Redeemer" (Jb.19:25)
- Psalms: "The Praise of Israel" (Ps.150:6)
- Proverbs: "The Wisdom of God" (Pr.8:22-23)
- Ecclesiastes: "The Great Teacher" (Ec.12:11)
- Song of Solomon: "The Fairest of Ten Thousand" (Song 5:10)
- Isaiah: "The Suffering Servant" (Is.53:11)
- Jeremiah: "The Maker of the New Covenant" (Je.31:31)
- Lamentations: "The Man of Sorrows" (La.3:28-30)
- Ezekiel: "The Glory of God" (Eze.43:2)
- Daniel: "The Coming Messiah" (Da.9:25)
- Hosea: "The Lover of the Unfaithful" (Hos.3:1)
- Joel: "The Hope of Israel" (Joel 3:16)
- Amos: "The Husbandman" (Am.9:13)
- Obadiah: "The Savior" (Ob.21)
- Jonah: "The Resurrected One" (Jon.2:10)
- Micah: "The Ruler in Israel" (Mic.5:2)
- Nahum: "The Avenger" (Nah.2:1)
- Habakkuk: "The Holy God" (Hab.1:13)
- Zephaniah: "The King of Israel" (Zep.3:15)
- Haggai: "The Desire of Nations" (Hag.2:7)
- Zechariah: "The Righteous Branch" (Zec.3:8)
- Malachi: "The Sun of Righteousness" (Mal.4:2)
- Matthew: "The King of the Jews" (Mt.2:2)
- Mark: "The Servant of the Lord" (Mk.10:45)
- Luke: "The Son of Man" (Lu.19:10)
- John: "The Son of God" (Jn.1:1)
- Acts: "The Ascended Lord" (Ac.1:10)
- Romans: "The Believer's Righteousness" (Ro.1:17)
- 1 Corinthians: "The Believer's Sanctification" (1 Co.1:30)
- 2 Corinthians: "The Believer's Sufficiency" (2 Co.12:9)
- Galatians: "The Believer's Liberty" (Ga.2:4)
- Ephesians: "The Exalted Head of the Church" (Ep.1:22)
- Philippians: "The Christian's Joy" (Ph.1:26)
- Colossians: "The Fullness of Deity" (Col.2:9)
- 1 Thessalonians: "The Believer's Comfort" (1 Th.4:16, 17)
- 2 Thessalonians: "The Believer's Glory" (2 Th.1:12)
- 1 Timothy: "The Christian's Preserver" (1 Ti.4:10)
- 2 Timothy: "The Christian's Rewarder" (2 Ti.4:8)
- Titus: "The Blessed Hope" (Tit.2:13)
- Philemon: "The Substitute" (Phile.17)
- Hebrews: "The High Priest" (He.4:15)
- James: "The Giver of Wisdom" (Js.1:5)
- 1 Peter: "The Rock" (1 Pe.2:6)

- 2 Peter: "The Precious Promise" (2 Pe.1:4)
- 1 John: "The Life" (1 Jn.)
- 2 John: "The Truth" (2 Jn.)
- 3 John: "The Way" (3 Jn.)
- Jude: "The Advocate" (Jude)
- Revelation: "The King of Kings and Lord of Lords" (Re.19:16)[4]

We wish to acknowledge two excellent sources that have helped tremendously in preparing the material on "The Introduction to the Holy Bible."

❖ Harold Lindsell and Charles J. Woodbridge. *A Handbook of Christian Truth*. Westwood, NJ: Fleming H. Revell Company, 1953.

❖ Norman Geisler. *A Popular Survey of the Old Testament*. Grand Rapids, MI: Baker Book House, 1977.

There are others, but these two have stirred numerous thoughts and provided excellent research and overview of the subjects covered in this particular Introduction.

---

[4] Norman Geisler. *A Popular Survey of the Old Testament*, pp.24-25.

OLD TESTAMENT CHRONOLOGY

Dates (B.C.)	Persons & Events	Contemporary Culture
Undatable Past(Gen.1–11)	Creation Adam Flood Babel	Prehistoric culture
2300–1800 (Gen.12–50)	The Patriarchs Abraham Isaac Jacob Joseph	Mesopotamia & Egypt
1800–1500 (Between Genesis & Exodus)	Israel enslaved in Egypt	Egypt
1500–1050 (Exodus-Judges)	Exodus & the conquest of Canaan	Various nations oppress Israel
1526–1406 1446	Moses Date of the Exodus	
1406–1390	Joshua, as leader of Israel	
1390–1050 1105 1075	The Judges Samuel Sampson	
1050–931	**THE UNITED KINGDOM** (Established 1050 B.C.) Saul (1050–1010) David (1010–970) Solomon (970–930)	Surrounding nations defeated by Israel
931	**THE DIVIDED KINGDOM**	

THE DIVIDED KINGDOM

JUDAH, The Southern Kingdom			ISRAEL, The Northern Kingdom			
Dates	Kings	Southern Prophets	Northern Prophets	Dates	Kings	Contemporary Culture
931–913	Rehoboam			931–910	Jeroboam I	Syrian Kingdom (971–732)
913–911	Abijam					
911–870	Asa		Elijah (875–848)	910–909	Nadab	
				909–886	Baasha	
				886–885	Elah	
				885	Zimri	
				885–880	Tibni	
872–848	Jehoshaphat	Obadiah (855–804?)		885–874	Omri	
				874–853	Ahab	
				853–852	Ahaziah	
848–841	Jehoram			852–841	Joram	
841	Ahaziah			841–814	Jehu	
841–835	Athaliah					
835–796	Joash	Joel(?)		814–798	Jehoahaz	

OLD TESTAMENT CHRONOLOGY

JUDAH, The Southern Kingdom			ISRAEL, The Northern Kingdom			
Dates (cont.)	Kings (cont.)	Southern Prophets (cont.)	Northern Prophets (cont.)	Dates (cont.)	Kings (cont.)	Contemporary Culture (cont.)
796–767	Amaziah		Jonah (785–775)	798–782	Jehoash	
792–740	Azariah (Uzziah)	Isaiah (740–681)	Amos (760–750)	793–753	Jeroboam II	
				753	Zechariah	
				752	Shallum	
750–735	Jotham		Hosea (750–715)	752–742	Menahem	
				742–740	Pekahiah	Fall of Syria (732 B.C.)
735–715	Ahaz	Micah (715?)		752–732	Pekah	Assyrian seige & conquest of Palestine (745–650 B.C.)
				732–722	Hoshea	
				722	FALL OF NORTHERN KINGDOM: EXILED BY ASSYRIA	
715–686	Hezekiah					
697–641	Manesseh					
641–639	Amon					
639–608	Josiah	Zephaniah (628–620)				
608	Jehoahaz	Jeremiah (626–586)				
608–598	Jehokiam	Habakkuk (605–600) Daniel (605–530)				Babylon Supremacy (625-539)
598–597	Jehoiachin					
597–586	Zedekiah	Ezekiel (593–571)				
586	FALL OF JERUSALEM: EXILED BYBABYLON					
538	RETURN: FIRST GROUP UNDER ZERRUBABEL					Media-Persian Rule (539–331)
520–515	SECOND TEMPLE	Zechariah 520–480) Haggai (515?)				
458	RETURN: SECOND GROUP UNDER EZRA (440–430)	Malachi (440–430)				
432	RETURN: THIRD GROUP UNDER NEHEMIAH					

NEW TESTAMENT CHRONOLOGY

(Jesus Christ was born before the death of Herod the Great [see Mt.2:1, 16]. Herod died in 4 B.C.; thus, we know that Jesus was born around 4–5 B.C. Please note: all dates are approximate. This is the reason why a span of years is given for most events. It is just impossible to know exactly when most of the New Testament events happened.)

Persons & Events	Dates	New Testament Books
Jesus' Birth	5–4 B.C.	
Jesus in the Temple as a child, 12 years old (Lk.2:42-52)	7–8 A.D.	
John the Baptist's ministry began	25–27 A.D.	
Jesus' Baptism	26–27 A.D.	
John the Baptist's death	28–29 A.D.	
Jesus' crucifixion & resurrection	28–30 A.D.	
Pentecost: The birth of the church	28–30 A.D.	
Paul's conversion	34–35 A.D.	
Death of Herod Agrippa I (see Acts 12:1-23)	44 A.D.	
	45–50 A.D.	Epistle of James
Paul's first missionary journey	48–49 A.D.	
	48–60 A.D.	Galatians (?)
Great Jerusalem Council	49–50 A.D.	
Paul's second missionary journey	50–51 A.D.	
Paul in Corinth	50–53 A.D.	
	50–52 A.D.	1 & 2 Thessalonians
Gallio as procounsel of Achaia (Acts 18:12f)	52 A.D.	
Paul's third missionary journey	54 A.D.	
Paul's ministry in Ephesus	54–57 A.D.	
	54–56 A.D.	1 Corinthians
	56–57 A.D.	2 Corinthians
	55–58 A.D.	Romans
Paul's arrest in Jerusalem	58–59 A.D.	

15

NEW TESTAMENT CHRONOLOGY

Persons & Events (Cont.)	Dates (cont.)	New Testament Books (cont.)
Paul's imprisonment in Caesarea	58–60 A.D.	
	58–62 A.D.	Gospel of Luke
Paul on the Island of Malta	60–61 A.D.	
Paul's imprisonment in Rome	60–63 A.D.	
	60–63 A.D.	Ephesians, Philippians, Colossians, Philemon
	62 A.D.	Acts of the Apostles
Paul's release from prison	63 A.D.	
	61–64 A.D.	1 Timothy
	63–67 A.D.	1 Peter
	61–68 A.D.	2 Peter
	64–66 A.D.	Titus
	64–67 A.D.	Hebrews
Peter's death	65–68 A.D.	
Paul's second imprisonment in Rome	65–68 A.D.	
	65–68 A.D.	2 Timothy
Paul's death	65–68 A.D.	
	50–70 A.D.	Matthew
	67–70 A.D.	Mark
	67–90 A.D.	Jude
Destruction of Jerusalem by Rome	70 A.D.	
	80–95 A.D.	Gospel of John
	85–95 A.D.	Epistles of John
	95–96 A.D.	Revelation

THE FIRST BOOK OF MOSES, CALLED

GENESIS

INTRODUCTION

AUTHOR: Moses, the great lawgiver and deliverer of Israel. Moses was the great leader who led Israel from Egyptian bondage and through the wilderness wanderings.

Moses' authorship is questioned by some commentators. It is true that *Genesis* is silent: the book does not name an author. But the evidence is strong—very strong—that Moses is the author. The great *Pulpit Commentary* says this in its Introduction to *Genesis*:

> There does not appear, however, to have been any serious questioning on the subject of the Mosaic authorship of the Pentateuch as a whole, or of Genesis as a part of that larger work, until the sixteenth century, when it began to be insinuated by Masius (1574), Spinoza (1670), and Anton Van Dale (1696), that not Moses, the Hebrew lawgiver, but Ezra, the priest-prophet of the Restoration, was the first composer of those parts of sacred Scripture. [1]

This means, of course, that the earlier Biblical commentators—those who lived and wrote before the *sixteenth century*—held that Moses was the author. Any serious suggestion that he might not be did not arise until the sixteenth century.

However, for several centuries now there has been a popular theory that is called "the documentary hypothesis." This theory says there are four major sources for the Pentateuch, each of which was written sometime between 900–400 B.C. These sources are said to be...

- *J* (for Jehovah or Yahweh). This represents the writer or source that used the Hebrew name *Jehovah* or *Yahweh* for God throughout the Pentateuch.
- *E* (for Elohim). This represents the writer or source that used the Hebrew name *Elohim* for God.
- *D* (for Deuteronomist). This represents the writer or source that recorded the different accounts of the law throughout the Pentateuch.
- *P* (for Priestly). This represents the writer or source that recorded the information dealing with the *priests*.

The first person to suggest this theory was a French physician, Jean Astruc, in 1752. Note that he was a physician, not a theologian. The theory was later picked up by the German historian and Biblical writer, J.G. Eichhorn in 1787. However, "the documentary hypothesis" was not thoroughly developed and popularized until Julius Wellhausen who lived in 1844-1918. [2]

The *NIV Study Bible* has an excellent summary about this theory:

> Each of these documents is claimed to have its own characteristics and its own theology, which often contradicts that of the other documents. The Pentateuch is thus depicted as a patchwork of stories, poems and laws. However, this view is not supported by conclusive evidence, and intensive archaeological and literary research has undercut many of the arguments used to challenge Mosaic authorship. [3]

The great weight of evidence points to Moses being the author of *Genesis*. The evidence can be summarized in the following points.

1. *Genesis* is the first book of the Pentateuch (the first five books of the Bible), and the Pentateuch is said to be written by Moses. In fact, the Pentateuch is sometimes simply called "Moses" (Jn.5:46; Lu.24:27, see 44).

2. Each of the five books of the Pentateuch says that Moses is the author, except for *Genesis* (Ex.17:14; 24:3-4; 34:27; Le.1:1; 4:1; 6:1, 8, 19, 24; 7:22, 28; 8:1; Nu.33:2; De.1:1; 17:18-19; 27:1-8; 28:58, 61; 29:19-20, 27; 30:10; 31:9-11, 24-26).

3. The Old Testament always refers without exception to Moses as the author of the Pentateuch (Jos.1:7-8; 8:31-32; 1 K.2:3; 8:9, 53; 2 K.10:31; 14:6; Ezr.6:18; Ne.13:1; Da.9:11-13; Mal.4:4).

4. The New Testament always refers to Moses as the author of the Pentateuch which includes Genesis (Mt.8:4; 19:7-8; 23:2; Mk.1:44; 7:10; 10:3-4; 12:19, 26; Lk.2:22; 5:14; 16:29-31; 20:37; 24:27, 44; Jn.1:17; 3:14; 5:45-46; 6:32; 7:19, 22-23; Ac.3:22; 13:39; 15:1, 5, 21; 26:22; 28:23; Ro.10:5, 19; 1 Co.9:9; 2 Co.3:15; He.8:5). The weight of the Scriptural evidence is that Moses is the author of the whole Pentateuch including *Genesis*.

5. The Talmud, the earliest writings of the Jews, says that Moses was the author of *Genesis*.

6. Moses was an eyewitness, an actual participant in the events of *Exodus* through *Deuteronomy*. For example, note his observation of twelve wells of water and seventy palm trees (Ex.15:27).

7. Moses was well acquainted with Egypt. The author of Genesis is familiar with Egyptian names, and *Genesis* actually has a larger number of Egyptian words than any other book in the Old Testament.

8. The ordinance of circumcision is said to be part of the law of Moses (Jn.7:23), and circumcision was instituted in Genesis 17:12, as well as in Ex.12:48 and in Le.12:3.

9. *Genesis* and *Exodus* form a whole; that is, Exodus is just incomplete without *Genesis*. It is *Genesis* that explains such questions as...

- how Israel got into Egypt
- how Israel was freed from Egyptian slavery and was formed as a nation
- how Israel became so involved with the promises and covenant relationship with God
- why the Exodus of Israel and the journey into the land of Canaan were so important

---

1 *The Pulpit Commentary*, Vol.1. HDM Spence and Joseph S. Exell, Editors. (Grand Rapids, MI: Eerdmans, 1950), p. 88.
2 Victor Hamilton. *The Book of Genesis*, Chapters 1-17. "The New International Commentary on the Old Testament." (Grand Rapids, MI: Eerdmans Publishing Co.,1990), p.13.
3 *NIV Study Bible*. (Grand Rapids, MI: Zondervan Corporation, 1985), p.2.

There is also this fact: in the Hebrew the first word in the *Book of Exodus* is "and" (Ex.1:1). It connects Exodus with some former writing. The weight of the evidence is that the same person wrote both Exodus and Genesis, and Moses is said to be the author of Exodus.

One final thing should be said about Moses writing Genesis. All the events in Genesis happened before Moses: they occurred many generations before his time. How then does he know about such events as the creation and such persons as the Patriarchs: Abraham, Isaac, Jacob, and Joseph? The following possibilities seem reasonable since God is a God of revelation.

1. God revealed *to Adam* the creation account (see DEEPER STUDY # 1—Ge.1:1-2:3 [Intro.]; pt.4—Ge.3:21 for discussion).

2. Adam and his descendents—the godly line—were led to preserve God's dealings with them. Each person, especially one who was truly godly, was bound to pass on—both by spoken and written word—the most significant events of their lives, which would be their relationship to God and His promises. Norman Geisler, who has written an excellent survey of the Old Testament, says this:

> *We can conclude that Moses, using the family records which had been passed on to him, compiled the Book of Genesis....Jewish history shows that family records were kept and passed on to later generations. Moses could have copied his material from such records just as Hezekiah's men copied from Solomon's writings to complete the Book of Proverbs (cf. Prov.25:1).*[4]

3. Moses was well educated in "all the wisdom of the Egyptians" (Ac.7:22). He was well prepared by God to take both the written and oral testimony of his forefathers and write the beginning history of the world, especially under the inspiration of God's Spirit. (See note—2 Ti.3:16.) Again, Norman Geisler has an excellent comment on this point:

> *Moses is the only person we know of from this early time period who had the ability to write this book. The rest of the Israelites were a nation of uneducated slaves, whereas Moses was a highly educated son of the king (Acts 7:22). Moses was the only one who had both the interest and information to write Genesis. Being Jewish Moses would have had access to the family records of his ancestors (cf. Gen.5:1; 10:1; 25:19; etc.) which were no doubt brought down to Egypt by Jacob (Gen.46). Since Moses was bent on delivering his people from Egypt, it is natural to assume that he was familiar with the promises of God passed down by his forefathers that God would indeed deliver them (cf. Gen.46:3-4; Exod.2:24)*[5]

DATE: Probably some time between 1450–1406 B.C. Perhaps sometime before 1487 B.C.
1. Moses lived 120 years (De.34:7).
2. Moses spent 40 years in Egypt (Ac.7:22-23).
3. Moses spent 40 years in Midian (Ex.2:15).
4. Moses spent 40 years leading Israel through the wilderness experiences (De.8:2f).

Now, we know with some accuracy when Moses lived:

> **"And it came to pass in the four hundred and eightieth year after the children of Israel were come out of the land of Egypt, in the fourth year of Solomon's reign over Israel, in the month Zif, which is the second month, that he began to build the house of the LORD" (1 K.6:1).**

The fourth year of Solomon's reign was about 966 B.C.; therefore, Moses led Israel out of Egypt around 1446 B.C. (480 years before Solomon's 4th year as king).[6] Based upon this information, Moses' life would be dated as follows:
⇒ Moses in Egypt 1526-1486 B.C.
⇒ Moses in Midian 1486-1446 B.C.
⇒ Moses leading Israel through the wilderness 1446-1406 B.C.

Moses had access to the records and writings of Israel only when he was with them. He was not with them in Midian, so he wrote Genesis either when he was living as the adopted son of Pharaoh in Egypt and was close by Israel and their writings, or else when he was with them in the wilderness.
⇒ Norman Geisler, who holds to the earlier date, has an excellent reason for this position.

> *There are three reasons for believing that Moses compiled Genesis during the first forty years of his life (before 1487 B.C.). During this period Moses came to faith in God and the desire to deliver his people (cf. Exod. 2:11f.; Heb. 11:24). He must have carefully studied Israel's history and God's promises to Abraham's descendants at this time. Later, while in Midian, Moses would not have had access (such as he had had in Egypt) to all the records of his people. By the third period of his life, Moses was busy as a leader and writer of the other books of the Law. It is more likely, then, that Genesis was compiled while his early interest in his people's past and their deliverance gave him access to the records of their history and the promises of God to deliver them.*[7]

⇒ However, a later date—during the wilderness wanderings—is also possible (1446-1406 B.C.). Moses unquestionably wrote the other four books of the Pentateuch—*Exodus, Leviticus, Numbers,* and *Deuteronomy*—during

---

[4] Norman Geisler. *A Popular Survey of the Old Testament*, p.38.
[5] Ibid., p.37.
[6] *NIV Study Bible*, p.2.
[7] Norman Geisler. *A Popular Survey of the Old Testament*, p.38.

this period. Apparently, he did what many great men have done down through history, he kept a diary of the events and compiled his notes into the various books as he found time.

There are also two other strong points for the later date:

⇒ Moses would have been much more mature spiritually during the wilderness wanderings. When he was a young man in Egypt, he seems to have lacked the spiritual maturity necessary for the Holy Spirit to inspire him to write Genesis. In fact, it was his having committed murder that forced him to flee Egypt (see Ex.2:11-15).

⇒ It was during the wilderness wanderings that God dealt with Moses time and again face to face (so to speak). If God Himself shared the creation story and any other earlier events of human history with Moses, it was more likely during these forty years of his life.

Whatever the case, Moses wrote Genesis either during the years he was in Pharaoh's court or during the years of the wilderness wanderings, either...

- around or before 1487 B.C.
- or 1447–1407 B.C.

TO WHOM WRITTEN: Israel in particular and the human race in general.

God is a God of love and truth; consequently His love is bound to lead Him to reveal the truth to all people everywhere...

- the truth of their origin: where they have come from
- the truth of their purpose: why they are on the earth
- the truth of their end and destiny: where they are going

Genesis was written to both Israel and the human race, to reveal the truth of their origin, purpose, and destiny. God's very purpose in creating man is for all people to know these three great truths.

PURPOSE: Three purposes can be gleaned from Genesis, a historical, doctrinal, and Christological purpose.[8]

1. The historical purpose: to encourage and strengthen Israel in its faith and trust in God. Remember, for about 430 years the children of Israel suffered the awful bondage of slavery in Egypt, and now during the time that Genesis was being written, they were suffering through the trials and temptations of the wilderness wanderings. The one thing the people needed above all else was to be encouraged and strengthened in their faith in God. Historically, Genesis was written to teach Israel five strong lessons.

   a. To teach Israel that there was only one living and true God, one God who had created and purposed all things (Ge. Chapter 1-11).

   b. To teach Israel its roots, that they had actually been chosen by God Himself through Abraham, appointed to be *the chosen line* of God's people.

   c. To teach Israel that *the promised seed*, the Savior, was to be sent into the world through them. They were *the chosen line* through whom God was going to save the world. Salvation—*the promised seed*—was to come through Israel.

   d. To teach Israel that they were to receive *the promised land*, the land of Canaan, and that God would be faithful to His Word and give them *the promised land*.

   e. To teach Israel that they must believe and follow God...
      - in conquering and overcoming the trials and enemies of life
      - in seeking after *the promised land*

2. The doctrinal or spiritual purpose: to teach all people everywhere...

   a. To teach that God is the Sovereign Creator: He is the Lord and Majesty of the universe, the Supreme Intelligence and Force of all creation, both visible and invisible (Genesis, Chapters 1-2).

   b. To teach that God created man and woman: He created them to pour out His grace upon them and to secure their personal fellowship and service, both now and forever (Genesis 1:26-2:25).

   c. To teach the origin of sin and death: why these two awful things exist and infect the lives of people so deeply (Genesis, Chapter 3).

   d. To teach God's mercy and grace: that God has mercy upon man and will pour out His grace upon him, if man will just repent and turn back to God (Genesis, Chapters 1-50. See the lives of Adam, Noah, Abraham, Isaac, and Jacob.)

   e. To teach the faithfulness of God and His Word: that what God says and promises will be fulfilled no matter what He has to do to overcome the terrible failings of men (Genesis, Chapters 9-50. See the failings of Noah, Abraham, Isaac, and Jacob.)

   f. To teach that all true believers—both ancient and present—are to receive *the promised land* (a symbol of heaven).

3. The Christological or Christ-centered purpose: to teach that *the promised seed* pointed to Jesus Christ as the Savior of the world, that Jesus Christ is *the promised seed* who came from the godly line of...

the woman (Ge.3:15)

- Seth (Ge.4:25)
- Shem (Ge.9:27; 11:10-26)
- Abraham (Ge.12:3; see Ro.9:7-9)
- Isaac (Ge.21:12)
- Jacob (Ge.25:23; see Ro.9:10-12)
- Judah (Ge.49:10)

---

8   The idea for this approach to the **PURPOSE** was gleaned from Norman L. Geisler's *A Popular Survey of the Old Testament*, p.40.

INTRODUCTION TO GENESIS

SPECIAL FEATURES:

1. *Genesis* is "The Great Book of Prehistoric Times" or "The Great Book of Creation." In fact the title, "The Book of the Creation of the World" was an actual title given to Genesis during the early history of the Jews and Jewish tradition (Talmudic times). It is the only written record of prehistoric times that is both accurate and satisfying to the human mind and heart. Man's mind seeks accuracy, and his heart craves a satisfying understanding lying behind the accuracy of facts. In Genesis God gives a glimpse of prehistoric times and reveals what lies behind the beginning of creation and history.

2. *Genesis* is "The Great Book of Beginnings." The very first word of *Genesis* is *Bereshith* which means "in the beginning." The Jews have sometimes even referred to the book simply as *Bereshith*. The Greeks called the book Genesis (genesis), which is the title the English speaking world has adopted. Genesis means origin, source, generation, beginning. It is a record of several major beginnings.

    a. The beginning of the universe, both of heaven and earth (Ge.1:1-11:31).
    b. The beginning of man and woman (Ge.1:26-31; 2:4-25).
    c. The beginning of God's covenant with man (Ge.2:15-17).
    d. The beginning of sin (Ge.3:1-13; 4:8-15).
    e. The beginning of salvation, of man's deliverance from sin and death through God's promised *seed*, the Savior of the world (Ge.3:14-21).
    f. The beginning of the family (Ge.4:1-15).
    g. The beginning of civilization and society (Ge.4:16-9:29).
    h. The beginning of the nations and races (Ge. Chapters 10-11).
    i. The beginning of Israel, God's chosen people (Ge. Chapters 12-50).
    j. The beginning of the hope for *the promised land* (Canaan, a symbol of heaven) (Ge. Chapters 12-50).

3. *Genesis* is "The Great Book of Generations." The word *generations* (toledot) means offspring, descendents, or history of a person. The word is used ten times by the author to divide the book under ten headings. The author begins each section with the words, "These are the generations." Genesis is often outlined by these sections. They are as follows:

    a. The generations of the heavens and earth (Ge.2:4-4:26).
    b. The generations or history of Adam (Ge.5:1-6:8).
    c. The generations or history of Noah (Ge.6:9-9:29).
    d. The generations or history of the sons of Noah (Ge.10:1-11:9).
    e. The generations or history of Shem (Ge.11:10-26).
    f. The generations or history of Terah (Abraham) (Ge.11:27-25:11).
    g. The generations or history of Ishmael (Ge.25:12-18).
    h. The generations or history of Isaac (Ge.25:19-35:29).
    i. The generations or history of Esau (Ge.36:1-43).
    j. The generations or history of Jacob (Ge.37:1-50:26).

Please note, *The Preacher's Outline & Sermon Bible®* does not strictly follow this division because it is sometimes difficult for the reader to connect what is being read with the given subject heading. For example, "the generations of Terah" covers fourteen chapters; yet the whole section has to do with Abraham, one of the sons of Terah.

4. *Genesis* is "The Great Book of Human Ancestry." (See Special Feature, point 3.)

5. *Genesis* is "The Great Book of Patriarchal History" or "The Great Book of the Patriarchs." The lives of the fathers of Israel, Abraham, Isaac, and Jacob are covered by Genesis.

6. *Genesis* is "The Great Book That Launches God's Grace Toward Man." Of course, creation and life itself with all their privileges are an act of grace, an act of God's favor toward man. *By grace* means much more than just creation and life, as wonderful as they are. Grace means that God favors man despite man's terrible sin and rebellion against God. God favors man by saving him from a destiny of corruption and death to a life of perfection that is to last forever. This glorious salvation was launched right after Adam's first sin and rebellion against God, launched when God began to seek and call out to Adam, "Where art thou?" (Ge.3:9). God became the seeking Savior, ready to launch His glorious plan of salvation and redemption, all through His wonderful grace. But this was not all: the theme of grace continued as God sacrificed the life and blood of an animal in order to secure "coats of skin and clothe" Adam and Eve in their nakedness (Ge.3:21). A life had to be sacrificed in order to clothe and save them. From then on, God is seen ever seeking and crying out to man "where art thou" in order to cover and forgive man's sin and failure. Even the chosen people of God, the patriarchal fathers themselves, demonstrated time after time an unbelievable tendency toward sin and rebellion that necessitated God's intervening grace.

7. *Genesis* is "The Great Book That Launches God's Plan of Salvation." (See Special Features, point 6.)

8. *Genesis* is "The Great Book That Begins the History of Redemption." (See Special Features, point 6.)

9. *Genesis* is "The Great Book That Begins the Trail of Blood and Sacrifice." (See Special Features, point 6; and see note—Ge.3:21, esp. pt.4.)

10. *Genesis* is "The Great Book That Establishes God's Covenant Relationship with Man." Genesis shows God's very special relationship with man, how God established His first four covenants with man at four crucial times in man's history.

These covenants are:

    a. The Edenic covenant whereby God met man's most basic needs (Ge.2:15-17).
    b. The Adamic covenant or the covenant with Adam whereby God promises redemption (Ge.3:15).
    c. The Noahic covenant or the covenant with Noah whereby God preserves the human race (Ge.6:18; 9:8-17).
    d. The Abrahamic covenant or the covenant with Abraham whereby God begins a new race (the Jews) to be *the chosen line* of God's people (Ge.12:1-3).

        It is important to note that the covenants with Adam and Noah were universal covenants; that is, they cover the relationship that exists between God and the whole human race. But the covenant with Abraham is a limited covenant; that is, it covers only the relationship that exists between God and His chosen people, the believers of the earth who diligently follow God (Ge.11:6).

11. *Genesis* is "The Great Book That Begins Man's Pilgrimage of Faith."
   ⇒ Adam, Abel, Enoch, Noah—*the godly line* of God's people—believed God: they demonstrated great faith in God (see notes—Ge.3:15; 3:21; 4:3-4; 5:21-24; 6:9-10).
   ⇒ Abraham, Isaac, and Jacob were men of great faith. Scripture declares:

> **"These all died *in faith*, not having received the promises but having seen them afar off, and were persuaded of them, and confessed that they were strangers and pilgrims on the earth. For they that say such things declare plainly that they seek a country...a better country, that is, an heavenly" (He.11:13-16).**

Man's life—his pilgrimage from birth right on through death and to whatever lies beyond—is either a pilgrimage into the unknown or *a pilgrimage of faith* in God's promises. Genesis is the story of men who walked the *pilgrimage of faith*.

12. *Genesis* is "The Great Book That Reveals and Deals with the Major Promises of God."
   ⇒ There is God's promise to send *the promised seed*, the Savior of the world, to crush the power of that "old serpent, called the devil" (Ge.3:15; see Re.12:9; 20:2).
   ⇒ There is God's promise to always see that *a godly line* of people exists so that He can fulfill his promises and purposes upon earth (Ge.3:15; 12:1-3).
   ⇒ There is God's promise to give *the promised land* of Canaan to Israel. But note: *the promised land* refers to both a physical inheritance and a spiritual inheritance. *The promised land* is a symbol of heaven which God has promised to all genuine believers who diligently seek after Him (Ge.12:1 see He.11:8-10, 13-14, 16; see notes—Ge.11:29; 12:1; Ro.4:13; Ga.3:16).

13. *Genesis* is "The Great Book of the Promised Seed," the Savior of the world. The *promised seed* is one of the major themes that runs throughout the whole Bible (see notes—Ge.3:15; Ga.3:6-7; 3:16).

14. *Genesis* is "The Great Book of Theological Pictures." Biblical doctrines are not developed in Genesis, but practically every doctrine that is developed in the New Testament is pictured or illustrated in Genesis.
   a. There are the names or doctrinal pictures of God as...
      • The Almighty God (Elohim, Ge.1:1)
      • The God of redemption and revelation, the covenant God who establishes a personal relationship with man (Jehovah or Yahweh, Ge.2:4; 2:7)
      • God Most High (El Elyon, Ge.14:18-20)
      • God Almighty (El Shaddai, Ge.17:1; see Ex.6:3)
      • The Everlasting God (El Olam, Ge.21:33)
      • God of Seeing (El Roi, Ge.16:13)
      • God, the God of Israel (El-elohe-Israel, Ge.33:20)
      • God of Bethel (El-Bethel, Ge.35:7)
      • God of Abraham (Ge.24:12; 28:13; 31:42; see Ex.3:6)
      • The Fear of Isaac (Ge.31:42, 53)
      • The Strong or Mighty One of Jacob (Ge.49:24; see Is.1:24; Ps.132:2)
      • The Lord God of Shem (Ge.9:26)
      • The Lord of all (Adonay, Ge.18:27; see Ex.23:17; Is.6:1; 10:16, 33)

   b. There are the doctrinal pictures of...
      • justification (Ge.15:6 see Ro.4:3, 20-23).
      • righteousness and the necessity of being clothed in righteousness by God (Ge.3:21)
      • creation (Ge, Chapters 1-2)
      • redemption (Ge.3:21)
      • salvation through the *promised seed*, the Savior of the world (Ge.3:15; 12:3)
      • heaven, the *promised land* (Ge.12:1)
      • believers, a godly line of people who follow God (Ge., Chapters 4-50)
      • mercy (Ge.4:15; 6:8; 18:26; 19:16)
      • election (Ge.25:21-23 see Ro.9:9-13)
      • judgment (Ge.6:1-7; 19:24 see 18:16-33)
      • death and the hope of conquering death through the promises of God, the *promised seed* (Ge.3:15; 5:24), and the *promised land* (Ge.12:1-3; 22:5; 47:29; 50:24 see He.11:13-14, 16, 17-19, esp. 19)
      • prayer (Ge.18:23; 25:21; 32:24-32)
      • human law (Ge.9:4-6)

   On and on the list could go, but the above list illustrates how Genesis is "The Great Book of Theological or Doctrinal Pictures."

15. *Genesis* is "The Great Book of Israel's Beginnings." From chapter twelve onward—from the selection of Abraham through Joseph—the book is simply a history of Israel's beginnings, the beginning of the Jewish nation, the nation chosen by God to be His witness to the world.

OUTLINE OF GENESIS

THE PREACHER'S OUTLINE AND SERMON BIBLE® is *unique*. It differs from all other Study Bibles and Sermon Resource Materials in that every Passage and Subject is outlined right beside the Scripture. When you choose any *Subject* below and turn to the reference, you have not only the Scripture, but you discover the Scripture and Subject *already outlined for you—verse by verse.*

For a quick example, choose one of the subjects below and turn over to the Scripture, and you will find this marvelous help for faster, easier, and more accurate use.

In addition, every point of the Scripture and Outline is *fully developed in a Commentary with supporting Scripture* at the bottom of the page. Again, this arrangement makes sermon preparation much easier and faster.

Note something else: The Subjects of *Genesis* have titles that are both Biblical and *practical*. The practical titles sometimes have more appeal to people. This *benefit* is clearly seen for use on billboards, bulletins, church newsletters, etc.

A suggestion: For the *quickest* overview of *Genesis*, first read *all the major titles* (I, II, III, etc.), then come back and read the subtitles.

OUTLINE OF GENESIS

THE BEGINNING OF THE WORLD: THE CREATION OF MANKIND AND OF THE GODLY SEED, Chapters 1-11

INTRODUCTION TO THE SEVEN DAYS OF CREATION, pp.25-44.

I. **CREATION OF THE HEAVENS AND THE EARTH, 1:1–2:3**

    A. The Basic Questions of Creation, 1:1-2
    B. The First Day: The Creation of Light, 1:3-5
    C. The Second Day: Creation of the Firmament (the Atmosphere and Air Space Encircling the Earth), 1:6-8
    D. The Third Day (Part 1): Creation of the Waters (Seas, Lakes, Rivers) and the Dry Land (Continents, Islands), 1:9-10
    E. The Third Day (Part 2): Creation of Plant Life or Vegetation, 1:11-13
    F. The Fourth Day: Creation and Distribution of Light Upon Earth to Regulate Day and Night, Seasons and Years, 1:14-19
    G. The Fifth Day: Creation of Water Creatures (Fish, Sea Life, Creeping Creatures) and Air Creatures (Birds, Winged Fowl, Insects, etc.), 1:20-23
    H. The Sixth Day (Part 1): Creation of Land Animals, 1:24-25
    I. The Sixth Day (Part 2): Creation of Man, Male and Female, 1:26-31
    J. The Seventh Day: Creation of a Day for Rest and Worship, 2:1-3

II. **ADAM, THE FIRST MAN (PART 1): THE BEGINNING OF MANKIND AND OF THE GODLY SEED— WHAT HAPPENED TO MAN AND THE EARTH, 2:4–3:24**

    A. The First Picture of the Earth Before Man: Prehistoric Times, 2:4-6
    B. The First Man: Adam, 2:7
    C. The First Garden and Its Purpose: Eden, Man's Ideal Place or Home, 2:8-14
    D. The First Charge or Covenant: Man's Purpose upon the Earth, 2:15-17
    E. The First Woman: Man's Companion, Eve, 2:18-25
    F. Man and Woman's First Steps Into Sin, 3:1-6
    G. The First Consequences of Sin: Man's Tragic Fall from Perfection, 3:7-13
    H. The First Judgment Upon Sin (Part 1): Judgment upon the Tempter, That Old Serpent Called the Devil, 3:14-15
    I. The First Judgment Upon Sin (Part 2): Judgment upon Woman, 3:16
    J. The First Judgment Upon Sin (Part 3): Judgment upon Man, 3:17-19
    K. The First Provision of God for Man: God Provides Life and Clothing (Righteousness) for Man, 3:20-21
    L. The First Act of Deliverance or Salvation: Man Is Saved from Living Forever as a Sinner in a Fallen World, 3:22-24

OUTLINE OF GENESIS

III. **ADAM, THE FIRST MAN (PART 2): THE BIRTH, DEVELOPMENT, AND CORRUPTION OF BOTH THE UNGODLY AND THE GODLY SEED (DESCENDANTS), 4:1–6:8**

    A. The First Children, Cain and Abel: False Vs. True Worship—the Beginning of False Worship, 4:1-7

    B. The First Murder, Cain Kills Abel: The Undeniable Truth of Judgment—Sin Cannot Be Hid, 4:8-15

    C. The First Civilization and Society (Part 1): The Development of the First Ungodly Seed or Descendants, 4:16-24

    D. The First Civilization and Society (Part 2): The Continuation of the Godly Seed or Descendants, 4:25-26

    E. The First Civilization and Society (Part 3): The Line of the Godly Seed or Descendants—Significant Events, 5:1-32

    F. The First Civilization and Society (Part 4): The Corruption of the Godly Line—Co-mingling with the Ungodly Line, 6:1-8

IV. **NOAH: THE MAN CHOSEN TO PRESERVE MANKIND AND THE GODLY SEED THROUGH WORLD DESTRUCTION (THE FLOOD), 6:9–9:29**

    A. Noah and the Rest of Mankind: A Great Contrast of Character—Why God Destroyed the Earth, 6:9-12

    B. Noah and the Ark: God's Great Demand for Faith—What Noah Had to Believe, 6:13-22

    C. Noah and the Last Week: God's Great Invitation and Noah's Great Obedience, 7:1-9

    D. Noah and the Flood: God's Great Judgment of the Earth, 7:10-24

    E. Noah and God: God's Great Preservation (Salvation) of Life, 8:1-14

    F. Noah and the Great Day: God Sent Noah Forth into the World to Begin a New Life, 8:15-22

    G. Noah and the New Beginning (Part 1): God Established a New World Order for Man, 9:1-7

    H. Noah and the New Beginning (Part 2): God Established a New Covenant with Man—The Noahic Covenant, 9:8-17

    I. Noah and the Human Race: The Future of the Human Race Foretold, 9:18-29

V. **NOAH'S SONS: THE THREE BRANCHES OF THE HUMAN RACE CHOSEN TO REPOPULATE AND TO SCATTER OVER THE EARTH, 10:1–11:9**

    A. The Growth of the Human Race and the Birth of Nations, 10:1-32

    B. The Scattering of the Human Race Over the Earth: The People's Tragic Mistake and Sin—The Secular City and False Worship (The Tower of Babel), 11:1-9

VI. **SHEM, NOAH'S SON: THE SON CHOSEN TO CARRY ON THE GODLY SEED, 11:10-32**

    A. The Preservation of the Promised Seed (Part 1), 11:10-26

    B. The Preservation of the Promised Seed (Part 2): The Beginning of a Great Life (Abram), 11:27-32

INTRODUCTION TO THE SEVEN DAYS OF CREATION

The Bible declares an astounding truth: the earth and the universe did not just happen by chance nor by some random accident.

⇒ The earth and the heavens did not originate *out of nowhere*.
⇒ Something—some particle or force, some matter or energy, some element or electrical impulse, some atom, proton, neutron, electron, chemical, gas, or something else—did not just appear *out of nothing*.
⇒ The earth and the universe did not evolve from some particle of dust, some gas, or some energy that just appeared. For something to appear *out of nothing* is against all the laws of nature and science.

The Bible declares this astounding truth: the earth and the heavens were created by a Sovereign Intelligence and Power who has revealed Himself to be the Supreme Person of the universe, to be ELOHIM, *GOD ALMIGHTY, the Supreme Lord and Majesty* of all! The Bible declares that the universe has been *deliberately and personally created* by God Himself. God, Elohim, is the Mighty God who alone has the *Intelligence and Power* to create a universe like ours, a universe…

- that stretches so far into the outer reaches of space
- that reaches out in unbelievable distances
- that includes an unbelievable number of worlds
- that reaches unfathomable dimensions
- that exceeds the comprehension and understanding of man

The Bible declares that God (Elohim) is the Creator, the Supreme Person, the Sovereign Lord and Majesty of the universe. Note how the Bible begins:

"In the beginning God" (Ge.1:1).

The stress is God. God was there in the beginning, already existing when the universe first began. He is the God of power who actually existed *before* the universe and who acted and created the universe. God (Elohim) is the subject, the Sovereign Person who stands behind all things. This is the great declaration of the very first chapter of Genesis. *This is immediately seen by quickly glancing at the underlined words of the Scripture below.*

(Please note: The Creation account needs to be looked at as a whole before it is studied in detail. It is much easier to grasp the whole account by getting an *overall view* before tackling the details. The Bible says that God created the universe in six days and rested on the seventh day [see the outlines of the Scripture below, A-J]. Each of the seven days will be studied in detail after gaining the overall view. Some key words are underlined in the Scripture to show how forcefully Scripture declares that God [Elohim] stands behind the universe.)

	CHAPTER 1	
	I. CREATION OF THE HEAVENS & THE EARTH, 1:1-2:3	
	A. The Basic Questions of Creation, 1:1-2	
1. When: In the beginning 2. Who created: God 3. What: Heavens & earth 4. How was the earth created: In stages a. Without form & void b. In darkness c. Covered by water d. By the Spirit's activity	In the beginning <u>God created</u> the heaven and the earth. 2 And the earth was without form, and void; and darkness was upon the face of the deep. And the spirit of <u>God moved</u> upon the face of the waters.	
	B. The First Day: Creation of Light, 1:3-5	
1. God's Word created light 2. God saw that His creation was *good*—fulfilled its function 3. God named the light Day & the darkness He named Night	3 And <u>God said</u>, Let there be light: and there was light. 4 And <u>God saw</u> the light, that it was good: and <u>God divided</u> the light from the darkness. 5 And <u>God called</u> the light Day, and the darkness he called Night. And the even-ing and the morning were the first day.	
	C. The Second Day: Creation of the Firmament (The Atmosphere & Air Space Encircling the Earth), 1:6-8	
	6 And <u>God said</u>, Let there be a firmament in the midst of the waters, and let it divide the waters from the waters. 7 And <u>God made</u> the firmament, and <u>divided</u> the waters which were under the firmament from the waters which were above the firmament: and it was so. 8 And <u>God called</u> the firmament Heaven. And the evening and the morning were the second day.	1. God's Word created the firmament (atmosphere & air space) 2. God made the firmament 3. God named the firmament Heaven
	D. The Third Day (Part 1): Creation of the Waters (Seas, Lakes, Rivers) & of Dry Land (Continents, Islands), 1:9-10	

INTRODUCTION TO THE SEVEN DAYS OF CREATION

1. God's Word created the waters & dry land
2. God named the dry land Earth & the waters Seas
3. God saw that His creation was *good*—fulfilled its function

1. God's Word created plant life or vegetation—each *after its kind*
2. God created all vegetation upon the earth
3. God's creative act was fulfilled—the earth became fruitful
4. God saw that His creation was *good*—fulfilled its function

1. God's Word created & distributed light upon the earth
2. God made the sun, moon, & stars that provide light for the earth
   a. God & God alone made them
   b. The reasons He made them
      1) To give light
      2) To rule over the day & night
3. God saw that His creation was *good*—fulfilled its function

9 And <u>God said</u>, Let the waters under the heaven be gathered together unto one place, and let the dry land appear: and it was so.
10 And <u>God called</u> the dry land Earth; and the gathering together of the waters called he Seas: and <u>God saw</u> that it was good.

E. The Third Day (Part 2): Creation of Plant Life or Vegetation, 1:11-13

11 And <u>God said</u>, Let the earth bring forth grass, the herb yielding seed, and the fruit tree yielding fruit after his kind, whose seed is in itself, upon the earth: and it was so.
12 And the earth brought forth grass, and herb yielding seed after his kind, and the tree yielding fruit, whose seed was in itself, after his kind: and <u>God saw</u> that it was good.
13 And the evening and the morning were the third day.

F. The Fourth Day: Creation & Distribution of Light Upon Earth to Regulate Day & Night, Seasons & Years, 1:14-19

14 And <u>God said</u>, Let there be lights in the firmament of the heaven to divide the day from the night; and let them be for signs, and for seasons, and for days, and years:
15 And let them be for lights in the firmament of the heaven to give light upon the earth: and it was so.
16 And <u>God made</u> two great lights; the greater light to rule the day, and the lesser light to rule the night: he made the stars also.
17 And <u>God set</u> them in the firmament of the heaven to give light upon the earth,
18 And to rule over the day and over the night, and to divide the light from the darkness: and <u>God saw</u> that it was good.
19 And the evening and the morning were the fourth day.

G. The Fifth Day: Creation of Water & Air Animals, 1:20-23

20 And <u>God said</u>, Let the waters bring forth abundantly the moving creature that hath life, and fowl that may fly above the earth in the open firmament of heaven.
21 And <u>God created</u> great whales, and every living creature that moveth which the waters brought forth abundantly, after their kind, and every winged fowl after his kind: and <u>God saw</u> that it was good.
22 And <u>God blessed</u> them, saying, Be fruitful, and multiply, and fill the waters in the seas, and let fowl multiply in the earth.
23 And the evening and the morning were the fifth day.

H. The Sixth Day (Part 1): Creation of Land Animals, 1:24-25

24 And <u>God said</u>, Let the earth bring forth the living creature after his kind, cattle, and creeping thing, and beast of the earth after his kind: and it was so.
25 And <u>God made</u> the beast of the earth after his kind, and cattle after their kind, and every thing that creepeth upon the earth after his kind: and <u>God saw</u> that it was good.

I. The Sixth Day (Part 2): Creation of Man, Male & Female, 1:26-31

26 And <u>God said</u>, Let us make man in our image, after our likeness: and let them have dominion over the fish of the sea, and over the fowl of the air, and over the cattle, and over all the earth, and over every creeping thing that creepeth upon the earth.
27 So <u>God created</u> man in his own image, in the image of <u>God created</u> he him; male and female created he them.
28 And <u>God blessed</u> them and <u>God said</u> unto them, Be fruitful, and multiply, and replenish the earth, and subdue it: and have dominion over the fish of the sea, and over the fowl of the air, and over

1. God's Word created water creatures and air creatures
2. God created every water creature & every air creature—each *after its kind*
3. God saw that His creation was *good*—fulfilled its function
4. God blessed the water creatures and air creatures

1. God's Word created land animals
2. God made land animals, each *after its kind*
3. God saw that His creation was *good*—fulfilled its function

1. God's Word created man
   a. God held a divine counsel to create man
   b. God created man in the image of the Godhead
   c. God created man with a very special purpose: To have dominion
      1) Over all animals
      2) Over all the earth
2. God & God alone created man, both male & female, with the highest dignity & honor: In His image
3. God blessed man
4. God gave man three great assignments
   a. To be fruitful & reproduce & fill the earth
   b. To subdue the earth

c. To have dominion—to rule—over all animal life	every living thing that moveth upon the earth.	**CHAPTER 2**	
5. God provided vegetation on the earth to feed man & animals	29 And <u>God said</u>, Behold, I have given you every herb bearing seed, which is upon the face of all the earth, and every tree, in the which is the fruit of a tree yielding seed; to you it shall be for meat.	**J. The Seventh Day: Creation of the Seventh Day— A Day of Rest & Sanctification or Worship, 2:1-3**	
a. Provided vegetation for man		<u>T</u>hus the heavens and the earth were finished, and all the host of them.	1. **God completed & perfected the creation of the heavens & earth**
b. Provided vegetation for animals	30 And to every beast of the earth, and to every fowl of the air, and to every thing that creepeth upon the earth, wherein there is life, I have given every green herb for meat: and it was so.	2 And on the seventh day <u>God ended</u> his work which he had made; and he rested on the seventh day from all his work which he had made.	2. **God rested on the seventh day from all His work**
6. God saw that His creation was *good*—fulfilled its function	31 And <u>God saw</u> every thing that he had made, and, behold, it was very good. And the evening and the morning were the sixth day.	3 And <u>God blessed</u> the seventh day, and sanctified it: because that in it he had rested from all his work which <u>God created and made</u>.	3. **God blessed the seventh day & set it apart as holy**

DEEPER STUDY # 1

(1:1-2:3) **Creation**: profound, impressive, stunning—here is the true account of creation in God's Holy Scripture; here is what God reveals to man about the origin of the universe and of life upon earth. God has much to say to man in the account of creation, and man desperately needs to heed the truth of what God says. Why? There are at least four reasons.

1. Man was not present—no man—when the universe was created; only God was there. Therefore, man cannot know—not for sure, not with absolute certainty—how the universe came into being. Only God can know. If we are to know, and know for sure, where the universe and man came from, God has to tell us. Science can discover much about our origin, but it cannot know with absolute certainty how the universe and life came into being. It cannot explain how something can come *out of nothing*. For something to come *out of nothing* is impossible according to natural law, impossible according to everything that is known in the physical and material universe. But God knows, for God was there. And God tells us in the Holy Scripture that He created the world. Therefore, man must heed what God reveals or else man will miss God, and he will have to give an account for his rejection and denial of God.

The account of creation, of just what happened, must have been given to man in one of two ways.

⇒ God must have shared the account of creation with Adam. Then the account must have been passed on down from generation to generation by believers (through writing and through word of mouth).
⇒ God must have re-shared the creation account with Moses when He called Moses to meet Him on Mount Sinai. It was on Mount Sinai that God gave *The Law* to Moses which included the creation account. (Remember: *The Law* means far more than the Ten Commandments. *The Law* refers to the first five books of the Bible which includes *Genesis* and the creation account. The first five books are sometimes called the Pentateuch, which includes *Genesis, Exodus, Leviticus, Numbers,* and *Deuteronomy.*)

2. Man owes his life to God. God is the Creator of the universe, the Sovereign Lord and Majesty of the universe. Man must heed this fact and worship and serve God as Creator. If man rejects God or neglects his Creator, then it is only logical that he will have to face his Creator in judgment (Jn.3:18; Ro.1:18-23; 2 Th.1:7-9; Ps.95:5-6).

3. Man suffers from disease and accident and from all kinds of trials and temptations. Man is corruptible by nature: he ages, deteriorates, and eventually dies. If man will heed what God reveals in the creation account, then man can be cared for and looked after by God. If man acknowledges God and confesses that God is his Creator and Lord, then man can have a personal relationship with God. Man can be absolutely secure in God's love and care, in God's joy and peace (Pr.3:5-6; Is.41:10; 1 Pe.5:7).

4. God is a God of love. Despite all the evil in the world, we can look at all the love, goodness, and beauty of the universe and know a striking truth: the Supreme Creator is a God of love. And a God of love is bound *to reveal* Himself and the basic truth of the universe to man. A God of love would never leave man in the dark, ever seeking and never able to find out where he has come from, why he is here on earth, and where he is going. A God who would leave man in the dark and not reveal Himself and the basic truth about life would be a God of hate, not a God of love. This is not the God of the Holy Scriptures. The God of the Holy Scriptures is not a God of hate; He is not a God who has left man groping and grasping about in the dark seeking after the truth of life. The God of the Holy Scriptures is a God of love. He is a loving God who has revealed the truth...

• about Himself
• about man
• about the universe

God (Elohim) declares that He is the great Creator, the Sovereign LORD and Majesty of the universe. Therefore, man must heed what God reveals both about Himself and about life in the creation account.

Now, what are the truths of creation that man must heed? What are the truths of creation that God declares in the Scripture? There are at least eight truths.

1. God is; God actually exists, and the universe has come from Him (1:1–2:3).
2. God created the universe by His Word (1:1–2:3).
3. God is the Supreme Intelligence of the universe (1:1–2:3).
4. God is a God of goodness and grace and a God of order (1:1–2:3).
5. God is a God of great will and purpose, a God who plans, foreordains, and predestines (1:1–2:3).
6. God is a God of revelation, a God who reveals His nature, just what He is like and what He has done (1:1–2:3).
7. God is a God of form, fullness, completeness, fulfillment, and satisfaction (1:1–2:3).
8. God is a God of enormous power, a God who created the universe in six days (1:1–2:3).

Please note: the outline uses the word *creation* as a title throughout the creation account. We do this because it is the natural way to read the chapter. However, the word *creation* may not technically describe what happened on a particular day. For example, on the third day, the waters were separated so that dry land could appear. Water and dry land were not technically created on the third day; they were separated. Nevertheless, as stated, we use the word *creation* to describe the event because it seems more natural and fitting in describing what God did.

Glance back to the Scripture and note the underlined words and you will see just how true this is, how natural and fitting the word *creation* describes what God did in each of the six days of creation. Note in verse one that "*God created.*" Then quickly read the first three words of each day's creation, "And *God said.*" What we have is this:

"*God created* the heaven and the earth" (v.1).

⇒ "*God said*, 'Let there be light'" on the first day (v.3).
⇒ "*God said*, 'Let there be a firmament [atmosphere]'" on the second day (v.6).
⇒ "*God said*, 'Let the waters...be gathered together...and let the dry land appear'" on the third day (v.9).
⇒ "*God said*, 'Let the earth bring forth grass, the herb [plants]...and the fruit tree'" also on the third day (v.11).
⇒ "*God said*, 'Let there be lights [sun, moon, and stars]'" on the fourth day (v.14).
⇒ "*God said*, 'Let the waters bring forth [the] creature...and fowl that may fly'" on the fifth day (v.20).
⇒ "*God said*, 'Let the earth bring forth the living creature'" on the sixth day (v.24).
⇒ "*God said*, 'Let us make man in our image'" also on the sixth day (v.26).

Also please note this: if the Gap Theory is true, then the word *recreation* or *restoration* would be more fitting in describing what happened in the six days of creation. (See DEEPER STUDY # 4, *Gap Theory*—Ge.1:2 for discussion of the theory.)

DEEPER STUDY # 2
(1:1–2:3) **Creation, Overview of; Charts of—God, Creator**: the first truth seen in the creation account is a stunning truth: *God is*; *God actually exists*, and the universe has come from Him. God (Elohim) is the great Creator of the universe, the Supreme Intelligence and Power of creation. God is the Majestic Person who created the universe. This is the whole point of the creation account: to stress that God is the Sovereign Lord and Creator of the universe. The universe did not just happen...
- by chance
- by some random happening
- by something—some particle or force, some matter or energy, some element or electrical impulse, some atom, proton, neutron, electron, chemical, gas, or something else—appearing *out of nothing*. As stated earlier, for something to appear *out of nothing* is against all the laws of nature and science

The Holy Scripture declares a stunning truth: the universe was created by God, by the Supreme Intelligence and Power of all being, of all that is, has been, or ever will be.

Now glance back to the Scripture and scan the underlined words: note how God is the *subject of creation*, how the creation account focuses upon God. The Bible unmistakably declares that God is God, that He alone is the only living and true God.
⇒ God existed before the universe.
⇒ God is the Supreme Intelligence who planned and purposed the universe.
⇒ God is the Sovereign Power who created the universe.
⇒ God is the only Person who was living, and He and He alone had the power to create the universe.

Immediately, before anything else is discussed, the Bible declares that God *is*, that He exists. The Bible stresses the undeniable truth that God truly exists, and that He created the universe. The creation account mentions God time and again, a striking number of times. Quickly glance back to the Scripture and note all the underlined words, all the acts of God. Chapter One declares that...
- God created *four times* (vv.1, 21, 27a, 27b)
- God said *ten times* (vv.3, 6, 9, 11, 14, 20, 24, 26, 28, 29)
- God saw *seven times* (vv.4, 10, 12, 18, 21, 25, 31)
- God called *three times* (vv.5, 8, 10)
- God made *three times* (vv.7, 16, 25)
- God divided *two times* (vv.4, 7)
- God blessed *two times* (vv.22, 28)
- God set *one time* (v.17)
- God moved *one time* (v.2)

God is also seen witnessing the fulfillment of His will fourteen times. God saw His creative act...
- "that it was good," seven times (vv.4, 10, 12, 18, 21, 25, 31)
- that "it was so," six times (vv.7, 9, 11, 15, 24, 30)
- that "there was," one time (v.3)

The Bible declares the truth as forcefully as it can be declared: God is; God exists; God is the great Creator of the universe. God is the Omnipotent (all powerful) and Omniscient (all knowing) Authority behind all creation. God is the Sovereign Lord and Majesty of the universe.

> **"Thou, even thou, art LORD alone; thou hast made heaven, the heaven of heavens, with all their host, the earth, and all things that are therein, the seas, and all that is therein, and thou preservest them all; and the host of heaven worshippeth thee" (Ne.9:6).**
> **"But without faith it is impossible to please him: for he that cometh to God must believe that he is, and that he is a rewarder of them that diligently seek him" (He.11:6).**

DEEPER STUDY # 3
(1:1-2:3) **Creation—God, Word of—God, Nature of**: the second truth seen in the creation account is an impressive truth: God created the universe *by His Word*. Quickly glance at the Scripture, at the first verse of each creative day, and note the underlined words, *"God said"* (vv.3, 6, 9, 14, 20, 24, 26. Also vv.11, 28, 29.)

God is so powerful, so absolutely powerful, that He can create by His Word. God simply spoke and things came into being. God's Word is what God used to create. His Word was the process, the method, the manner, the means, and the way God created. There was *nothing existing*: no material, no substance, no element, no matter, no energy, no atom, no neutron, no proton, no electron, no gas, no energy. There was only God. God willed the universe, and He did as He willed. He carried out His will by simply speaking, and once He had spoken, it was done and done immediately: the universe was created. Everything was created instantaneously by the power of God's Word. There was "no variation, neither shadow of turning" from what God willed and spoke (Js.1:17). Scripture emphatically declares this phenomenal truth.

> **"By the word of the LORD were the heavens made; and all the host of them by the breath of his mouth" (Ps.33:6).**
> **"For he spake, and it was done; he commanded, and it stood fast" (Ps.33:9).**
> **"Let them praise the name of the LORD: for he commanded, and they were created" (Ps.148:5).**
> **"Through faith we understand that the worlds were framed by the word of God, so that things which are seen were not made of things which do appear" (He.11:3).**

Thought 1. Matthew Henry says:

> *O the power of the word of God! He spoke, and it was done, done really, effectually, and for perpetuity...he commanded, and it stood fast: with him it was dictum, factum—a word, and a world.*[1]

Thought 2. Note a significant point: God did not have to speak in order to create, *but He did*. God could have just thought the universe into being, but instead He spoke the universe into being. He used His Word to create. The point is unmistakable: God holds His Word in the highest regard possible, counts His Word of the utmost importance. This is also seen in five other striking facts.
1) The *Word of God* is what God uses to make man into a new creature. If a man is to be *born again*—if he is to become spiritually alive to God, a new creature, a new man before God—it has to be by the *Word of God*. A person has to hear the Word of God and heed it. He has to let God's Word recreate his spirit and make him into a new creature.

> **"Being born again, not of corruptible seed, but of incorruptible, by the word of God, which liveth and abideth for ever" (1 Pe.1:23).**
> **"Jesus answered and said unto him, Verily, verily, I say unto thee, Except a man be born again, he cannot see the kingdom of God. Nicodemus saith unto him, How can a man be born when he is old? can he enter the second time into his mother's womb, and be born? Jesus answered, Verily, verily, I say unto thee, Except a man be born of water and of the Spirit, he cannot enter into the kingdom of God. That which is born of the flesh is flesh; and that which is born of the Spirit is spirit" (Jn.3:3-6).**
> **"Therefore if any man be in Christ, he is a new creature: old things are passed away; behold, all things are become new" (2 Co.5:17).**
> **"And that ye put on the new man, which after God is created in righteousness and true holiness" (Ep.4:24).**

2) The *Word of God* is what God uses to grow and mature man spiritually.

> **"And now, brethren, I commend you to God, and to the word of his grace, which is able to build you up, and to give you an inheritance among all them which are sanctified" (Ac.20:32).**

---

1 Matthew Henry. *Matthew Henry's Commentary*, Vol.1. (Old Tappan, NJ: Fleming H. Revell, n.d.), p.4.

"Study to show thyself approved unto God, a workman that needeth not to be ashamed, rightly dividing the word of truth" (2 Ti.2:15).

"All scripture is given by inspiration of God, and is profitable for doctrine, for reproof, for correction, for instruction in righteousness" (2 Ti.3:16).

"For the word of God is quick, and powerful, and sharper than any twoedged sword, piercing even to the dividing asunder of soul and spirit, and of the joints and marrow, and is a discerner of the thoughts and intents of the heart" (He.4:12).

"As newborn babes, desire the sincere milk of the word, that ye may grow thereby: if so be ye have tasted that the Lord is gracious" (1 Pe.2:2-3).

3) The *Word of God and its proclamation* is the very way God has chosen to save people and to accomplish His will upon earth.

"It pleased God by the foolishness of preaching [the Word] to save them that believe" (1 Co.1:21).

"For I am not ashamed of the gospel of Christ: for it is the power of God unto salvation to every one that believeth; to the Jew first, and also to the Greek" (Ro.1:16).

"So then faith cometh by hearing, and hearing by the word of God" (Ro.10:17).

"For this cause also thank we God without ceasing, because, when ye received the word of God which ye heard of us, ye received it not as the word of men, but as it is in truth, the word of God, which effectually worketh also in you that believe" (1 Th.2:13).

"So shall my word be that goeth forth out of my mouth: it shall not return unto me void, but it shall accomplish that which I please, and it shall prosper in the thing whereto I sent it" (Is.55:11).

4) The *Word of God* shall endure forever, even longer than the heavens and the earth, the universe itself.

"For ever, O Lord, thy word is settled in heaven" (Ps.119:89).

"The grass withereth, the flower fadeth: but the word of our God shall stand for ever" (Is.40:8).

"For verily I say unto you, Till heaven and earth pass, one jot or one tittle shall in no wise pass from the law, till all be fulfilled" (Mt.5:18).

"Heaven and earth shall pass away, but my words shall not pass away" (Mt.24:35).

"But the word of the Lord endureth for ever" (1 Pe.1:25).

5) The *Word of God*—the whole counsel of God's Word—has been given to the world to be preached and taught.

"For I have not shunned to declare unto you all the counsel of God" (Ac.20:27).

"All scripture is given by inspiration of God, and is profitable for doctrine, for reproof, for correction, for instruction in righteousness [that is, for all of life]" (2 Ti.3:16).

"Study to show thyself approved unto God, a workman that needeth not to be ashamed, rightly dividing the word of truth" (2 Ti.2:15).

"The counsel of the LORD standeth for ever, the thoughts of his heart to all generations" (Ps.33:11).

DEEPER STUDY # 4
(1:1-2:3) **Creation—God, Intelligence of—God, Nature of**: the third truth seen in the creation account is a profound truth: God is *the Supreme Intelligence of the universe*. To speak and to create requires intelligence. A person has to be able to think in order to form words and to make things. "God said"; He spoke; and "God created," "made," "divided," and "set" the universe and the things of the universe in place. The very fact that He spoke and made things shows that He is intelligent. How intelligent is God? Note exactly what Scripture says:

"God said, 'Let there be light': and there was light" (Ge.1:3).

God is so intelligent that He can do this: God can think thoughts within His mind; He can think of light and He can think the thought through and plan for light. He can plan all the minute details that are necessary to create light and to bring light into existence.

How intelligent is God? The day by day account of creation tells us exactly how intelligent God is.
⇒ God *thought of light* and planned all the details for the creation of light.

"And God said, 'Let there be light': and there was light" (Ge.1:3).

⇒ God *thought of the firmament or atmosphere* surrounding the earth, and He planned all the details for the creation of the atmosphere.

"And God said, 'Let there be a firmament [atmosphere]'...and it was so" (Ge.1:6, 7).

⇒ God *thought of dry land*, and He planned all the details for the creation of dry land.

"And God said…'let the dry land appear': and it was so" (Ge.1:9).

⇒ God *thought of vegetation*, and He planned all the details for the creation of vegetation.

"And God said, 'Let the earth bring forth grass, the herb [plant] yielding seed, and the fruit tree'…and it was so" (Ge.1:11).

⇒ God *thought of the heavenly bodies*—the sun and the moon and the stars—and He planned all the details for the creation of the heavenly bodies.

"And God said, 'Let there be lights in the firmament of the heaven'…and it was so" (Ge.1:14, 15).

⇒ God *thought of sea and water creatures* and of birds, and He planned all the details for the creation of sea and water creatures and of birds.

"And God said, 'Let the waters bring forth abundantly the moving creature that hath life, and fowl that may fly above the earth'…and God saw that it was good" (Ge.1:20, 21).

⇒ God *thought of earth animals and of man*, and He planned all the details for the creation of earth animals and of man.

"And God said, 'Let the earth bring forth the living creature after his kind, cattle [livestock, domestic animals], and creeping thing, and [wild] beast of the earth after his kind': and it was so" (Ge.1:24).

"And God said, 'Let us make man in our image, after our likeness'…so God created man in His own image, in the image of God created He him; male and female created He them" (Ge.1:26, 27).

Now, how intelligent is God? He is the Supreme Intelligence of the universe. When "God said"—when He spoke the universe and life into existence—His Word revealed that He is the Supreme Intelligence of the universe. The universe—all the heavenly bodies and life itself—exists only because God Himself, the Supreme Intelligence of the universe, thought and planned and spoke the universe into being.

Thought 1. This means a most wonderful thing: God has supreme knowledge. Nothing escapes His attention. God knows all about us: all about our hurt, pain, suffering, loneliness, and emptiness—all the trials and temptations, all the problems and difficulties that roll in upon us and threaten to engulf us. God knows all, and He can work out the plans to deliver us. God knows—knows exactly—how to deliver us. He knows how to create better things and a better way for us to live and experience the fullness of life. God knows how to create whatever is needed to meet our needs.

"Hast thou not known? hast thou not heard, that the everlasting God, the LORD, the Creator of the ends of the earth, fainteth not, neither is weary? there is no searching of his understanding. He giveth power to the faint; and to them that have no might he increaseth strength. Even the youths shall faint and be weary, and the young men shall utterly fall; but they that wait upon the LORD shall renew their strength; they shall mount up with wings as eagles; they shall run, and not be weary; and they shall walk, and not faint" (Is.40:28-31).

"He revealeth the deep and secret things: he knoweth what is in the darkness, and the light dwelleth with him" (Da.2:22).

"Doth not he see my ways, and count all my steps?" (Jb.31:4).

"For his eyes are upon the ways of man, and he seeth all his goings" (Jb.34:21).

"He healeth the broken in heart, and bindeth up their wounds. He telleth the number of the stars; he calleth them all by their names. Great is our Lord, and of great power: his understanding is infinite" (Ps.147:3-5).

"I am come that they might have life, and that they might have it more abundantly" (Jn.10:10).

"For in him dwelleth all the fulness of the Godhead bodily. And ye are complete in him, which is the head of all principality and power" (Col.2:9-10).

"Neither is there any creature that is not manifest in his sight: but all things are naked and opened unto the eyes of him with whom we have to do. Seeing then that we have a great high priest, that is passed into the heavens, Jesus the Son of God, let us hold fast our profession. For we have not an high priest which cannot be touched with the feeling of our infirmities; but was in all points tempted like as we are, yet without sin. Let us therefore come boldly unto the throne of grace, that we may obtain mercy, and find grace to help in time of need" (He.4:13-16).

"For if our heart condemn us, God is greater than our heart, and knoweth all things" (1 Jn.3:20).

DEEPER STUDY # 5
(1:1-2:3) Creation—Days of Creation—God, Nature: the fourth truth seen in the creation account is a most wonderful truth: God is *a God of goodness and grace and a God of order*. (Also see DEEPER STUDY # 6, *Day Six*—Ge.1:1-2:3 for more

INTRODUCTION TO THE SEVEN DAYS OF CREATION

discussion.) This is seen in God's purpose for creating man and in the seven days of creation, in their sequence and order. Note these two significant facts:

1. God is a God of goodness and grace. The summit of God's creation is man. God wanted to shower His goodness and grace upon a creature who would freely choose to love and fellowship with Him. God wanted a creature who could know and experience all the wonders of God's goodness and grace, a creature upon whom God could pour all His glory and blessings. It is true that God created the universe for His own benefit; Scripture definitely teaches this. But it is also true that God created the universe for man's benefit. Scripture also teaches this. All of God's creation, the whole universe, was created for God's benefit, yes, but it was also created for man's benefit. God wants man to experience all the splendor and facets of His eternal glory throughout the whole universe (Ep.2:7).

2. God is a God of order. Before God could create man, He had to create a place for man and make provision for man. He had to create the heavens and earth and everything else that would be needed to sustain man's life. This is the reason the things created followed a natural sequence. Each day of creation was based upon what was created the day before. Each creative act was necessary before the next creative act could take place. God followed an orderly procedure in creation; He met the needs of man in an orderly fashion. Day by day He created exactly what was needed.

The point is this: God always acts in an orderly fashion, never disorderly. God is a God of order. God has inter-connected and inter-related everything in creation. Everything created on the six days of creation was essential to man's life. Man could not survive on earth if any of the creative acts had been omitted or if some catastrophe destroyed what was created on any of the days. All of creation is inter-connected and inter-related; everything is needed to sustain life upon earth. Therefore, God's creative acts, day by day, followed an orderly pattern. Each day's creation built upon what was created the day before. Creation followed a natural sequence: each day met some great need of man. The following chart will show this.

THE NATURAL SEQUENCE AND ORDER OF CREATION

Days of Creation	What Was Created	The Need Met/The Provision Made/The Primary Benefit for Man
1st Day (vv.3-5)	Light	Needed to provide light and warmth to stimulate growth
2nd Day (vv.6-8)	Atmosphere (Air) Water	Needed to provide air and water to sustain life and growth
3rd Day (vv.9-13)	Dry Land Vegetation (Plants)	Needed to provide a place to live, and to give food, variety, and beauty for life upon the earth
4th Day (vv.14-19)	Lights (Sun, Moon, & Stars)	Needed to provide the seasons and days and years for man, animals, and vegetation, and to give variety and beauty to the universe
5th Day (vv.20-23)	Water Animals Birds	Needed to *populate the waters* and sky, to help carry on the reproduction of the food chain, and to provide animal life for companionship, variety, and beauty for man
6th Day (vv.24-31)	Land animals	Needed to *populate the earth*, to help carry on the reproduction of the food chain, and to provide animal life for companionship, variety and beauty for man
	Man	Needed to populate the earth and to *freely* love, worship, serve, and fellowship with God
7th Day (Ch.2:1-3)	The Sabbath Day	Needed to provide a concentrated day of worship and fellowship between God and man and to give a day of rest from a week's labor

Thought 1. Note: man's ability to experience all of God's goodness and grace has been marred by sin and by having to live in a corruptible world. When, then, shall God's purpose for man be fulfilled?

1) God's goodness and grace are experienced to some degree now, in this life. Man experiences the goodness and grace of God by living upon the earth created by God. All the beauty and all the good things of life are gifts from God.

> **"Every good gift and every perfect gift is from above, and cometh down from the Father of lights, with whom is no variableness, neither shadow of turning" (Js.1:17).**
> **"O taste and see that the LORD is good: blessed is the man that trusteth in him" (Ps.34:8).**

2) In addition, man can now experience the goodness and grace of God through His Son, the Lord Jesus Christ. Man can now receive the forgiveness of sins and experience the fullness of life that is in Christ Jesus.

> **"In whom we have redemption through his blood, the forgiveness of sins, according to the riches of his grace" (Ep.1:7).**

"I am come that they might have life, and that they might have it more abundantly" (Jn.10:10).

"For in him dwelleth all the fulness of the Godhead bodily. And ye are complete in him, which is the head of all principality and power" (Col.2:9-10).

3) The fullness of God's goodness and grace will be fully known and experienced in the glorious day of redemption. God is going to do a marvelous thing for His Son, the Lord Jesus Christ, and for His followers, the believers of the earth. God is going to recreate the heavens and the earth and perfect them. The new heavens and earth are to become the home of the Lord Jesus Christ and His followers. Believers are to serve Christ throughout the universe, throughout the new heavens and earth, in the glorious day of redemption. It is then that believers will experience the goodness and grace of God...

- in all the splendor and brilliance of His glory
- in all the richness and fullness of His glory (See note, *Rewards*—Lu.16:10-12; DEEPER STUDY # 4—Ro.8:17; Tit.3:6; 1 Pe.1:4; Re.14:13)

"But the day of the Lord will come as a thief in the night; in the which the heavens shall pass away with a great noise, and the elements shall melt with fervent heat, the earth also and the works that are therein shall be burned up. Seeing then that all these things shall be dissolved, what manner of persons ought ye to be in all holy conversation and godliness, looking for and hasting unto the coming of the day of God, wherein the heavens being on fire shall be dissolved, and the elements shall melt with fervent heat? Nevertheless we, according to his promise, look for new heavens and a new earth, wherein dwelleth righteousness" (2 Pe.3:10-13).

"And I saw a new heaven and a new earth: for the first heaven and the first earth were passed away; and there was no more sea" (Re.21:1).

"Of old hast thou laid the foundation of the earth: and the heavens are the work of thy hands. They shall perish, but thou shalt endure: yea, all of them shall wax old like a garment; as a vesture shalt thou change them, and they shall be changed: but thou art the same, and thy years shall have no end" (Ps.102:25-27).

"And all the host of heaven shall be dissolved, and the heavens shall be rolled together as a scroll: and all their host shall fall down, as the leaf falleth off from the vine, and as a falling fig from the fig tree" (Is.34:4).

"Lift up your eyes to the heavens, and look upon the earth beneath: for the heavens shall vanish away like smoke, and the earth shall wax old like a garment, and they that dwell therein shall die in like manner: but my salvation shall be for ever, and my righteousness shall not be abolished" (Is.51:6).

"For, behold, I create new heavens and a new earth: and the former shall not be remembered, nor come into mind" (Is.65:17).

"For as the new heavens and the new earth, which I will make, shall remain before me, saith the LORD, so shall your seed and your name remain [believers]" (Is.66:22).

Thought 2. God wants man to know His goodness and grace. God wants man to experience all the splendor and facets of His glory and grace throughout all the ages. This is the very reason God saves us and gives us eternal life, the very reason He is going to create a new heavens and earth.

"But God, who is rich in mercy, for his great love wherewith he loved us, even when we were dead in sins, hath quickened us together with Christ, (by grace ye are saved;) and hath raised us up together, and made us sit together in heavenly places in Christ Jesus: [note why] that in the ages to come he might show the exceeding riches of his grace in his kindness toward us through Christ Jesus" (Ep.2:4-7).

"For the promise, that he should be the heir of the world, was not to Abraham, or to his seed, through the law, but through the righteousness of faith" (Ro.4:13).

"The Spirit itself beareth witness with our spirit, that we are the children of God: and if children, then heirs; heirs of God, and joint-heirs with Christ; if so be that we suffer with him, that we may be also glorified together" (Ro.8:16-17).

"For the earnest expectation of the creature [creation] waiteth for the manifestation of the sons of God. For the creature was made subject to vanity, not willingly, but by reason of him who hath subjected the same in hope, because the creature itself also shall be delivered from the bondage of corruption into the glorious liberty of the children of God. For we know that the whole creation groaneth and travaileth in pain together until now" (Ro.8:19-22).

"That being justified by his grace, we should be made heirs according to the hope of eternal life" (Tit.3:7).

"For unto the angels hath he not put in subjection the world to come, whereof we speak. But one in a certain place testified, saying, What is man, that thou art mindful of him? or the son of man, that thou visitest him? Thou madest him a little lower than the angels; thou crownedst him with glory and honour, and didst set him over the works of thy hands: thou hast put all things in subjection under his feet. For in that he put all in subjection under him, he left nothing that is not put under him. But now we see not yet all things put under him" (He.2:5-8).

DEEPER STUDY # 6

(1:1-2:3) **Creation—God, Nature—Foreordination—Predestination**: the fifth truth seen in the creation account is a most assuring truth: God is *a God of great will and purpose*, a God who plans, foreordains, and predestines. This, too, is seen in the six days of creation. But it is seen by reversing the six days and thinking back to God's mind and thoughts before He ever created the universe. Picture God's mind and thoughts; picture Him thinking over what He wanted. In order to get what He wanted, He had to think and plan it through; then He had to will and purpose it, ordain and predestine it. God wanted man and the universe; therefore, God thought and planned about how to create man and the universe. He thought the plan of creation through step by step. Then God willed and purposed, ordained and predestined man and the universe.

The following chart will show how creation reveals that God is a God of great will and purpose, a God who plans, foreordains, and predestines. Remember: we are looking at God before He created man and the universe; we are looking at His mind and thoughts as He thought through creation. We are looking at what God wanted and at what He knew before He ever acted and actually created.

GOD'S MIND AND THOUGHTS IN PLANNING CREATION

(Seen by Reversing the Six Days of Creation)

What God Planned and Knew Before Creation	The Reasons for the Order of Creation
God wanted and planned the creation of a creature (man) upon whom He could shower His goodness and grace, a creature who would *freely* choose to love, worship, serve, and fellowship with Him.	Man would naturally be the last thing that God would create. Why? Because man would need a number of things to sustain his life, and these would need to exist before man was created.
God knew that man would need other creatures that would immediately surround him, creatures that could help carry on the reproduction of the food chain and provide companionship, variety, and beauty for him *upon the earth*.	Land animals would naturally be the thing created right before man. Why? Because they are the closest creatures surrounding man, the creatures more closely akin to man, the creatures which share the earth with man.
God knew that man would also need other creatures to fill the air and the waters, creatures that could also help carry on the food chain and provide companionship, variety, and beauty for man.	Water animals and air animals [birds, winged fowl] are a little farther removed from man, so they would logically be created right before the land animals.
God knew that both man and animal would need lights upon earth (sun, moon, and stars) to govern their lives and their seasons, their days and their years, and to give variety and beauty to the universe.	Light *upon earth* would be needed right before the animals and man were created. Why? So that they could see to move about, and so that the life of all things upon earth could be regulated. If man and animals were in total darkness upon earth, and if there were no days or seasons to regulate growth and life upon earth, neither man nor animals could exist.
God knew that both man and animal would need a place to live and the necessary food to sustain life.	A place to live and food to eat were needed before the heavenly bodies were visible upon earth. Why? Because without dry land and vegetation there would be no reason for regulating seasons or days or years.
God knew that both man and animal would need air to breathe and water to drink.	The atmosphere (air to breathe) and water to drink were bound to be created before the dry land and vegetation. Why? Because vegetation and all life upon earth are dependent upon air to breathe and water for survival.
God knew that both man and animal would need light to provide warmth and to stimulate the growth of all things.	Light has to precede everything—light has to be the first thing created—for light is absolutely essential for the warmth and growth of life.

Now, how was God going to get what He wanted—man and the universe? And how was He going to make sure that things were created in the right order and sequence? God knew that each thing was dependent upon other things being created. God knew that creation would be a chaotic mess and things could not exist unless He created things in an orderly manner and in sequence. God knew that sequence and order were an absolute necessity if man and the universe were to survive. How, then, was God going to make sure that things were created in the right order and sequence? There was only one way. God had...

- to will and purpose creation
- to plan and think through creation
- to foreordain and predestine creation

How do we know this? By the order and sequence of creation. The six days of creation, the order and sequence of what God created on each of the days, show us. Creation reveals that God is a God of great will and purpose, a God who plans and thinks through, foreordains and predestines what He *wants* and *wills*.

Thought 1. As stated above, God wanted and planned the creation of man upon whom He could shower His grace and goodness, a creature who would *freely choose* to love, worship, serve, and fellowship with God.

1) This is the reason God saves us, chooses us, and predestines us in Christ.

> "According as he hath chosen us in him before the foundation of the world, that we should be holy and without blame before him in love; having predestinated us unto the adoption of children by Jesus Christ to himself, according to the good pleasure of his will, to the praise of the glory of his grace, wherein he hath made us accepted in the beloved" (Ep.1:4-6).
>
> "Ye have not chosen me, but I have chosen you, and ordained you, that ye should go and bring forth fruit, and that your fruit should remain: that whatsoever ye shall ask of the Father in my name, he may give it you" (Jn.15:16).

2) This is the reason God demands that we love Him with all our hearts.

> "Jesus said unto him, Thou shalt love the Lord thy God with all thy heart, and with all thy soul, and with all thy mind. This is the first and great commandment" (Mt.22:37-38).

3) This is the reason God works all things out for the good of those who love Him and are called according to His purpose.

> "And we know that all things work together for good to them that love God, to them who are the called according to his purpose. For whom he did foreknow, he also did predestinate to be conformed to the image of his Son, [note why] that he might be the firstborn among many brethren. Moreover whom he did predestinate, them he also called: and whom he called, them he also justified: and whom he justified, them he also glorified" (Ro.8:28-30).

Thought 2. This is a most wonderful truth. God has a purpose and a plan for every human life. All human life is precious to God. But there is a problem: most persons do not surrender their lives to God and His purpose. The will and purpose of God cannot be worked out in their lives. The result is tragic: most persons miss the purpose and plan of God for their lives, and they die without ever having fulfilled their purpose for being on earth.

If we will surrender our lives to God, then God can work out His purpose and plan in our lives. We can know the salvation of God in Christ and the fullness of life that God has purposed and planned for us.

> "'For I know the plans that I have for you,' declares the LORD, 'plans for welfare and not for calamity to give you a future and a hope' " (Je.29:11, NAS).
>
> "I know the plans I have in mind for you—it is Yahweh who speaks—plans for peace, not disaster, reserving a future full of hope for you" (Je.29:11, J.B.)
>
> "But seek ye first the kingdom of God, and his righteousness; and all these things shall be added unto you" (Mt.6:33).
>
> "According as he hath chosen us in him before the foundation of the world, that we should be holy and without blame before him in love; having predestinated us unto the adoption of children by Jesus Christ to himself, according to the good pleasure of his will" (Ep.1:4-5).
>
> "But ye are a chosen generation, a royal priesthood, an holy nation, a peculiar people; that ye should show forth the praises of him who hath called you out of darkness into his marvellous light: which in time past were not a people, but are now the people of God: which had not obtained mercy, but now have obtained mercy" (1 Pe.2:9-10).

DEEPER STUDY # 7

(1:1-2:3) **Creation—God, Nature—Man, Purpose of**: the sixth truth seen in the creation account is a glorious truth: God is *a God of revelation*, a God who reveals His nature, just what He is like and what He has done. This, of course, is seen in some of the above notes. But it is especially seen in the six days of creation and in what other Scriptures say about God and His six creative acts. When we look closely at the six days of creation, they seem to teach some great truths about God. The following chart will show this. The chart may also help in understanding and applying the creation account to our hearts and ministries. Perhaps it will help us in our understanding of God, of His glorious nature and of His great purposes for man. He created us, and He had some of the greatest purposes imaginable for putting us here upon earth. (Note: much more thought needs to be put into this subject, the subject of: "What Scripture Stresses and Teaches About God in His Creative Acts." Perhaps the following study will stir some believer(s) to dig much deeper than a pressing schedule has presently allowed.)

INTRODUCTION TO THE SEVEN DAYS OF CREATION

WHAT SCRIPTURE STRESSES AND TEACHES ABOUT GOD IN HIS CREATIVE ACTS			
Day	**What Was Created**	**Primary Provision and Benefit**	**What Scripture Stresses and Teaches About God**
1st Day	Light	Provides light and warmth to stimulate growth	God's nature: is light (1 Ti.6:16; Js.1:17; 1 Jn.1:5; Mic.7:8)
2nd Day	Heavens: the Firmament or Atmosphere (Air) Water	Provides air and water to sustain life	God's being: ⇒ is infinite, clearly seen in the height of the heavens (Jb.22:12) ⇒ is glorious, declared glorious by the heavens (Ps.19:1) ⇒ is great, declared by the creation of the heavens and the waters (Ps.104:1-3; Is.48:13)
3rd Day	Dry land (the fertile earth) Vegetation	Provides a place to live and food and beauty for life	1) God's right: is sovereign over all—the Sovereign Owner of all land (the earth) and all that is upon the land (Ps.24:1; 50:12; 89:11; 1 Co.10:26) 2) God's creative design: is intelligent and good (Ps.33:4-5; 104:5-9; Ec.1:4-7)
4th Day	Lights (sun, moon and stars)	Provides seasons and days and years	1) God's glory: ⇒ is full of splendor and brilliance, grace and glory (Ps.84:11; 97:6) ⇒ shines within and upon believers now, while upon the earth (2 Co.4:6; see 1 Pe.2:9; Re.22:5; Ps.18:28) ⇒ shall shine in and upon believers in heaven throughout all of eternity (Re.22:5; Is.60:19-20) 2) God's Word and its power (Ps.33:6; 62:11; He.11:3)
5th Day	Water animals Birds	Provides animals to populate the water and air, to help carry on the reproduction of the food chain, and to give kinship, variety, and beauty	God's power: is strong enough to create life (Jb.12:7-10; Ac.4:24; 14:15)
6th Day	Land animals Man	Provides animals to populate the earth, to help carry on the reproduction of the food chain, and to give kinship, variety, and beauty Provides the free moral creature desired by God: ⇒ the creature who can freely choose to love, worship, serve, and fellowship with God ⇒ the creature upon whom God can pour out His goodness and grace throughout all eternity	1) God's power: is all-embracing and sufficient to create all things, including all animals and man (Ge.2:18-22; Jb.33:4; Is.45:12; Ac.17:24-26) 2) God's purpose for man: ⇒ to love God (De.6:5; 10:12; Mt.22:37-38; Jude 21) ⇒ to worship God (Ne.9:6; Ps.5:7; 95:6; 96:9; Mt.4:10; Jn.4:24; Re.14:7; 15:4) ⇒ to fellowship with God (Ps.73:28; 145:18; Is.43:10-13; Mt.18:20; Ac.17:24-28; Js.4:8; 1 Jn.1:3; Re.3:20) ⇒ to serve God (Ge.1:24-30; 2:15-17; Ex.23:25; Ps.2:11; 8:6-8; 40:8; 100:2-3; He.12:28) ⇒ to know and experience the goodness and grace of God throughout all eternity (Ps.84:11; Ro.8:16-17; Ep.1:3-14, esp. 4-6, 9; 2:7, see v.4-10; 3:11-12; Tit.3:7; He.2:6-8)

DEEPER STUDY # 8

(1:1–2:3) **Creation—God, Creator**: the seventh truth seen in the creation account is that God is a *God of form*, fullness, completeness, fulfillment, and satisfaction.
⇒ God forms that which is formless
⇒ God fills that which is unfilled and empty
⇒ God completes that which is incomplete and unfinished
⇒ God fulfills that which is unfulfilled and lacking
⇒ God satisfies that which is unsatisfied and displeasing

This, too, is seen in the six days of creation. Glance at verse two which says that "the earth was without form, and void" (Ge.1:2). That is, the earth was…
• "without form": formless, unshaped, undeveloped, unfinished
• "void": empty, barren, and desolate

But note what God did in the six days of creation. He moved from the "formless and empty" to form and fill up the universe. In fact, a close study of the six days reveals that…
• God "*forms*" the universe on the first three days
• God "*fills up*" or gives "*fulness*" to the universe on the last three days

This is clearly seen in the following chart.

FORMING THE UNIVERSE		FILLING UP OR GIVING FULNESS TO THE UNIVERSE	
1st Day	Light (v.3)	4th Day	Lights (sun, moon, and stars) (v.14)
2nd Day	Water (v.7)	5th Day	Water creatures and birds (vv.20-21)
	Firmament or atmosphere (air)		
3rd day	Dry land (vv.9-10)	6th Day	Land creatures (land animals and man)
	Vegetation (vv.11-12)		

Note that this particular outline shows God *forming* the universe then *filling* it. God is seen *completing* the creation He had earlier begun. He *fulfills and satisfies* His plan and purpose for creation. The six days of creation reveal God to be a God of form, fullness, completeness, fulfillment, and satisfaction.

(Perhaps this chart will help in grasping the overall view of the six days of creation. Many commentators follow this outline of creation, such as Griffith Thomas in his commentary on *Genesis*; Derek Kidner in *The Tyndale Old Testament Commentaries*; the *NIV Study Bible*; and the great *Pulpit Commentary*.)

DEEPER STUDY # 9

(1:1–2:3) **Evolution—Creation, Days of—Geologic Ages—Fossils—Earth, Age of—Flood, The Great**: the eighth truth seen in the creation account is an astounding truth: God is a God of enormous power, a God who created the universe in six days. The word *day* (yom) is used in Scripture to refer both to a literal day of twenty four hours and to a longer period of time. An example of this is "the day of the Lord" which includes a host of events that are to occur over a long period of time (see Is.4:2; Zec.14:6-7; 1 Th.5:2). Even the six days of creation are referred to as the *day of creation*.

> **"These are the generations of the heavens and of the earth when they were created, in the day that the LORD God made the earth and the heavens" (Ge.2:4).**

How, then, are we to understand the word *day* in the creation account? Did God actually create the world in six twenty-four hour days? Or does each day stand for and represent ages—long, long periods of time—what science calls *geological ages*? There are essentially three positions that need to be considered.

I. THE POSITION OF SIX DAY CREATIONISM

The persons who hold to this position say that creation actually took place in six twenty-four hour days: the Bible uses the word "day" because it meant *day*.

A. There are at least eight significant arguments spelled out by those who hold to this position.

1. The word *day*, when it refers to a specific number like first or second, always means a 24 hour day (Ge.1:5, 8, 13, 19, 23, 31).

2. Only days have mornings and evenings, not geological ages (Ge.1:5, etc.). To say that "morning and evening" is figurative language picturing long ages of time is stretching the rules of grammar.

"Evening" nowhere in the Scripture bears this meaning...neither does "morning"...[and] "day" never means "period."[2]

3. God actually named the light "day" and the darkness "night," and then He actually ended the day with darkness and the night with light (vv.5, 17-18). It is most unlikely—possible, but most unlikely—that God would call each creative period a day with light and darkness dividing it.

4. Note that God created plant life on the third day (vv.11-13). This plant life could not have survived without sunlight which was not visible upon earth until the fourth day (vv.14-19). To say that the *days of creation* are ages is to say that plant life existed for thousands, perhaps millions, of years without the light of the sun, moon, and stars, and without the regulation of the seasons which they control.

5. Genesis 1:14 definitely says that God divided days, seasons, and years. This division is bound to mean twenty-four hour days and not geological ages.

6. Other Scriptures definitely say that God made the earth in six literal days and that the Sabbath day is for rest (Ex.20:8-11; 31:14-17).

7. Note that God rested on the seventh day (Ge.2:1-2). If the seventh day is a geological age, then God would still be resting, for the sixth day stopped all activity for God. To some minds, saying that God is still resting would mean that God is far removed from the earth and is not active in the affairs of the world.

8. Note that God created the universe in six days and rested on the Sabbath day, and then He blessed and sanctified the Sabbath day. This means that He set aside the day for man to rest and worship. The only analogy that makes sense for man working six days and resting one day is to take the days as literal days. To say that the days are ages makes no sense as an analogy.

B. Now, note: if the twenty-four hour day position is correct, *what about the geological and fossil evidence that points to the earth being millions, perhaps billions, of years old*? For example, geology says that it takes millions of years for the rock formations within the earth's core to form, and that it takes ages for coal, oil, diamonds, uranium, gold, and the other minerals and ores to form. And some fossils—the skeletons and imprints of plant life and animals upon rock formations—lie hundreds of feet within the earth's crust. Science tells us that it would take millions of years for erosion to bury the fossil remains that deeply and then millions more, in some cases, for rivers to cut a furrow or river bed back down through the earth to expose the fossil remains. The theory of evolution is based primarily upon the evidence of fossil remains.

What about this? Is the earth millions or billions of years old? Were plants and animals upon earth millions or billions of years before man? The geological formations, mineral deposits, and fossil remains and imprints seem to indicate so. If scientists are correct, then creation could not have taken place within six twenty-four hour days. The days of creation would have to refer to geological days or ages. But, as asked, what about the scientific evidence? Is it accurate or is science missing something in its investigation and research of the earth's geology and of the origin of things? There are at lease five answers given by the six day creationists to the scientific evidence.

1. The six day creationists say that God created by *Fiat Creation* or *Immediate Creation*. The rock formations and mineral deposits (such as coal, oil, gold, diamonds, and uranium) were formed immediately when God created the earth's crust. Simply stated, the earth's crust was created as a solid mass, in a fully formed and completed state. The rock formations and mineral deposits were put in place from the first, from the very moment of creation.

⇒ But what about the light that reaches the earth from distant stars and suns? Light travels 186,000 miles per second; thus, we know that the light now reaching earth from some of the distant stars has been traveling for millions and billions of years. This, again, would point toward the days of creation being geological ages. But, the six day creationists say that the answer is *Fiat Creation* or *Immediate Creation*. When God created the universe, He created a varied and beautiful universe for both Himself and man, for both of their pleasure and enjoyment. Different stars and suns were in varying stages of development: some were completed; others were in various stages of gaseous, solid, and fiery development even as some are today.

⇒ But what about the fossil remains and imprints within the earth's crust? They seemingly point to plant and animal life being upon earth millions of years before man. Where did the fossil strata of the earth come from? This question is answered in the next point (pt.2).

2. The six day creationists say that *The Great Flood* was a universal flood with catastrophic effects upon the earth's crust. Are they correct? Unquestionably, any universal flood would have catastrophic and devastating effects upon the earth's crust. Note what Ge.7:11 says about *The Great Flood*:

"In the six hundredth year of Noah's life, in the second month, the seventeenth day of the month, the same day were all the fountains of the great deep broken up, and the windows of heaven were opened" (Ge.7:11).

When the reader studies the flood passage in *The Preacher's Outline & Sermon Bible*, he will read the following description of *The Great Flood*:

First, God's power violently broke up the earth's crust and burst loose all the earth's subterranean waters. Earthquakes must have taken place all over the earth. Note exactly what Scripture says...
• All the fountains of the great deep [were] broken up" (v.11).

The idea is that all the waters underneath the earth's crust—all the caverns, springs, rivers, lakes, and perhaps seas of water—were *violently broken up*. The crust of the earth cracked under the violence of quake after

---

2 H.C. Leupold. *Genesis*, Vol.1. (Grand Rapids, MI: Baker Book House, 1942), p.56.

quake and the waters burst loose and shot forth from under the crust of the earth. The picture is this: the subterranean water from beneath the earth and the water from the great oceans were violently discharged by quake after quake and hurled from their beds, churning and surging forth in huge, gigantic tidal waves.

Second, God's power opened up the floodgates of heaven: a violent, torrential downpour fell from the sky. Heavy rains—torrential downpours never witnessed before nor since—fell upon the earth. The torrential downpours continued, without any break whatsoever, for forty days and forty nights.

Note this: the torrential rain apparently stopped after forty days, but the waters flooded the earth for 150 days (Ge.8:2-3). This is significant, in particular when considering the core and the surface of the earth. The breaking up of the earth's crust and the violent quaking of the earth's surface, and the churning and surging of the waters continued for 150 days, even over the highest mountain peaks. It would continue for almost a year over the rest of the earth. This kind of violent quaking, movement, and erosion of the earth's core and land masses would drastically affect the shape and geological formations of the earth. The surface and inner core of the earth was apparently so changed that it was like a new earth. Nothing, absolutely nothing—no mountain, no valley, no body of water, no island, no continent, no land mass—could possibly be the same after so violent a quaking and flooding of the earth.

⇒ Just imagine the force required to break up all the subterranean waters around the world, the enormous quaking of the earth's core required to burst loose and shoot forth all the underground water under the earth's crust.

⇒ Just imagine the change over the earth's surface as the torrential rain fell for forty days and nights without stopping: all the erosion and washing away of mountains, all the valleys that filled up with the sediment from higher ground.

Just imagine the change within the earth's core and over the earth's surface as the force of the subterranean waters burst forth and as the force of the torrential rains flooded the earth. Imagine how drastic a change must have taken place...

• as mountains and hills eroded and literally washed away from the onslaught of the rushing water
• as valleys and crevices were filled up with the soil and debris from the higher elevations
• as quakes shifted and shot up mounds of dirt and hills and, most likely, even mountains

Again, nothing could ever be the same, not after such a violent quaking and forceful burst of water shot forth both from beneath the earth and from above the earth. Most if not all of the earth—both the core and the surface, both the rock formations and mineral deposits—was changed forever. As stated, two sources of water had changed it:

⇒ All the subterranean water had been broken up and shot forth by quake after quake—broken up by the power of God Himself.

⇒ Torrential downpours had fallen upon the earth—the very floodgates of the sky had been opened by God Himself.

"Behold, he withholdeth the waters, and they dry up: also he sendeth them out, and they overturn the earth" (Jb.12:15).

Thought 1. Think of the shifting and changing of the earth's core and surface that must have taken place under the violence of the surging and raging of the flood. The appearance—the geological change—of the earth must have been so drastically changed that the earth was totally different from what it had been, just like a brand new earth, both within its core and without on its surface.

But that was not all: verse twenty-four tells us that the waters flooded the earth for 150 days. The waters—the worldwide oceans—actually rose and surged and raged to their highest peak for 150 days. (Note: the aftershocks of such massive earthquakes that were necessary to burst loose the subterranean waters would continue on for days and weeks. This probably means that the core of the earth was also undergoing eruptions for 150 days. The impact of this violence upon the earth—upon the geological and fossil formations—would be tremendous.)

Any person who has ever worked around the pressure and force of water knows that it drastically changes its environment. The pressure and force of the great flood, the worldwide torrential rain and bursting loose of the earth's crust and shooting forth of all the subterranean waters—the awesome judgment of God—was bound to drastically change the earth forever thereafter, both its core and surface. This was the awesome judgment of God upon the earth in Noah's day. (See note—Ge.7:24 for more discussion.)

The point is this: the great flood has to be a factor when scientists are researching the origin of the earth. Just think! The smaller and weaker animals and plants would die and be uprooted first in a great flood or mad rush of water. They would thereby be the first buried under the eroding soil. The small and weaker would lie in the lower or deeper strata of the earth. This is the reason, when science studies the geological formations, they find the smaller and weaker—the less developed and simpler forms of life—in the lower strata of the earth. This is one of the reasons evolutionists think there has been a development of life from the simpler to the more complex. But the six day creationists would say this: the geological formations and fossil imprints within the earth's crust are actually due to the titanic upheaval and rearrangement of the earth's crust caused by *The Great Flood*. (See notes—Ge.7:10-12; 7:24 for more discussion.)

H.C. Leupold says this:

"Note should be taken of the tremendous geological possibilities that lie behind the breaking open of the fountains of the great deep. The vastness of these eruptions must be in proportion to the actual depth of the Flood....The Flood was of astounding power and magnitude....Such eruptions from subterranean sources must

have caused a rush of waters upon the earth comparable to the highest tidal wave. Such waves in turn must have been capable of producing effects of almost incalculable magnitude. So, then, the effects caused by the waters of the great deep (1:2), as they surged about on the earth in process of formation, together with the effects brought about by this great Flood, seem to us an entirely adequate explanation for geological formations of every kind, as they are now to be observed."[3]

John Whitcomb, a scholar in the Old Testament, and Henry Morris, an outstanding 20th century scientist, are two of the major exponents of the six day creationists' position. They say this:

> *Although there may be considerable latitude of opinion about details, the Biblical record does provide a basic outline of earth history, within which all the scientific data ought to be interpreted.*
> ⇒ *It describes an initial Creation, accomplished by processes which no longer are in operation and which, therefore, cannot possibly be understood in terms of present physical or biological mechanisms.*
> ⇒ *It describes the entrance into this initial Creation of the supervening God on the 'whole creation,' resulting from the sin and rebellion of man...against his Creator.*
>
> *[It is] the record of the great Flood [which] plainly asserts that it was so universal and cataclysmic in its cause, scope and results that it also marked a profound hiatus [break] in terrestrial history. Thus the Creation, the Fall [of Adam into sin], and the Flood constitute the truly basic facts, to which all the other details of early historical data must be referred.*
> *Thus, it seems most reasonable to attribute the formations of the crystalline basement rocks, and perhaps some of the Pre-Cambrian non-fossiliferous sedimentaries, to the Creation period, though later substantially modified by the tectonic upheavals of the Deluge period. The fossil-bearing strata were apparently laid down in large measure during the Flood, with the apparent sequences attributed not to evolution but rather to hydrodynamic selectivity, ecologic habitats, and differential mobility and strength of the various creatures.*[4]

3. The six day creationists say this about the fossil records and evolution: the fossil records are weak when it comes to proving evolution. (Also see point III "The Position of Science and the Bible.") Note what several scholars who are familiar with the latest research have to say:

James Montgomery Boice says this about the six day creationists:

> *Creationists believe that their views are reinforced by additional considerations:*
> *Present-day conditions are forming very few potential fossil deposits, and most of these are unusual. Nothing comparable to the known fossil beds of ancient times is being formed today, which makes us think that some past catastrophe was necessary to produce them.*
> *The facts of geology do not support the view of essentially harmonious strata with the older levels on the bottom and the most recent on the top. There is a tendency in this direction, but the facts reflect a far more unruly situation. A universal flood accounts for these facts more adequately than the theory of lengthy geological ages and slow evolutionary development.*
> *The existence of huge fossil deposits containing thousands of large complex species, such as the mammoth deposits in Siberia, are best explained either by the Flood or by the abnormal weather conditions that must have followed it.*[5]

As John Whitcomb and Henry Morris say above:

> *The fossil-bearing strata were apparently laid down in large measure during the Flood, with the apparent sequences attributed not to evolution but rather to hydrodynamic selectivity, ecologic habitats, and differential mobility and strength of the various creatures.*[6]

M.R. DeHaan says this about evolution and the change within the species of plants and animals:

> *There is, of course, evolution and change within the various species of plants and animals, but never a crossing over from one into the other—never a gradual process by which a plant became a fish or a fowl. This is the error which modern man makes. He recognizes the fact that the effect of climate, food, environment, and natural enemies have caused great changes in plants and animals, resulting in diversities so great that they have lost much of their resemblance to one another, but one species never evolves into another.*
> *Just an example: There are many different kinds of oak trees in the world—all the offspring of a single acorn—a single seed. Through generations of change they have evolved or degenerated into various kinds or varieties. Depending on soil and minerals, rainfall, heat, and climate, they have by inherent, divinely created natural powers adapted themselves to these varying environments so that some acorns are huge in size, and in other areas small. Some are light brown, others dark; thick-shelled and thin-shelled; sweet or bitter. Almost limitless are the changes which may occur due to different conditions. But they are all oak trees bearing only acorns. Think of the varieties of apples produced by cultivation, careful selective pollination and crossing, but man still has not been able to grow an orange on an apple tree. All these changes and adaptations occur only within the*

---

3 H.C. Leupold. *Genesis*, Vol.1, p.296.
4 John Whitcomb. *The Genesis Flood*. (Phillipsburg, NJ: Presbyterian and Reformed Publishing Co., 1961), p.327.
5 James Montgomery Boice. *Genesis*, Vol.1. (Grand Rapids, MI: Zondervan Publishing House, 1982), p.59.
6 John Whitcomb. *The Genesis Flood*, p.327.

limits of the species. And this the Word of God asserts in Genesis 1, that He made the fruit tree yielding its fruit after its kind (species), the birds after their kind, and the various animals after their kind. And the missing link between the species has never been found, for it does not exist.[7]

There is much which goes under the name of evolution which is not evolution, but should be called development or improvement instead. The Bible statement, "Let it bring forth after its kind," does not preclude the development of a wide range of varieties within that particular species or kind. Unfortunately a great deal of misunderstanding has resulted from use of the term 'evolution' to denote mere improvement of a species or the development of new varieties of the same species. There are many varieties of the same species; for instance, there are different kinds of apples, or different kinds of pickles. We have within the canine or dog species many varieties: foxes, wolves, and dingoes, from the diminutive Mexican Chihuahua to the massive St. Bernard, or Great Dane, but they are all dogs. So there are many varieties of cats within the feline kind, such as the different breeds of domestic cats: Siamese, Angora, and Maltese, not to mention other members of the family such as lions, leopards, tigers, wild cats, etc. But all are still cats. All the varieties of apples came from one original kind of apple, but by culture and scientific pollination and grafting were developed into greatly improved different varieties. But this is not evolution; this is merely improvement, development, and cultivation.

Evolution teaches the change or transmutation by means of a slow process of one species into another, from a lower to a higher, resulting in an entirely new kind, such as a fish into a mammal, or a goat into a cow, or a hippopotamus into a horse, or a monkey into a man. This is quite a different thing than cultivating new varieties of the same species. Not one single proven example of an evolution from one species to another has ever been found. The missing link is a link which is entirely in the realm of supposition without one single speck of tangible proof. We therefore do not reject an 'evolution' which refers to a development or improvement within the species, but we do reject an evolution which assumes a transgression of the basic, inviolable law of God, "Let it bring forth after its kind."

Today science must abide by that law, "like produces like"; or "everything after its kind." Not one example of evolution of a lower order of beings into a higher has yet been found. The whole theory is built upon speculative and dubious findings of parts of organisms in a state of decay and only remotely related to each other. Science today itself defines a species as a group capable of reproducing offspring of any two parents. This fertility determines and proves that the parents were of the same species. Members of two different species usually cannot interbreed, but even in the rare cases where two very closely related species can reproduce, the resulting offspring is sterile and the evolutionist theory is stopped at its outset. As an example we have the mule, which is the offspring of a jackass and a mare, but is completely sterile and cannot reproduce, thus making impossible the emergence of a new species. Since members of different species (kinds in Bible language) do not interbreed, there can be no evolution. Without a change or production of a new species, there can be no evolution; therefore, the theory of evolution is not only unscriptural but it is utterly unscientific, unproven and contrary to all scientific facts and logic.[8]

4. The six day creationists also say that evolution is disproven by the first two laws of thermodynamics. And there is no question about this argument: those who hold to the theory of evolution have to deal with the first two laws of thermodynamics. Whitcomb and Morris say that "These two laws provide the very foundation upon which the great superstructure of modern science and technology has been erected"[9]

⇒ The first law deals with the conservation of energy. Simply stated, energy changes, but it is never lost. Energy is neither being created nor lost within our present universe. It changes form, but the total amount of energy within the universe remains constant.

⇒ The second law says that energy does, however, decrease in its useful work. This law is called *entropy*.

What these two laws mean is this: the energy of everything is running down, changing form, and becoming more and more useless and disorderly. The energy never ceases to exist, but it always changes form and the change is always in a decreasing direction, a form that is less than its original form. Simply stated, the universe itself and all things within the universe are running down, wearing out, and becoming more and more useless and disorderly.

Note how these two basic laws of modern science stand opposed to the theory of evolution. Evolution says that the progress of energy and life—of all creatures and things—is…

- upward
- forward
- always increasing
- developing
- gaining more and more energy, order, usefulness, and development

Whitcomb and Morris go on to say this about chromosome and gene mutations:

The plain facts of the situation, therefore, are that evolution has been simply assumed as the universal principle of change in nature, despite the fact that there is no experimental evidence supporting it and despite the still more amazing fact that universal experience and experimentation have demonstrated this universal principle of change to be its very opposite: namely, that of deterioration! Truly, this is one of the most astounding paradoxes to be found in all the history of scientism!

7   M.R. DeHaan. *Genesis and Evolution.* (Grand Rapids, MI: Zondervan Publishing House, 1962), p.22.
8   Ibid., pp.69-71.
9   John Whitcomb. *The Genesis Flood*, p.222.

The two scholars make this conclusion about evolution:

And the whole difficulty arises from man's refusal to accept God's emphatic statement that the creation of the world and of its living creatures was accomplished by processes no longer in operation. A real understanding of origins requires, as we have repeatedly emphasized, divine revelation. God in grace has provided this revelation, but men have refused to believe it, in effect making God a liar. No wonder they ultimately arrive at contradictions and irreconcilables in their reasonings!"[10]

Evolution is the great "escape mechanism" of modern man. This is the pervasive philosophic principle by which man either consciously or sub-consciously seeks intellectual justification for escape from personal responsibility to his Creator and escape from the 'way of the Cross' as the necessary and sufficient means of his personal redemption.[11]

5. There is the answer given by many of those who hold to the Gap or Recreation Theory. Some persons who hold to the Gap Theory are also six day creationists, but they use different arguments for their position (see DEEPER STUDY # 4, *Gap Theory*—Ge.1:2 for discussion).

II. THE POSITION OF THE SIX DAYS BEING LONGER PERIODS OF TIME OR GEOLOGICAL AGES

Those who hold to this position say that God took age after age to create the universe, that the days of creation refer to geological ages. This position is an attempt to reconcile the theories of science with the Biblical revelation.

A. There are at least four major arguments for holding this position.
1. Scripture uses the word *day* (yom) as an indefinite period of time (see Is.4:2; Zec.14:6-7; 1 Th.5:2). Even the creation account itself speaks of *the six days of creation* as being one day.

> **"These are the generations of the heavens and of the earth when they were created, in the day that the LORD God made the earth and the heavens" (Ge.2:4).**

2. The Hebrew does not use the definite article when referring to "the first day," "the second," and so on (vv.3, 8, 13, 19, 23, 31). It simply says "first day" and "second day." This is more indefinite language, leaving the door open for a longer period of time for each of the creative acts.
3. The science of astronomy seems to refute a six day creation period. Light travels 186,000 miles per second. This means that the light which we see at night from distant stars has been traveling toward the earth for millions and billions of years.
In addition, astronomers tell us that all the bodies in outer space and the earth itself are flying through space, moving further and further apart from one another. If they are moving away from one another, this must mean that they were once much closer together and most likely were comprising one huge mass of energy. This is the basis for the popular "Big Bang Theory" on the origin of the universe that we often hear about. From all indications, astronomers tell us, there was a huge mass or some form of energy that exploded and gave rise to the universe and sent the various bodies flying apart throughout space. This would mean the universe is billions of years old. We would know this because of the distance the suns and stars are from one another today and the speed at which they are traveling away from one another.
4. The science of geology seems to refute six day creationism. The rock formations and fossil remains within the earth's crust indicate that both plant life and animals have been on earth for millions of years, much longer than man. To say what six day creationists say, that the earth—plant life and animals—were only about 24-72 hours older than man, seems impossible.
In addition, geologists tell us that the simpler forms of life lie in the lowest and deepest strata of the earth, that there is a progression from the simpler to the more complex development of life as one moves up in the earth's crust. For example, the order of the fossil remains seems to be...
- first, algae, protozoa, and sponges
- second, fish, reptiles, and amphibians
- third, land animals of ancient times such as dinosaurs
- fourth, land animals of today
- fifth, man[12]

Now, note the progression from the simplest life form to the most complex. This is one of the main arguments of evolution. But for now the point is this: if the fossil remains are accurate, it would take millions and billions of years for life to develop from the simplest form to the most complex form, for man to evolve from the simplest form of life that appeared on earth. Consequently, the six *days* of creation must refer to six geological ages.

B. There are at least three groups who hold to the theory of geological ages.
1. The theistic evolutionists: these persons believe in God, but they also accept the theory of evolution to varying degrees. They say that God *was behind* all creation, but they also accept the theories of evolution except where evolution may conflict with clear Biblical teaching. To them, Scripture does not say when nor how God created, only that He did

---

10 John Whitcomb. *The Genesis Flood,* p.227.
11 Ibid., p.328.
12 James Montgomery Boice. *Genesis,* Vol.1, p.39. Boice has an excellent discussion on the theories of creation, pp.37-68.

create the universe. Therefore, science can help us tremendously in our understanding of the universe and life, how both began and developed throughout the ages.

2. The progressive creationists: three facts will give a picture of who the progressive creationists are.

⇒ They believe in science and the great help it can be in understanding the universe and life. Therefore, they make a deliberate effort to reconcile Scripture with science.

⇒ They believe that God created the world and created it in an orderly fashion, but that He did it throughout the geological ages, as science suggests. To them, Scripture actually says nothing about when God created nor how He created. Consequently, the latest theories of science could be correct, including the "Big Bang" theory of creation and the development of higher and more complex life from lower and simpler forms.

⇒ However, the geological ages overlap and creation is still happening all throughout space including upon earth. For example, the birth of stars and suns throughout the universe and the sudden appearance of some plant life upon earth.

3. Some of those who suggest that the Gap Theory may be correct also suggest that the days of creation may actually be geological ages. Harold Lindsell and Charles Woodbridge say this:

> The first chapter of Genesis seems to teach that the universe is only a few thousand years old. Geologists insist that it is millions of years old. Hence findings of science appear to contradict the Biblical record. Many students claim to have lost their faith in God because of this seeming contradiction.
>
> But Genesis does not teach anything that contradicts true science.. Gen.1:1 describes the original creation of material substance which occurred in the distant past. Gen.1:2 reads: "And the earth was without form, and void." The Hebrew word "was" in this text may be translated 'became.' The world may have become waste and void as the result of some cataclysmic judgment of God. Atomic energy was stored in the original mass, and such a vast destruction is by no means inconceivable. Nothing is said in Genesis about the length of time which elapses between the first creative work of God (1:1) and the commencement of His word of re-creation (1:2). An indefinite period may have intervened.
>
> Again, in referring to the various "days" of creation, which many have interpreted as "creative periods," the indefinite article 'a' is suggested in the Hebrew in each case: e.g. "a first day," "a second day." (See Genesis 1:5,8,13.) No intimation is given of the length of time which may have occurred between these creative periods.
>
> The Genesis record leaves ample time for all truly scientific eras. One need not be alarmed nor deceived when he hears pseudo-scientists attack the Bible on the ground that it denies the findings of geology. Genesis and true geology are in full accord.[13]

III. THE POSITION OF SCIENCE AND THE BIBLE

The scholar Norman Geisler has an excellent statement on the conflicts that sometimes seem to exist between science and the Bible. The statement is lengthy, but it is so well stated that it will be applicable throughout the centuries to come if Jesus tarries. For this reason, it is quoted in full here. Some parts are outlined by us for simplicity. (Also see above [point I, B] for more discussion on the position of science and the Bible.)

HOW CAN GENESIS BE RECONCILED WITH MODERN SCIENCE?

1. *Some general principles of reconciliation between science and Scripture.* There is no contradiction between the facts of Genesis and the facts of science. There is a difference between *some interpretations* of Genesis and *some theories* of science. Since God is revealed in both His *Word* (Scripture) and His *world* (science) (Ps.19:1; Ro.1:19), there is *really* no contradiction between them. When the Bible and science *appear* to be in conflict, we must remember that scientific theories change, and they may be wrong today. In addition, there is more than one way to interpret the early chapters of Genesis. Finally, through the years science has come to support many things in the Bible that it once taught were untrue.

2. *Some areas where science supports the Bible.*

⇒ Archaeology has discovered thousands of things that prove the historical accuracy of the Bible.

⇒ Astronomy agrees with Genesis that the world had a beginning.

⇒ Geology supports the order of creation presented in Genesis 1, following its approach that the universe came first, the world was formed next, that life began in the sea, with the lower forms of life appearing first, and that man is the highest and latest form of life to appear.

⇒ Physics (the second Law of Thermodynamics) shows the world is running out of available energy. Hence the world cannot be eternal but must have had a beginning.

⇒ Mathematics (the Law of Probability) shows that the world did not happen by chance but was designed by an intelligent power.

⇒ Biology teaches that each creature reproduces its own kind.

⇒ Anthropology shows that there is only one race of mankind (see Ac.17:26) with different ethnic groupings within it. This indicates a common ancestor for all men.

3. *Evolution and creation are a serious area of conflict between science and the Bible.* The Bible teaches that God created matter, life, and man (Ge.1:1, 21, 26). It also teaches that God made the basic kinds of organisms like fish, fowl, plants and beasts (Ge.1) and that each organism reproduces after its own kind (Ge.1:11, 12, 21). Finally, the Bible says that man and woman were specially created by God from the earth (Ge.2:7f.). What the facts of science indicate about the origin of life and man is that the most basic forms (*phyla*) began suddenly and abundantly and that new forms of life began in the fossil record in the same way. Science reveals that there are

---

13   Harold Lindsell and Charles Woodbridge. *A Handbook of Christian Truth*, p.82.

different kinds of life forms in which small developments and changes may occur by means of limited cross-breeding and mutations (called *microevolution*). But science also reveals that no large changes are observable (called *macro-evolution*) and that at the known rate of mutation over the estimated scientific time scale of a half billion years, the odds against things happening by chance alone are 1 followed by 3 million zeros to 1 (this is admitted by the famous evolutionist Julian Huxley in his book, *Evolution in Action*). Our conclusion in the light of the facts of Scripture and science is that although evolution is *theoretically* possible, it is *scientifically* highly improbable and *biblically* untenable (since the Bible clearly teaches that God created the different kinds of organisms, including man).

4. *"The age of the world and of mankind is another area of conflict between the Bible and modern science.* Science says the world is billions of years old while some Bible scholars say the world was created about 4004 B.C. The facts of the matter are simply these: the Bible does not say how old the world or mankind is; there are gaps in the genealogical tables of Genesis 5 and 11 of such a nature that one cannot simply add up all the ages and get 4000 years B.C. (cf. 1 Chron.3:11f. and Matt.1:8); and scientific methods of dating are not absolute but subject to change. Therefore, the so-called contradiction between the Bible and modern science is only a conflict in opinion and not a contradiction in fact"[14]

(We wish to acknowledge five excellent sources that have helped greatly in preparing the Introductory material on Genesis and on "The Seven Days of Creation." There are many other excellent commentaries, but these have stirred numerous thoughts and provided excellent research and overview of the subjects covered in the above Introductory material.)

❖ Derek Kidner. *Genesis*. "Tyndale Old Testament Commentaries." Downers Grove, IL: Inter-Varsity Press, 1979.

❖ H.C. Leupold. *Genesis*, Vol.1. Grand Rapids, MI: Baker Book House, 1942.

❖ James Montgomery Boice. *Genesis, An Expositional Commentary*, Vol.1. Grand Rapids, MI: Zondervan Publishing House, 1938.

❖ John C. Whitcomb and Henry M. Morris. *The Genesis Flood*. Phillipsburg, NJ: Presbyterian and Reformed Publishing Co., 1961.

❖ Norman Geisler. *A Popular Survey of the Old Testament*. Grand Rapids, MI: Baker Book House, 1977.

---

[14] Norman Geisler. *A Popular Survey of the Old Testament*, pp.43-44.

THE BEGINNING OF THE WORLD: THE CREATION OF MANKIND AND OF THE GODLY SEED,

Chapters 1-11

DIVISION I

CREATION OF THE HEAVENS AND THE EARTH, 1:1–2:3

(1:1-2:3) **DIVISION OVERVIEW**: **Creation, of Universe—Universe, Source—God, Creator**: the Bible declares an astounding truth: the earth and the universe did not just happen by chance nor by some random accident.

⇒ The earth and the heavens did not originate *out of nowhere*.

⇒ Something—some particle or force, some matter or energy, some element or electrical impulse, some atom, proton, neutron, electron, chemical, gas, or something else—did not just appear *out of nothing*.

⇒ The earth and the universe did not evolve from some particle of dust, some gas, or some energy that just appeared. For something to appear *out of nothing* is against all the laws of nature and science.

The Bible declares this astounding truth: the earth and the heavens were created by a Sovereign Intelligence and Power who has revealed Himself to be the Supreme Person of the universe, to be ELOHIM, *GOD ALMIGHTY, the Supreme Lord and Majesty* of all! The Bible declares that the universe has been *deliberately and personally created* by God Himself. God, Elohim, is the Mighty God who alone has the *Intelligence and Power* to create a universe like ours, a universe …

• that stretches so far into the outer reaches of space
• that reaches out in unbelievable distances
• that includes an unbelievable number of worlds
• that reaches unfathomable dimensions
• that exceeds the comprehension and understanding of man

The Bible declares that God (Elohim) is the Creator, the Supreme Person, the Sovereign Lord and Majesty of the universe. Note how the Bible begins:

"In the beginning God." (Ge.1:1)

The stress is God. God was there in the beginning, already existing when the universe first began. He is the God of power who actually existed *before* the universe and who acted and created the universe. God (Elohim) is the subject, the Sovereign Person who stands behind all things. This is the great declaration of the very first chapter of *Genesis*.

CREATION OF THE HEAVENS AND THE EARTH, 1:1–2:3

A. **The Basic Questions of Creation, 1:1-2**

B. **The First Day: Creation of Light, 1:3-5**

C. **The Second Day: Creation of the Firmament or Expanse (The Atmosphere and Air Space Encircling the Earth), 1:6-8**

D. **The Third Day (Part 1): Creation of the Waters (Seas, Lakes, Rivers) and of Dry Land (Continents, Islands), 1:9-10**

E. **The Third Day (Part 2): Creation of Plant Life or Vegetation, 1:11-13**

F. **The Fourth Day: Creation and Distribution of Light Upon Earth to Regulate Day and Night, Seasons and Years, 1:14-19**

G. **The Fifth Day: Creation of Water Creatures (Fish, Sea Life, Creeping Creatures) and Air Creatures (Birds, Winged Fowl, Insects, etc.), 1:20-23**

H. **The Sixth Day (Part 1): Creation of Land Animals, 1:24-25**

I. **The Sixth Day (Part 2): Creation of Man, Male and Female, 1:26-31**

J. **The Seventh Day: Creation of a Day for Rest and Worship, 2:1-3**

CHAPTER 1

I. CREATION OF THE HEAVENS & THE EARTH,[DS1] **1:1–2:3**

A. The Basic Questions of Creation, 1:1-2

1. When: In the beginning
2. Who created: God[DS2]
3. What: Heavens & earth[DS3]
4. How was the earth created: In stages[DS4]
   a. Without form & void
   b. In darkness
   c. Covered by water
   d. By the Spirit's activity
	In the beginning God created the heaven and the earth.
	2 And the earth was without form, and void; and darkness was upon the face of the deep. And the spirit of God moved upon the face of the waters.

DIVISION I

CREATION OF THE HEAVENS AND THE EARTH, 1:1–2:3

A. The Basic Questions of Creation, 1:1-2

(1:1-2) **Introduction—Creation**: profound, impressive, stunning—the opening words of Scripture are astounding.

"In the beginning God created the heaven and the earth" (Ge.1:1).

A person who reads and thinks—truthfully thinks—about this great statement is captivated by its astounding declaration. Why? Because he realizes that the basic questions of creation are captured in the divine statement. There is so much being said, so much to think about, so much to learn.

The Bible declares that God is behind everything. The universe is not eternal nor did it just happen. The universe did not just come into being by chance. Something did not come *out of nothing*. *Nothing* did not produce nor give rise to *something*. There is a Creator—a Supreme Person, a Supreme Intelligence and Force—who has created the universe, and the Creator has given the universe purpose and meaning.

⇒ Scripture does not argue God's existence; it declares God's existence.
⇒ Scripture does not argue that the heavens and earth have a Creator; it declares that *God created* the heavens and the earth.

Note a significant fact: the first two verses of Scripture answer the most basic questions concerning creation. They answer the very questions that man asks about his own personal origin and about the origin and roots of the universe. This is, *The Basic Questions of Creation*.

1. When was the universe created: "In the beginning" (v.1).
2. Who created the universe: "God created [it]" (v.1).
3. What was created: "the heavens and the earth," that is, the universe, (v.1).
4. How was the earth created: in stages:
   a. Without form and void (v.2).
   b. In darkness (v.2).
   c. Covered by water (v.2).
   d. By the Spirit's activity (v.2).

(1:1-2) **Another Outline**: if a person holds to the *Gap Theory* between verses one and two, then he might prefer the following outline of Scripture. (See DEEPER STUDY #4, *Gap Theory*—Ge.1:2.)

1. When was the universe created: "In the beginning" (v.1).
2. Who created the universe: "God created it" (v.1).
3. What was created: "the heaven and the earth," that is, the universe, (v.1).
4. What happened to the original creation: judgment and destruction (v.2).
   a. The earth became an empty waste and ruin.
   b. The earth was covered with darkness and water.
   c. The Spirit of God began to move upon the face of the waters.

DEEPER STUDY # 1

(1:1-2:3) **Creation—Man, Needs of**: profound, impressive, stunning—here are the very first words that God wants to say to man; here are the beginning words of the Holy Bible.

"In the beginning God created the heaven and the earth" (Ge.1:1).

This is the first thing that God reveals to man, the very first thing that God wants man to know: where man and his world have come from. God wants man to know the origin of the universe and of life upon earth. But why? Why is it that God wants man to know the origin of all things *before knowing anything else*? Because of the nature of man. The nature of man has three basic needs that only God can meet, and God wants to meet these needs.

1. There is the need for life, the need to conquer death. By nature, man lives only for a few years and then he dies. Man's life is like a vapor that quickly appears and just as quickly disappears. His life is like a leaf that quickly forms in the spring of the year, but just as quickly floats to the ground upon the fall winds and returns to the dust of the earth. God wants to meet man's need for life; God wants to conquer death for man. But to do this, man must know that he and the world have come from the hand of God, that he belongs to God—all he is and has belongs to the worship and service of God. This is the first reason man must know his origin, that he has come from the hand of God.

2. There is the need of man to improve his life upon earth, the need to conquer the devastating evils of the world and of the human heart and of society.

By nature the world is corruptible, and this corruption causes all kinds of evil and devastation such as tornadoes, hurricanes, earthquakes, starvation, homelessness, poverty, and a host of other natural disasters and social ills. In addition, man finds his own heart and even the hearts of nations filled with evil, the evil of...

- greed
- prejudice
- selfishness
- lust

- immorality
- pride
- hatred
- assault

- murder
- war
- bitterness
- drunkenness

- lying
- cheating
- stealing

Simply stated, the ravages of evil sweep the earth. The crying need of the human heart is for deliverance, deliverance from the rampaging evil that enslaves the human heart and the societies and communities of the world. God wants to meet man's need to improve his life upon earth. God wants to conquer the devastating evil of man's heart and of this world. But to do this, man must know that God exists and that God will deliver him from this corruptible world. Man must acknowledge God and surrender his life—all he is and has—to God, so that God can deliver him. This is the second reason why man must know his origin, that he has come from the hand of God.

3. There is the need to satisfy man's thirst for knowledge, to satisfy his drive to *know how* to lengthen his years and to improve his life upon earth. By nature man is an inquisitive creature. He wants to know; therefore, he asks questions. And when he asks questions, he searches and searches for answers. This is how man progresses, how he develops his technology and science, how he lengthens his days and improves his life upon earth. This is the reason man is always searching for his roots. Man wants to know where he and the universe have come from. He wants to know the origin of his world and of life itself. Therefore, man asks:

⇒ Has the *universe* always existed or did it have a beginning? Will the *universe* exist on and on, forever?

⇒ Has *life* always existed or did it have a beginning? Will *life* exist on and on, forever?

Man's destiny depends upon knowing the answer to these questions. If the universe is not eternal, then it will someday run down and life will cease to exist. Man will no longer exist as a species within the universe. But even if the universe continues on and on, man must ask the second question: will human life continue to exist within the universe? To learn the answers to these questions, man knows that he has to find out where he has come from. Therefore, he searches for his origin, his roots, for the very cause of existence. Man has to find out...

- Is the universe, that is, the basic energy and matter of the universe, eternal? If not, what gave rise to the universe and what is it that keeps it going? What gave rise to human life and what is it that keeps it going?

- If the universe is not eternal, then what is the great energy that brought the universe and life into being?

Man feels this: if he can discover the basic energy and power, the raw force that lies at the very core of the universe and of life, then he can perhaps harness that energy and power. If he can harness the raw energy and power of the universe, then he can *lengthen his years and improve his life upon earth.*

The point is this: man is an inquisitive creature. He wants to know where he has come from, why he is here, and where he is going. And God wants to meet man's need, man's thirst for knowledge and purpose. Therefore, God has spoken to man, given man the Word of God, the Holy Bible. God has revealed the great underlying truth to man, and the very first truth that man needs to know is the origin of all things. Man needs to know that both he and the universe have come from the very hand of God Himself.

However, two tragic and terrible things often happen with man and his technology and science.

1. Man tends to forget that he can lengthen his life only for a certain number of years. True, man can live longer through good health, medicine, and science. But man never will be able to live forever, not by his own efforts, not through human technology and science. Therefore, man's efforts to lengthen his life and to discover the basic material and energy of physical life will always come up short. There is *only one discovery* that can lengthen life permanently and eternally. That is the great discovery of Jesus Christ, God's Son. Man must discover Christ and trust Christ to save him from death. Man must trust Christ to give him eternal life (see Jn.3:16-18; 5:24; 10:10).

2. Man can improve his life and make himself comfortable with the things developed through technology and science. But material things do not satisfy nor fulfill the human soul, not completely, not perfectly. Material things cannot erase...

- greed
- selfishness
- drunkenness
- murder

- prejudice
- pride
- bitterness
- loneliness

- lust
- hoarding
- hatred
- emptiness

- immorality
- drugs
- war
- purposelessness

The material things of this world cannot erase the host of evil that rises up and enslaves the human heart. Material things just cannot significantly improve human life, not the real issues of human life. What, then, can? Christ and love.

When man is willing to trust Christ and to live like Christ says to live, that is, to love, then human life and relationships among people will improve significantly.

The point is this: God meets the need of man to know about the origin of the universe and of human life. In the Holy Scripture—with the very first words—God immediately tells man where man and the universe have come from. God declares that He is the basic intelligence and raw energy and power behind the existence of all things. God Himself is the Supreme Intelligence and Force that made all things. He is the Supreme Mind and Energy, the Supreme Person and Power, the Sovereign LORD and Majesty who created all things.

This is the reason the Bible begins with God Himself, begins with God creating the heavens and the earth. Man must know God, know Him *personally*. God alone has created man and the universe. Therefore, God alone can meet man's basic needs...

- God alone can deliver man from death
- God alone can deliver man from the terrible and devastating evils of the world
- God alone can improve man's life and world on a permanent basis
- God alone can reveal what existed before the universe and man, for God alone was there. No man can reach back before the first matter and energy, before the first atom came into being. Only God was there. Therefore, only God can know what existed back in the annals of eternity. Only God can reveal the truth, exactly how the universe and man came into being

1 (1:1) **"In the Beginning"—Creation**: When did the universe come into being? When did it first begin? When was *matter* first formed and *energy* first activated? When were the heavens and earth created? The Bible tells us, and it tells us in the simplest of ways, in a way that all nations of people can understand. The heavens and earth were created *in the beginning* (bereshith). There was a beginning for the universe. Neither the world nor human life are eternal. The universe has not always existed. The phrase *in the beginning* means there was a time when everything *first started*, when the universe *first began*. The idea is the absolute beginning of things, the absolute beginning of time. The great scholar H.C. Leopold says that it means "the absolute beginning of created things"[1]. Note two significant facts.

a. The universe had a beginning. There was a time when the world did not exist, and then all of a sudden—*out of nowhere and out of nothing*—the world began. The things of the world had a beginning. There was a beginning to the things...

- that surround man
- that man handles and deals with and possesses
- that constitute man's own being
- that are physical and material
- that compose the substances of the world
- that make up all matter and all energy

As stated, all things had a beginning. There was a time when there was nothing, no heavens and no earth, no physical matter and no physical energy, no atoms, electrons, protons, or neutrons and no hydrogen nor any other gaseous substance. There was nothing in the physical and material world or dimension of being. Then, all of a sudden, *out of nowhere and out of nothing*, the universe began to be made. The process of time began. There was a beginning. The universe—material and physical things—began. The physical world and dimension of being was launched. When? "In the beginning"—in the absolute beginning of creation.

> **"And, Thou, Lord, in the beginning hast laid the foundation of the earth; and the heavens are the works of thine hands" (He.1:10).**
> **"In the beginning God created the heaven and the earth" (Ge.1:1).**

b. Nothing whatsoever is said about how long ago the universe was created. No dates are given to determine the age of the heavens and earth. There is not even a hint given as to the age of either.

> **Thought 1.** Man must heed this passage of Scripture. He must know where he has come from and why he is here. He can never fulfill his purpose upon earth unless he knows who put him here and why he was placed here.
> This passage also stands as a dramatic warning to man. Since man had a beginning, he also has an ending; therefore, he must prepare to face the Person who gave him his beginning. Man must repent and prepare to face his Creator.

> **"Remember now thy Creator in the days of thy youth, while the evil days come not, nor the years draw nigh, when thou shalt say, I have no pleasure in them" (Ec.12:1).**
> **"And saying, Repent ye: for the kingdom of heaven is at hand" (Mt.3:2).**
> **"Repent ye therefore, and be converted, that your sins may be blotted out, when the times of refreshing shall come from the presence of the Lord" (Ac.3:19).**
> **"Repent therefore of this thy wickedness, and pray God, if perhaps the thought of thine heart may be forgiven thee" (Ac.8:22).**
> **"And the times of this ignorance God winked at; but now commandeth all men every where to repent" (Ac.17:30).**

[1] H.C. Leupold. *Genesis*, Vol.1, p.39.

Thought 2. Jesus Christ, *God the Son*, is the beginning and the ending of all things. It is to Him that man must repent and turn.

> "In the beginning was the Word [Jesus Christ], and the Word was with God, and the Word was God. The same was in the beginning with God" (Jn.1:1-2).
> "I am Alpha and Omega, the beginning and the ending, saith the Lord, which is, and which was, and which is to come, the Almighty" (Re.1:8).
> "And unto the angel of the church of the Laodiceans write; These things saith the Amen, the faithful and true witness, the beginning of the creation of God" (Re.3:14).
> "And he said unto me, It is done. I am Alpha and Omega, the beginning and the end. I will give unto him that is athirst of the fountain of the water of life freely" (Re.21:6).
> "I am Alpha and Omega, the beginning and the end, the first and the last" (Re.22:13).
> "And he is the head of the body, the church: who is the beginning, the firstborn from the dead; that in all things he might have the preeminence" (Col.1:18).

Thought 3. This is a universal truth: there was a beginning; consequently, there will be an ending. Everything that begins has an ending. The world and all that is in the world shall pass away. The physical and material things of the world change their form, pass on, deteriorate, decay, and waste away. Even man himself changes, ages, and wastes away. He dies. There is an end to all that begins, including man.

> "In the beginning God created the heaven and the earth" (Ge.1:1).
> "When I begin, I will also make an end" (1 S.3:12).
> "Remember the former things of old: for I am God, and there is none else; I am God, and there is none like me, declaring the end from the beginning, and from ancient times the things that are not yet done, saying, My counsel shall stand, and I will do all my pleasure" (Is.46:9-10).
> "And, Thou, Lord, in the beginning hast laid the foundation of the earth; and the heavens are the works of thine hands: they shall perish; but thou remainest; and they all shall wax old as doth a garment; and as a vesture shalt thou fold them up, and they shall be changed: but thou art the same, and thy years shall not fail" (He.1:10-12).
> "And as it is appointed unto men once to die, but after this the judgment" (He.9:27).
> "But the day of the Lord will come as a thief in the night; in the which the heavens shall pass away with a great noise, and the elements shall melt with fervent heat, the earth also and the works that are therein shall be burned up. Seeing then that all these things shall be dissolved, what manner of persons ought ye to be in all holy conversation [behavior] and godliness, looking for and hasting unto the coming of the day of God, wherein the heavens being on fire shall be dissolved, and the elements shall melt with fervent heat? Nevertheless we, according to his promise, look for new heavens and a new earth, wherein dwelleth righteousness" (2 Pe.3:10-13).

2 (1:1) **Creation—God, Creator:** Who created the universe? God. This is clearly stated. As mentioned earlier, man is an inquisitive creature. He wants to know; therefore, he asks questions and searches and searches for answers. When man looks at the world and himself, he wonders where he and the world have come from. What is the origin of man and of the world? Note three significant points now covered by this profound but simply stated phrase:

"In the beginning God created...." (Ge.1:1).

a. First, the Hebrew name for God is *Elohim.* (See DEEPER STUDY # 2—Ge.1:1 for discussion.)

b. Second, God was there *in the beginning.* "*In the beginning*" there was the Supreme Person—the Supreme Presence, the Supreme Being, the Supreme Intelligence, the Supreme Force—who had the intelligence and power to create the universe. That Someone was God. God existed before the beginning; He preceded the beginning. God began the beginning. All that followed is due to Him. This means three significant things.

  1) God is the *Almighty God,* the God of all might and power. He is the Sovereign Majesty and Supreme Master of the universe. He existed before anything else; therefore, everything owes its existence to God. This includes man. Man owes his life—all he is and has—his obedience, worship, and service to God.

  2) God is *self-existent and eternal.* God existed before anything else. Nothing created God; nothing gave life to God. On the contrary, God created the universe and all matter and all atoms and all energy and force within the universe. God created all life including the life of man; therefore, man owes his life—all he is and has—his obedience, worship, and service to God.

  3) God is totally *self-sufficient.* God possesses everything that He needs within Himself, within His very own being and personality. He is perfect—perfect in an absolute sense—within Himself. But man is not self-sufficient; therefore, man must cast his life—all he is and has—upon God. Man must obey, worship, and serve God in total dependence, trusting God to provide for all of his needs.

c. Third, the fact that God was there "*in the beginning*"—that He was there before the universe ever existed—disproves, refutes, and destroys six beliefs of men.

  1) God's existence *disproves atheism and skepticism or agnosticism.* Atheism is the belief that there is no God, no Supreme Being. Skepticism or agnosticism is the belief that a person just cannot know whether or not there is a God. Atheism and skepticism are wrong. The Bible, God's written revelation, declares unequivocally: "In the beginning God"—God does exist. He is the Sovereign Majesty of the universe, the Supreme Intelligence and Force of the universe.

"The fool hath said in his heart, There is no God. They are corrupt, they have done abominable works, there is none that doeth good" (Ps.14:1).

"The fool hath said in his heart, There is no God. Corrupt are they, and have done abominable iniquity: there is none that doeth good. God looked down from heaven upon the children of men, to see if there were any that did understand, that did seek God. Every one of them is gone back: they are altogether become filthy; there is none that doeth good, no, not one" (Ps.53:1-3).

"Let them be confounded and troubled for ever; yea, let them be put to shame, and perish: that men may know that thou, whose name alone is JEHOVAH, are the most high over all the earth" (Ps.83:17-18).

"For thus saith the Lord that created the heavens; God himself that formed the earth and made it; he hath established it, he created it not in vain, he formed it to be inhabited: I am the Lord; and there is none else. I have not spoken in secret, in a dark place of the earth: I said not unto the seed of Jacob, Seek ye me in vain: I the Lord speak righteousness, I declare things that are right" (Is.45:18-19).

2) God's existence *disproves pantheism*. Pantheism believes in God, but not in a personal God. God is nothing more than the force and energy of the universe, the basic, underlying force and energy of all things. Stated another way, pantheism says that God is not a person, but rather that God is within everything, within everything as the force and energy that gives life and being to all things. For example, take a tree. The force and energy that makes a tree live and grow is said to be God. God is nothing more than the impersonal energy and force that gives life to the tree and causes it to grow.

The Bible strongly denies this belief. The Bible unequivocally declares that God is a *person*, the Supreme Person and Majestic Lord of the universe, and that God existed *before* the universe. God existed before the forces and energies of the universe ever came into being or were activated. Therefore, God is above and beyond all matter and all energy. God is both *before the universe* and *supreme over the universe*. And God longs for a personal relationship with man.

"All nations whom thou hast made shall come and worship before thee, O Lord; and shall glorify thy name. For thou art great, and doest wondrous things: thou art God alone. Teach me thy way, O Lord; I will walk in thy truth: unite my heart to fear thy name. I will praise thee, O Lord my God, with all my heart: and I will glorify thy name for evermore. For great is thy mercy toward me: and thou hast delivered my soul from the lowest hell" (Ps.86:9-13).

"Ye are my witnesses, saith the Lord, and my servant whom I have chosen: that ye may know and believe me, and understand that I am he: before me there was no God formed, neither shall there be after me. I, even I, am the Lord; and beside me there is no saviour. I have declared, and have saved, and I have showed, when there was no strange god among you: therefore ye are my witnesses, saith the Lord, that I am God. Yea, before the day was I am he; and there is none that can deliver out of my hand: I will work, and who shall let [hinder] it?" (Is.43:10-13).

"Thus saith the Lord the King of Israel, and his redeemer the Lord of hosts; I am the first, and I am the last; and beside me there is no God. And who, as I, shall call, and shall declare it, and set it in order for me, since I appointed the ancient people? and the things that are coming, and shall come, let them show unto them. Fear ye not, neither be afraid: have not I told thee from that time, and have declared it? ye are even my witnesses. Is there a God beside me? yea, there is no God; I know not any" (Is.44:6-8).

3) God's existence *refutes and destroys polytheism*. Polytheism is the belief that there are many gods. But the Bible is clear: "In the beginning God." There was God and God alone—one God, not many gods. The Lord God is one God. He and He alone is the Sovereign Majesty of the universe. Polytheism is a false belief of man, formed by man's own imagination and human ideas about God.

"Thou shalt have no other gods before me. Thou shalt not make unto thee any graven image, or any likeness of any thing that is in heaven above, or that is in the earth beneath, or that is in the water under the earth: thou shalt not bow down thyself to them, nor serve them: for I the Lord thy God am a jealous God, visiting the iniquity of the fathers upon the children unto the third and fourth generation of them that hate me" (Ex.20:3-5).

"Unto thee it was showed, that thou mightest know that the Lord he is God; there is none else beside him" (De.4:35).

"Wherefore thou art great, O Lord God: for there is none like thee, neither is there any God beside thee, according to all that we have heard with our ears" (2 S.7:22).

"We know that an idol is nothing in the world, and that there is none other God but one. For though there be [many] that are called gods, whether in heaven or in earth, (as there be gods many, and lords many,) but to us there is but one God, the Father, of whom are all things" (1 Co.8:4-6).

"For there is one God, and one mediator between God and men, the man Christ Jesus; who gave himself a ransom for all, to be testified in due time" (1 Ti.2:5-6).

"One God and Father of all, who is above all, and through all, and in you all" (Ep.4:6).

4) God's existence *disproves and destroys materialism*. Materialism is the belief that the universe is all there is; the world and the things of the world are all that exist. The basic, underlying energy and force of matter, whatever it is, is the supreme energy and force. Materialism says there is no god, not a personal God. The greatest and most supreme thing in the universe is the very basic energy and force that causes all matter to exist and function. Therefore, the universe and its forces and energies are all there is. Beyond this universe, beyond the material and physical world, there is nothing. There is no other world, no spiritual world, and no heaven or hell. There is only this world, only the material and physical world.

The Bible declares in no uncertain terms: "No! A thousand times no!" "In the beginning God." God existed prior to the material and physical universe. *There is more to life than just this world and its materialism, more to life than just the things of this world*. There is God, and man is answerable to God. The belief of materialism is wrong.

"Lay not up for yourselves treasures upon earth, where moth and rust doth corrupt, and where thieves break through and steal: but lay up for yourselves treasures in heaven, where neither moth nor rust doth corrupt, and where thieves do not break through nor steal: for where your treasure is, there will your heart be also" (Mt.6:19-21).

"But seek ye first the kingdom of God, and his righteousness; and all these things [shelter, food, clothing] shall be added unto you" (Mt.6:33).

"For what is a man profited, if he shall gain the whole world, and lose his own soul? or what shall a man give in exchange for his soul?" (Mt.16:26).

"For what is a man advantaged, if he gain the whole world, and lose himself, or be cast away?" (Lu.9:25).

"And the world passeth away, and the lust thereof: but he that doeth the will of God abideth for ever" (1 Jn.2:17).

"So then because thou art lukewarm, and neither cold nor hot, I will spue thee out of my mouth. Because thou sayest, I am rich, and increased with goods, and have need of nothing; and knowest not that thou art wretched, and miserable, and poor, and blind, and naked" (Re.3:16-17).

5) God's existence *disproves and destroys humanism*. Humanism is the belief that man himself is the ultimate being in the universe. There is no God, no supreme being who rules over man and the universe. Man is his own authority and determines his own destiny, and man has the reasoning power to control and rule over both himself and nature. Humanism declares that man himself is his own supreme being.

The Bible is emphatic: "In the beginning God." God existed before man ever appeared on the scene. Therefore, God is *before, above, and beyond man*. God is far, far superior to man. The Bible emphatically declares that God is the Supreme Majesty of the universe, not man. Humanism is wrong, dead wrong.

"Thou shalt have no other gods before me [not even oneself]. Thou shalt not make unto thee any graven image, or any likeness of any thing that is in heaven above, or that is in the earth beneath, or that is in the water under the earth: thou shalt not bow down thyself to them, nor serve them: for I the Lord thy God am a jealous God, visiting the iniquity of the fathers upon the children unto the third and fourth generation of them that hate me; and showing mercy unto thousands of them that love me, and keep my commandments" (Ex.20:3-6).

"Hear, O Israel: The Lord our God is one Lord: and thou shalt love the Lord thy God [not oneself] with all thine heart, and with all thy soul, and with all thy might" (De.6:4-5).

"Have ye not known? have ye not heard? hath it not been told you from the beginning? have ye not understood from the foundations of the earth? It is he [God] that sitteth upon the circle of the earth, and the inhabitants thereof are as grasshoppers; that stretcheth out the heavens as a curtain, and spreadeth them out as a tent to dwell in: that bringeth the princes to nothing; he maketh the judges of the earth as vanity. Yea, they shall not be planted; yea, they shall not be sown: yea, their stock shall not take root in the earth: and he shall also blow upon them, and they shall wither, and the whirlwind shall take them away as stubble. To whom then will ye liken me, or shall I be equal? saith the Holy One. Lift up your eyes on high, and behold who hath created these things, that bringeth out their host by number: he calleth them all by names by the greatness of his might, for that he is strong in power; not one faileth" (Is.40:21-26).

"I am the Lord, and there is none else, there is no God beside me: I girded thee, though thou hast not known me: that they may know from the rising of the sun, and from the west, that there is none beside me. I am the Lord, and there is none else. I form the light, and create darkness: I make peace, and create evil [disaster, NIV]: I the Lord do all these things" (Is.45:5-7).

"Tell ye, and bring them near; yea, let them take counsel together: who hath declared this from ancient time? who hath told it from that time? have not I the Lord? and there is no God else beside me; a just God and a Saviour; there is none beside me. Look unto me, and be ye saved, all the ends of the earth: for I am God, and there is none else. I have sworn by myself, the word is gone out of my mouth in righteousness, and shall not return, That unto me every knee shall bow, every tongue shall swear. Surely, shall one say, in the Lord have I righteousness and strength: even to him shall men come; and all that incensed against him shall be ashamed" (Is.45:21-24).

"And Jesus answered him, The first of all the commandments is, Hear, O Israel; The Lord our God is one Lord: and thou shalt love the Lord thy God with all thy heart, and with all thy soul, and with all thy mind, and with all thy strength: this is the first commandment. And the second is like, namely this, Thou shalt love thy neighbour as thyself. There is none other commandment greater than these" (Mk.12:29-31).

6) God's existence *disproves and destroys secularism.* Secularism is similar to humanism. It is just another name cloaked in the same belief as humanism. It is the belief that this world and the things of this world are all there is. Man is not a spiritual being, and he is not answerable to a supreme God. Therefore, man is to focus upon this life and this life alone. He is to make himself as comfortable and as happy as he can, and he is to get as much out of this life as he can. Man is *to eat, drink, and be merry, for tomorrow he dies.*

But again, the Bible disproves secularism: "In the beginning God." God exists; God has always existed, He exists now, and He will always exist. Therefore, man is answerable to God. *Man must live for God, not for this world and its possessions and pleasures.*

"For thou shalt worship no other god [many worship the world itself]: for the Lord, whose name is Jealous, is a jealous God" (Ex.34:14).

"And take heed to yourselves, lest at any time your hearts be overcharged with surfeiting [self-indulgence], and drunkenness, and cares of this life, and so that day come upon you unawares" (Lu.21:34).

"Wherefore come out from among them, and be ye separate, saith the Lord, and touch not the unclean thing; and I will receive you, and will be a Father unto you, and ye shall be my sons and daughters, saith the Lord Almighty" (2 Co.6:17-18).

"Teaching us that, denying ungodliness and worldly lusts, we should live soberly, righteously, and godly, in this present world; looking for that blessed hope, and the glorious appearing of the great God and our Saviour Jesus Christ" (Tit.2:12-13).

"Ye adulterers and adulteresses, know ye not that the friendship of the world is enmity with God? whosoever therefore will be a friend of the world is the enemy of God" (Js.4:4).

"Love not the world, neither the things that are in the world. If any man love the world, the love of the Father is not in him. For all that is in the world, the lust of the flesh, and the lust of the eyes, and the pride of life, is not of the Father, but is of the world" (1 Jn.2:15-16).

DEEPER STUDY # 2

(1:1) **God** (Elohim): Elohim is the general or universal name for God in the Hebrew language. It means the Almighty God, the God of all might and strength. It means the Strong and Mighty, the Omnipotent, the One with supreme power and intelligence, the One who is always there, the Faithful One, the One who is to be reverenced and feared (see note—Ge.1:3). God's (Elohim's) power in creation is to strike reverence and fear in the heart of man. The word is used about 2570 times in the Bible. The word *Elohim* is a plural noun which suggests the Trinity. (See note 4, pt.1d—Ge.1:2 for a discussion on all three persons being involved in creation. Also see note 2—Ge.2:4; note 1—Ge.2:7 for a discussion of Jehovah or Yahweh as a name for God. See Ge.14:18; 15:2; 17:1; 21:33; 22:14; Ex.3:14-15; 4:10-11; 1 S.1:3.)

Thought 1. The very name of God, *Elohim*, says three things to us.
1) God (Elohim) is the One with the power to create the universe.
2) God (Elohim) is the One upon whom we can depend to deliver us. He is always there, always faithful, and He has the power and strength to always help us.
3) God (Elohim) is the Omnipotent One, the Sovereign Majesty of the universe; therefore, we are to worship and serve Him in all reverence and fear.

---

3 (1:1) **Creation—God, Creator:** What was created? God created the heavens and the earth, that is, the universe. When science uses its massive telescopes and other instruments to scan and measure the universe above and the earth below, man sees the most amazing facts.
⇒ *The earth* is only 8,000 miles in diameter and only 25,000 miles in circumference. The earth measures less than one grain of sand on all the seashores of the earth in comparison to the universe.
⇒ Our earth is within a *solar system,* a system of nine other planets that revolve around the sun (ten planets counting the earth). The largest planet of our solar system is Jupiter. It is so large that it is 1300 times the size of earth.
⇒ Our sun is so large that it is about 864,000 miles in diameter. The sun could hold 1,300,000 earths. And, if we could just imagine the distance, the sun is 93,000,000 miles away from the earth. But this is only the beginning.
⇒ Our solar system is only one solar system of millions that make up what science calls a *galaxy.* There are millions and millions of solar systems that are just like our nine planets revolving around the sun—millions and millions of solar systems that make up our galaxy. And our galaxy has billions and billions of stars scattered all throughout the heavens, over 200 billion. Such facts stagger our imagination. Just think of this: there is one star so big, a star called Betelguese, that it is 215 million miles in diameter. How big is that? The sun could sit in the star's center and the earth could revolve around the sun in its present orbit without ever touching the sides of this enormous star.[2]
⇒ When we stand out at night and look up into the heavens, we see what we call the *Milky Way.* The Milky Way is the name of our own galaxy, the galaxy of stars of which the earth is a part. When we look up at the *Milky Way* on a starry night, what we see is the reflected light of billions and billions of stars being reflected across the night sky, billions and billions of stars that are a part of our own galaxy. But imagine this: there are millions of galaxies, untold billions and billions of stars in the far regions of outer space.

---

2   William W. Orr. *How We May Know That God Is.* (Wheaton, IL: VanKampen Press. n.d.), p.29.

⇒ But this is not all. Science tells us that the galaxies are moving away from each other at an incredible speed, a speed that exceeds millions of miles per hour. Just imagine! The stars and galaxies of the heavens are moving away from each other, traveling millions and millions of miles every hour. We live in what is called an *expanding universe*, an ever growing universe. As stated, the heavens, the galaxies of our universe, are expanding more and more—moving farther and farther away from each other, flying away at the incredible speed of millions of miles per hour. Profound, impressive, stunning. When we stand back and gaze up at the stars in heaven and think about the enormity of it all, we stand in stark amazement at the glory of the heavens above. But this is not all.

⇒ When we focus in upon the small and minute world of the earth and universe, we stand in stark amazement at the glory of the small and minute world. There is the small world of the busy ant and the minute world of all the other small creatures that fascinate us. But there is much more to the small and minute world than just what is visible to the naked eye. For example, what are the smallest particles of existence? What do things consist of? What is it that makes things exist? What are the basic elements and building blocks of existence and of life itself? Science has discovered a great deal, enough to tell us that the universe and life are made up of atoms and electrons and protons and neutrons and a host of other minute particles—minute particles that are invisible and even today far, far beyond man's understanding. Man has yet to discover the basic raw element and force of the universe.

Someday, if the world stands long enough, man may be able to discover the basic element, the raw matter and energy of life and existence or being. If that day ever comes, man will make a startling discovery. The declaration of the Bible is true: behind it all is God. This is the clear declaration of Scripture:

"In the beginning [in the *very beginning*] God created the heaven and the earth" (Ge.1:1).
"And he is before all things, and by him all things consist [hold together]" (Col.1:17).

Where did the heavens and earth come from? What is the origin of the universe? No clearer declaration could be made. It can be stated no simpler: God created the universe. The heavens and earth exist because God brought them into being. Note four significant facts.

a. God was there when the heavens and the earth were created. Before anything was ever made, God existed. His presence and power were present everywhere, just as they are now. God has always been living, eternally. And God is living now, and He shall live forever. On and on God shall live, eternally.

Thought 1. Applying this to us, we must always remember that God is present with us. He surrounds us and wants to make Himself known to us. He wants us to experience His presence and power, to know Him personally. The problem is that so few have drawn near to God; so few seek to know God.

"But if from thence thou shalt seek the Lord thy God, thou shalt find him, if thou seek him with all thy heart and with all thy soul" (De.4:29).
"Seek ye the Lord while he may be found, call ye upon him while he is near" (Is.55:6).
"And ye shall seek me, and find me, when ye shall search for me with all your heart" (Je.29:13).
"God that made the world and all things therein, seeing that he is Lord of heaven and earth, dwelleth not in temples made with hands; neither is worshipped with men's hands, as though he needed any thing, seeing he giveth to all life, and breath, and all things; and hath made of one blood all nations of men for to dwell on all the face of the earth, and hath determined the times before appointed, and the bounds of their habitation; that they should seek the Lord, if haply they might feel after him, and find him, though he be not far from every one of us: for in him we live, and move, and have our being; as certain also of your own poets have said, For we are also his offspring" (Ac.17:24-28).

b. God created the universe *out of nothing* (ex nihilo). (See Deeper Study #3—Ge.1:1 for discussion.)

c. There is purpose in creation. Things did not just happen by chance nor at random; the universe did not just come into being, did not just appear. The universe did not just begin *out of nothing*. *God was there.* This fact—that God was there—means that He thought up the universe. The idea of the universe was in His mind, and He desired it. Therefore, He planned and willed it, and He brought it into being. God was there before the universe was ever made. It was His mind and thoughts, His intelligence and power that created the universe. Therefore, there is purpose to the universe. God has some awesome purpose, some great and glorious reason for creating the universe and life. (See note 4—Ge.1:28; outline and notes—Ge.2:15-17 for discussion.)

Thought 1. There is more to life than just the physical and material...
• more to life than the things of this world
• more to life than comfort and pleasure
• more to life than money and power
• more to life than position and prestige
• more to life than recognition and fame

There is God and His presence, God and His purpose for life. Life is to be full of purpose, meaning, and significance. Life is not to be empty and lonely and alienated from God. God created the universe and gave man life so that man could be fulfilled and satisfied and live forever. God gave man life so that man could live in the fullness of God's...
• love, joy, and peace
• longsuffering, gentleness, and goodness
• faith, meekness, and control (Ga.5:22-23)

God gave man life so that man could fellowship, worship, and serve God in all the fullness of life forever and ever.

> **"Ye are my witnesses, saith the Lord, and my servant whom I have chosen: that ye may know and believe me, and understand that I am he: before me there was no God formed, neither shall there be after me" (Is.43:10).**
> **"For I know the thoughts that I think toward you, saith the Lord, thoughts of peace, and not of evil, to give you an expected end [a future and a hope]" (Je.29:11).**
> **"For I know the plans that I have for you, declares the Lord, plans for welfare and not for calamity to give you a future and a hope" (Je.29:11, NASB).**
> **"I am come that they might have life, and that they might have it more abundantly" (Jn.10:10).**
> **"Brethren, I count not myself to have apprehended: but this one thing I do, forgetting those things which are behind, and reaching forth unto those things which are before, I press toward the mark for the prize of the high calling of God in Christ Jesus" (Ph.3:13-14).**

d. The heavens and earth reveal some things about God. Scholars call this *natural revelation*. Very simply stated, when we stand back and look at the heavens and earth, they tell us a great deal about who God is and what God is like. This is to be expected; in fact, it could not be otherwise. Since God created the world, the world is bound to have God's stamp upon it. The world, that is, nature, is bound to show us some things about God. Romans 1:20 states it well:

> **"For the invisible things of him from the creation of the world are clearly seen, being understood by the things that are made, even his eternal power and Godhead [deity]; so that they are without excuse."**

Note that this verse in Romans clearly states what can be known about God: His *"eternal power"* and *"Godhead,"* that is, His deity. Creation definitely reveals God. The whole universe, its presence and its nature, declares God. But note a fact often overlooked; man can look at nature and see *more* than the simple fact that God is Creator. Man can see *more* than a Supreme Being behind creation. He can see "the invisible things" of God. This means at least two things.

1) Man can see the *"eternal power,"* the Supreme Intelligence and Force (or Energy and Power) of God. Man can look at the creation of the earth and outer space, of plants and animals, of men and women; he can look and clearly see their...
   * bodies and structure
   * variety and beauty
   * arrangement and order
   * purpose and laws

   When man looks at such things and reasons with an honest spirit, he sees clearly that the world was made by a Creator. But, as stated above, he sees much more. He sees that the Creator is a God of supreme...
   * life and being
   * glory and honor
   * beauty and majesty
   * purpose and meaning
   * design and order (law)
   * value and worth (morality)
   * energy and power (the Supreme Force)
   * intelligence and knowledge
   * mystery (things not understood; secrets undiscovered)

2) Man can see the *"Godhead,"* that is, the deity of God. When he looks at nature and reasons with an honest spirit, he clearly sees that the Creator is a God who...
   * cares and provides for what He has created
   * gives life and has interest in life
   * regenerates, replenishes, and carries things on
   * deserves worship and obedience (God is the Creator of life and purpose and being. He is the Supreme Person of law and order. Consequently, He demands that all His subjects serve and obey Him)

Thought 1. Note what Scripture says: man is without excuse (Ro.1:20). This fact is shocking. Man has every evidence imaginable within creation directing him to God; yet man rejects the knowledge of God within creation. Therefore, man is without excuse. Man has no defense, no answer, and no reason that can justify his rejection of God.

> **"Nevertheless he left not himself without witness, in that he did good, and gave us rain from heaven, and fruitful seasons, filling our hearts with food and gladness" (Ac.14:17).**
> **"For the invisible things of him from the creation of the world are clearly seen, being understood by the things that are made, even his eternal power and Godhead; so that they are without excuse" (Ro.1:20).**
> **"Through faith we understand that the worlds were framed by the word of God, so that things which are seen were not made of things which do appear" (He.11:3).**
> **"But without faith it is impossible to please him: for he that cometh to God must believe that he is [exists], and that he is a rewarder of them that diligently seek him" (He.11:6).**
> **"The heavens declare the glory of God and the firmament showeth His handiwork" (Ps.19:1).**
> **"The heavens declare his righteousness, and all the people see his glory" (Ps.97:6).**

Thought 2. God is the Creator of the universe, the Supreme Intelligence and Force of all that is. Therefore, God is the Owner of all. He immediately possesses all the rights to the world. This includes man. God is the rightful Owner of man's life; He deserves all the rights and all the say so in a man's life. Man owes his life, all that he is and has, to God.

> "I beseech you therefore, brethren, by the mercies of God, that ye present your bodies a living sacrifice, holy, acceptable unto God, which is your reasonable service" (Ro.12:1).
> "What? know ye not that your body is the temple of the Holy Ghost which is in you, which ye have of God, and ye are not your own? For ye are bought with a price: therefore glorify God in your body, and in your spirit, which are God's" (1 Co.6:19-20).

Thought 3. God possesses Supreme Intelligence and Power. Therefore, He has the intelligence and power to help us through any and all trials, no matter how severe and terrible.

> "I will lift up mine eyes unto the hills, from whence cometh my help, My help cometh from the Lord, which made heaven and earth" (Ps.121:1-2).
> "Fear thou not; for I am with thee: be not dismayed; for I am thy God: I will strengthen thee; yea, I will help thee; yea, I will uphold thee with the right hand of my righteousness" (Is.41:10).
> "Let your conversation [behavior, conduct] be without covetousness; and be content with such things as ye have: for he hath said, I will never leave thee, nor forsake thee. So that we may boldly say, The Lord is my helper, and I will not fear what man shall do unto me" (He.13:5-6).

Thought 4. When we look at the beauty of heaven above or of the earth below, we should make it a habit...
- to remember that God did it all; He created the universe in all its majesty and beauty
- to praise and thank God for all His works within the universe
- to pray that God will help us to fulfill our purpose as His creatures, to worship and serve Him ever so faithfully, day by day

---

DEEPER STUDY # 3

(1:1) Creation: there are two Hebrew words used for creation in chapter one, *bara* and *asah*. This fact is sometimes used to support the argument for a prehistoric creation (see DEEPER STUDY # 4, *the Gap Theory*—Ge.1:2).

1. The word *created* (bara) is used three times in chapter one: the creation of heaven and earth (Ge.1:1); of sea and winged fowls (Ge.1:21); and of man (Ge.1:27). Two significant facts need to be noted about the word *bara*.
⇒ The word *bara* is used only of God, only when God Himself creates.
⇒ The word *bara* is used only when God is creating something new, only when He is creating something for the very first time, creating something *out of nothing*. That is, there is no existing material. Verse one definitely teaches that God created the world *out of nothing* (ex nihilo). Only God existed prior to the earth. No material existed along with God. God alone is eternal. He and He alone is the Sovereign Majesty of the universe.

2. The word *create* (asah) is entirely different. It means to make, to mould, to form things out of material already existing. Two quotes are worthy of note.

> *To assert that a world as intricate as ours emerged from chaos by chance is about as sensible as to claim that Shakespeare's dramas were composed by rioting monkeys in a print shop.*[3]

> *The probability of life originating from accident is comparable to the probability of the unabridged dictionary resulting from an explosion in a printing shop.*[4]

---

[4] **(1:2) Creation—God, Creator—Unshaped Earth Theory**: How was the *earth* created? Note that the focus now centers upon the earth. The earth is to be the primary concern of man, for the earth is man's primary home, and man is responsible for caring and looking after the earth, for subduing it (Ge.1:28). Therefore, the Scripture now focuses upon the earth, the primary dwelling place of man, the primary place for which man is responsible.

This is a highly controversial verse. There are two basic positions and interpretations of the verse, but each person has to decide for himself which position he takes. There are strong arguments for both interpretations. (Please note: the outline beside verse two follows the KJV interpretation, for this is the text that is outlined by *The Preacher's Outline and Sermon Bible®*. The KJV translates verse 2 after *The Unshaped or Undeveloped Earth Theory*. The outline for *The Divine Judgment or Gap Theory* is given in DEEPER STUDY # 4—Ge.1:2.)

There is *The Unshaped or Undeveloped Earth Position*. This position says that the earth was created in stages just as chapter one of Genesis says.
⇒ Verse one launches the first stage of creation: God created the earth right along with the heavens. He used His supreme power to hang both the earth and the other heavenly bodies in space at the same time.
⇒ Verse two simply describes what the earth looked like in the first stage of creation, what it looked like before the seven days of creation took place, before God created light, vegetation, animals, and man.

---

3 Merrill C. Tenney. *Living Quotations for Christians*, ed. by Sherwood Eliot Wirt and Kersten Beckstrom. (New York, NY: Harper & Row, Publishers, 1974), p.46
4 Edwin Conklin. *Living Quotations for Christians*, p.45.

Four points need to be noted about this position.

a. The earth was *without form and void* (tohu va bohu, v.2). This simply means that the earth was like so many other planets scattered throughout space...
- unshaped and unformed
- barren and empty
- desolate and destitute
- undeveloped and unfinished
- unfruitful and unproductive

> **"I beheld the earth, and, lo, it was without form, and void; and the heavens, and they had no light" (Je.4:23).**

This could also mean that the earth went through the various states of gaseous development, a co-mingling of the gases and solid elements that make up the planets and stars of space. Science tells us that there are heavenly bodies being formed even now, each in some state of gaseous or solid development. As stated, this could be what is meant by being "without form and void." The earth merely went through the various formative stages of development, both the gaseous and solid stages. If so, this would mean that God created the atoms and other basic elements of the universe and allowed them to form through the natural laws that He had set in motion. So far as we can tell, this is certainly the way stars and worlds are being formed in the far regions of outer space today. Just think what beauty God beholds on a daily basis—the beauty of His creative works—the beauty of forming stars as light reflects the rainbow colors upon the various gases and elements. If this is what happened, then all of the statements here in verse two took place over a long period of time.

How could a blanket of darkness be covering the earth when the heavenly bodies (sun, moon, and stars) had already been created in verse one? Scripture tells us: because a heavy mist—thick clouds and dense fog—covered the earth (Ge.2:4-6, esp.6).

b. The earth was wrapped in a blanket of darkness (v.2). The whole earth, not just part of it, was covered in darkness. The idea is that of...
- absolute and total darkness
- full and complete darkness
- thick and heavy darkness
- pitch darkness, the deep black of darkness

c. The earth was covered by water (v.2). There was a time in ages past when the whole earth was covered by water. Note the phrase *the deep*: this is simply a description of the *waters* mentioned in the next sentence. H.C. Leupold, the great Lutheran theologian and writer, says that the Hebrew word for *deep* pictures the earth as being covered with "surging, raging, primeval waters".[5] The face of the earth was not that of peace and tranquility. The surface of the earth was covered with water, the churning and tossing to and fro of huge gigantic waves, the surging back and forth of "raging, primeval waters." Remember that the earth was also covered in a blanket of darkness. The picture is that of an eerie mist and cloudiness hanging over churning, gigantic waves and "raging, primeval waters"—all taking place under the cover of pitch black darkness. (What a terrifying, yet fascinating, place the earth must have been at that historic time.)

d. The earth was created by the Spirit of God, that is, the Holy Spirit.

> **"The Spirit of God moved upon the face of the waters" (Ge.1:2).**

The word *move* has the idea of "a vibrant moving, a protective hovering....This 'hovering' was not a single and instantaneous act. It rather describes a continued process".[6] The picture is that of the Spirit of God hovering over the earth, caring for it and protecting it, until He is ready to act on its behalf. But the picture is also that of the Spirit of God being ready to launch the second stage of creation. He is hovering, ready to move and to shape and form and make the earth fruitful and productive. He is ready to move and create life to live upon the earth.

Note that the Spirit of God is active in creation as well as God the Father. This is declared throughout Scripture. In fact, Scripture declares that all three persons of the Godhead were actively involved in creation.

⇒ God the Father was involved in creation.

> **"In the beginning God created the heaven and the earth" (Ge.1:1).**

⇒ God the Holy Spirit was involved in creation.

> **"And the earth was without form, and void; and darkness was upon the face of the deep. And the Spirit of God moved upon the face of the waters" (Ge.1:2).**
> **"By the word of the Lord were the heavens made; and all the host of them by the breath of his mouth [the Holy Spirit]" (Ps.33:6).**
> **"Thou sendest forth thy spirit, they [all the works of God] are created: and thou renewest the face of the earth" (Ps.104:30).**
> **"By his spirit he hath garnished [cleared, NASB] the heavens; his hand hath formed the crooked serpent" (Jb. 26:13).**

---

5 H.C. Leupold. *Genesis*, Vol.1, p.47.
6 Ibid., pp.48, 51.

⇒ God the Son, the Lord Jesus Christ, was involved in creation.

> "In the beginning was the Word, and the Word was with God, and the Word was God. The same was in the beginning with God. All things were made by him; and without him was not any thing made that was made" (Jn.1:1-3).

> "But to us there is but one God, the Father, of whom are all things, and we in him; and one Lord Jesus Christ, by whom are all things, and we by him" (1 Co.8:6).

> "For by him were all things created, that are in heaven, and that are in earth, visible and invisible, whether they be thrones, or dominions, or principalities, or powers: all things were created by him, and for him" (Col.1:16).

> "Who being the brightness of his glory, and the express image of his person, and upholding all things by the word of his power, when he had by himself purged our sins, sat down on the right hand of the Majesty on high" (He.1:3).

Thought 1. God created as He wished and willed. He began the process of creation and moved step by step, clearly showing that with Him all things are possible. He repeated and repeated the creative act, moving from the first stage of creating the unformed earth on through to the sixth day of creation. By repeating and repeating His creative power, God hammers into the mind of man two great truths.
1) God is God (Elohim. See note 6—Ge.1:1 for discussion.)
2) It is God who has created. He alone has the power to create; therefore, He is worthy of all praise, and He is to be exalted above all.

> "Stand up and bless the Lord your God for ever and ever: and blessed be thy glorious name, which is exalted above all blessing and praise. Thou, even thou, art Lord alone; thou hast made heaven, the heaven of heavens, with all their host, the earth, and all things that are therein, the seas, and all that is therein, and thou preservest them all; and the host of heaven worshippeth thee" (Ne.9:5-6).

Thought 2. God created the earth stage by stage. He had the power to take an unshaped and unformed earth and shape and form it. He had the power to take a lifeless and unpopulated earth and create life and populate it. Thereby, God is the Sovereign Lord and Majesty of the universe. As Sovereign Lord, God reveals three wonderful truths to us.
1) God has the power to take a person and make a new creation out of him. And God has the power to take that new person, that new creation, and move him along stage by stage until he reaches the climactic moment of redemption and perfection—all at the return of the Lord Jesus Christ.

> "Therefore if any man be in Christ, he is a new creature: old things are passed away; behold, all things are become new" (2 Co.5:17).

> "Being confident of this very thing, that he which hath begun a good work in you will perform it until the day of Jesus Christ" (Ph.1:6).

> "I know whom I have believed, and am persuaded that he is able to keep that which I have committed unto him against that day" (2 Ti.1:12).

> "Who [believers] are kept by the power of God through faith unto salvation ready to be revealed in the last time" (1 Pe.1:5).

> "Now unto him that is able to keep you from falling, and to present you faultless before the presence of his glory with exceeding joy, to the only wise God our Saviour, be glory and majesty, dominion and power, both now and ever. Amen" (Jude 24-25).

2) God also has the power to take the present universe, which is corrupted, and destroy it and make a new heavens and earth.

> "But the day of the Lord will come as a thief in the night; in the which the heavens shall pass away with a great noise, and the elements shall melt with fervent heat, the earth also and the works that are therein shall be burned up. Seeing then that all these things shall be dissolved, what manner of persons ought ye to be in all holy conversation and godliness, looking for and hasting unto the coming of the day of God, wherein the heavens being on fire shall be dissolved, and the elements shall melt with fervent heat? Nevertheless we, according to his promise, look for new heavens and a new earth, wherein dwelleth righteousness. Wherefore, beloved, seeing that ye look for such things, be diligent that ye may be found of him in peace, without spot, and blameless" (2 Pe.3:10-14).

> "And I saw a new heaven and a new earth: for the first heaven and the first earth were passed away; and there was no more sea. And I John saw the holy city, new Jerusalem, coming down from God out of heaven, prepared as a bride adorned for her husband. And I heard a great voice out of heaven saying, Behold, the tabernacle of God is with men, and he will dwell with them, and they shall be his people, and God himself shall be with them, and be their God. And God shall wipe away all tears from their eyes; and there shall be no more death, neither sorrow, nor crying, neither shall there be any more pain: for the former things are passed away. And he that sat upon the throne said, Behold, I make all things new. And he said unto me, Write: for these words are true and faithful" (Re.21:1-5).

> "For, behold, I create new heavens and a new earth: and the former shall not be remembered, nor come into mind" (Is.65:17).

"For as the new heavens and the new earth, which I will make, shall remain before me, saith the Lord, so shall your seed and your name remain [the seed and name of believers]" (Is.66:22).

"For the earnest expectation of the creature [creation] waiteth for the manifestion of the sons of God. For the creature [creation] was made subject to vanity [by the sins of man], not willingly, but by reason of him who hath subjected the same in hope, because the creature [creation] itself also shall be delivered from the bondage of corruption into the glorious liberty of the children of God. For we know that the whole creation groaneth and travaileth in pain together until now" (Ro.8:19-22).

3) God has the power to quicken dead, lifeless matter and give it life. He has the power to quicken the dead spirit of man. He has the power to "quicken the dead, and call those things which be not as though they were" (Ro.4:17).

"And you hath he quickened, who were dead in trespasses and sins" (Ep.2:1).

"And you, being dead in your sins and the uncircumcision of your flesh, hath he quickened together with him, having forgiven you all trespasses" (Col.2:13).

There is *The Divine Judgment or Gap Position*. (See DEEPER STUDY # 4—Ge.1:2 for discussion.)

DEEPER STUDY # 4

(1:2) **Creation—God, Creator—Gap Theory—Divine Judgment Theory—Recreation Theory—Restitution Theory—Satan, Fall of**: the second major position on creation is known by at least four names, but the most used name is probably *The Gap Theory*. The other names by which the theory is known are *The Recreation Theory, The Restitution Theory*, or *The Divine Judgment Theory*. Each of the names stresses some major point of the theory.

Briefly stated, the Gap theory says that the word "*was*" (v.2) should be translated "*became.*" The earth was created perfect in verse one. But in verse two the earth is seen as a waste and void. Thus between verse one and verse two there is a huge gap of time, an unknown number of centuries. Between the two verses something happened—something with *catastrophic* consequences. What? What caused the earth to "become a waste and void"? It is usually said that Satan's fall occurred at this time, and his rebellion against God caused a catastrophic judgment to fall upon the earth. (See Is.14:12; see Eze.28:12.) Thus verse one describes a perfect creation, and verse two describes what happened to the earth after a great judgment fell upon it. Verse three begins the recreation of the earth by the Spirit of God who had been hovering over the earth. There are several arguments used to support this position.

1. The word *was* can be translated *became*. Therefore, these two verses should read:

"In the beginning God created the heaven and the earth. And the earth *became* without form and void [empty]" (Ge.1:1-2).

2. The Bible clearly says that the earth was created "not in vain [empty, as a waste]" (Is.45:18). Therefore, when God created the earth, it must have been perfect. The earth must have reflected the very perfection of God's nature, the perfection of all His glory and majesty. This logical argument is also added: a perfect and loving God cannot create an imperfect universe. A perfect and loving God can create only a perfect world.

"For thus saith the Lord that created the heavens; God himself that formed the earth and made it; he hath established it, he created it not in vain [empty, as a waste], he formed it to be inhabited: I am the Lord; and there is none else" (Is.45:18).

3. The Bible teaches that Satan (Lucifer) was the most exalted angel in all of heaven, that God had created him to rule as the highest of all created beings. But Satan did the same thing that all men have done: he sinned and fell. He rebelled against God. Therefore, just as man was cast out of the Garden of Eden, so Satan was cast from his exalted position before God. And just as men are to face the eternal judgment of God, so is Satan. Satan is to be condemned to an eternity of hell—soon, very soon, just as all men who reject God are to be condemned.

When was Satan cast from his exalted position before God? The *Gap Theory* says in the dateless past, someplace in the ages between verses one and two. And Satan's fall caused a catastrophic judgment to fall upon the earth. Apparently, part of his rule and reign was the earth and the physical and material universe. Therefore, when judgment fell upon Satan, judgment also fell upon all that he ruled over, which included the earth. It was then that the earth became "without form and void [empty, a waste]" (Ge.1:2).

"How art thou fallen from heaven, O Lucifer, son of the morning! how art thou cut down to the ground, which didst weaken the nations! For thou hast said in thine heart, I will ascend into heaven, I will exalt my throne above the stars of God: I will sit also upon the mount of the congregation, in the sides of the north: I will ascend above the heights of the clouds; I will be like the most High. Yet thou shalt be brought down to hell, to the sides of the pit" (Is.14:12-15).

"Moreover the word of the Lord came unto me, saying, Son of man, take up a lamentation upon the king of Tyrus [a type of Satan, Lucifer], and say unto him, Thus saith the Lord GOD; Thou sealest up the sum, full of wisdom, and perfect in beauty. Thou hast been in Eden the garden of God; every precious stone was thy covering, the sardius, topaz, and the diamond, the beryl, the onyx, and the jasper, the sapphire, the emerald, and the carbuncle, and gold: the workmanship of thy tabrets and of thy pipes was prepared in thee in the day that thou wast created. Thou art the anointed cherub that covereth; and I have set thee so: thou wast upon the holy mountain of God; thou hast walked up and down in the midst of the stones of rie. Thou wast perfect in thy ways from the day that thou wast created, till iniquity was found in thee. By the multitude of thy merchandise they have filled the midst of thee with violence, and thou hast sinned: therefore I will cast thee as profane out of the mountain of God: and I will destroy thee, O covering cherub, from the midst of the stones of fire. Thine heart was lifted up because of thy beauty, thou hast corrupted thy wisdom by reason of thy brightness: I will cast thee to the ground, I will lay thee before kings, that they may behold thee. Thou hast defiled thy sanctuaries by the multitude of thine iniquities, by the iniquity of thy traffic; therefore will I bring forth a fire from the midst of thee, it shall devour thee, and I will bring thee to ashes upon the earth in the sight of all them that behold thee" (Eze.28:11-18).

4. The Bible teaches that Satan has some control over the earth: he has access to influence the world and man. History and the destruction and devastation of nature and the evil of men show that the domain of Satan includes the earth, at least to some degree. God certainly did not create the universe and then put Satan and his evil forces in charge of it. This would be absolutely contrary to God's nature. Therefore, Satan's fall and control over the earth had to take place after the earth and universe were created. Again, the only time this could have happened was between verse one and verse two. God created a perfect heavens and earth, and then when Satan fell, the earth "became without form and void" because it was under the domain of Satan. (See DEEPER STUDY # 1, *Satan*—Rev.12:9 for more discussion.)

⇒ Scripture calls Satan the god of this world.

"But if our gospel be hid, it is hid to them that are lost: in whom the god of this world hath blinded the minds of them which believe not, lest the light of the glorious gospel of Christ, who is the image of God, should shine unto them" (2 Co.4:3-4).

⇒ Scripture calls Satan the prince of this world.

"Now is the judgment of this world: now shall the prince of this world be cast out" (Jn.12:31).
"Hereafter I will not talk much with you: for the prince of this world cometh, and hath nothing in me" (Jn.14:30).
"Of judgment, because the prince of this world is judged" (Jn.16:11).

⇒ Scripture calls Satan the prince of the power of the air.

"Wherein in time past ye walked according to the course of this world, according to the prince of the power of the air, the spirit that now worketh in the children of disobedience" (Ep.2:2).

⇒ Scripture calls Satan the ruler of the darkness of this world.

"For we wrestle not against flesh and blood, but against principalities, against powers, against the rulers of the darkness of this world, against spiritual wickedness in high places" (Ep.6:12).

⇒ Satan is the king of a kingdom.

"And if Satan cast out Satan, he is divided against himself; how shall then his kingdom stand?" (Mt.12:26).
"Again, the devil taketh him up into an exceeding high mountain, and showeth him all the kingdoms of the world, and the glory of them; and saith unto him, All these things will I give thee, if thou wilt fall down and worship me" (Mt.4:8-9).

⇒ Satan has his grip upon the whole world.

"And we know that we are of God, and the whole world lieth in wickedness" (1 Jn.5:19).

5. The earth shows some signs that it has suffered some prehistoric catastrophe. Most of us have seen pictures or read of prehistoric animals that were found frozen with their internal organs intact. They apparently suffered some catastrophe that immediately fell upon them and froze them or else their internal organs would have decayed. This points to an unexpected and immediate catastrophe that caught the world of the animals off guard. The fall of Satan would explain the catastrophe.

6. The words *without form and void* (tohu va bohu) are used together in only two other places (Is.34:11; Je.4:23). In both cases they point to a condition brought by God's judgment. Therefore, it is argued that to be consistent, we must conclude that the earth became "without form and void" here in verse two because of some judgment of God. The only prehistoric judgment revealed by Scripture is that of Satan when he fell.

7. The gap, the indefinite period of time between verses one and two, can be used to explain the scientific discoveries that point to a prehistoric earth. The fossil discoveries of prehistoric animals and vegetation and the centuries needed for mineral deposits to develop—all these can be explained as having taken place during the ages between verses one and two.

8. The earth had to be created perfect because a perfect God was creating it. A perfect God could never create anything "without form and void."

9. The structure of the creation account sets verses one and two off from the rest of the account of creation. Genesis 1:1-2 is just different from Genesis 1:3-31, significantly different.

⇒ Verse three is where the seven days of creation begin, not verses one and two.

⇒ Verse three is where Scripture begins to declare that "God said," and where the six days of creation begin. And note how each of the days of creation begin with the very same words "God said" (Ge.1:3, 6, 9, 14, 20, 24). This sets the actual creation of the universe off from verses one and two—markedly so—according to the Gap Theory.

⇒ Each day of creation is also set off by what is said at the close of the day's account. Note the words, "And the evening and the morning were the first [second, third, fourth, fifth and sixth] day" (vs.5, 8, 13, 19, 23, 31).

The very structure of the creation account is hereby said to point to two different creations of the universe. Verses one and two are said to be the record of the original creation, and verses three to twenty-three gives the record of the *recreation of the earth* after some catastrophic judgment fell upon the earth.

10. The Bible says that God instructed man to "be fruitful, and multiply, and replenish the earth" (Ge.1:28). Note the word *replenish*. To replenish means to fill again, to repopulate, not to populate for the first time.

11. The Bible says that when the foundations of the earth were laid, "the morning stars [angels] sang together, and all the sons of God shouted for joy" (Jb. 38:7). An undeveloped and unshaped earth would not be reason for singing a song of joy nor for rejoicing in God's sovereignty, in His supreme intelligence and power.

	B. The First Day: Creation of Light, 1:3-5
1. God's Word created light	3 And God said, Let there be light: and there was light.
2. God saw that His creation was *good*—fulfilled its function	4 And God saw the light, that it was good: and God divided the light from the darkness.
3. God named the light Day & the darkness He named Night	5 And God called the light Day, and the darkness he called Night. And the evening and the morning were the first day.

DIVISION I

CREATION OF THE HEAVENS AND THE EARTH, 1:1–2:3

B. The First Day: Creation of Light, 1:3-5

(1:3-5) **Introduction**: remember the stage of creation the earth was in. It was hanging in space, unshaped and unformed, undeveloped and unfinished. The face of the whole earth was covered with "surging, raging, primeval waters";[1] and a heavy, dense fog (mist) hung over the waters. The earth was also wrapped in a blanket of pitch black darkness. Picture the scene: it is an eerie one. It is the picture of a primeval earth, an earth that had not yet been fully developed and formed, an earth that had an eerie, dense fog (mist) hanging over churning, gigantic waves and raging, primeval waters—all blanketed under the cover of pitch black darkness.

Now God is ready to move to the next stage of creation. He is ready to launch what is known as *the six days of creation*, the time that He took to create the universe. (See Introduction to the Seven Days of Creation, DEEPER STUDY # 9—Ge.1:1-2:3.) This is *The First Day: Creation of Light*."

  1. God's Word created light (v.3).
  2. God saw that His creation was *good*—fulfilled its function (v.4).
  3. God named the light Day and the darkness He named Night (v.5).

[1] (1:3) **Light—Creation—Word of God**: God's Word created light. The phrase *let there be* is one word in the Hebrew (hayah). It is a strong, active imperative. God is commanding "light to become," to come into existence. Light is not eternal; it has not always been in existence. Light came into existence just like everything else in the universe. God created light.

Now, what is light? Light is a radiating energy that radiates out from some body. In the case of the earth, light radiates out from the body of the sun. Science tells us that there are billions of suns and stars (a star is a sun) scattered all throughout the universe, billions of stars that radiate and give off light. Science also tells us that heavenly bodies, suns and stars, are being born and formed and dying all the time. Scattered all throughout the universe—all throughout outer space—there are billions of stars in various stages of birth and growth and death. These stages range all the way...

  • from the first stage where gases begin to form and create intense heat
  • over to the formation of a solid mass or heavenly body of volcanic flame
  • over to the burning out of the volcanic flame and the eventual death of the sun

Now, refer back to verse one: "In the beginning God created the heaven and the earth." God had already created the heavens, the stars and suns, of the universe in verse one. What, then, does it mean here in verse three when it says that "God said, 'Let there be light': and there was light"? It can mean one of four things.

a. *Let there be light*: this can mean that God created cosmic light throughout the whole universe. It is possible that the universe was in a stage of incompleteness just as the earth was. God had not yet finished or completed the stars in outer space. The heavenly bodies had been created just as the earth had, in a rough stage of development. All heavenly bodies were in a gaseous stage, but now God was ready to create light. Therefore, he *completed* some—just some—of the stars, causing the gases and solid elements (atoms, protons, neutrons, electrons, or whatever the most basic elements are that form stars) to form into solid mass, into their completed form.

Very simply stated, when God said, "Let there be light," He completed the formation of *some stars*. Throughout the universe, sun after sun began to give off their light and heat and beauty. God said, "'Let there be light': and there was light" (Ge.1:3).

b. *Let there be light*: this can mean that God created the heaven and the earth by what we call *natural law* or *the laws of nature*. Perhaps God created the atoms, protons, neutrons, electrons, gases, or chemicals—whatever the most minute particles or mass and energy are. Perhaps God then set in motion the natural laws that are to govern the heavenly bodies. This would mean that the stars and suns began in a gaseous stage and then developed into a solid state of mass and gas just as they do today throughout the far reaches of space. When God said. "Let there be light," He was setting in motion the natural law that would take matter and energy and develop suns and stars that would give off light, matter and energy that would continue to develop suns and stars throughout all the ages. This is certainly what happens today, for

---

[1] H.C. Leupold. *Genesis*, Vol.1, p.47.

science tells us an amazing thing: the gases, particles, and molecules floating about in outer space are interacting and being compressed together. They are being compressed with such force that a flaming mass of enormous temperature is being created. Thereby new stars are being born and formed all throughout the universe. Of course, the laws that cause this phenomena to happen were created and set in motion by God.

c. *Let there be light*: this can mean that God created light completely independent of heavenly bodies (that is, suns and stars). When God created the heaven and the earth, perhaps He just hung them in space (v.1). Perhaps the laws which govern their functioning were not yet created or put into motion. The heavenly bodies were just hanging there in space, but they were not yet performing their function, not rotating, not set in motion, not flying through space. But when God said, *Let there be light*, the combustible energy that radiates light was given to some of the stars and suns. The physical laws which govern them were put into operation, and the stars of the universe began to operate. They began to perform the function for which they were created: they gave off light.

d. *Let there be light*: this can mean that the clouds and dense fog (mist) that hung over the earth began to evaporate and thin out. They evaporated and thinned out enough to allow the first rays of light to hit the earth. If this is what happened, then it took three more days before all the clouds and mist were completely gone and the sun, moon, and stars were able to be seen from the earth. (See outline and notes—Ge.1:14-19 for more discussion.)

Note: this is the position taken by those who hold to the *Gap Theory*. (See DEEPER STUDY # 4—Ge.1:2 for more discussion.) The Gap Theory says that the fall of Satan was so devastating that God had to severely judge Satan and his domain of rule. Part of Satan's rule had included the earth. Therefore, verse two is a description of how severely God had to judge the earth. Part of the judgment included the blanket of darkness that engulfed the earth. God commanded the sun to withhold its light from the earth. How? By covering the earth with thick, dense fog and clouds. This idea is taken from the following Scriptures.

> "Who laid the foundations of the earth, that it should not be removed for ever. Thou coveredst it with the deep as with a garment: the waters stood above the mountains. At thy rebuke they fled; at the voice of thy thunder they hasted away. They go up by the mountains; they go down by the valleys unto the place which thou hast founded for them. Thou hast set a bound that they may not pass over; that they turn not again to cover the earth" (Ps.104:5-9. Note: this passage could and most likely does refer to The Great Flood in Noah's day.)

> "Behold, the Lord maketh the earth empty, and maketh it waste, and turneth it upside down, and scattereth abroad the inhabitants thereof" (Is.24:1).

> "For thus saith the Lord that created the heavens; God himself that formed the earth and made it; he hath established it, he created it not in vain, he formed it to be inhabited: I am the Lord; and there is none else" (Is.45:18).

> "I beheld the earth, and, lo, it was without form, and void; and the heavens, and they had no light. I beheld the mountains, and, lo, they trembled, and all the hills moved lightly. I beheld, and, lo, there was no man, and all the birds of the heavens were fled. I beheld, and, lo, the fruitful place was a wilderness, and all the cities thereof were broken down at the presence of the Lord, and by his fierce anger" (Je.4:23-26).

> "For this they willingly are ignorant of, that by the word of God the heavens were of old, and the earth standing out of the water and in the water: whereby the world that then was, being overflowed with water, perished: but the heavens and the earth, which are now, by the same word are kept in store, reserved unto fire against the day of judgment and perdition of ungodly men" (2 Pe.3:5-7).

Thought 1. Light is the most pure and brilliant thing known to man. It is often used to picture a scene full of glory and splendor. Light is often spellbinding and awe inspiring.

> "The light of the eyes rejoiceth the heart: and a good report maketh the bones fat" (Pr.15:30).
> "Truly the light is sweet, and a pleasant thing it is for the eyes to behold the sun" (Ec.11:7).

Thought 2. Scripture declares that God is light. Light is what God is within Himself, within His being and nature and within His character. God dwells in the splendor and glory of light. Wherever He is, the splendor and glory of light shines out of His being. In fact, there is not even a need for the sun when God's glory is present. The glory of His presence just beams forth the most brilliant light imaginable, so brilliant and glorious that it would consume human flesh. God's nature of light is the light of His *holiness*. God is holy, full of the light and splendor of holiness. (See note 5—1 Jn.1:5 for more discussion.)

1) God is the infinite and eternal light.

> "This then is the message which we have heard of him, and declare unto you, that God is light, and in him is no darkness at all" (1 Jn.1:5).

2) God is the Father of lights.

> "Every good gift and every perfect gift is from above, and cometh down from the Father of lights, with whom is no variableness, neither shadow of turning" (Js.1:17).

3) God lives in the inaccessible light.

> "Who only hath immortality, dwelling in the light which no man can approach unto; whom no man hath seen, nor can see: to whom be honour and power everlasting. Amen" (1 Ti.6:16).

4)   Believers shall live eternally with God in His holy city. His holy city shall be the capital of the new heavens and earth, and we shall all live there in the splendor of God's light and glory forever and ever.

> **"And the city had no need of the sun, neither of the moon, to shine in it: for the glory of God did lighten it, and the Lamb is the light thereof. And the nations of them which are saved shall walk in the light of it: and the kings of the earth do bring their glory and honour into it" (Re.21:23-24).**
> **"And there shall be no night there; and they need no candle, neither light of the sun; for the Lord God giveth them light: and they shall reign for ever and ever" (Re.22:5).**

Thought 3. God does not want man dwelling in darkness, but in light. Life cannot exist in darkness—it is impossible. Therefore, God created light so that man can live and walk upon earth.

This is also true in the spiritual realm of life. God does not want man living in spiritual darkness, but in spiritual light. God does not want man walking in the dark, stumbling, fumbling, groping, and grasping about, wondering...

*   where he has come from
*   why he is here upon earth
*   where he is going

God does not want man in spiritual darkness. God knows that man cannot exist—he cannot live, not eternally, not forever—if he walks in spiritual darkness.

Therefore, God has given man *the Light of life* so that he can live and walk, so that he can see and know the truth about the world and man. God has given man *the Light of life* so that man can see and know where he has come from, why he is here upon earth, and where he is going.

What is that *Light of life*? It is Jesus Christ, the Son of God. (See DEEPER STUDY # 1—Jn.8:12.)

> **"In him was life; and the life was the light of men" (Jn.1:4).**
> **"And this is the condemnation, that light [Jesus Christ] is come into the world, and men loved darkness rather than light, because their deeds were evil" (Jn.3:19).**
> **"Then spake Jesus again unto them, saying, I am the light of the world: he that followeth me shall not walk in darkness, but shall have the light of life" (Jn.8:12).**
> **"As long as I am in the world, I am the light of the world" (Jn.9:5).**
> **"Then Jesus said unto them, Yet a little while is the light with you. Walk while ye have the light, lest darkness come upon you: for he that walketh in darkness knoweth not whither he goeth. While ye have light, believe in the light, that ye may be the children of light" (Jn.12:35-36).**
> **"I am come a light into the world, that whosoever believeth on me should not abide in darkness" (Jn.12:46).**
> **"The night is far spent, the day is at hand: let us therefore cast off the works of darkness, and let us put on the armour of light [Christ and His teachings]" (Ro.13:12).**
> **"For God, who commanded the light to shine out of darkness, hath shined in our hearts, to give the light of the knowledge of the glory of God in the face of Jesus Christ" (2 Co.4:6).**
> **"Wherefore he saith, Awake thou that sleepest, and arise from the dead, and Christ shall give thee light" (Ep.5:14).**

2 **(1:4) Light—Creation:** God saw that His creation was *good*—light fulfilled its function. The picture is that God looked at the *light* and saw that it was *good*. The word *good* refers to the value, the purpose, and the function of something. Hence, God looked and saw that the light was *good*: it was valuable, very valuable; it fulfilled its purpose and its function. What is the purpose and function of light? Note the statement: "God divided the light from the darkness." Unless light existed—unless light was divided from darkness—the earth would be in total darkness.

⇒   If the earth had no sun, the earth would be engulfed in total darkness.
⇒   If the earth was still covered by a heavy dense fog (clouds and mist), the earth would be blanketed in total darkness.

Light has at least five basic functions or purposes.

⇒   Light divides darkness to give some light to the earth and universe.
⇒   Light makes things grow. Life cannot exist without light. Man, animals, green plants, and algae—all are dependent upon light in order to live upon the earth. Green plants and algae convert light into energy, and they grow thereby (the process is known as photosynthesis). Without light there would be no plants upon earth to feed man and animal. Light is an absolute essential for life and growth.
⇒   Light gives heat and warmth.
⇒   Light gives color and beauty to things.
⇒   Light enables man and animals to see; light exposes things—all the universe and all the earth—so that man and animals can see and carry out their function in a world of variety and beauty.

When "God saw the light, [He saw] that it was *good*." Light fulfilled its function. Light was exactly as God had planned; it was designed and perfectly fitted for its purpose; it was useful and profitable; it was functioning just as God had willed.

Thought 1. The creation of light enables man to see two things.
1) Light enables man to see the beauty of God's creation. It enables man to see the great work of God in creation, the great intelligence and power of God (see note 3—Ge.1:1; also see notes, "Introduction to the Seven Days of Creation"—Ge.1:1-2:3).
2) Light enables man to see how to carry on his work. It enables man to fulfill his purpose upon earth. But note: just being able to see and to work does not mean that a man will fulfill his purpose upon earth. A man has to be responsible. He has to follow the Lord Jesus Christ, the Son of God Himself, to reap purpose, meaning, and significance in life. He has to use his skills—his abilities and talents—as Christ has instructed him. Then and only then can man fulfill his purpose and function upon earth.

God gave man life and sent His Son into the world to show man how to live and function. Therefore, man has to do what God says, or else man will never have meaning and purpose—not eternal meaning and purpose. Man will never be able to live and function with God—not eternally, not forever—unless man lives as Christ says.

Thought 2. God created light, divided the light from the darkness, and He did it for man. God will do the same things for man spiritually. God will give man light in the midst of darkness...
• the light of order in the midst of dark chaos
• the light of purpose in the midst of dark emptiness
• the light of fellowship in the midst of dark loneliness
• the light of knowledge in the midst of dark ignorance

God will create light within the dark, chaotic heart of man so that man may *know God*—so that man may feel and sense the glory of God within his very own being.

"And have put on the new man, which is renewed in knowledge after the image of him that created him" (Col.3:10).

Thought 3. Light and darkness can never again be joined or reconciled, not within nature. The same is true spiritually.

"Be ye not unequally yoked together with unbelievers: for what fellowship hath righteousness with unrighteousness? and what communion hath light with darkness?" (2 Co.6:14. See DEEPER STUDY #2—Jn.8:12.)

Thought 4. God created light. Light is one of the great words of Scripture.
1) God is light and in Him is no darkness at all (1 Jn.1:5).
2) Jesus Christ is the Light of the world—the very embodiment of the heavenly light (Jn.8:12; 9:5).
3) The light of the knowledge of God is seen in the face of Jesus Christ (2 Co.4:6).
4) Jesus Christ "lights every man" who comes into the world (Jn.1:9).
5) Believers are said to become "children of light" through belief in the Light, Jesus Christ Himself (Jn.12:36).
6) Believers have been transferred from the dominion of darkness into the Kingdom of Christ, the inheritance of light (Col.1:13).
7) Before they come to Christ, believers are not only in darkness but are an embodiment of darkness. But when they come to Christ, believers are placed in the Light and become an embodiment of the Light itself (Ep.5:8).
8) Believers are the light of the world (Mt.5:14-16).
9) Believers are to set their light on a candlestick—to make their light conspicuous (Mt.5:15).
10) Evil-doers shun the light (Jn.3:20f).
11) The creation of light is a picture of the expulsion of spiritual darkness (Ge.1:2f).

3 (1:5) **Light—Darkness—Creation**: God named the light *Day*, and the darkness He named *Night*. Note two facts.
a. God, not man, named the light and darkness. This is very significant. It shows that God is the Lord of both day and night, not man. Light and darkness are both part of God's creation. Both are *good*; both have their purpose and function in God's creation.

Thought 1. This means that man owes his body and life to God both during the day and the night. Man is to serve God in the day and in the night. He is not to abuse either the day or the night...
• by being lazy, slothful, or complacent
• by harming his body, mind, or spirit
• by neglecting, ignoring, or denying God
• by partying, drinking, or taking drugs
• by being conceited, haughty, or prideful
• by carousing, going too far, or being immoral
• by showing prejudice, favoritism, or partiality

Thought 2. God is the Lord of both day and night. Therefore, there is no need to fear the day or the night. God is able to take care of us in the light and in the dark. Believers can live every moment of every day and every moment of every night knowing that God is looking after them. We can know that we are in the *safekeeping* of God. We are always under the watchful eye of God—day and night.

"Are not two sparrows sold for a farthing? and one of them shall not fall on the ground without your Father. But the very hairs of your head are all numbered. Fear ye not therefore, ye are of more value than many sparrows" (Mt.10:29-31).

"For the which cause I also suffer these things: nevertheless I am not ashamed: for I know whom I have believed, and am persuaded that he is able to keep that which I have committed unto him against that day" (2 Ti.1:12).

"And the Lord shall deliver me from every evil work, and will preserve me unto his heavenly kingdom: to whom be glory for ever and ever. Amen" (2 Ti.4:18).

"Go ye therefore, and teach all nations, baptizing them in the name of the Father, and of the Son, and of the Holy Ghost: teaching them to observe all things whatsoever I have commanded you: and, lo, I am with you alway, even unto the end of the world" (Mt.28:19-20).

"The Lord is my strength and my shield; my heart trusted in him, and I am helped: therefore my heart greatly rejoiceth; and with my song will I praise him" (Ps.28:7).

"But I am poor and needy; yet the Lord thinketh upon me: thou art my help and my deliverer; make no tarrying, O my God" (Ps.40:17).

"Behold, he that keepeth Israel shall neither slumber nor sleep" (Ps.121:4).

"Fear thou not; for I am with thee: be not dismayed; for I am thy God: I will strengthen thee; yea, I will help thee; yea, I will uphold thee with the right hand of my righteousness" (Is.41:10).

"And even to your old age I am he; and even to hoar [gray] hairs will I carry you: I have made, and I will bear; even I will carry, and will deliver you" (Is.46:4).

b. God has given a very special function to both day and night. The earth rotates and spins on its axis as it flies through space. It takes about twenty-four hours for every part of the earth to rotate and face the sun. When a part of the earth rotates and faces the sun, it is called day. When the other part of the earth faces away from the sun, it is called night.

The point is this: each (day and night) follows in the steps of the other, in the succession of time. Time is divided between day and night.

⇒ The day gives the light for work and for the fulfilling of man's function upon earth.
⇒ The night gives the darkness for rest and the renewing of strength.

Thought 1. Spiritually, there is a message for us in the creation of day and night.
1) The day shows man there is a new beginning, a new day, a new start, a new arising.
   ⇒ The beginning of a new day points toward the beginning of a new life. We can start life all over again: we can be *born again* and be spiritually renewed. We can become a *new creature*, a *new man* in Christ.

   "Jesus answered and said unto him, Verily, verily, I say unto thee, Except a man be born again, he cannot see the kingdom of God. Nicodemus saith unto him, How can a man be born when he is old? can he enter the second time into his mother's womb, and be born? Jesus answered , Verily, verily, I say unto thee, Except a man be born of water and of the Spirit, he cannot enter into the kingdom of God" (Jn.3:3-5).

   "Therefore if any man be in Christ, he is a new creature: old things are passed away; behold, all things are become new" (2 Co.5:17).

   "And that ye put on the new man, which after God is created in righteousness and true holiness" (Ep.4:24).

   "And have put on the new man, which is renewed in knowledge after the image of him that created him" (Col.3:10).

   "Being born again, not of corruptible seed, but of incorruptible, by the word of God, which liveth and abideth for ever" (1 Pe.1:23).

   ⇒ The beginning of a new day, the awakening out of sleep, points toward the resurrection of the body.

   "Verily, verily, I say unto you, The hour is coming, and now is, when the dead shall hear the voice of the Son of God: and they that hear shall live" (Jn.5:25).

   "And this is the will of him that sent me, that every one which seeth the Son, and believeth on him, may have everlasting life: and I will raise him up at the last day" (Jn.6:40).

   "Jesus said unto her, I am the resurrection, and the life: he that believeth in me, though he were dead, yet shall he live" (Jn.11:25).

   "For as in Adam all die, even so in Christ shall all be made alive" (1 Co.15:22).

   "Knowing that he which raised up the Lord Jesus shall raise up us also by Jesus, and shall present us with you" (2 Co.4:14).

   "For the Lord himself shall descend from heaven with a shout, with the voice of the archangel, and with the trump of God: and the dead in Christ shall rise first: then we which are alive and remain shall be caught up together with them in the clouds, to meet the Lord in the air: and so shall we ever be with the Lord" (1 Th.4:16-17).

   "Marvel not at this: for the hour is coming, in the which all that are in the graves shall hear his voice, and shall come forth; they that have done good, unto the resurrection of life; and they that have done evil, unto the resurrection of damnation" (Jn.5:28-29).

   "And have hope toward God, which they themselves also allow, that there shall be a resurrection of the dead, both of the just and unjust" (Ac.24:15).

"But God will redeem my soul from the power of the grave: for he shall receive me" (Ps.49:15).

"Thou, which hast showed me great and sore troubles, shalt quicken me again, and shalt bring me up again from the depths of the earth" (Ps.71:20).

"And many of them that sleep in the dust of the earth shall awake, some to everlasting life, and some to shame and everlasting contempt" (Da.12:2).

"I will ransom them from the power of the grave; I will redeem them from death: O death, I will be thy plagues; O grave, I will be thy destruction" (Ho.13:14).

2) The night shows man that there is a time to stop and end one's activity and lie down and evaluate one's daily life. This points toward the end of life when there is to be a stoppage of life, a lying down of the human body, a time when man can no longer work, a time when man is to be judged for how he has lived upon earth.

"For the wages of sin is death; but the gift of God is eternal life through Jesus Christ our Lord" (Ro.6:23).

"For to be carnally minded is death; but to be spiritually minded is life and peace" (Ro.8:6).

"Who shall be punished with everlasting destruction from the presence of the Lord, and from the glory of his power" (2 Th.1:9).

"And as it is appointed unto men once to die, but after this the judgment" (He.9:27).

"Lord, make me to know mine end, and the measure of my days, what it is; that I may know how frail I am" (Ps.39:4).

Thought 2. The creation of day and night teaches two challenging lessons:
1) We are to work for God by day.

"I must work the works of him that sent me, while it is day: the night cometh, when no man can work" (Jn.9:4).

"Therefore, my beloved brethren, be ye stedfast, unmovable, always abounding in the work of the Lord, forasmuch as ye know that your labour is not in vain in the Lord" (1 Co.15:58).

"Whatsoever ye do, do it heartily, as to the Lord, and not unto men; knowing that of the Lord ye shall receive the reward of the inheritance: for ye serve the Lord Christ" (Col.3:23-24. See outline and notes—Ep.6:5-9.)

"If ye be willing and obedient, ye shall eat the good of the land" (Is.1:19).

"And ye shall serve the Lord your God, and he shall bless thy bread, and thy water; and I will take sickness away from the midst of thee" (Ex.23:25).

2) We are to rest in God by night. We are to meditate in God's Word day and night.

"But his delight is in the law of the Lord; and in his law doth he meditate day and night" (Ps.1:2).

"O how love I thy law! it is my meditation all the day" (Ps.119:97).

"And these words, which I command thee this day, shall be in thine heart: and thou shalt teach them diligently unto thy children, and shalt talk of them when thou sittest in thine house, and when thou walkest by the way, and when thou liest down, and when thou risest up" (De.6:6-7).

	C. The Second Day: Creation of the Firmament (the Atmosphere & Air Space Encircling the Earth), 1:6-8
1. God's Word created the firmament (atmosphere & air space)	6 And God said, Let there be a firmament in the midst of the waters, and let it divide the waters from the waters.
2. God made the firmament	7 And God made the firmament, and divided the waters which were under the firmament from the waters which were above the firmament: and it was so.
3. God named the firmament Heaven	8 And God called the firmament Heaven. And the evening and the morning were the second day.

DIVISION I

CREATION OF THE HEAVENS AND THE EARTH, 1:1–2:3

C. The Second Day: Creation of the Firmament (the Atmosphere and Air Space Encircling the Earth), 1:6-8

(1:6-8) **Introduction**: remember what the earth was like: surging, raging waters covered the whole earth. No land rose above the waters; no land was exposed; no land could be seen. There was only the primeval waters with churning, gigantic waves raging back and forth over the face of the earth. Also covering the earth were heavy, thick clouds, fog, and mist, all of which engulfed the earth in pitch black darkness (Ge.2:4-6, esp. 6). This is the picture of prehistoric earth, an earth covered by waters, waters that surged back and forth and waters in the form of clouds, fog, and mist hanging right above the surging waters. The whole earth was covered in water, its face and its atmosphere. The earth was one massive, unending ocean of water covered with high rising clouds, fog, and mist—all blanketed in pitch black darkness.

Now, the second day of creation takes place. Now God is ready to divide the waters. He is ready to create the physical laws that will cause the clouds, fog, and mist to leave the face of the earth and rise up and hang in the sky above the earth. God is now ready to create the firmament, that is, the atmosphere, the air, the expanse, the space between the clouds above and the earth below. This is, *The Second Day: Creation of the Firmament (the Atmosphere and Air Space Encircling the Earth)*.

1. God's Word created the firmament (atmosphere and air space) (v.6).
2. God made the firmament (atmosphere and air space) (v.7).
3. God named the firmament Heaven (the atmosphere and air space, the lower heaven) (v.8).

1 (1:6) **Firmament—Creation**: God's Word created the firmament. The firmament is the atmosphere, the air, the expanse, the space that encircles the earth. H.C. Leupold, the great Lutheran theologian and Hebrew scholar, says that the word *firmament* (ragia) comes from the Hebrew root that means "to hammer or to spread out".[1] What God did was spread out the clouds and fog that covered the earth. God caused the clouds and fog to leave the face of the earth and rise up and hang in the sky above. God set in motion the physical laws that created...

- an air space
- an atmosphere
- an expanse
- a clear sky above the earth

How did God do this? By His Word. Note the Scripture: "God said, 'Let there be a firmament'" (v.6). God used the power of His Word; God spoke the firmament—the atmosphere and clear sky—into being.

This was absolutely necessary if life was to exist upon the earth. As long as clouds and dense fog hung over the earth, the sun and its light would never be able to penetrate the earth and do its work. Neither would suitable vegetation ever grow, nor would man ever be able to see and function. God had to create the firmament. He had to divide the clouds and fog from the waters upon earth. He had to set in motion the physical laws that *form and keep* the clouds above the surface of the earth.

Thought 1. The creation of the firmament (atmosphere and air space) shows the great being and power of God. By clearing out the clouds and fog, man is able to see the enormous universe of which he is a part. He can see

---

1 H.C. Leupold. *Genesis*, Vol.1, p.59.

both the lower sky (atmosphere) where the birds fly (v.20), and the higher sky (outer space) where the heavenly bodies are (vv.14-15).
⇒ Man is able to observe the spectacular beauty of the heavens above.
⇒ Man is able to think upon the air space, the atmosphere, that encircles the earth and that allows him to breath and survive.

The firmament, the atmosphere and clear sky above, should stir man to worship and praise God. It should cause man to thank God for His great being and power.

"The heavens declare the glory of God; and the firmament showeth his handiwork" (Ps.19:1).
"The heavens declare his righteousness, and all the people see his glory" (Ps.97:6).
"Praise ye the Lord. Praise God in his sanctuary: praise him in the firmament of his power" (Ps.150:1).
"Nevertheless he left not himself without witness, in that he did good, and gave us rain from heaven, and fruitful seasons, filling our hearts with food and gladness" (Ac.14:17).
"For the invisible things of him from the creation of the world are clearly seen, being understood by the things that are made, even his eternal power and Godhead; so that they are without excuse" (Ro.1:20).

Thought 2. God has created the firmament, the atmosphere and air space that encircles the earth. It is this that enables man to breath and survive upon earth. God's care and provision should stir man to bless the Lord from the depths of his soul.

"Bless the Lord, O my soul. O Lord my God, thou art very great; thou art clothed with honour and majesty. Who coverest thyself with light as with a garment: who stretchest out the heavens like a curtain: who layeth the beams of his chambers in the waters: who maketh the clouds his chariot: who walketh upon the wings of the wind....Who laid the foundations of the earth, that it should not be removed for ever. Thou coveredst it with the deep as with a garment: the waters stood above the mountains....He watereth the hills from his chambers: the earth is satisfied with the fruit of thy works" (Ps.104:1-3, 5-6, 13).
"It is he that buildeth his stories in the heaven, and hath founded his troop in the earth; he that calleth for the waters of the sea, and poureth them out upon the face of the earth: The Lord is his name" (Am. 9:6).

Thought 3. God's Word created the firmament, the atmosphere that surrounds the earth. God spoke, and what God commanded happened. There was no variation nor shadow of turning from what He said. Once He had spoken, nothing could stop the firmament or atmosphere from coming into being. What He said took place: the firmament was created exactly as He said. God's Word is sure. All the promises and all the warnings of His Word stand and shall never be changed. What God has said will come to pass, both the promises and the warnings. His Word to man will come to pass just as the firmament came into being when He spoke. God's Word is sure and stedfast. His Word never fails.

"For ever, O Lord, thy word is settled in heaven" (Ps.119:89).
"The grass withereth, the flower fadeth: but the word of our God shall stand for ever" (Is.40:8).
"For verily I say unto you, Till heaven and earth pass, one jot or one tittle shall in no wise pass from the law, till all be fulfilled" (Mt.5:18).
"Heaven and earth shall pass away, but my words shall not pass away" (Mt.24:35).
"But the word of the Lord endureth for ever. And this is the word which by the gospel is preached unto you" (1 Pe.1:25).
"Blessed be the Lord, that hath given rest unto his people Israel, according to all that he promised: there hath not failed one word of all his good promise, which he promised by the hand of Moses his servant" (1 K.8:56).
"The works of his hands are verity [truth] and judgment; all his commandments are sure" (Ps.111:7).
"For I am the Lord: I will speak, and the word that I shall speak shall come to pass; it shall be no more prolonged: for in your days, O rebellious house, will I say the word, and will perform it, saith the Lord God" (Eze.12:25).
"For all the promises of God in him [Jesus Christ] are yea, and in him Amen, unto the glory of God by us" (2 Co.1:20).

Thought 4. God knows that man must have an atmosphere in order to *breathe and live* upon the earth. Therefore, God created the atmosphere or air space to sustain life.
The same is true spiritually. In the Scripture the Hebrew word for *breath of God (pneuma)* means *the Spirit of God.* God knows that man cannot live spiritually without the breath or Spirit of God. No person can live with God unless he has the divine nature of God—the very breath of God, the very presence of the Holy Spirit living within his heart. Therefore, God has made it possible for man to be created anew, to be born again and to become a new man and a new creature. God has made it possible for His breath or Spirit, for His divine nature, to

live within the heart of man. God can make a new man, a new person, a new creature out of a person. A person can start life all over again.

> "Jesus answered and said unto him, Verily, verily, I say unto thee, Except a man be born again, he cannot see the kingdom of God....Jesus answered, Verily, verily, I say unto thee, Except a man be born of water and of the Spirit, he cannot enter into the kingdom of God" (Jn.3:3, 5).
>
> "Therefore if any man be in Christ, he is a new creature: old things are passed away; behold, all things are become new" (2 Co.5:17).
>
> "And that ye put on the new man, which after God is created in righteousness and true holiness" (Ep.4:24).
>
> "And have put on the new man, which is renewed in knowledge after the image of him that created him" (Col.3:10).
>
> "Being born again, not of corruptible seed, but of incorruptible, by the word of God, which liveth and abideth for ever" (1 Pe.1:23).
>
> "Whereby are given unto us exceeding great and precious promises: that by these ye might be partakers of the divine nature, having escaped the corruption that is in the world through lust" (2 Pe.1:4).
>
> "What? know ye not that your body is the temple of the Holy Ghost which is in you, which ye have of God, and ye are not your own? For ye are bought with a price: therefore glorify God in your body, and in your spirit, which are God's" (1 Co.6:19-20).
>
> "[God] who hath also sealed us, and given the earnest of the Spirit in our hearts" (2 Co.1:22).
>
> "In whom [Jesus Christ] ye also trusted, after that ye heard the word of truth, the gospel of your salvation: in whom also after that ye believed, ye were sealed with that holy Spirit of promise" (Ep.1:13).

---

2 (1:7) **Firmament—Creation**: God made the firmament, the atmosphere and air. The reason for repeating and re-emphasizing this creative act of God is twofold.

a. There is a need to stress that God and God alone created the atmosphere and air space encircling the earth. The atmosphere and air space did not just happen...

- by chance
- by random
- by some impersonal force or energy in the universe
- by physical laws that were already in existence

The atmosphere was created by God and by God alone. God Himself spoke the physical laws into being; God Himself made the laws that caused the clouds and fog to arise from the earth and hang in the sky above. God created the laws of nature that put a circle of air and atmosphere around the earth. God Himself stands behind the atmosphere and the physical laws that govern it.

b. There is a need to stress that God fulfills His Word. He completes what He begins. God continued to exercise His power until the atmosphere and air space completely encircled the earth.

⇒ In verse 6 God said, "Let there be a firmament in the midst of the waters." He only *spoke* the Word.

⇒ In verse 7, God made the firmament. That is, God's Word began to operate and carry out what God had said. And the power of God's Word operated all day long, operated until the whole earth was completely encircled with an atmosphere and air space.

Note the words, "and it was so" (v.7). What God said was done. He commanded and it happened. His Word could not be resisted. God and God alone is the Sovereign Lord of the universe; He and He alone has supreme intelligence and knowledge, power and energy. Therefore, when God planned the atmosphere and air space for the earth, He said, "Let there be a firmament" (v.6) and "it was so" (v.7). The power and energy of God's Word went to work and created the firmament, created the atmosphere and air space that encircles the earth. Note that the words "and it was so" are used six times in the creation account (vv.7, 9, 11, 15, 24, 30).

Thought 1. What God began, He completed. What God said, He did. He began the process and the act of creating the atmosphere, and He went about finishing it. This emphasis, this double statement of fact in verses six and seven, gives great confidence to believers. God will complete the work of salvation He has begun in us.

> "Being confident of this very thing, that he which hath begun a good work in you will perform it until the day of Jesus Christ" (Ph.1:6).
>
> "For it is God which worketh in you both to will and to do of his good pleasure" (Ph.2:13).
>
> "Faithful is he that calleth you, who also will do it" (1 Th.5:24).
>
> "But the Lord is faithful, who shall stablish you, and keep you from evil" (2 Th.3:3).
>
> "I know whom I have believed, and am persuaded that he is able to keep that which I have committed unto him against that day" (2 Ti.1:12).
>
> "If we believe not, yet he abideth faithful: he cannot deny himself" (2 Ti.2:13).
>
> "Who are kept by the power of God through faith unto salvation ready to be revealed in the last time" (1 Pe.1:5).
>
> "Now unto him that is able to keep you from falling, and to present you faultless before the presence of his glory with exceeding joy" (Jude 24).

Thought 2. God did not open up the atmosphere above earth to make us feel the great distance of space, to make us feel that God is off in outer space someplace far removed from us, to make us feel that God cannot be reached or approached. On the contrary, God opened up the atmosphere...
• so that we can see all the heavens above, all the glory, power, and goodness of God
• so that we can know there is an open space, an open door, right into the presence of God. We can draw near God; we have open access into His very presence

> "But it is good for me to draw near to God: I have put my trust in the Lord GOD, that I may declare all thy works" (Ps.73:28).
> "Make a joyful noise unto the Lord, all ye lands. Serve the Lord with gladness: come before his presence with singing. Know ye that the Lord he is God: it is he that hath made us, and not we ourselves; we are his people, and the sheep of his pasture" (Ps.100:1-3).
> "Let us draw near with a true heart in full assurance of faith, having our hearts sprinkled from an evil conscience, and our bodies washed with pure water" (He.10:22).
> "Draw nigh to God, and he will draw nigh to you. Cleanse your hands, ye sinners; and purify your hearts, ye double minded" (Js.4:8).

Thought 3. Scripture declares that God uses the firmament for several reasons.
⇒ To reveal the glory and power and knowledge of God.

> "The heavens declare the glory of God; and the firmament showeth his handiwork. Day unto day uttereth speech, and night unto night showeth knowledge" (Ps.19:1-2).

⇒ To water the earth and make things grow.

> "Thou visitest the earth, and waterest it: thou greatly enrichest it with the river of God, which is full of water: thou preparest them corn, when thou hast so provided for it. Thou waterest the ridges thereof abundantly: thou settlest the furrows thereof: thou makest it soft with showers: thou blessest the springing thereof" (Ps.65:9-10).
> "He watereth the hills from his chambers: the earth is satisfied with the fruit of thy works" (Ps.104:13).

⇒ To hold the snow and hail to use as an instrument of judgment.

> "Hast thou entered into the treasures of the snow? or hast thou seen the treasures of the hail, which I have reserved against the time of trouble, against the day of battle and war?" (Jb. 38:22-23).

Thought 4. The waters below and the waters above illustrate worldly Egypt and heavenly or spiritual Canaan. Scripture uses this picture.

> "For the land, whither thou goest in to possess it, is not as the land of Egypt, from whence ye came out, where thou sowedst thy seed, and wateredst it with thy foot [by some irrigation method], as a garden of herbs: but the land, whither ye go to possess it, is a land of hills and valleys, and drinketh water of the rain of heaven: a land which the Lord thy God careth for: the eyes of the Lord thy God are always upon it, from the beginning of the year even unto end of the year" (De.11:10-12).

Note what has been said in the above verse:
⇒ The watering of crops from the waters of the earth (by irrigation methods) are pictured as coming only from the earth. They are symbolic of worldly Egypt.
⇒ The waters that come from the rain of heaven are pictured as coming from God. They are symbolic of heavenly or spiritual Canaan.

The point is this: we are not to look to the world and its ways and provisions to sustain us and to give us life. We are to look to heaven and to God. It is He who cares and looks after us. God and God alone can give us life, both abundant and eternal life. God and God alone can give us the water from heaven that lasts forever.

> "Jesus answered and said unto her, If thou knewest the gift of God, and who it is that saith to thee, Give me to drink; thou wouldest have asked of him, and he would have given thee living water" (Jn.4:10).
> "But whosoever drinketh of the water that I shall give him shall never thirst; but the water that I shall give him shall be in him a well of water springing up into everlasting life" (Jn.4:14).
> "In the last day, that great day of the feast, Jesus stood and cried, saying, If any man thirst, let him come unto me, and drink. He that believeth on me, as the scripture hath said, out of his belly shall flow rivers of living water. (But this spake he of the Spirit, which they that believe on him should receive: for the Holy Ghost was not yet given; because that Jesus was not yet glorified)" (Jn.7:37-39).
> "And the Spirit and the bride say, Come. And let him that heareth say, Come. And let him that is athirst come. And whosoever will, let him take the water of life freely" (Re.22:17).

3 (1:8) **Firmament—Heavens—Creation**: God names the firmament—the atmosphere and air space—*Heaven*. The word *heaven* (shamayim) literally means *the heights, the upper regions*. It means both the atmosphere and air space surrounding the earth and the far reaches of outer space. It means the whole universe, all outer space, all the heavens above. Note two points.

a. What God had just created on this second day of creation was the atmosphere and air space that encircles the earth. God did not have to create space, the distance between the suns and stars of the universe. Space (distance) already existed; it naturally existed when God created and hung the suns and stars in space. What God had to create was an atmosphere and air space that encircled the earth. Life upon earth had to breathe, so God had to create the atmosphere and air space. But note: what God names is both the atmosphere and outer space, both the space immediately above the earth and the outer reaches of space. God calls both "heaven." To help man in his understanding, man has often thought in terms of three heavens:

⇒ The *first heaven* is the atmosphere and air space encircling the earth, the heaven or sky where birds fly.
⇒ The *second heaven* is outer space where the heavenly bodies are. It is where all the suns and stars and planets of the material universe operate.
⇒ The *third heaven* is the place where God is, the place where He and all believers live and are to live eternally. The third heaven is the spiritual world, the spiritual dimension of being.

b. God, not man, named the atmosphere encircling the earth and outer space. This is significant. It means that God is the Sovereign Lord of the heavens. Both the atmosphere of the earth and the distances of outer space are creations of God. Both are under His dominion, no matter how far out the outer regions of space extend. God is above, before, and over all.

Thought 1. Man cannot get away from God. God's authority reaches everywhere, even beyond the far regions of outer space. This fact stands as both an encouragement and a warning to man.
⇒ It is an encouragement to believers who trust God. It means that God is everywhere and is able to look after us even when we travel to the far regions of space.
⇒ It is a warning to unbelievers. It means that no matter how much a person may try to escape God's presence and authority, God is still there. Even if a person travels to the far regions of outer space, God's authority and presence will still be there.

"**Know therefore this day, and consider it in thine heart, that the Lord he is God in heaven above, and upon the earth beneath: there is none else**" (De.4:39).
"**Whither shall I go from thy spirit? or whither shall I flee from thy presence? If I ascend up into heaven, thou art there: if I make my bed in hell, behold, thou art there**" (Ps.139:7-8).
"**The eyes of the Lord are in every place, beholding the evil and the good**" (Pr.15:3).
"**Thus saith the Lord, The heaven is my throne, and the earth is my footstool: where is the house that ye build unto me? and where is the place of my rest?**" (Is.66:1).
"**Can any hide himself in secret places that I shall not see him? saith the Lord. Do not I fill heaven and earth? saith the Lord**" (Je.23:24).

Thought 2. Scripture declares that God is in the height of heaven, above the firmament and air space encircling the earth, even above the far reaches of outer space.

"**Is not God in the height of heaven? and behold the height of the stars, how high they are!**" (Jb. 22:12).

Thought 3. When we stand out on a clear night and scan the heavens, as vast and enormous as they are, they are but a speck in comparison to God. God is still above and beyond all we see. God is...

• infinite	• eternal	• majestic
• transcendent	• omniscient	• glorious
• encompassing	• omnipotent	• holy
• sovereign	• omnipresent	• pure

"**Who is like unto thee, O Lord, among the gods? who is like thee, glorious in holiness, fearful in praises, doing wonders?**" (Ex.15:11).
"**Canst thou by searching find out God? canst thou find out the Almighty unto perfection?**" (Jb. 11:7).
"**He hath made every thing beautiful in his time: also he hath set the world in their heart, so that no man can find out the work that God maketh from the beginning to the end**" (Ec.3:11).
"**Hast thou not known? hast thou not heard, that the everlasting God, the Lord, the Creator of the ends of the earth, fainteth not, neither is weary? there is no searching of his understanding**" (Is.40:28).
"**Of old hast thou laid the foundation of the earth: and the heavens are the work of thy hands. They shall perish, but thou shalt endure: yea, all of them shall wax old like a garment; as a vesture shalt thou change them, and they shall be changed**" (Ps.102:25-26).
"**O the depth of the riches both of the wisdom and knowledge of God! how unsearchable are his judgments, and his ways past finding out! For who hath known the mind of the Lord? or who hath been his counsellor? Or who hath first given to him, and it shall be recompensed unto him**

again? For of him, and through him, and to him, are all things: to whom be glory for ever. Amen" (Ro.11:33-36).

"Now unto the King eternal, immortal, invisible, the only wise God, be honour and glory for ever and ever. Amen" (1 Ti.1:17).

"Who only hath immortality, dwelling in the light which no man can approach unto; whom no man hath seen, nor can see: to whom be honour and power everlasting. Amen" (1 Ti.6:16).

"And, Thou, Lord, in the beginning hast laid the foundation of the earth; and the heavens are the works of thine hands: they shall perish; but thou remainest; and they all shall wax old as doth a garment; and as a vesture shalt thou fold them up, and they shall be changed: but thou art the same, and thy years shall not fail" (He.1:10-12).

"To the only wise God our Saviour, be glory and majesty, dominion and power, both now and ever. Amen" (Jude 25).

	D. The Third Day (Part 1): Creation of the Waters (Seas, Lakes, Rivers) & the Dry Land (Continents, Islands), 1:9-10
1. God's Word created the waters & dry land	9 And God said, Let the waters under the heaven be gathered together unto one place, and let the dry land appear: and it was so.
2. God named the dry land *Earth* & the waters *Seas* 3. God saw that His creation was *good*—fulfilled its function	10 And God called the dry land Earth; and the gathering together of the waters called he Seas: and God saw that it was good.

DIVISION I

CREATION OF THE HEAVENS AND THE EARTH, 1:1–2:3

D. The Third Day (Part 1): Creation of the Waters (Seas, Lakes, Rivers) and the Dry Land (Continents, Islands), 1:9-10

(1:9-10) **Introduction—Earth, Primeval**: remember what the earth looked like. The whole earth was covered with water. Churning, gigantic waves rushed to and fro over the face of the earth. The earth had also been blanketed with a heavy mist of thick clouds and dense fog. It had been impossible to see any distance whatsoever from any place on earth. But on the second day of creation, God had set in motion the physical laws that caused the clouds and fog to leave the earth and hang in the sky above. God created the firmament, that is, the atmosphere, the air space, the expanse, the clear sky right above the earth. But note: apparently, the earth was still blanketed with thick clouds hanging several hundred feet above the earth. It was still impossible to see the sun, moon, and stars in outer space (see note—Ge.1:14-19 for discussion). In addition, there was no dry land—no continent, no island—no land whatsoever could be seen. There was only the surging, raging waters covering the surface of the earth.

Now, the third day of creation is ready to be launched. God is now ready to create the physical laws that will cause the dry land to appear and that will provide water and vegetation to sustain life upon planet earth. This is, *The Third Day (Part 1): Creation of the Waters (Seas, Lakes, Rivers) and the Dry Land (Continents, Islands)*. God also created plant life on the third day, but this will be seen in the next outline.

1. God's Word created the waters and dry land (v.9).
2. God named the dry land *Earth* and the waters *Seas* (v.10).
3. God saw that His creation was *good*—fulfilled its function (v.10).

1 (1:9) **Earth—Sea—Creation**: God's Word created the waters and dry land. Again, picture the earth. Its whole surface was completely engulfed with churning, raging waters. Not a single island, not even a mountain peak, rose above the water. No land whatsoever could be seen. All land was submerged under the turbulent waters. The earth was nothing but a worldwide ocean.

Imagine the scene.

⇒ What power, what gigantic force, could possibly strike the earth and completely reshape its surface?
⇒ What energy could possibly cause all the *continents* with their massive and towering mountains to thrust up out of the waters? What power could fire and lift up all the continents and mountains for thousands and thousands of feet and cause them to remain there? What titanic energy could possibly cause such a reshaping of the earth's crust?
⇒ What power could cause all the *islands* and their elevations to erupt and fire up out of the waters? What gigantic power could cause such a reshaping of the earth's crust?
⇒ What awesome force could cause all the *ravines, crevices, forges, depressions, hollows, and caverns*—all the beds for the rivers, lakes, and oceans—to form and receive and hold all the water that covered the earth's surface?

What force could cause such a reshaping of the earth's crust? God. God spoke. He commanded the waters to gather together and the dry land to appear. When God commanded, gigantic upheavals took place all over the earth.

⇒ Massive volcanic eruptions caused whole land masses to fire and thrust up out of the waters.
⇒ Titanic depressions were created in the earth's crust: depressions were created to receive and hold what seemed to be a limitless tonnage of onrushing, raging waters.

The point is this: God created the waters and dry land of the earth. The waters (seas, lakes, and rivers) and the dry land did not just happen by chance. The continents and waters of the earth do not exist because of some eternal or static physical laws, physical laws that produce water and that govern volcanic eruptions and depressions in the earth's crust. Whatever physical laws caused the volcanic eruptions and depressions—whatever physical forces exist that have such power—those laws or forces were created by God. All physical laws were spoken into being by God. All physical laws were created and put into operation by God. The gigantic upheavals in the earth's crust happened because God commanded the surface of the earth to be reshaped.

⇒ God commanded the waters to gather into one place. (By "one place" is meant the depths, ravines, and hollows of the earth's crust.)
⇒ God commanded the dry land to fire and thrust upward in gigantic eruptions.

God spoke. God said, "Let the waters...be gathered together unto one place, and let the dry land appear" (v.9). And note what happened: "it was so" (v.9). The dry land masses of the earth with their towering mountain peaks and elevations erupted in the most gigantic upheaval imaginable, and the waters—millions and millions of tons—rushed madly into the depths and ravines of the earth.

Thought 1. Scripture gives a graphic description of what happened, a vivid illustration of the power of God that did such an astounding thing:

> **"Then the channels of waters were seen, and the foundations of the world were discovered at thy rebuke, O LORD, at the blast of the breath of thy nostrils" (Ps.18:15).**
> **"You laid the foundations of the earth, that it should not be moved forever. You covered it with the deep as with a garment; the waters stood above the mountains. At Your rebuke they fled; at the voice of Your thunder they hastened away. The mountains rose, the valleys sank down to the place which You appointed for them" (Ps.104:5-8, Amp.).**
> **"When he gave to the sea his decree, that the waters should not pass his commandment: when he appointed the foundations of the earth" (Pr.8:29).**
> **"But I am the LORD thy God, that divided the sea, whose waves roared: The LORD of hosts is his name" (Is.51:15).**
> **"Fear ye not me? saith the LORD: will ye not tremble at my presence, which have placed the sand for the bound of the sea by a perpetual decree, that it cannot pass it: and though the waves thereof toss themselves, yet can they not prevail; though they roar, yet can they not pass over it?" (Je.5:22).**

Thought 2. The waters of the earth show the amazing intelligence and power of God. The waters are all interconnected and intertwined. They may be underground or above ground, but by deposit, flow, and evaporation, they all have a common source and receptacle. Only the intelligence and power of God could connect and interrelate all the waters of the earth.

> **"All the rivers run into the sea; yet the sea is not full; unto the place from whence the rivers come, thither they return again" (Ec.1:7).**

Thought 3. The waters of creation are often used in Scripture to symbolize both life and the trials and afflictions of life.
1) There is the picture of the water of life.

> **"I indeed baptize you with water unto repentance: but he that cometh after me is mightier than I, whose shoes I am not worthy to bear: he shall baptize you with the Holy Ghost, and with fire" (Mt.3:11).**
> **"Jesus answered, Verily, verily, I say unto thee, except a man be born of water and of the Spirit, he cannot enter into the kingdom of God" (Jn.3:5).**
> **"Jesus answered and said unto her, If thou knewest the gift of God, and who it is that saith to thee, Give me to drink; thou wouldest have asked of him, and he would have given thee living water" (Jn.4:10).**
> **"Jesus answered and said unto her, Whosoever drinketh of this water [from the earth] shall thirst again: but whosoever drinketh of the water that I shall give him shall never thirst; but the water that I shall give him shall be in him a well of water springing up into everlasting life" (Jn.4:13-14).**
> **"In the last day, that great day of the feast, Jesus stood and cried, saying, If any man thirst, let him come unto me, and drink. He that believeth on me, as the scripture hath said, out of his belly shall flow rivers of living water" (Jn.7:37-38).**

2) There is the picture of the trials and afflictions of life.

> **"Deep calleth unto deep at the noise of thy waterspouts: all thy waves and thy billows are gone over me. Yet the LORD will command his lovingkindness in the daytime, and in the night his song shall be with me, and my prayer unto the God of my life" (Ps.42:7-8).**
> **"I sink in deep mire, where there is no standing: I am come into deep waters, where the floods overflow me. I am weary of my crying: my throat is dried: mine eyes fail while I wait for my God....Deliver me out of the mire, and let me not sink: let me be delivered from them that hate me, and out of the deep waters. Let not the waterflood overflow me, neither let the deep swallow me up, and let not the pit shut her mouth upon me" (Ps.69:2-3, 14-15).**

2 (1:10) **Earth—Sea—Creation**: God named the dry land *Earth* and the waters He named *Seas*. Note that it is not man who names the dry land and waters, but God. This is significant; it means that God owns both land and sea. He is the Owner, the Lord and Master, of all the land and of all the seas of the earth. As the Owner of planet earth, it was His right, His prerogative, to call them what He wished. And God chose to name the dry land *Earth* and the waters *Seas*.

Thought 1. Man is only the trustee of the land and waters of the earth. Man is only a temporary trustee, a trustee who is so temporary that he, as an individual, lasts only seventy or so years—at most—providing no accident or disease snatches his life away.

1) Man must look after the dry land and the waters of the earth and diligently care for them. He must conserve both the land and water of the earth. The land and water belong to God, not to man. God holds man responsible for the way he uses the reserves of planet earth.

> "Now therefore, if ye will obey my voice indeed, and keep my covenant, then ye shall be a peculiar treasure unto me above all people: for all the earth is mine" (Ex.19:5).
> "The land shall not be sold for ever: for the land is mine [God's]; for ye are strangers and sojourners with me" (Le.25:23).
> "But who am I, and what is my people, that we should be able to offer so willingly after this sort? for all things come of thee, and of thine own have we given thee" (1 Chr.29:14).
> "The earth is the LORD's, and the fulness thereof; the world, and they that dwell therein" (Ps.24:1).

2) God owns and oversees both land and sea. Therefore, God is able to take care of man when he is upon the land and the sea. God can use His land and sea to provide for man. He can also deliver man through the dangers and storms that rage across both land and sea.

> "And, behold, I am with thee, and will keep thee in all places whither thou goest, and will bring thee again into this land; for I will not leave thee, until I have done that which I have spoken to thee of" (Ge.28:15).
> "Be merciful unto me, O God, be merciful unto me: for my soul trusteth in thee: yea, in the shadow of thy wings will I make my refuge, until these calamities be overpast" (Ps.57:1).
> "Behold, he that keepeth Israel shall neither slumber nor sleep" (Ps.121:4).
> "For thou hast been a strength to the poor, a strength to the needy in his distress, a refuge from the storm, a shadow from the heat, when the blast of the terrible ones is as a storm against the wall" (Is.25:4).
> "Fear thou not; for I am with thee: be not dismayed; for I am thy God: I will strengthen thee; yea, I will help thee; yea, I will uphold thee with the right hand of my righteousness" (Is.41:10).
> "When thou passest through the waters, I will be with thee; and through the rivers, they shall not overflow thee: when thou walkest through the fire, thou shalt not be burned; neither shall the flame kindle upon thee" (Is.43:2).

3 (1:10) **Earth—Seas—Creation**: God saw that His creation was *good*—the dry land and the seas fulfilled their function. The word *good* means that the dry land and waters of the earth were valuable: they had a very specific purpose for being created. What are the purposes for which the land and waters were created?
⇒ To provide a place for both man and animals to live, both land and sea animals
⇒ To provide a place for the food to grow and for the water to sit and flow so that life might be sustained upon planet earth.

Thought 1. Man owes his life, his very existence, to God. It is the land and the waters—all created by God—that keep man alive. Without God's creative hand that made the land and the water, man could not survive.

Thought 2. The creation of land and water is a most wonderful gift from God.
⇒ The land gives man a place to live and to produce food to eat.
⇒ The waters provide both water to drink and food to eat.
⇒ Both land and water give variety and add to the interest and the beauty of man's home upon planet earth.

> "The sea is his, and he made it: and his hands formed the dry land. O come, let us worship and bow down: let us kneel before the LORD our maker" (Ps.95:5-6).
> "And he said unto them, I am an Hebrew; and I fear the LORD, the God of heaven, which hath made the sea and the dry land" (Jonah 1:9).

Thought 3. Several things should stir man to praise God.
⇒ The provision of dry land as a home.
⇒ The provision of day land that bears so much growth to provide food and beauty and variety.
⇒ The provision of water to drink.
⇒ The provision of water to provide food, commercial ventures, beauty, and recreation.

Thought 4. God knows that man must have water to drink and dry land as a home in order to sustain his life upon earth. The same is true spiritually.

1) Man must have the spiritual water, the living water, of Christ in order to live eternally with God.

> **"Jesus answered and said unto her, If thou knewest the gift of God, and who it is that saith to thee, Give me to drink; thou wouldest have asked of him, and he would have given thee living water....Jesus answered and said unto her, Whosoever drinketh of this water shall thirst again: but whosoever drinketh of the water that I shall give him shall never thirst; but the water that I shall give him shall be in him a well of water springing up into everlasting life" (Jn.4:10, 13-14).**

Note five facts about the living water of Christ.

⇒ The living water comes from Christ. He, and He alone, is its source.

⇒ The living water keeps a man from ever thirsting again. His inner thirst is gone forever. It is quenched and fully satisfied.

⇒ The living water is "a well of water" placed *in* the man. The "well of water" is not placed outside the man, not placed anywhere out in the world, not in his home, church, club, land, lake, or in his business. It is placed *in* him.

⇒ The living water springs up and continues to spring up and bubble, flowing on and on. It is ever in motion.

⇒ The living water springs up into everlasting life. It will never end.

> **"In the last day, that great day of the feast, Jesus stood and cried, saying, If any man thirst, let him come unto me, and drink. He that believeth on me, as the scripture hath said, out of his belly shall flow rivers of living water" (Jn.7:37-38).**
>
> **"For the Lamb which is in the midst of the throne shall feed them, and shall lead them unto living fountains of waters: and God shall wipe away all tears from their eyes" (Re.7:17).**
>
> **"And he said unto me, It is done. I am Alpha and Omega, the beginning and the end. I will give unto him that is athirst of the fountain of the water of life freely" (Re.21:6).**
>
> **"And the Spirit and the bride say, Come. And let him that heareth say, Come. And let him that is athirst come. And whosoever will, let him take the water of life freely" (Re.22:17).**
>
> **"For with thee is the fountain of life: in thy light shall we see light" (Ps.36:9).**
>
> **"Therefore with joy shall ye draw water out of the wells of salvation" (Is.12:3).**
>
> **"Ho, every one that thirsteth, come ye to the waters, and he that hath no money; come ye, buy, and eat; yea, come, buy wine and milk without money and without price" (Is.55:1).**
>
> **"And the LORD shall guide thee continually, and satisfy thy soul in drought, and make fat thy bones: and thou shalt be like a watered garden, and like a spring of water, whose waters fail not" (Is.58:11).**

2) Man must look beyond this *corruptible earth* to the eternal home of the new heavens and earth in order to live eternally with God.

> **"For the promise, that he should be the heir of the world [new heavens and earth], was not to Abraham, or to his seed, through the law, but through the righteousness of faith" (Ro.4:13).**
>
> **"For he looked for a city which hath foundations, whose builder and maker is God" (He.11:10).**
>
> **"But now they desire a better country, that is, an heavenly: wherefore God is not ashamed to be called their God: for he hath prepared for them a city" (He.11:16).**
>
> **"But ye are come unto mount Sion, and unto the city of the living God, the heavenly Jerusalem, and to an innumerable company of angels" (He.12:22).**
>
> **"For here have we no continuing city, but we seek one to come" (He.13:14).**
>
> **"But the day of the Lord will come as a thief in the night; in the which the heavens shall pass away with a great noise, and the elements shall melt with fervent heat, the earth also and the works that are therein shall be burned up. Seeing then that all these things shall be dissolved, what manner of persons ought ye to be in all holy conversation [behavior] and godliness, looking for and hasting unto the coming of the day of God, wherein the heavens being on fire shall be dissolved, and the elements shall melt with fervent heat? Nevertheless we, according to his promise, look for new heavens and a new earth, wherein dwelleth righteousness" (2 Pe.3:10-13).**
>
> **"And I saw a new heaven and a new earth: for the first heaven and the first earth were passed away; and there was no more sea. And I John saw the holy city, new Jerusalem, coming down from God out of heaven, prepared as a bride adorned for her husband. And I heard a great voice out of heaven saying, Behold, the tabernacle of God is with men, and he will dwell with them, and they shall be his people, and God himself shall be with them, and be their God. And God shall wipe away all tears from their eyes; and there shall be no more death, neither sorrow, nor crying, neither shall there be any more pain: for the former things are passed away" (Re.21:1-4).**

	E. The Third Day (Part 2): Creation of Plant Life or Vegetation, 1:11-13
1. God's Word created plant life or vegetation—each "after its kind"	11 And God said, Let the earth bring forth grass, the herb yielding seed, and the fruit tree yielding fruit after his kind, whose seed is in itself, upon the earth: and it was so.
2. God created all vegetation upon earth	
3. God's creative act was fulfilled—the earth became fruitful	12 And the earth brought forth grass, and herb yielding seed after his kind, and the tree yielding fruit, whose seed was in itself, after his kind: and God saw that it was good.
4. God saw that His creation was *good*—fulfilled its function	13 And the evening and the morning were the third day.

DIVISION I

CREATION OF THE HEAVENS AND THE EARTH, 1:1–2:3

E. The Third Day (Part 2): Creation of Plant Life or Vegetation, 1:11-13

(1:11-13) **Introduction—Earth, Primeval**: the third day of creation is still taking place. These three verses cover the last part of the day. Remember, the whole earth had been covered with churning, raging waters. But at the beginning of this third day, the surface of the earth was reshaped. God struck the whole planet with a gigantic, convulsive upheaval:

⇒ All the dry land of the earth—the continents and islands—fired up out of the waters.

⇒ All the waters rushed down into the depths of the earth: into the depressed beds—valleys, crevices, and ravines-that had been formed for the rivers, lakes, and oceans of the world.

Now the dry land and waters of the earth were placed in their proper boundaries. They were ready to provide a home for the life which God was about to create. At last, in this second part of the third day, God can create the first living things for planet earth: that of vegetation or plant life. This is *The Third Day (Part 2): Creation of Plant Life or Vegetation*.

1. God's Word created plant life or vegetation—each "after its kind" (v.11).
2. God created all vegetation upon earth (v.11).
3. God's creative act was fulfilled—the earth became fruitful (vv.11-12).
4. God saw that His creation was *good*—fulfilled its function (vv.12-13).

1 (1:11) **Plant Life—Vegetation—Creation**: God's Word created vegetation. "God said, 'Let the earth bring forth [vegetation]'" (v.11). Note that God did not directly create fully grown plant life. Rather, He commanded the earth to produce the vegetation; the vegetation came out of the earth itself. God created the laws of nature that caused the earth to produce vegetation. The earth itself gave life to vegetation. God said—God spoke—and the physical laws that give birth and growth to plant life were launched. The earth, in obedience to God's Word, brought forth vegetation.

> "If I were hungry, I would not tell thee: for the world is mine, and the fulness thereof" (Ps.50:12).
> "The heavens are thine, the earth also is thine: as for the world and the fulness thereof, thou hast founded them" (Ps.89:11).
> "For the earth is the Lord's, and the fulness thereof" (1 Co.10:26).

2 (1:11) **Plant life—Vegetation—Creation**: God created all vegetation upon earth. This is the point of the broad classification given by Scripture. The King James Version gives three broad classes in the translation of the Hebrew text: grass, herbs or plants, and trees. The great commentators Keil and Delitzsch, Leupold and *The Pulpit Commentary* all agree with this translation and classification.

⇒ *Grass* (deshe): note that the chief characteristic of this classification is that it does not bear seed. The other two classifications do. The root meaning of the Hebrew word "deshe" means green or damp. This would include all damp and all green plants that carpet and hug the earth. It would include mosses, lichens, algae, fungi, ferns—plants which reproduce by spores (cryptogamous plants)—plants which carpet and lie immediately upon or under the surface of the earth.

⇒ *Herbs or Plants* (esebh) which yield seed: this includes all seed-bearing plants such as grains, vegetables, bushes, shrubs, flowers, weeds, grass—all plant life between the ground-hugging plants and the towering trees.

⇒ *Fruit- or seed-bearing trees*: by fruit the Hebrew means all trees that bear seed, not just the trees that bear fruit for eating. This would include trees that bear cones, nuts, berries, and other forms of seed.

Now, note a significant fact: plant life comes out of the earth. God created the physical laws that cause the earth to produce vegetation. This ties plant life to its environment: all plant life comes from a single source, the earth. This means that all vegetation upon the earth is interrelated. All plant life has some common elements, some common chemicals, some similarities.

But all plants have an independent existence, an independent character and purpose of their own. Note the words "*after its kind.*" This means that all plants and vegetation reproduce themselves. All plant life has some means to carry on its own species, its own kind of life. Some reproduce when their seeds fall to the ground, and others reproduce through spores: all vegetation has the power to bring forth the same kind of life as the parent bush. "After its kind" means that all plant life reproduces and propagates its own *species*. The point is this: each plant is interrelated to all others because each comes from the earth, a single source. But each is also independent; each has a distinct existence, character, and purpose that belongs to it and it alone.

Thought 1. The earth and all its plant life are the Lord's. He is the rightful Owner and Sovereign Lord of it all. Man is only the trustee of the earth and its fruitfulness. This means several practical things:
1) Man is to constantly give thanks for the fruitfulness of the earth.
2) Man is to acknowledge God's ownership and worship God as the Creator.
3) Man is to be responsible and careful. He is to be using the plant resources of the earth.
4) Man is to give an account for how he treats the earth and its resources.

"**For the kingdom of heaven is like unto a man that is an householder, which went out early in the morning to hire labourers into his vineyard [the world]**" (Mt.20:1).

"**Hear another parable: there was a certain householder, which planted a vineyard [the world], and hedged it round about, and digged a winepress in it, and built a tower, and let it out to husbandmen, and went into a far country**" (Mt.21:33).

"**Moreover it is required in stewards [over the earth], that a man be found faithful**" (1 Co.4:2).

"**So God created man in his own image, in the image of God created he him; male and female created he them. And God blessed them, and God said unto them, Be fruitful, and multiply, and replenish the earth, and subdue it: and have dominion over the fish of the sea, and over the fowl of the air, and over every living thing that moveth upon the earth. And God said, Behold, I have given you every herb bearing seed, which is upon the face of all the earth, and every tree, in the which is the fruit of a tree yielding seed; to you it shall be for meat [food]**" (Ge.1:27-28).

"**Thou madest him to have dominion over the works of thy hands; thou hast put all things under his feet**" (Ps.8:6).

"**The earth is the LORD's, and the fulness thereof; the world, and they that dwell therein**" (Ps.24:1).

"**If I were hungry, I would not tell thee: for the world is mine, and the fulness thereof**" (Ps.50:12).

3 (1:11-12) **Plant Life—Vegetation—Creation**: God's creative act was fulfilled: the earth became fruitful (v.11ᶜ-12). Note the words, "and it was so" (v.11c). "God said, 'Let the earth bring forth [plant life]...*and it was so*...And the earth brought forth [plant life]' " (vv.11-12). The earth had been...
- empty
- barren
- unfruitful
- colorless

But now the earth was dramatically changed. The earth became alive, full of all kinds of grass, shrubs, flowers, trees, and fruit. The earth was filled with color; it was made green, lush, and fruitful.

Now, note the significant point: "the earth brought forth [plant life]" (v.12). But God was the source, the first cause, the Creator. The earth produced vegetation only because God had spoken and set in motion the laws of nature that give birth to plant life. Originally—at the first—there was *no seed* and no plant life: no eternal substance, matter, element, or particle to give birth to the vegetation of the earth. In the beginning there was only God. God created the vegetation, the earth, and all that is therein. True, the earth now produces the plant and the seed, but in the beginning, God spoke and created all matter and all energy. God Himself created the matter and substances and set in motion the physical laws that gave birth to plant life. The earth brought forth plant life only because God had created matter and "quickened" the earth to bear vegetation.

Thought 1. The earth flourishes with vegetation because of God's love and care for man. God loves and cares for us. This is the reason He has created and given an abundance of plant life to fill the earth. We must, in return, show love and care for God. We must love Him and demonstrate care for the earth He has created. (See previous note 2 for verses.)

4 (1:12-13) **Plant Life—Vegetation—Creation**: God saw that His creation was "good," the vegetation of the earth fulfilled its function and purpose. What is the function of the earth's vegetation? The major functions are...

- to provide food
- to supply oxygen to the atmosphere
- to help in controlling climate
- to keep the dry land from eroding away
- to decay and provide the fossil fuels of the earth
- to capture energy from light and convert it to chemical energy (photosynthesis). It is the chemical energy that makes life possible upon earth.

Thought 1. Man must praise God for the environment of the earth, for the bountiful plant life that flourishes upon planet earth. But man must also protect the environment; he must protect all plant life upon earth. Each plant is interrelated with other plants. Each has its own purpose and function to fulfill upon earth. To destroy one species of plant is to break the chain of life existing within the world. It is to destroy the purpose for which the plant life existed. The result is dangerous, and if enough vegetation is destroyed upon earth, the result can become life threatening. Human life could conceivably become extinct through the abuse of the earth's plant life. This is clearly seen in the destruction of the rain forests of the earth that is taking place in the 20th century.

The great need is for man to praise God for the environment of the earth, for the bountiful plant life that flourishes upon planet earth. Man's need is to give thanks and protect plant life, not destroy it.

Thought 2. Man must have vegetation to sustain his life upon earth. The same is true spiritually. Man must have the food of God, that is, the bread of God, to sustain him while upon earth if he wishes to live with God forever.

"And Jesus said unto them, I am the bread of life: he that cometh to me shall never hunger; and he that believeth on me shall never thirst" (Jn.6:35).

"Verily, verily, I say unto you, He that believeth on me hath everlasting life" (Jn.6:47).

"This [Christ] is the bread which cometh down from heaven, that a man may eat thereof, and not die. I am the living bread which came down from heaven: if any man eat of this bread, he shall live for ever: and the bread that I will give is my flesh, which I will give for the life of the world" (Jn.6:50-51).

"As the living Father hath sent me, and I live by the Father: so he that eateth me, even he shall live by me. This is that bread which came down from heaven: not as your fathers did eat manna, and are dead: he that eateth of this bread shall live for ever" (Jn.6:57-58).

| 1. God's Word created & distributed light upon the earth | F. The Fourth Day: Creation & Distribution of Light Upon Earth to Regulate Day & Night, Seasons & Years, 1:14-19

14 And God said, Let there be lights in the firmament of the heaven to divide the day from the night; and let them be for signs, and for seasons, and for days, and years: 15 And let them be for lights in the firmament of the heaven to give light upon the earth: and it was so. | 16 And God made two great lights; the greater light to rule the day, and the lesser light to rule the night: he made the stars also. 17 And God set them in the firmament of the heaven to give light upon the earth, 18 And to rule over the day and over the night, and to divide the light from the darkness: and God saw that it was good. 19 And the evening and the morning were the fourth day. | 2. God made the sun, moon, & stars that provide light for the earth

a. God & God alone made them
b. The reason He made them
  1) To give light

  2) To rule over the day & night

3. God saw that His creation was *good*—fulfilled its function |

DIVISION I

CREATION OF THE HEAVENS AND THE EARTH, 1:1–2:3

F. The Fourth Day: Creation and Distribution of Light Upon Earth to Regulate Day and Night, Seasons and Years, 1:14-19

(1:14-19) **Introduction—Earth, Prehistoric**: remember what the earth had looked like. It was hanging in space unformed and unfinished.

⇒ The earth was enveloped in total darkness. A blanket of heavy mist, thick clouds, and dense fog engulfed the earth (see note 4, pt.a.2)—Ge.1:2 for discussion).

⇒ In addition, the whole surface of the earth was covered with water—one massive worldwide ocean with huge, surging, raging waves (see note 4, pt.a.3)—Ge.1:2 for discussion).

But God had begun to form the earth, to create the things that would be needed to sustain life.

⇒ On the first day, God had created light. The heavy mist that had engulfed the earth began to evaporate—just enough to let the rays of light begin to penetrate and reach the earth (vv.3-5).

⇒ On the second day, God had created the firmament, that is, the atmosphere or air space that hangs right above the earth. God had lifted the heavy mist, clouds, and fog—apparently lifted them up into the sky several hundred feet. The clouds still encircled the earth, but there was a clear air space between the clouds and the earth (v.6-8).

⇒ On the third day, God had created the waters—the seas, lakes, and rivers—and He had created the dry land. There was a worldwide convulsive upheaval of the earth's crust, a convulsive upheaval that fired and shot the land masses of the earth upward. The waters of the worldwide ocean rushed madly into the ravines and depressed valleys of the world. Thereby the continents and islands and the fresh and salt waters of the earth were created.

In addition, on this third day God had created all the plant life—all the grasses, flowers, bushes, vegetables, and trees—in all their color, beauty, and provision to feed and sustain life.

Now, we come to *The Fourth Day: Creation and Distribution of Light Upon Earth to Regulate the Seasons, Days, and Years*.
1. God's Word created and distributed light upon the earth (vv.14-15).
2. God made the sun, moon, and stars that provide light for the earth (vv.16-18).
3. God saw that His creation was *good*—fulfilled its function (vv.18-19).

1 (1:14-15) **Light—Creation—Sun—Moon—Stars**: God's Word created and distributed light upon earth. "God said, 'Let there be lights in the firmament [the sky or outer space] of the heaven'" (v.14). The word *lights* (meoroth) means light-bearers or luminaries. It refers to the heavenly bodies: the sun, moon, and stars (v.16). Now note verses 14 and 15; note closely what God is doing.

⇒ God is not creating the sun, moon, and stars. They had already been created when "God created the heaven and the earth" (v.1).

⇒ God is not creating light—day and night—throughout the universe. Light had already been created when "God said, 'Let there be light'" (v.3).

What then is God creating on this fourth day of creation? These two verses tell us: God is creating and distributing light *upon earth*. He is not dealing with light throughout the universe; He is dealing with light upon earth. Remember: the earth had been covered with a thick layer of clouds and dense fog (see note 4, pt.1b—Ge.1:2 for discussion). On the first day of creation, when God created light—cosmic light, light throughout the universe—the light had apparently begun to penetrate the clouds and foggy mist covering the earth. But the light and heat from the sun had not yet evaporated enough of the clouds and mist to be visible upon earth, not enough to give or regulate day and night, seasons and years. But now,

are made to evaporate so that the sun, moon, and stars become visible to the earth. They can now carry out their work upon earth.

What is the work, what are the functions, of the sun, moon, and stars? Five major works or functions are given by Scripture.

a. The sun divides the day from the night; it provides a period of light and of darkness (v.14, 18. See vv.4-5.) This is a particular function of the sun, for light upon earth comes from the sun. The earth is round, and it revolves on an axis at about 1000 m.p.h. Each rotation takes 23 hours, 56 minutes, and 4.1 seconds—just about 24 hours. Therefore, about one half of the earth faces the sun all the time. When a part of the earth rotates and faces the sun, the light from the sun gives man a time for work. When a part of the earth rotates and faces away from sun, the darkness gives man a time for rest.

> **Thought 1.** The division of the day from the night was absolutely essential. Man needs both.
> ⇒ By day, man gains a sense of purpose and satisfaction from his work, from feeling good about his work.
> ⇒ By night, man rests his body and renews his strength.
>
> Thus, God's creation and distribution of light upon earth was absolutely essential. Both day and night had to be created in order to sustain life upon earth.

b. The heavenly bodies serve as *signs* for the earth (v.14). The word *signs* (othoth) means something that is engraved or marked.
  ⇒ The heavenly bodies are signs that men use for direction, whether upon land or sea; signs that guide a compass by day or night.
  ⇒ The heavenly bodies are signs that indicate weather conditions.

> **"He answered and said unto them, When it is evening, ye say, It will be fair weather: for the sky is red. And in the morning, It will be foul weather to day: for the sky is red and lowering. O ye hypocrites, ye can discern the face of the sky; but can ye not discern the signs of the times?" (Mt.16:2-3).**

  ⇒ The heavenly bodies are signs that declare the glory of God and point a person to God.

> **"The heavens declare the glory of God; and the firmament showeth his handiwork" (Ps.19:1).**
> **"The heavens declare his righteousness, and all the people see his glory" (Ps.97:6).**
> **"For the invisible things of him from the creation of the world are clearly seen, being understood by the things that are made, even his eternal power and Godhead; so that they are without excuse" (Ro.1:20).**

  ⇒ The heavenly bodies are signs that control the oceans and their tides day by day and month by month.

> **Thought 1.** The moon is said to be a lesser light, and it is. It is smaller and the light it gives is only a reflective light from the sun. But despite its smaller size and borrowed light, its function is essential to the earth. Its value is enormous: it gives light at night and controls part of the signs, and it influences the tides of the seas. But note: the moon is not as gifted nor does it impact the earth as much as the sun. The same is true of believers. Among believers, there are those gifted less than others. Yet, God says every believer is essential to the body of Christ (1 Co.12:14-24). Every believer is of enormous size and value to the world. The amount of light (gifts) does not determine value. Value is determined by the use of light (gifts), of what a person does with what he has.
>
> > **"For the kingdom of heaven is as a man travelling into a far country, who called his own servants, and delivered unto them his goods. And unto one he gave five talents, to another two, and to another one; to every man according to his several ability; and straightway took his journey" (Mt.25:14-15).**
> > **"He said therefore, A certain nobleman went into a far country to receive for himself a kingdom, and to return. And he called his ten servants, and delivered them ten pounds, and said unto them, Occupy till I come" (Lu.19:12-13).**
> > **"But it shall not be so among you: but whosoever will be great among you, let him be your minister" (Mt.20:26).**
> > **"But he that is greatest among you shall be your servant" (Mt.23:11).**

c. The heavenly bodies provide *seasons* for the earth (v.14). How were seasons created? Note two significant facts.
  1) The earth not only rotates on its own axis, but it also rotates around the sun. Its journey or orbit around the sun is about 583,400,000 miles (or 938,900,000 km). The earth travels along in its orbit about 66,000 m.p.h. (or 106,000 km). It takes about 365 days for the earth to revolve around the sun. This is how we measure our years. One year is one trip or revolution of the earth around the sun.
  2) The axis of the earth tilts about 23 1/2 degrees. It is this tilt and the earth's revolving around the sun that creates the seasons of the year. Because of the tilt, different parts of the earth face the sun more directly at different times during the year. Of course, the more directly a place faces the sun, the warmer it is, and the more indirectly, the cooler it is. It is this, the warmth and coolness of the earth's surface, that gives seasons to the earth.

What is the purpose of seasons upon earth? Seasons provide...

- periods for agriculture, for farming

- periods for the migration of animals

    "Yea, the stork in the heaven knoweth her appointed times; and the turtle and the crane and the swallow observe the time of their coming; but my people know not the judgment of the LORD" (Je.8:7).

- periods for religious festivals and other celebrations upon earth

    "Thus saith the LORD of hosts; The fast of the fourth month, and the fast of the fifth, and the fast of the seventh, and the fast of the tenth, shall be to the house of Judah joy and gladness, and cheerful feasts; therefore love the truth and peace" (Zec.8:19).

- periods for variety and beauty

Thought 1. The temperature of the sun's surface is enormous: about 9300° F. The temperature at the center is an unimaginable 29 million degrees. The sun is one mass of volcanic fire. It is 864,000 miles in diameter. The fiery, red furnace is so large it could hold 1,300,000 earths. And if we could imagine the distance, it is 93,000,000 miles away from earth. If the earth were closer to the sun, it would be too hot for life; and if it were farther away, it would be too cold for life. God has created the heavenly bodies just right to sustain life, to give light, seasons, days, and years.[1]

Thought 2. The sun's rising and setting determines day and night; its movement toward the axis of the earth determines summer and winter, the seasons of the earth. God created a purpose for every movement of the sun and of the earth. So it is with man. God created man and created him with purpose. His every movement should, therefore, have purpose. He should be able to say with Ecclesiastes:

"To every thing there is a season, and a time to every purpose under the heaven" (Ec.3:1).

d. The heavenly bodies provide "day and years" for the earth. As stated, one day is one revolution of the earth around its own axis, about 24 hours. One year is one revolution of the earth around the sun, about 365 days. The earth would not have days and nights nor years if it were not for the heavenly bodies, in particular the sun.
The days give light upon earth so that man can see to walk and work.

    "I must work the works of him that sent me, while it is day: the night cometh, when no man can work" (Jn.9:4).
    "Jesus answered, Are there not twelve hours in the day? If any man walk in the day, he stumbleth not, because he seeth the light of this world" (Jn.11:9).

The years give man a way to measure time, a larger measure of time. This enables him to keep a better record of time and to better know and measure the seasons and events of life.

Thought 1. The stress of this creative act is purpose. The lights of heaven do not give light and control day and night, time, and seasons for themselves, but for man—to enable man to fulfill his purpose upon earth. (See outline and notes—Ge.2:15-17 for discussion on the purpose of man.)

Thought 2. The lights of the heavens go about fulfilling their function day by day and night by night. They follow the laws set up by God to control their being—ever so *consistently and faithfully*. What a lesson for believers!

e. The heavenly bodies provide light upon earth (v.15). (See note 2—Ge.1:4 for a full discussion.)

Thought 1. See note 2, Thought 3—Ge.1:4 for thought and application.

Thought 2. The lights of heaven are created to give light. Their light is clearly seen by all. Believers are called "the light of the world" (Mt.5:14-16). They are to let their light shine as the lights of the heavens so that the world can clearly see and not stumble. How much the world needs the clear sight and witness of believers.

Thought 3. The greatest thing that heavenly lights do is fulfill their function *consistently*. No man worries about their failing to fulfill their function. If they did fail, just think of the devastation! The greatest thing that a man can do is to be consistent in fulfilling his function on earth—to let his light shine.

    "Ye are the light of the world. A city that is set on an hill cannot be hid. Neither do men light a candle, and put it under a bushel, but on a candlestick; and it giveth light unto all that are in the house. Let your light so shine before men, that they may see your good works, and glorify your father which is in heaven" (Mt.5:14-16).

---

[1] *Funk & Wagnalls New Encyclopedia*, Vol.24. (USA: Funk & Wagnalls, Inc.: 1971; 1975; 1979; 1983).
  William Orr. *How We May Know That God Is*, p.29.

Now note the words, "And it was so" (v.15). What God said was done. He commanded light to be distributed upon earth, and it happened. His Word could not be resisted. When God spoke, the light of the sun reached the earth by day and the light of the moon and stars reached the earth by night. The earth received the light it needed to sustain life.

2 (1:16-18) **Creation—Astrology—Sun—Moon—Stars**: God made the sun, moon, and stars that provide light for the earth. Note: these verses tell us where the light came from that God distributed upon the earth. The light came from three sources:

⇒ a great light, which is the sun
⇒ a lesser light, which is the moon
⇒ the stars

Why is this being mentioned here, when the sun, moon, and stars had already been created (v.1), and when light had already been diffused throughout the universe (v.3)? There are two reasons.

a. There is a need to stress that God and God alone created the sun, moon, and stars. They exist only because God created them. They are not eternal; they have not always existed. They did not come into being...

• by chance
• by random
• by some impersonal mass or energy that is eternal in the universe
• by physical laws that were already in existence

The sun, moon, and stars were created by God and God alone. He Himself created the laws of nature that gave birth to build and set in motion the heavenly bodies.

b. There is a need to stress the reason why God created the sun, moon, and stars. Note this carefully: He made the heavenly bodies to give light upon earth, to rule over the day and the night, to divide light from darkness. Why repeat this from verse 14-15? Why re-stress this? Because of man's tendency to worship and to seek his fate and destiny in the sun, moon, and stars. The heavenly bodies are to rule over the day and the night, not over man's life. God never intended the heavenly bodies to rule over man's life. He made them only to rule over the day and the night.

> **Thought 1.** Astrology and the worship of the heavenly bodies are false beliefs and false worship.
> ⇒ The person who reads his fate and destiny in the heavenly bodies reads in vain.
> ⇒ The person who joys or stumbles because of what he reads in the stars does so in vain.
> ⇒ The person who worships the sun, moon, or stars worships in vain.
>
> The heavenly bodies were created by God only to rule over the day and night, not over people's lives. There is only one God who is to rule over our lives, God Himself. And there are only two persons who determine our fate and destiny: ourselves and God.
>
> > **"Thou art wearied in the multitude of thy counsels. Let now the astrologers, the stargazers, the monthly prognosticators, stand up, and save thee from these things that shall come upon thee. Behold, they shall be as stubble; the fire shall burn them; they shall not deliver themselves from the power of the flame: there shall not be a coal to warm at, nor fire to sit before it. Thus shall they be unto thee with whom thou hast laboured, even thy merchants, from thy youth: they shall wander every one to his quarter; none shall save thee" (Is.47:13-15).**
> > **"Thus saith the LORD, Learn not the way of the heathen, and be not dismayed at the signs of heaven; for the heathen are dismayed at them" (Je.10:2).**
> > **"Regard not them that have familiar spirits, neither seek after wizards, to be defiled by them: I am the LORD your God" (Le.19:31).**
> > **"Daniel answered in the presence of the king, and said, The secret which the king hath demanded cannot the wise men, the astrologers, the magicians, the soothsayers, show unto the king; but there is a God in heaven that revealeth secrets, and maketh known to the king Nebuchadnezzar what shall be in the latter days. Thy dream, and the visions of thy head upon thy bed, are these" (Da.2:27-28).**
> > **"The king cried aloud to bring in the astrologers, the Chaldeans, and the soothsayers. And the king spake, and said to the wise men of Babylon, Whosoever shall read this writing, and show me the interpretation thereof, shall be clothed with scarlet, and have a chain of gold about his neck, and shall be the third ruler in the kingdom" (Da.5:7).**
> > **"And I will cut off witchcrafts out of thine hand; and thou shalt have no more soothsayers" (Mi.5:12).**
> > **"For the idols have spoken vanity, and the diviners have seen a lie, and have told false dreams; they comfort in vain: therefore they went their way as a flock, they were troubled, because there was no shepherd" (Zec.10:2).**
> > **"But the fearful, and unbelieving, and the abominable, and murderers, and whoremongers, and sorcerers, and idolaters, and all liars, shall have their part in the lake which burneth with fire and brimstone: which is the second death" (Re.21:8).**
>
> **Thought 2.** Day and night are reminders of the need for daily worship, worship both in the morning and at night (Ps.1:2). As the sun rules the day and the moon the night, so man must rule his worship of God by day and night.

No one else can do it for him, certainly not the stars of heaven. God set them for one purpose and one purpose only...
- to give light upon earth
- to rule over day and night

> "This book of the law shall not depart out of thy mouth; but thou shalt meditate therein day and night, that thou mayest observe to do according to all that is written therein: for then thou shalt make thy way prosperous, and then thou shalt have good success" (Jos.1:8).
> "But his delight is in the law of the LORD; and in his law doth he meditate day and night" (Ps.1:2).
> "Stand in awe, and sin not: commune with your own heart upon your bed, and be still" (Ps.4:4).
> "Let the words of my mouth, and the meditation of my heart, be acceptable in thy sight, O LORD, my strength, and my redeemer" (Ps.19:14).
> "When I remember thee upon my bed, and meditate on thee in the night watches" (Ps.63:6).
> "My meditation of him shall be sweet: I will be glad in the LORD" (Ps.104:34).
> "I will meditate in thy precepts, and have respect unto thy ways" (Ps.119:15).
> "My hands also will I lift up unto thy commandments, which I have loved; and I will meditate in thy statutes" (Ps.119:48).
> "Mine eyes prevent [precede] the night watches, that I might meditate in thy word" (Ps.119:148).
> "I remember the days of old; I meditate on all thy works; I muse [meditate] on the work of thy hands" (Ps.143:5).

Thought 3. The lights of the heavens rule over the day and night, not man. They are not created to worship nor to determine the fate and destiny of man. They are created to show man when to rest and when to work. How loud is the cry for performance and consistency in man's work and witness! The night is coming when no man can work.

> "Whatsoever thy hand findeth to do, do it with thy might; for there is no work, nor device, nor knowledge, nor wisdom, in the grave, whither thou goest" (Ec.9:10).
> "I must work the works of him that sent me, while it is day: the night cometh, when no man can work" (Jn.9:4).
> "Not slothful in business; fervent in spirit; serving the LORD" (Ro.12:11).
> "Therefore, my beloved brethren, be ye stedfast, unmoveable, always abounding in the work of the LORD, forasmuch as ye know that your labour is not in vain in the LORD" (1 Co.15:58).
> "As we have therefore opportunity, let us do good unto all men, especially unto them who are of the household of faith" (Ga.6:10).
> "Wherefore I put thee in remembrance that thou stir up the gift of God, which is in thee by the putting on of my hands" (2 Ti.1:6).
> "For God is not unrighteous to forget your work and labour of love, which ye have showed toward his name, in that ye have ministered to the saints, and do minister. And we desire that every one of you do show the same diligence to the full assurance of hope unto the end: that ye be not slothful, but followers of them who through faith and patience inherit the promises" (He.6:10-12).
> "Wherefore the rather, brethren, give diligence to make your calling and election sure: for if ye do these things, ye shall never fall" (2 Pe.1:10).

3 (1:18-19) **Light—Creation**: God saw that His creation was *good*—light upon the earth fulfilled its function. (See note 2—Ge.1:4 for discussion.)

	G. The Fifth Day: Creation of Water Creatures (Fish, Sea Life, Creeping Creatures) & Air Creatures (Birds, Winged Fowl, Insects, etc.), 1:20-23	whales, and every living creature that moveth, which the waters brought forth abundantly, after their kind, and every winged fowl after his kind: and God saw that it was good.	ture & every air creature—each "after its kind"
1. God's Word created water creatures and air creatures[DS1]	20 And God said, Let the waters bring forth abundantly the moving creature that hath life, and fowl that may fly above the earth in the open firmament of heaven.	22 And God blessed them, saying, Be fruitful, and multiply, and fill the waters in the seas, and let fowl multiply in the earth.	**3. God saw that His creation was _good_—fulfilled its function** **4. God blessed the water creatures and air creatures**
2. God created every water crea-	21 And God created great	23 And the evening and the morning were the fifth day.	

DIVISION I

CREATION OF THE HEAVENS AND THE EARTH, 1:1–2:3

G. The Fifth Day: Creation of Water Creatures (Fish, Sea Life, Creeping Creatures) and Air Creatures (Birds, Winged Fowl, Insects, etc.), 1:20-23

(1:20-23) **Introduction—Birds—Fish—Water Creatures**: remember what the earth looked like. God had hung the heavens and the earth in space. But the first picture we get of the earth is that of an earth that is without form and void. The earth was incomplete, unfinished, and empty. The earth—the whole earth—was covered with water, with one massive ocean of surging, raging water and with huge waves being tossed to and fro all across the surface of the earth. In addition, the earth was blanketed in pitch black darkness because of a dense fog and heavy, thick clouds that hung over the surging, raging waters. But God was ready to create; He was now ready to prepare the earth to sustain life. God, therefore, launched _The Seven Great Days of Creation_. So far, we have studied four of the great days of creation. Thus far we have seen God...

- create light (Ge.1:3-5)
- create the firmament (the atmosphere and air space right above the earth) (Ge.1:6-8)
- create the waters (seas, lakes, rivers) and dry land (continents, islands) (Ge.1:9-10)
- create plant life or vegetation (Ge.1:11-13)
- create and distribute light upon earth to regulate day and night and the seasons and years (Ge.1:14-19)

Now, the fifth day of creation is launched. This is a very significant day, for the first animal life is now to be created. This is _The Fifth Day: Creation of Water Creatures and Air Creatures._
1. God's Word created water creatures and air creatures (v.20).
2. God created every water creature and every air creature—each "after its kind" (v.21).
3. God saw that His creation was _good_—fulfilled its function (v.21).
4. God blessed the water creatures and air creatures (vv.22-23).

[1] (1:20) **Fish—Birds—Creation**: God's Word created water creatures and air creatures. What God now created was totally different from all other creation. The creation of animal life was distinctive and unique. This is seen in three facts.
a. In the Hebrew this verse reads, "Let the waters teem with swarms of living creatures [souls], and let birds fly above the earth in the open expanse of the heavens" (Ge.1:20, NAS). The waters did not produce the living creatures of the sea and air. God Himself created the animals of the sea and air. There was nothing within the waters, air, or land that could create or bring forth sea and air creatures, no...

- energy
- force
- power
- gas
- chemical
- matter
- substance
- element
- particle

God Himself—His Word, the power of His command—created both sea and air creatures.

> **Thought 1.** God's Word is power, unlimited power. It was God's Word that created, that had the power to create the creatures of the water and air. Scripture declares that God's Word is unlimited power, that God's Word can do anything.
> ⇒ God's Word can set the hardest heart afire or else pound it like a hammer until it breaks and surrenders to Christ.
>
> **"Is not my word like as a fire? saith the LORD; and like a hammer that breaketh the rock in pieces?" (Je.23:29).**
>
> ⇒ God's message—the gospel of Christ—can save everyone who believes.
>
> **"For I am not ashamed of the gospel of Christ: for it is the power of God unto salvation to every one that believeth; to the Jew first, and also to the Greek" (Ro.1:16).**

⇒ God's Word can pierce like a sword, divide asunder both spirit and soul, thoughts and motives.

> **"For the word of God is quick, and powerful, and sharper than any twoedged sword, piercing even to the dividing asunder of soul and spirit, and of the joints and marrow, and is a discerner of the thoughts and intents of the heart" (He.4:12).**

⇒ God's Word can cleanse the way of a person.

> **"Wherewithal shall a young man cleanse his way? by taking heed thereto according to thy word" (Ps.119:9).**
> **"Now ye are clean through the word which I have spoken unto you" (Jn.15:3).**
> **"Sanctify them through thy truth: thy word is truth" (Jn.17:17).**

b. The word *create* (bara, v.21) is used for the first time since verse one. In the first four days of creation, God used existing material, something that was created when He created the heavens and the earth. He simply took what He had already created and rearranged or reformed it in order to create whatever He wished. For example:

⇒ On the first day: God rearranged or forced the light of the heavenly bodies down upon earth. He created or caused light to begin penetrating through the clouds and fog upon earth.

⇒ On the second day: God rearranged the fog and clouds, caused them to rise from the earth and hang in space. He created the atmosphere or air space between the clouds and earth.

⇒ On the third day: God reformed the waters and dry land. Both water and land (under the water) already existed, but He created new ravines and depressions for the waters, and He created the continents and islands by causing a massive, worldwide eruption of the earth upward.

⇒ On the third day: God also formed plant life or vegetation out of the earth itself. The earth already existed, but God had the earth to give birth to plant life.

⇒ On the fourth day: God took the light that already existed and distributed it upon earth. He caused the light of the heavenly bodies to reach the earth and to govern its days and nights, and its seasons and years.

The point is this: everything created up to this point was a matter of God taking something He had already created and focusing, rearranging, or reforming it. But not now, not in the creation of animal life. Water and air creatures were to be different, distinctive, and unique—so much so that a special creative act of God was needed. The *bara creation* of God was needed.

⇒ The Hebrew word *bara* means the creation of something new, completely new. It is the creation of something *out of nothing*. No material, no matter, no substance, nothing whatsoever is used. God's Word and command alone created animal life. He created water and air creatures *out of nothing*.

As pointed out, this is the first time the Hebrew word *bara* (create) is used since God created (bara) the heavens and earth (v.1). This is definitely showing that the creation of water and air creatures was different from all former creation.

> **Thought 1.** God can do anything. His power is unlimited. He can create life *out of nothing*, by the sheer power of His Word.

> > **"I know that thou canst do every thing, and that no thought can be withholden from thee" (Jb. 42:2).**
> > **"But our God is in the heavens: he hath done whatsoever he hath pleased" (Ps.115:3).**
> > **"Yea, before the day was I am he; and there is none that can deliver out of my hand: I will work, and who shall let [hinder] it?" (Is.43:13).**
> > **"But Jesus beheld them, and said unto them, With men this is impossible; but with God all things are possible" (Mt.19:26).**
> > **"For with God nothing shall be impossible" (Lu.1:37).**
> > **"Now unto him that is able to do exceeding abundantly above all that we ask or think, according to the power that worketh in us" (Ep.3:20).**

c. The Hebrew term *moving creature* means *living souls*. (See DEEPER STUDY # 1—Ge.1:20 for discussion.)

> **Thought 1.** God is the God of progression and perfection. He wills to move forward and to go higher. Therefore, He moved forward and created a higher form of existence, that of water and air creatures.
> There is a lesson in God's progressive and forward movement. Within creation, believers should always move upward and advance forward, learning to grow more and more in Christ. Believers should walk day by day learning all they can about Christ. Believers should mature in Christ until they reach the highest form of life, that of being perfected in Christ Jesus. (Note: too few move forward and grow.)

> > **"They go from strength to strength, every one of them in Zion appeareth before God" (Ps.84:7).**
> > **"But the path of the just is as the shining light, that shineth more and more unto the perfect day" (Pr.4:18).**

"And now, brethren, I commend you to God, and to the word of his grace, which is able to build you up, and to give you an inheritance among all them which are sanctified" (Ac.20:32).

"And I, brethren, could not speak unto you as unto spiritual, but as unto carnal, even as unto babes in Christ. I have fed you with milk, and not with meat: for hitherto ye were not able to bear it, neither yet now are ye able" (1 Co.3:1-2).

"That we henceforth be no more children, tossed to and fro, and carried about with every wind of doctrine, by the sleight of men, and cunning craftiness, whereby they lie in wait to deceive; but speaking the truth in love, may grow up into him in all things, which is the head, even Christ" (Ep.4:14-15).

"As ye have therefore received Christ Jesus the Lord, so walk ye in him" (Col.2:6).

"Meditate upon these things; give thyself wholly to them; that thy profiting [growth] may appear to all" (1 Ti.4:15).

"For when for the time ye ought to be teachers, ye have need that one teach you again which be the first principles of the oracles of God; and are become such as have need of milk, and not of strong meat" (He.5:12).

"Therefore leaving the principles of the doctrine of Christ, let us go on unto perfection; not laying again the foundation of repentance from dead works, and of faith toward God" (He.6:1).

"As newborn babes, desire the sincere milk of the word, that ye may grow thereby" (1 Pe.2:2).

"And beside this, giving all diligence, add to your faith virtue; and to virtue knowledge" (2 Pe.1:5).

"But grow in grace, and in the knowledge of our Lord and Saviour Jesus Christ. To him be glory both now and for ever" (2 Pe.3:18).

"He that saith he abideth in him ought himself also so to walk, even as he walked" (1 Jn.2:6).

DEEPER STUDY # 1

(1:20) **Soul** (nephesh): the Hebrew says, "Let the waters teem with swarms of 'living souls.'" This is the first time the word *"soul"* is used in Scripture. This fact indicates that the thing now being created was different and distinctive from all other creation.

The *soul* is the breath, life, consciousness, and animation of animals. The soul is the essence and being of animals. Animals are *soulish creatures*, creatures that breathe, possess conscious life, and are animated. It is this that distinguishes animals from vegetation. The world of vegetation lives and animals live, but there is a difference in their living. Animals are...

- *breathing beings*
- *conscious beings*
- *animated beings*

The essence of their being is *breath and consciousness and animation*. Animals are *"living souls"* (nephesh) *"that hath life"* (Ge.1:20). The point is this: the things now being created were different from the vegetation God had just created. The things now created were *"living souls"—soulish creatures*. The "living souls" were animals: water and air creatures that breathe and possess consciousness and live by being animated and moving about.

---

2 (1:21) **Fish—Birds—Creation**: God created every water creature and every air creature—each "after its kind." Why is God's creative act being repeated? To stress that God and God alone created every living creature in the waters and air of the earth. Note the creatures mentioned.

⇒ The *great whales* or *great creatures* (tanninim): the Hebrew word actually means the great creatures of the seas and waters. This would include the whales, crocodiles, sharks, and other large creatures.

⇒ Every living creature that moves in the water: this would include all the small fish and the creeping creatures of the waters such as crabs, lobster, and shrimp.

⇒ Every winged fowl: this would include all living creatures that have wings such as birds, chickens, ostriches, and insects.

There is not a creature in the water or air that God did not create. All that makes up an animal—the chemicals, the molecules, the cells, the DNA, the substance, whatever the basic element is, whatever the raw matter and energy of animal life is—God created it. God created the raw substance of life; He created the water and air creatures of the earth. And note: this verse emphatically declares that He created *every one* of them. God is the Source, the Origin, behind all water and air creatures. He stands as the great Creator of all living creatures both in the water and air.

Now, note one other fact: God created every creature "after its kind." This means that all water creatures and air creatures have the power to reproduce themselves. All animal life has some means...

- to carry on its species, its kind of animal life
- to bring forth the same kind of animal life, the same kind of life as the parent animal
- to propagate its own species

Thought 1. Just think of all the beautiful birds and fish of the earth—all the variety and beauty of water and air creatures. God is a God of beauty and variety.

Think of another fact as well: how much companionship the creatures of the sea and air provide for us. Just think...

- how empty the waters and air would be without any life whatsoever
- how empty the earth would be without any fish or birds

God is to be praised for giving us the companionship—all the variety and beauty—of water and air creatures. We should be constantly thanking and praising God for His glorious creation of animal life.

> "The fowl of the air, and the fish of the sea, and whatsoever passeth through the paths of the seas. O LORD our Lord, how excellent is thy name in all the earth!" (Ps.8:8-9).
> "O LORD, how manifold are thy works! in wisdom hast thou made them all: the earth is full of thy riches. So is this great and wide sea, wherein are things creeping innumerable, both small and great beasts [creatures]" (Ps.104:24-25).

Thought 2. God is the God of order and of supreme intelligence. He creates an abundance of water and air creatures, species after species. And He creates each "after its kind," with the ability to reproduce itself. God thought, planned, willed, and acted—all with supreme intelligence.

How much more is man to be a person of order and intelligence: to think, plan, will, and act. Man is to order his steps and life after God, to live as God commands.

> "Order my steps in thy word: and let not any iniquity have dominion over me" (Ps.119:133).
> "This I say then, Walk in the Spirit, and ye shall not fulfil the lust of the flesh" (Ga.5:16).
> "I therefore, the prisoner of the Lord, beseech you that ye walk worthy of the vocation wherewith ye are called" (Ep.4:1).
> "See then that ye walk circumspectly, not as fools, but as wise" (Ep.5:15).
> "As ye have therefore received Christ Jesus the Lord, so walk ye in him" (Col.2:6).
> "But if we walk in the light, as he is in the light, we have fellowship one with another, and the blood of Jesus Christ his Son cleanseth us from all sin" (1 Jn.1:7).
> "He that saith he abideth in him ought himself also so to walk, even as he walked" (1 Jn.2:6).

3 (1:21) **Fish—Birds—Creation**: God saw that His creation was good—the water and air creatures fulfilled their function and purpose. Again, the word *good* means that the sea and air creatures of the earth were valuable: they had a specific purpose for being created. There are at least four *major reasons* why God created sea and air creatures:
- ⇒ To populate and give life to His creation, both the waters and the sky of the earth.
- ⇒ To help carry on the reproduction of the food chain.
- ⇒ To give variety and beauty to the earth's water and sky; to show forth His glorious handiwork.
- ⇒ To provide companionship for man.

The importance of these purposes is clearly seen when we picture an earth without fish or birds. Just imagine how empty the oceans, lakes, and rivers would be without fish, without any water life whatsoever. How empty the earth would be without birds, without any winged fowl at all. What an emptiness would fill the waters (oceans, lakes, and rivers) and sky of the earth.

Thought 1. God is the God of variety, diversity, and beauty. Kind after kind, species after species, class after class were created—an infinite variety and diversity, each with its own beauty and purpose. How clearly man could see the power of God within creation if man would just take time and look. How often God expects to be seen and praised in creation!

> "Thou, even thou, art LORD alone; thou hast made heaven, the heaven of heavens, with all their host, the earth, and all things that are therein, the seas, and all that is therein, and thou preservest them all; and the host of heaven worshippeth thee" (Ne.9:6).
> "But ask now the beasts, and they shall teach thee; and the fowls of the air, and they shall tell thee: or speak to the earth, and it shall teach thee: and the fishes of the sea shall declare unto thee. Who knoweth not in all these that the hand of the LORD hath wrought this? In whose hand is the soul of every living thing, and the breath of all mankind" (Jb. 12:7-10).
> "The fowl of the air, and the fish of the sea, and whatsoever passeth through the paths of the seas" (Ps.8:8).
> "He hath made every thing beautiful in his time: also he hath set the world in their heart, so that no man find out the work that God maketh from the beginning to the end" (Ec.3:11).
> "And saying, Sirs, why do ye these things? We also are men of like passions with you, and preach unto you that ye should turn from these vanities unto the living God, which made heaven, and earth, and the sea, and all things that are therein" (Ac.14:15).

4 (1:22-23) **Fish—Birds—Creation**: God blessed the water and air creatures. What is the blessing?

First, there is the blessing and privilege of life; the privilege of being animated, soulish creatures; the privilege of living upon the earth, an earth full of variety, beauty, and provision. (Remember: the earth was not corrupted until after man's fall.)

> "And God said, Let the waters bring forth abundantly the moving creature that hath life, and fowl that may fly above the earth in the open firmament of heaven" (Ge.1:20).

Second, there is the blessing and privilege of reproducing, of being fruitful and multiplying, of populating the waters and the air, of carrying on their particular species. Note: the power to reproduce is infused into the very nature of the creature. The creatures—the fish and birds, the water and air creatures—have the power themselves to reproduce and to continue their species. But note the crucial point: God placed the power of reproduction into the animal. The power of reproduction was created by God. God commanded the creatures of both water and air to reproduce.

Thought 1. God is the God of life. He wills life to go on, to be fruitful and multiply, and He has made provision for reproduction. Man is to honor God and His will: he is to worship God and to respect and preserve life.

> **"But ask now the beasts, and they shall teach thee; and the fowls of the air, and they shall tell thee: or speak to the earth, and it shall teach thee: and the fishes of the sea shall declare unto thee. Who knoweth not in all these that the hand of the LORD hath wrought this? In whose hand is the soul of every living thing, and the breath of all mankind" (Jb. 12:7-10).**
>
> **"I know that, whatsoever God doeth, it shall be for ever: nothing can be put to it, nor any thing taken from it: and God doeth it, that men should fear before him" (Ec.3:14).**

Thought 2. God is the God of life and hope. The day is coming when pain and death will be no more. Animal will no longer feed upon animal. Neither man nor animal will be savage and take the life of another creature: all life will live together in peace. In that day there will be no struggle, no slaughtering, no assaults, no killing, no war. The earth will be recreated and made perfect. All creatures will live in a perfect state of being, just as they did before sin and evil corrupted the earth.

> **"The wolf also shall dwell with the lamb, and the leopard shall lie down with the kid; and the calf and the young lion and the fatling together; and a little child shall lead them. And the cow and the bear shall feed; their young ones shall lie down together: and the lion shall eat straw like the ox. And the sucking child shall play on the hole of the asp, and the weaned child shall put his hand on the cockatrice' den. They shall not hurt nor destroy in all my holy mountain: for the earth shall be full of the knowledge of the LORD, as the waters cover the sea" (Is.11:6-9).**
>
> **"Because the creature itself also shall be delivered from the bondage of corruption into the glorious liberty of the children of God. For we know that the whole creation groaneth and travaileth in pain together until now" (Ro.8:21-22).**
>
> **"But the day of the Lord will come as a thief in the night; in the which the heavens shall pass away with a great noise, and the elements shall melt with fervent heat, the earth also and the works that are therein shall be burned up. Seeing then that all these things shall be dissolved, what manner of persons ought ye to be in all holy conversation [behavior] and godliness, looking for and hasting unto the coming of the day of God, wherein the heavens being on fire shall be dissolved, and the elements shall melt with fervent heat? Nevertheless we, according to his promise, look for new heavens and a new earth, wherein dwelleth righteousness. Wherefore, beloved, seeing that ye look for such things, be diligent that ye may be found of him in peace, without spot, and blameless" (2 Pe.3:10-14).**
>
> **"And I saw a new heaven and a new earth: for the first heaven and the first earth were passed away; and there was no more sea....And God shall wipe away all tears from their eyes; and there shall be no more death, neither sorrow, nor crying, neither shall there be any more pain: for the former things are passed away. And he that sat upon the throne said, Behold, I make all things new. And he said unto me, Write: for these words are true and faithful. And he said unto me, it is done. I am Alpha and Omega, the beginning and the end. I will give unto him that is athirst of the fountain of the water of life freely. He that overcometh shall inherit all things; and I will be his God, and he shall be my son" (Re.21:1, 4-7).**

	H. The Sixth Day (Part 1): Creation of Land Animals, 1:24-25
1. God's Word created land animals	24 And God said, Let the earth bring forth the living creature after his kind, cattle, and creeping thing, and beast of the earth after his kind: and it was so.
2. God made land animals, each after its kind	25 And God made the beast of the earth after his kind, and cattle after their kind, and every thing that creepeth upon the earth after his kind: and God saw that it was good.
3. God saw that His creation was *good*—fulfilled its function	

DIVISION I

CREATION OF THE HEAVENS AND THE EARTH, 1:1–2:3

H. The Sixth Day (Part 1): Creation of Land Animals, 1:24-25

(1:24-25) **Introduction**: remember what prehistoric earth looked like. It was a primeval earth: the whole earth was blanketed in pitch black darkness and covered with water, the surging, raging waves of one massive ocean. There was also a heavy mist, a dense fog and thick clouds, hanging over the earth, apparently several hundred feet thick—so thick that it blocked out all light from the sun. The primeval earth was hanging in space unfinished and incomplete, empty and unfruitful. But then God began to move; God began to create exactly what was needed to sustain life upon the earth.

⇒ God created light (Ge.1:3-5).
⇒ God created the firmament (the atmosphere and air space right above the earth) (Ge.1:6-8).
⇒ God created the waters (seas, lakes, rivers) and dry land (continents and islands) (Ge.1:9-10).
⇒ God created plant life or vegetation (Ge.1:11-13).
⇒ God created and distributed light upon the earth to regulate day and night and the seasons and years (Ge.1:14-19).
⇒ God created water animals and air animals (Ge.1:20-23).

Now, we come to the sixth day of creation, to the most important day of all—by far the most important day. Why? Because God now creates both land animals and man. Man is to be the summit of God's creation. Once man is created, God will create no more. But man is not created until the last half of the day. Before man, the earth must be filled and populated with land animals. This is the subject that is under discussion now: *The Sixth Day (Part 1): Creation of Land Animals.*
1. God's Word created land animals (v.24).
2. God made land animals, each after its kind (v.25).
3. God saw that His creation was *good*—fulfilled its function (v.25).

1 (1:24) **Animals—Creation**: God's Word created land animals. Note five important facts.
a. Animals were created from the earth: "God said, 'Let the earth bring forth the living creature'" (v.24). It was the earth that brought forth the animals: the earth was commanded to produce the animals, commanded by God. The phrase *bring forth* (totse) means to produce, to cause to come forth. What is meant by these words? Three facts should be noted.
1) God did not say how He was going to use the earth in creating animals, not in this passage. In this particular passage, the Scripture does not say how the earth brought forth animal life. All that God said was: "Let the earth *bring forth* the living creature" (v.24). But note the next point.
2) Scripture is unmistakably clear: "God made the [animals] of the earth" (v.25. See pt. 5 below.) All theories that point toward animals coming from some source other than from God are totally wrong. The Holy Scripture declares in no uncertain terms: "God made the [animals] of the earth" (v.24).
3) Scripture is clear about how the earth played a part in man's creation. Man was created *out of the earth*.

"God formed man of the dust of the ground" (Ge.2:7).

What is meant by being formed is clearly and unmistakably stated: "Out of it [the ground] wast thou taken: for dust thou art, and unto dust shalt thou return" (Ge.3:10). The earth was the substance, the material, the elements, the particles that God used in creating man.

The point is this: this is how the earth served God in creating land animals. The animals of the earth were created *out of the earth*. The earth was the substance and material, the elements and particles that God used to form and create animals. In fact, Scripture clearly states this:

"And out of the ground the Lord God formed [molded] every beast of the field, and every fowl of the air" (Ge.2:19).

"And out of the ground the Lord God formed [molded] every beast of the field, and every fowl of the air" (Ge.2:19).

Thought 1. The earth served God. God told the earth to "bring forth" animal life, and the earth did. The earth had a very, very special task to perform for God—by God's appointment. How much more should man serve God. Man's task is to serve God while upon this earth. Scripture is clear about this.

"And ye shall serve the LORD your God, and he shall bless thy bread, and thy water" (Ex.23:25).
"And now, Israel [in reality, all people], what doth the LORD thy God require of thee, but to fear the LORD thy God, to walk in all his ways, and to love him, and to serve the LORD thy God with all thy heart and with all thy soul" (De.10:12).
"Serve the LORD with fear, and rejoice with trembling" (Ps.2:11).
"Wherefore we receiving a kingdom which cannot be moved, let us have grace, whereby we may serve God acceptably with reverence and godly fear" (He.12:28).

b. Animals were created as living souls, as soulish creatures. Note what was created: *living creatures*. The Hebrew word for *creature* (nephesh) is soul. God created *living souls*. Animals are *living souls* (see DEEPER STUDY # 1, *Soul*—Ge.1:20 for discussion).
c. Animals were created in three classes.
⇒ *Cattle* (behemah): the domestic animals; animals that can be tamed and used in the service of man such as cattle, oxen, camels, horses, dogs, sheep, and donkeys.
⇒ *Creeping things* (remes): the smaller animals that glide along on their bellies or else creep along with small feet. The creepers would include such animals as snakes, worms, ants, and insects.
⇒ *Beast of the earth* (chayyah haarets): the wild animals, the daring and untamed animals such as lions, bears, wolves, and elephants.

Thought 1. God is a God of wisdom. God grouped the animals into the three classes that men most naturally think of them. Just think of the number, beauty, and variety of animals. Their number, kinds, shapes, nature, and beauty all speak of the glory of God.

"Thou, even thou, art LORD alone; thou hath made heaven, the heaven of heavens, with all their host, the earth, and all things that are therein, the seas, and all that is therein, and thou preservest them all; and the host of heaven worshippeth thee" (Ne.9:6).
"And when they heard that, they lifted up their voice to God with one accord, and said, Lord, thou art God, which hast made heaven, and earth, and the sea, and all that in them is" (Ac.4:24).

d. Animals were created with the power to reproduce "after their kind." This means that all land animals have some means...
• to carry on their species, their kind of animal life
• to bring forth the same kind of animal life, the same kind of life as the parent animal
• to propagate their own species

e. Animals were created by God's Word, by the power of His Word. Note the words, "And it was so." When God spoke to the earth, the earth brought forth animal life. What God said was done. What He commanded was carried out. Once He had spoken, nothing could stop the creation of animal life.

"The works of his hands are verity and judgment; all his commandments are sure" (Ps.111:7).
"But our God is in the heavens: he hath done whatsoever he hath pleased" (Ps.115:3).
"For ever, O LORD, thy word is settled in heaven" (Ps.119:89).
"For with God nothing shall be impossible" (Lu.1:37).

2 (1:25) **Animals—Creation**: God made land animals, each *after its kind*. Why is Scripture again declaring God to be the source of animal life? Why is the origin of animals being repeated and reemphasized? There are at least two reasons.
a. There is a need to stress that God and God alone created the animals of the earth. Animal life did not just happen. The basic substance of animal life did not come *out of nothing*, not the cells of animals, neither the DNA of animals, nor the hydrogen of animals, nor the molecules of animals. Whatever the basic element of animal life is—whatever man may yet discover to be the basic substance of life, whatever the raw matter and energy of life is—that basic substance did not just begin to form and mold animal life. Animal life did not just happen...
• by chance
• by random
• by some impersonal force or energy bringing the basic cells and DNA together to form animal life
• by some physical laws that were already in existence and that just began to form animal life

Animal life was created by God and by God alone. Whatever the basic substances are that make up animal life—whatever raw forces and laws cause animal life—they were all created and put into operation by God. God and God alone, by the power of His omnipotent Word, created animal life. God and God alone commanded the earth to bring forth animal life.

b. There is a need to stress that God made animals after "*their own kind*" and only after "their own kind." Note how this is clearly stated after each of the three classes of animals. God made...

- the wild animals "after their kind"
- the domestic animals "after their kind"
- the creeping animals "after their kind"

What does this mean? It means that God gave animals the power to reproduce *their own kind.* All animal life has some means...

- to carry on its species, its kind of animal life
- to bring forth the same kind of animal life, the same kind of life as the parent animal
- to propagate its own species

Does this also mean that species can only reproduce within their own species? That the theory of evolution is wrong? That there was not and has not been any crossover or transmutation of species? Up to the present time, the fossil record of the earth has not revealed any crossover or transmutation of one species to another species. The fossil record has indicated development and adaptation among some animals within species, but there has not been any discovery that shows development from one species to another species. In fact, the very opposite is the case. Fossil remains have now been studied for decade after decade with the most scientific technology available, but no crossover of species has ever been found. There has not even been a gradual development or a slow transition from one species to another. (Keep in mind that development and adaptation within species or certain groups of animals have been found, but not crossovers or transmutations.) What has been found is the sudden appearance of major groups of animals, not gradual development and crossovers. Between the major groups or species there are nothing but gaps and missing links, multitudes of them. Will missing links ever be found? Will the fossil record or any other discovery ever turn up enough evidence of crossovers, of gradual development, between species and major groups of animals? Three facts point strongly against it.

⇒ One hundred years of research has not been able to find significant evidence of gradual development between major animal groups. There is no evidence of crossover between species of animals. As asked, will fossil research ever produce such evidence? How can it, when it has been searching for over one hundred years? Significant evidence of crossovers would have certainly been discovered by now. But the missing links and gaps remain.

⇒ The study of life by astrophysics and by bio-chemistry shows that the probability of evolution is almost zero, if not zero. From the factual and honest study of science, it just seems impossible that life could have come from gases, protons, neutrons, and electrons appearing *out of nothing* and developing into a single cell and then continuing to develop into the complex form of man. The true facts point toward each species reproducing its own species.

⇒ The Holy Scripture declares that God made and molded animals "after their kind." Each species, each major group, was created to reproduce only *its own kind.*

(Note: James Montgomery Boice has an excellent discussion on the various views of creation, including the view of evolution. See his book: *Genesis*: *An Expositional Commentary*, Vol.1, p.37-38.)

> **"For the invisible things of him from the creation of the world are clearly seen, being understood by the things that are made, even his eternal power and Godhead; so that they are without excuse; because that, when they knew God, they glorified him not as God, neither were thankful; but became vain in their imaginations, and their foolish heart was darkened. Professing themselves to be wise, they became fools, and changed the glory of the incorruptible God into an image made like to corruptible man, and to birds, and fourfooted beasts, and creeping things" (Ro.1:20-23).**
>
> **"All things were made by him; and without him was not any thing made that was made" (Jn.1:3).**
>
> **"[God] who created all things by Jesus Christ" (Ep.3:9).**
>
> **"For by him were all things created, that are in heaven, and that are in earth, visible and invisible, whether they be thrones, or dominions, or principalities, or powers: all things were created by him, and for him: and he is before all things, and by him all things consist" (Col.1:16-17).**
>
> **"Thou art worthy O Lord, to receive glory and honour and power: for thou hast created all things, and for thy pleasure they are and were created" (Re.4:11).**

Thought 1. God gave the animals a kinship with the earth. He created the animals out of the earth (see note—Ge.1:24). As fellow creatures of God and of God's earth, man is obligated to care for the animals, even as God Himself would care for them.

Thought 2. The believer now sees a great truth confirmed in the creation of land animals: God is definitely a God of order (progression and perfection) and a God of caring, of personal involvement. The fact that God created in an upward move—advanced forward—by making a higher form of creation is now clear (see note—Ge.1:20-23). Creation of beings with souls moves not only from one form to another, step by step, but creation of life moves upward to a higher order of being (see note and DEEPER STUDY # 1—Ge.1:20; note 3—1:25). And God Himself is actively involved in every move. Just imagine all the forms of life on earth alone—the innumerable number and the intricate detail of each and all combined! How infinite God is—the God of order (progression and perfection) and the God of caring, of personal involvement!

The believer bows, unable to comprehend God; he trusts God and submissively worships God.

"Thou art worthy, O Lord, to receive glory and honour and power: for thou hast created all things, and for thy pleasure they are and were created" (Re.4:11).

"Saying with a loud voice, Fear God, and give glory to him; for the hour of his judgment is come: and worship him that made heaven, and earth, and the sea, and the fountains of waters" (Re.14:7).

"Sing unto him, sing psalms unto him, talk ye of all his wondrous works" (1 Chr.16:9).

"Give unto the LORD the glory due unto his name; worship the LORD in the beauty of holiness" (Ps.29:2).

"O come, let us worship and bow down: let us kneel before the LORD our maker" (Ps.95:6).

"O worship the LORD in the beauty of holiness: fear before him, all the earth" (Ps.96:9).

[3] (1:25) **Animals—Creation**: God saw that His creation was good—the animals of the earth fulfilled their function. The word *good* means that the land animals of the earth were valuable: they had a specific purpose for being created. There are at least four *major reasons* why God created land animals:

⇒ To populate and give life to His creation, to the earth.
⇒ To help carry on the reproduction of the food chain.
⇒ To give variety and beauty to the earth; to show forth His glorious handiwork.
⇒ To provide companionship for man.

The importance of these purposes is clearly seen when we picture an earth without land animals. Just imagine how empty the land of the earth would be without any animal life whatsoever. What an emptiness would fill the land of the earth.

Thought 1. God is the God of variety, diversity, and beauty. Kind after kind, species after species, class after class were created—an infinite variety and diversity, each with its own beauty and purpose. How clearly man could see the power of God if he would just take time and look. How often God expects to be seen and praised in creation!

"Thou, even thou, art LORD alone; thou hast made heaven, the heaven of heavens, with all their host, the earth, and all things that are therein, the seas, and all that is therein, and thou preservest them all; and the host of heaven worshippeth thee" (Ne.9:6).

"But ask now the beasts, and they shall teach thee; and the fowls of the air, and they shall tell thee: or speak to the earth, and it shall teach thee: and the fishes of the sea shall declare unto thee. Who knoweth not in all these that the hand of the LORD hath wrought this? In whose hand is the soul of every living thing, and the breath of all mankind" (Jb. 12:7-10).

"He hath made every thing beautiful in his time: also he hath set the world in their heart, so that no man find out the work that God maketh from the beginning to the end" (Ec.3:11).

"And saying, Sirs, why do ye these things? We also are men of like passions with you, and preach unto you that ye should turn from these vanities unto the living God, which made heaven, and earth, and the sea, and all things that are therein" (Ac.14:15).

Thought 2. God "approved" and judged His own work. How much more will He judge man's behavior toward the earth and man's duty toward the earth? The way man treats the earth and the creatures of the earth is important to God—critically important.

"For the earnest expectation of the creature waiteth for the manifestation of the sons of God. For the creature was made subject to vanity, not willingly, but by reason of him who hath subjected the same in hope, because the creature itself also shall be delivered from the bondage of corruption into the glorious liberty of the children of God. For we know that the whole creation groaneth and travaileth in pain together until now. And not only they, but ourselves also, which have the firstfruits of the Spirit, even we ourselves groan within ourselves, waiting for the adoption, to wit, the redemption of our body" (Ro.8:19-23).

"For the kingdom of heaven is like unto a man that is an householder, which went out early in the morning to hire labourers into his vineyard [the world]" (Mt.20:1).

"Hear another parable: there was a certain householder, which planted a vineyard [the world], and hedged it round about, and digged a winepress in it, and built a tower, and let it out to husbandmen, and went into a far country" (Mt.21:33).

"Moreover it is required in stewards, that a man be found faithful" (1 Co.4:2).

"So God created man in his own image, in the image of God created he him; male and female created he them. And God blessed them, and God said unto them, Be fruitful, and multiply, and replenish the earth, and subdue it: and have dominion over the fish of the sea, and over the fowl of the air, and over every living thing that moveth upon the earth. And God said, Behold, I have given you every herb bearing seed, which is upon the face of all the earth, and every tree, in the which is the fruit of a tree yielding seed; to you it shall be for meat" (Ge.1:27-28).

"Thou madest him to have dominion over the works of thy hands; thou hast put all things under his feet" (Ps.8:6).

"The earth is the LORD's, and the fulness thereof; the world, and they that dwell therein" (Ps.24:1).

"If I were hungry, I would not tell thee: for the world is mine, and the fulness thereof" (Ps.50:12).

Thought 3. God had created animals for man (Ge.2:18f). Man should, therefore, be pleased with the animal creation of God, and act responsibly toward them.

Thought 4. God cares for all animals, even for the little sparrow that falls to the ground. Think how much more He cares for us.

"Behold the fowls of the air: for they sow not, neither do they reap, nor gather into barns; yet your heavenly Father feedeth them. Are ye not much better than they?" (Mt.6:26).

"Are not five sparrows sold for two farthings, and not one of them is forgotten before God? But even the very hairs of your head are all numbered. Fear not therefore: ye are of more value than many sparrows" (Lu.12:6-7).

"And the Lord shall deliver me from every evil work, and will preserve me unto his heavenly kingdom: to whom be glory for ever and ever" (2 Ti.4:18).

"So that we may boldly say, The Lord is my helper, and I will not fear what man shall do unto me" (He.13:6).

"And he said, My presence shall go with thee, and I will give thee rest" (Ex.33:14).

"Fear thou not; for I am with thee: be not dismayed; for I am thy God: I will strengthen thee; yea, I will help thee; yea, I will uphold thee with the right hand of my righteousness" (Is.41:10).

"When thou passest through the waters, I will be with thee; and through the rivers, they shall not overflow thee: when thou walkest through the fire, thou shalt not be burned; neither shall the flame kindle upon thee" (Is.43:2).

"The LORD is my strength and my shield; my heart trusted in him, and I am helped: therefore my heart greatly rejoiceth; and with my song will I praise him" (Ps.28:7).

"But I am poor and needy; yet the Lord thinketh upon me: thou art my help and my deliverer; make no tarrying, O my God" (Ps.40:17).

	I. The Sixth Day (Part 2): Creation of Man, Male & Female,[DS1] 1:26-31	over the fish of the sea, and over the fowl of the air, and over every living thing that moveth upon the earth.	b. To subdue the earth[DS3] c. To have dominion—to rule—over all animal life

1. God's Word created man
   a. God held a divine counsel to create man
   b. God created man in the image of the Godhead[DS2]
   c. God created man with a very special purpose: To have dominion
     1) Over all animals
     2) Over all the earth
	26 And God said, Let us make man in our image, after our likeness: and let them have dominion over the fish of the sea, and over the fowl of the air, and over the cattle, and over all the earth, and over every creeping thing that creepeth upon the earth.	29 And God said, Behold, I have given you every herb bearing seed, which is upon the face of all the earth, and every tree, in the which is the fruit of a tree yielding seed; to you it shall be for meat.	5. God provided vegetation upon the earth to feed man & animals
			   a. Provided vegetation for man

2. God & God alone created man, both male & female: Created them with the highest dignity & honor, in His image 3. God blessed man 4. God gave man three great assignments a. To be fruitful & reproduce & fill the earth	27 So God created man in his own image, in the image of God created he him; male and female created he them. 28 And God blessed them, and God said unto them, Be fruitful, and multiply, and replenish the earth, and subdue it: and have dominion	30 And to every beast of the earth, and to every fowl of the air, and to every thing that creepeth upon the earth, wherein there is life, I have given every green herb for meat: and it was so. 31 And God saw every thing that he had made, and, behold, it was very good. And the evening and the morning were the sixth day.	b. Provided vegetation for animals 6. God saw that His creation was *good*—fulfilled its function

DIVISION I

CREATION OF THE HEAVENS AND THE EARTH, 1:1–2:3

I. The Sixth Day (Part 2): Creation of Man, Male and Female, 1:26-31

(1:26-31) **Introduction**: when God created the universe, He created it in stages. At first, He simply hung the stars and the earth in space. They were all incomplete, unfinished, and unproductive. The earth itself was covered with one massive ocean: the whole earth lay under a sea of surging, raging waves. In addition, there was a heavy mist—a dense fog and thick clouds—that encircled the earth. Just imagine! The earth was encircled with a thick mass of clouds that apparently rose several thousand feet up into the sky. This would mean that the earth was engulfed in pitch black darkness (see note 4—Ge.1:2 for more discussion). This was primeval earth; this was the way our planet looked before God began the six days of creation. But God did not create the earth to remain in a primeval stage. He created the earth to be the home for man. Therefore, God launched His great creative acts; God launched the six great days of creation:

⇒ On the first day: God created light (Ge.1:3-5).
⇒ On the second day: God created the firmament (the atmosphere and air space right above earth) (Ge.1:6-8).
⇒ On the third day: God created the waters, dry land, and vegetation (Ge.1:9-13).
⇒ On the fourth day: God distributed light upon the earth to regulate day and night and the seasons and years (Ge.1:14-19).
⇒ On the fifth day: God created water and air creatures (Ge.1:20-23).
⇒ On the sixth day, during the first half of the day: God created land animals (Ge.1:24-25).

Now, on the second half of the sixth day, the final act of creation is to take place. This creative act is to be the crown and summit of God's creation. After this act of creation, the earth will be completely filled with creatures created by God. There will be no more creation, not upon the earth. The earth will have the creature that is to be its *ruler and protector:* man. Man is the climactic creation of God. Man is the creature whom God planned and purposed eternally—long, long before the earth was ever founded. This is the subject of this great passage of Scripture, the passage that covers God's climactic act of creation: *The Sixth Day (Part 2): Creation of Man, Male and Female.*

1. God's Word created man (v.26).
2. God and God alone created man, both male and female: created them with the highest dignity and honor, in His very own image (v.27).
3. God blessed man (v.28).
4. God gave man three great assignments (v.28).
5. God provided vegetation upon the earth to feed man and animals (vv.29-30).
6. God saw that His creation was *good*—fulfilled its function (v.31).

DEEPER STUDY # 1

(1:26-31) **Man, Creation of—Animals**: man is the crowning summit and climax of God's creation. He is not just an animal. Man is a special being, a distinctive being that was formed in the mind of God. This is the critical truth that man must know in order to understand himself.

⇒ Man is of the earth, but he is also of God.
⇒ Man is of the physical world, but he is also of the spiritual world. Man is flesh, but he is also spirit.
⇒ Man is related to the animals of the earth, but he is also related to God.

In man, both flesh and spirit are brought together. In man, both earth and heaven are represented. In man, both now and eternity are desired. In man, both the physical world and the spiritual world are experienced. (See notes— Ro.8:28-39, see 8:2; 1 Co.3:1-3. See Ro.8:1, 5f; Gal.5:17.)

How is man related to the animals, and how does he differ from the animals? Man shares the following with animals according to the creation account.

1. *Creation*: man is made out of the dust of the earth, the same as animals (Ge.2:7, 19. See note—Ge.1:24.)
2. *Sustenance*: man lives *of* the earth, just as animals live (Ge.1:29-30).
3. *Reproduction*: man carries on the human race by the same process that animals carry on their species—by reproducing (Ge.1:22, 28).
4. *Nature*: animals were created for man (akin to, associate to man). There is a very close association between man and animals (Ge.2:18-19, see 6:19f; 8:18-19).

Man differs from animals in at least four significant ways. (It should be noted that despite all the similarities between man and animals, the stress of Genesis is upon the distinctiveness of man. Man *is* the crowning summit and climax of God's creation [Ps.8:5-8].)

1. Man is different from animals in *the mind and the heart of God*. There was a "Divine Counsel" held to discuss man's creation (see DEEPER STUDY # 2—Ge.1:26). God holds man very dear to His heart (Pr.8:31; Jn.3:16).
2. Man is different from animals in *the words of Scripture*. "Let us make [man]" stresses a more direct and distinctive act of God than "let the earth bring forth [animals]" (see Ge.1:24, 26). The words point toward a being of dignity, intelligence, and power being created—a being who is to master the earth for God.
3. Man is different from animals in the way God created him. God breathed His own breath—His own Spirit and life—into man (Ge.2:7).
4. Man is different from animals by *office*. He is given dominion "over all the earth," including dominion over all animals (see DEEPER STUDY # 3—Ge.1:28, see 2:19; Ps.8:4-8; Js.3:7).

1 (1:26) **Man—Creation—Earth—Trinity**: God's Word created man. Man exists because God spoke man into existence. God used the power of His Word to create man. God simply spoke and man came into being. God spoke and the laws that caused man to form went into operation. God spoke, and the basic elements—the atoms, molecules, protons, neutrons, electrons, genes, DNA, and whatever basic element is ever discovered that makes up human life—came into being. God spoke, and the power of His Word formed and created man. There are three very special points in this verse.

a. God held a very special conference, a divine counsel, to create man. Note what God said, "Let *us* make man...in *our* image...after *our* likeness." This is plural. God is speaking to Christ, His Son, and to the Holy Spirit. How do we know this?

⇒ First, because Jesus Christ revealed the Trinity to us (Jn.14:16-17, 26). God the Father, God the Son, and God the Holy Spirit do exist. All three exist in perfect unity. They are all of one mind and purpose. Therefore, they are bound to discuss and decide things together just as any unified family does.

⇒ Second, because Scripture reveals that all three Persons of the Godhead were involved in creation (Ge.1:1; 1:2; Jn.1:3; Col.1:16; Heb.1:1-2). The Godhead would have certainly discussed the plans and work of creation while they were creating the earth. It is illogical to think they would not discuss their work.

⇒ Third, because God uses the plural here in Genesis. God says, "Let *us* make man in *our* image, after *our* likeness." God is not telling angels nor any other heavenly creature that they are to work together in creating man. God, not heavenly beings, is creating man. Man is the creation of God and of God alone. God the Father, God the Son, and God the Holy Spirit—the complete Godhead, all that God is—created His crown and glory: man.

⇒ Fourth, because God made man in His own image. God did not make man in the image of angels nor of any other heavenly being. This is not the stress of this creative act. The stress is this: God was making man in His *own* image and in *His image* alone. "Let us make man" is referring to God the Father talking with God the Son and with God the Holy Spirit. Man bears the very image of God Himself. Man was created...

• in the image of God the Father
• in the image of God the Son
• in the image of God the Holy Spirit

The point is this: God held a very special conference, a divine counsel, to create man. The Holy Spirit, who inspires Scripture, is using the plural "let us" to tell us this. This is not to say that the full doctrine of the Trinity is taught here. Such is foolishness. God would never be known as a Trinitarian Being if we read only the Genesis account of creation and ignored the New Testament. But when we read and notice the plural, the seed of the Trinity is planted in our minds. And we know what is meant because of the revelation of Jesus Christ and of the Scripture as a whole. We know that the Holy Spirit has inspired Scripture, that He has deliberately led the writer of Genesis to use the plural. Why? To show the great dignity and honor of man. Man was given the glorious privilege of being created by *all the Godhead*. God held a great counsel to plan man's creation. Man's creation was to be so special, so climactic—the very crown and glory of creation—that God called a very special conference to discuss the matter, a divine counsel that involved...

• God the Father
• God the Son
• God the Holy Spirit

(See DEEPER STUDY # 3—Ge.3:22 for more discussion.)

Thought 1. All three persons of the Godhead consulted and became personally involved in the creation of man. When the believer really meditates upon this glorious truth, his heart should throb with excitement. He sees that

God planned him with a very special plan and that God cares for him and loves him with a very special care and love. God the Father, God the Son, and God the Holy Spirit were all involved in planning and creating him. God's plan for his creation was so important that it necessitated the fulness of God's presence and love and care.

"Thou sendest forth thy spirit [the Holy Spirit], they are created: and thou renewest the face of the earth" (Ps.104:30).

"All things were made by him [Christ]; and without him was not any thing made that was made" (Jn.1:3).

"For by him [Christ] were all things created, that are in heaven, and that are in earth, visible and invisible, whether they be thrones, or dominions, or principalities, or powers: all things were created by him, and for him" (Col.1:16).

"God, who at sundry times and in divers manners spake in time past unto the fathers by the prophets, hath in these last days spoken unto us by his Son, whom he hath appointed heir of all things, by whom also he [God] made the worlds" (He.1:1-2).

Thought 2. In the beginning, God held a very special conference, a divine counsel to create man. Today, God holds a very special hope for man: redemption. Since the fall of man into sin and death, God (the whole Godhead) has been actively involved in the recreation and redemption of man. In the initial creation, God sent forth both His Son and His Spirit to create man. Now, in the recreation—necessitated by the fall of man—God sends forth both His Son and His Spirit to recreate man (the new birth). All three persons of the Godhead are actively involved in the redemption of man, in the recreation of man, just as they were in the initial creation of man. All three persons of the Godhead are seeking the redemption of man.

"For God so loved the world, that he gave his only begotten Son, that whosoever believeth in him should not perish, but have everlasting life" (Jn.3:16).

"And I will pray the Father, and he shall give you another Comforter [the Holy Spirit], that he may abide with you for ever; even the Spirit of truth; whom the world cannot receive, because it seeth him not, neither knoweth him: but ye know him; for he dwelleth with you, and shall be in you. I will not leave you comfortless: I will come to you" (Jn.14:16-18).

"Nevertheless I tell you the truth; It is expedient for you that I go away: for if I go not away, the Comforter will not come unto you; but if I depart, I will send him unto you. And when he is come, he will reprove the world of sin, and of righteousness, and of judgment: of sin, because they believe not on me; of righteousness, because I go to my Father, and ye see me no more; of judgment, because the prince of this world is judged. I have yet many things to say unto you, but ye cannot bear them now. Howbeit when he, the Spirit of truth, is come, he will guide you into all truth: for he shall not speak of himself but whatsoever he shall hear, that shall he speak: and he will show you things to come. He shall glorify me: for he shall receive of mine, and shall show it unto you. All things that the Father hath are mine: therefore said I, that he shall take of mine, and shall show it unto you" (Jn.16:7-15).

"For as many as are led by the Spirit of God, they are the sons of God. For ye have not received the spirit of bondage again to fear; but ye have received the Spirit of adoption, whereby we cry, Abba, Father. The Spirit itself beareth witness with our spirit, that we are the children of God: and if children, then heirs; heirs of God, and joint-heirs with Christ; if so be that we suffer with him, that we may be also glorified together" (Ro.8:14-17).

b. God created man to be a very special creature: man was created in God's very own image, after God's very own likeness (see pt.a. above for discussion).

c. God created man for a very special purpose: to have dominion over all the earth. God planned and created man with a very special honor and responsibility: to look after all that He had created (see Deeper Study # 3—Ge.1:28 for discussion).

DEEPER STUDY # 2

(1:26) **Man—Creation—Spirit**: God created man in the image of the Godhead. Note exactly what Scripture says:

"And God said, 'Let us make man in our image, after our likeness' " (v.26).
"So God created man in his own image, in the image of God created he him" (v.27).

What is meant by man being created in "the image and likeness of God"? Whatever it means, it is that which distinguishes man from all other life. Nowhere else does God say that He created a being in "his own image, after his own likeness." Only man is "in the image, in the likeness of God." (See note—Ge.5:1-2 for more discussion.)

1. It is unlikely that it means the *soul* of man. The Bible says that all living creatures are souls. They are created as *living souls*. All living creatures possess the breath, the consciousness, and the animation of life. (See Deeper Study # 1, *Soul*—Ge.1:20 for more discussion.)

2. It is unlikely that it means the ability to reason. Apparently, animals have some ability to reason and even to learn to varying degrees. Animals show some ability to think when facing problems or an enemy, or in going through the innumerable experiences of life.

3. It is unlikely that it means the ability to be moral and just. Animals—in particular some animals, both individually and within family groups—have rules and acts that lead to moral and virtuous behavior among themselves and even toward others. There seems to be some exercise of right and wrong among some animals.

However, this needs to be pointed out: man is far superior to animals both mentally and morally. Man is far superior both as a rational being (a being that reasons) and as a moral being (a being that is to live in justice, to relate to others as he should). (Note how being *spiritually and mentally renewed* in Christ affects the rational and moral powers of man. Man can be *created* in real righteousness and *true* holiness—delivered from the legalistic bondage of man-made righteousness and holiness, from a man-made religion of rules and rituals [Ep.4:24; Col.3:10].)

What, then, does God mean when He says that man was created "in the image, in the likeness of God"? It means at least five things.

1. God is perfect, so He created man just like Himself, perfect. This, of course, refers to the *original creation* of man. When God first created man, man was created just like God, created in perfection, created without any flaw or defect whatsoever. He had a perfect body and mind, perfect health and intelligence. Man knew no sickness, disease, or accidents; and he had no inability to learn. He experienced no pain or suffering. He sensed no alienation, no emptiness, or loneliness. Man never shed a tear of sadness, sorrow, or grief. And above all, man was free of sin and corruption, free to live forever and never to die. Man was created perfect, in the very "image and likeness" of God's perfection.

> **"Be ye therefore perfect, even as your Father which is in heaven is perfect"** (Mt.5:48).
> **"Having the understanding darkened, being alienated from the life of God through the ignorance that is in them, because of the blindness of their heart"** (Ep.4:18).
> **"Whom we preach, warning every man, and teaching every man in all wisdom; that we may present every man perfect in Christ Jesus"** (Col.1:28).

2. God is light, full of the glory, splendor, and brilliance of light. Thus, God created man and clothed him with the glory of His light (see note 1, pt.2—Ge.3:7; 3:21).

> **"This then is the message which we have heard of him, and declare unto you, that God is light, and in him is no darkness at all"** (1 Jn.1:5).
> **"[God] who coverest thyself with light as with a garment"** (Ps.104:2).

3. God is holy: sinless, righteous, pure, and moral. Thus God created man holy, sinless, righteous, pure, and moral. God made man to be distinctive—set apart from all other creatures—in life and behavior, to live a godly life.

> **"Because it is written, Be ye holy; for I am holy"** (1 Pe.1:16, see Lev.11:45).
> **"Follow peace with all men, and holiness, without which no man shall see the Lord"** (He.12:14).
> **"Seeing then that all these things shall be dissolved, what manner of persons ought ye to be in all holy conversation and godliness"** (2 Pe.3:11).

4. God is love: devoted, loyal, loving, merciful, gracious, and compassionate. So God created man as a creature of love, devotion, loyalty, mercy, grace, and compassion.

> **"Beloved, let us love one another: for love is of God; and every one that loveth is born of God, and knoweth God. He that loveth not knoweth not God; for God is love"** (1 Jn.4:7-8).
> **"And we have known and believed the love that God hath to us. God is love; and he that dwelleth in love dwelleth in God, and God in him"** (1 Jn.4:16).

5. God is Spirit, eternal Spirit; God is Life, eternal Life; God is the only Person who has lived forever, who never had a beginning and shall never have an ending. Therefore...
- God created man and gave him a *spirit, an immortal breath, a life that lives forever just like God*

God went beyond what He had made when He created the animals as living souls and gave them an earthly life and a temporal breath. God made man a *spirit that is just like Himself, just like His very own life*. Apparently, no animal is a spirit; animals are only souls. As living souls, they are enabled by varying degrees to breathe, to reason, and to relate. But none of them have the inherent power to breathe eternally, nor the drive and ability to reason after God nor to relate to God. But man does have that power, that drive and ability. Man is spirit, even as God is Spirit. Man is not only body and soul as are the animals of creation. Man is not only a breathing, living soul for this earth. Man is a spirit, an immortal being.

In light of this, there are at least two distinguishing marks of God's image within man, two distinguishing marks of man as a spirit.

1. God's image within man is *the power of immortality*. Man lives beyond this earth, lives forever hereafter just like God. As mentioned above, according to the Bible, no animal is a spirit; animals are only souls. As souls they are enabled to breathe, that is, to live. But none of them have the inherent power to breathe eternally. But man does have that power. Man is a spirit, even as God is Spirit. *Man is not only a living and breathing soul like the animals which are made for this earth, man is a spirit, an immortal being made both for this earth and for eternity.*

> **"And this is life eternal, that they might know thee the only true God, and Jesus Christ, whom thou hast sent"** (Jn.17:3).

2. God's image within man is both the *drive and the ability (choice) to worship*. Man not only has the soulish ability to reason and to relate, but he has...

- an unquenchable *spiritual drive and ability* to reason after God
- an unquenchable drive and ability to relate to God

Again, as mentioned above, no earthly animal has this spiritual drive and ability. The Bible does ascribe to souls varying abilities, but no animal soul has the drive and ability to *reason after God* nor to *relate to God*. Worship is a spiritual drive and ability, an ability of spirit only, of man only. Just like animals, *man knows and understands the things* of this earth; but *man is to know, believe, and understand* God first and foremost (Is.43:10). Man is to worship God. God is Spirit, and man, who is created as spirit, is to worship God in spirit and in truth.

> **"God is a Spirit: and they that worship him must worship him in spirit and in truth" (Jn.4:24).**
> **"Ye are my witnesses, saith the Lord, and my servant whom I have chosen: that ye may know and believe me, and understand that I am he: before me there was no God formed, neither shall there be after me" (Is.43:10).**

There are two very significant facts to be noted about the image of God within man, about man as a spiritual being.
1. The rebellion of man against God (man's fall) affected God's image within man. God had created man as an immortal being. As an immortal being upon earth, man had two rights:
⇒ the right to live on this earth
⇒ the right to live with God forever

When man exercised his ability and choice and turned against God, he lost both rights. Man could no longer live on the earth forever, nor could he live with God forever. In his rebellion against God, man was saying...

- that he preferred a different world other than God's world
- that he preferred a different god (his own will) other than God Himself

Man thereby condemned himself to leave this earth (to die, Ge.2:17; 3:1f; 3:19) and to be separated from God eternally (Jn.3:18). Note that man was already created as an immortal being. Thus, he would continue on; he would exist forever, but...

- he was to be placed somewhere else other than this earth (he had chosen such)
- he was to be separated from God forever

This was man's choice (see note 3 and DEEPER STUDY # 2—Ge.2:16-17). The image of God—the power of immortality and the drive and ability to worship and live with God—was marred eternally.
2. The image of God within man can be renewed.
   a. Man can be "born again"—made spiritually alive to God, just as spiritually alive as he was in the beginning—never to perish.

> **"Jesus answered and said unto him, Verily, verily, I say unto thee, Except a man be born again, he cannot see the kingdom of God....Jesus answered, Verily, verily, I say unto thee, Except a man be born of water and of the Spirit, he cannot enter into the kingdom of God" (Jn.3:3, 5).**
> **"Being born again, not of corruptible seed, but of incorruptible, by the word of God, which liveth and abideth for ever" (1 Pe.1:23).**
> **"Whosoever believeth that Jesus is the Christ is born of God: and every one that loveth him that begat loveth him also that is begotten of him" (1 Jn.5:1).**

   b. Man can partake of God's divine nature, "put on the new man."

> **"And that ye put on the new man, which after God is created in righteousness and true holiness" (Ep.4:24).**
> **"And have put on the new man, which is renewed in knowledge after the image of him that created him" (Col.3:10).**
> **"Whereby are given unto us exceeding great and precious promises: that by these ye might be partakers of the divine nature" (2 Pe.1:4).**

   c. Man can be renewed, regenerated, or recreated in Christ Jesus.

> **"Therefore if any man be in Christ, he is a new creature: old things are passed away; behold, all things are become new" (2 Co.5:17).**
> **"For he hath made him to be sin for us, who knew no sin; that we might be made the righteousness of God in him" (2 Co.5:21).**
> **"Who his own self bare our sins in his own body on the tree, that we, being dead to sins, should live unto righteousness: by whose stripes ye were healed" (1 Pe.2:24).**
> **"Not by works of righteousness which we have done, but according to his mercy he saved us, by the washing of regeneration, and renewing of the Holy Ghost" (Tit.3:5).**

---

d. Man can partake of God's divine nature and be assured of living forever in the new heavens and earth.

> "And as we have borne the image of the earthy, we shall also bear the image of the heavenly" (1 Co.15:49).
>
> "Whereby are given unto us exceeding great and precious promises: that by these ye might be partakers of the divine nature" (2 Pe.1:4).
>
> "But the day of the Lord will come as a thief in the night; in the which the heavens shall pass away with a great noise, and the elements shall melt with fervent heat, the earth also and the works that are therein shall be burned up. Seeing then that all these things shall be dissolved, what manner of persons ought ye to be in all holy conversation and godliness, looking for and hasting unto the coming of the day of God, wherein the heavens being on fire shall be dissolved, and the elements shall melt with fervent heat? Nevertheless we, according to his promise, look for new heavens and a new earth, wherein dwelleth righteousness" (2 Pe.3:10-13).
>
> "And I saw a new heaven and a new earth: for the first heaven and the first earth were passed away; and there was no more sea" (Re.21:1).

Thought 1. God said, "Let us make man in *our image, after our likeness*" (Ge.1:26). By these words *God is showing* that man is the crowning glory of His creation: the being that embraces all the dignity and nobility of God's mind, the being that towered high and far above all else, the being that was purposed to master and control all of God's creation and was given the phenomenal powers to do just that.

Thought 2. God held man very dear to His heart. God planned and created man with a very special grace and care: in His own image, after His own likeness. Man is the crowning summit and climax of God's creation.

---

2 (1:27) **Man—Creation**: God and God alone created man, both male and female, created them with the highest dignity and honor, in His image. Why is God's creation of man being repeated? Why is Scripture again declaring that God made man in His own image? Note exactly what the verse says:

> "So God created man in his own image, in the image of God created he him; male and female created he them" (v.27).

There are three reasons why God's creation of man is being re-emphasized.

a. There is a need to stress that God and God alone created man. Human life did not just happen to come into being. The basic substance of human life did not come *out of nothing*—not the cells of man, nor the DNA, atoms, or molecules of man. Whatever the basic element of human life is—whatever man may yet discover to be the basic substance of life; whatever the raw matter and energy of life is—that basic substance did not just begin to form and mold life. Human life did not just happen...

- by chance
- by random
- by some impersonal force or energy bringing the basic cells and DNA together to form human life
- by some physical laws that were already in existence and just began to form human life

Human life was created by God and by God alone. Whatever the basic substances are that make up human life, whatever raw forces and laws cause human life, they were all created and put into operation by God. God and God alone, by the power of His omnipotent Word, created human life. God and God alone commanded human life to come into existence.

Thought 1. God alone created man. Man must not reject and deny God; he must not neglect and ignore God. To do so leads to rejection by God, for God is the Creator of man. Man is the creature. The creature must never rebel against the Creator. Such rebellion will only lead to judgment and condemnation. Man must, therefore, acknowledge God as his Creator. Man must serve and worship God as the Creator, as the Source and Giver of life, the Sovereign LORD and Majesty of the universe.

> "And forgettest the Lord thy maker, that hath stretched forth the heavens, and laid the foundations of the earth?" (Is.51:13).
>
> "Have we not all one father? hath not one God created us?" (Mal.2:10).
>
> "Know ye that the Lord he is God: it is he that hath made us, and not we ourselves; we are his people, and the sheep of his pasture. Enter into his gates with thanksgiving and into his courts with praise: be thankful unto him, and bless his name. For the Lord is good; his mercy is everlasting; and his truth endureth to all generations" (Ps.100:3-5).

Thought 2. The creature should always serve its Creator. A Creator who is so considerate that He gives the creature a free will deserves to be worshipped and served forever. A Creator who loves so much that He gives the creature the capacity to love freely deserves to be loved and adored. This God has done. God has given us both a free will and the capacity to love freely; therefore, God is to be worshipped and served forever. God is to be loved and adored by us all.

b. There is a need to stress the great dignity and honor of man. Man was created in the very image and likeness of God. Man is the crown and summit of God's creation. Man is the creature to whom God has given His Spirit—His very own immortal breath, His life that lives forever. Therefore, man lives forever just like God. Man never ceases to exist.

Thought 1. This is one thing man needs to know: he has been created in the image, in the very likeness, of God. He is an immortal creature: he shall exist forever and ever. Man must, therefore, make sure—absolutely sure—that he is going to live with God. The one thing he must not do is to live separated and apart from God. Man must not miss out on the glorious privilege of living forever with God.

"For God so loved the world, that he gave his only begotten Son, that whosoever believeth in him should not perish, but have everlasting life" (Jn.3:16).

"He that believeth on the Son hath everlasting life: and he that believeth not the Son shall not see life; but the wrath of God abideth on him" (Jn.3:36).

"Verily, verily, I say unto you, If a man keep my saying, he shall never see death" (Jn.8:51).

"And whosoever liveth and believeth in me shall never die. Believest thou this?" (Jn.11:26).

"For we know that if our earthly house of this tabernacle were dissolved, we have a building of God, an house not made with hands, eternal in the heavens" (2 Co.5:1).

"And this is the record, that God hath given to us eternal life, and this life is in his Son. He that hath the Son hath life; and he that hath not the Son of God hath not life" (1 Jn.5:11-12).

"Then shall the dust return to the earth as it was: and the spirit shall return unto God who gave it" (Ec.12:7).

Thought 2. God has given man His very own Spirit, the very breath of His own being.

"The spirit of God hath made me, and the breath of the Almighty hath given me life" (Jb. 33:4).

Thought 3. God has given great dignity to man. God has crowned man with glory and honor.

"For thou hast made him a little lower than the angels, and hast crowned him with glory and honour" (Ps.8:5).

Thought 4. God's image that presently rests upon man is only a shadow. It is like a picture upon a stamp. The picture is not the person. It is only a picture, only an image of the person. But note: it is an image; it is a likeness.

Why has God given man an image, a likeness, of Himself? So that man will walk by faith and *freely choose* to love and worship God. God has given man enough of Himself to cause man to hunger and seek after God. Man has just enough of God's image to drive him to seek after immortality and live forever.

"But if from thence thou shalt seek the Lord thy God, thou shalt find him, if thou seek him with all thy heart and with all thy soul" (De.4:29).

"Seek the Lord, and his strength: seek his face evermore" (Ps.105:4).

"Seek ye the Lord while he may be found, call ye upon him while he is near" (Is.55:6).

"For thus saith the Lord unto the house of Israel, Seek ye me, and ye shall live" (Am. 5:4).

"Seek ye the Lord, all ye meek of the earth, which have wrought his judgment; seek righteousness, seek meekness: it may be ye shall be hid in the day of the Lord'S anger" (Zep.2:3).

"That they should seek the Lord, if haply they might feel after him, and find him, though he be not far from every one of us" (Ac.17:27).

Thought 5. Jesus Christ alone is the *exact image* of God (He.1:3, see Ph.2:6-8).

c. There is a need to stress that God made *both male and female*, both man and woman, in His own image. Woman was created by God as much as man was; she was made in the image of God as much as man was. Woman was given as much dignity and honor as man was. Woman is as much the crown and summit of God's creation as man is.

Thought 1. Men and societies that downgrade and enslave women are wrong, terribly wrong. Women are created in the image of God; therefore, women are to be esteemed and honored as much as the men. They are to be allowed to fulfill their function upon earth with dignity and honor just as much as men are. God created woman to walk as a companion to man, not as a slave.

"So God created man in his own image, in the image of God created he him; male and female created he them. And God blessed them, and God said unto them, Be fruitful, and multiply, and replenish the earth, and subdue it: and have dominion over the fish of the sea, and over the fowl of the air, and over every living thing that moveth upon the earth" (Ge.1:27-28).

"And the Lord God said, It is not good that the man should be alone; I will make him an help meet [helper, companion] for him" (Ge.2:18).

"Who can find a virtuous woman? for her price is far above rubies" (Pr.31:10).

"Greet Priscilla and Aquila my helpers in Christ Jesus" (Ro.16:3).

"Greet Mary, who bestowed much labour on us" (Ro.16:6).

"Salute Tryphena and Tryphosa, who labour in the Lord" (Ro.16:12).

"[A woman is to be received]…well reported of for good works; if she have brought up children, if she have lodged strangers, if she have washed the saints' feet, if she have relieved the afflicted, if she have diligently followed every good work" (1 Ti.5:10).

Thought 2. God created both male and female. Each one came from God. He created one as much as He created the other. Each one was created *for* God as well as *by* God.

Each one is as important to God as the other, to His plan and purpose for the world. Very simply stated, both male and female were created *by* and *for* God; therefore each one is created *to* God. Each one, both male and female, is to live *to* God's glory, serving and worshiping God as the Creator, the Lord and Sovereign of all life.

"Serve the Lord with gladness: come before his presence with singing. Know ye that the Lord he is God: it is he that hath made us, and not we ourselves; we are his people, and the sheep of his pasture" (Ps.100:2-3).

---

3 (1:28) **Man, Purpose—Marriage—Earth—Creation—Animals—Science**: God blessed man and woman. This is a picture of a meeting that God held with man and woman soon after both had been created. Imagine how Adam (the first man) felt right after he had been created, when all of a sudden he was standing upon earth, experiencing the very first moments of life. He was aware of himself and of all his surroundings, the beauty and fruitfulness of the earth, but everything was strange, a complete puzzle. Who was he? Where was he? What was he to do? All these questions needed to be answered and answered soon after he was created. The same was bound to be true with Eve (the first woman) as well.

This is the picture of what was happening in verses 28-30. God was meeting face to face with man and woman, blessing them and explaining who they were and why they were created and placed upon earth. Note that God blessed man and woman. What was the blessing? God blessed man and woman with…

- the privilege of God's presence, of fellowship with God
- the privilege of life, both life abundant and life eternal
- the privilege of being created in the image of God, of being the crown and summit of His creation
- the privilege of living upon earth with all its provisions for food and beauty
- the privilege of being male and female, of having the companionship of one another
- the privilege of reproduction, of filling the earth with their own species
- the privilege of having animals as fellow companions on earth
- the privilege of ruling and reigning over all the creatures of earth
- the privilege of work, of finding satisfaction and fulfillment in subduing the earth—through research, discovery, development, and growth

Thought 1. Note: the blessings and privileges are given to every man and woman. But every person has to claim the privileges, diligently work at using them more and more for the benefit of oneself and of society—all in obedience to God.

Thought 2. Note that God's blessing was personal: "And God blessed them and said to them" (v.28). God spoke to man and woman personally, face to face. To be blessed by God means that God…

- keeps us
- makes His face to shine upon us
- is gracious to us
- lifts up His countenance upon us
- and gives us peace

"The Lord bless thee, and keep thee: the Lord make his face shine upon thee, and be gracious unto thee: the Lord lift up his countenance upon thee, and give thee peace" (Nu.6:24-26).

---

4 (1:28) **Man, Purpose—Marriage—Earth—Creation—Animals—Science**: God gave man and woman three great assignments or purposes.

a. First, man and woman were to reproduce and fill the earth. This was to be a most wonderful assignment. Man and woman were to establish the closest bond imaginable—a relationship of love, care, trust, and loyalty with each other. They were to walk, work, and worship hand in hand as they journeyed through life together. The relationship they built was to serve as the basis for all other relationships upon earth and within the societies and nations of earth. All groups upon earth—whether societies or nations—were to walk together in love, care, trust, and loyalty.

Note: God had created many animals, but He created only one man and one woman. Why? There were at least four reasons.

⇒ To establish the family: to institute the rule and principle of one man and one woman for each other. There was to be no separation or divorce—no split families, no children without a father or mother—when God first created man and woman.

⇒ To build a much stronger love, trust, and loyalty within man and woman. Love, trust, and loyalty are weakened and destroyed when intimate relationships are carried on with other persons. When love, trust, and loyalty are weakened within the strongest bond known to man, that of the family, they are weakened in all the other relationships of life: at work, at play, with one's country.

⇒ To teach man that all people are of one blood, from one source. Therefore, all people—all races and nations—are to live in peace and unity, working together to subdue the earth. There was to be no prejudice, discrimination, violence, greed, selfishness, or war upon earth—not originally, not when God first created man.

⇒ To teach that man is as important as woman and woman is as important as man, that all succeeding generations of men and women are to be as highly esteemed as the first man and woman were. There is to be no abuse and no enslavement of women or men in God's creation. Both are involved in the mission of God for the earth.

"And he answered and said unto them, Have ye not read, that he which made them at the beginning made them male and female, and said, For this cause shall a man leave father and mother, and shall cleave to his wife: and they twain shall be one flesh? Wherefore they are no more twain, but one flesh. What therefore God hath joined together, let no man put asunder" (Mt.19:4-6).

Thought 1. Note how far away man has gotten, how far he has fallen, from God's original assignments. Note all the...

- prejudice
- discrimination
- overpopulation
- violence
- hatred
- war
- selfishness
- greed
- enslavement
- child and spousal abuse
- leadership abuse
- government abuse

b. Second, man and woman were to subdue the earth. (See DEEPER STUDY # 3—Ge.1:28 for discussion.)

c. Third, man and woman were to have dominion over all the animals. Dominion means to rule over, to master, to control, to manage, to look after and care for. Originally, when God first created the animals and man, there was apparently no savagery among animals. Neither man nor animal ate other animals (Ge.1:30, see 9:3). Man and animal lived side by side in peace and apparently with some affection for each other—at least among the higher order of animals. But man was the ruler, the dominating force, the leader among all the creatures of the earth.

But note what has happened since the fall of man and the world into corruption. Animals live in a world of savagery, having to struggle for food and fight for survival against other animals. However God promises a new age and a new day, a new earth and a new world, when perfection and peace shall reign upon the earth. The lamb will lie down with the lion. A renovated earth, a new heavens and earth, is coming.

"The wolf also shall dwell with the lamb, and the leopard shall lie down with the kid; and the calf and the young lion and the fatling together; and a little child shall lead them. And the cow and the bear shall feed; their young ones shall lie down together: and the lion shall eat straw like the ox. And the sucking child shall play on the hole of the asp, and the weaned child shall put his hand on the cockatrice' den. They shall not hurt nor destroy in all my holy mountain: for the earth shall be full of the knowledge of the Lord, as the waters cover the sea" (Is.11:6-9).

"The wolf and the lamb shall feed together, and the lion shall eat straw like the bullock: and dust shall be the serpent's meat. They shall not hurt nor destroy in all my holy mountain, saith the Lord" (Is.65:25).

"And in that day will I make a covenant for them with the beasts of the field, and with the fowls of heaven, and with the creeping things of the ground: and I will break the bow and the sword and the battle out of the earth, and will make them to lie down safely" (Ho.2:18).

"And he [God] shall judge among the nations, and shall rebuke many people: and they shall beat their swords into plowshares, and their spears into pruninghooks: nation shall not lift up sword against nation, neither shall they learn war any more" (Is.2:4).

"Of the increase of his government and peace there shall be no end, upon the throne of David, and upon his kingdom, to order it, and to establish it with judgment and with justice from henceforth even for ever. The zeal of the Lord of hosts will perform this" (Is.9:7).

"But they shall sit every man under his vine and under his fig tree; and none shall make them afraid: for the mouth of the Lord of hosts hath spoken it" (Mi.4:4).

DEEPER STUDY # 3

(1:28) **Man, Purpose—Earth—Creation—Science**: God commanded man to *subdue* the earth. Verse twenty-eight says, "Have dominion...over all the earth." This is a large assignment, very large. Note four significant facts.

1. *To subdue and to have dominion over* the earth means...
- to rule and master the earth
- to look after and care for the earth
- to investigate, research, and discover the earth's resources
- to develop and use the resources of the earth
- to manage the earth with all its provisions and resources

2. God gave the earth to both man and woman, put the earth under their care. The earth was...
- both a gift and a duty
- both an inheritance and a responsibility
- both an estate and an obligation
- both a trust and a task

The earth is under the care of man and woman. God gave the earth to them as a gift, as an inheritance, as a trust. The earth is now their estate, their home and property. But the earth is also their responsibility. It is the task of man and woman—their duty and obligation—to look after the earth. God has placed them over the earth, over His creation. Therefore, it is their duty to manage the earth for God.

Thought 1. The environment matters to God; therefore, God has placed man in charge—to look after—the environment. The environment must matter to man. Man must not pollute the air and water; he must not contaminate and destroy the earth nor the heavens above.

3. God was meeting two of man's most basic needs in this assignment. Man has the basic needs...
   - to be loved and challenged
   - to love and commit his life to a meaningful purpose

God's provision of the earth meets man's need. When a person really realizes that God has given him the earth as an inheritance, that person knows that God loves him. He knows that God looks after him with the deepest care and love. In response, man should love God. God's great gift of the earth should stir man to respond to God, to love God even as God has loved him.

Also, God's assignment to subdue the earth meets man's need for a meaningful purpose. When a person really realizes that God has given the earth to look after and manage, that person is challenged with the greatest of purposes. He is challenged to commit his life to work diligently and to make all the contributions he can to develop the earth and its societies. He is challenged to love the earth and those who work with him in caring for the earth. He is challenged to give himself to the great purpose for which God put him upon earth: that of subduing and managing the earth *for God*.

Note: when a person works diligently at his job, works diligently to do all he can to make the earth a better place, that person senses *great purpose, fulfillment, and satisfaction*. These three great things—a *sense of purpose, fulfillment, and satisfaction*—come from...
   - knowing God in a personal way
   - knowing why God has put us on earth
   - committing our lives to God and His great purpose for man: to subdue and develop the earth to its fullest

4. Man's ability to subdue the earth has been marred and weakened—considerably so. Note three significant facts.
   a. God's original purpose, when He first created man, was this: man was to have a perfect life, living in perfect surroundings. He was to live in utopia. Man was to be in perfect fellowship with God, experiencing purpose and fulfillment in subduing the earth. Man was to be perfectly happy—perfectly satisfied—as he went about his work in developing and managing the earth. Man was to use all the scientific research and technology imaginable; he was to investigate, discover, and develop all the resources of the earth. He was to learn about his world and gain all the knowledge he could to make true progress. Apparently, he possessed a mind that was perfect in its capacity to learn, and he was subject only to God (Ge.2:15-17).
   b. It was sin that marred and weakened man's sovereignty and ability to subdue the earth. Since man's fall into sin, the earth, even man himself, is in a rage of violence and suffering...
      - Nature runs wild with natural disaster after natural disaster: hurricanes, typhoons, cyclones, tornadoes, floods, volcanic eruptions, earthquakes, dangerous lightning, violent storms, locust plagues, famines, and on and on. Nature constantly runs wild.
      - Man runs wild with violent act after violent act: child abuse, wife abuse, husband abuse, rape, assaults, maiming, murder, war, robbery, cheating, stealing, lying, assassination, terrorist acts, arson, and on and on.
      - The earth is full of disease, pestilence, and accidents—all causing suffering and destroying life and huge sections of the earth and its resources.

   The point is this: the earth—its nature—is far from being under the control of man. It used to be under control when God first created man. But not now, not since man's rebellion against God, not since man's terrible fall into sin. Sin has marred and weakened man's rule and sovereignty over the earth.
   c. But God has promised to restore man's rule and sovereignty over the earth, in fact, over the whole universe. How? Through Jesus Christ. Jesus Christ has secured the right to rule and reign over the earth. He is going to return to the earth, establish His government, and restore man to his original position of dominion and sovereignty—right along with Himself.

   "And the Lord said, Who then is that faithful and wise steward, whom his lord shall make ruler over his household, to give them their portion of meat in due season? Blessed is that servant, whom his lord when he cometh shall find so doing. Of a truth I say unto you, that he will make him ruler over all that he hath" (Lu.12:42-44).

   "The Spirit itself beareth witness with our spirit, that we are the children of God: and if children, then heirs; heirs of God, and joint-heirs with Christ; if so be that we suffer with him, that we may be also glorified together" (Ro.8:16-17).

   "For the creature [creation] was made subject to vanity, not willingly, but by reason of him who hath subjected the same in hope, because the creature [creation] itself also shall be delivered from the bondage of corruption into the glorious liberty of the children of God. For we know that the whole creation groaneth and travaileth in pain together until now. And not only they, but ourselves also, which have the firstfruits of the Spirit, even we ourselves groan within ourselves, waiting for the adoption, to wit, the redemption of our body" (Ro.8:20-23).

"Do ye not know that the saints shall judge [oversee, manage, rule] the world? and if the world shall be judged by you, are ye unworthy to judge the smallest matters? Know ye not that we shall judge angels? how much more things that pertain to this life?" (1 Co.6:2-3).

"If we suffer, we shall also reign with him: if we deny him, he also will deny us" (2 Ti.2:12).

"But one in a certain place testified, saying, What is man, that thou art mindful of him? or the son of man, that thou visitest him? Thou madest him a little lower than the angels; thou crownedst him with glory and honour, and didst set him over the works of thy hands: thou hast put all things in subjection under his feet. For in that he put all in subjection under him, he left nothing that is not put under him. But now we see not yet all things put under him. But we see Jesus, who was made a little lower than the angels for the suffering of death, crowned with glory and honour; that he by the grace of God should taste death for every man" (He.2:6-9).

"But the day of the Lord will come as a thief in the night; in the which the heavens shall pass away with a great noise, and the elements shall melt with fervent heat, the earth also and the works that are therein shall be burned up. Seeing then that all these things shall be dissolved, what manner of persons ought ye to be in all holy conversation [behavior] and godliness, looking for and hasting unto the coming of the day of God, wherein the heavens being on fire shall be dissolved, and the elements shall melt with fervent heat? Nevertheless we, according to his promise, look for new heavens and a new earth, wherein dwelleth righteousness" (2 Pe.3:10-13).

"And hast made us unto our God kings and priests: and we shall reign on the earth" (Re.5:10).

"And I saw a new heaven and a new earth: for the first heaven and the first earth were passed away; and there was no more sea....And God shall wipe away all tears from their eyes; and there shall be no more death, neither sorrow, nor crying, neither shall there be any more pain: for the former things are passed away" (Re.21:1, 4).

"And there shall be no more curse: but the throne of God and of the Lamb shall be in it; and his servants shall serve him: and they shall see his face; and his name shall be in their foreheads. And there shall be no night there; and they need no candle, neither light of the sun; for the Lord God giveth them light: and they shall reign for ever and ever" (Re.22:3-5).

Thought 1. Man desperately needs to do two things.
1) Man needs to repent, to turn back to God.

"Then Peter said unto them, Repent, and be baptized every one of you in the name of Jesus Christ for the remission of sins, and ye shall receive the gift of the Holy Ghost" (Ac.2:38).

"Repent ye therefore, and be converted, that your sins may be blotted out, when the times of refreshing shall come from the presence of the Lord" (Ac.3:19).

"Repent therefore of this thy wickedness, and pray God, if perhaps the thought of thine heart may be forgiven thee" (Ac.8:22).

"If my people, which are called by my name, shall humble themselves, and pray, and seek my face, and turn from their wicked ways; then will I hear from heaven, and will forgive their sin, and will heal their land" (2 Chr.7:14).

"Let the wicked forsake his way, and the unrighteous man his thoughts: and let him return unto the Lord, and he will have mercy upon him; and to our God, for he will abundantly pardon" (Is.55:7).

"But if the wicked will turn from all his sins that he hath committed, and keep all my statutes, and do that which is lawful and right, he shall surely live, he shall not die" (Eze.18:21).

"Cast away from you all your transgressions, whereby ye have transgressed; and make you a new heart and a new spirit: for why will ye die, O house of Israel?" (Eze.18:31).

2) Man needs to seek God for wisdom in seeking to subdue and control the earth. Our ability to manage the earth and its corrupt nature has been weakened and marred, but we need to work like trojans to subdue all that we can. All the violence and corruption—both within nature and within man—need to be controlled to the best of our ability. God can give us wisdom as we work to control it, if we will only ask Him.

"Ask, and it shall be given you; seek, and ye shall find; knock, and it shall be opened unto you: for every one that asketh receiveth; and he that seeketh findeth; and to him that knocketh it shall be opened" (Mt.7:7-8).

"If any of you lack wisdom, let him ask of God, that giveth to all men liberally, and upbraideth [scolds] not; and it shall be given him. But let him ask in faith, nothing wavering. For he that wavereth is like a wave of the sea driven with the wind and tossed. For let not that man think that he shall receive any thing of the Lord. A double minded man is unstable in all his ways" (Js.1:5-8).

"Do not err, my beloved brethren. Every good gift and every perfect gift is from above, and cometh down from the Father of lights, with whom is no variableness, neither shadow of turning" (Js.1:16-17).

[5] (1:29-30) **Food—Vegetation—Plant Life—Creation**: God provided the vegetation of the earth to feed man and animal. Remember: God is meeting with man, sharing who man is and why he has been created and placed upon earth (see note 3—Ge.1:28 for more discussion). Note several facts.

a. Man and animal were to be vegetarians in the original creation of the perfect earth. There was no such thing as eating flesh. Eating flesh came only after the fall (Ge.9:3).

b. Man and animal were given an abundance of food: vegetables, berries, and fruit. They were given every plant that bore seed and every tree that bore fruit.

c. All the land of the earth was fruitful. There was vegetation and plant life everywhere, and there was more than enough. Note the words, "upon the face of *all the earth*" (v.29). Apparently, there were no barren nor desolate lands upon earth.

c. Since the fall of man into sin, the earth and its fruitfulness have been affected. Man has abused and continues to abuse the earth and its plant life or vegetation, even to the point of threatening the survival of future generations. Man is rapidly destroying the earth's plant life by housing and commercial developments and by pollution. Man is polluting and bulldozing the lands of the earth so rapidly that the earth's resources are tragically being depleted. They are being depleted by...

- polluting the air and causing acid rain
- destroying the rain forests and other plant life
- dumping chemical and toxic wastes in threatening places
- failing to recycle usable materials

Thought 1. The grace and care of God is clearly seen in this passage. God has provided for man, provided enough vegetation and fruitfulness to feed all people. Man has but one responsibility:

"But seek ye first the kingdom of God, and his righteousness; and all these things [food, shelter, clothing] shall be added unto you" (Mt.6:33).

"Thy righteousness is like the great mountains; thy judgments are a great deep: O Lord, thou preservest man and beast" (Ps.36:6).

Thought 2. The earth and its nature that brings forth fruitfulness and food is given by God. Man is given the responsibility to "subdue the earth"—to use the earth to bring forth as much harvest as needed. God is to be praised and trusted for what food is necessary to feed the earth. But while praising and trusting God, man is to work for his bread.

"For even when we were with you, this we commanded you, that if any would not work, neither should he eat. For we hear that there are some which walk among you disorderly, working not at all, but are busybodies. Now them that are such we command and exhort by our Lord Jesus Christ, that with quietness they work, and eat their own bread. But ye, brethren, be not weary in well doing" (2 Th.3:10-13).

"And that ye study to be quiet, and to do your own business, and to work with your own hands, as we commanded you; that ye may walk honestly toward them that are without, and that ye may have lack of nothing" (1 Th.4:11-12).

Thought 3. God has given food for man to sustain his life. Man should not seek food to consume it upon his lust. He should seek only the amount of food that is necessary to sustain his life.

"And they tempted God in their heart by asking meat for their lust" (Ps.78:18).

"But Daniel purposed in his heart that he would not defile himself with the portion of the king's meat, nor with the wine which he drank" (Da.1:8, see 1:8-15).

Thought 4. Man should receive food by giving thanks to God for it.

"And when he had thus spoken, he took bread, and gave thanks to God in [the] presence of them all: and when he had broken it, he began to eat" (Ac.27:35).

6 (1:31) **Man—Creation**: God saw that His creation was *good*—everything created during the six days of creation, including man, fulfilled its function. This verse refers to all of God's creation. It refers to man, yes, but God is also looking back over everything He has created. Note two facts.

a. Man was able to fulfill his purpose and function upon earth. Man was created in *the image of God*: he had the very breath—the immortal life—of God. Therefore, man was...

- able to worship, fellowship, and commune with God (vv.26-27)
- able to populate the earth (v.28)
- able to serve God by subduing, developing, and managing the earth (v.28)
- able to be fed and sustained by the resources of the earth (vv.29-30)

b. God looked at everything He had made, and "behold, it was very good" (v.31). The word "behold" calls attention to how good—how perfect—God's creation was. God was extremely pleased with His creation. Everything was very good, perfect in every detail. Everything was exactly as God had planned it: everything was perfect in sustaining man upon the earth, perfect in providing a home for man as he went about fulfilling his God-given purpose upon the earth.

Thought 1. God looked back upon His work and evaluated it—a tremendous lesson for man as He works and serves. Man should be able to say, "I thought on my ways, and turned my feet unto thy [God's] testimonies" (Ps.119:59).

Thought 2. God looked back and saw everything—that it fulfilled its function. God Himself sets a dynamic example for man: everything was good and fulfilled its function. Everything in a man's life should be purposeful, looked after to the ultimate degree (Col.3:17, 23).

"And ye shall serve the Lord your God, and he shall bless thy bread, and thy water; and I will take sickness away from the midst of thee" (Ex.23:25).

"And now, Israel, what doth the Lord thy God require of thee, but to fear the Lord thy God, to walk in all his ways, and to love him, and to serve the Lord thy God with all thy heart and with all thy soul" (De.10:12).

"Serve the Lord with fear, and rejoice with trembling" (Ps.2:11).

"For whether we live, we live unto the Lord; and whether we die, we die unto the Lord: whether we live therefore, or die, we are the Lord's" (Ro.14:8).

"And that he died for all, that they which live should not henceforth live unto themselves, but unto him which died for them, and rose again" (2 Co.5:15).

"And whatsoever ye do in word or deed, do all in the name of the Lord Jesus, giving thanks to God and the Father by him" (Col.3:17).

"And whatsoever ye do, do it heartily, as to the Lord, and not unto men" (Col.3:23).

"Wherefore we receiving a kingdom which cannot be moved, let us have grace, whereby we may serve God acceptably with reverence and godly fear" (He.12:28).

Thought 3. What God made, He saw. He sees all that He has ever made. This is a great assurance to the righteous when they have need. This is also a clear warning to the wicked when they are sinning. Nothing escapes His sight or His presence (Ps.139:1-16).

"For mine eyes are upon all their ways: they are not hid from my face, neither is their iniquity hid from mine eyes" (Je.16:17).

"I know the things that come into your mind, every one of them" (Eze.11:5).

"And they consider not in their hearts that I remember all their wickedness: now their own doings have beset them about; they are before my face" (Ho.7:2).

"For God shall bring every work into judgment, with every secret thing, whether it be good, or whether it be evil" (Ec.12:14).

"For there is nothing covered, that shall not be revealed; neither hid, that shall not be known" (Lu.12:2).

"Therefore judge nothing before the time, until the Lord come, who both will bring to light the hidden things of darkness, and will make manifest the counsels of the hearts: and then shall every man have praise of God" (1 Co.4:5).

Thought 4. At the end of life, a man should be able to look back over his life and say just what God said: "It was very good!"

Thought 5. God saw: "It was very good"—fulfilled its function (v.31). What God began, He completed. This is also true in salvation. God will complete our salvation.

"Being confident of this very thing, that he which hath begun a good work in you will perform it until the day of Jesus Christ" (Ph.1:6).

"Faithful is he that calleth you, who also will do it" (1 Th.5:24).

"Nevertheless I am not ashamed: for I know whom I have believed, and am persuaded that he is able to keep that which I have committed unto him against that day" (2 Ti.1:12).

"Who are kept by the power of God through faith unto salvation ready to be revealed in the last time" (1 Pe.1:5).

"Now unto him that is able to keep you from falling, and to present you faultless before the presence of his glory with exceeding joy, to the only wise God our Saviour, be glory and majesty, dominion and power, both now and ever. Amen" (Jude 24-25).

CHAPTER 2

J. The Seventh Day: Creation of a Day for Rest & Worship, 2:1-3

1. God finished the creation of the heavens & earth	Thus the heavens and the earth were finished, and all the host of them.
2. God rested on the seventh day from all His work	2 And on the seventh day God ended his work which he had made; and he rested on the seventh day from all his work which he had made.
3. God blessed the seventh day & set it apart as holy	3 And God blessed the seventh day, and sanctified it: because that in it he had rested from all his work which God created and made.

DIVISION I

CREATION OF THE HEAVENS AND THE EARTH, 1:1–2:3

J. The Seventh Day: Creation of a Day for Rest and Worship, 2:1-3

(2:1-3) **Introduction**: remember what the earth looked like when God first hung it in space. It was unshaped and unformed, undeveloped and unfinished. God's great plan of creation was to create the world in stages. There were to be seven great days of creation. Hanging there in space, the whole earth was covered with an ocean of water. Turbulent waves—surging, raging waters—covered primeval earth. There was also a heavy mist hanging over the whole earth: a ring of dense fog and thick clouds rising several thousand feet up encircled the earth. The sun—all light—was blocked off from reaching the earth. The earth was engulfed in a blanket of pitch black darkness.

But God had a great plan to remedy the situation, a plan that was going to create the earth in stages, in what is known as *The Seven Days of Creation*. We have already looked at the first six days.

⇒ On the first day: God created light (Ge.1:3-5).
⇒ On the second day: God created the firmament (the atmosphere and air space above earth) (Ge.1:6-8).
⇒ On the third day: God created the waters, dry land, and vegetation (Ge.1:9-13).
⇒ On the fourth day: God distributed light upon the earth to regulate day and night and the seasons and years (Ge.1:14-19).
⇒ On the fifth day: God created water and air creatures (Ge.1:20-23).
⇒ On the sixth day, during the first half of the day: God created land animals (Ge.1:24-25).
⇒ On the sixth day, during the second half of the day: God created man, male and female (Ge.1:26-31).

Now, for a crucial question: why would God choose to create the world in stages, in seven days, instead of just creating everything all at once? The seventh day of creation tells us.

⇒ God intended man to measure time by days and weeks. And He intended man to take one day a week, the seventh day, for rest and worship.

Therefore God launched time, He began time, right along with His creative acts. All earthly activity was to be measured by days and weeks, and man was to take one of the seven days, the seventh day, to rest and worship. This is the reason God did not create the world in one moment of time; this is one of the reasons why God created the earth in stages, in seven days.

Now we come to the final day of creation: *The Seventh Day: Creation of a Day for Rest or Worship*.

1. God finished the creation of the heavens and earth (v.1).
2. God rested on the seventh day from all His work (v.2).
3. God blessed the seventh day and set it apart as holy (v.3).

1 (2:1) **Creation—Heavens—Earth**: God finished the creation of the heavens and the earth. The Hebrew reads, "And finished were the heavens and the earth." The word *finished* is stressed: creation is completed; God has now completed His plan of creation. The word *finished* means both *completed* and *perfected. Creation was now completed and the product was perfected.*

The universe had begun as an idea in God's mind. God had set out to bring His idea of the world into being. He had created it step by step.

⇒ God had now created all the basic elements of the universe—all the atoms, protons, neutrons, and electrons, whatever the most basic substance is that makes up matter—God had created all matter and energy within the universe. The creation of matter and energy was both finished and perfected.

110

⇒ God had now organized all matter and energy to form the heavens and the earth. The arrangement and organization was now finished.

⇒ God had now created everything that was necessary to maintain life upon earth. Light, air, water, dry land, vegetation, day and night, seasons and years had all been completed.

God's plan of creation was now finished, completed, and perfected. This is strongly emphasized in this verse. Note the phrase "all the hosts of them." This is a military picture. The idea is that "all the hosts" of creation were now finished and perfected:

⇒ all the atoms and elements
⇒ all the matter and energy
⇒ all the gases and chemicals
⇒ all the stars and planets
⇒ all the plant life and vegetation

All the hosts of creation had now been commanded and ordered, arranged and organized, marshalled and placed where they belonged. The innumerable hosts of creation had been finished, completed, and perfected just as God willed.

Thought 1. God finished, completed, and perfected all the works of creation. God always completes and perfects what He begins. Therefore, He will complete and perfect the work of salvation within the life of every believer, until the glorious day of redemption.

"Being confident of this very thing, that he which hath begun a good work in you will perform *it* until the day of Jesus Christ" (Ph.1:6).
"For it is God which worketh in you both to will and to do of *his* good pleasure" (Ph.2:13).
"Faithful *is* he that calleth you, who also will do *it*" (1 Th.5:24).
"For the which cause I also suffer these things: nevertheless I am not ashamed: for I know whom I have believed, and am persuaded that he is able to keep that which I have committed unto him against that day" (2 Ti.1:12).
"If we believe not, *yet* he abideth faithful: he cannot deny himself" (2 Ti.2:13).
"Who are kept by the power of God through faith unto salvation ready to be revealed in the last time" (1 Pe.1:5).
"Now unto him that is able to keep you from falling, and to present *you* faultless before the presence of his glory with exceeding joy" (Jude 24).
"To the only wise God our Saviour, *be* glory and majesty, dominion and power, both now and ever. Amen." (Jude 25).

2 (2:2) **Sabbath—Sunday—Creation**: God rested on the seventh day from all His work.

a. Note the word *ended*. In the Hebrew it means to declare an end to; to declare finished.[1] The idea is that God declared His work of creation to be finished.

Thought 1. The rejoicing of God, Christ, the Holy Spirit, and of the heavenly host of angelic beings must have been one of the most spectacular events ever witnessed in all of eternity. God's declaration that the creation of the universe was now completed must have stirred excitement—as much excitement, praise, and worship as has ever been witnessed in all the annals of eternity.

b. Note the word *rested* (shabhath). It means to stop or cease from working. The idea is not that God rested from all work after creation. God does not need rest like man needs rest: He was not tired, burdened, pressured, or exhausted from His work in creation. Verse two clearly tells us what God rested from or stopped doing: "He rested...from all His work which He had made [or created]." The word *work* (melakhah) means a special work, a very special job or task. The special work or task undertaken by God was creation; therefore, the work that God rested from was the work of creation. The meaning can be stated several ways.

⇒ God *had finished* His creative work; therefore, He rested, ceased from His creative work.
⇒ God *had completed* the work which He had just been doing, the work of creation; therefore, He rested, ceased from the work of creation.
⇒ God *had ended* the special work He had set out to do; therefore, he rested, ceased from that special work.
⇒ God *had completed and perfected* His work of creation; therefore, He stepped aside with a sense of quiet peace and accomplishment over His creative work.

The point is this: God did not rest or cease from working. He only rested and ceased from the work that He had been doing that week. His work for that week—the work of creation—was completed. The rest of God was not...

- inactivity
- laziness
- slackness
- idleness
- slumber
- shirking duty

"Hast thou not known? hast thou not heard, *that* the everlasting God, the LORD, the Creator of the ends of the earth, fainteth not, neither is weary? *there is* no searching of his understanding" (Is.40:28).

---

[1] H.C. Leupold. *Genesis*, Vol.1, p.102.

The rest of God was a sense of quiet peace and accomplishment over the creative work He had just completed. The picture is descriptive: God took a day, the seventh day, to stand back and enjoy His creative work. No doubt all the heavenly host joined in His celebration and declaration that the work of creation, the six great days of creation, was now completed. The seventh day of God's rest—*the rest of God*—is an inner sense of…

- peace
- accomplishment
- fulfillment
- satisfaction
- completeness
- success
- purpose
- meaning
- assurance
- confidence
- approval
- security

God was very pleased with His work. Standing there on the seventh day, He felt that He had done a very good job. God had a deep sense of peace, satisfaction, and accomplishment. He was at rest with what He had done. (See note, *Rest*—He.4:1 for more discussion.)

> **Thought 1.** Man is to follow the example of God. Man is to set aside a day when he rests from his labor. But throughout the week man must also labor even as God labored, diligently and faithfully. Man should be able to do as God did: stand on his day of rest and look back over the previous week, and have a deep sense of accomplishment. He should be able…
> - to feel like he has done a good job
> - to feel satisfied and fulfilled because he has worked diligently
> - to feel purpose because he has contributed to meet the needs of people and society and to make the world a better place to live
>
> The great tragedy is this: few people have this rest of God, the rest of fulfillment, satisfaction, and purpose in life. Too few work diligently upon the job. Too few do all they can to meet the needs of people and of society. Most just routinely do their work, use as little energy and effort as possible, and selfishly do as little work as possible.
>
> > "His lord said unto him, Well done, good and faithful servant; thou hast been faithful over a few things, I will make thee ruler over many things: enter thou into the joy of thy lord" (Mt.25:23).
> > "Moreover it is required in stewards, that a man be found faithful" (1 Co.4:2).
> > "Servants, be obedient to them that are *your* masters according to the flesh, with fear and trembling, in singleness of your heart, as unto Christ; Not with eyeservice, as menpleasers; but as the servants of Christ, doing the will of God from the heart; With good will doing service, as to the Lord, and not to men:" (Ep.6:5-7).
> > "And whatsoever ye do in word or deed, *do* all in the name of the Lord Jesus, giving thanks to God and the Father by him" (Col.3:17).
> > "Let as many servants as are under the yoke count their own masters worthy of all honour, that the name of God and *his* doctrine be not blasphemed" (1 Ti.6:1).
> > "*Exhort* servants to be obedient unto their own masters, *and* to please *them* well in all *things*; not answering again" (Tit.2:9).
> > "Servants, *be* subject to *your* masters with all fear; not only to the good and gentle, but also to the froward" (1 Pe.2:18).
> > "Whoso keepeth the fig tree shall eat the fruit thereof: so he that waiteth on his master shall be honoured" (Pr.27:18).
> > "Whatsoever thy hand findeth to do, do *it* with thy might; for *there is* no work, nor device, nor knowledge, nor wisdom, in the grave, whither thou goest" (Ec.9:10).

[3] (2:3) **Sabbath—Sunday**: God blessed the seventh day and set it apart as holy. Note how clearly—beyond any question—God sets the seventh day apart.

> "And God blessed the seventh day, and sanctified it: because that in it he had rested from all his work which God created and made" (Ge.2:3).

There can be no question about what God is doing with the seventh day. He is setting the day apart from all the other days of the week. Four significant things show this.

a. God blessed the seventh day. Note: it is *the day itself* that is blessed. No other day was blessed, just the seventh day. The seventh day alone was honored with God's blessing.

b. God sanctified the seventh day. The word "sanctified" means *to set apart and make holy*. God actually consecrated the day and declared it holy. This is very significant: it means that the seventh day was being set apart as a permanent day. The seventh day was to have a permanence that the other six days did not have. Any kind of work could be done on the other six days, but not on the seventh day. The work done on the seventh day was to be the same week by week. It was to be a day set apart for a very special purpose. It was to be a day different from the other six days, a day that was to never pass away, a day that was to be given over to the *work of holiness*.

> **Thought 1.** Note a clear fact: the seventh day is consecrated and declared *holy* by God. The very fact that God Himself does this means that the day is consecrated and holy. No matter how much man abuses the day of rest and worship, it is still consecrated and holy to God and His true followers.

What an indictment against man! How desperately we need to quit abusing the day of rest and worship. Many rest, but few give the day over to holiness.

c. God rested and worshipped on the seventh day. No doubt, all the heavenly host rejoiced with God as He celebrated His glorious work of creation. The heavenly host—all the angels, seraphim, and cherubim of God—were bound to be praising and blessing God for His marvelous work. God is...
- the Sovereign Creator
- the Supreme Intelligence and Power
- the LORD and Majesty of the universe

God is worthy of all glory and majesty, all dominion and power, all praise and thanksgiving, all worship and honor. The first seventh day, the great day of God's rest, must have been one of the most glorious days of worship ever experienced in all eternity.

d. God set the day apart as a day of celebration and commemoration. God sanctified and made the day holy, set it apart as a very special day and as a permanent day. Now note: the day was not set apart for God; it was set apart for man. God does not need a permanent day of rest. To say or think so would be foolish. The day of rest and holiness is set apart for man. Man needs the day for two very specific purposes.

1) Man needs a day when he can rest, both physically and spiritually. Man needs a day when he can experience a quiet peace and sense of accomplishment over his work of the past week. (See note 2—Ge.2:2 for more discussion.)

2) Man needs a day for worship and blessing, for praise and thanksgiving. Man needs a day that is set apart for him to concentrate upon God. Man's attention span is short and the focus of his emotions does not last very long. Therefore, man needs one day out of every seven when he can focus his attention and emotions upon God, one day when he can concentrate upon God without major distractions. Man needs one day a week to worship God, to worship...
- by praising God as the Creator of the universe
- by thanking God for life: the privilege and provision of life
- by acknowledging God as the Lord and Majesty of the universe
- by blessing God for the privilege of work and health throughout the week
- by serving God in the spirit of holiness and righteousness
- by asking God to meet his needs and the needs of others

Thought 1. Just imagine how God would bless the person who observed the day of rest and worship as He intends it to be observed!

"Blessed *is* the man *that* doeth this, and the son of man *that* layeth hold on it; that keepeth the sabbath from polluting it, and keepeth his hand from doing any evil" (Is.56:2).

"If thou turn away thy foot from the sabbath, *from* doing thy pleasure on my holy day; and call the sabbath a delight, the holy of the LORD, honourable; and shalt honour him, not doing thine own ways, nor finding thine own pleasure, nor speaking *thine own* words: Then shalt thou delight thyself in the LORD; and I will cause thee to ride upon the high places of the earth, and feed thee with the heritage of Jacob thy father: for the mouth of the LORD hath spoken *it*" (Is.58:13-14).

"Blessed *are* they that dwell in thy house: they will be still praising thee. Selah" (Ps.84:4).

"Surely goodness and mercy shall follow me all the days of my life: and I will dwell in the house of the LORD for ever" (Ps.23:6).

"One *thing* have I desired of the LORD, that will I seek after; that I may dwell in the house of the LORD all the days of my life, to behold the beauty of the LORD, and to enquire in his temple" (Ps.27:4).

"Blessed *is the man whom* thou choosest, and causest to approach *unto thee, that* he may dwell in thy courts: we shall be satisfied with the goodness of thy house, *even* of thy holy temple" (Ps.65:4).

Thought 2. Man is to faithfully observe and keep the Sabbath day.

"Remember the sabbath day, to keep it holy" (Ex.20:8).

"Six days thou shalt work, but on the seventh day thou shalt rest: in earing time and in harvest thou shalt rest" (Ex.34:21).

"Blessed *is* the man *that* doeth this, and the son of man *that* layeth hold on it; that keepeth the sabbath from polluting it, and keepeth his hand from doing any evil" (Is.56:2).

Thought 3. There is a difference between the Sabbath as observed by the Jews and others and Sunday as observed by Christian believers. The Sabbath is the last day of the week. It was a day when Jesus the Messiah was in the tomb, a day of great sadness for the true Christian believer. However, Sunday is the first day of the week. It is a day of great joy, for it was the day of Jesus' resurrection, the day that He triumphed over death. It is called the Lord's Day and is celebrated as a day of rest and joy, a glorious day for searching the soul and meditating upon God. It is the day of worship and of Christian fellowship celebrated by believers worldwide (Ac.20:7; 1 Co.16:2).
⇒ It was Jesus' custom to worship on the Sabbath (Lu.4:16).
⇒ It was Paul's custom to worship on Sunday (Ac.17:2).

⇒ God's people are not to neglect worship (He.10:25; see Ac.16:13).

⇒ God's people are to remember the Sabbath day, to keep it holy (Ex.20:8; 31:14; 34:21).

⇒ God's people are promised a special blessing for keeping the Sabbath day holy (Is.56:2; 58:13-14).

⇒ Polluting the Sabbath will bring the judgment of God upon a people (Eze.20:13; 22:8, 15; see Nu.15:32-35; Je.17:27; Eze.20:13; 22;8, 15).

⇒ Buying and selling are not to take place on the Sabbath (Ne.10:31; 13:15).

⇒ Helping the needy is lawful on the Sabbath (Mt.12:12; see Jn.7:23; 9:14).

⇒ Early believers worshipped on the day that Christ arose from the dead, that is, on Sunday, the first day of the week (Ac.20:7; 1 Co.16:2).

DIVISION II

ADAM, THE FIRST MAN (PART 1): THE BEGINNING OF MANKIND AND OF THE GODLY SEED—WHAT HAPPENED TO MAN AND THE EARTH, 2:4–3:24

(2:4–3:24) **DIVISION OVERVIEW: Man—History—Civilization**: this section of *Genesis* records the early history of man. It covers the very beginning of man upon earth. It is the beginning of mankind and of the godly seed or of the true followers of God. From this point on everything focuses upon man...

- how man got his start upon earth (Ge.2:4-25)
- how man began to sin against God and to die (Ge.3:1-13)
- how God went about saving man from sin and death (Ge.3:14-24)

This is clearly seen by glancing over the Scripture and the Major Headings of the outlines below (A,B,C, etc.). Note how clearly the very earliest history of man is covered. Note that everything discussed is a first, the very first time the event took place or happened upon earth.

ADAM, THE FIRST MAN (PART 1): THE BEGINNING OF MANKIND AND OF THE GODLY SEED—WHAT HAPPENED TO MAN AND THE EARTH, 2:4–3:24

A. The First Picture of the Earth Before Man: Prehistoric Times, 2:4-6

B. The First Man: Adam, 2:7

C. The First Garden and Its Purpose: Eden, Man's Ideal Place or Home, 2:8-14

D. The First Charge or Covenant: Man's Purpose upon the Earth, 2:15-17

E. The First Woman: Man's Companion, Eve, 2:18-25

F. The First Temptation and Sin: Man's Fall from Perfection—Man and Woman's First Steps into Sin, 3:1-6

G. The First Consequences of Sin: Man's Tragic Fall from Perfection, 3:7-13

H. The First Judgment Upon Sin (Part 1): Judgment upon the Tempter, That Old Serpent Called the Devil, 3:14-15

I. The First Judgment Upon Sin (Part 2): Judgment upon Woman, 3:16

J. The First Judgment Upon Sin (Part 3): Judgment upon Man, 3:17-19

K. The First Provision of God for Man: God Provides Life and Clothing (Righteousness) for Man, 3:20-21

L. The First Act of Deliverance or Salvation: Man Is Saved from Living Forever as a Sinner in a Fallen World, 3:22-24

	II. ADAM, THE FIRST MAN (PART 1): THE BEGINNING OF MANKIND & OF THE GODLY SEED— WHAT HAPPENED TO MAN & THE EARTH, 2:4–3:24	earth when they were created, in the day that the LORD God made the earth and the heavens,	**earth**
		5 And every plant of the field before it was in the earth, and every herb of the field before it grew: for the LORD God had not caused it to rain upon the earth, and there was not a man to till the ground.	**2. The LORD God Himself created the universe**
	A. The First Picture of the Earth Before Man: Prehistoric Times, 2:4-6		**3. The LORD God created the earth & the heavens in stages** a. Before field shrubs & plants b. Before rain c. Before man
1. The LORD God created the universe, the heavens & the	4 These are the generations of the heavens and of the	6 But there went up a mist from the earth, and watered the whole face of the ground.	d. At first, the earth was encircled by a heavy mist of dense fog & thick clouds

DIVISION II

ADAM, THE FIRST MAN (PART 1): THE BEGINNING OF MANKIND AND OF THE GODLY SEED—WHAT HAPPENED TO MAN AND THE EARTH, 2:4–3:24

A. The First Picture of the Earth Before Man: Prehistoric Times, 2:4-6

(2:4-6) **Introduction**: man has always wondered about prehistoric times. What was the earth like in the earliest days? What existed and what did not exist? How did vegetation and life upon earth get their start? What is the origin of plants and of life? These four verses give a picture of prehistoric earth. They are actually a brief review of the account of creation covered in the first chapter of Genesis. These four verses lay the groundwork for explaining what has happened to the earth and the heavens, to man and his world, since God created the universe. This is, *The First Picture of the Earth Before Man: Prehistoric Times*.

1. The LORD God created the universe, the heavens and the earth (v.4).
2. The LORD God Himself created the universe (v.4).
3. The LORD God created the earth and the heavens in stages (vv.5-6).

1 (2:4) **Creation—Universe**: the LORD God created the heavens and the earth. This is the account of the heavens and of the earth "when they were created." The Hebrew word *account* (toledoth) means generations, story, history, account. This is the true account of how the earth and heavens came into being. This is the true account—a brief review—of the origin of prehistoric earth. This is a brief review of chapter one of Genesis. Note the words "when they were created." The stress is that they *were created*: the universe did not just come into being by itself. The heavens and the earth did not just happen...

- by chance
- by some random happening
- by something—some force or matter, some gas or energy—appearing *out of nothing*

For something to appear *out of nothing* is against all the laws of nature and science.

What is the truth about the origin of the universe, of the heavens and the earth? The truth is that the LORD God Himself created the universe, both the earth and the heavens. And in this declaration there is a stunning truth: the stunning truth is that God truly exists. Man's denial and rejection of the truth cannot do away with God. God *is*—God *exists*—and God Himself created both the earth and the heavens.

> "Stand up and bless the LORD your God for ever and ever: and blessed be thy glorious name, which is exalted above all blessing and praise. Thou, even thou, art LORD alone; thou hast made heaven, the heaven of heavens, with all their host, the earth, and all things that are therein, the seas, and all that is therein, and thou preservest them all; and the host of heaven worshippeth thee" (Ne.9:5-6).
> "The fool hath said in his heart, There is no God. They are corrupt, they have done abominable works, there is none that doeth good" (Ps.14:1).
> "The fool hath said in his heart, There is no God. Corrupt are they, and have done abominable iniquity: there is none that doeth good. God looked down from heaven upon the children of men, to see if there were any that did understand, that did seek God. Every one of them is gone back: they are altogether become filthy; there is none that doeth good, no, not one" (Ps.53:1-3).
> "Let them be confounded and troubled for ever; yea, let them be put to shame, and perish: that men may know that thou, whose name alone is JEHOVAH, art the most high over all the earth" (Ps.83:17-18).
> "God that made the world and all things therein, seeing that he is Lord of heaven and earth, dwelleth not in temples made with hands; neither is worshipped with men's hands, as though he needed any thing, seeing he giveth to all life, and breath, and all things; and hath made of one blood all nations of men for to dwell on all the face of the earth, and hath determined the times before appointed, and the bounds of their habitation; that they should seek the Lord, if haply they might feel after him, and find

him, though he be not far from every one of us; for in him we live, and move, and have our being; as certain also of your own poets have said, For we are also his offspring" (Ac.17:24-28).

2 (2:4) **God, Names of—Jehovah—Yahweh—Creation**: the LORD *God* Himself made the universe. Note the name used for God in these verses: the LORD God (Jehovah Elohim). The name for God changes or rather is enlarged here in chapter two of Genesis. *God* (Elohim) is combined with *LORD* (Jehovah or Yahweh). In chapter one, where the creative power and might of God needed to be stressed, just the general name for God, *Elohim*, was used. Elohim is the name that stresses His power and might as the Creator and Sovereign Majesty of the universe. (See DEEPER STUDY # 2—Ge.1:1 for the full meaning of Elohim.) Now, in recording the early history of man upon earth, *Jehovah or Yahweh* is combined with the creative name of God: it was the *LORD* God—Jehovah (Yahweh) Elohim—who created the universe. Why the combined names? Why combine Jehovah or Yahweh with Elohim? Why is it now necessary to say that it was the LORD God who stands behind creation? Because Jehovah is the *personal name* of God, the *revealing and redemptive* name of God. God is about ready...
- to *reveal Himself* to man
- to establish a *personal relationship* with man
- to *redeem* man from his fall into sin and death

This passage is laying the foundation for what is to follow: the early history of man upon earth. The early history explains the relationship between God and man:
⇒ what happened to man and his world
⇒ how man became alienated and cut off from God
⇒ how God went about redeeming man from his fall into sin and death.

It is time for God to be revealed as *Jehovah*, as the *Lord God* of the universe. The universe was created by a *personal God*, a God who created the world so that He might establish a personal relationship with His creation, in particular with man. Simply stated, the Lord God—Jehovah Elohim—is the name that describes what God is about to do upon earth: *establish a personal relationship* with man and *redeem man* from his terrible plunge into sin and death. (See note 1, pt.c—Ge.2:7 for more discussion.)

Thought 1. The very name of God describes His glorious character, exactly what He is like.

1) God is the LORD *God*—Jehovah Elohim—*the personal God*: the only living and true God, the only God who can establish a personal relationship with man. His very purpose for creating the earth was to establish a personal relationship with us—with every one of us. This is the declaration of Scripture from beginning to end.

"And the LORD God called unto Adam, and said unto him, Where art thou?" (Ge.3:9).
"But if from thence thou shalt seek the LORD thy God, thou shalt find him, if thou seek him with all thy heart and with all thy soul" (De.4:29).
"Come now, and let us reason together, saith the LORD: though your sins be as scarlet, they shall be as white as snow; though they be red like crimson, they shall be as wool" (Is.1:18).
"For thus saith the LORD that created the heavens; God himself that formed the earth and made it; he hath established it, he created it not in vain, he formed it to be inhabited: I am the LORD; and there is none else" (Is.45:18).
"Ho, every one that thirsteth, come ye to the waters, and he that hath no money; come ye, buy, and eat; yea, come buy wine and milk without money and without price" (Is.55:1).
"Seek ye the LORD while he may be found, call ye upon him while he is near" (Is.55:6).
"And ye shall seek me, and find me, when ye shall search for me with all your heart" (Je.29:13).
"Come unto me, all ye that labour and are heavy laden, and I will give you rest" (Mt.11:28).
"God that made the world and all things therein, seeing that he is Lord of heaven and earth, dwelleth not in temples made with hands; neither is worshipped with men's hands, as though he needed any thing, seeing he giveth to all life, and breath, and all things; and hath made of one blood all nations of men for to dwell on all the face of the earth, and hath determined the times before appointed, and the bounds of their habitation; that they should seek the Lord, if haply they might feel after him, and find him, though he be not far from every one of us; for in him we live, and move, and have our being; as certain also of your own poets have said, For we are also his offspring" (Ac.17:24-28).
"Behold, I stand at the door, and knock: if any man hear my voice, and open the door, I will come in to him, and will sup [fellowship] with him, and he with me" (Re.3:20).
"And the Spirit and the bride say, Come. And let him that heareth say, Come. And let him that is athirst come. And whosoever will, let him take the water of life freely" (Re.22:17).

2) God is the LORD *God*—Jehovah Elohim—*the revealing God*: the only living and true God, the only God who can reveal Himself and the truth about man and the world. The LORD God alone can reveal where man has come from, why man is here, and where man is going. The LORD God alone can tell man why there is evil, suffering, and death upon earth. He alone can reveal how man can be delivered from evil and death.
Note: the LORD God reveals the truth in four ways.
a) The LORD *God* has revealed the truth through His Son, the Lord Jesus Christ.

"I will raise them up a Prophet [the Lord Jesus Christ] from among their brethren, like unto thee, and will put my words in his mouth; and he shall speak unto them all that I shall command him" (De.18:18).

"For thus saith the LORD that created the heavens; God himself that formed the earth and made it; he hath established it, he created it not in vain, he formed it to be inhabited: I am the LORD; and there is none else. I have not spoken in secret, in a dark place of the earth: I said not unto the seed of Jacob, Seek ye me in vain: I the LORD speak righteousness, I declare things that are right" (Is.45:18-19).

"I have many things to say and to judge of you: but he [God] that sent me is true; and I speak to the world those things which I have heard of him" (Jn.8:26).

"Jesus saith unto him, Have I been so long time with you, and yet hast thou not known me, Philip? he that hath seen me hath seen the Father; and how sayest thou then, Show us the Father?" (Jn.14:9).

b) The LORD *God* reveals the truth through the Holy Spirit.

"Howbeit when he, the Spirit of truth, is come, he will guide you into all truth: for he shall not speak of himself; but whatsoever he shall hear, that shall he speak: and he will show you things to come" (Jn.16:13).

"But as it is written, Eye hath not seen, nor ear heard, neither have entered into the heart of man, the things which God hath prepared for them that love him. But God hath revealed them unto us by his Spirit: for the Spirit searcheth all things, yea, the deep things of God" (1 Co.2:9-10).

c) The LORD *God* reveals the truth through His Word, the Holy Bible.

"Study to show thyself approved unto God, a workman that needeth not to be ashamed, rightly dividing the word of truth" (2 Ti.2:15).

"For this cause also thank we God without ceasing, because, when ye received the word of God which ye heard of us, ye received it not as the word of men, but as it is in truth, the word of God, which effectually worketh also in you that believe" (1 Th.2:13).

"All scripture is given by inspiration of God, and is profitable for doctrine, for reproof, for correction, for instruction in righteousness" (2 Ti.3:16).

"For ever, O LORD, thy word is settled in heaven" (Ps.119:89).

"For verily I say unto you, Till heaven and earth pass, one jot or one tittle shall in no wise pass from the law, till all be fulfilled" (Mt.5:18).

"For the prophecy came not in old time by the will of man: but holy men of God spake as they were moved by the Holy Ghost" (2 Pe.1:21).

"And now, brethren, I commend you to God, and to the word of his grace, which is able to build you up, and to give you an inheritance among all them which are sanctified" (Ac.20:32).

d) The LORD *God* reveals the truth through nature.

"Nevertheless he left not himself without witness, in that he did good, and gave us rain from heaven, and fruitful seasons, filling our hearts with food and gladness" (Ac.14:17).

"For the invisible things of him from the creation of the world are clearly seen, being understood by the things that are made, even his eternal power and Godhead; so that they are without excuse" (Ro.1:20).

"Through faith we understand that the worlds were framed by the word of God, so that things which are seen were not made of things which do appear" (He.11:3).

"But without faith it is impossible to please him: for he that cometh to God must believe that he is [exists], and that he is a rewarder of them that diligently seek him" (He.11:6).

"The heavens declare the glory of God and the firmament showeth His handiwork" (Ps.19:1).

"The heavens declare his righteousness, and all the people see his glory" (Ps.97:6).

3) God is the LORD *God*—Jehovah Elohim—*the redemptive God*: the only living and true God, the only God who can truly redeem and save man from sin, death, and hell.

"Into thine hand I commit my spirit: thou hast redeemed me, O LORD God of truth" (Ps.31:5).

"He sent redemption unto his people: he hath commanded his covenant for ever: holy and reverend is his name" (Ps.111:9).

"Fear not: for I have redeemed thee, I have called thee by thy name; thou art mine" (Is.43:1).

"Even as the Son of man came not to be ministered unto, but to minister, and to give his life a ransom for many" (Mt.20:28).

"Blessed be the Lord God of Israel; for he hath visited and redeemed his people" (Lu.1:68).

"In whom we have redemption through his [Christ's] blood, the forgiveness of sins, according to the riches of his grace" (Ep.1:7).

"[God] who hath delivered us from the power of darkness, and hath translated us into the kingdom of his dear Son: in whom we have redemption through his blood, even the forgiveness of sins" (Col.1:13-14).

"For this is good and acceptable in the sight of God our Saviour; who will have all men to be saved, and to come unto the knowledge of the truth. For there is one God, and one mediator between God and men, the man Christ Jesus; who gave himself a ransom for all, to be testified in due time" (1 Ti.2:3-6).

"Forasmuch as ye know that ye were not redeemed with corruptible things, as silver and gold, from your vain conversation [behavior] received by tradition from your fathers; but with the precious blood of Christ, as of a lamb without blemish and without spot" (1 Pe.1:18-19).

3 (2:5-6) **Creation**: the LORD God created the heavens and the earth in stages (vv.5-6). Note that the heavens and the earth were created:

⇒ before the field plants and shrubs
⇒ before rain
⇒ before man

The brief picture of prehistoric earth painted by verses five and six is this: the earth was encircled with a heavy mist of dense fog and thick clouds. It was this that watered the earth. Note this: apparently the light and heat from the sun and other heavenly bodies could not reach the earth at this time. When God created the earth, it was a barren planet hanging in space, and it was encircled by a thick, heavy layer of clouds, fog, and mist. There was little light and heat and no growth, not at first, not when God first created the planet earth. The LORD God created the universe in stages and on successive days.

Now, note the emphasis laid upon the prehistoric earth:

⇒ The earth and the heavens—the universe—was created by the LORD God Himself.
⇒ The universe—the earth and the heavens—was created in stages by the LORD God.

The fact that God is—that God exists—that it was He Himself who created the universe, is the emphasis and stress of prehistoric earth, of these three verses.

Thought 1. God created the earth stage by stage. He had the power to take an unshaped and unformed earth and shape and form it. He had the power to take a lifeless and unpopulated earth and create life and populate it. Thereby God is the Sovereign Lord of the universe. As Sovereign Lord, God reveals two wonderful things to us.

1) God has the power to take a person and make a new creation out of him. And God has the power to take that new person, that new creation, and move him along stage by stage until he reaches the climactic moment of redemption at the return of the Lord Jesus Christ.

"Therefore if any man be in Christ, he is a new creature: old things are passed away; behold, all things are become new" (2 Co.5:17).

"Being confident of this very thing, that he which hath begun a good work in you will perform it until the day of Jesus Christ" (Ph.1:6).

"I know whom I have believed, and am persuaded that he is able to keep that which I have committed unto him against that day" (2 Ti.1:12).

"Who [believers] are kept by the power of God through faith unto salvation ready to be revealed in the last time" (1 Pe.1:5).

"Now unto him that is able to keep you from falling, and to present you faultless before the presence of his glory with exceeding joy, to the only wise God our Saviour, be glory and majesty, dominion and power, both now and ever. Amen" (Jude 24-25).

2) God has the power to quicken dead, lifeless matter and give it life. Therefore, God has the power to quicken the dead spirit of man. He has the power to "quicken the dead, and call those things which be not as though they were" (Ro.4:17).

"And you hath he quickened, who were dead in trespasses and sins" (Ep.2:1).

"And you, being dead in your sins and the uncircumcision of your flesh, hath he quickened together with him, having forgiven you all trespasses" (Col.2:13).

	B. The First Man: Adam, 2:7
1. The LORD God formed man 2. Man was formed from the dust of the ground 3. God breathed His own breath of life into man 4. Man became a living soul	7 And the LORD God formed man of the dust of the ground, and breathed into his nostrils the breath of life; and man became a living soul.

DIVISION II

ADAM, THE FIRST MAN (PART 1): THE BEGINNING OF MANKIND AND OF THE GODLY SEED—WHAT HAPPENED TO MAN AND THE EARTH, 2:4–3:24

B.   The First Man: Adam, 2:7

(2:7) **Introduction**: this is the summit of God's creation, the phenomenal creation of man. God took two things and made man: the dust of the ground and His own breath of life. He formed Adam out of the dust of the ground, and He breathed His own breath into the nostrils of Adam. Thus the believer knows a wonderful truth: he has been made by God Himself, by the Sovereign Lord and Majesty of the universe. As the Psalmist says, "I am fearfully and wonderfully made" (Ps.139:14). When we study and meditate upon the teachings of Scripture, we are able to say with Elihu, "There is a spirit in man....the spirit of God hath made me, and the breath of the Almighty hath given me life....I also am formed out of the clay" (Jb. 32:8; 33:4, 6). This is a great study on *The First Man: Adam*.

1. The LORD God formed man (v.7).
2. Man was formed from the dust of the ground (v.7).
3. God breathed His own breath of life into man (v.7).
4. Man became a living soul (v.7).

1 (2:7) **Man—Creation**: the LORD God formed man. This is exactly what Scripture says: "And the Lord God formed man." Three significant facts are being stated in this declaration.

a. God and God alone formed man. Man was not formed by impersonal forces nor did he just appear *out of nothing*. Neither did man evolve from other creatures that had come *out of nothing*. Impersonal forces did not *form* man: not cells, not DNA, not atoms, not molecules, not hydrogen, not protons, not neutrons, not electrons. Whatever is discovered to be the basic substance and energy of human life, that substance did not form man. But note: all these substances *are* a part of man; they are what constitute and make up the body and physical life of man. However the basic substances are not what formed man. The energy and power that formed man is the Supreme Intelligence of the universe, the LORD God of the universe. The LORD God formed man. The LORD God created the substances and then He took the substances and used them to create man. Man was created and formed by God and by God alone.

b. God *formed* (yatsar) man. The word "*formed*" means to mold, to shape, to form. It is the picture of a potter who has an image in his mind that he wants to create. Therefore, he takes some clay and molds and forms the clay into the image of his mind. Note: the potter has the idea of what he wants to create, and he has both the intelligence and power to form his creation. So it was with God. God is the Master Craftsman who had the idea of man within His mind. God also had both the intelligence and power to create man, both the omniscience (all knowledge) and omnipotence (all power) to do what He wanted. God wanted to create man; therefore, God *formed* man. God molded and shaped man just like a potter who forms the creation of his mind. Man is the creation of God, of God's mind, of God's intelligence and power, of God's omniscience and omnipotence.

> **Thought 1.** This gives great dignity and honor to man. Man is the product of God's mind, of His thought and heart. Man's creation—man's very body, mind, and spirit—came from the heart of God, from the intelligence and power of God Himself. We are the creation of God's very own heart, His very own mind and power. We have been created with all the dignity and honor possible—created by the very intelligence and power of God Himself. We are the creation of the Sovereign LORD and Majesty of the universe.

> > "When I consider thy heavens, the work of thy fingers, the moon and the stars, which thou hast ordained: what is man, that thou art mindful of him? and the son of man, that thou visitest him? For thou hast made him a little lower than the angels, and hast crowned him with glory and honour. Thou madest him to have dominion over the works of thy hands; thou hast put all things under his feet" (Ps.8:3-6).
> > "I will praise thee; for I am fearfully and wonderfully made....my substance was not hid from thee, when I was made in secret, and curiously wrought in the lowest parts of the earth" (Ps.139:14-15).
> > "What is man, that thou shouldest magnify him? and that thou shouldest set thine heart upon him? And that thou shouldest visit him every morning, and try him every moment?" (Jb. 7:17-18).
> > "Thou madest him a little lower than the angels; thou crownedst him with glory and honour, and didst set him over the works of thy hands" (He.2:7).

120

c. It was the LORD God—Jehovah Elohim—who formed man. This is the *personal name* of God, the name that stresses...
- God's *personal relationship* to man
- God's *revelation* to man
- God's *redemption* of man

When this name—the LORD God—is used, God's *personal relationship* with man is being stressed. God's creation of man was very, very special. It was a matter that had the personal attention and care of God. God Himself was personally involved in the creation of man, involved in a far different way than when He created the rest of the world. In creating man, God was creating the creature...
- who was to be the summit of His creation upon earth
- who was to have the ability to freely choose to worship and serve God
- who was to oversee the universe for God throughout all of eternity

Therefore a very special relationship, a personal relationship, was bound to be established by the LORD God between Himself and man, between Himself and the creature He was putting in charge of His world. God stood before man as God, as the great Creator and Sustainer of life. But God also stood before man as LORD, as the Supreme Master of man's life, as the Supreme Lord and Master...
- who loves and cares for man
- who watches over and looks after man
- who seeks after and saves man
- who is personally related to man as Lord and Master
- who reveals Himself, communicates and fellowships with man

This is why the name *LORD God* is used in the creation of man. The LORD God was establishing a personal relationship with the creature He was now creating: man was to be very, very special to God. There was to be a personal relationship, a close bond, between God and man forever. God—the LORD God—was to stand before man as man's Lord. Man was to be the subject of God forever and ever. (See note 2—Ge.2:4 for more discussion.)

Thought 1. God created man to know Him, to worship Him, and to serve Him.
1) God created man to know Him.

"Know ye that the LORD he is God: it is he that hath made us, and not we ourselves; we are his people, and the sheep of his pasture" (Ps.100:3).
"I have created him for my glory, I have formed him; yea, I have made him....Ye are my witnesses, saith the LORD, and my servant whom I have chosen: that ye may know and believe me, and understand that I am he: before me there was no God formed, neither shall there be after me." (Is.43:7, 10).
"But let him that glorieth glory in this, that he understandeth and knoweth me, that I am the LORD which exercise lovingkindness, judgment, and righteousness, in the earth: for in these things I delight, saith the LORD" (Je.9:24).
"And this is life eternal, that they might know thee the only true God, and Jesus Christ, whom thou hast sent" (Jn.17:3).

2) God created man to worship Him.

"O come, let us worship and bow down: let us kneel before the LORD our maker" (Ps.95:6).
"O worship the LORD in the beauty of holiness: fear before him, all the earth" (Ps.96:9).
"Then saith Jesus unto him, get thee hence, Satan: for it is written, Thou shalt worship the Lord thy God, and him only shalt thou serve" (Mt.4:10).
"God is a Spirit: and they that worship him must worship him in spirit and in truth" (Jn.4:24).
"Saying with a loud voice, Fear God, and give glory to him; for the hour of his judgment is come: and worship him that made heaven, and earth, and the sea, and the fountains of waters" (Re.14:7).

3) God created man to serve Him.

"And God said, Let us make man in our image, after our likeness: and let them have dominion over the fish of the sea, and over the fowl of the air, and over the cattle, and over all the earth, and over every creeping thing that creepeth upon the earth. So God created man in his own image, in the image of God created he him; male and female created he them. And God blessed them, and God said unto them, Be fruitful, and multiply, and replenish the earth, and subdue it: and have dominion over the fish of the sea, and over the fowl of the air, and over every living thing that moveth upon the earth" (Ge.1:26-28).
"The LORD hath made all things for himself: yea, even the wicked for the day of evil" (Pr.16:4).
"According as he hath chosen us in him before the foundation of the world, that we should be holy and without blame before him in love: having predestinated us unto the adoption of children

by Jesus Christ to himself, according to the good pleasure of his will, to the praise of the glory of his grace, wherein he hath made us accepted in the beloved" (Ep.1:4-6).

"That ye might walk worthy of the Lord unto all pleasing, being fruitful in every good work, and increasing in the knowledge of God" (Col.1:10).

"But ye are a chosen generation, a royal priesthood, an holy nation, a peculiar people; that ye should show forth the praises of him who hath called you out of darkness into his marvellous light" (1 Pe.2:9).

"Thou art worthy, O Lord, to receive glory and honour and power: for thou hast created all things, and for thy pleasure they are and were created" (Re.4:11).

2 (2:7) **Man—Creation**: man was formed from the dust of the ground. The material used to *form* the body of man was lowly stuff—stuff that is both humble and base, of little worth and value. What was it? Dust, the dirt of the ground. Isaiah and Job say *clay* (Is.64:8; Job 33:6). Martin Luther translates the Hebrew *lump of earth*.[1] The idea of Scripture seems to be that a mixture of water and dirt was used to form the body of man. Imagine! Our bodies are made of the same substance—of the same chemical elements—as the earth itself. Physically, we are nothing more than *lowly and base dirt*, nothing more than the grains of dirt and dust that lie upon the ground. No better description of the lowliness of man's creation has ever been written than the statements made by Matthew Henry:

⇒ "The matter was despicable. He [man] was made of the dust of the ground, a very unlikely thing to make a man of."

⇒ "[Man was made] next to nothing."

⇒ "He [man] was made of the dust, the small dust, such as is upon the surface of the earth."

⇒ "He [man] was not made of gold-dust, powder of pearl, or diamond dust, but common dust, dust of the ground."

⇒ "He [Adam] is said to be of the earth...dusty, 1 Co.15:47. And we also are of the earth, for we are his offspring, and of the same mould."

⇒ There is such an affinity between the earth and our earthly bodies that "our mother's womb, out of which we were born, is called the earth."

"My substance was not hid from thee, when I was made in secret, and curiously wrought in the lowest parts of the earth [womb]" (Ps.139:15).

⇒ Our bodies are called houses of clay and our foundations are said to be in the earth.

"How much less in them that dwell in houses of clay, whose foundation is in the dust, which are crushed before the moth?" (Jb.4:19).

⇒ "Our fabric [flesh, body] is earthly, and the fashioning of it like that of an earthen vessel."

"Remember, I beseech thee, that thou hast made me as the clay; and wilt thou bring me into dust again?" (Jb.10:9).

⇒ "Our food is out of the earth."

"As for the earth, out of it cometh bread" (Jb.28:5).

⇒ Our bodies decay and corrupt and are eaten by the worms of the earth.

"I have said to corruption, Thou art my father: to the worm, Thou art my mother, and my sister" (Jb.17:14).

⇒ "Our fathers are in the earth, and our own final tendency [destiny] is to it; and what have we then to be proud of."[2]

Thought 1. Indeed! What do we have to be proud of? Nothing. Absolutely nothing, for we are made of nothing more than a handful of dust. From dust we have come, and to dust we shall return. Before we know it, our bodies will be nothing more than a small cup of dust lying someplace within the ground of the earth.

Thought 2. The point of Scripture is this: we come from the humblest of beginnings. Our origin is that of dust, lowly dirt and dust. Our bodies are fragile and frail. They are as nothing; therefore, we must depend upon God to look after us, and we must seek the glory and dignity that God alone can give. No matter how much glory and dignity we achieve upon earth, we shall soon be nothing more than a handful of dust. Our origin and beginning upon earth was humble. Therefore, we must walk humbly before God, depending upon God to make us eternal and glorious beings—beings who shall arise out of the dirt of the earth and live forever. We must depend upon God to give us a body that will never age or pass away, a body that will never die, but that will live forever.

---

1 H.C. Leupold. *Genesis*, Vol.1, p.115.
2 *Matthew Henry's Commentary*, Vol.1, p.14.

"For God so loved the world, that he gave his only begotten Son, that whosoever believeth in him should not perish, but have everlasting life" (Jn.3:16).

"Verily, verily, I say unto you, He that heareth my word, and believeth on him that sent me, hath everlasting life, and shall not come into condemnation; but is passed from death unto life" (Jn.5:24).

"Marvel not at this: for the hour is coming, in the which all that are in the graves shall hear his voice, and shall come forth; they that have done good, unto the resurrection of life; and they that have done evil, unto the resurrection of damnation" (Jn.5:28-29).

"Being born again, not of corruptible seed, but of incorruptible, by the word of God, which liveth and abideth for ever" (1 Pe.1:23).

Thought 3. Every person is made of the same substance, of the dust of the ground. No person has any more value or worth than any other person—not on the basis of the stuff from which he is made. All come from dust and all shall return to dust. This is significant: it means...

- that no person is above another person
- that no person is worth more than any other person
- that no person has any right to put any other person down

There is no place for pride, prejudice, discrimination, jealousy, enslavement, partiality, or favoritism among people. There is no place for any mistreatment of any person upon earth.

"These things also belong to the wise. It is not good to have respect of persons in judgment" (Pr.24:23).

"He will surely reprove you, if ye do secretly accept persons" (Jb.13:10).

"Have we not all one father? hath not one God created us? why do we deal treacherously every man against his brother, by profaning the covenant of our fathers?" (Mal.2:10).

"Judge not, that ye be not judged" (Mt.7:1).

"Love worketh no ill to his neighbor: therefore love is the fulfilling of the law" (Ro.13:10).

"Are ye not then partial in yourselves, and are become judges of evil thoughts?" (Js.2:4).

"There is one lawgiver, who is able to save and to destroy: who art thou that judgest another?" (Js.4:12).

3 (2:7) **Man—Creation**: God breathed His own breath of life into man. Man is not just dust, not just physical substance. Man is far more than just a physical body. Man is a spirit. God has given man His very own breath. The picture is this...

- the body of the first man, Adam, was lying upon the ground before God. It had just been formed by God from the dust of the earth. Adam was lifeless—just a human body lying there upon the ground—never having breathed. Then all of a sudden—in descriptive terms—God leaned over and breathed His own breath into Adam's nostrils. Adam received the breath of God, and when he did, the result was astounding: he arose from the ground and became a living soul.

Now, what is the breath of God? What is there about God's breath that caused God to breathe His own breath into man? The breath of God is at least two things. (See DEEPER STUDY # 2—Ge.1:26 for discussion on the image of God within man.)

a. The breath of God is *the Spirit of God*. This is seen in the Hebrew word for spirit, *ruach*. The word *ruach* means wind, breath, air, spirit. When God breathed into the nostrils of Adam, He was not just breathing air into Adam's lungs so that Adam could live. If this was all God was doing—giving life to Adam—He did not have to breathe His own breath into Adam. God could have simply spoken the word and caused Adam to become a living soul just like He did when He created the animals. What God was doing was symbolizing and picturing for all generations to come this one fact: God has given man His Spirit, the very Spirit of God Himself. God has actually breathed into man His very own Spirit. This means a most wonderful thing: God has connected Himself to man in the most intimate way possible. God has put within man His very own Spirit. Man is related to God, bound to God, connected to God. Both God and man have the same breath, the very same Spirit. Man has within his body the very breath and Spirit of God Himself.

b. The breath of God is the life of God. When God breathed into man, God gave His very own life to man. What is the life of God? It is life that lives on and on, the life of eternity, the power to live eternally. God's breath is not temporal; God's breath lives forever. God's breath never ceases to exist. Therefore, man was to breathe and live forever; man was to live eternally with God. Man was given the very breath of God Himself, the power of immortality, the power to live forever.

But note this about the Spirit of life—the Spirit of God—that has been given to man: man was created a spiritual being, but his spirit has been marred by his fall into sin (see DEEPER STUDY # 2, latter part—Ge.1:26 for discussion).

Thought 1. God made no other creature like He made man. God gave no other creature His breath, neither His Spirit nor His life of immortality. This makes man's creation distinctive, of the highest order and being, of the highest honor and glory, of the highest worth and value.

"The spirit of God hath made me, and the breath of the Almighty hath given me life" (Jb.33:4).

"For thou hast made him a little lower than the angels, and hast crowned him with glory and honour" (Ps.8:5).

Thought 2. There is a sense in which man is a paradox. He was created with all the dignity and honor possible—created by the hand of God and given the very breath of God. Yet, he was also created out of the most base and lowly stuff of all: dirt. In one sense man has every reason to glory; in another sense he has every reason to be humble. What is to be man's attitude? Man is to glory: there is nothing wrong with glorying. Man is to be humble: there is nothing wrong with being humble. It is the reason or object for glorying and for being humble that makes man right or wrong.

⇒ Man is to worship and glory in God—that God gave him life and the dignity and honor (privilege) of life.

⇒ Man is to walk humbly before God and before men, for God has made all men from the same material, from the dust of the earth itself. (Je.9:24; see 1 Co.1:31; 2 Co.10:17; Ro.11:36; Ga.1:5; 2 Ti.4:18; He.13:21; 1 Pe.5:11).

The duty of man is this: to present his body to God as "a living sacrifice" and as "the temple of the Holy Spirit" (Ro.12:1; 1 Co.6:19).

"And God said, Let us make man in our image, after our likeness....So God created man in His own image" (Ge.1:26-27).

"I will praise thee; for I am fearfully and wonderfully made....my substance was not hid from thee, when I was made in secret, and curiously wrought in the lowest parts of the earth" (Ps.139:14-15).

"I beseech you therefore, brethren, by the mercies of God, that ye present your bodies a living sacrifice, holy, acceptable unto God, which is your reasonable service" (Ro.12:1).

"What? know ye not that your body is the temple of the Holy Ghost which is in you, which ye have of God, and ye are not your own? For ye are bought with a price: therefore glorify God in your body, and in your spirit, which are God's" (1 Co.6:19-20).

Thought 3. There is one thing man needs to know: he has been created in the image, in the very likeness, of God. He is an immortal creature: he shall exist forever and ever. Man must, therefore, make sure—absolutely sure—that he is going to live with God. The one thing he *must not do* is live apart from God. Man must not miss out on the glorious privilege of living forever with God.

"For God so loved the world, that he gave his only begotten Son, that whosoever believeth in him should not perish, but have everlasting life" (Jn.3:16).

"He that believeth on the Son hath everlasting life: and he that believeth not the Son shall not see life; but the wrath of God abideth on him" (Jn.3:36).

"Verily, verily, I say unto you, If a man keep my saying, he shall never see death" (Jn.8:51).

"And whosoever liveth and believeth in me shall never die. Believest thou this?" (Jn.11:26).

"For we know that if our earthly house of this tabernacle were dissolved, we have a building of God, an house not made with hands, eternal in the heavens" (2 Co.5:1).

"And this is the record, that God hath given to us eternal life, and this life is in his Son. He that hath the Son hath life; and he that hath not the Son of God hath not life" (1 Jn.5:11-12).

"Then shall the dust return to the earth as it was: and the spirit shall return unto God who gave it" (Ec.12:7).

4 (2:7) **Creation**: man became a living soul. Remember: *soul* (nephesh) means an *animated, breathing, conscious, and living being*. It does not mean the spirit of man. God had just breathed His Spirit and life into man. Once God did this, man became a living soul—an animated, breathing, conscious, and living creature. He was a living soul just like all the other creatures of earth (see note 3, *Soul*—Ge.1:20 for more discussion). However, there was one distinctive difference between the animals and man: man was given the very breath of God Himself, the very Spirit and life of God.

Note: man did not become a living soul until God breathed His Spirit and life into man. This is significant, very significant:

⇒ It means that man is the only living spirit upon earth. Man is both a spiritual and soulish or animate being.

⇒ It means that animals are only living souls or non-spiritual beings.

⇒ It means that vegetation is only an *inanimate being*.

Another way to say the same thing is this:

⇒ Vegetation (plant life) lives, but it is inanimate.

⇒ Animals live, but they are only animate or soulish creatures. They are not spiritual creatures; they do not have the breath or spirit of God within them; they do not worship God.

⇒ Man lives, but he is both an animate and a spiritual creature. Man is both soul and spirit. Man is an animal, a soulish creature, but he is also a spiritual creature, a creature who worships God. Man is made both of earth and heaven.

This is the distinctiveness of man. Man is the summit of God's creation: the creature who possesses both soul and spirit. He is the creature who has been given *the very breath of God, the very spirit and life of God Himself.*

⇒ Man is the creature who has been created both of earth and heaven.

⇒ Man is the creature who can choose to live either for the earth or for God.

Thought 1. Why has God given His own breath to man, given man His own Spirit and life? So that man can freely choose to love and worship God. God has given man (despite man's fall) enough of Himself to make man hunger and seek after God. Man has a sense, a consciousness, that he has lost God's Spirit and lost the power to live eternally with God; he has just enough awareness of God to seek after immortality with God, to seek after God and the privilege of living forever with God.

"But if from thence thou shalt seek the LORD thy God, thou shalt find him, if thou seek him with all thy heart and with all thy soul" (De.4:29).
"Seek the LORD, and his strength: seek his face ever more" (Ps.105:4).
"Seek ye the LORD while he may be found, call ye upon him while he is near" (Is.55:6).
"For thus saith the LORD unto the house of Israel, Seek ye me, and ye shall live" (Am. 5:4).
"Seek ye the LORD, all ye meek of the earth, which have wrought his judgment; seek righteousness, seek meekness: it may be ye shall be hid in the day of the LORD'S anger" (Zep.2:3).
"That they should seek the Lord, if haply they might feel after him, and find him, though he be not far from every one of us" (Ac.17:27).

Thought 2. What a shame that man cleaves to this earth and its worldliness.

"He that refuseth instruction despiseth his own soul" (Pr.15:32).

God breathed His Spirit into man. How often and how intensely that spirit within man should breathe after God.

"Blessed are they which do hunger and thirst after righteousness: for they shall be filled" (Mt.5:6).

	C. The First Garden & Its Purpose: Eden, Man's Ideal Place or Home,[DS1] 2:8-14	Eden to water the garden; and from thence it was parted, and became into four heads.	water & irrigation[DS2]
1. A real place, a garden planted by God	8 And the LORD God planted a garden eastward in Eden; and there he put the man whom he had formed.	11 The name of the first is Pison: that is it which compasseth the whole land of Havilah, where there is gold;	
2. Eden met man's need for a home: A very special place to live		12 And the gold of that land is good: there is bdellium and the onyx stone.	
3. Eden met man's need for beauty & food & for spiritual surroundings	9 And out of the ground made the LORD God to grow every tree that is pleasant to the sight, and good for food; the tree of life also in the midst of the garden, and the tree of knowledge of good and evil.	13 And the name of the second river is Gihon: the same is it that compasseth the whole land of Ethiopia.	
4. Eden met man's need to live forever: The tree of life		14 And the name of the third river is Hiddekel: that is it which goeth toward the east of Assyria. And the fourth river is Euphrates.	
5. Eden met man's need to exercise his free will—his ability to choose: The tree of knowing good & evil			
6. Eden met man's need for	10 And a river went out of		

DIVISION II

ADAM, THE FIRST MAN (PART 1): THE BEGINNING OF MANKIND AND OF THE GODLY SEED—WHAT HAPPENED TO MAN AND THE EARTH, 2:4–3:24

C. The First Garden and Its Purpose: Eden, Man's Ideal Place or Home, 2:8-14

(2:8-14) **Introduction—Eden, Garden of**: picture the scene: man had just been created. The LORD God Himself had just formed man from the dust of the ground, and had breathed the very breath of God into the nostrils of man (Ge.2:7). Man stood there upon earth for the very first time in human history, stood there in the midst of all the lush green of the forest and the radiant reds, oranges, yellows, blues, purples, whites and all the other colors of the flowers and bushes that displayed their wild beauty. God now had...

- the universe which He had planned and purposed
- the man whom He had planned and purposed
- the perfection—the perfect man and the perfect universe—which He had planned and purposed

But something else was needed. Man needed a residence, a home, a place to live. This passage of Scripture describes the place where man had his beginnings upon earth, the place where man was to live. It covers the features which God designed for man's residence or home. The place is called *The Garden of Eden*, the most beautiful and bountiful paradise man could ever imagine. Eden was man's paradise, his utopia.

Note that God's glorious goodness is seen in His design of the Garden. The features of the Garden clearly show that God cares deeply for man—for man's welfare, provision, security, joy, and happiness. The Garden shows that God designed the ideal place for man's residence or home. This passage covers *The First Garden and Its Purpose: Eden, Man's Ideal Place or Home.*

1. A real place, a Garden planted by God (v.8).
2. Eden met man's need for a home: a very special place to live (v.8).
3. Eden met man's need for beauty and food and for spiritual surroundings (v.9).
4. Eden met man's need to live forever: the tree of life (v.9).
5. Eden met man's need to exercise his free will—his ability to choose: the tree of knowing good and evil (v.9).
6. Eden met man's need for water and irrigation (v.10).

DEEPER STUDY # 1

(2:8-14) **Adam vs. Christ**: this note is discussed as DEEPER STUDY # 2 because it stands as a separate study to preach and teach, and to include it here would interrupt the study of this passage. (See DEEPER STUDY # 2—Ge.2:10-14 for discussion.)

---

1 (2:8) **Garden of Eden**: the Garden of Eden was a real place, a real Garden planted by God Himself. However, the reality of the Garden has been denied by some persons.
- ⇒ *Secular man* considers the Garden of Eden to be a fictitious story, just a fairy tale or fable. He thinks the Garden is just the Biblical author's imagination of how man first began his life upon earth. Secular man says that the Biblical author simply pictures man beginning his life in a perfect environment and later failing and beginning to corrupt the earth.
- ⇒ *Religious man* often looks upon the Garden of Eden as a symbol or type of the ideal environment or ideal earth. He thinks that the Garden is the dream of the ideal earth and environment toward which man should work. Religious man often says that the task of man is to strive to make the earth a Garden of Eden, the utopian paradise for which man dreams.

But note: this is not what this passage says, nowhere close to what it says. This passage clearly teaches that the Garden of Eden was a real, historical place—a real, historical Garden created by God Himself. How can we say this so confidently, so positively? Because of three clear facts.

a. The specific direction of the Garden is given: the Garden was planted in the East, in the land of Eden. When Moses wrote this, he was leading Israel in the wilderness wanderings throughout the great Arabian desert. East of the Arabian desert would point toward the Arab nations of the Middle East, specifically toward the great fertile plains of the Tigris and Euphrates rivers.

Note: the direction being pointed to is not a fictitious or symbolic land. It is a specific direction and a well known land.

b. The general location of the Garden is given (vv.10-14). Real lands are mentioned: Havilah, Ethiopia, and Assyria. Real rivers are also given: Pison, Gihon, Hiddekel or the Tigris, and the Euphrates. Apparently, the Garden was someplace close to where the Tigris and Euphrates join. This would place the Garden in what is known today as southern Iraq.

The point to note is this: the Garden of Eden—man's paradise—lay toward the East and was located around four rivers that flowed through lands or countries well known to the people of that day. There is nothing fictitious or imaginary about the direction or location of the Garden of Eden. It was a real, historical place, a real, historical Garden.

c. Note a third fact as well. The very context of this section of Scripture points toward the Garden being historical. What is being discussed in this section of Genesis is creation, the beginnings of the universe and of man upon earth. If the earth and the universe are real and man is real—if the account of creation is accurate—then the Garden of Eden, man's paradise upon earth, must be a real, historical place. Part of man's beginnings upon earth is bound to include a discussion of his first environment and home. This is only logical; this is only to be expected.

Thought 1. Why is it important to stress that the Garden of Eden was a real, historical place?
1) If the Garden was a fictitious place, then it means that the fall of man is a fable. Why? Because the fall of man took place in the Garden of Eden. Therefore, if the Garden is unreal, then it means there is no such thing as sin, as man being lost in sin and separated from God. If the Garden of Eden never existed—not really—then man falling into sin never took place.
2) If the Garden is just a symbol or type of paradise—of the ideal environment or ideal earth—then redemption through Christ is not necessary. Man does not need God nor Christ to save him and his world. Man is perfectly capable of creating the perfect environment himself. All man has to do is work and work for the ideal earth, and eventually he will bring paradise and utopia to earth—all by his own energy, efforts, works, and goodness.

"Wherefore, as by one man [Adam] sin entered into the world, and death by sin; and so death passed upon all men, for that all have sinned" (Ro.5:12).
"Thy first father hath sinned, and thy teachers have transgressed against me" (Is.43:27).
"For all have sinned, and come short of the glory of God" (Ro.3:23).
"For by grace are ye saved through faith; and that not of yourselves: it is the gift of God: not of works, lest any man should boast" (Ep.2:8-9).
"Not by works of righteousness which we have done, but according to his mercy he saved us, by the washing of regeneration, and renewing of the Holy Ghost; which he shed on us abundantly through Jesus Christ our Saviour; that being justified by his grace, we should be made heirs according to the hope of eternal life" (Tit.3:5-7).

2 (2:8) **Man, Needs; Responsibility—Home—Environment—Garden of Eden**: the Garden of Eden met man's need for a home, his need for a very special place to live. Man needs a place that he can call home, a place...
• where he can be centrally located
• where he can experience the closest and most intimate love, caring, sharing, communication, and relationships
• where he can be employed and fulfill his duties and responsibilities and make his contribution to society
• where he can give birth to and rear a family
• where he can feel settled and secure, quiet and at peace
• where he can settle down at night and relax, rest, sleep, and revive his strength for the next day's duties

God knew man's need, that man needed a place where he could be centrally located, a place that he could call home. Therefore, God met man's need: God created the Garden of Eden, the most beautiful paradise imaginable; then He took man and put him into the Garden. Note two facts.

a. The word *garden* (gan) means a place that is enclosed, protected, and sheltered. It even has the idea of being covered, of being perfectly protected (He., ganan) (*Pulpit Commentary*, Vol.1, p.43). The word *Eden* (edhen) means a place of delight, of pleasure, of bliss. Eden means a paradise.

The point is this: the Garden of Eden was different from the rest of the earth. The earth was perfect with a perfect and unthreatening environment, and it overflowed with an abundance of beauty and fruit. But the idea of Scripture is that the Garden of Eden far exceeded the earth in beauty and provision. The Garden gave man a place—some land, some acreage—where he could live and establish a home and community; a place that was enclosed, protected, and sheltered from the elements of nature and of the weather; a place that provided the covering—the perfect home and provision—that man needed. The Garden of Eden was a paradise for man.

b. God took man and put man into the Garden. As stated above, the Garden differed from the rest of the earth. From the beginning, man knew the difference between the Garden and the rest of the land outside. Man knew that God had blessed and cared for him in a most excellent way: God had given him a place that far exceeded the rest of the earth. As

Matthew Henry points out: God did not put man in a palace made of silver and gold, nor in a house made of ivory, but in the most beautiful and artful place of all: nature—a Garden furnished and adorned by God Himself.[1]

Thought 1. Man often blames his shortcomings and failures upon his environment. But note how man began his life upon earth: in a perfect environment, in a paradise upon earth. God was as good to man as He could be: He gave man a perfect nature and a perfect environment so that man could have an abundance of life, a life that far exceeded anything for which man could ask. But as we shall see in Chapter Three of Genesis, man still fell into sin. He still came short and failed. Man cannot—not the first man, nor any other man—use his environment as an excuse to sin, fail, or come short. Environment, of course, has an influence upon every one of us; but a person is basically responsible for his own behavior and actions. Adam—the first man upon earth, the father of us all— clearly illustrates this. We would all fail and come short even if we had a perfect environment and world. Our problem with failure and sin is not a bad environment; our problem is the heart: the desire and craving to do what we want and to have what we want no matter what effect our behavior has upon the earth and others. We are without excuse.

> "For the invisible things of him from the creation of the world are clearly seen, being understood by the things that are made, even his eternal power and Godhead; so that they are without excuse" (Ro.1:20).
> "For all have sinned, and come short of the glory of God" (Ro.3:23).
> "For we ourselves also were sometimes foolish, disobedient, deceived, serving divers [many] lusts and pleasures, living in malice and envy, hateful, and hating one another" (Tit.3:3).
> "If we say that we have no sin, we deceive ourselves, and the truth is not in us" (1 Jn.1:8).
> "Who can bring a clean thing out of an unclean? not one" (Jb. 14:4).
> "Most men will proclaim every one his own goodness: but a faithful man who can find?" (Pr.20:6).
> "Who can say, I have made my heart clean, I am pure from my sin?" (Pr.20:9).
> "Surely I am more brutish than any man, and have not the understanding of a man" (Pr.30:2).
> "But we are all as an unclean thing, and all our righteousnesses are as filthy rags; and we all do fade as a leaf; and our iniquities, like the wind, have taken us away" (Is.64:6).

Thought 2. The environment of Eden shows what God's will is for the environment of the earth. God wants us to protect and look after the environment, not to destroy it. But think about what we do: all the pollution, garbage, junk, and nuclear waste; all the devastating effects pollution has upon the rivers, lakes, seas, sky, air, and lands of the earth. And why? Because of the selfishness (personal and economic selfishness), extravagance, and sin of the human heart.

3 (2:9) **Man, Needs of**: the Garden of Eden met man's need for beauty and food and for spiritual surroundings. God caused *every tree* (kol ets)—all kinds of trees—to grow within the Garden. The idea is an enormous number and all manner of trees "pleasant to the sight and good for food." The Garden was apparently a huge forest of trees, shrubs, and vegetation. It was furnished both to provide for Adam's *need* and *pleasure*. The beauty and provision of the Garden met to some degree the three basic needs of man.

a. The Garden provided *beauty, discovery, and encounter* for man. Every tree, bush, shrub, flower, and plant imaginable was there: each with its own height and width, leaf and bark, color and fragrance. The Garden's beauty and immense size gave man the very provision he needed to meet his mental, emotional, and aesthetic needs.

b. The Garden provided *food and shelter* for man. Every species of vegetation, fruit, berry, and nut was there— everything to satisfy the taste and nourishment of man.

c. The Garden provided *spiritual surroundings, a spiritual environment*. The Garden's beauty and provision was bound to give man a sense of awe and worship—to stir praise and thanksgiving from man. No surroundings and no environment can fully meet man's need for worship. Only God can fully meet man's spiritual need. But the Garden was so beautiful and so conducive to worship that it was bound to pull and stir man to worship God. (See notes Ge.2:15-17 for God's full provision in meeting man's needs. Also see note—Col.2:9-10 for more discussion.)

Thought 1. Most people seek the fullness of life from three things:
⇒ the possessions of the earth
⇒ the pleasures of the earth
⇒ the power of the earth

People seek to get what they want from their surroundings and environment. But the earth and the things of the earth cannot meet man's basic need. As important as the earth and the physical are, man's basic need is much deeper than what appears on the surface—much deeper than the physical and material. Man is spirit; consequently, his basic need is spiritual (see notes—Ge.1:26; 2:15-17; Ep.1:3. The Ephesian note will aid greatly in understanding the importance of the spiritual vs. the material world.)

Thought 2. God makes an unusual promise to man. God will see to it that any person has sufficient food, shelter and clothing. *But*, there is a condition. The person has to "seek...first the kingdom of God and His righteousness" (Mt.6:33; see 6:24-34).

---

[1] *Matthew Henry's Commentary*, Vol.1, p.15.

Thought 3. When one receives an abundance, three results should immediately follow.
⇒ God should be acknowledged.
⇒ God should be praised.
⇒ The abundance should be shared.

4 (2:9) **Man, Needs—Eternal Life—Tree of Life**: the Garden of Eden met man's need to live forever. How? God planted a fruit tree within the Garden and gave it the power of everlasting life. What is this tree? Here are all the Scripture verses that refer to it:

> **"And out of the ground made the LORD God to grow every tree that is pleasant to the sight, and good for food; the tree of life also in the midst of the Garden, and the tree of knowledge of good and evil" (Ge.2:9).**
> **"And the LORD God said, Behold, the man is become as one of us, to know good and evil: and now, lest he put forth his hand, and take also of the tree of life, and eat, and live for ever" (Ge.3:22).**
> **"He that hath an ear, let him hear what the Spirit saith unto the churches; To him that overcometh will I give to eat of the tree of life, which is in the midst of the paradise of God" (Re.2:7).**
> **"In the midst of the street of it, and on either side of the river, was there the tree of life, which bare twelve manner of fruits, and yielded her fruit every month: and the leaves of the tree were for the healing of the nations" (Re.22:2).**
> **"Blessed are they that do his commandments, that they may have right to the tree of life, and may enter in through the gates into the city" (Re.22:14).**
> **"And by the river upon the bank thereof, on this side and on that side, shall grow all trees for meat [food], whose leaf shall not fade, neither shall the fruit thereof be consumed: it shall bring forth new fruit according to his months, because their waters they issued out of the sanctuary: and the fruit thereof shall be for meat, and the leaf thereof for medicine" (Eze.47:12).**

Here are the facts given about the tree:
⇒ The tree is named "the tree of life." It sat in the middle of the Garden of Eden (Ge.2:9).
⇒ If Adam, the first man upon earth, had eaten of the tree, he would have lived forever. Apparently, he had never eaten of the tree when he was in the Garden (Ge.3:22).
⇒ Ezekiel the prophet predicted this about the tree of life: when Christ returned, there would be trees growing that would continually provide—never cease to provide—food and medicine for the citizens of His kingdom (Eze.47:12).
⇒ The overcomers in the great tribulation will be given the right to the tree of life (Re.2:7).
⇒ The tree of life will be in the New Jerusalem, the capital of the new heavens and earth. The tree of life will sit in the middle of the main street of the capital and grow on both banks of the major river that flows through the capital. Note that this verse, just as Ezekiel's, refers to the tree of life being many trees—a type or species of tree—and not just one tree (Re.22:2).

Now, what is the tree of life? On the basis of the facts revealed in Scripture, the tree is a real tree that bears life-giving fruit, fruit that gives a person everlasting life, that keeps a person from ever dying. But note this: the tree of life exists only in a perfect world, only where perfection exists...
• only in the perfection of the Garden of Eden
• only in the New Jerusalem, the capital of the new heavens and earth (see note—Rev.22:1-5 for more discussion)

When God planted *the tree of life* in the Garden of Eden, the tree was to keep Adam from dying. Adam was to eat of its fruit and live forever. But, as shall be seen, Adam never ate of the tree of life. He chose to eat the fruit of the forbidden tree. The result was catastrophic: man was expelled from the Garden and not allowed to eat the fruit of the tree of life (see notes—Ge.3:22-24).

The point to see in the present passage is this: God planted the tree of life right in the midst of the Garden, in the most prominent and conspicuous spot where it would always be easily seen. It was planted right where Adam would always be reminded that he had to eat of the tree in order to live forever. God gave man every opportunity imaginable...
• *to choose* life over death
• *to choose* God's presence over alienation
• *to choose* eternity with God over separation from God
• *to choose* peace over division
• *to choose* obedience over disobedience and rebellion
• *to choose* freedom over enslavement and bondage
• *to choose* righteousness over unrighteousness
• *to choose* good over evil
• *to choose* purpose over uselessness
• *to choose* fulfillment over emptiness
• *to choose* perfection over corruption
• *to choose* God over self and Satan

> **"See, I have set before thee this day life and good, and death and evil" (De.30:15).**
> **"I call heaven and earth to record this day against you, that I have set before you life and death, blessing and cursing: therefore choose life, that both thou and thy seed may live" (De.30:19).**

Thought 1. God loves man—all of us. He showed Adam His love by providing the tree of life—the very possibility of living forever. God shows us His love by providing eternal life through His Son, the Lord Jesus Christ.

"For God so loved the world, that he gave his only begotten son, that whosoever believeth in him should not perish, but have everlasting life" (Jn.3:16).
"He that believeth on the Son hath everlasting life: and he that believeth not the Son shall not see life; but the wrath of God abideth on him" (Jn.3:36).
"And this is the will of him that sent me, that every one which seeth the Son, and believeth on him, may have everlasting life: and I will raise him up at the last day" (Jn.6:40).
"But God commendeth his love toward us, in that, while we were yet sinners, Christ died for us" (Ro.5:8).
"But [God's purpose] is now made manifest by the appearing of our Saviour Jesus Christ, who hath abolished death, and hath brought life and immortality to light through the gospel" (2 Ti.1:10).
"And this is the record, that God hath given to us eternal life, and this life is in his Son. He that hath the Son hath life; and he that hath not the Son of God hath not life" (1 Jn.5:11-12).

5 (2:9) **Man, Needs—Tree of Knowledge of Good and Evil**: the Garden of Eden met man's need to exercise his free will, his ability to choose. God planted a second fruit tree in the Garden. Several facts are also given about this tree.
a. It was in the center of the Garden (Ge.3:3).
b. It was *good* for food and *pleasant* to the eyes (Ge.3:6).
c. It was the only tree from which Adam and Eve were instructed not to eat. God used the tree for man to exercise his freedom of choice, his spiritual drive and ability (See DEEPER STUDY # 2—Ge.1:26).
⇒ Man was to choose God by obeying Him (see note—Ge.2:16; see 2:16-17; 3:2-3).
⇒ If man chose to disobey God by eating of the tree's fruit, man would know evil—what it is to be disobedient. He would experience evil personally and die, that is, be separated from God spiritually, physically, and eternally.

d. It was one of the two trees chosen to exercise man's choice between life and death (separation from God). Adam, the first man—the forefather of the human race—did just what we do: he chose to go his own way, to do his own thing—to disobey God. He rejected the tree of life and ate of the tree of knowledge of good and evil. (See notes—Ge.2:16-17; 3:1-6; see 3:8-9; He.9:27.)

Several things need to be said at this point about both the tree of life and the tree of the knowledge of good and evil. Are the trees figurative or literal? To hold that they are literal is neither naive nor magical.
a. Something—some object, some act—had to be chosen for man to exercise his ability or choice *for God* and for life with Him. Note this: man was within nature, within the most beautiful Garden of the world. The Garden had the most excellent trees of the world, and the trees bore the most luscious fruit in the world. One of man's basic needs and drives was to satisfy his hunger with the luscious fruit so richly provided. What better way for man to exercise his ability or choice for God than through the flesh, than to have a commandment involving the fruit needed to meet his physical need for food?
In fact, forbidding fruit within such an environment as the Garden of Eden would be *the very thing* for God to do—the natural, expected thing.
b. No tree, within itself, has the power to give life or death. No tree or fruit has such inherent power. Any fruit that has such power would have such power only because God gave it life-producing qualities, chemicals, or juices. We all know this.
Scripture says this is exactly what God did: God gave life producing qualities to the tree of life and death producing, corruptible qualities to the tree of the knowledge of good and evil. Note three significant points about this fact:
⇒ First, this is exactly what Scripture says. It is the *literal statement* of the account of Genesis.
⇒ Second, God is God—Elohim, Almighty God, the God of all might and power (see DEEPER STUDY # 2—Ge.1:1). God can decree such power to any food He wishes.
⇒ Third, as stated in point one, any person is hard pressed to choose a better method for man to exercise his choice for God and eternity, hard pressed to choose a better method when man is within a garden such as the Garden of Eden.

c. Now having said the above, there is one other possibility about the life and death qualities of the trees. It is possible that the trees and their fruit were the objects (vehicle, method, manner) chosen for man to exercise his spiritual choice to live with God or apart from God. It is possible that God's Word decreed life or death for man—based upon man's choice. It is possible that the trees possessed no qualities or chemicals or juices to give life or death, that they were only the objects used for man to exercise his freedom to choose to obey God. God, His Word, decreed that to eat of the tree of life gave life; to eat of the other tree brought death. The trees were only the things used to bring about what God had already said. The power of life and death rested in what God had decreed and man chose to do, not in the trees themselves. (See note 3 and DEEPER STUDY # 2—Ge.2:16-17.)

"See, I have set before thee this day life and good and death and evil" (De.30:15).
"I call heaven and earth to record this day against you, that I have set before you life and death, blessing and cursing: therefore choose life, that both thou and thy seed may live" (De.30:19).

130

"And if it seem evil unto you to serve the Lord, choose you this day whom ye will serve...but as for me and my house, we will serve the Lord" (Jos.24:15).

"And Elijah came unto all the people, and said, How long halt ye between two opinions? if the Lord be God, follow him" (1 K.18:21).

6 (2:10-14) **Man, Needs—Garden of Eden**: the Garden of Eden met man's need for water and irrigation. God caused a river to flow through Eden, apparently a great river. It was large enough to irrigate the whole Garden and to break out into four major rivers. The purpose for listing the four rivers and several of the surrounding lands was...
- to show that the Garden of Eden had been a real Garden
- to show that the first man, Adam, was a real person
- to show that the account of Genesis is not only accurate, but it is truth
- to show the truth of how God created man and placed man in the Garden and the truth of what happened to man

Note the facts given:

The Rivers	The Facts
Pison	It flowed through the land of Havilah, the Havilah that is known for its gold, bdellium (a valuable gem), and the onyx stone.
Gihon	It flowed through the land of Ethiopia.
Hiddekel or Tigris	It flowed along the east side of Assyria.
Euphrates	It flowed from the highlands of Armenia down into the Persian Gulf.
	It was known as "the great river," the most important river in Western Asia.

Now, where was the Garden of Eden located? Note that two of the rivers are known today, the Tigris and the Euphrates, but two are not known. Most likely, the catastrophic flood in Noah's day rearranged the earth's geography and eliminated the two unknown rivers. But note this as well: the flood was so catastrophic that it most likely rearranged the beds and channels of the Tigris and Euphrates. To think otherwise would be unrealistic, for the devastation and rearrangement of the geography of the earth's surface by torrential rains and severe floods are too well known today. Therefore, it is impossible to say just where the Garden of Eden was located. The closest that we can say with accuracy is that it was someplace in the lands that surround the Tigris and Euphrates rivers, lands that actually cover several nations of the world such as Armenia, Turkey, Syria, Iraq, and Iran. H.C. Leupold thinks that it may have been in the Armenian highlands;[2] others think that it may have been in southern Iraq (see NIV, Ge.2:8).

Now, back to the major thrust of this point: God caused a great river to flow through Eden, a river that separated into four other rivers as it flowed out of Eden. This shows the glorious goodness and care of God. God made every provision for man, even to seeing that man had water to drink and an irrigation system to water the growth of the Garden.

Thought 1. God makes two great promises to man today.
1) God will provide all the necessities of life for man if man will first seek Him and His righteousness.

"But seek ye first the kingdom of God, and his righteousness; and all these things shall be added unto you" (Mt.6:33).

2) God has provided a living water that gives man eternal life, a living water that is found in His Son, the Lord Jesus Christ.

"But whosoever drinketh of the water that I shall give him shall never thirst; but the water that I shall give him shall be in him a well of water springing up into everlasting life" (Jn.4:14).

"And Jesus said unto them, I am the bread of life: he that cometh to me shall never hunger; and he that believeth on me shall never thirst" (Jn.6:35).

"He that believeth on me, as the scripture hath said, out of his belly shall flow rivers of living water. (But this spake he of the Spirit, which they that believe on him should receive: for the Holy Ghost was not yet given; because that Jesus was not yet glorified)" (Jn.7:38-39).

"And he said unto me, It is done. I am Alpha and Omega, the beginning and the end. I will give unto him that is athirst of the fountain of the water of life freely" (Re.21:6).

"And the Spirit and the bride say, Come. And let him that heareth say, Come. And let him that is athirst come. And whosoever will, let him take the water of life freely" (Re.22:17).

"Therefore with joy shall ye draw water out of the wells of salvation" (Is.12:3).

"And the LORD shall guide thee continually, and satisfy thy soul in drought, and make fat thy bones: and thou shalt be like a watered garden, and like a spring of water, whose waters fail not" (Is.58:11).

"In that day there shall be a fountain opened...for sin and for uncleanness" (Zec.13:1).

---

2 H.C. Leupold. *Genesis*, Vol.1, p.126.

DEEPER STUDY # 2

(2:10) Adam vs. Christ—Gethsemane vs. The Garden of Eden—The Cross vs. the Tree of the Knowledge of Good and Evil: there is a strong contrast between the *first Adam* in his Garden of Eden and the *second Adam*, the Lord Jesus Christ, in His Garden of Gethsemane. (The idea for the contrast was stirred by James Montgomery Boice.[3] Remember that our Lord was facing the critical decision of the cross in the Garden of Gethsemane.

The First Adam in His Garden of Eden	The Second Adam, the Lord Jesus Christ, in His Garden of Gethsemane
Adam was in a perfect Garden within a perfect world (Ge.1:1; 2:8-9).	Christ was in a barren, desert-like garden in an imperfect world (Ge.3:17-18; Ro.8:19-22).
Adam was in a Garden of beauty and joy (Ge.2:8-10).	Christ was in a place of heaviness and sorrow (Mt.26:37).
Adam was seeking to fulfill his own desires and cravings (Ge.2:17; 3:6).	Christ was seeking to do the will of God (Mt.26:39; He.10:7-10).
Adam disobeyed God and sinned and brought death to the human race (Ge.2:17; 3:1f; Ro.5:12).	Christ obeyed God and died for man and brought life to the human race (Jn.3:16; Ro.5:8; 1 Pe.2:24; 3:18).

There is also a strong contrast between the tree of the knowledge of good and evil and the tree of the cross. (The idea for this contrast was stirred by Arthur Pink.[4])

The Tree of the Knowledge of Good and Evil	The Tree of the Cross
The tree was planted by God (Ge.2:8-9).	The tree of the cross was made by man (Jn.19:15-16).
The tree was pleasant to the eyes (Ge.3:6).	The tree of the cross was a repulsive, cursed tree (Ga.3:13).
Man was commanded to turn away from this tree (Ge.2:17).	Man is commanded to come near this tree (Jn.12:32).
Eating of its fruit resulted in death (Ge.2:17; 3:1f; Ro.5:12).	Eating of this fruit—of Christ Himself—results in life (Jn.6:53-54; see Jn.6:51,58).

---

[3] James Montgomery Boice. *Genesis,* Vol.1, p.104f.
[4] Arthur Pink. *Gleanings in Genesis.* (Chicago, IL: Moody Press, 1922), p.27f.

	D. The First Charge or Covenant: Man's Purpose Upon the Earth,[DS1] 2:15-17

1. To know the goodness & grace of God
2. To serve God by working & taking care of the garden
3. To choose life with God: Love, worship, & fellowship[DS2]
   a. The incentive to choose life with God
   b. The one prohibition
 	
   c. The result of disobedience: Death[DS3]
	15 And the LORD God took the man, and put him into the garden of Eden to dress it and to keep it.
	16 And the LORD God commanded the man, saying, Of every tree of the garden thou mayest freely eat:
	17 But of the tree of the knowledge of good and evil, thou shalt not eat of it: for in the day that thou eatest thereof thou shalt surely die.

DIVISION II

ADAM, THE FIRST MAN (PART 1): THE BEGINNING OF MANKIND AND OF THE GODLY SEED—WHAT HAPPENED TO MAN AND THE EARTH, 2:4–3:24

D. The First Charge or Covenant: Man's Purpose Upon the Earth, 2:15-17

(2:15-17) **Introduction—Man, Purpose—Creation, Purpose**: above all other verses in the creation account, these verses show why God created man. Very simply stated, God wants to live with a being who chooses—freely chooses—to live with Him. God wants to live with a being who has the ability to choose to live with Him and who *will choose* to live with Him. God wants to live with a being who has freedom of choice, a being...

- who will choose to know God, to know the goodness and grace of God
- who will choose to serve God
- who will choose to live with God: to love, worship, and fellowship with God

God does not want to coerce man; God does not want man to be a robot that has been run off an assembly line and programmed to serve and worship God. God wants man to have freedom of choice, the ability to choose to live either with God or apart from God.

This is clearly seen by looking at the nature of man revealed in these verses.

⇒ Man is seen *to be highly intelligent and physically strong*. He is made responsible for thinking, planning, and cultivating the Garden (v.15).

⇒ Man is seen *to have the ability to communicate* with others. God is seen talking and sharing with him (vv.16-17).

⇒ Man is seen *to have the ability to will and to choose*. He possesses freedom of will (vv.16-17).

⇒ Man is seen *to have needs and drives* that have to be met both by his environment and by God. His environment has to provide work, food, and beauty for him. God has to provide instructions, directions, love, worship, fellowship, and purpose, meaning, and significance for him (vv.15-17).

⇒ Man is seen *to be a spiritual being* who requires spiritual direction and godly fellowship for his life (vv.15-17).

⇒ Man is seen *to be a being who is very capable of responding* to others, of loving and of expressing appreciation to others. God is here interacting with him (vv.15-17).

⇒ Man is seen *to have been a being of perfection and of immortality*, a being who was morally perfect, physically perfect, and spiritually perfect. Man was originally a being who was not corrupted and did not die and had never been separated from God.

⇒ Man is seen *to be a being who has desires and urges* that push him toward that which appeals to the flesh and which looks attractive and beneficial. The trees in the Garden and the prohibition governing the tree of the knowledge of good and evil show this (vv.16-17).

⇒ Man is seen *to be a being of curiosity*—a being who has the drive to know more and more, even if the knowledge leads to evil (see the development of war weapons) (v.17).

Much is revealed about the nature of man in these three brief verses, and much more could be added to the list above. But enough has been given to make the point: God has created man with freedom of choice. God wants to live with persons who choose to live with Him. God does not want persons with Him who do not want to be with Him. God wants to share His grace and goodness with those who want to experience His grace and goodness. This is the discussion of this informative passage of Scripture. These verses cover *The First Charge or Covenant: Man's Purpose Upon Earth.*

1. To know the goodness and grace of God (v.15).
2. To serve God by working and taking care of the Garden (or world) (v.15).
3. To choose life with God: love, worship, and fellowship (vv.16-17).

(2:15-25) **Another Outline**: the purpose of man.
 1. Purpose 1: kinship—to be like God (1:26).
 2. Purpose 2: dominion and authority—to rule over God's creation (1:28).
 3. Purpose 3: worship (2:3).
 4. Purpose 4: fellowship and enjoyment (2:8; see 3:8f).
 5. Purpose 5: service and work (2:15).
 6. Purpose 6: obedience and loyalty (2:16-17).
 7. Purpose 7: companionship (2:18-25).

DEEPER STUDY # 1
(2:15-17) **Covenant**: a covenant is a specific agreement between two or more persons. There are three types of covenants seen in the Bible.
 1. An agreement between two or more persons who freely agree to the terms of the contract or covenant (Ge.21:32).
 2. An agreement imposed by a superior party demanding obedience from the weaker party (Eze.17:13-14). This is also seen when God demands obedience from man by issuing certain commandments (Ge.2:16-17; Jos.23:16).
 3. An unconditional agreement or promise—what might be called a covenant of mercy or grace—whereby God obligates Himself to help or to reconcile sinful man (De.7:6-8; Ps.89:3-4; see Ge.3:15).

The word covenant is used about 253 times in the Old Testament and twenty times in the New Testament. Many of these are used in reference to the ark of the covenant that sat in the holy of holies, the inner sanctuary of the Jewish tabernacle which was the worship center of Israel.
 H.C. Leupold says that covenants made by God...
 • *"[Are] the most solemn and binding form of...promise,*
 • *"[Are] given for man's double assurance and because of man's carnal weakness...*
 • *"[Are] not to be put on a parallel with human covenants in which two contracting parties meet on the same level and make mutual pledges...*
 • *"Emanate [come] from God...He makes them, He fixes the terms and the conditions, He in sovereign freedom binds Himself"*[1].

Scholars differ as to the actual number of covenants in the Bible. However, Scripture discusses at least nine covenants or promises and charges. (See outlines and notes of each at the references given for additional information.)
 ⇒ The covenant of Eden whereby God meets man's most basic needs (Ge.2:15-17).
 ⇒ The covenant with Adam whereby God promises redemption (Ge.3:15).
 ⇒ The covenant with Noah whereby God preserves the human race (Ge.9:8-17).
 ⇒ The covenant with Abraham whereby God begins a new race (the Jewish race) to be the chosen line of God's people (Ge.12:1-3; 15:9-21; 17:1-27).
 ⇒ The covenant with Moses whereby God promises that Israel can be His chosen people (Ex.19:5-6).
 ⇒ The covenant with God's priestly servants whereby God promises to establish an everlasting priesthood (Nu.25:12-13; Mal.2:4-5; Eze.44:15).
 ⇒ The covenant with Israel whereby God promises to gather Israel back to the promised land (from being scattered all over the earth) (De.30:1-3).
 ⇒ The covenant with David whereby God promises to send the Messiah through David's family. The Messiah was to be "the Son of David" (2 S.7:16; 23:5).
 ⇒ The covenant with believers whereby God reconciles man to Himself through Christ (Je.31:31-34; see He.8:6-13, esp. 8. See Is.42:6; 49:8; 2 Co.3:6-18; He.7:22; 8:6-13.)

---

1 (2:15) **Man, Purpose—Creation, Purpose**: Man's purpose is to know the goodness and grace of God. Why did God create man? Why does man exist? What is the purpose of life? As stated, man's purpose is to know the goodness and grace of God. God wants to share the riches of His goodness and grace with man—the overflowing riches of His goodness and grace. This is clearly seen in what God did for the first man, Adam.
 God made a paradise—the Garden of Eden—for man. The Garden was the most perfect paradise imaginable. Remember: the earth was perfect, but God wanted a place that would be very, very special for man—a place of unmatched splendor, beauty, provision, fellowship, and perfection. The Garden of Eden far exceeded the outside world. Adam could compare the two, for he had lived in the outside world for some time. Just how long is unknown, but he had been there and walked about (Ge.2:8, 15).
 But note what happened (v.15): God took Adam and placed him in the Garden of Eden. He had been outside the Garden, but God wanted him within its boundaries. God wanted Adam to know and experience paradise, the great gift of God, the glorious goodness and grace of God.
 The point is this: God created the most glorious home imaginable for man, paradise itself, the Garden of Eden. Man already had a perfect earth, but a perfect earth could not hold nor adequately show the infinite goodness and grace of God. Therefore, God created paradise itself—a place where man could behold all the splendor, beauty, provision, fellowship, and perfection of God's goodness and grace.

 Thought 1. God's purpose for man has not been defeated despite the sin of Adam. God will not allow His purpose to be defeated, not ever—not by anything nor by anyone. Everything that was lost by Adam's sin has been

---

[1] H.C. Leupold. *Genesis*, Vol.1, p.336.

regained by Christ. How? By Christ's death. Remember: God's purpose for creating man is to show man the riches of His goodness and grace. No greater love could ever be shown than for God to give His Son to die for the sins of man. This is exactly what happened in the death of Christ. The summit of goodness and grace is seen in this: God gave His Son to bear the condemnation, punishment, and judgment for man's sin. When a man believes that *Christ died for him*, God takes that man's belief and counts it as the death of Christ. God counts the man as having died with Christ. The man's punishment has therefore been paid: he has died with Christ. Consequently, he is freed from sin: he stands perfect and acceptable to God. By Christ—by faith in Christ—man is freed from sin; man is able to be restored to perfection and righteousness.

> "But God, who is rich in mercy, for his great love wherewith he loved us, Even when we were dead in sins, hath quickened us together with Christ, (by grace ye are saved;) And hath raised us up together, and made us sit together in heavenly places in Christ Jesus: That in the ages to come he might show the exceeding riches of his grace in his kindness toward us through Christ Jesus" (Ep.2:4-7).
> "And he believed in the Lord; and he counted it to him for righteousness" (Ge.15:6).
> "Even as Abraham believed God, and it was accounted to him for righteousness" (Ga.3:6).
> "Who his own self bare our sins in his own body on the tree, that we, being dead to sins, should live unto righteousness: by whose stripes ye were healed" (1 Pe.2:24).

But how about paradise? How can a perfect earth and a perfect paradise be restored? By the promise and power of God. God has promised to recreate a new heavens and a new earth, to create a paradise throughout the whole universe for man. The day is coming when God will show the riches of His goodness and grace beyond anything we can ask or think. When? In the glorious day of redemption and of eternity.

> "That in the ages to come he might show the exceeding riches of his grace in his kindness toward us through Christ Jesus" (Ep.2:7).
> "For I reckon that the sufferings of this present time are not worthy to be compared with the glory which shall be revealed in us. For the earnest expectation of the creature waiteth for the manifestation of the sons of God. For the creature was made subject to vanity, not willingly, but by reason of him who hath subjected the same in hope, Because the creature itself also shall be delivered from the bondage of corruption into the glorious liberty of the children of God. For we know that the whole creation groaneth and travaileth in pain together until now" (Ro.8:18-22).
> "But the day of the Lord will come as a thief in the night; in the which the heavens shall pass away with a great noise, and the elements shall melt with fervent heat, the earth also and the works that are therein shall be burned up. Seeing then that all these things shall be dissolved, what manner of persons ought ye to be in all holy conversation and godliness, Looking for and hasting unto the coming of the day of God, wherein the heavens being on fire shall be dissolved, and the elements shall melt with fervent heat? Nevertheless we, according to his promise, look for new heavens and a new earth, wherein dwelleth righteousness" (2 Pe.3:10-13).

Thought 2. Note that God put Adam in the Garden. The greatest thing in all the world is to be called and placed by God. No matter where it is, the place God chooses for us is the best place to be.

2 (2:15) **Man, Purpose—Labor—Work—Employment**: man's purpose is to serve God by working and taking care of the Garden—the paradise in which he lives. God had given Adam the Garden—the most perfect, beautiful, and bountiful paradise imaginable—and God expected Adam to work and keep up the Garden. Note three significant facts.

a. Man was to look after the Garden. He was to *dress* (abhadh) it. The word means to work, till, cultivate, dress, and serve the Garden. Man was also to *keep* (shamar) the Garden. This word means to watch over, to guard, to keep, to look after, to take care of. The point is this: man was made responsible—personally responsible—for the Garden of Eden. The Garden was paradise: it was the most perfect, beautiful, and bountiful place imaginable, but it had to be looked after and cared for. This duty was placed upon man. Man was...

- to till and cultivate the land
- to dress the orchards, shrubs, and flowers
- to feed and provide for himself
- to keep the growth under control
- to look after and care for the animals

Simply stated, man was to keep paradise as paradise. God had created the Garden, the most perfect, beautiful, and bountiful paradise imaginable; it was up to man to keep the Garden perfect, beautiful, and bountiful.

b. Man was created to be a responsible person and an active, working person. Man was not made to be irresponsible nor to be inactive, idle, slothful, complacent, or lazy. He was made to work and to work hard.

> "And God blessed them, and God said unto them, Be fruitful, and multiply, and replenish the earth, and subdue it: and have dominion over the fish of the sea, and over the fowl of the air, and over every living thing that moveth upon the earth" (Ge.1:28).
> "Not slothful in business; fervent in spirit; serving the Lord" (Ro.12:11).

"Servants, obey in all things your masters according to the flesh; not with eyeservice, as menpleasers; but in singleness of heart, fearing God: And whatsoever ye do, do it heartily, as to the Lord, and not unto men; Knowing that of the Lord ye shall receive the reward of the inheritance: for ye serve the Lord Christ" (Col.3:22-24).

"For even when we were with you, this we commanded you, that if any would not work, neither should he eat" (2 Th.3:10).

"And ye shall serve the Lord your God, and he shall bless thy bread, and thy water; and I will take sickness away from the midst of thee" (Exo.23:25).

"I went by the field of the slothful, and by the vineyard of the man void of understanding; And, lo, it was all grown over with thorns, and nettles had covered the face thereof, and the stone wall thereof was broken down" (Prov.24:30-31).

"By much slothfulness the building decayeth; and through idleness of the hands the house droppeth through" (Ec.10:18)

c. Man was created to have a strong sense of purpose and of self-worth. Man is a mental and emotional creature. Man needs strong purpose in life, to feel that he is worthwhile, that what he does matters and is significant and counts for something. Man also needs strong self-image, to feel that he is somebody, a person who matters to other people. Both purpose and self-image come—to a great degree—from the work that a man does. If a man's work is significant, then he has a reason for getting up in the morning and living, and he feels worthwhile and has a strong purpose and self-image. This is the way God made man. This is the reason God charged man to work and to look after the Garden and the world. Man needs to think, plan, discover, work, and do something profitable. From such mammoth responsibility, man's sense of purpose and self-worth are somewhat met. (Note: mental and emotional needs—purpose and self-worth—are only partially met by the physical world and responsibility within it. The most satisfying sense of purpose and self-worth comes from having one's spiritual needs met. This is discussed in the next note—Ge.2:16-17.)

Thought 1. Paradise has been lost and the earth has been corrupted. Adam's sin and fall destroyed both. But Jesus Christ has promised to restore both. He has promised...

• to recreate a new heavens and earth, a perfect universe.

• to create the most perfect, beautiful, and bountiful paradise imaginable—a city that will glisten with all the jewels and glory of God Himself—a city that will be the summit of perfection and provision—a city that will be the very city of God and Christ—a city that will serve as the capital of the universe, and be named the City of God, the Holy City, the New Jerusalem.

The point is this: every person should make sure he is acceptable to God, that he is to be a citizen of the new heavens and earth, of the coming paradise of God (see outline and notes—Rev.21:1-22:5 for more discussion).

"But the day of the Lord will come as a thief in the night; in the which the heavens shall pass away with a great noise, and the elements shall melt with fervent heat, the earth also and the works that are therein shall be burned up. Seeing then that all these things shall be dissolved, what manner of persons ought ye to be in all holy conversation and godliness, Looking for and hasting unto the coming of the day of God, wherein the heavens being on fire shall be dissolved, and the elements shall melt with fervent heat? Nevertheless we, according to his promise, look for new heavens and a new earth, wherein dwelleth righteousness" (2 Pe.3:10-13).

"And I saw a new heaven and a new earth: for the first heaven and the first earth were passed away; and there was no more sea. And I John saw the holy city, new Jerusalem, coming down from God out of heaven, prepared as a bride adorned for her husband. And I heard a great voice out of heaven saying, Behold, the tabernacle of God is with men, and he will dwell with them, and they shall be his people, and God himself shall be with them, and be their God. And God shall wipe away all tears from their eyes; and there shall be no more death, neither sorrow, nor crying, neither shall there be any more pain: for the former things are passed away. And he that sat upon the throne said, Behold, I make all things new. And he said unto me, Write: for these words are true and faithful" (Re.21:1-5).

"Of old hast thou laid the foundation of the earth: and the heavens are the work of thy hands. They shall perish, but thou shalt endure: yea, all of them shall wax old like a garment; as a vesture shalt thou change them, and they shall be changed: But thou art the same, and thy years shall have no end" (Ps.102:25-27).

"And all the host of heaven shall be dissolved, and the heavens shall be rolled together as a scroll: and all their host shall fall down, as the leaf falleth off from the vine, and as a falling fig from the fig tree" (Is.34:4).

"For, behold, I create new heavens and a new earth: and the former shall not be remembered, nor come into mind" (Is.65:17).

"For as the new heavens and the new earth, which I will make, shall remain before me, saith the Lord, so shall your seed and your name remain" (Is.66:22).

Thought 2. Paradise has been lost, and the earth has been corrupted, but the earth has not been destroyed. We still have our minds and bodies and we still have the earth upon which to live. Therefore, the charge of God still stands: man's purpose upon earth is still the same. We are to look after and take care of the earth. We are to cultivate it and keep it, watching ever so closely over its welfare. The earth—its soil, air, water, and growth—is to be preserved and protected, both for succeeding generations and for God.

"And God blessed them, and God said unto them, Be fruitful, and multiply, and replenish the earth, and subdue it: and have dominion over the fish of the sea, and over the fowl of the air, and over every living thing that moveth upon the earth" (Ge.1:28).

"And whatsoever ye do, do it heartily, as to the Lord, and not unto men; Knowing that of the Lord ye shall receive the reward of the inheritance: for ye serve the Lord Christ" (Col.3:23-24).

"Moreover it is required in stewards, that a man be found faithful" (1 Co.4:2).

"Therefore, my beloved brethren, be ye stedfast, unmovable, always abounding in the work of the Lord, forasmuch as ye know that your labour is not in vain in the Lord" (1 Co.15:58).

"As every man hath received the gift, even so minister the same one to another, as good stewards of the manifold grace of God" (1 Pe.4:10).

"If ye be willing and obedient, ye shall eat the good of the land" (Is.1:19).

3 (2:16-17) **Man, Purpose**: man's purpose is to choose to live with God—to love, worship, and fellowship with Him. Why did God create man? Why did God put man upon earth and not immediately into heaven? These two verses show us: God wants a being who chooses—freely chooses—to live with Him. God wants a creature with freedom of choice, a creature who *wills* to live with Him—who wills to love, worship, and fellowship with Him *supremely*. Note three significant points.

a. There was the great incentive for man to choose life with God. Man was given every tree in the Garden except one. Man had everything:

⇒ a home in paradise
⇒ perfection: he was sinless
⇒ all the trees and food of paradise
⇒ the tree of life, of immortality (Ge.2:9)
⇒ the love, presence, and fellowship of God

Man had the attraction, the appeal, the pull of all this. Man had the attraction and the right to *all the fruit* in the Garden. There was *only one fruit* he could not touch—only one fruit among *all the fruit*. There was no excuse for man ever choosing any fruit—or anything—over God. Man had the greatest incentive in all the world for choosing God. By choosing God, man had everything: every tree—all of the abundance and benefits of paradise itself.

"How shall we escape, if we neglect so great salvation; which at the first began to be spoken by the Lord, and was confirmed unto us by them that heard him" (He.2:3).

b. There was the great choice—the great test—that had to be made. It involved one simple prohibition. How was God going to *arrange* for man to exercise his freedom of choice, his will? How was God going to test man's choice—his love and loyalty—for God? Man had to be tested to show that he loved God above all else, that he wanted to live with God. The test was essential; otherwise, man would be nothing more than a robot. Note three significant facts.

1) There had to be something for man to choose other than God. If a man was to make a choice for God, the opportunity to turn away from God had to be present. Something—some object, some act—had to be chosen for man to exercise his ability or choice *for God* and for life with Him. Note this: man was within nature, within the most beautiful Garden of the world. The Garden had the most excellent trees of the world, and the trees bore the most luscious fruit in the world. One of man's basic needs and drives was to satisfy his hunger with the luscious fruit so richly provided. What better way for man to exercise his ability or choice for God than through the flesh, than to have a commandment involving the fruit needed to meet his physical need for food?

In fact, forbidding fruit within such an environment as the Garden of Eden would be the very thing for God to do—the natural, expected thing.

2) God gave man a choice, a very simple and easy choice. God set *only one* restriction, and that one restriction was *only upon one* tree. Adam could eat from every tree in the Garden except one, the tree of the knowledge of good and evil. Note: the command in the Hebrew is in the strongest language possible: you *must not*, *absolutely must not*, eat of the tree.

3) God gave man this choice for a very specific reason: man is a spiritual being. Man was created with a need for God. Every thinking and honest person knows this, knows it down deep within his heart. But man not only needs God, man has the ability to live with God. Man can have his need met; man can seek after and come to know God. It is a matter of choice: man has to choose to live with God. The decision is up to man.

This is the reason God gave Adam this command. Adam needed God's Word—needed God to speak with him—needed God to fellowship and interact with him. Man needed God's Word, needed God to tell him in simple terms what to do and what not to do. It is in seeking after and in obeying God that man interacts and fellowships with God. This is clearly seen in Adam.

God simply said, "You may eat from every tree in the garden, but you may not eat from this one tree" (Ge.2:16-17). God spoke, set the course for man's life. Adam was to simply do what God said. Adam was to choose the life God had laid out for him.

⇒ Obeying meant choosing life with God forever; disobeying meant choosing death, separation from God forever (Ge.2:17; see DEEPER STUDY # 1—Heb.9:27; see Jn.3:18).
⇒ Obeying meant choosing fellowship with God; disobeying meant separating oneself from God.
⇒ Obeying meant choosing to serve God; disobeying meant choosing to serve self and Satan.
⇒ Obeying meant choosing to acknowledge God; disobeying meant rebelling against and ignoring God.
⇒ Obeying meant choosing to honor God; disobeying meant dishonoring God.

Thought 1. Adam had to choose; he had to make a decision. The tree was there. If he left the *forbidden fruit* alone, he would be obeying God and choosing to live with God. If he ate the fruit, he would be disobeying God and choosing to walk his own way in life.

The same is true with us. We have to choose; we have to make a decision. Jesus Christ, God's Son, has come to earth. He is there. If we ignore, neglect, deny, or rebel against Him, we disobey God and choose to live without God. If we receive Jesus Christ as our Savior, we obey God and choose to live with God.

> **"But as many as received him, to them gave he power to become the sons of God, even to them that believe on his name" (Jn.1:12).**
> **"For God so loved the world, that he gave his only begotten Son, that whosoever believeth in him should not perish, but have everlasting life" (Jn.3:16).**
> **"And this is his commandment, That we should believe on the name of his Son Jesus Christ, and love one another, as he gave us commandment" (1 Jn.3:23).**
> **"I call heaven and earth to record this day against you, that I have set before you life and death, blessing and cursing: therefore choose life, that both thou and thy seed may live" (De.30:19).**
> **"And if it seem evil unto you to serve the Lord, choose you this day whom ye will serve; whether the gods which your fathers served that were on the other side of the flood, or the gods of the Amorites, in whose land ye dwell: but as for me and my house, we will serve the Lord" (Jos.24:15).**
> **"But I trusted in thee, O Lord: I said, Thou art my God" (Ps.31:14).**

Thought 2. Man does not live by bread alone, but by every Word that comes out of the mouth of God. Life—true fellowship, worship, and service—with God is found by living in the Word of God and letting the Word live itself out in us.

> **"But he answered and said, It is written, Man shall not live by bread alone, but by every word that proceedeth out of the mouth of God" (Mt.4:4).**
> **"All scripture is given by inspiration of God, and is profitable for doctrine, for reproof, for correction, for instruction in righteousness: That the man of God may be perfect, thoroughly furnished unto all good works" (2 Ti.3:16-17).**
> **"That which we have seen and heard declare we unto you, that ye also may have fellowship with us: and truly our fellowship is with the Father, and with his Son Jesus Christ" (1 Jn.1:3).**
> **"I have chosen the way of truth: thy judgments have I laid before me" (Ps.119:30).**

c. There was the result of disobedience: death. The Hebrew literally says, "Dying, you shall die." If man disobeys God—fails to choose life with God—he dies. Death is sure, absolute, certain. It cannot be stopped.

In the Bible death means separation—separation from God. (See DEEPER STUDY # 2, *Death*—Ge.2:17 for more discussion.) If a man chooses to live without God, then he will not live with God. He will die—be separated, cut off from God. This is exactly what Adam chose. He turned away from God—away from God's Word—and turned to his own will and way in life. He did his own thing. As a result, he died.

> **"Many will say to me in that day, Lord, Lord, have we not prophesied in thy name? and in thy name have cast out devils? and in thy name done many wonderful works? And then will I profess unto them, I never knew you: depart from me, ye that work iniquity." (Mt.7:22-23).**

Thought 1. Note that death is to be feared by those who choose not to live with God. God warns man time and again.

> **"And as it is appointed unto men once to die, but after this the judgment" (He.9:27).**
> **"And then will I profess unto them, I never knew you: depart from me, ye that work iniquity" (Mt.7:23).**
> **"But the children of the kingdom shall be cast out into outer darkness: there shall be weeping and gnashing of teeth" (Mt.8:12).**
> **"The Son of man shall send forth his angels, and they shall gather out of his kingdom all things that offend, and them which do iniquity" (Mt.13:41).**
> **"Then said the king to the servants, Bind him hand and foot, and take him away, and cast him into outer darkness; there shall be weeping and gnashing of teeth" (Mt.22:13).**
> **"And shall cut him asunder, and appoint him his portion with the hypocrites: there shall be weeping and gnashing of teeth" (Mt.24:51).**
> **"And these shall go away into everlasting punishment: but the righteous into life eternal" (Mt.25:46).**
> **"And if thy hand offend thee, cut it off: it is better for thee to enter into life maimed, than having two hands to go into hell, into the fire that never shall be quenched...And if thy foot offend thee, cut it off: it is better for thee to enter halt into life, than having two feet to be cast into hell, into the fire that never shall be quenched...And if thine eye offend thee, pluck it out: it is better for thee to enter into the kingdom of God with one eye, than having two eyes to be cast into hell fire" (Mk.9:43, 45, 47).**

"He that believeth on the Son hath everlasting life: and he that believeth not the Son shall not see life; but the wrath of God abideth on him" (Jn.3:36).

"But unto them that are contentious, and do not obey the truth, but obey unrighteousness, indignation and wrath" (Rom.2:8).

"If any man defile the temple of God, him shall God destroy; for the temple of God is holy, which temple ye are" (1 Co.3:17).

"Who shall be punished with everlasting destruction from the presence of the Lord, and from the glory of his power" (2 Th.1:9).

"The Lord knoweth how to deliver the godly out of temptations, and to reserve the unjust unto the day of judgment to be punished" (2 Pe.2:9).

"But the heavens and the earth, which are now, by the same word are kept in store, reserved unto fire against the day of judgment and perdition of ungodly men" (2 Pe.3:7).

"Raging waves of the sea, foaming out their own shame; wandering stars, to whom is reserved the blackness of darkness for ever" (Jude 13).

"And whosoever was not found written in the book of life was cast into the lake of fire" (Re.20:15).

"But the fearful, and unbelieving, and the abominable, and murderers, and whoremongers, and sorcerers, and idolaters, and all liars, shall have their part in the lake which burneth with fire and brimstone: which is the second death" (Re.21:8).

DEEPER STUDY # 2

(2:16-17) **Man, Nature of—Sin, Meaning of**: there are at least six more significant facts that need to be looked at in this brief passage.

1. Adam's nature. Adam had been created *innocent*, with an innocent human nature. He did not know evil. He had never tasted or experienced evil; therefore, the pull and taste of evil from experience was not within him. Adam had no idea what evil would taste or feel like. He was innocent, perfectly innocent; therefore, he did not know the difference between good and evil.

The point is this: God created Adam with the ability, the power, the capacity not to sin. True, Adam had the power to sin, but he also had the power not to sin.

But if Adam chose to sin, he would then know good and evil; he would lose the power not to sin. How? By sinning. By sinning he would become a sinful being. He could never again be innocent or perfect. He would be a being who had fallen below what God wanted, a being with a fallen human nature—a nature that is corruptible and that dies (see Deeper Study # 1—Mt.6:19; note—1 Co.15:50; Deeper Study # 1—2 Pe.1:4 for discussion).

2. Adam's moral nature. Adam was given a choice. He had free choice, freedom of will. He was a *free being*. But more than this, Adam was a free *moral being*. His morality is seen in the decision he had to make. If he obeyed God, he was moral and just; if he disobeyed God, he was immoral and unjust.

3. The nature of sin, morality, and justice. Morality and justice are essentially obeying God. Sin—immorality and injustice—is essentially disobeying God.

4. Man's need for God's Word. Man needs God's Word, desperately needs it. Living by God's Word is the only way man can ever live abundantly and eternally. This is the reason God had to give man (Adam) His Word, His commandment. This is clearly seen by noting the difference between animals and man. Animals are soulish beings (see Deeper Study # 1—Ge.1:20 for discussion). They are not given God's Word to live by. They are not spiritual beings. They are not immortal nor do they have the choice—drive and ability—to live with God. Animals do not have the capacity to love, worship, or fellowship with God. They act only as the physical—their flesh, mind, and urges—dictate. They desire only this world and are driven to live and act only for this world. Therefore, they never know anything but this world.

But not so man. God made man a spiritual being, that is...

- a being who is *immortal*
- a being with the choice—the *need, drive, and ability*—to choose life with God, both now and eternally (see Deeper Study # 2—Ge.1:26).

God meets man's spiritual need by giving man God's Word: "Of every tree of the garden thou mayest freely eat: but of the tree of the knowledge of good and evil, thou shalt not eat of it" (Ge.2:16-17). By this Word from God, man exercises his ability to choose to live with God. He keeps his spirit alive by obeying and doing what God says. In doing what God says, man lives with God—loves, worships, and fellowships with Him. Consequently, God gives man life, both now and eternally.

5. God's great love and care for man is shown in these verses.

   a. Man was placed in the most beautiful surrounding and environment imaginable. The surroundings clearly showed man just how good it was to live in fellowship with God, and the beautiful surroundings attracted and pulled man to God (v.15).

   b. Man had every need met by God through his environment and the commandment (the Word of God) given him (vv.15-17).

   c. Man was given every tree in the Garden. Only one tree was withheld (vv.16-17).

   d. Man was clearly told the consequences of his behavior. The warning of death was given if he rejected God (v.17).

   e. Man was given a magnificent opportunity to respond, to love, and show appreciation to God (v.16-17). He could have chosen God, chosen to live with God and to love, worship, and fellowship with God.

6. What God did for man. Up to this point, three significant steps have been taken with man since his creation.

a. Man was created a spiritual being; that is, he was created in the image and likeness of God. This means at least two things:
   ⇒ Man has the need and drive for immortality.
   ⇒ Man has the need and ability (choice) to live with God—to love, worship, and fellowship with God.

b. Man was placed in an environment that met his needs. To varying degrees his environment met his physical, mental, and spiritual needs.

c. Man was given God's Word to live by. God's Word was the course man was to follow throughout his life. In obeying God's Word, man was to exercise and keep his spirit alive and active. The vehicle chosen for God's Word and commandment was that which was most natural to man—his environment—the fruit from one of the trees for which he was responsible.

DEEPER STUDY # 3

(2:17) **Death**: the basic meaning of death is *separation*. Death does not mean what some people think: ceasing to exist. Death never means extinction, annihilation, non-existence, or inactivity.

The Bible speaks of three deaths.

1. Physical death: the *separation* of a man's spirit or life from the body. This is what men commonly call death. It is when a person ceases to exist on this earth and is buried (1 Co.15:21-22; Heb.9:27).

> **"For since by man came death, by man came also the resurrection of the dead. For as in Adam all die, even so in Christ shall all be made alive" (1 Co.15:21-22).**
> **"And as it is appointed unto men once to die, but after this the judgment" (He.9:27).**

2. Spiritual death: the *separation* of man's spirit from God while he is still living and walking upon earth. This death is the *natural state* of a man on earth without Christ. Man is seen as still in his sins and *dead* to God (Ep.2:1; 4:18; 1 Jn.5:12).

Spiritual death speaks of a person who is dead while he still lives (1 Ti.5:6). He is a natural man living in this present world, but he is said to be dead to the Lord Jesus Christ and to God and to spiritual matters.

a. A person who wastes his life in riotous living is spiritually dead.

> **"It was meet that we should make merry, and be glad: for this thy brother was dead, and is alive again; and was lost, and is found" (Lu.15:32).**

b. A person who has not partaken of Christ—allowed Christ to live within him—is spiritually dead.

> **"Then Jesus said unto them, Verily, verily, I say unto you, Except ye eat the flesh of the Son of man, and drink his blood, ye have no life in you" (Jn.6:53).**

c. A person who does not have the Spirit of Christ is said to be spiritually dead.

> **"But ye are not in the flesh, but in the Spirit, if so be that the Spirit of God dwell in you. Now if any man have not the Spirit of Christ, he is none of his" (Rom.8:9).**

d. A person who lives in sin is said to be spiritually dead.

> **"And you hath he quickened, who were dead in trespasses and sins" (Ep.2:1).**
> **"And you, being dead in your sins and the uncircumcision of your flesh, hath he quickened together with him, having forgiven you all trespasses" (Col.2:13).**

e. A person who is alienated from God is said to be spiritually dead.

> **"Having the understanding darkened, being alienated from the life of God through the ignorance that is in them, because of the blindness of their heart: Who being past feeling have given themselves over unto lasciviousness, to work all uncleanness with greediness" (Ep.4:18-19).**

f. A person who sleeps in sin is spiritually dead.

> **"Wherefore he saith, Awake thou that sleepest, and arise from the dead, and Christ shall give thee light" (Ep.5:14).**

g. A person who lives in sinful pleasure is spiritually dead, dead while he lives.

> **"But she that liveth in pleasure is dead while she liveth" (1 Ti.5:6).**

h. A person who does not have the Son of God is spiritually dead.

> **"He that hath the Son hath life; and he that hath not the Son of God hath not life" (1 Jn.5:12).**

i. A person who does great religious works but does the wrong works is spiritually dead.

> **"And unto the angel of the church in Sardis write; These things saith he that hath the seven Spirits of God, and the seven stars; I know thy works, that thou hast a name that thou livest, and art dead" (Re.3:1).**

3. Eternal death: the *separation* of man from God's presence forever. This is the second death, an eternal state of being *dead to God* (1 Co.6:9-10; 2 Th.1:9). It is spiritual death, separation from God, that is prolonged beyond the death of the body. It is called the "second death" or eternal death.

> **"For to be carnally minded is death; but to be spiritually minded is life and peace" (Rom.8:6).**
> **"And to you who are troubled rest with us, when the Lord Jesus shall be revealed from heaven with his mighty angels, In flaming fire taking vengeance on them that know not God, and that obey not the gospel of our Lord Jesus Christ: Who shall be punished with everlasting destruction from the presence of the Lord, and from the glory of his power" (2 Th.1:7-9).**
> **"And whosoever was not found written in the book of life was cast into the lake of fire" (Re.20:15).**

1. God's plan to create woman	**E. The First Woman: Man's Companion, Eve, 2:18-25**	caused a deep sleep to fall upon Adam, and he slept: and he took one of his ribs, and closed up the flesh instead thereof;	a. God put Adam to sleep & took a rib from him
a. Because it was not good for man to be alone	18 And the LORD God said, It is not good that the man should be alone; I will make him an help meet for him.		b. God created woman from the rib of Adam
b. Because man needed a helper, a companion		22 And the rib, which the LORD God had taken from man, made he a woman, and brought her unto the man.	4. **Man & woman were brought together by God: The facts governing the union**
2. **Man's need for woman**	19 And out of the ground the LORD God formed every beast of the field, and every fowl of the air; and brought them unto Adam to see what he would call them: and whatsoever Adam called every living creature, that was the name thereof.		a. The union was of God
a. God reemphasizes that He is the Creator of all man's companions, of all living creatures			b. Woman was equal to man in being
b. God shows man that man is superior to animals		23 And Adam said, This is now bone of my bones, and flesh of my flesh: she shall be called Woman, because she was taken out of Man.	c. Man was created before woman
1) In authority			
2) In intelligence			d. Marriage is the first institution of society
3) In being & person: A spiritual being	20 And Adam gave names to all cattle, and to the fowl of the air, and to every beast of the field; but for Adam there was not found an help meet for him.	24 Therefore shall a man leave his father and his mother, and shall cleave unto his wife: and they shall be one flesh.	1) To leave parents
			2) To cleave
			3) To be one flesh
c. God's purpose: To show man his great need for woman		25 And they were both naked, the man and his wife, and were not ashamed.	5. **Man & woman were created perfect, innocent, and without shame**
3. **Woman's creation by God**	21 And the LORD God		

DIVISION II

ADAM, THE FIRST MAN (PART 1): THE BEGINNING OF MANKIND AND OF THE GODLY SEED—WHAT HAPPENED TO MAN AND THE EARTH, 2:4–3:24

E. The First Woman: Man's Companion, Eve, 2:18-25

(2:18-25) **Introduction**: this is a precious passage of Scripture. There is within its words…
- the experience of need and desire (on Adam's part)
- the experience of caring and love (on God's part)
- the experience of promise and provision (by God)
- the experience of anticipation and excitement (by Adam)
- the experience of warmth and tenderness (by both Adam and Eve). (See outlines and notes—Ep.5:22-33 for more discussion.)

This is a great study on *The First Woman: Man's Companion, Eve.*
1. God's plan to create woman (v.18).
2. Man's need for woman (vv.19-20).
3. Woman's creation by God (vv.21-22).
4. Man and woman were brought together by God: the facts governing the union (vv.22-24).
5. Man and woman were created perfect, innocent, and without shame (v.25).

[1] (2:18) **Woman—Creation—Eve**: God planned woman. Woman was as much the creation of God as was man.

"So God created man in his own image, in the image of God created he him; male and female created he them" (Ge.1:27).

Note that the creation of woman is discussed in great detail in the present passage. Why? The primary reason seems to be this: to establish and set the relationship between man and woman forever.
⇒ Man and woman are related to each other—intimately so. They are bound together and they are totally dependent upon each other. One cannot exist without the other. Man and woman need each other, desperately need each other. God needed to reveal this fact for all generations.
⇒ Man and woman are different persons—distinct individuals. Each has a distinctive role upon earth; each was created for a different purpose. Each must fulfill his or her role in order to survive and to have a full and complete life. God also needed to reveal this fact for all generations.

Again, why does the Bible discuss the creation of woman in detail? To show that man and woman are related to each other—intimately so—but at the same time, to show that they are different from one another. Each is distinctive and unique with a distinctive role and purpose upon earth.

Note this: God planned woman's creation (v.18). It is God Himself who is planning and speaking in this event. The plan for woman's creation…

- was not just an afterthought
- was not an inferior plan
- was not of less importance
- was not given less attention and thought than the creation of man

On the contrary, the very opposite was true. This passage shows that great attention and thought were given to the creation of woman. The plan for woman's creation was worked out in great detail.

Note why God created woman. His purpose is clearly stated.

a. Woman was created because it was not good for man to be alone. The phrase "not good" means incomplete, unfinished, unfulfilled, deficient. Standing by himself—standing alone—man is...

- incomplete
- unfinished
- unfulfilled
- deficient
- lonely

Therefore, it was not good for man to be alone. Without woman, man would have no suitable companion for love and comfort. Neither would he be able to reproduce, nor to work and subdue the earth as God had instructed (see Ge.1:28). Without woman, man would have no person with whom to share life, not someone of his own nature. And since the corruption of the earth by sin, man would soon die out and be an extinct species.

The point is this: man was only half of God's plan for human life. Woman was the other half. God's plan was not complete until woman was created. Woman was as much a part of God's plan for human life as man was. Therefore, it was not good that man should be alone. Man was incomplete and deficient without woman. Man needed woman, desperately needed her. God knew this when He first began to plan for human life upon earth. Consequently, God planned the creation of woman, planned to create her right along with man.

Thought 1. The same problems afflict and plague man today:
⇒ loneliness
⇒ emptiness
⇒ deficiency
⇒ incompleteness
⇒ unfulfillment

God did not create man and woman to suffer such afflictions. But too many of us do, all because of sin. Is there an answer—deliverance—to these problems? Is there such a thing as a complete and fulfilled life—a life of purpose, meaning, and significance? Yes! Scripture declares there is. Scripture declares that Jesus Christ came to earth for this very purpose: to give us life, both abundant and eternal life. All we have to do is this: turn to Christ and follow Him. It is when we turn to Christ and follow Him that He gives us the life for which we long.

> **"In him was life; and the life was the light of man" (Jn.1:4).**
> **"Verily, verily, I say unto you, He that heareth my word, and believeth on him that sent me, hath everlasting life, and shall not come into condemnation; but is passed from death unto life" (Jn.5:24).**
> **"I am come that they might have life, and that they might have it more abundantly" (Jn.10:10).**
> **"Come unto me, all ye that labour and are heavy laden, and I will give you rest" (Mt.11:28).**
> **"Peace I leave with you, my peace I give unto you: not as the world giveth, give I unto you. Let not your heart be troubled, neither let it be afraid" (Jn.14:27).**
> **"Casting all your care upon him; for he careth for you" (1 Pe.5:7).**
> **"These things have I spoken unto you, that my joy might remain in you, and that your joy might be full" (Jn.15:11).**

b. God planned woman because man needed a helper, a companion—a *suitable* helper and companion. The Hebrew word *meet* or *suitable* (keneghdo) means fit, corresponding to, adapted to, agreeing with, counterpart, opposite, equal to. It means that the woman...

- was created as a suitable helper for man
- was created as a fit helper for man
- was adapted to the nature of man
- corresponded to the nature of man
- agreed with the nature of man
- was like the nature of man
- was an opposite and equal being for man

Another way to say the same thing is this: God planned woman...

- to be the counterpart to man
- to be of the very same nature as man
- to be of the very same rank as man
- to be suited to man mentally, physically, and morally

143

Note three significant points in this fact.

1) God's plan included the creation of woman just as His plan had included the creation of man. God created woman to be a true helper and companion for man. Man, of course, was to provide the same help and companionship for her. There is nothing in the plan of God about superiority and inferiority, nothing about a superior or inferior rank for woman nor for man. The idea that woman is inferior to man—a lesser being—has not come from God nor from His Word, the Holy Bible. It has come from depraved, sinful humanity and society.

2) The primary reason God planned the creation of woman was "for him"—for man (v.18). Man was incomplete—incomplete in an absolute sense—without woman. He was totally deficient. Creation was not finished with just man upon earth. Man needed woman, desperately needed her. Therefore, woman was created first and foremost *for man*. Woman was created to be the helper, the companion, the partner of man. Companionship—being the partner of man—is woman's primary function upon earth. This function exceeds all other purposes.

3) God created the first two humans to be the *parents of the human race*. They were to be companions, to live and work together as partners, helping each other every way they could. *As the parents of the human race*, they were to picture just what God wants the race to be: one family. This is one of the major points or revelations God is making in this passage. Man and woman are to be companions to each other, true companions, living and working together as one family, as God's family. The human race is to live together in peace—in the love, joy, and peace of a family.

Thought 1. It is God's plan for man and woman to help each other. This requires two things:
1) The willingness to help.
2) The willingness to receive and accept the offered help.

> "Wherefore receive ye one another, as Christ also received us to the glory of God" (Ro.15:7).
> "Bear ye one another's burdens, and so fulfil the law of Christ" (Ga.6:2).
> "Two are better than one; because they have a good reward for their labour. For if they fall, the one will lift up his fellow: but woe to him that is alone when he falleth; for he hath not another to help him up" (Ec.4:9-10).

Thought 2. There is no record of Adam complaining about his loneliness. He fellowshipped with God. God was all he knew, all he had. He made it enough. When and if we are forced to be alone, God will make His presence enough.

> "Lo, I am with you alway, even unto the end of the world" (Mt.28:20).
> "Let your conversation [behavior] be without covetousness; and be content with such things as ye have: for he hath said, I will never leave thee, nor forsake thee" (He.13:5).
> "And he said, My presence shall go with thee, and I will give thee rest" (Ex.33:14).
> "I have redeemed thee, I have called thee by thy name; thou art mine. When thou passest through the waters, I will be with thee; and through the rivers, they shall not overflow thee: when thou walkest through the fire, thou shalt not be burned; neither shall the flame kindle upon thee" (Is.43:1-2).

Thought 3. Several thoughts are applicable at this point.
1) A home should have rivers of communication and sharing running through its rooms. Yet, so many homes are like dried up deserts.
2) A person can be in the midst of a crowd or in the center of a family and still be all alone.

Thought 4. Note the picture painted of God in verse 18: God sees and cares. He saw Adam's need, and He sees our need. The picture is that of a fatherly care. If we walk with God as Adam walked, God will meet our need.

> "Casting all your care upon him; for he careth for you" (1 Pe.5:7).
> "But my God shall supply all your need according to his riches in glory by Christ Jesus" (Ph.4:19).

2 (2:19-20) **Man—Needs**: man's need for woman, for companionship. Note what the Bible now does: it switches from God's decision to create woman to God's creation of animals and to His instructing man to name the animals. Why? Why inject the creation and naming of animals right in the middle of God's creation of woman? There are at least three reasons.

a. God needed to reemphasize a critical fact: He is the Creator of all man's companions, of all living creatures. Man needed to learn this, to have it driven into his mind. If man was to have a special companion—a companion with his very own nature—God was the One who had to create her. Man had to depend upon God to give him the companion who would be a perfectly suitable partner.

Thought 1. This is still God's emphasis, even today: every man and woman should depend upon God to give them the very companion they need.

Thought 2. Note: some critics of the Bible say this is a second account—an entirely different account—of creation. Nothing could be further from the truth. The critics use the tense of "*God formed*" and say that it is a plain past tense. But many Biblical scholars point out that the Hebrew tense can be just as accurately, if not more accurately, translated "*God had formed*" (the pluperfect tense). Note what the great old commentary of Keil and Delitzsch says:

Our modern style of expressing the same thought would be simply this: "God brought to Adam the beasts which he had [already] formed."[1]

b. God shows man that he is superior to the animals. This is true in three significant areas.
1) Man has *superior authority over animals.* His authority is seen in the fact that God brought the animals to Adam to be named. The animals did not name man; man named the animals. God had given man dominion over the earth. God now turned over the animal world for man to begin exercising that authority. The animal world was thereafter under man's authority and keeping. (See note d—Ge.1:28 for more discussion.)
   Note: Scripture says that God brought the animals to Adam. Two logical questions need to be asked.
   First, how did God bring the animals? By having angels escort the animals to Adam? By some movement upon their hearts to go to Adam? Scripture does not say, but it is more natural to say that God moved upon the animals' hearts—gave them an intuitive sense—to go to Adam.
   Second, did all the animals of the earth go to Adam? Many Bible scholars say no, that only the animals in the Garden of Eden were named. However, note the Scripture: the indication seems to be that God created *every animal* and man named *every animal.* But note this: water animals such as fish are not mentioned.

   Thought 1. Man's authority over the world is seen from the beginning of known history. History reveals two significant things about man's authority:
   1) Man has used his authority for good in that he has made some progress in building up his world through medicine and technology.
   2) Man has also used his authority for depraved purposes: for the destruction of human life, nature, the environment, and the air and water we breathe and drink.

2) Man has *superior intelligence over animals.* The Hebrew words for *calling and naming* the animals have the idea of study and concentrated thought—study and thought that tries to match the names to the nature of an animal. Man's superior intelligence is seen in the following facts:
   • Man was able to control the animals so that he could name them. He held authority over them because of his superior intelligence.
   • Man was able to study, reason, and concentrate much longer than animals—long enough to give names to the animals, names that matched the animals' nature.
   • Man was able to research the nature of each animal. Then he demonstrated creativity by formulating names to match their nature.
   • Man was able to speak, to attach words to his thoughts, to vocalize his ideas.

   Thought 1. Down through the centuries, man has used his intelligence in both responsible and irresponsible ways, both for good and bad.
   1) Responsibly, man has sought to better his welfare upon earth both materially and mentally.
      ⇒ Materially he has sought to make himself more comfortable and healthy.
      ⇒ Mentally he has sought to learn more and more in order to better the life of all men and to control more and more of the natural world.

   2) Irresponsibly, man has turned much of his advancement in science and technology toward selfish ends, toward indulgence, extravagance, power, and authority over others—the selfishness that deprives others, that enslaves and destroys them.

3) Man has a *superior being and person* over animals. Man is a spiritual being. Apparently, as Adam began to associate with the animals, a fact began to dawn upon him; he realized something. There was not a suitable helper or companion for him. All the animals had mates, for God had created them with companions and with the capacity to reproduce. But not Adam. There was no companion for Adam. As he studied the nature of the animals and named them, a longing for companionship with a superior being must have arisen within his heart. Thus, Adam came to realize his need for a spiritual companion just like himself.

   Thought 1. There is a close association between man and animal, but there is also a vast difference between the two. Man and animal can to some degree communicate, play together, and enjoy each other. But in every case—without exception—man has to lower himself and meet the animal on its level. Never can the animal raise itself and meet man on his level. This is what Adam saw and sensed ever so deeply. There was no creature capable of being a companion to him. Adam needed woman, a being equal in person and nature with him.[2]

(Please note: all the *Thoughts* under point two above deal with man's supremacy over the world, not with the creation of woman. A person can take this point and teach a separate lesson on the *Supremacy of Man Over the Earth.* When dealing with the creation of woman, remember what God is doing in point 2 [vv.19-20]: showing man his great need for woman, for a companion just like himself. Despite man's great authority over the animal world, he still had no companion like himself, no companion with his superior nature.)

---

[1] Keil and Delitzsch. *Commentary on the Old Testament,* Vol.1. (Grand Rapids, MI: Eerdmans Publishing Co., n.d.), p.87.
[2] Arnold Toynbee in the tenth volume of his great history. James Montgomery Boice. *Genesis,* Vol.1, p.108.

c. God's purpose was to show man his great need for woman, for a companion just like himself. Picture Adam studying and observing the animals. As he researches their nature, at some point it dawns upon him that every living animal has a companion just like itself—except him. He realizes that creation is incomplete, that another act of creation is needed, a very special act of creation: God needs to create a companion for him. Note two significant points.

1) This method of showing Adam his need for woman was bound to have a tremendous impact upon Adam. It was bound to make Adam love and appreciate his dear wife far more than if God had created her at the same time he was created. When God created Eve, Adam was longing for her—longing with an intense desire. He knew how desperately he needed a companion who was just like himself, a companion with his very own nature.

2) This method of showing Adam his need for woman was God's way of showing man a fact that was to always be remembered: man and woman were created as equal beings, as two beings who were to be equal companions to one another, the counterpart to each other. Man was the stronger person *physically*. Therefore, God knew (as history has proven) that in many, if not all, societies man would tend to dominate the woman. Therefore, God needed to show man that woman is equal—equal by the very nature of her creation.

⇒ Woman was to be created by God as a unique individual just as man was.

⇒ Woman was to be taken from the body of man himself; therefore, she was to be made out of the same stuff as man (v.22).

⇒ Man was to hold the woman ever so dear to his heart—loving and respecting her ever so deeply—for she came both from God's hand and from man's very own body. She was of the *very same spiritual being* as Adam and of the *very same physical being* as Adam. She was both of God and of man.

The point is this: man and woman are equal in person and being. They differ only in that they have different roles and purposes upon earth (see notes—Ge.2:18; Ep.5:22-33 for more discussion).

Thought 1. Man has used his spiritual being in both good and bad ways. He has looked at the world in all its vastness, beauty, and design; and he has studied and researched its origin, wondering where everything has come from. He has asked: "Is there a Creator, a Supreme Intelligence and Force, a Personal God who has made the world and created man and woman?" Man has often seen the power and intelligence of God revealed in nature; he has seen that God does indeed exist. But man has too often become vain in his imagination and professed himself to be *too wise* to believe in a God beyond himself. As a result man has changed the image of the incorruptible God into the image of corruptible man. Man has too often claimed to be his own god (humanism and secularism).

"Because that, when they knew God, they glorified him not as God, neither were thankful; but became vain in their imaginations, and their foolish heart was darkened. Professing themselves to be wise, they became fools, and changed the glory of the incorruptible God into an image made like to corruptible man, and to birds, and fourfooted beasts, and creeping things" (Ro.1:21-23).

"For the heart of this people is waxed gross, and their ears are dull of hearing, and their eyes have they closed; lest they should see with their eyes, and hear with their ears, and understand with their heart, and should be converted, and I should heal them" (Ac.28:27).

"In whom the god of this world hath blinded the minds of them which believe not, lest the light of the glorious gospel of Christ, who is the image of God, should shine unto them" (2 Co.4:4).

"Having the understanding darkened, being alienated from the life of God through the ignorance that is in them, because of the blindness of their heart" (Ep.4:18).

"And God saw that the wickedness of man was great in the earth, and that every imagination of the thoughts of his heart was only evil continually" (Ge.6:5).

"The wicked, through the pride of his countenance, will not seek after God: God is not in all his thoughts" (Ps.10:4).

"They know not, neither will they understand; they walk on in darkness: all the foundations of the earth are out of course" (Ps.82:5).

"The LORD knoweth the thoughts of man, that they are vanity" (Ps.94:11).

Thought 2. The world and the things of the world can never satisfy the soul of man. Nothing can satisfy the spiritual hunger of man except God. Man's soul will always be incomplete, unfulfilled, dissatisfied, and restless until it comes to know God—know Him personally.

"Come unto me, all ye that labour and are heavy laden, and I will give you rest" (Mt.11:28).

"I am come that they might have life, and that they might have it more abundantly" (Jn.10:10).

"Come now, and let us reason together, saith the LORD: though your sins be as scarlet, they shall be as white as snow; though they be red like crimson, they shall be as wool" (Is.1:18).

"Ho, every one that thirsteth, come ye to the waters, and he that hath no money; come ye, buy, and eat; yea, come buy wine and milk without money and without price" (Is.55:1).

"Behold, I come quickly: blessed is he that keepeth the sayings of the prophecy of this book" (Re.22:7).

Thought 3. Some persons give more attention and affection to animals than to their own spouses or children. They substitute animals for those who are supposed to be their loved ones. How unlike God!

Thought 4. Note an extremely important point: the reason for man's superior authority is his superior intelligence, and the reason for his superior intelligence is his superior being, his spirit. It is his spirit, the image and likeness of God, that gives man superior intelligence and authority. All man's investigation and research into the world of nature should begin from this basis. Man is a spiritual being, a being made in the image and likeness of God.

3 (2:21-22) **Woman—Eve—Creation**: woman's creation by God. Woman's creation is a picture of the closeness—the great companionship—that God wants between husband and wife as they live and work together upon earth. The closeness and intimacy—the bond between man and woman—is immediately seen in the facts given.

a. God put Adam to sleep and took a rib from him. God did not create woman like He did man and the animal kingdom, independent of each other. Just like a surgeon, God carefully put Adam to sleep and Adam slept. The Hebrew word *slept* (tardemah) means a *deep, deep sleep*. God tenderly and meticulously operated upon Adam and removed a rib from his body.

b. God created the woman from the rib of Adam. God created woman out of the very body and being of man. Simply stated, God performed surgery upon man, took one of his ribs, and made woman out of that rib. Fantastic! Unbelievable! Unimaginable! No, not really—not when we look at the beautiful and meaningful reasons why God created woman this way. This is not a fable about the origin of the female species of humanity, not a myth as to how woman appeared upon earth and began her journey down through the centuries. The Biblical account is a simple explanation of exactly what happened. It is an accurate account. But why? Why would God not just form woman out of the dust of the ground as He did with man?

A careful study of this passage shows why. It shows that God had several beautiful and meaningful reasons for creating woman in this manner:
⇒ Woman came *out of man's need*. Therefore, she was to come *"out of man's"* being (vv.18, 21-23).
⇒ Woman was to be the object of man's *cleaving*. Therefore, woman was made out of man's being in order to cause a *natural clinging*, a reaching out for one another's own being, one another's own flesh (vv.23-24).
⇒ Woman was to be *one flesh* with man. Therefore, she was made out of the very flesh of man so that man and woman would have *identical natures* and stand as the *counterpart* to one another (vv.22-23).
⇒ Woman came *out of man's flesh* so that both would cherish and nurture the other. No person hates his own flesh. The very opposite is true: he cherishes, protects, and cares for it.

> **"So ought men to love their wives as their own bodies. He that loveth his wife loveth himself. For no man ever yet hated his own flesh; but nourisheth and cherisheth it, even as the Lord the church" (Ep.5:28-29).**

⇒ Woman is the *glory and crown of creation*, the being who brings more refinement to the world than any other creature.

> **"The woman is the glory of man" (1 Co.11:7).**

Woman is the glory and crown of both man and nature. Note this: the animals had just been created by God (Ge.1:20-25). *After* their creation, man was created out of the dust of the ground. He who was created *after* was more excellent and of more glory than the animals. But woman was made *after* man, and she was not taken out of the dust, but out of man himself. Woman's creation may, therefore, be said...
• to be more excellent and more glorious than man's, for she was twice removed from the dust of the earth
• to bring more refinement, beauty, and glory to the earth
• to be the summit, the crowning glory of creation

Woman was created from the rib taken from the very chest of man, that which protects his heart. Woman is that which gives so much meaning to man, that which brings warmth, tenderness, and encouragement to man. She is either a protective or destructive force in his life.

4 (2:22-24) **Marriage—Woman—Man**: man and woman were brought together by God. This passage is both dramatic and informative. The New Testament bases most of its teachings on the relationship between man and woman upon the experience recorded here (see 1 Co.11:2, 7-9, 11-12; 1 Ti.2:12-15). Remember: before this, Adam had no companion, no human being with whom to share his life. It was while he was researching and studying the animals that his great need for companionship struck him. The animals had mates and companions of their own kind, but not Adam. Adam was all alone: there was no creature who had his flesh and nature, no one with whom he could share life.

But now, there stood Eve. Just imagine the scene. The first two human beings standing there face to face with each other for the very first time in human history. Imagine the experience, the first sight and touch of each other! The emotions, the excitement! The moment must have been one of the most dramatic and exciting moments of human experience.

As stated, the passage lays the basis for the relationship between man and woman upon earth. Note these facts.

a. The union and relationship between man and woman was wrought by God.
⇒ God created both man and woman: man first, then woman (vv.7, 22).
⇒ God brought man and woman together (v.22b).
⇒ God established the law of marriage (v.24).

b. Woman was equal to man in being and person. She was made of the same flesh and blood, the very same material as Adam. She was *"like Adam"* in every respect: in the physical, mental, and spiritual being. She was "taken out of man"—

out of the very same stuff or substance as man was (v.23. See note, pt.b.—Ge.2:18; also see DEEPER STUDY # 2—Ge.1:26; 1:27; 2:21-22 for more discussion.)

c. Man was created and formed first, sometime before woman (v.23; see 18; see 1 Ti.2:13; see 1 Co.11:8-9). This does not mean superiority and inferiority, but *order and priority*. Neither man nor woman is superior or inferior to the other, not in being or person. As persons, man and woman are equal in God's eyes, and they are to be equal in each other's eyes.

What Scripture is saying is this: God created in an orderly fashion. He structured order within the family and within society. He arranged for man to be first in the order of the family and society, then the woman, and then the child. If there is to be order within any structure or organization, someone has to be first—someone has to be the head or leader of the structure or organization.

However, the Bible is clear in its instructions to the head: true order and priority are not found in domination, but in voluntary submissiveness and love. (See outlines and notes—1 Co.11:3; 11:7-10; Ep.5:22-24; 1 Ti.2:12-14.)

Thought 1. The order and relationship between man and woman are clearly shown in this Scripture: woman...
- was created for man
- was created out of man
- was presented *to* man

But again: the point of this passage is not to declare some supposed superiority of man over woman. The point is to declare that God created a *partner for man*, a partner who was desperately needed in order to carry out the will of God for the earth. The partnership is between two *equal persons and beings*, but their *functions and purposes* upon earth differ.

"**Let the deacons be the husbands of one wife, ruling their children and their own houses well**" (**1 Ti.3:12**).

"**Wives, submit yourselves unto your own husbands, as unto the Lord**" (**Ep.5:22**).

"**Husbands, love your wives, even as Christ also loved the church, and gave himself for it**" (**Ep.5:25**).

"**Likewise, ye wives, be in subjection to your own husbands; that, if any obey not the word, they also may without the word be won by the conversation [behavior] of the wives**" (**1 Pe.3:1**).

Thought 2. Note that *man* (ish) names woman after himself because she had been taken out of his body. He names her *woman* or *womb-man* (isha or ishshah).

d. Marriage is established as the first institution upon earth, the first institution established for society. Note three laws or rules of the marriage bond.
1) There is to be a *leaving of parents*, a permanent separation from parents by the man and woman. The union between husband and wife is to be the primary and strongest relationship between persons. It is to be so strong that the man and woman will leave their parents, be married, and build a family of their own. (See DEEPER STUDY # 2—Mt.19:5 for more discussion.)
2) There is to be a *cleaving to each other*. The union is to be intimate and permanent—as lasting as *one flesh*. The marriage bond is to endure as long as the flesh lives. (See note 7—Mt.19:5 for more discussion.)
3) There is to be *one flesh*. Man and woman—husband and wife—are to become one flesh. He is to be hers and she is to be his—so much so that they are as one flesh, as one person. Simply stated, there is to be a physical intimacy and a spiritual union so binding that they become as "one flesh"—as one person in body, mind, and spirit. (See note 6—Mt.19:5 for more discussion.)

Thought 1. God brought the woman to the man. God provided for the need of Adam. Note two lessons.
1) We must depend upon God to meet our need for a wife or for godly companionship.
2) God wants a voice in choosing our companion and spouse.

"**What therefore God hath joined together, let not man put asunder**" (**Mk.10:9**).

"**So ought men to love their wives as their own bodies. He that loveth his wife loveth himself**" (**Ep.5:28**).

"**Marriage is honorable in all, and the bed undefiled: but whoremongers and adulterers God will judge**" (**He.13:4**).

"**Let thy fountain be blessed: and rejoice with the wife of thy youth**" (**Pr.5:18**).

"**Whoso findeth a wife findeth a good thing, and obtaineth favour of the LORD**" (**Pr.18:22**).

5 (2:25) **Man—Woman**: man and woman were created perfect, innocent, and without shame. This verse is laying the groundwork for what is to follow in the next passage: the fall of man.

Note that man and woman were naked, yet they were not embarrassed or ashamed. Why? Because they had nothing about which to be ashamed. They were perfect beings, completely innocent. They had done nothing wrong. They sensed no guilt or shame whatsoever. They belonged to one another: their bodies belonged to the other, and together they belonged to God. They stood before God and before each other in perfection—perfectly innocent and free of any sense of shame, guilt, wrong, or failure. They were perfect beings in a perfect world, being everything they should be to each other and to God. There was no sin, guilt, or shame—nothing whatsoever to hide from each other nor from God.

"Blessed are the pure in heart: for they shall see God" (Mt.5:8).

"That ye may be blameless and harmless, the sons of God, without rebuke, in the midst of a crooked and perverse nation, among whom ye shine as lights in the world" (Ph.2:15).

"And the Lord make you to increase and abound in love one toward another, and toward all men, even as we do toward you: to the end he may stablish your hearts unblameable in holiness before God, even our Father, at the coming of our Lord Jesus Christ with all his saints" (1 Th.3:12-13).

"And the very God of peace sanctify you wholly; and I pray God your whole spirit and soul and body be preserved blameless unto the coming of our Lord Jesus Christ" (1 Th.5:23).

"Now the end of the commandment is charity [love] out of a pure heart, and of a good conscience, and of faith unfeigned" (1 Ti.1:5).

"Wherefore, beloved, seeing that ye look for such things, be diligent that ye may be found of him in peace, without spot, and blameless" (2 Pe.3:14).

"Now unto him that is able to keep you from falling, and to present you faultless before the presence of his glory with exceeding joy, to the only wise God our Saviour, be glory and majesty, dominion and power, both now and ever" (Jude 24-25).

Thought 1. Note two significant things about the family as an institution.
1) God established the family as the first institution of society. He will later establish the worship center (tabernacle, temple, and church) and the government.
2) All institutions of society find their roots in the family. The home gave rise...
   - to government: when rules and laws were needed between families and tribes
   - to worship: when the need for fellowship with God and for instruction of children arose
   - to education: when the need to instruct and teach children arose
   - to health care: when the physical care of the family members arose[3]

---

[3] James Montgomery Boice. *Genesis*, Vol.1, p.113.

		the garden, God hath said, Ye shall not eat of it, neither shall ye touch it, lest ye die.	
	CHAPTER 3	4 And the serpent said unto the woman, Ye shall not surely die:	5. **Step 4: Thinking that one will be more fulfilled, that one will gain & benefit more**
	F. The First Temptation & Sin: Man's Fall from Perfection—Man & Woman's First Steps into Sin, 3:1-6	5 For God doth know that in the day ye eat thereof, then your eyes shall be opened, and ye shall be as gods, knowing good and evil.	
1. The serpent	Now the serpent was more subtle than any beast of the field which the LORD God had made. And he said unto the woman, Yea, hath God said, Ye shall not eat of every tree of the garden?	6 And when the woman saw that the tree was good for food, and that it was pleasant to the eyes, and a tree to be desired to make one wise, she took of the fruit thereof, and did eat, and gave also unto her husband with her; and he did eat.	6. **Step 5: Looking & desiring—lusting**
2. Step 1: Being confronted with suggestive, enticing, & tempting thoughts			7. **Step 6: Committing the sin: Taking & eating the forbidden fruit**
3. Step 2: Entertaining, harboring, & discussing the suggestive thoughts	2 And the woman said unto the serpent, We may eat of the fruit of the trees of the garden:		8. **Step 7: Leading others to sin: Being a stumblingblock**
4. Step 3: Doubting the consequences of God's Word	3 But of the fruit of the tree which is in the midst of		

DIVISION II

ADAM, THE FIRST MAN (PART 1): THE BEGINNING OF MANKIND AND OF THE GODLY SEED—WHAT HAPPENED TO MAN AND THE EARTH, 2:4–3:24

F. The First Temptation and Sin: Man's Fall from Perfection—Man and Woman's First Steps into Sin, 3:1-6

(3:1-6) **Introduction**: the world is full of lawlessness, crime, immorality, adultery, drugs, drunkenness, lying, stealing, cheating, greed, covetousness, extravagance, indulgence, murder, assaults, war—all kinds of sin and evil. But this has not always been true. There was a time when the world was perfect, a time when there was not a single act of violence or evil upon earth. In fact, an evil deed had never been committed. The earth was perfect; both man and woman were sinless. They knew only harmony and peace, satisfaction and fulfillment, love, joy, and peace—all the fullness of life prevailed. Perfection ruled and reigned.

What happened? What destroyed the perfection and caused such devastation and lawlessness upon earth? What corrupted the heart of man?

This is the discussion of this Scripture, a passage that reveals the naked truth about temptation and sin. This is, *The First Temptation and Sin: Man's Fall from Perfection—Man and Woman's First Steps into Sin.*

1. The serpent (v.1).
2. Step 1: being confronted with suggestive, enticing, and tempting thoughts (v.1).
3. Step 2: entertaining, harboring, and discussing the suggestive thoughts (v.2).
4. Step 3: doubting the consequences of God's Word (v.3).
5. Step 4: thinking that one will be more fulfilled, that one will gain and benefit more (vv.4-5).
6. Step 5: looking and desiring—lusting (v.6).
7. Step 6: committing the sin: taking and eating the forbidden fruit (v.6).
8. Step 7: leading others to sin: being a stumblingblock (v.6).

1 (3:1) **Satan—Serpent**: this event of the serpent tempting the woman is a shocking scene, a drastic turn of events. God had just created the universe and it was all good. Scripture is pointedly clear about this: God was well pleased—perfectly satisfied—with His creation, for it was perfect. It had to be perfect, for He is God, the Sovereign LORD and Majesty of the universe, and God cannot create anything imperfect. God had also created the Garden of Eden for man, the most perfect place imaginable for man to live. Everything was ideal and perfect: man was in utopia, in paradise. Man could want nothing more.

But then it happened. Out of nowhere, something terrible happened: evil appeared in the form of an evil creature. Where in the world did the creature come from? Was not man in the Garden of Eden, in paradise itself?

"Yes!" The answer to these questions is, "Yes. God did create all things good, and He did give man paradise in which to live."

But, if this is so, who is this evil creature and where did he come from? How did he get upon earth and into the Garden of Eden, the paradise of earth? Other passages of Scripture tell us. Note seven points.

a. Scripture tells us that the devil, Satan himself, is called the serpent.

> **"And the great dragon was cast out, that old serpent, called the Devil, and Satan, which deceiveth the whole world: he was cast out into the earth, and his angels were cast out with him" (Re.12:9; see vv.14-15; 20:2).**

Does this mean that Satan possessed or energized a real living serpent and spoke through the creature? Some outstanding commentators hold to this position.[1] Or does it mean that Satan actually transformed himself into a serpent (NIV)? Or does it mean that the serpent is only a reference to Satan, whose very name is "that old serpent, called the Devil, and Satan" (Re.12:9)? That is, could this just be a picture of Satan himself? Some outstanding scholars hold this position.[2] Is it possible to know which is meant? Is Scripture clear about how Satan tempted man? Some very dear commentators hold that Scripture allows for either interpretation.[3] (See note—Ge.3:14 for more discussion.)

In determining just who or what the serpent was, these facts need to be noted about the Scripture.

1) The serpent—when first created—apparently walked upright and was a most magnificent creature (Ge.3:14). This is either symbolic language referring to Satan (note that v.15 is definitely symbolic, for it definitely refers to Satan) or it is literal language referring to an actual serpent. If it is literal, then v.15 switches to symbolic language.

2) The craftiness of the serpent is compared to the craftiness of the beast of the field. Scripture says the serpent was more *subtle* (crafty, clever, shrewd) than any of the animals upon earth (Ge.3:1). This is either a comparison of Satan's craftiness to the craftiness of the animals, or of the craftiness of one animal to the craftiness of the other animals.

3) Scripture gives examples where Satan had the power to use people as his tools and speak through them.
   ⇒ Peter (Mt.16:22-23).
   ⇒ Demon-possessed people (Mt.8:28-34; Acts 16:16-18).

4) All creation was created perfect by God, even the serpent. If we say that the serpent was a literal serpent used as an evil tool by Satan, then we have a problem explaining how creation was perfect: how could an animal be used as an evil tool in a world of perfect animals? This is the reason some interpreters say that Satan actually transformed or clothed himself as a serpent.[4]

b. Jesus Christ Himself tells us that Satan was behind the tragic fall of man.

"Ye are of your father the devil, and the lusts of your father ye will do. He was a murderer from the beginning, and abode not in the truth, because there is no truth in him. When he speaketh a lie, he speaketh of his own: for he is a liar, and the father of it [in tempting Eve]" (Jn.8:44).

c. Paul also says that Satan was behind the fall of man.

"But I fear, lest by any means, as the serpent beguiled Eve through his subtlety, so your minds should be corrupted from the simplicity that is in Christ....And no marvel; for Satan himself is transformed into an angel of light" (2 Co.11:3, 14).

"And the God of peace shall bruise Satan under your feet shortly" (Ro.16:20; see Ge.3:15 for the specific event to which Paul refers).

d. Scripture says that Satan had been the most exalted angel ever created by God, that God had created him to rule as the highest of all created beings. His particular reign and rule for God was over the earth and the universe, over the *physical and material world* and dimension of being. But Satan did the same thing that all men have done: he sinned and fell. He began to look at himself, and he began to want to live like he wanted instead of like God wanted. He wanted...
   • to rule and reign over the universe like he wanted
   • to rule without answering to God
   • to possess the ultimate authority over the world
   • to be the supreme ruler of the earth and physical universe

Satan wanted the very same thing that human nature has wanted down through history: to be one's own person; to do one's own thing; to control one's own life. Satan wanted what so many power-hungry men have wanted down through history: to be the sovereign ruler over nations and over the lives of people. This is what Scripture means when it reveals what Satan said in Is.14:13-14:
   • "Thou hast said in thine heart...
   • "I will ascend into heaven [God's position, rule, and authority over the universe]...
   • "I will exalt my throne above the stars of God...
   • "I will sit also upon the mount of the congregation [be honored, praised, adored, worshipped by the congregation of others]...
   • "I will ascend above the heights of the clouds; I will be like the most High [God Himself]" (Is.14:13-14).

Simply stated, Satan rebelled against God. Consequently, God had no choice but to cast Satan down from his exalted position in heaven. Originally, when Satan ruled as the highest of all created beings...
   • his name was Lucifer, which means *star of the morning*.
   • he was the anointed cherub who covered the very throne of God Himself. He was the angel in charge of the glory of God's very own throne throughout the physical and material universe.

Note how the following Scriptures have a double reference referring both to an earthly king and to Satan himself.

1 H.C. Leupold. *Genesis,* Vol. 1, p.142; Derek Kidner. *Genesis.* "Tyndale Old Testament Commentaries." (Downers Grove, IL: Inter-Varsity Press, 1979), pp.67, 70.
2 W.H. Griffith Thomas. *Genesis, a Devotional Commentary.* (Grand Rapids, MI: Eerdmans Publishing Co., 1946). p.47.
3 *Matthew Henry's Commentary*, p.21.
4 *NIV Study Bible*, Gen.3:1.

"How art thou fallen from heaven, O Lucifer, son of the morning! how art thou cut down to the ground, which didst weaken the nations! For thou hast said in thine heart, I will ascend into heaven, I will exalt my throne above the stars of God: I will sit also upon the mount of the congregation, in the sides of the north: I will ascend above the heights of the clouds; I will be like the most High. Yet thou shalt be brought down to hell, to the sides of the pit" (Is.14:12-15).

"Moreover the word of the LORD came unto me, saying, Son of man, take up a lamentation upon the king of Tyrus, and say unto him, Thus saith the LORD GOD; Thou sealest up the sum, full of wisdom, and perfect in beauty. *Thou hast been in Eden the garden of God*; every precious stone was thy covering, the sardius, topaz, and the diamond, the beryl, the onyx, and the jasper, the sapphire, the emerald, and the carbuncle, and gold: the workmanship of thy tabrets and of thy pipes was prepared in thee in the day that thou wast created. Thou art the anointed cherub that covereth; and I have set thee so: thou wast upon the holy mountain of God; thou hast walked up and down in the midst of the stones of fire. Thou was perfect in thy ways from the day that thou wast created, till iniquity was found in thee. By the multitude of thy merchandise they have filled the midst of thee with violence, and thou hast sinned: therefore I will cast thee as profane out of the mountain of God: and I will destroy thee, O covering cherub, from the midst of the stones of fire. Thine heart was lifted up because of thy beauty, thou hast corrupted thy wisdom by reason of thy brightness: I will cast thee to the ground, I will lay thee before kings, that they may behold thee. Thou hast defiled thy sanctuaries by the multitude of thine iniquities, by the iniquity of thy traffic; therefore will I bring forth a fire from the midst of thee, it shall devour thee, and I will bring thee to ashes upon the earth in the sight of all them that behold thee. All they that know thee among the people shall be astonished at thee: thou shalt be a terror, and never shalt thou be any more" (Eze.28:11-19).

Note one other significant fact: Jesus Christ Himself said that the Isaiah passage was speaking about Satan. He quoted Is.14:12 in referring to Satan in Lu.10:18.

⇒ Note Isaiah 14:12.

"How art thou fallen from heaven, O Lucifer, son of the morning! how art thou cut down to the ground, which didst weaken the nations!" (Is.14:12).

⇒ Note Luke 10:18.

"And he said unto them, I beheld Satan as lightning fall from heaven" (Lu.10:18).

e. The Bible teaches that Satan has some control over the earth. He has access to influence the world and man. History, the destruction and devastation of nature, and the terrible evil of men—all this—show that the domain of Satan includes the earth and the universe, that is, the physical and material world or dimension of being.

The question arises, when did Satan get access and control of the earth and universe? God certainly did not create the universe and put Satan and his evil forces in charge of it. The only living and true God—the Supreme LORD and Majesty of the universe who is the God of perfection and love—could never create evil nor put evil in charge of His perfect creation. This would be totally against God's nature. This is discussed in the next point, point six. For now, the fact to see is the control and authority of Satan in the world. Scripture says this:

⇒ Scripture calls Satan the god of this world.

"But if our gospel be hid, it is hid to them that are lost: in whom the god of this world hath blinded the minds of them which believe not, lest the light of the glorious gospel of Christ, who is the image of God, should shine unto them" (2 Co.4:3-4).

⇒ Scripture calls Satan the prince of this world.

"Now is the judgment of this world: now shall the prince of this world be cast out" (Jn.12:31). "Hereafter I will not talk much with you: for the prince of this world cometh, and hath nothing in me" (Jn.14:30). "Of judgment, because the prince of this world is judged" (Jn.16:11).

⇒ Scripture calls Satan the prince of the power of the air.

"Wherein in time past ye walked according to the course of this world, according to the prince of the power of the air, the spirit that now worketh in the children of disobedience" (Ep.2:2).

⇒ Scripture calls Satan the ruler of the darkness of this world.

"For we wrestle not against flesh and blood, but against principalities, against powers, against the rulers of the darkness of this world, against spiritual wickedness in high places" (Ep.6:12).

⇒ Satan is the king of a kingdom.

"And if Satan cast out Satan, he is divided against himself; how shall then his kingdom stand?" (Mt.12:26).

"Again, the devil taketh him up into an exceeding high mountain, and showeth him all the kingdoms of the world, and the glory of them; and saith unto him, All these things will I give thee, if thou wilt fall down and worship me" (Mt.4:8-9).

⇒ Satan has his grip upon the whole world.

"And we know that we are of God, and the whole world lieth in wickedness" (1 Jn.5:19).

f. The Bible teaches that Satan struggles and fights against God and His will. Satan's purpose in fighting against God is twofold.
  1) Satan's purpose is power and worship, to receive as much of the power and worship of the universe as possible (Is.14:12-17; Eze.28:11-17). He goes about this in at least three ways.
    ⇒ He opposes and disturbs God's work in the world (Is.14:12-17; Eze.28:11-17; Job 1:6; 2:1-6; Mt.4:10; Mk.1:13; Lu.4:8; Rev.12:7-9).
    ⇒ He discourages believers through various strategies (see notes—Lu.22:31; Ep.6:10-12).
    ⇒ He arouses God's justice against people by leading people to sin and to deny and rebel against God. And when they do, God's justice has to act and judge people to the fate of their choice: that of living with Satan eternally (see note—Jn.13:31-33).

  2) Satan's purpose is to hurt and cut the heart of God. Why? Because God has judged and condemned him for rebelling against God. Therefore, Satan does all he can to get back at God. The best way he can do this is to turn the hearts of people away from God and lead them to sin and to follow the way of evil. (See notes, pt.3—Re.12:3-4; pt.2—Re.12:7-9; pt.2—Re.12:10-11 for more discussion.)

The point is this: when did evil enter the world? How did Satan get access to and control of the world? This much can be said: God would certainly not create the universe and then put Satan in charge of it. This would be totally contrary to the nature of the Sovereign LORD and Majesty of the universe, the Sovereign LORD whose very nature is love and perfection. Satan's history must, therefore, precede man. Satan's creation and fall happened before man was ever created. In the eons of past history when Satan was created as the highest of angelic beings, he must have been placed in charge of the earth, even as man was later to be. But...
  • just as man was to sin and fall, so Satan sinned and fell
  • just as God has not yet utterly destroyed man, so God did not utterly destroy Satan—not yet
  • just as God still has a purpose for man, so God still had a purpose for Satan

Satan was to be used by God to test man, to give man the opportunity to choose God, to exercise his free will to obey and follow God instead of disobeying and rejecting God (see notes—Ge.2:16-17; 3:1 for discussion). Remember that we as sinful human beings still have the right to roam about the universe. So Satan, as a sinful spiritual being, still has the right to roam about the earth and universe. God's purpose for creation will not be stopped, neither by man nor by Satan and his evil spirits, not until God's purpose is completed and fulfilled. God is going to have a race of people with free wills, a race of people who will choose to love and follow Him supremely.

The point is this: the best explanation as to where Satan and evil entered the world is that of the Scripture, that of the Holy Bible—not the conjectures of men—as covered in the above points.

g. Man had to be tempted in order to exercise his free will *for God*. God had to create a situation whereby man could exercise his will and choose to obey and follow God. As already seen, there was no better way than to demand that man not eat from one of the trees in the Garden (see note 5—Ge.2:9 for more discussion). But remember this: man was created perfect, perfectly sinless and innocent. Man had no idea what temptation and sin were. Man had perfect access and fellowship with God. In his perfect state of innocence and sinlessness, there was no way man was going to act against God. Thus, for man to exercise his free will, something other than God telling Adam not to eat from a single tree was needed. Temptation was needed: the arousal of a suggestive thought.

This is the reason God allowed Satan to tempt Eve. Satan's temptation was needed for man to exercise his will for God, needed so that man could reject his own desire and choose to obey and follow God. But note this: Satan had the right to tempt Eve, but he did not have the power to make Eve sin. Eve was sinless and innocent: she chose to sin. She exercised her own free will by choosing to follow Satan and his evil lusts. The temptation was from Satan arousing lust within her, but the sin was of her own free will and choice.

[2] (3:1) **Temptation—Thoughts—Satan—Eve**: the first step in temptation and sin involves the thoughts: suggestive, enticing, and tempting thoughts. Several striking things are immediately noticed about Eve and the temptation that attacked her.
    ⇒ Eve was alone. She had gone off without her husband, Adam.
    ⇒ Eve was where she did not belong. She was standing by the forbidden tree.
    ⇒ Eve was apparently thinking about the tree and its delicious looking fruit.
    ⇒ Eve was not keeping a watchful eye against temptation.

What makes us say this—that Eve was thinking about the delicious fruit? Note what Satan said to Eve, "Yea—indeed—has God said, 'you must not eat from every tree of the garden'?" The very first words, "Yea—indeed," strongly suggest that Eve was thinking about the tree. At that very moment, while she was thinking about it, Satan attacked and just continued her thoughts: "Yea—indeed [how good it looks]—has God said; 'You must not eat from every tree of the garden'?"

Note that Satan misquoted God's Word. God had said that man *could eat from every tree* in the garden except one. God was good, extremely good. Man had everything he could ever want: all the fruit except one tree. All the trees would benefit man, but the forbidden tree would destroy him. But note what Satan did: he questioned Eve, "Yea—indeed—has God said, 'You *must not eat from every tree*'?" The thought was planted in Eve's mind, the suggestive thought...

- that she was missing out on something
- that the most delicious fruit was the very thing being forbidden
- that something good was being withheld and kept from her
- that she must not miss what looked good and would probably feel and taste good

This is the first step in temptation, the step that involves our thoughts, the thoughts of suggestion. The suggested thought is...

- that we are missing something that looks good, feels good, and tastes good
- that perhaps God's Word is causing us to miss something that is delicious

Thought 1. Too many of us get alone or away from loved ones and go places we should not. Tragically, even some husbands and wives do this.

"I beseech you therefore, brethren, by the mercies of God, that ye present your bodies a living sacrifice, holy, acceptable unto God, which is your reasonable service. And be not conformed to this world: but be ye transformed by the renewing of your mind, that ye may prove what is that good, and acceptable, and perfect, will of God" (Ro.12:1-2).

"Wherefore come out from among them, and be ye separate, saith the LORD, and touch not the unclean thing; and I will receive you, and will be a Father unto you, and ye shall be my sons and daughters, saith the LORD Almighty" (2 Co.6:17-18).

3 (3:2) **Thoughts—Temptation—Sin**: the second step in temptation and sin involves discussing our thoughts: actually entertaining, harboring, and discussing the suggestive thoughts. We may discuss the thoughts within our own minds or verbally with someone else. Very practically, what happens with a suggestive thought that begins to tempt us is this: the suggestive thought flies across our minds. At that point it should be rejected and not entertained or harbored and discussed. A tempting thought—a thought that suggests we sin, that we disobey God's Word—should never be harbored or entertained. As we move about in a sinful world—whether sitting, walking, standing, or riding...

- we cannot always keep from being tempted, but we can always flee the temptation
- we cannot always keep the appealing thing from crossing our eyes, but we can keep from looking
- we cannot help the first look, but we can control the second look
- we cannot always keep the thoughts from crossing our minds, but we can keep them from roosting there
- we cannot always keep the first suggestive thought of temptation from entering our minds, but we can push the thought out. We can turn our thoughts and mind to something else, in particular to quoting Scripture

But note: this is not what Eve did. Eve did three things.

a. Eve entertained, harbored, and discussed the suggestive thought. It was at this point that Eve began to sin, for she turned away from the great goodness of God. Note that she omits the word "every" or "all" from "every tree" (Ge.2:16). She simply says, "We may eat of the fruit of the trees." God's glorious goodness in giving *all the trees* to her is being dimmed in her mind. Her thoughts have slipped from God's goodness: she is no longer focused upon all that God has done for her. She has turned her thoughts away from God and His goodness and is now harboring and discussing the suggestive thoughts. Sin actually begins when the suggestive thoughts are harbored and thought about. It is then that God and His goodness are being rejected, ignored, neglected, and pushed aside.

b. Eve began to feel that God's command was too strict and restrictive. This is seen in her words, "Neither shall you touch it." God never said this (Ge.2:17). God simply said, "You shall not [must not] eat of it." Eve was not completely trusting God at this point. She was thinking—rationalizing—that touching the tree would be all right. Perhaps she should not eat of it, but touching it could not hurt anything. Eve's thoughts were running back and forth discussing God's Word, just what He had said. She was entertaining and harboring the tempting thought; she was rationalizing and justifying her intentions. She was thinking how restrictive God's Word was, doubting God's goodness, that God had not provided the very best for her. Eve was right in the midst of sinning, sinning by questioning and doubting the great goodness of God.

c. Eve began to think about the consequence of the sin. She lightened the consequences some when she said, "lest you die" or "you will die." This is not what God had said. God had pulled no punches: He had said that man would "surely die" (Ge.2:17). Again, Eve was rationalizing; a chain of thoughts was running through her mind about God's Word. She was wavering: wondering and questioning exactly what God had said. She should have fled the first suggestive and tempting thought. Instead, she was entertaining, harboring, and discussing the suggestive thought. She had forgotten the great goodness of God. She was no longer thinking about God and all that He had done for her. She was slipping further and further away from God, rationalizing her behavior more and more.

4 (3:3) **Word of God—Doubt—Temptation**: the third step in temptation and sin involves doubt: doubting the consequences of God's Word. The suggestive and tempting thought was roosting in Eve's mind. She had allowed her mind to hesitate, stop, and embrace the suggestive thought. She was now dallying with the temptation, harboring and

rationalizing her behavior. She was wondering and questioning if she could get away with it, wondering if she should experiment with the fruit. Then suddenly, unbelievably, Satan thrust the lie into her mind: "You shall not surely die" (v.4). Eve doubted that the consequences would ever happen to her.

Such thoughts as these often attack us and no doubt they attacked Eve:

⇒ "The warning was given to Adam, not to me—not directly. The judgment—if I am to be judged—is bound to be less than death."
⇒ "Certainly, God would not condemn me and leave Adam alone, without a wife, without a companion and helper to help him."
⇒ "God is so good, He'll forgive me. I'll just taste the fruit this time, then ask God to forgive me."
⇒ "God surely would not condemn me for doing it just one time."
⇒ "I'll make it up to God. I can go ahead and do it, and then serve God as never before, and He will forgive and accept me."
⇒ "Surely God would not let me die; there is still so much to do and accomplish in life and for God."
⇒ "In the final analysis—when everything is said and done—God just would never reject me, not permanently, not to everlasting death."

But Eve was wrong. We shall see in the next outline that God's Word stood. Adam and Eve were condemned to die, and they died. Satan lied, suggested a downright lie to Eve. As we shall see in the next note, Eve accepted the lie: she doubted God's Word. She rationalized and felt that the warning of God's Word would not apply to her, not completely—not fully—not in the full weight of its judgment.

Thought 1. God's warning about sin and its consequences stand. There is no escape from the judgment upon sin.

"For the wages of sin is death; but the gift of God is eternal life through Jesus Christ our LORD" (Ro.6:23).

"And to you who are troubled rest with us, when the LORD Jesus shall be revealed from heaven with his mighty angels, in flaming fire taking vengeance on them that know not God, and that obey not the gospel of our LORD Jesus Christ: who shall be punished with everlasting destruction from the presence of the LORD, and from the glory of his power" (2 Th.1:7-9).

"For if after they have escaped the pollutions of the world through the knowledge of the LORD and Saviour Jesus Christ, they are again entangled therein, and overcome, the latter end is worse with them than the beginning. For it had been better for them not to have known the way of righteousness, than, after they have known it, to turn from the holy commandment delivered unto them" (2 Pe.2:20-21).

"For God giveth to a man that is good in his sight wisdom, and knowledge, and joy: but to the sinner he giveth travail" (Ec.2:26).

"Behold, all souls are mine; as the soul of the father, so also the soul of the son is mine: the soul that sinneth, it shall die" (Eze.18:4; see 18:20).

Thought 2. The declaration of God's Word and of God's Son is clear: the choice is ours.

"I said therefore unto you, that ye shall die in your sins: for if ye believe not that I am he, ye shall die in your sins" (Jn.8:24).

[5] (3:4-5) **Fullness, Spiritual—Temptation**: the fourth step in temptation and sin involves personal fulfillment: thinking that one will be more fulfilled, that one will gain and benefit more if one eats of the *forbidden fruit* (v.5). This is the final step in temptation. When we have allowed our minds to get this far with suggestive and enticing thoughts, it is difficult—if not impossible—to turn back from sin.

a. There is the thought that we have *needs that cannot be met any other way*, the thought that the temptation will meet our needs more than what God has given us.

This is exactly what Satan said to Eve: "God knows that when you eat of this tree, your needs are going to be met far more than if you don't eat of it. God has not provided the best for you, not in the most fulfilling way."

b. There is the thought that our *eyes will be opened*, that we will never know if we don't experience it. This is what Satan said to Eve: "If you eat of the tree—do this thing—you will know more about it, how good it feels and tastes. You must do it to know. You cannot know whether it is good or bad until you actually experience it."

c. There is the thought of position, power, strength, self-sufficiency, independence, and individuality, of being one's own person and determining one's own destiny and fate. The raw thought—the underlying basis to the thought—is what Satan promised Eve: "You shall be as gods. If you do this thing, you will be your own person—independent, individualistic—you will gain position and power. Do it: do your own thing; do what you want when you want. It is worth it."

⇒ "Being your own person brings fulfillment and satisfaction, strong ego and self-image. It brings excitement, stimulation, and pleasure.
⇒ "Being your own person makes you as god: you can determine your own life and destiny."

d. There is the thought that we can know good and evil, that we can determine what is good and evil for ourselves. Satan told Eve...

- that she could determine what she should and should not do herself
- that she could discern good and evil apart from God's Word
- that she needed to go ahead and do what she wanted, and by doing her own thing, she would learn (gain the power) to govern and direct her life more and more
- that the only way she could ever learn to choose the fullest of lives—discern good and evil—would be if she went ahead and did what she wanted
- that she did not need God to tell her what to do, but she could gain the knowledge herself by doing what she wanted

Thought 1. We must understand the attack of Satan through temptation.
1) Satan has all kinds of strategies to attack us.

> **"Put on the whole armour of God, that ye may be able to stand against the wiles [strategies] of the devil" (Ep.6:11; see 6:10-18).**

2) Satan uses all kinds of devices or schemes to get an advantage over us.

> **"Lest Satan should get an advantage of us: for we are not ignorant of his devices" (2 Co.2:11).**

3) Satan is cunning; he seeks to deceive us just as he did Eve.

> **"But I fear, lest by any means, as the serpent beguiled Eve through his subtlety, so your mind should be corrupted from the simplicity that is in Christ" (2 Co.11:3).**

4) Satan is as a roaring lion. He goes about seeking to devour all who will follow him.

> **"Be sober, be vigilant; because your adversary the devil, as a roaring lion, walketh about, seeking whom he may devour" (1 Pe.5:8).**

5) Satan will tempt us when we have great need and are most susceptible to fall into sin.

> **"Then was Jesus led up of the Spirit into the wilderness to be tempted of the devil. And when he had fasted forty days and forty nights, he was afterward an hungered. And when the tempter came to him, he said, If thou be the Son of God command that these stones be made bread. But he answered and said, It is written, Man shall not live by bread alone, but by every word that proceedeth out of the mouth of God" (Mt.4:1-4).**

6) Satan will take a person who does not understand the Word and snatch the Word out of the person's heart. (This shows the critical importance of studying and learning God's Word.)

> **"When any one heareth the word of the kingdom, and understandeth it not, then cometh the wicked one, and catcheth away that which was sown in his heart. This is he which received seed by the way side" (Mt.13:19).**

6 (3:6) **Temptation—Eve—Sin—Worldliness—Lust**: the fifth step in temptation and sin is looking and desiring and lusting. Scripture clearly says:

> **"For all that is in the world, the lust of the flesh, and the lust of the eyes, and the pride of life, is not of the Father, but is of the world" (1 Jn.2:16).**

A simple chart shows what happened to Eve.

The Statement of Scripture	What Happened to Eve
The lust of the flesh	Eve saw that the tree was *good for food*
The lust of the eyes	Eve saw that the tree was pleasant, pleasing, and *attractive to the eyes*
The pride of life	Eve saw that the tree was desirable for gaining *knowledge, experience, and wisdom*

(See outline and notes, pt.2—1 Jn.2:15-16 for detailed discussion of these sins of worldliness.)

a. Eve's flesh lusted after the tree. She saw that the tree was good for food. She should have stayed away from the tree and controlled her eyes, never looking at it. But she went out alone and went to the tree, a place she should have never gone. She gave the tempter an open door, a wide open chance, to tempt her. As soon as he tempted her, she should have fled the temptation. But as has been seen, she thought about the temptation, harbored and discussed the thoughts of the sin. Now she was looking at the forbidden fruit and her flesh was lusting, craving, and desiring it. She wanted it.

"Now the works of the flesh are manifest, which are these; adultery, fornication, uncleanness, lasciviousness, idolatry, witchcraft, hatred, variance, emulations, wrath, strife, seditions, heresies, envyings, murders, drunkenness, revellings, and such like: of the which I tell you...that they which do such things shall not inherit the kingdom of God" (Ga.5:19-21).

b. Eve's eyes lusted after the tree. Eve saw that the tree was pleasant, pleasing, and attractive. The fruit—forbidden fruit—appealed to her. She was apparently so attracted that she experienced what we sometimes experience: a lustful craving, a hungering, an unstoppable urge to reach out and take the forbidden fruit.

Thought 1. What are the sins most often committed by the lust of the eyes? Scripture mentions these:
⇒ There is the lust of the eyes for sex.

"But I say unto you, That whosoever looketh on a woman to lust after her hath committed adultery with her already in his heart" (Mt.5:28).
"For this cause God gave them up unto vile affections: for even their women did change the natural use into that which is against nature: and likewise also the men, leaving the natural use of the woman, burned in their lust one toward another; men with men working that which is unseemly, and receiving in themselves that recompense of their error which was meet. And even as they did not like to retain God in their knowledge, God gave them over to a reprobate mind, to do those things which are not convenient [natural, normal]" (Ro.1:26-28).
"Having eyes full of adultery, and that cannot cease from sin; beguiling unstable souls: an heart they have exercised with covetous practices; cursed children" (2 Pe.2:14).
"I made a covenant with mine eyes; why then should I think upon a maid?" (Jb. 31:1).

⇒ There is the lust of the eyes after all kinds of evil.

"But if thine eye be evil, thy whole body shall be full of darkness. If therefore the light that is in thee be darkness, how great is that darkness!" (Mt.6:23).

⇒ There is the lust of the eyes after the things of other people.

"He sitteth in the lurking places of the villages: in the secret places doth he murder the innocent: his eyes are privily [secretly] set against the poor" (Ps.10:8).
"And he said unto them, Take heed, and beware of covetousness: for a man's life consisteth not in the abundance of the things which he possesseth" (Lu.12:15).

⇒ There is the lust of the eyes after all the pleasures and possessions of the world.

"And whatsoever mine eyes desired I kept not from them, I withheld not my heart from any joy; for my heart rejoiced in all my labor: and this was my portion of all my labor" (Ec.2:10).

⇒ There is the lust of the eyes after wine, drugs, and alcoholic drinks.

"Who hath woe? who hath sorrow? who hath contentions? who hath babbling? who hath wounds without cause? who hath redness of eyes? They that tarry long at the wine; they that go to seek mixed wine. Look not thou upon the wine when it is red, when it giveth his color in the cup, when it moveth itself aright" (Pr.23:29-31).

⇒ There is the lust of the eyes after other gods.

"Ye shall make you no idols nor graven image, neither rear you up a standing image [to look upon], neither shall ye set up any image of stone in your land, to bow down unto it: for I am the LORD your God" (Le.26:1).

c. Eve lusted after the pride of life. She saw that the tree was desirable for gaining knowledge, experience, and wisdom. Eve wanted to determine what was good for her and what was bad (evil). She wanted the full knowledge, experience, and wisdom—the fullness of life—apart from God. Life—the wisdom and fullness of life—apart from God is impossible, absolutely impossible. But Eve was deceived. She had given herself over to the grip of temptation and sin. Eve wanted knowledge, experience, wisdom, authority, power, position, independence, self-sufficiency—all apart from God. She was lusting after the pride of life.

"I am clean without transgression, I am innocent; neither is there iniquity in me" (Jb. 33:9).
"When pride cometh, then cometh shame: but with the lowly is wisdom" (Pr.11:2).
"Pride goeth before destruction, and an haughty spirit before a fall" (Pr.16:18).
"An high look, and a proud heart, and the plowing of the wicked, is sin" (Pr.21:4).
"He that is of a proud heart stirreth up strife: but he that putteth his trust in the LORD shall be made fat" (Pr.28:25).
"Jesus said unto them, If ye were blind, ye should have no sin: but now ye say, We see; therefore your sin remaineth" (Jn.9:41).

"Let nothing be done through strife or vainglory [empty glory]; but in lowliness of mind let each esteem other better than themselves. Look not every man on his own things, but every man also on the things of others" (Ph.2:3-4).

Thought 1. We must not exalt ourselves: we must not seek recognition, position, authority, power, money, wealth, possessions, knowledge, wisdom, experience—anything apart from God. We must not act self-sufficient and independent, exalting ourselves above others. We must not live as though we do not need God.
1) God warns us against pride and conceit.

"Be of the same mind one toward another. Mind not high things, but condescend to men of low estate. Be not wise in your own conceits" (Ro.12:16).
"And if any man think that he knoweth any thing, he knoweth nothing yet as he ought to know" (1 Co.8:2).
"Be not wise in thine own eyes: fear the LORD, and depart from evil" (Pr.3:7).
"When pride cometh, then cometh shame: but with the lowly is wisdom" (Pr.11:2).
"Pride goeth before destruction, and an haughty spirit before a fall" (Pr.16:18).
"An high look, and a proud heart, and the plowing of the wicked, is sin" (Pr.21:4).
"Woe unto them that are wise in their own eyes, and prudent in their own sight!" (Is.5:21).

2) God warns against self-sufficiency and self-exaltation.

"And whosoever shall exalt himself shall be abased; and he that shall humble himself shall be exalted" (Mt.23:12).
"And I will say to my soul, Soul, thou hast much goods laid up for many years; take thine ease, eat, drink, and be merry. But God said unto him, Thou fool, this night thy soul shall be required of thee: then whose shall those things be, which thou hast provided" (Lu.12:19-20).
"Wherefore let him that thinketh he standeth take heed lest he fall" (1 Co.10:12).
"Though thou exalt thyself as the eagle, and though thou set thy nest among the stars, thence will I bring thee down, saith the LORD" (Ob.4).
"He that trusteth in his own heart is a fool: but whoso walketh wisely, he shall be delivered" (Pr.28:26).

3) God warns us against spiritual pride.

"The Pharisee stood and prayed thus with himself, God, I thank thee, that I am not as other men are, extortioners, unjust, adulterers, or even as this publican" (Lu.18:11).
"Jesus said unto them, If ye were blind, ye should have no sin: but now ye say, We see; therefore your sin remaineth" (Jn.9:41).
"I am clean without transgression, I am innocent; neither is there iniquity in me" (Jb. 33:9).

7 (3:6) **Temptation—Eve—Sin**: the sixth step in temptation and sin is committing the sin, actually taking and eating the forbidden fruit. Remember: sin had already taken place in Eve's heart.
⇒ Eve had already been thinking and harboring the thoughts of the forbidden fruit (see note 6, pt.a.—Ge.3:6).
⇒ Eve had already questioned and forgotten God and His goodness.
⇒ Eve had already looked, desired, and lusted after the forbidden fruit.

The point is this: Eve had already sinned inwardly, within her thoughts. Now she was to sin outwardly; she was to actually commit the act. We cannot always tell when a person is sinning inwardly, within his heart. The silent sins—the sins of the mind and heart—are often not seen. Eve's sin until now could not be seen by man's eye. But now, the sin of her heart—her lustful cravings—is ready to break out into the open. Eve reached up and took the forbidden fruit and ate it. Eve...
• disobeyed God's Word
• rebelled against God's Word
• ignored God's Word
• rejected God's Word
• acted against God's Word
• opposed God's Word
• took a stand against God's Word

Eve sinned. Note what sin was: disobedience, disobeying the Word of God. God had said, you must not eat this fruit, for it will bring death—sure death—to you. But Eve turned away from God; she refused to listen to God. She rejected His warning and disobeyed His Word. She went ahead and did the forbidden thing.

Thought 1. It is difficult, very, very difficult, to turn away from temptation and sin...
• when we go to worldly places where temptation and sin swirl about
• when we allow suggestive thoughts to enter our minds
• when we think and think about the enticing fruit
• when we harbor the tempting thoughts

If we put ourselves in the presence of sinful fruit, there is no way to keep from thinking about the sinful fruit, and if the sinful fruit is available—right there before us, being offered to us—we cannot stop ourselves. We will sin and fall. Putting ourselves in the presence of sinful fruit is *always*—without exception—playing with fire.

Temptation has to be defeated when it first strikes. We must stay away from worldly places and people and things—as much as possible—and we must reject any and all suggestive thoughts that fly across our minds. This was Eve's failure, and it is always our failure when we sin. We must always—without a single exception—*flee temptation*.

> "Flee fornication" (1 Co.6:18).
> "Flee from idolatry" (1 Co.10:14).
> "Flee these things" (1 Ti.6:11).
> "Flee also youthful lusts" (2 Ti.2:22).

8 (3:6) **Temptation—Eve—Sin—Stumblingblock**: the seventh step in temptation and sin is leading others to sin. Note the simplicity and brevity of Scripture as it now states what happened: Eve gave the fruit to her husband *who had joined her*, and he also ate the forbidden fruit. Why does Scripture not spell out Adam's experience of temptation? Because Adam's temptation was the same as Eve's. The steps to temptation and sin are the same for all of us. Eve used the same arguments with Adam that Satan had used with her.

⇒ Eve presented the suggestive, enticing, and tempting thought to Adam.
⇒ Adam entertained, harbored, and discussed the thought.
⇒ Adam then began to doubt the consequence of God's Word. And note, Eve was standing before him the same as always: the penalty of death had not fallen upon her. What God had said had not happened to her.
⇒ Eve tempted Adam by sharing that he could experience more and be more fulfilled by eating the forbidden fruit.
⇒ Adam looked, desired, and lusted after the forbidden fruit.
⇒ Adam ate of the fruit.

Note two significant points.

First, Eve was a stumblingblock to Adam. She was supposed to be a helper to him, but she was his temptress, a stumblingblock to his doing the will of God.

Second, Adam was not deceived in his sin: he knew exactly what he was doing. Adam willingly and deliberately sinned. This was not true with Eve: she was deceived. But Adam deliberately and knowingly...

• disobeyed God's Word
• rejected God's Word
• rebelled against God

Consequently, Adam stood in the greater wrong. A person who knows and deliberately does wrong is always more guilty than the person who is deceived and does wrong. Both do wrong, but the deliberate and willing sinner is far more guilty of wrongdoing. This is exactly what Scripture says:

> "And Adam was not deceived, but the woman being deceived was in the transgression" (1 Ti.2:14).

This is the reason Scripture can say that sin entered the world through the man, Adam. He was the one who knowingly and deliberately brought sin into the world.

> "Wherefore, as by one man sin entered into the world, and death by sin; and so death passed upon all men, for that all have sinned" (Ro.5:12).

Thought 1. This is one of the most serious sins ever committed by a person. Scripture warns us—severely warns us—we must not be a stumblingblock to others.

> "Then said he unto the disciples, It is impossible but that offences will come: but woe unto him, through whom they come! It were better for him that a millstone were hanged about his neck, and he cast into the sea, than that he should offend one of these little ones" (Lu.17:1-2).
> "Let us not therefore judge one another any more: but judge this rather, that no man put a stumblingblock or an occasion to fall in his brother's way" (Ro.14:13).
> "But if thy brother be grieved with thy meat, now walkest thou not charitably. Destroy not him with thy meat, for whom Christ died" (Ro.14:15).
> "It is good neither to eat flesh, nor to drink wine, nor any thing whereby thy brother stumbleth, or is offended, or is made weak" (Ro.14:21).
> "Give none offence, neither to the Jews, nor to the Gentiles, nor to the church of God" (1 Co.10:32).
> "Giving no offence in any thing, that the ministry be not blamed" (2 Co.6:3).

Thought 2. We desperately need to heed what God teaches us in this experience of Adam and Eve. We must observe and learn the seven steps involved in temptation and sin. Learning the steps will help us greatly in combatting temptation and sin. Knowing the steps—having them in mind ready for recall—will enable us to stop any tempting thoughts that attack us. The steps will make us more aware of temptation and sin, about how temptation and sin attack us.

1) We must reject every suggestive, enticing, and tempting thought.
2) We must not entertain, harbor, or discuss any suggestive thought.
3) We must not doubt the consequences of God's Word. What God has said cannot be broken; His Word will be fulfilled. God has no favorites. He shows no partiality, no matter who we are.
4) We must never think that forbidden fruit will give us more fulfillment, that we will gain and benefit more by doing the forbidden thing.
5) We must never look and desire, never lust after the forbidden fruit, no matter how attractive and appealing it may be.
6) We must never commit sin, never take and eat the forbidden fruit.
7) We must never lead others to sin, never be a stumblingblock to others.
8) We must never doubt God's Word and goodness. We must know—always trust—that God will meet our needs in the most beneficial way possible.

"Neither yield ye your members as instruments of unrighteousness unto sin: but yield yourselves unto God, as those that are alive from the dead, and your members as instruments of righteousness unto God" (Ro.6:13).

"There hath no temptation taken you but such as is common to man: but God is faithful, who will not suffer you to be tempted above that ye are able; but will with the temptation also make a way to escape, that ye may be able to bear it" (1 Co.10:13).

"Blessed is the man that endureth temptation: for when he is tried, he shall receive the crown of life, which the LORD hath promised to them that love him" (Js.1:12).

"The LORD knoweth how to deliver the godly out of temptations, and to reserve the unjust unto the day of judgment to be punished" (2 Pe.2:9).

"Ye therefore, beloved, seeing ye know these things before, beware lest ye also, being led away with the error of the wicked, fall from your own stedfastness" (2 Pe.3:17).

	G. The First Consequences of Sin: Man's Tragic Fall from Perfection, 3:7-13	him, Where art thou? 10 And he said, I heard thy voice in the garden, and I was afraid, because I was naked; and I hid myself.	5. The disturbed relationships & the severe divisions caused by sin
1. The sense of being naked—of being imperfect & corruptible, short of God's glory & righteousness 2. The attempt to cover sin	7 And the eyes of them both were opened, and they knew that they were naked; and they sewed fig leaves together, and made themselves aprons.	11 And he said, Who told thee that thou wast naked? Hast thou eaten of the tree, whereof I commanded thee that thou shouldest not eat?	a. Sin disturbs man's relationship with God b. Sin disturbs man's relationship with others & causes a division between him & others
3. The running away & hiding from God	8 And they heard the voice of the LORD God walking in the garden in the cool of the day: and Adam and his wife hid themselves from the presence of the LORD God amongst the trees of the garden.	12 And the man said, The woman whom thou gavest to be with me, she gave me of the tree, and I did eat.	1) Adam blamed Eve 2) Adam blamed God
4. The alienation from God & the breaking of God's heart	9 And the LORD God called unto Adam, and said unto	13 And the LORD God said unto the woman, What is this that thou hast done? And the woman said, The serpent beguiled me, and I did eat.	3) Eve blamed the serpent, the devil

DIVISION II

ADAM, THE FIRST MAN (PART 1): THE BEGINNING OF MANKIND AND OF THE GODLY SEED—WHAT HAPPENED TO MAN AND THE EARTH, 2:4–3:24

G. The First Consequences of Sin: Man's Tragic Fall from Perfection, 3:7-13

(3:7-13) **Introduction**: there was a time when there was no evil—no sin whatsoever—upon earth, a time when the whole world was perfect, clothed in perfection. But the day came when sin entered the world. This we saw in the last passage (Ge.3:1-6). When sin first entered the world, catastrophic consequences began immediately to take place. This passage covers *The First Consequences of Sin: Man's Tragic Fall from Perfection* (Ge.3:7-13). Note how sin affected Adam and Eve's image of themselves. Sin crushed and devastated their self-image. All five of these consequences are tendencies or traits of a low self-image.

1. The sense of being naked—of being imperfect and corruptible, short of God's glory and righteousness (v.7).
2. The attempt to cover sin (v.7).
3. The running away and hiding from God (v.8).
4. The alienation from God and the breaking of God's heart (v.9).
5. The disturbed relationships and the severe divisions caused by sin (vv.10-13).

(3:7-24) **Another Outline**: There are seven consequences of sin seen in this chapter.

1. Shame, 3:7
2. Guilt and fear, 3:8
3. Alienation from God, 3:9
4. Division - disturbed relationships, 3:10-13
5. Judgment, 3:14-19
6. Death, 3:19
7. Separation - expulsion from perfection, 3:22-24

[1] (3:7) **Sin, Results—Man, Fall of—Imperfection—Glory of God, Short of—Shame—Unrighteousness**: there is the sense of being naked—of being imperfect and corruptible, short of God's glory and righteousness. As soon as Adam and Eve sinned, their eyes were opened and they immediately knew something: they were stark naked. What does this mean? It probably means two things.

a. The clothing of perfection and innocence was stripped away. Note the statement: their eyes "were opened and they knew that they were naked" (v.7). This could not mean their physical eyes, for the eyes of their body had been opened since their creation. It must mean, therefore, the eyes of their heart and mind, of their conscience. Before their sin, Adam and Eve were *morally* perfect and innocent, sinless and righteous. But when they sinned, a radical change took place within their hearts and minds. They immediately knew that something was wrong, tragically wrong—something terrible had happened. They no longer felt perfect or innocent, sinless or righteous. Within their hearts and minds they sensed guilt and shame, and they knew—beyond all question—they had done wrong. They knew *both good and evil*, for they had eaten *the fruit of evil*. They had turned away from God, disobeyed His Word and rebelled against Him. The consequence of sin had taken effect: sin had stripped them naked. They were now…

- imperfect, not perfect
- guilty of rebelling against God, not innocent
- sinful, not sinless
- unrighteous, not righteous

The radical change within their hearts and minds was traumatic. Their hearts and minds had never known anything but perfection. But now their sin had changed all that.

⇒ They had perfect peace, but sin made them feel disturbance.
⇒ They had perfect security, but sin made them feel insecure.
⇒ They had perfect comfort, but sin made them feel restless.
⇒ They had perfect goodness, but sin made them feel bad and evil.
⇒ They had perfect joy, but sin made them feel sad.
⇒ They had perfect love, but sin made them feel rejected.
⇒ They had perfect strength, but sin made them feel weak.
⇒ They had perfect control, discipline, and obedience; but sin made them feel guilt and shame.

Adam and Eve stood there, having just sinned, stripped of all the perfection and innocence of their being. They knew—sensed and felt within their minds and hearts—that they were naked. The clothing of their perfection and innocence was now stripped away.

> **Thought 1.** Every human being—every thoughtful and honest person—senses and knows that he is imperfect, that he often comes short of what he should be and do. This is what the Bible calls *sin* or *unrighteousness*. We just fail to do the right thing and often do the wrong thing. This sense and knowledge of sin—of unrighteousness, of being short—entered the world through Adam. But there is glorious news: God has counteracted the sin of Adam. God has provided a way for us to be saved from sin and death. How? Through His Son, the Lord Jesus Christ.
>
>> **"Wherefore, as by one man sin entered into the world, and death by sin; and so death passed upon all men, for that all have sinned" (Ro.5:12).**
>>
>> **"For God so loved the world, that he gave his only begotten Son, that whosoever believeth in him should not perish, but have everlasting life" (Jn.3:16).**
>>
>> **"Who his own self bare our sins in his own body on the tree, that we, being dead to sins, should live unto righteousness: by whose stripes ye were healed" (1 Pe.2:24).**
>>
>> **"For Christ also hath once suffered for sins, the just for the unjust, that he might bring us to God, being put to death in the flesh, but quickened by the Spirit" (1 Pe.3:18).**

b. The clothing of God's glory and righteousness was stripped away. Remember, Adam had been created in the image and likeness of God. Scripture tells us that "God is light" (1 Jn.1:5) and that "[God] covers Himself with light as with a garment" (Ps.104:2). God's glory is so brilliant and full of so much splendor and light that it has stricken a terrifying fear in men when they have witnessed it. An example is the shepherds at the birth of Christ (Lu.2:9-10; see Is.6:1f). Remember also the transfiguration of Christ: the glory of God changed the whole countenance of Christ. His face shone like the sun and His clothes became as white as light itself (Mt.17:2f).

Just imagine what the "image and likeness of God" is like in His glory, in the brilliance and splendor of the light of His presence. The point is this: Adam and Eve had been created in the "image of likeness of God." This was bound to include—at least to some degree—some of the glory and righteousness of God's being. In their perfect bodies and within their perfect environment (the Garden of Eden) some of God's glory and righteousness must have dwelt within and shone out of their bodies. The image and likeness of God—some of His glory and righteousness—must have covered and clothed Adam and Eve in their perfect state of being.

But note what happened when they sinned: they immediately became *naked*. They lost the covering of God's glory and righteousness. They had turned away from God, rejected His way of life, the way of perfection, glory, and righteousness. Apparently, sin caused a radical change within their bodies and countenance, a change so radical that the glory, light, and righteousness of God was stripped away from them. Their bodies were radically changed...

• from perfection to imperfection
• from incorruption to corruption
• from glory to dishonor
• from power to weakness
• from spiritual to natural bodies (see 1 Co.15:42-44)

> **Thought 1.** Scripture declares two significant facts about our spiritual nakedness, about our having lost God's glory.
> 1) It is sin that causes us to come short of God's glory.
>
>> **"For all have sinned, and come short of the glory of God" (Ro.3:23).**
>
> 2) Believers shall receive a perfect body when Christ returns. The glory of God will once again return and *be manifested* in the bodies of believers.
>
>> **"For in this we groan, earnestly desiring to be clothed upon with our house [body] which is from heaven" (2 Co.5:2).**
>>
>> **"[This] is the resurrection of the dead. It is sown in corruption; it is raised in incorruption: it is sown in dishonor; it is raised in glory: it is sown in weakness; it is raised in power: it is sown a natural body; it is raised a spiritual body. There is a natural body, and there is a spiritual body" (1 Co.15:42-44).**
>>
>> **"And as we have borne the image of the earthy, we shall also bear the image of the heavenly" (1 Co.15:49).**

"For our conversation [citizenship] is in heaven; from whence also we look for the Saviour, the Lord Jesus Christ: who shall change our vile [lowly] body, that it may be fashioned like unto his glorious body, according to the working whereby he is able even to subdue all things unto himself" (Ph.3:20-21).

2 (3:7) **Sin—Guilt—Shame**: there is the attempt to cover one's sin and shame. This is always true of the person who sins: he tries to hide and cover his sin to keep others from finding out. Why? Because of shame. He is ashamed of his sin and failure, so he does not want people to know about it. This was true of Adam and Eve. Immediately, when they partook of the forbidden fruit, they felt shame and guilt. Before, they felt no shame, none whatsoever. But now, they felt deep, intense shame. Remember, we see and experience so much sin and shame that we become hardened and immune to both. But not Adam and Eve. They had never seen nor experienced wrong-doing. This was the first sin and shame ever seen or experienced by man. The shame they felt must have been the most intense and terrifying shame imaginable. This is what made them cover themselves with aprons made from fig leaves. They were trying to cover the shame and guilt they were feeling.

Thought 1. Everyone needs to ask himself the same questions Job asked hundreds of years after Adam and Eve:

"[Have] I covered my transgressions as Adam, by hiding mine iniquity in my bosom?" (Jb.31:33).

Remember this: Adam and Eve had lost the covering of God's glory, light, and righteousness. They were feeling naked and unclothed. They felt what we feel when we are naked and unclothed and ready to go out and move about in public: the instinctive move to reach for clothing and to dress ourselves.

But note this: why did they cover only the sexual organs? There are at least two reasons.

First, it was the only part of the body that leaves could reasonably cover. A person's movement would be greatly hindered if leaves were wrapped around his legs, shoulders and arms, and over his head and face. To cover these body parts would not make much sense—not with aprons of leaves.

Second, the great Lutheran expositor H.C. Leupold is probably right in what he says: Adam and Eve covered that part of the body from which human nature comes. They covered the reproductive organs. Why? Because they instinctively felt that human life was now contaminated by sin. It was from that part of the body that fallen mankind was now to be born. Therefore, Adam and Eve were instinctively led to cover that which best represents the fallen, corrupted nature of man.[1]

Thought 1. Some may argue against the inner, instinctive sense of nakedness and sin. For example, there have been tribes of natives in the jungles of the world who wear no clothing whatsoever and feel no shame. Similarly, there are many people in technological cultures who walk about in the presence of their spouses or sexual partners who feel no shame. There are even nudist colonies scattered around the world, people who live together and wear no clothes, and they sense no shame.

Why do these have no instinctive sense of shame? Because we can adjust and condition ourselves to accept nudity. As human beings, we are creatures of conditioning. We can harden our sensitivity and consciences against sin and shame. Remember, Adam and Eve had not had time to condition themselves against anything. They had just committed the very first sin upon earth. They felt immediate and intense shame. Consequently, they tried to do what we do when we sin: they tried to cover and hide their sin. They instinctively—because of a convicting conscience—tried to cover their nakedness.

"Wherefore, as by one man sin entered into the world, and death by sin; and so death passed upon all men, for that all have sinned" (Ro.5:12).

"For it is a shame even to speak of those things which are done of them in secret" (Ep.5:12).

"Who can understand his errors? cleanse thou me from secret faults" (Ps.19:12).

"Draw me not away with the wicked, and with the workers of iniquity, which speak peace to their neighbors, but mischief is in their hearts" (Ps.28:3).

"Woe to the rebellious children, saith the LORD, that take counsel, but not of me; and that cover with a covering, but not of my spirit, that they may add sin to sin" (Is.30:1).

Thought 2. James Montgomery Boice has an excellent discussion on how we go about trying to cover and conceal our sin. His discussion is based upon C.S. Lewis' discussion in Lewis' *The Problem of Pain* (pp.47-48). Boice says the following:[2]

1) We try to conceal our shame and sin by "looking on the outside of things rather than on what is within." Just as Adam and Eve, we dress ourselves up to cover our sin, who we really are. We dress up as much as possible to attract attention instead of rejection. We also compare ourselves to others and their goodness or sinfulness so that we will feel that our failures are not so bad after all. We are as good and no worse than anyone else.

2) We try to conceal our shame and sin by "focusing on corporate sin rather than our wrongdoing." Boice admits there are corporate or social sins and guilt. But the institutions of society, government, and business are formed and operated by us. They are, therefore, sinful—short of what they should be—because of our sin and shortcomings. Society and its institutions are merely extensions of ourselves.

3) We try to conceal our shame and sin by "assuming that time conceals sin." This is seen when we refer to sins that we committed a long time ago. The sins fade in our memory and we refer back to them, not remembering the terrible hurt and pain they caused. They cut the heart of God, who is eternal and who always

---

1 H.C. Leupold. *Genesis*, Vol.1, p.154.
2 James Montgomery Boice. *Genesis,* Vol.1, pp.147-148.

knows about our terrible sins and depraved nature. In addition, our sins often hurt others far more deeply than we can imagine. Yet, too often, we refer to our past sins, sometimes even jokingly. We think that time has taken care of our sins and diminished our guilt and shame. But not so—not in the eyes of God. Christ and Christ alone can take care of sin.

4) We try to conceal sin by "thinking that there is safety in numbers." If everyone does it, then I can do it. It must not be so bad a thing. God certainly will not be too harsh with me when everyone else is doing it. He would not reject me—not in the final analysis—not for doing something everyone else is doing.

3 (3:8) **Hiding—Fleeing—Conceal—Concealment—Sin—Shame—Guilt**: there is the running away and hiding from God. Note two significant facts in this point.

a. It was apparently the habit of God to appear to Adam and Eve and share with them in fellowship and communion. Remember: fellowship was one of the primary reasons God had created man (see notes—Ge.2:15; 2:16-17). Therefore, God "walking in the garden in the cool of the day" is to be expected. This was His habit, His custom, to come to Adam and Eve and fellowship with them. Does this mean that God appeared to them in bodily form? Several things can be said in seeking the answer to this question.

⇒ This seems to be the picture painted by verse 8.

⇒ God—apparently in the person of Jesus Christ—did appear to men throughout the Old Testament (see DEEPER STUDY # 2—Ge.16:7). This could easily be the way God appeared to Adam and Eve and fellowshipped with them. In the future—when the new heavens and earth are created—Scripture emphatically declares that all believers will have face to face fellowship with God. Why would God have done any less for Adam in his perfect world? Adam and Eve were created perfect and placed in a perfect world. Consequently, they must have had face to face contact with God.

The comments of H.C. Leupold—because of his great scholarship—are helpful at this point:

> Yahweh God is represented as "walking about in the Garden." The almost casual way in which this is remarked indicates that this did not occur for the first time just then....That God had repeatedly done this is quite feasible....There is extreme likelihood that the Almighty assumed some form analogous to the human form which was made in His image. Nor is there anything farfetched [to say that]...our first parents had freely met with and conversed with their heavenly Father.[3]

b. Adam and Eve ran away and hid themselves from God. What an abrupt change! They had often heard God walking about and calling out to them in the garden. Their hearts had always leaped with joy, excitement, and great expectation when they heard the sound of His strong, yet tender and welcoming voice. They had always run to meet Him, just as a child runs to meet his father who has been away for awhile.

But not now, not this time. Something terrible had happened since God's last visit. Adam and Eve...

• had turned away from God
• had disobeyed God
• had rebelled against God
• had decided to do what they wanted instead of what God wanted
• had chosen to follow self and Satan instead of following God

The result had been catastrophic: their whole being—both inwardly and outwardly, both spirit and body—had been marred and corrupted. They were stripped naked: no longer perfect and innocent. They no longer possessed the glow of God's glory, light, and righteousness. They were now separated, cut off, alienated from God. This is the reason Adam and Eve fled and tried to hide from God. They did not want...

• to face God
• to face the fact of their sin
• to give an account for their behavior
• to suffer the judgment and punishment

Very simply stated, they did not want to face the consequences of their sin. God had made it clear: if you partake of the forbidden fruit, *you shall die*. No doubt, God had explained exactly what He meant by *death*, just as He has to explain death (that it means separation not annihilation) to us in the Holy Scriptures. Adam and Eve knew exactly what lay ahead. It was this—the judgment and punishment of death—that made them flee and hide from God.

Thought 1. Man still tries to run away from God, to hide from Him. He tries to run and hide...

• by staying away from church
• by refusing to sit under the preaching of God's Word
• by never seeking God
• by never reading and studying the Bible and by never praying
• by refusing to allow loved ones and neighbors to talk about God
• by denying the existence of God
• by ignoring God
• by neglecting God
• by pushing thoughts about God out of his mind
• by denying there is such a thing as sin, guilt, or conscience

---

[3] H.C. Leupold. *Genesis*, Vol.1, p.155.

- by stressing the physical world of science, technology, philosophy, and psychology and minimizing or denying the spiritual world

On and on the list could go. People try to hide behind everything imaginable to keep from facing God. But no person—not a single person—can hide from God. Everyone of us will have to face God—someday, someplace—we will all have to stand face to face with Him. No person can hide from Him. He sees us, no matter where we are and what we are doing, good or bad.

> "Whither shall I go from thy spirit? or whither shall I flee from thy presence? If I ascend up into heaven, thou art there: if I make my bed in hell, behold, thou art there. If I take the wings of the morning, and dwell in the uttermost parts of the sea; Even there shall thy hand lead me, and thy right hand shall hold me. If I say, Surely the darkness shall cover me; even the night shall be light about me. Yea, the darkness hideth not from thee; but the night shineth as the day: the darkness and the light are both alike to thee" (Ps.139:7-12).
>
> "The eyes of the LORD are in every place, beholding the evil and the good" (Pr.15:3).
>
> "Can any hide himself in secret places that I shall not see him? saith the LORD. Do not I fill heaven and earth? saith the LORD" (Je.23:24).
>
> "And before him shall be gathered all nations: and he shall separate them one from another, as a shepherd divideth his sheep from the goats: and he shall set the sheep on his right hand, but the goats on the left. Then shall the King say unto them on his right hand, Come, ye blessed of my Father, inherit the kingdom prepared for you from the foundation of the world....Then shall he say also unto them on the left hand, Depart from ye, ye cursed, into everlasting fire, prepared for the devil and his angels" (Mt.25:32-34, 41).
>
> "So then every one of us shall give account of himself to God" (Ro.14:12).
>
> "For we must all appear before the judgment seat of Christ; that every one may receive the things done in his body, according to that he hath done, whether it be good or bad" (2 Co.5:10).
>
> "And I saw the dead, small and great, stand before God; and the books were opened: and another book was opened, which is the book of life: and the dead were judged out of those things which were written in the books, according to their works" (Re.20:12).

4 (3:9) **God, Love—Alienation—Reconciliation, Need for**: there is the alienation (separation) from God and the breaking of God's heart. Adam's sin separated (alienated) man from God and broke God's heart. The separation is seen in Adam running away and hiding from God's voice, and the broken heart of God is seen in His seeking after Adam (v.9). Note that Adam is not seeking after God, but God is seeking after Adam.

Note God's question: "Adam, where are you?" This is a startling question, for God knew exactly where Adam was. God knows everything. What, then, is God doing?

a. This is the call of *the seeking Savior*. God's heart had been broken by Adam's sin. In His infinite knowledge...

- God saw all the ages, centuries, decades, years, and days of sin and shame that lay ahead for fallen man: acts of lying, stealing, cheating, killing, wars, maiming, immorality—all the broken homes and lives—all the pain and hurt and suffering that would be borne by men, women, and children down through the days and centuries of history.
- God saw the great price He would have to pay to complete His purpose upon earth. God saw that He would have to give His Son to pay the penalty for man's sin.

As stated, God's heart was broken—broken because He saw the terrible sin of man and the great price He, as God, would have to pay to save man from sin. God is love—His very nature is love—therefore, God set out to demonstrate His love. God went after Adam, went seeking after him: "Adam, where are you?" This is the call of God as the seeking Savior.

> "And sent forth his servants to call them that were bidden to the wedding: and they would not come" (Mt.22:3).
>
> "What man of you, having an hundred sheep, if he lose one of them, doth not leave the ninety and nine in the wilderness, and go after that which is lost, until he find it?" (Lu.15:4).
>
> "For the Son of man is come to seek and to save that which was lost" (Lu.19:10).
>
> "Behold, I stand at the door, and knock: if any man hear my voice, and open the door, I will come in to him, and will sup with him, and he with me" (Re.3:20).

Thought 2. Arthur W. Pink says, *"This was not the voice of the policeman, but the call of a yearning love. Dark as is the background here, it only serves more clearly to reveal the riches of God's grace. Highly favored as our first parents were, blest with everything the heart could desire, only a single restriction placed upon their liberty in order to test their loyalty and fidelity to their Maker—how fearful then their fall, how terrible their sin! What wonder if God had consigned them to 'everlasting chains under darkness,' as He did the angels when they sinned? What wonder if His wrath had instantly consumed them? Such would have been no undue severity. It would simply have been bare justice. It was all they deserved. But no. In His infinite condescension and abundant mercy, God deigned to be the Seeker, and came down to Eden crying, Where art thou?"*[4]

---

4 Arthur Pink. *Gleanings in Genesis*, p.41.

b. This is the call of *godly conviction*. God knew exactly where Adam was. The question, "Adam, where are you?" was not for God's information; it was to stir Adam to think about where he was. He was running away and hiding from God. God was calling out to Adam in order to arouse conviction within him. Adam needed to think about what he was doing: he was running away and hiding from the only Person...

- who could reconcile and help him
- who could correct, rectify, and salvage the situation
- who could give Him guidance and direction, peace and security, love and joy, hope and life upon this earth
- who could save and restore him to his former position of perfection, glory, and righteousness
- who could tell him how to escape the judgment of death that was to soon fall upon and snatch him from this world

Remember: Adam had lost his being of perfection, glory, and righteousness. There was no longer a glow within his heart nor shining in his body. He had been stripped naked of perfection, glory, and righteousness. Remember also that Adam had lived in a perfect world. The only way he could have known what death meant was for God to explain the meaning to him. This is, apparently, what God did. Adam knew that he was to die.

Adam needed to think about these things; he needed to sense conviction, sense his need for God, sense his need to be reconciled to God. Adam needed to seek after God, not run away from Him.

> **"For mine iniquities are gone over mine head: as an heavy burden they are too heavy for me" (Ps.38:4).**
> **"For I acknowledge my transgressions: and my sin is ever before me" (Ps.51:3).**
> **"And when he [the Holy Spirit] is come, he will reprove the world of sin, and of righteousness, and of judgment" (Jn.16:8).**
> **"But Paul cried with a loud voice, saying, Do thyself no harm: for we are all here. Then he called for a light, and sprang in, and came trembling, and fell down before Paul and Silas, and brought them out, and said, Sirs, what must I do to be saved? And they said, Believe on the Lord Jesus Christ, and thou shalt be saved, and thy house" (Ac.16:28-31).**

c. This is the call of *God's justice*. Adam's sin was a terrible sin against God. In fact, Adam's sin was the same terrible sin that we commit against God. Adam did the same terrible thing that we do when we sin:

$\Rightarrow$ turned away from God
$\Rightarrow$ disobeyed God
$\Rightarrow$ rebelled against God

He refused to live for God, refused to do what God said. He rebelled against God, committed the most violent act a person can ever commit: that of rebellion.

When God created Adam, He told Adam the penalty of sin: the penalty was death. Therefore, God's call to Adam was a summons to judgment. Adam was to appear before the court of God and face the sentence of death. He had to bear the judgment for his rebellion and insurrection against God.

Thought 1. A person may try to run away and hide from God. He may deny, ignore, and neglect God. But the day is coming when God will call him and everyone else before His court of justice. And every person—all who ran away and tried to hide from God—will be judged...

- judged because they turned away from God
- judged because they disobeyed God
- judged because they rebelled against God

> **"When the Son of man shall come in his glory, and all the holy angels with him, then shall he sit upon the throne of his glory: and before him shall be gathered all nations: and he shall separate them one from another, as a shepherd divideth his sheep from goats" (Mt.25:31-32).**
> **"And to you who are troubled rest with us, when the Lord Jesus shall be revealed from heaven with his mighty angels, in flaming fire taking vengeance on them that know not God, and that obey not the gospel of our Lord Jesus Christ" (2 Th.1:7-8).**
> **"And as it is appointed unto men once to die, but after this the judgment" (He.9:27).**
> **"The Lord knoweth how to deliver the godly out of temptations, and to reserve the unjust unto the day of judgment to be punished" (2 Pe.2:9).**
> **"But the heavens and the earth, which are now, by the same word are kept in store, reserved unto fire against the day of judgment and perdition of ungodly men" (2 Pe.3:7).**
> **"Behold, the Lord cometh with ten thousands of his saints, to execute judgment upon all, and to convince all that are ungodly among them of all their ungodly deeds which they have ungodly committed, and of all their hard speeches which ungodly sinners have spoken against him" (Jude 14-15).**
> **"And I saw the dead, small and great, stand before God; and the books were opened: and another book was opened, which is the book of life: and the dead were judged out of those things which were written in the books, according to their works. And the sea gave up the dead which were in it; and death and hell delivered up the dead which were in them: and they were judged every man according to their works" (Re.20:12-13).**
> **"Behold, I will send for many fishers, saith the LORD, and they shall fish them [sinners]; and after will I send for many hunters, and they shall hunt them [sinners] from every mountain, and from every**

hill, and out of the holes of the rocks. For mine eyes are upon all their ways: they are not hid from my face, neither is their iniquity hid from mine eyes" (Je.16:16-17).

5 (3:10-13) **Excuses—Sin—Division—Relationships**: there is the disturbed relationships and the severe divisions caused by sin. Note two significant facts.

a. Sin disturbs a man's relationship with God, and sin causes a division between him and God. This has already been seen when Adam ran away and hid from God. The perfect relationship he had known with God no longer existed. He had shared and fellowshipped face to face with God, but not now. Adam now feared God (v.10). Note why he feared God: because he was naked. Adam was...

- no longer perfect and innocent
- no longer full of God's glory and righteousness
- no longer like God
- no longer in the image and likeness of God

Adam was now totally different from God. A wall of disturbed feelings and division separated Adam from God. Adam was the sinner, and God was the perfect and holy God, the glorious and righteous God. Adam was now naked, stripped of God-likeness. If he faced God, he would have to bear the penalty and judgment for sin, for having disturbed the relationship between himself and God. He would be judged and condemned for sin, for causing the great division—the great alienation and separation—between himself and God. This is the reason Adam feared God.

Simply stated, he was naked before God, alienated and separated from God. He had disturbed the relationship between himself and God, created a great gulf—a terrifying division—between man and God. And Adam was to be judged for his terrible sin.

> **Thought 1.** Sin has caused a great gulf—a terrifying division—between us and God. Our relationship with God has been so disturbed by sin that we are doomed, doomed unless we cast ourselves totally upon God and commit all we are and have to follow God. Sin separates us from God.
>
> > **"This people draweth nigh unto me with their mouth, and honoreth me with their lips; but their heart is far from me" (Mt.15:8).**
> > **"This I say therefore, and testify in the Lord, that ye henceforth walk not as other Gentiles [sinners] walk, in the vanity of their mind, having the understanding darkened, being alienated from the life of God through the ignorance that is in them, because of the blindness of their heart: who being past feeling have given themselves over unto lasciviousness, to work all uncleanness with greediness" (Ep.4:17-19).**
> > **"If I regard iniquity in my heart, the Lord will not hear me" (Ps.66:18).**
> > **"But your iniquities have separated between you and your God, and your sins have hid his face from you, that he will not hear" (Is.59:2).**
> > **"And there is none that calleth upon thy name, that stirreth up himself to take hold of thee: for thou hast hid thy face from us, and hast consumed us, because of our iniquities" (Is.64:7).**

b. Sin disturbs man's relationship with others and causes severe division (v.11-13). God asked Adam two questions: Who told you that you were naked? Have you disobeyed me; have you eaten the forbidden fruit? Note three facts.

1) Adam blamed Eve (v.12). In essence, he said: "The woman gave me the fruit. I did not eat it until she enticed me to eat it. I would have never touched it if she had not enticed me."

> **Thought 1.** This is the way of sin, blaming others and trying to escape as much guilt as possible. Whatever happens to us—no matter the circumstances—we often lay the major blame at the feet of...
> - husband
> - wife
> - parent
> - in-laws
> - employer
> - employees
> - government
> - economy
> - conditions
> - situations or circumstances

2) Adam blamed God (v.12). Note how insidious this is: "The woman *you* gave to be with me, she enticed me to eat the forbidden fruit" (v.12). Emphasize the word *"you"* and the fact is clearly seen. This is the depth of sin: blaming God for our failure, shortcoming, circumstances, sickness, disease, death—for whatever evil and bad thing happens to us. Yet, this is exactly what Adam did and what we sometimes do. We often ask why God let such a terrible thing happen to us, as though God caused the temptation or tragedy. But note: God did not tempt Adam, nor does God tempt us and cause bad things to happen to us. It was Adam's sin and it is our own sin that causes corruption and death in the world.

Adam desired and craved the forbidden fruit. He knew exactly what he was doing. Scripture is clear about this: he was not deceived by anyone (1 Ti.2:14). He and he alone made the choice to eat the forbidden fruit.

> **"Let no man say when he is tempted, I am tempted of God: for God cannot be tempted with evil, neither tempteth he any man: but every man is tempted, when he is drawn away of his own lust, and enticed. Then when lust hath conceived, it bringeth forth sin: and sin, when it is finished, bringeth forth death" (Js.1:13-15).**

"From whence come wars and fightings among you? come they not hence, even of your lusts that war in your members? Ye lust, and have not: ye kill, and desire to have, and cannot obtain: ye fight and war, yet ye have not, because ye ask not. Ye ask, and receive not, because ye ask amiss, that ye may consume it upon your lusts" (Js.4:1-3).

3) Eve blamed the serpent, the devil. She simply said, "The serpent deceived me" (v.13). Note: this was the truth, but Eve still chose—made the decision—to eat the forbidden fruit.

Note this also: Eve did not accept blame for her sin any more than Adam did. She blamed someone else, the devil. By so doing, she plummeted to the depth of sin that Adam had fallen into: she indirectly charged God with being the cause of the sin. She was saying that God could have kept the devil from tempting her, that it was He, God, who had allowed the devil to enter the Garden and entice her.

Thought 1. Note how progressive sin is—how sin just grows and grows once it has been committed:
⇒ Adam and Eve ate the forbidden fruit.
⇒ Adam blamed Eve, and Eve blamed the devil.
⇒ Then, Adam and Eve both blamed God.

Note also how the relationships between all the parties were tragically affected.
⇒ Adam and Eve's love and oneness of spirit were greatly disturbed.
⇒ Love and oneness of spirit with God was greatly disturbed.

They were both fallen from their perfect state. They were now blaming each other, criticizing and accusing each other. What a terrible and devastating tragedy sin is!

"Therefore thou are inexcusable, O man, whosoever thou art that judgest: for wherein thou judgest another, thou condemnest thyself; for thou that judgest doest the same things" (Ro.2:1).

"If I justify myself, mine own mouth shall condemn me: if I say, I am perfect, it shall also prove me perverse" (Jb. 9:20).

"Most men will proclaim every one his own goodness: but a faithful man who can find?" (Pr.20:6).

"There is a generation that are pure in their own eyes, and yet is not washed from their filthiness" (Pr.30:12).

"Yet thou sayest, Because I am innocent, surely his anger shall turn from me. Behold, I will plead with thee, because thou sayest, I have not sinned" (Je.2:35).

Thought 2. We must confess and repent of our sins. God has provided salvation—eternal life—for us, but we must be honest and quit blaming others. We must do just what Scripture says: repent and confess our sins.

"Repent ye: for the kingdom of heaven is at hand" (Mt.3:2).

"I tell you, Nay: but, except ye repent, ye shall all likewise perish" (Lu.13:3).

"Then Peter said unto them, Repent, and be baptized every one of you in the name of Jesus Christ for the remission of sins, and ye shall receive the gift of the Holy Ghost" (Ac.2:38).

"Repent ye therefore, and be converted, that your sins may be blotted out, when the times of refreshing shall come from the presence of the Lord" (Ac.3:19).

"Repent therefore of this thy wickedness, and pray God, if perhaps the thought of thine heart may be forgiven thee" (Ac.8:22).

"And the times of this ignorance God winked at; but now commandeth all men every where to repent" (Ac.17:30).

"If we confess our sins, he is faithful and just to forgive us our sins, and to cleanse us from all unrighteousness" (1 Jn.1:9).

"If my people, which are called by my name, shall humble themselves, and pray, and seek my face, and turn from their wicked ways; then will I hear from heaven, and will forgive their sin, and will heal their land" (2 Chr.7:14).

"Let the wicked forsake his way, and the unrighteous man his thoughts: and let him return unto the LORD, and he will have mercy upon him; and to our God, for he will abundantly pardon" (Is.55:7).

"But if the wicked will turn from all his sins that he hath committed, and keep all my statutes, and do that which is lawful and right, he shall surely live, he shall not die" (Eze.18:21).

	H. The First Judgment upon Sin (Part 1): Judgment upon the Tempter, That Old Serpent Called the Devil, 3:14-15
1. He was cursed above all creatures	14 And the LORD God said unto the serpent, Because thou hast done this, thou art cursed above all cattle, and above every beast of the field; upon thy belly shalt thou go, and dust shalt thou eat all the days of thy life:
2. He was to crawl upon his belly, that is, to be detested, degraded, & miserable—always	
3. He was to eat dust: To be defeated & humiliated—always	
4. He was to be the object of enmity—enmity was to be waged between him & the woman & her seed	15 And I will put enmity between thee and the woman, and between thy seed and her seed; it shall bruise thy head, and thou shalt bruise his heel.
5. He was to be crushed by one particular seed or descendant of the woman	

DIVISION II

ADAM, THE FIRST MAN (PART 1): THE BEGINNING OF MANKIND AND OF THE GODLY SEED—WHAT HAPPENED TO MAN AND THE EARTH, 2:4–3:24

H. The First Judgment upon Sin (Part 1): Judgment upon the Tempter, That Old Serpent Called the Devil, 3:14-15

(3:14-15) **Introduction**: Adam sinned, and when he sinned he immediately suffered terrible consequences. The consequences of sin are covered in the former passage (Ge.3:7-13). Now comes the judgment upon sin. Sin is to be judged; perfect justice is to be executed. It was true in the beginning with Adam; it will be true with us in the final judgment of all men. This passage covers the first judgment ever pronounced upon earth. It covers *The First Judgment upon Sin (Part 1): Judgment upon the Tempter, That Old Serpent, Called the Devil.* (See note 1—Ge.3:1 for a discussion on just who or what the serpent was, a creature serpent or Satan Himself.)

1. He was cursed above all creatures (v.14).
2. He was to crawl upon his belly: to be detested, degraded, and miserable—always (v.14).
3. He was to eat dust: to be defeated and humiliated—always (v.14).
4. He was to be the object of enmity—enmity was to be waged between him and the woman and her seed (v.15).
5. He was to be crushed by one particular seed or descendant of the woman (v.15).

1 (3:14) **Judgment—Satan—Serpent**: the tempter was cursed above all creatures. Two points need to be considered in this part of the judgment.

a. Was the serpent a literal serpent or a reference to Satan himself? This has already been discussed in a previous note (see note 1—Ge.3:1).

1) James Montgomery Boice holds that the serpent is to be understood as literal. However, before the curse, he walked upright and was a most magnificent creature. Boice says:

There is something very striking in this literal judgment. We do not know what the serpent looked like before this judgment, though he must have been a beautiful and upright creature, perhaps the most splendid of all the creatures. Nor do we know precisely when the judgment here pronounced was executed, though it was probably at this point. What we can know—because we can put ourselves in their place—is the horror of Adam and Eve as they heard the voice of God and witnessed the terrifying transformation of this once beautiful creature into the hissing, slithering, dangerous creature we know as a snake today. They must have recoiled in mortal fear, recognizing that God had every right to pronounce this same or even a more terrible judgment on themselves. They must have expected that He would do so, and the devil must also have expected this judgment.[1]

2) Other scholars hold that the serpent was literal, but he was a reptile from the beginning, not necessarily a magnificent, upright creature.[2]

3) Scripture says this when referring to Satan and these two verses of judgment upon the serpent (vv.14-15):

"And the God of peace shall bruise Satan under your feet shortly. The grace of our Lord Jesus Christ be with you" (Ro.16:20; this is clearly a reference to Ge.3:15).

---

1 James Montgomery Boice. *Genesis*, Vol.1, p.159.
2 Derek Kidner. *Genesis*, p.70.

"And the great dragon was cast out, that old serpent, called the Devil, and Satan, which deceiveth the whole world: he was cast out into the earth, and his angels were cast out with him" (Re.12:9).

"And he laid hold on the dragon, that old serpent, which is the Devil, and Satan, and bound him a thousand years" (Re.20:2).

4) The present passage of Genesis 3:14-15 definitely refers to Satan. Therefore, if the serpent is to be understood in a literal sense, then the passage must have a double reference. It must refer to both the serpent as a creature and to Satan who is "that old serpent, called the Devil" (Re.12:9). This will be clearly seen as we discuss the specifics of the judgment upon the tempter.

⇒ For example, in the third judgment, the serpent is condemned to *eat dust* (v.14ᶜ). Snakes do not eat dust. This is symbolic language meaning that the tempter is to *eat the dust* of defeat and humiliation.

⇒ Another example is the reference to the seed of the woman and the seed of the serpent (v.15). This curse of God is not talking about all the little snakes crawling all over the world. It is referring to the followers of that "old serpent, called the Devil" (Re.12:9). As stated, the judgment definitely refers to Satan. If a serpent creature is also involved, then the judgment has a double reference to both Satan and the serpent creature (see note 2—Ge.3:1 for more discussion).

b. The tempter was cursed above all creatures. All creation was affected by the sin and fall of man:
⇒ All creatures were cursed and condemned. But note: the serpent and tempter were *cursed above all* other creatures.
⇒ Man and woman were condemned (vv.16-19).
⇒ The earth with its vegetation was cursed (vv.17-19).

The point is this: the judgment upon the tempter was the most severe judgment pronounced by God. Note exactly what Scripture says: "Because you have done this—because you are the tempter, because you tempted and led man to sin—you are cursed *above all other creatures*" (v.14).

Man's sin was most tragic, and the judgment he brought upon himself was terrible, but a way of salvation was to be offered to man. The earth also was to suffer a terrible corruption under the curse of God, but it, too, is to be delivered from the bondage of corruption and made incorruptible (Ro.8:19-21). But not the tempter. He is doomed forever. Scripture never says—not anywhere, not in any passage or verse—that the tempter will ever be saved and freed from the judgment pronounced upon him. In fact, Scripture declares the very opposite.

⇒ The tempter is to eat dust (be defeated and humiliated) *all the days* of his life (v.14).
⇒ The tempter will eat dust in the future world, during the millennial reign of Christ upon the earth.

"And he laid hold on the dragon, that old serpent, which is the Devil, and Satan, and bound him a thousand years, and cast him into the bottomless pit, and shut him up, and set a seal upon him, that he should deceive the nations no more, till the thousand years should be fulfilled: and after that he must be loosed a little season" (Re.20:2-3).

"The wolf and the lamb shall feed together, and the lion shall eat straw like the bullock: and dust shall be the serpent's meat. They shall not hurt nor destroy in all my holy mountain, saith the LORD" (Is.65:25).

⇒ The tempter, "that old serpent, called the Devil," is doomed to an eternity in the lake of fire.

"And the devil that deceived them was cast into the lake of fire and brimstone, where the beast and the false prophet are, and shall be tormented day and night for ever and ever" (Re.20:10; see 19:20).

The point is this: the tempter was cursed above all created creatures. There is no hope for him. He will never be freed from his judgment and condemnation, never freed because of his terrible atrocity against God and man.

2 (3:14) **Judgment—Satan—Serpent**: the tempter was cursed to crawl upon his belly all the days of his life. This means he was cursed to be detested, degraded, and miserable.
⇒ A crawling creature (e.g., a serpent) is the picture of a being that is detested, degraded, repulsive, contemptible, and scorned—an abomination (Le.11:42).
⇒ A body that bows low and clings to the ground is a picture of misery (Ps.44:25).

Note that this curse could apply either to the serpent or the devil. Most people despise, detest, and scorn both. Even if this judgment is directed at the snake as an earthly creature, its main thrust is leveled at the devil who is the prime tempter of man. It is he—"that old serpent, called the Devil"—that God is primarily judging and condemning. It was the devil who desired, planned, and initiated the temptation, sin, and fall of man. The devil is condemned to be...

- despised
- detested
- hated
- degraded
- repulsive

- contemptible
- scorned
- miserable
- abhorred
- disgusting

Thought 1. One of the names given Satan is *Beelzebub*. The name means the god of flies, the god of filth, or the god of dung. Satan is known as the god of unclean spirits (see DEEPER STUDY # 1—Mk.3:22).

3 (3:14) **Judgment—Satan—Serpent**: the tempter was cursed to eat dust all the days of his life. This means he is cursed to be defeated and humiliated. In the Scripture, *to eat or lick dust* means to be defeated, to be humiliated.

> **"They that dwell in the wilderness shall bow before him; and his enemies shall lick the dust"** (Ps.72:9).
> **"And kings shall be thy nursing fathers, and their queens thy nursing mothers: they shall bow down to thee with their face toward the earth, and lick up the dust of thy feet; and thou shalt know that I am the LORD: for they shall not be ashamed that wait for me"** (Is.49:23).
> **"They shall kick the dust like a serpent, they shall move out of their holes like worms of the earth: they shall be afraid of the LORD our God, and shall fear because of thee"** (Mi.7:17).

Donald Grey Barnhouse says,

> *To eat dust is to know defeat, and that is God's prophetic judgment upon the enemy. He will always reach for his desires and fall just short of them. There will be continuous aspiration, but never any attainment.*[3]

Again, if the judgment is against the serpent as a creature, the major wrath is still thrust against the devil. "That old serpent, called the Devil" is condemned to be...

- defeated
- smashed
- overthrown
- triumphed over
- smashed

- humiliated
- disgraced
- shamed
- debased

> **Thought 1.** Satan has been defeated and always will be. His final destiny is utter destruction in the lake of fire.

> **"And the seventy returned again with joy, saying, Lord, even the devils are subject unto us through thy name"** (Lu.10:17).
> **"And he laid hold on the dragon, that old serpent, which is the Devil, and Satan, and bound him a thousand years, and cast him into the bottomless pit, and shut him up, and set a seal upon him, that he should deceive the nations no more, till the thousand years should be fulfilled: and after that he must be loosed a little season"** (Re.20:2-3).
> **"And the devil that deceived them was cast into the lake of fire and brimstone, where the beast and the false prophet are, and shall be tormented day and night for ever and ever"** (Re.20:10).

4 (3:15) **Judgment—Seed, The—Jesus Christ—Satan—Serpent**: the tempter was to be the object of enmity: enmity was to be waged between him and the woman and her seed throughout history. The word *enmity* (ebhah) means hatred, antagonism, hostility. In the Bible it is always used to refer to the enmity between people, not animals. This fact alone, as well as the rest of this part of the judgment, points to the tempter being the devil and not just a serpent.[4]

a. There is always to be enmity between the tempter and the woman.

1) It is God who puts enmity between the serpent and man. It is God who stirs man to oppose evil. It is God who says "I will put enmity." Enmity is usually sinful, but enmity against evil is a virtue. Believers are to always be angry at sin and stand against all evil. (See note—Ep.4:26-27 for more discussion on *Anger*.)

2) This enmity actually began when woman was first created. James Montgomery Boice points out that Satan hated woman from the moment she was created. But now—from the moment of this judgment—woman was to hate Satan. She might love her sin, but she would also hate it. As Boice says,

> *When we sin, we often find that we like the sin but want to escape sin's consequences. We would like to destroy ourselves in comfort, like the addict destroying himself in the dreamlike stupor of debilitating drugs or booze. We would like to go to hell happy.*[5]

3) Woman was to also hate the destruction Satan and his evil wrought upon her family through divorce, illness, accident, drugs, alcohol, war, and death. History shows that woman, by her more delicate and parental nature, is much more sensitive to sin and its effects upon human families and society. She usually hates and attacks injustice and evil with a greater diligence—not always, but usually.

4) Note another fact as well: Satan would never be able to dominate the woman entirely. He had attempted to conquer the human race by getting the woman and man to act selfishly—to do their own thing—against God. This they did—acted selfishly—sought to do what they wanted. But in this act of selfishness, Satan doomed himself, for man would forever act selfishly. Man would forever tend to selfishly put himself before anyone and everything, including Satan. Satan may want the human race to do his bidding, but most men usually seek their own desires and lusts. In the words of Donald Grey Barnhouse,

> *[Satan] does not want the good of the race nor does the race want his good. Each, in fact, selfishly desires his own good. Therefore, there can be no...coalition between man and Satan. A few may become the children of the devil, but the majority are...addicted to the love of their own interests.*[6]

3 Donald Grey Barnhouse. *Genesis,* Vol. 1. (Grand Rapids, MI: Zondervan Publishing House, 1970), p.22.
4 H.C. Leupold. *Genesis,* Vol.1, p.164.
5 James Montgomery Boice. *Genesis,* Vol.1, p.162.
6 Donald Grey Barnhouse. *Genesis,* p.23.

The point is this: even the selfishness of Satan and the selfishness of the woman (mankind) was cursed to enmity. God put enmity (antagonism) between the selfishness of Satan and the selfishness of the woman—selfishness acting against selfishness. God used the very thing Satan injected into the human race—selfishness—to doom Satan to defeat. Satan would never be able to conquer the human race because most of the race would always act selfishly, seek after their own desires, even before the desires of Satan.

b. There is always to be enmity between the seed (offspring) of the tempter and the seed of the woman. Who is the seed (offspring) of the tempter or serpent?

The serpent's seed could not be all the snakes of future generations which were yet to be born. Such an interpretation just makes no sense. In addition, as stated above, the word *enmity* always refers to hostility between persons, not creatures. It is also doubtful, very doubtful, that the serpent's seed would be referring to the demons who serve under Satan. Satan does not bear demons as *offspring*: demons are not increasing in numbers. They were all created by God as angelic beings and fell from their exalted position when Satan fell. Who then is the seed or offspring of "that old serpent, called the Devil?" Who are the children and descendants of the devil? Scripture tells us: the seed or offspring of the devil are...

- Persons who live after the lusts of the flesh

   "Ye are of your father the devil, and the lusts of your father ye will do" (Jn.8:44).

- Persons who are enemies of God, those who deny, curse, neglect, and ignore God

   "For if, when we were enemies, we were reconciled to God by the death of his Son, much more, being reconciled, we shall be saved by his life" (Ro.5:10; see Ro.5:6-9).
   "And you, that were sometime alienated and enemies in your mind by wicked works, yet now hath he reconciled" (Col.1:21).

- Persons who are adulterers and adulteresses

   "Ye adulterers and adulteresses, know ye not that the friendship of the world is enmity with God? whosoever therefore will be a friend of the world is the enemy of God" (Js.4:4).

- Persons who commit sin

   "He that committeth sin is of the devil; for the devil sinneth from the beginning. For this purpose the Son of God was manifested, that he might destroy the works of the devil" (1 Jn.3:8).

- Persons who are unrighteous and do not love others

   "In this the children of God are manifest, and the children of the devil: whosoever doeth not righteousness is not of God, neither he that loveth not his brother" (1 Jn.3:10).

The seed (offspring) of the devil refers to the ungodly men and women upon earth, and the seed of the woman refers to the godly men and women of earth. There are two seeds upon earth, two offsprings, two descendants:
   ⇒ Those who follow after righteousness and those who follow after unrighteousness.
   ⇒ Those who follow after the way of God and those who follow after the way of self and the devil.
   ⇒ Those who follow after the good of God and those who follow after the sin and evil of the devil.
   ⇒ Those who follow after God Himself and those who follow after the devil himself.

The godly seed of the woman is in a struggle against the ungodly seed of the devil. This verse—Genesis 3:15—is a prophecy of human history. History is to be a great struggle between good and evil among men and nations. History is to be a stage upon which the play of conflict is to be acted out, a conflict between the godly and the ungodly—between the good and the evil—upon the earth. There is a good and godly seed upon earth, and there is an evil and ungodly seed upon earth. There is a godly humanity and an ungodly humanity upon earth, and there always will be.

But note this: God will not let Satan triumph. There will always be godly people upon earth. No matter how much Satan tries to destroy godliness upon earth, God will make sure there are always some godly people someplace upon earth. Satan and his followers will never be free from the enmity they feel toward the godly, the true followers of God. The ungodly will burn with enmity against true godliness as long as the earth stands.

   "They shall put you out of the synagogues: yea, the time cometh, that whosoever killeth you will think that he doeth God service. And these things will they do unto you, because they have not known the Father, nor me" (Jn.16:2-3).
   "Remember the word that I said unto you, The servant is not greater than his lord. If they have persecuted me, they will also persecute you; if they have kept my saying, they will keep yours also" (Jn.15:20).
   "These things have I spoken unto you, that ye should not be offended. They shall put you out of the synagogues: yea, the time cometh, that whosoever killeth you will think that he doeth God service. And these things will they do unto you, because they have not known the Father, nor me. But these things have I told you, that when the time shall come, ye may remember that I told you of them. And these things I said not unto you at the beginning, because I was with you" (Jn.16:1-4).
   "That no man should be moved by these afflictions: for yourselves know that we are appointed thereunto" (1 Th.3:3).

"For unto you it is given in the behalf of Christ, not only to believe on him, but also to suffer for his sake" (Ph.1:29).

"Yea, and all that will live godly in Christ Jesus shall suffer persecution" (2 Ti.3:12).

"Marvel not, my brethren, if the world hate you" (1 Jn.3:13).

"Beloved, think it not strange concerning the fiery trial which is to try you, as though some strange thing happened unto you: but rejoice, inasmuch as ye are partakers of Christ's sufferings; that, when his glory shall be revealed, ye may be glad also with exceeding joy. If ye be reproached for the name of Christ, happy are ye; for the spirit of glory and of God resteth upon you: on their part he is evil spoken of, but on your part he is glorified" (1 Pe.4:12-14).

5 (3:15) **Seed, The—Jesus Christ—Judgment—Satan—Serpent—Covenant, Adamic—Reconciliation**: the tempter was to be crushed by one particular seed or descendant of the woman. This is a glorious promise: some descendant of the woman was to destroy the serpent. The serpent would strike the descendant's heel and bruise him, but the descendant would strike the final and fatal blow. The descendant would crush the serpent's head. This is definitely a promise of the Savior, the Lord Jesus Christ. Note: this is the first promise of the Savior in the Bible, and the promise is unconditional: the Savior would come and He would destroy the serpent (tempter) in order to reconcile man with God. This is what is known as the *Adamic covenant*, God's unconditional promise to Adam and man, the unconditional promise to send the Savior to deliver man.

Verse fifteen is also known as the *Protevangelium*, which means the very first declaration of the gospel. Note several facts.

a. The New Testament clearly tells us who *the promised seed* is. The seed may sometimes refer to the descendants of humanity or Israel, but the primary meaning of *the promised seed* is singular: it is Christ Jesus Himself.

> "Now to Abraham and his seed were the promises made. He saith not, And to seeds, as of many; but as of one, And to thy seed, which is Christ" (Ga.3:16).

b. *The promised seed* is said to be the seed of the woman, not of the man. This points toward the virgin birth—the incarnation—of Christ.

c. The devil—from this point on—would try to destroy the seed of the woman. But note: God never said which woman would bear the seed. Satan was always left guessing. In fact, Satan has tried from the very beginning to destroy the seed of the woman. He has been waging war against the *Seed* of God, the Savior of the world, ever since God promised to save the world. The great Baptist preacher W.A. Criswell points this out by tracing some of the attempts of the devil throughout the Bible.[7] For clarity the attempts are put in chart form.

The Seed or Line Through Whom the Promised Seed Was to Come	The Strategies of Satan to Destroy the Seed or Devour the Child and God's Great Deliverance
⇒ There was the line of Abel, Adam's Son.	⇒ Satan led Cain to kill Abel, but God gave Adam another son, Seth (Ge.4:1f).
⇒ There was the early line of the godly seed.	⇒ Satan led the godly line to mix with the ungodly and led them into such vile wickedness that God had to destroy the earth. But God raised up Noah (Ge.6:5f).
⇒ There was the line of Abraham, Isaac, and Jacob.	⇒ Satan led Esau to threaten to kill his brother, Jacob. But God protected Jacob (Ge.27:41f).
⇒ There was the line of the children of Israel.	⇒ Satan led Pharoah to attempt to kill all the male babies of Israel. But God saved Moses (Ex.1:8f).
⇒ There was the line of David.	⇒ Satan led several of David's sons into sin, led them to commit murder and disqualify themselves from the godly line. But God always kept at least one son of David alive (2 S.13f).
⇒ There was the line of the sons of David.	⇒ Satan led Jehoram, one of Jehosophat's sons, to kill all his brothers. But God caused sons to be born to Jehoram to carry on the line (2 Chr.21:1f).
⇒ There was the line of Jehoshophat's sons.	⇒ Satan led an enemy to come in and kill all the sons but one—Ahaziah (2 K.8:25f).

---

7 W.A. Criswell. *Expository Sermon On Revelation*, Vol.4. (Grand Rapids, MI: Zondervan Publishing House, 1969), pp.86-87.

The Seed or Line Through Whom the Promised Seed Was to Come (continued)	**The Strategies of Satan to Destroy the Seed or Devour the Child and God's Great Deliverance** (continued)
⇒ There was the line of Ahaziah.	⇒ Satan led Jehu to kill Ahaziah, and the queen's mother, Athaliah, took over the throne and killed all the sons but one. God led the wife of the high priest to save one small baby, Joash. At this point the line of the promised seed rested in the saving of this one little baby's life (2 K.9:11f).
⇒ There was the line of the chosen people.	⇒ Satan led King Ahasuerus to plan to exterminate all of God's people. But God gave him a most restless and frightening night of sleep. The king, therefore, spared the chosen line (The Book of Esther).
⇒ There was the line of the Promised Seed, Jesus Himself, at His birth.	⇒ Satan led King Herod to slay all the babies in Bethlehem in an attempt to kill the promised child. But God warned Joseph and told Joseph to flee with the child (Mt.2:1f).
⇒ There was the line of the Promised Seed, Jesus Himself, at his temptation.	⇒ Satan tempted Jesus to cast Himself down from the pinnacle of the temple, to secure the loyalty and worship of the people by a spectacular sign instead of the cross. But Jesus chose God's way, the way of the cross, instead of Satan's way (Mt.4:1f).
⇒ There was the line of the Promised Seed, Jesus Himself, at his hometown, Nazareth.	⇒ Satan led the citizens of Nazareth to try to cast Jesus off the cliff of a hill, but Jesus escaped (Lu.4:29).
⇒ There was the line of the Promised Seed, Jesus Himself, in facing the religionists.	⇒ Satan led the religionists to hate Jesus and to plot His death time and again (Jn.7:1f). But Jesus escaped time and again.
⇒ There was the line of the Promised Seed, Jesus Himself, on the cross.	⇒ Satan led the world to put Jesus on the cross and to kill Him. But God raised Jesus from the dead (Jn.19:1f).

This is how Satan has attempted to hurt God, by doing all he could to devour the woman and her godly descendants down through the centuries. He did all he could to keep the Savior, the Lord Jesus Christ, from being born. Now that Christ has come, Satan does all he can to turn people away from repentance and from following the Lord. Even when people do repent and turn to follow Christ, Satan does all he can to turn the followers of the Lord away from Him.

d. *The promised seed* of the woman, the Lord Jesus Christ, was to crush the head of the serpent. Jesus Christ crushed Satan when He died upon the cross.

1) Christ crushed Satan's head by never giving in to the devil's temptations (Mt.4:1-11) and by never sinning (2 Co.5:21; He.4:15; 7:26; 1 Pe.1:19; 2:22). Christ lived a perfect life; he was perfectly righteous. Therefore, He became the Perfect Man, the Ideal Man, the Ideal Righteousness…
   * whom all men are to trust
   * whom all men are to follow
   * whom all men are to use as the *pattern* for their lives (see note—Mt.8:20)

Satan was defeated in that an Ideal Righteousness was now provided for man. Man could now become acceptable to God by putting on the righteousness of Christ *through faith* (2 Co.5:21; Ep.4:23-24. See Deeper Study # 2, *Justification*—Ro.4:22; 5:1.)

2) Christ crushed Satan's head by dying *for man*, by bearing all of man's guilt and punishment for sin. In behalf of man, Christ took all of man's sins upon Himself and bore the judgment of God against sin. He is the *Ideal Man*, so His death becomes the Ideal Death. Just as His *Ideal Righteousness* stands for and covers every man, so His Ideal Death stands for and covers every man. Consequently, the penalty and punishment for sins has now been paid. Man no longer has to die and be separated from God (see Deeper Study # 1, *Death*—He.9:27). The way to live forever in the presence of God is now open. Satan's power is broken and destroyed.

> **"Forasmuch then as the children are partakers of flesh and blood, he also himself likewise took part of the same; that through death he might destroy him that had the power of death, that is, the devil; and deliver them who through fear of death were all their lifetime subject to bondage" (He.2:14-15).**

"Now is the judgment of this world: now shall the prince of this world be cast out. And I, if I be lifted up from the earth, will draw all men unto me. This he said, signifying what death he should die" (Jn.12:31-33. See Jn.14:30, esp. v.28-31; 16:11.)

"Who hath delivered us from the power of darkness, and hath translated us into the kingdom of his dear Son: in whom we have redemption through his blood, even the forgiveness of sins" (Col.1:13-14).

3) Christ crushed Satan's head by being raised from the dead. Again, as the Ideal Man, Christ's resurrection becomes the *Ideal Resurrection*. His resurrection stands for and covers every man. Note two facts.
   a) It was the *perfect spirit of holiness* (perfect righteousness) that raised up Christ from the dead. Death could not hold perfection, for death is the result of sin. Christ, being perfect, was bound to arise.
   b) When Christ arose, He triumphed over Satan, openly showing that death is the work of Satan. Death is not to be the natural experience of man. Death was never the purpose of God; life is the purpose of God. The resurrection of Christ openly shows this.

   "God, who hath raised him from the dead..and having spoiled principalities and powers, he made a show of them openly, triumphing over them in it" (Col.2:12, 15).

4) Christ crushed Satan's head by His Incarnation, that is, by coming into the world and being revealed as the Son of God. Think about it: the fact that the Son of God came into the world destroys the works of the devil. As soon as the Son of God appeared on the scene, His coming meant that the works of the devil were to be destroyed.

   "For this purpose the Son of God was manifested, that he might destroy the works of the devil" (1 Jn.3:8).

   "For God so loved the world, that he gave his only begotten Son, that whosoever believeth in him should not perish, but have everlasting life. For God sent not his Son into the world to condemn the world; but that the world through him might be saved" (Jn.3:16-17; see Jn.3:18-21).

5) Christ crushed Satan's power to charge men with sin. Satan's power *to charge men with sin* is now "cast out." Men now have the power to escape the penalty of sin. Christ took the sins of men upon Himself and paid the penalty for their sin. He died for the sins of the world.

   "Who his own self bare our sins in his own body on the tree, that we, being dead to sins, should live unto righteousness: by whose stripes ye were healed" (1 Pe.2:24).

   "Who shall lay any thing to the charge of God's elect? It is God that justifieth" (Ro.8:33).

6) Satan's power *to cause death* is now "cast out." Men no longer have to die. Christ died *for man*, became man's substitute in death.

   "Forasmuch then as the children are partakers of flesh and blood, he also himself likewise took part of the same; that through death he might destroy him that had the power of death, that is, the devil; and deliver them who through fear of death were all their lifetime subject to bondage" (He.2:14-15.)

7) Satan's power *to cause men to be separated from God* is now cast out. Men no longer have to go to hell and be separated from God. Christ was separated from God *for man* (see note—Mt.27:46-49). Man can now be reconciled to God and live forever.

   "For Christ also hath once suffered for sins, the just for the unjust, that he might bring us to God, being put to death in the flesh, but quickened by the Spirit" (1 Pe.3:18).

   "But if the Spirit of him that raised up Jesus from the dead dwell in you, he that raised up Christ from the dead shall also quicken your mortal bodies by his Spirit that dwelleth in you" (Ro.8:11).

8) Satan's power *to enslave men* with the habits of sin and shame is now *cast out*. By His death, Christ made it possible for man to be freed from sin. The believer, cleansed by the blood of Christ, becomes a holy temple unto God, a temple fit for the presence and power of God's Spirit. Man can now conquer the enslaving habits of sin by the power of God's Spirit.

   "What? know ye not that your body is the temple of the Holy Ghost which is in you, which ye have of God, and ye are not your own? For ye are bought with a price: therefore glorify God in your body, and in your spirit, which are God's" (1 Co.6:19-20).

   "Greater is he that is in you, than he that is in the world" (1 Jn.4:4).

	I. The First Judgment upon Sin (Part 2): Judgment upon Woman, 3:16
1. She was to experience many forms of pain	16 Unto the woman he said, I will greatly multiply thy sorrow and thy conception; in sorrow thou shalt bring forth children; and thy desire shall be to thy husband, and he shall rule over thee.
2. She was to have a yearning desire for a husband	
3. She was to live in subjection to her husband	

DIVISION II

ADAM, THE FIRST MAN (PART 1): THE BEGINNING OF MANKIND AND OF THE GODLY SEED—WHAT HAPPENED TO MAN AND THE EARTH, 2:4–3:24

I.   The First Judgment upon Sin (Part 2): Judgment upon Woman, 3:16

(3:16) **Introduction**: remember, man and woman had just sinned. "That old serpent, called the Devil and Satan" had seduced the woman to take the forbidden fruit, and the man had deliberately chosen to follow the woman into sin. The judgment of God had just been pronounced upon the devil. Now, it was time for man and woman to stand before God, time for them to hear the terrible judgment they had brought upon themselves. As the specifics of the judgment are studied, three facts need to be kept in mind.

First, God's judgment is always *just* and *equitable*, perfectly fair. God always judges a person impartially. A person receives exactly what he deserves, nothing more, nothing less. God's judgment always matches a person's sin. A person will never be judged for more wrong than he has done. The judgments pronounced upon Adam and Eve match their sin. Note this as we study these judgments.

Second, God's judgment is always full of *wisdom, purpose, and mercy*. While man is on earth, God always *wisely* pronounces judgment for the *purpose* of arousing the person to repent and turn to God for *mercy*.

God judges Adam and Eve—man and woman—for the purpose of arousing and stirring them...
* to return to God
* to flee and stay away from sin lest worse judgment come upon them
* to trust the mercy and grace of God
* to stay close to God

Third, Adam and Eve stand as the representative heads of the human race. This is clearly seen in every judgment pronounced upon them. The judgments pronounced upon Adam and Eve are passed on down through their children. The judgments are still being borne by the human race. Adam and Eve stand as the father and mother of the human race. We bear the human and fleshly nature—the fallen nature—of Adam and Eve. Consequently, we bear the judgment of our father and mother, of Adam and Eve. The first judgment is upon the person who sinned first, the woman. This passage is, *The First Judgment upon Sin (Part 2): Judgment upon Woman.*
1. She was to experience many forms of pain (v.16).
2. She was to have a yearning desire for a husband (v.16).
3. She was to live in subjection to her husband (v.16).

1 (3:16) **Judgment—Woman—Eve**: the woman was to experience many *forms of pain*. This verse does not refer only to the pain of childbearing, as it is often interpreted. The great scholar H.C. Leupold points this out: "The conjunction [the word 'and'] before 'conception' is to be taken in the sense of 'and in particular.'"[1] The judgment is this:

"I will greatly multiply your sorrow and in particular [the sorrow of your] conception" (v.16).

Note the word *sorrow* (itstsebhon). It means trouble, sorrow, and pain.[2] Three particular sorrows are mentioned.

a. There is the sorrow caused by woman's very nature. God created woman with a more tender, delicate, and sensitive nature than man. Consequently, when she fell into sin, she was bound to feel and suffer greater sorrow. But note: God says He is going to intensify this sorrow, and when we look at the life of woman, this is exactly what we see. Because of her nature, the woman usually feels things more deeply than man. She usually experiences sorrow more than man, and she usually feels for others more than man. She seems to understand the feelings, needs, trouble, sorrow, and pain of others more deeply. But as commendable as this trait is, it often causes trouble, sorrow, and pain for her, both physically and mentally. Because she feels more deeply, she often suffers more.

⇒   Woman had turned away from God and sought the pleasure of life on her own. The judgment was fair: she would thereafter live as she had chosen. The pleasure of God's perfection would no longer rest upon her. She would now walk through life bearing imperfection and its fruits: trouble, sorrow, and pain. The perfect body and nature God had given her would now suffer the trouble, sorrow, and pain of the imperfect life she had chosen.

---
1   H.C. Leupold. *Genesis*, Vol.1, p.171.
2   William Wilson. *Wilson's Old Testament Word Studies.* (McLean, VA: MacDonald Publishing Company, n.d.), p.406.

⇒ Woman had also led another person to turn away from God and seek the pleasure of life apart from God. Therefore, she was judged to feel for others, to suffer their sorrow and pain more keenly than man. (Note how true this is, in particular with her own family and close friends.)

The mercy of God is seen in this: sorrow and pain often, and always should, arouse a person to call upon God for help. Sorrow and pain stirs repentance, trust, dependence, and hope in God. This is probably one of the reasons women seemingly turn to God more easily and sooner than most men.

b. There is the unique pain of childbirth which the woman has to bear. The travail of childbirth is painful, so painful it is often used in Scripture to picture severe suffering and grief (Jn.16:21; 1 Th.5:3; Re.12:2; Mi.4:10). God commanded man and woman to bear children right after they were created (Ge.1:27-28). They were in paradise—the Garden of Eden—a perfect place in which there was no sorrow or pain. The pain of childbearing did not enter the world until after the fall of woman into sin. It is a part of the judgment of sin upon woman. Bearing children was now, after the sin of the woman, to involve pain and travail.

Note: the judgment is just and fair. The woman had chosen to live her life apart from God and His perfection. Therefore, God judged her to bear what she had sown. She would now bear children in an imperfect and corruptible world, a world of sorrow and pain. But note the mercy of God in this: every time a woman bears a child, her pain is to stir her to cry out in trust and dependence upon God for her and her child. Her pain in childbirth should cause her to turn to God for help.

c. The woman's sorrow and pain is also deeper than the man's in rearing children. In sorrow the woman *brings forth* children (v.16). The phrase *bring forth* means more than just conception and birth. It means bringing up and rearing children. By her very nature—more tender, delicate, and sensitive nature—the woman feels and suffers greatly for her children when they suffer or go astray.

This judgment is just and fair. The very sin the woman introduced into the world literally breaks the heart of many mothers. Many sons and daughters sin, and when they do, the mother usually suffers much more of the sorrow and pain than the father. The woman—by her very nature—has to bear more of the sorrow and pain when children...

- speak sharply
- react
- rebel
- fall into sin

But again, note the wisdom and mercy of God. Woman's deep sorrow and pain over her children is to arouse her...

- to cry out to God and to seek, trust, and depend upon God for help
- to be more diligent in helping and teaching her children to live like they should

As stated above, the woman's judgment is just and fair. She turned away from God and His perfection of life, turned away to pursue the pleasure of life in her own strength and will. Her judgment allowed her to do just that: to live apart from God, to live in an imperfect world, a world of fleshly pleasures, but also a world of corruption, sorrow, and pain. Consequently, the judgment upon woman was the suffering of many forms of pain. A woman in travail has sorrow, because her hour is come. But as soon as she has delivered the child, she does not remember the anguish, for joy floods her heart because a child is born into the world (Jn.16:21).

> **"Now no chastening [judgment] for the present seemeth to be joyous, but grievous: nevertheless afterward it yieldeth the peaceable fruit of righteousness unto them which are exercised thereby" (He.12:11).**
> **"Thou shalt also consider in thine heart, that, as a man chasteneth [judges] his son, so the LORD thy God chasteneth [judges] thee" (De.8:5).**
> **"Behold, happy is the man whom God correcteth: therefore despise not thou the chastening of the Almighty" (Jb.5:17).**
> **"Before I was afflicted I went astray: but now have I kept thy word" (Ps.119:67).**

2 (3:16) **Judgment—Woman—Eve—Marriage—Wife**: the woman was to have a yearning desire toward a husband.
The word *desire* (teshuqah) means longing, yearning, desiring. By nature, the woman longs, yearns, and desires to settle down with a husband. This is not merely sexual attraction. The attraction involves all of life for the woman: it is an attraction that is deeper and involves more of life than that of man. Of course, man is attracted to woman, very much so, but the desire of woman to settle down with a husband is usually more intense than man's. Most parents of teenagers notice that daughters and girls spend much more time talking about boys than boys do about girls. Even adult women talk more about their husbands and men than men do about them. The very center of conversation among a group of women—young, single, or married—is often men, far more often than the conversation of men.

This desire and longing often leads to sorrow and pain for the woman, terrible sorrow and pain, much more so than for the man. This fact is seen in such facts as these:

⇒ There are more women in the world than men, considerably more. The desire of many women for a husband and family can never be fulfilled, not in godly obedience to God's command of one wife for one husband. Many women are forced to go through life single and alone. Many are forced to handle all the affairs of life alone and to suffer loneliness when they would prefer to have a husband.

⇒ Woman is usually more attached to man than man is to the woman. This means that man is usually...
- slower to become attached
- more easily led astray
- less likely to stay attached

This, of course, means that man causes far more broken hearts and broken homes than woman. But it also means that the woman usually suffers more trouble, sorrow, and pain than man.

But note: this is a just and fair judgment.

⇒ It was the woman who enticed and led the man astray; therefore, she is now to be led and enticed by a deeper attraction for the man.

⇒ It was the woman who acted independently of the man who was to be her perfect companion in the perfect world. Therefore, she was now to have a deeper attraction and pull to be next to him, more so than he would with her.

⇒ It was the woman who sought pleasure and fulfillment apart from the man. Therefore, she was now judged to long and yearn for the pleasure and fulfillment of his presence—again, more so than the man.

But note the mercy of God in this judgment. The woman's desire for a husband would stir her to be as attractive as possible, to settle down, and to have a family. Her desire, longing, and yearning would tend to pull man to her and hold the family together in a much closer bond.

Thought 1. The *Song of Solomon* often expresses the desire of woman, her longing and yearning, for man.

> **"I opened to my beloved; but my beloved had withdrawn himself, and was gone: my soul failed when he spake: I sought him, but I could not find him; I called him, but he gave me no answer" (Song 5:6).**
> **"Whither is thy beloved gone, O thou fairest among women? whither is thy beloved turned aside? that we may seek him with thee....I am my beloved's, and my beloved is mine: he feedeth among the lilies" (Song 6:1,3).**
> **"I am my beloved's, and his desire is toward me" (Song 7:10).**
> **"By night on my bed I sought him whom my soul loveth: I sought him, but I found him not. I will rise now, and go about the city in the streets, and in the broad ways I will seek him whom my soul loveth: I sought him, but I found him not. The watchmen that go about the city found me: to whom I said, Saw ye him whom my soul loveth?" (Song 3:1-3).**

3 (3:16) **Judgment—Woman—Eve—Wife—Marriage:** the woman was to live in subjection to her husband. When a person says anything about the subjection of woman to man—in fact, the subjection of anyone to another person—he has to be careful. The very thought of a person subjecting to another person arouses reaction. This should not be, for we are all subject to some authority, rule, and order every day. Someone holds authority and is ultimately responsible for the order of things no matter where we are: in the office, shop, school, church, or any other place. Rule, authority, law, and order is necessary—absolutely necessary—for any body of people to live and function together. Why should it be any different in the *home*? Note the word *home*. This is the key. God's judgment is not as some people declare and as some societies live: the general subjection of woman to man. Note the Scripture: it is as clear as can be:

"He [the husband] shall rule over thee [the wife]" (v.16).

This judgment applies to every man individually, not to *all men over all women*. It means *every wife* is subject to her *own husband*, not subject to all men. The judgment is not that all men are to rule over all women; the judgment is that each husband will hereafter rule over his wife and her alone. This is exactly what the New Testament says:

"Wives, submit yourselves unto your own husbands, as unto the Lord. For the husband is the head of the wife, even as Christ is the head of the church" (Ep.5:22-23).

When God judged woman to be under the rule of man, God was not condemning her to be...

- of less ability or worth
- of less competence or value
- of less brilliance or advantage

God's judgment dealt with function and order within the family. Because of sin, the family was no longer to be perfect where every member would live perfect lives free from problems. The family was now to know selfishness, difficulties, trouble, reaction, rebellion—all sorts of disorder and sin. The family needed someone to be the head, someone to be responsible for rule and order within the family. The head was to be the man, not the woman. The woman was to be ruled over by her husband, and she was to submit to his authority. This was part of her judgment.

Note: the judgment is a *just and fair judgment*. The woman had acted independently of God and of man. She had taken matters—the rule of her own life—into her own hands. She craved control—independence, authority, rule—over her own life. In addition, she enticed the man...

- to walk away from God
- to walk out from under the rule of God
- to act independently of God
- to rebel against God

The judgment is, therefore, just and fair: the woman is now to be under the authority and rule of her husband. This does not mean man is to be domineering and demanding. It simply means that by reaching out for the forbidden fruit, Eve had acted alone, taken control, and put matters into her own hands. She had sought an independence that was never intended to be between man and woman. Thus, the judgment is that she is to be under the very authority that she had attempted to take unto herself. She was to thereafter live under the authority of her husband. (See note—Ep.5:22-24 for more discussion.)

There is mercy in this: her submissiveness arouses respect and love within her husband. How? Her submissiveness attracts her husband to her. Her submissiveness...

- honors her husband within the home and before the world
- shows respect for her husband and family before the world
- eliminates differences, arguments, and disorderliness that would otherwise arise

The woman's submissiveness actually becomes a part of her attraction. A submissive spirit is soft, tender, warm, precious—always attractive to a caring, interested, or pursuing husband.

Thought 1. Remember this: in most societies women are tragically dominated—sometimes enslaved—by husbands and in some cases by men in general. Domination and enslavement—unequal opportunity in society and in the workplace—are not the judgment of God. This is due to sin and selfishness. God is clear: the husband is to *love* his wife, sacrificially love her, love her to the point that he would sacrifice all he is and has—including his own will and way—for her. The woman is condemned to be the subjected party within the family, but the family is to be ruled in love, sacrificial love.

"Wives, submit yourselves unto your own husbands, as it is fit in the Lord" (Col.3:18).

"Let the woman learn in silence with all subjection. But I suffer not a woman to teach, not to usurp authority over the man, but to be in silence. For Adam was first formed, then Eve" (1 Ti.2:11-13).

"Even so must their wives be grave, not slanderers, sober, faithful in all things" (1 Ti.3:11).

"That they may teach the young women to be sober, to love their husbands, to love their children" (Tit.2:4).

"Likewise, ye wives, be in subjection to your own husbands; that, if any obey not the word, they also may without the word be won by the conversation [behavior] of the wives" (1 Pe.3:1).

"She looketh well to the ways of her household, and eateth not the bread of idleness" (Pr.31:27).

	J. The First Judgment upon Sin (Part 3): Judgment upon Man, 3:17-19	eat of it all the days of thy life;	most basic necessity of life, food
1. He was condemned to live in a cursed world, a world of imperfection & corruption	17 And unto Adam he said, Because thou hast hearkened unto the voice of thy wife, and hast eaten of the tree, of which I commanded thee, saying, Thou shalt not eat of it: cursed is the ground for thy sake; in sorrow shalt thou	18 Thorns also and thistles shall it bring forth to thee; and thou shalt eat the herb of the field;	
2. He was condemned to struggle for survival, condemned to struggle against nature for the		19 In the sweat of thy face shalt thou eat bread, till thou return unto the ground; for out of it wast thou taken: for dust thou art, and unto dust shalt thou return.	3. He was condemned to die[DSI]

DIVISION II

ADAM, THE FIRST MAN (PART 1): THE BEGINNING OF MANKIND AND OF THE GODLY SEED—WHAT HAPPENED TO MAN AND THE EARTH, 2:4–3:24

J. The First Judgment upon Sin (Part 3): Judgment upon Man, 3:17-19

(3:17-19) **Introduction**: the first man upon earth sinned, tragically sinned, and he refused to accept the responsibility for his sin. Like so many today, he blamed his wife for his sin. He accused her of leading him into sin, of causing him to sin. It is true, she did approach and entice him to sin, but Adam himself stood guilty before God. In fact, he was guilty of at least three sins. Adam failed in at least three areas.

⇒ First, Adam did not try to lead Eve back to God. Just think what a failing this is! He did not *even try* to lead his wife to repentance, did not even bring up the subject of her returning to God. He did not even suggest that she confess and beg God for forgiveness and restoration.

⇒ Second, Adam listened to Eve's enticements and persuasions. He did not stop her from talking about and presenting the forbidden fruit to him. He stood there and listened to her persuasive arguments, to her enticements and seduction. Note, this is exactly what God says: *Because you have listened to the voice of your wife*, you are to be judged (v.17.) Adam failed—tragically failed—by listening to his wife, by not stopping her from talking about the forbidden fruit.

⇒ Third, Adam himself chose to eat the forbidden fruit. He blamed his wife, but Eve did not force him to eat the forbidden fruit. Adam *willfully chose*—made a *deliberate decision*—to sin. He knew exactly what he was doing. He was not deceived; his eyes were wide open when he sinned (1 Ti.2:14). He was guilty, willfully and deliberately guilty, of...

• rejecting God
• rebelling against God
• disobeying God
• turning away from God

Adam was, therefore, to be judged. He stood before God guilty, guilty of the most terrible sin: Adam had willfully and deliberately turned away from God. This is the great discussion of this passage: *The First Judgment upon Sin (Part 3): Judgment upon Man.*

1. He was condemned to live in a cursed world, a world of imperfection and corruption (v.17).
2. He was condemned to struggle for survival, condemned to struggle against nature for the most basic necessity of life, food (vv.17-18).
3. He was condemned to die (v.19).

Note one other fact: all of the judgments upon man fell upon the woman as well. There may be one difference, an emotional and psychological difference. In *judgment two*, man may be judged to suffer the pressure of providing the food and other necessities for the family more than the woman. Woman, of course, often senses the pressure of necessities, in particular if she is a single parent without a husband. But perhaps judgment two is condemning man to have a nature that suffers the pain of more pressure and stress than the woman. Man's shorter life span may be an indication of this.

1 (3:17) **Judgment—World—Adam—Man**: man was condemned to live in a cursed world, a world of imperfection and corruption. The Hebrew text says: "Cursed be the ground *because of you*," "on account of you." God cursed the earth because of Adam's sin.

Why? Why would the earth have to suffer a curse when it was Adam who sinned? Very simply stated, the earth was Adam's home. Adam and the earth were *interrelated*. Adam was now imperfect, a fallen creature. God could not let imperfect Adam continue on in a perfect world. Imperfection is not compatible with, not able to live with, perfection. Imperfection and sin do not belong with perfection and righteousness. Therefore, God had to curse the earth as part of the judgment upon Adam. The earth belonged to Adam and Adam belonged to the earth; they were as closely related as they could be. Therefore, whatever fall Adam suffered, the earth had to suffer the same fall as well.

Scripture explains what happened even more in Romans 8:19-22. This is an important passage for understanding what happened. Because of its importance, the Scripture, outline, and commentary of Romans 8:19-22 are being repeated here. Note what Romans says: all creation—the whole universe, not just the earth—was corrupted by sin.[1]

(Romans 8:19-22)

The creation suffers & struggles for deliverance from corruption	19 For the earnest expectation of the creature waiteth for the manifestation of the sons of God.
1. Creation is subject to corruption	20 For the creature was made subject to vanity, not willingly, but by reason of him who hath subjected the same in hope.
2. Creation will be delivered	21 Because the creature itself also shall be delivered from the bondage of corruption into the glorious liberty of the children of God.
3. Creation groans in labor for deliverance	22 For we know that the whole creation groaneth and travaileth in pain together until now.

Note that the creation suffers and struggles for deliverance from corruption. The word *creation* refers to everything *under* man: animal, plant, and mineral. All creation is pictured as living and waiting expectantly for the day when the sons of God will be glorified. The words *earnest expectation* (apokaradokia) means to watch with the neck out-stretched and the head erect. It is a persistent, unswerving expectation, an expectation that does not give up but keeps looking until the event happens. Note three facts revealed about the universe in which man lives.

a. Creation is subject to corruption. This is clearly seen by men; and what men see is constantly confirmed by such authorities as the botanist, zoologist, geologist, and astronomers of the world. All of creation, whether mineral, plant, or animal, suffers just as men do. All creation suffers hurt, damage, loss, deterioration, erosion, death, and decay; all creation struggles for life. It is full of *vanity* (mataios), that is, condemned to futility and frustration, unable to realize its purpose, subject to corruption. Note the two things said about creation in this verse (v.20).

1) Creation was condemned to vanity—futility and frustration—by God. Creation did not willingly choose to be condemned to corruption. The world was made to be the home of man, the place where he was to live. Therefore, when man sinned, his world was doomed to suffer the consequences of sin with him. Man's world was cursed right along with him.

> "Cursed is the earth for thy sake [because of you]" (Ge.3:17).
> "The earth mourneth and fadeth away, the world languisheth and fadeth away [for] the haughty people of the earth do languish. The earth also is defiled under the inhabitants thereof; because they have transgressed the laws, changed the ordinance, broken the everlasting covenant. Therefore hath the curse devoured the earth" (Is.24:4-6).
> "How long shall the land mourn, and the herbs of every field wither, for the wickedness of them that dwell therein?" (Je.12:4).

Thought 1. Just picture the enormous hurt and damage and decay that takes place in our world. Think about...
- the disease and savagery of the animal world
- the hurt and damage that so easily happens in the plant world
- the destruction and deterioration that takes place in the mineral world

Think about the earthquakes, tornados, storms, diseases, starvation, attacks, and struggles for survival that take place. And these are only a few of the myriad happenings that show the corruption of the world.

2) Creation has been subjected to corruption "in hope." The news of Scripture is glorious: the situation of the world is neither hopeless nor final. Creation has the same *hope of redemption and of renovation* as man. The world was made for man; therefore, all creation will be ultimately delivered from corruption just as man will be delivered from corruption.

b. Creation will be delivered from corruption. This is the wonderful news of the glorious gospel. Note a most significant point: whatever happens to man is bound to happen to his world. Man is the summit of God's creation; therefore, all that is under man is intertwined, interwoven, and interrelated to him. Man and his world are one and the same; they are dependent upon each other. This is enormously significant: since man and his world are interrelated, it means that the world will experience whatever man experiences. When man fell, his world was bound to fall with him. But this is the glorious news as well. When man is liberated from corruption, his world will be liberated as well. God had to subject man's world to man's fate, but God also had to subject man's world "in hope." Creation will experience the glorious hope

---

1 *Romans.* "The Preacher's Outline &Sermon Bible," Vol.7, Ro.8:18-27, pp.157-158.

of *living forever* with man, of being completely and perfectly renovated. There will be a "new heavens and a new earth" (see Ps.96:11-13; 98:7-9; Is.11:6-9; Re.5:13).

> "But the day of the Lord will come as a thief in the night; in the which the heavens shall pass away with a great noise, and the elements shall melt with fervent heat, the earth also and the works that are therein shall be burned up. Seeing then that all these things shall be dissolved, what manner of persons ought ye to be in all holy conversation and godliness, looking for and hasting unto the coming of the day of God, wherein the heavens being on fire shall be dissolved, and the elements shall melt with fervent heat? Nevertheless we, according to his promise, look for new heavens and a new earth, wherein dwelleth righteousness" (2 Pe.3:10-13).
>
> "And I saw a new heaven and a new earth: for the first heaven and the first earth were passed away" (Re.21:1; see He.12:26-27).
>
> "For, behold, I create new heavens and a new earth: and the former shall not be remembered, nor come into mind" (Is.65:17).
>
> "For as the new heavens and the new earth, which I will make, shall remain before me, saith the LORD, so shall your seed and your name remain" (Is.66:22).

c. Creation groans in labor for deliverance. Note that *all creation* suffers together: all creation is interrelated, intertwined, and interconnected. The whole universe is dependent upon its various parts for survival. The earth could not survive without the heavens, and the heavens would have no purpose apart from God's creation of man and his earth. This does not mean that man is to be egocentric or egotistical, nor that man is the only rational being within the universe. It simply means that man and his earth are the focal point of God's unbelievable creation, of His eternal plan and purpose in Christ. Being the center of creation *before God* is not a truth to make man proud, but to make him humble—a truth to cause him to bow in worship and praise, appreciation and thankfulness—a truth to make him carry the gospel to the far ends of the universe if there are rational beings there. Being the summit of God's creation is not a gift of privilege, not presently, but of enormous responsibility.

Note the word *groaneth* and *travaileth*. The picture is that of a woman giving birth. Creation experiences "birth pangs" under its struggle to survive. And note: it has been experiencing the "birth pangs" *until now*, that is, from the fall of man up until this present moment.

In conclusion, the whole scene of these four verses is that creation awaits a renovated world. Creation resents evil and struggles against decay and death. It fights for survival. It struggles against the bondage of being slaughtered or changed.

The idea expressed is that creation awaits the Day of Redemption: anxiously, expectantly, longingly, and eagerly awaits for its deliverance from corruption. Creation moans and groans and cries for the unveiling of the Son of God. God cursed the earth because of man's sin, yes, but God has also given the greatest hope imaginable to the earth—yea to the whole universe—the hope of eternal redemption.

> "Because the creature itself also shall be delivered from the bondage of corruption into the glorious liberty of the children of God" (Ro.8:21).
>
> "Nevertheless we, according to his promise, look for new heavens and a new earth, wherein dwelleth righteousness" (2 Pe.3:13).
>
> "And there shall be no more curse: but the throne of God and of the Lamb shall be in it; and his servants shall serve him: and they shall see his face; and his name shall be in their foreheads. And there shall be no night there; and they need no candle, neither light of the sun; for the Lord God giveth them light: and they shall reign for ever and ever" (Re.22:3-5).

2 (3:17c-19a) **Judgment—Labor—Needs—Necessities—Adam**: man was condemned to struggle for survival, condemned to struggle against nature for the most basic necessities of life. Note three things about this particular judgment upon man:

a. Man was condemned to suffer *sorrow* in meeting his most basic need: food. The word *sorrow* (itstsebhon) means pain, misery, toil, arduous labor, strenuous work. Before the fall of man into sin, his labor was not a strain. He was never miserable. His work and activity were always a pleasure and joy. Both he and his world were perfect; therefore, he never experienced the pain of aching muscles, nor of mental and physical exhaustion. But not now, not after his sin. Man now has to suffer...

- the pain of stress, pressure, tension
- the pain of toil, labor, and work
- the pain of mental and physical fatigue

And note: he has to suffer this pain *all the days* of his life. The ground—nature itself—had been cursed because of man's sin. Consequently, man is condemned to struggle for survival, to struggle against the forces of nature for the very basic necessities of life.

b. Man was condemned to struggle against the thorns and thistles of the earth. Before man's sin and fall, the earth had produced every good fruit and plant imaginable for man. Nature was completely under control. All of man's necessities were abundantly met. But not now, not since man's sin. Nature is no longer under control. It produces thorns and thistles and all kinds of problems for man. Man always has to struggle against nature—struggle to control nature—in order to protect his most basic necessity, the very food he eats.

Imagine! Just to eat—just to meet his most basic necessity—man would have to struggle and fight to control nature itself.

Note: the idea in this particular judgment is not just thorns and thistles, not just man struggling against thorns and thistles in order to eat. The idea is that nature is no longer under control; nature is no longer going to produce plenty for man, not naturally, not orderly, not regularly. Man has been condemned to struggle against nature—against the thorns and thistles of nature—against all of nature in order to meet his most basic need, that of eating. Food—man's most basic need—is just an example of *all the basic necessities* he needs. Man has to struggle against nature for all his necessities—shelter, clothing, and food. He could live without shelter and clothing, but he could not live without food. Apparently, God chose to talk about the struggle for food because it was the most basic need Adam had. But, again, the point is this: nature is no longer under control, no longer perfect. Nature is, therefore, to produce both good and bad things, to be both under control and uncontrollable. Man had to struggle against nature for survival, struggle to meet his most basic needs, even his need for food.

c. Man was condemned to sweat in order to eat, in order to control nature and meet his most basic need. The point is twofold.

1) Man's struggle against nature is strenuous and difficult. Man has been condemned to *sweat*—to work hard—in order to have anything. This is true even in securing his most basic necessity, food. The struggle against the earth—against nature and its irregular and uncontrolled features—is a strenuous and difficult struggle. Man's needs, his most basic needs, are to be met by sweat, tears, and toil.

2) Man's struggle against nature has to go on and on, to last all of his life, until he returns to the ground. Everything man has and owns—even food—is uncertain since the fall of Adam. Some happening—some quick, some uncontrolled event in nature—can snatch away everything a man has. Man is condemned to struggle for survival all the days of his life.

Thought 1. God's mercy is seen even in the midst of this judgment. Man's hard labor and sweat will produce results. He will be able to feed himself, to meet the necessities of life. But note: he must labor and labor diligently in order to have his necessities met.

"And the LORD God took the man, and put him into the garden of Eden to dress it and to keep it" (Ge.2:15).

"Cursed is the ground for thy sake; in sorrow shalt thou eat of it all the days of thy life; thorns also and thistles shall it bring forth to thee; and thou shalt eat the herb of the field; in the sweat of thy face shalt thou eat bread" (Ge.3:17^c-19^a).

"Servants [employees], be obedient to them that are your masters [employers] according to the flesh, with fear and trembling, in singleness of your heart, as unto Christ" (Ep.6:5).

"Servants, obey in all things your masters according to the flesh; not with eyeservice, as menpleasers; but in singleness of heart, fearing God" (Col.3:22).

"Let as many servants as are under the yoke count their own masters worthy of all honour, that the name of God and his doctrine be not blasphemed" (1 Ti.6:1).

"Exhort servants to be obedient unto their own masters, and to please them well in all things; not answering again" (Tit.2:9).

"Servants, be subject to your masters with all fear; not only to the good and gentle, but also to the froward" (1 Pe.2:18).

"I went by the field of the slothful, and by the vineyard of the man void of understanding; and, lo, it was all grown over with thorns, and nettles had covered the face thereof, and the stone wall thereof was broken down" (Pr.24:30-31).

"By much slothfulness the building decayeth; and through idleness of the hands the house droppeth through" (Ec.10:18).

"That ye be not slothful, but followers of them who through faith and patience inherit the promises" (He.6:12).

3 (3:19^b) **Death—Judgment—Man**: man was condemned to die. Remember: Adam and the world were created perfect. In a perfect world, there is perfect fellowship and sharing between God and man. God must have discussed *death* with Adam when He warned Adam about sin and its consequence of death. God is bound to have shared with Adam what sin and death meant, its terrible tragedy and consequences. Just as we understand all about the tragedy and consequence of sin today, so Adam understood. God would not have left him in the dark even as He has not left us in the dark. Note three significant points about this judgment of death.

a. Adam himself brought death and corruption to the world. God had warned Adam: if he ate of the forbidden fruit, he would surely die (Ge.2:17). Adam turned away from God; he disobeyed and rejected God's Word.

⇒ Adam set in motion the law of disobedience, of disorder, and of imbalance which results in corruption.

From the point of Adam's sin onward, he and all that were in the world were to experience...

- aging
- deterioration
- decay
- disorder
- imbalance
- wearing away
- wasting away
- returning to dust

b. The judgment upon Adam was a judgment upon all mankind. Adam was the father of the human race. History, experience, and the Bible—all three—proclaim the judgment of the earth's curse and of man's death. Adam stands as a figurehead, as a representative man, for all men (see note—Ro.5:12-14 for more discussion).

c. Adam was condemned to death. What does *death* mean? What does it mean *to die*? (See DEEPER STUDY #3—Ge.2:17 for discussion.)

DEEPER STUDY # 1

(3:19) **Jesus Christ—Judgment**: Matthew Henry gives an excellent description of how the death of Jesus Christ answered the judgment passed upon the sin of our first parents, Adam and Eve.[2] Matthew Henry asks:

1. Did sin bring travailing pain into the world? Scripture declares...
   - that Christ's death was "the travail of His soul" (Is.53:11)
   - that the pain of death that held Him was a *pain* (odinai) just like the *travail* (odinai) of a woman (Ac.2:24). Note how the two Hebrew words are the same

2. Did sin bring subjection into the world? Christ was made "under the law," subject to the law, for the very purpose of dying for the transgressions of the law (Ga.4:4-5).

3. Did sin bring the curse upon the world and man? Christ was made a curse for us (Ga.3:13).

4. Did sin bring thorns upon earth? Christ wore a crown of thorns for us (Mk.15:17).

5. Did sin bring sweat into the world? Christ sweated drops of blood for us (Lu.22:44; see He.12:4).

6. Did sin bring sorrow into the world? Christ was the man of sorrows. His death involved so much agony that the sorrow of His soul almost killed Him (Mt.26:38; Mk.14:34).

7. Did sin bring death into the world? He was obedient to death, even to the death of the cross (Ph.2:8).

---

2 *Matthew Henry's Commentary*, Vol.1, pp.33-34.

	K. The First Provision of God for Man: God Provides Life & Clothing (Righteousness) for Man, 3:20-21
1. Adam names the woman, Eve: He believes God's provision for birth & life 2. God provides clothing for man & woman, clothing through sacrifice	20 And Adam called his wife's name Eve; because she was the mother of all living. 21 Unto Adam also and to his wife did the LORD God make coats of skins, and clothed them.

DIVISION II

ADAM, THE FIRST MAN (PART 1): THE BEGINNING OF MANKIND AND OF THE GODLY SEED—WHAT HAPPENED TO MAN AND THE EARTH, 2:4–3:24

K. The First Provision of God for Man: God Provides Life and Clothing (Righteousness) for Man, 3:20-21

(3:20-21) **Introduction**: the first judgment has just been pronounced upon man and woman. Both man and his world have been judged to suffer under the corruption of imperfection. Man, tragically, is to be struggling for survival in a hostile and evil world, a world that will eventually snatch his life away. Man is condemned to the most awful fate imaginable, the doom of death and eternal separation from God—unless God can save him. This is the subject of this great passage: *The First Provision of God for Man: God Provides Life and Clothing (Righteousness) for Man.*

1. Adam names the woman, Eve: he believes God's provision for birth and life (v.20).
2. God provides clothing for man and woman, clothing through sacrifice (v.21).

1 (3:20) **Eve—Life—Faith—Belief—Salvation**: Adam names the woman, Eve: he believes God's provision for birth and life. This is the first time the name *Eve* appears in Scripture. We sometimes overlook this fact, so much so that we often refer to *Eve* when discussing the creation and the fall of man and woman into sin. But Scripture never refers to the woman as *Eve* in these accounts. She has been called *female* (Ge.1:27); a *help-meet* or *suitable helper* (Ge.2:18); *wife* (Ge.2:24-25; 3:8, 17, 20-21); and usually *woman* (Ge.2:22-23; 3:1-2, 4, 6, 12-13, 15-16). But now Adam names his wife, and the name he gives her is very significant. The name *Eve* (chavvah) means to live, to give life, or the mother of all living. Different commentators give the Hebrew word different shades of meaning, such as to breathe, to propagate life, and to quicken seed.[1] But the fundamental meaning of the name is *life*. *Eve* means to give life, to spring forth life, to propagate life. Note the latter part of the verse. This is exactly why Adam named his wife Eve: she was the mother of all living.

As stated, this is very significant. When Adam named his wife *Eve*, he was acting in faith. Remember: Eve had no children; no child was yet born. Adam did not even know what pregnancy and giving birth involved, not yet, for no pregnancy or birth had ever taken place upon earth. By naming his wife *Eve*, Adam was showing that he accepted and believed God's Word, God's promise. What Word, what promise?

a. First, there was God's promise made in verses 15 and 16, the promise that Eve would *bear seed and bring forth children.*

⇒ Note the promise made in verse 15 where God is judging Satan. God says there will be enmity—hostility—between the devil's seed (followers) and the woman's seed (believers). God clearly says that the woman will be bearing seed or children.

⇒ Note the promise made in verse 16 where God is judging the woman. God clearly says that she shall conceive and "bring forth children."

b. Second, there was God's promise made in the latter part of verse 15, the promise that Eve would bring forth a seed—one particular child—who would crush the head of the serpent or Satan. In speaking to the serpent or Satan, God clearly said,

"It [the seed, the Savior, which is singular] shall bruise [or crush] thy head, and thou shalt bruise his heel" (Ge.3:15b).

The point is this: Adam believed the Word of God; he believed these two promises of God. Remember, as pointed out, Adam and Eve had no children, not yet. They had no experience in bearing children; they had no way to know that they could even bear children, not after they had sinned. The only way Adam could know his wife was going to bear children was for God to tell him. This God did; this is clearly stated in the two Scriptures covered above (vv.15-16). Adam believed God, believed the Word and promises of God. Therefore, he named his dear wife Eve, which means *life*. His wife

---

[1] *The Pulpit Commentary*, Vol.1, p.72.

was to bring forth children, and more importantly, she was to bear *the promised seed* or Savior who would save them and their children.

Note this also: faith—true faith—always involves repentance. A person who truly believes God always repents. He always turns away from sin and turns to God, completely and fully. This means that Adam repented of his sin, truly repented.

Thought 1. Adam is a dynamic example for us, a dynamic example of faith. He knew nothing—absolutely nothing—about the birth process. He had...

- never *seen* a pregnant woman before
- never *touched* a baby
- never *heard* a baby cry

All Adam had was the sheer Word and promise of God, that God would give life to the world, both the life of other human beings and the life of one particular person, the Savior.

The same promise is given to us. We already have life upon earth as human beings, but just as Adam and Eve were condemned to die, so we are doomed to die. However, we do not have to die. We can have the life of the Savior. We can be saved from the judgment of death just as Adam and Eve were. We can live forever through the cross of *the promised seed*, the Lord Jesus Christ. How? By doing what Adam did: believing and accepting the Word and promise of God. We have the very same thing Adam had, God's Word and promise of life. All we have to do is believe—truly believe—and commit our lives to God's Word and promise about Jesus Christ.

"In him was life; and the life was the light of men" (Jn.1:4).
"For God so loved the world, that he gave his only begotten Son, that whosoever believeth in him should not perish, but have everlasting life" (Jn.3:16).
"Verily, verily, I say unto you, He that heareth my word, and believeth on him that sent me, hath everlasting life, and shall not come into condemnation; but is passed from death unto life" (Jn.5:24).
"I am come that they might have life, and that they might have it more abundantly" (Jn.10:10).
"Jesus said unto her, I am the resurrection, and the life: he that believeth in me, though he were dead, yet shall he live" (Jn.11:25).
"But these are written, that ye might believe that Jesus is the Christ, the Son of God; and that believing ye might have life through his name" (Jn.20:31).
"But [God's grace] is now made manifest by the appearing of our Saviour Jesus Christ, who hath abolished death, and hath brought life and immortality to light through the gospel" (2 Ti.1:10).
"And this is the record, that God hath given to us eternal life, and this life is in his Son. He that hath the Son hath life; and he that hath not the Son of God hath not life" (1 Jn.5:11-12).

2 **(3:21) Sacrifice—Necessities—Needs—Righteousness**: God provides clothing for man and woman, clothing through sacrifice. Note that God Himself makes the clothing for Adam and Eve, and that He Himself actually clothes them. This verse, as much as any, shows the enormous love and care of God for man and woman. Note exactly what God did.

a. God Himself met the need of man and woman for the raw, basic necessities of life. The world had been corrupted by sin. It was now afflicted with the disorder and confusion of nature, with harsh and dangerous weather. Man and woman were soon to be expelled from the Garden of Eden out into the world. The only clothing they had was made of fig leaves, and fig leaves would never last nor protect them from severe weather. They needed one of the very basic necessities of life, that of clothing. But they had no idea how they could meet their need; they had no idea how to secure heavier clothing that would last and be more protective. They had been living in a perfect world where there was no harsh weather nor any need for heavy clothing.

But note this: God knew. God knew how sin had corrupted the earth, how cold the weather would sometimes get and how violent nature and weather would sometimes react. God knew that fig leaves would never last nor provide the protection Adam and Eve needed; therefore, God provided for their need. God Himself made clothes for man and woman, and God Himself put the clothing across their shoulders. Imagine this tender act, actually laying the skins upon their shoulders. God showed man and woman both how to make clothing and how to clothe themselves.

A question needs to be asked at this point: Why did God do this? There are at least two reasons.

⇒ God wanted to show His great love and care for man and woman. God loves and cares for us; therefore, God always reaches out to show us His love and care.
⇒ God wanted to teach man and woman that He would take care of their necessities. God will always meet our needs if we will trust and follow after Him. Adam and Eve needed to know this great lesson as they stepped out and began their journey together in the harsh and violent world of sin and evil.

This is the same lesson we need to learn. God will meet our needs, our necessities—always—just as He met Adam's and Eve's. But He can help us only if we let Him, only if we trust and follow Him, only if we do what He says:

"But seek ye first the kingdom of God, and his righteousness; and all these things [food, shelter, clothing] shall be added unto you" (Mt.6:33; see 6:25-33).
"But my God shall supply all your need according to his riches in glory by Christ Jesus" (Ph.4:19).
"Casting all your care upon him; for he careth for you" (1 Pe.5:7).

"And ye shall serve the LORD your God, and he shall bless thy bread, and thy water; and I will take sickness away from the midst of thee" (Ex.23:25).

"Oh how great is thy goodness, which thou hast laid up for them that fear thee; which thou hast wrought for them that trust in thee before the sons of men!" (Ps.31:19).

"Be merciful unto me, O God, be merciful unto me: for my soul trusteth in thee: yea, in the shadow of thy wings will I make my refuge, until these calamities be overpast" (Ps.57:1).

"For thou hast been a strength to the poor, a strength to the needy in his distress, a refuge from the storm, a shadow from the heat, when the blast of the terrible ones is as a storm against the wall" (Is.25:4).

"Fear thou not; for I am with thee: be not dismayed; for I am thy God: I will strengthen thee; yea, I will help thee; yea, I will uphold thee with the right hand of my righteousness" (Is.41:10).

b. God taught man and woman that sin causes the most terrible things imaginable, even death. Note what God used to clothe man and woman: the skins of animals. Imagine Adam and Eve standing there as the animals were slaughtered. They had never seen blood nor the agony, pain, and suffering of death before. They must have stood there in shock, stricken with the horror and devastation of sin. When the animals were slaughtered, Adam and Eve learned the terrible results of sin.

1) Adam and Eve learned that the animal kingdom was thrown into utter disorder and confusion. They learned that sin had caused terrible suffering and pain for the animal world of the earth.

2) Adam and Eve learned that the whole world—all of life and nature, including their own personal lives—was thrown into utter confusion and disorder. Sin leads to corruption and death.

3) Adam and Eve learned what death meant. An awesome fear must have gripped their hearts. God had warned them, if they sinned, they would die. Now, Adam and Eve knew exactly what death meant. Every death they witnessed in the future would forever remind them...

• that they, too, were soon to die
• that they must trust God for life beyond death

4) Adam and Eve learned what mercy meant and how dependent they were upon the mercy of God. God had warned them: if they sinned, they would die. But note: their death was delayed. They were allowed to live upon earth for some years and to prove their trust in God and their worthiness to live with God throughout eternity.

"And many of them that sleep in the dust of the earth shall awake, some to everlasting life, and some to shame and everlasting contempt" (Da.12:2).

"And these shall go away into everlasting punishment: but the righteous into life eternal" (Mt.25:46).

"Labour not for the meat which perisheth, but for that meat which endureth unto everlasting life, which the Son of man shall give unto you: for him hath God the Father sealed" (Jn.6:27).

"And I give unto them eternal life; and they shall never perish, neither shall any man pluck them out of my hand" (Jn.10:28).

"To them who by patient continuance in well doing seek for glory and honour and immortality, eternal life" (Ro.2:7).

"But now being made free from sin, and become servants to God, ye have your fruit unto holiness, and the end everlasting life. For the wages of sin is death; but the gift of God is eternal life through Jesus Christ our Lord" (Ro.6:22-23).

"For to be carnally minded is death; but to be spiritually minded is life and peace" (Ro.8:6).

"Laying up in store for themselves a good foundation against the time to come, that they may lay hold on eternal life" (1 Ti.6:19).

"In hope of eternal life, which God, that cannot lie, promised before the world began" (Tit.1:2).

"And this is the promise that he hath promised us, even eternal life" (1 Jn.2:25).

"Keep yourselves in the love of God, looking for the mercy of our Lord Jesus Christ unto eternal life" (Jude 21).

c. God met the need of man and woman to cover their shame. When Adam and Eve sinned, they were immediately affected emotionally and spiritually: they immediately felt guilt and shame.

Before they sinned, they were perfect: they had no sense of guilt, shame, sin, evil, wrong, or nakedness—no sense of anything negative whatsoever. As discussed in an earlier passage, Adam and Eve had most likely been clothed with the shining light of glory and perfection (see notes—Ge.1:26; 3:7). But sin changed all this: sin corrupted man and woman, stripped them of glory and perfection. They became conscious and aware of sin, that they had done wrong and were guilty of wrong-doing. They felt guilt and shame; they became aware of their nakedness. Remember: they had rushed into the bushes and made aprons of fig leaves.

The point is this: after their confession and repentance—after they had been reconciled with God—God clothed Adam and Eve. God Himself clothed their shame. This taught Adam and Eve two things:

⇒ God alone could cover their feelings of shame and guilt.
⇒ God alone could make them feel right within their hearts, within their inner soul and spirit.

Thought 1. This, of course, points to the righteousness of Jesus Christ, the righteousness which must clothe every person who wishes to become acceptable to God. The only way a person can have his guilt and shame covered is to be clothed in the righteousness of Christ. The righteousness of Jesus Christ alone...

- can cover the guilt and shame of sin
- can clothe a person with the righteousness that God accepts

> **"For he hath made him to be sin for us, who knew no sin; that we might be made the righteousness of God in him" (2 Co.5:21).**
> **"And that ye put on the new man, which after God is created in righteousness and true holiness" (Ep.4:24; see Ro.13:14; Col.3:10; Is.61:10).**
> **"Whom God hath set forth to be a propitiation through faith in his blood, to declare his righteousness for the remission of sins that are past, through the forbearance of God" (Ro.3:25).**

d. God taught man and woman that the sacrifice of life was necessary to clothe their shame. Again, note how God clothed Adam and Eve: by slaughtering several animals—by taking the life and shedding the blood of others. The life of animals had to be sacrificed in order to clothe the shame and guilt that man and woman felt. Adam and Eve were bound to grasp this fact as they stood there witnessing the slaughter. Remember: they had been perfect in intelligence, and sin had not yet had time to affect their minds too much. Adam and Eve were certainly able to see and reason about what was happening: a life was being taken in order to clothe them. A life was being substituted in order to cover the shame and guilt they felt, in order to reconcile them to God.

Note another fact as well. Scripture does not say this, but common sense and logic would certainly point to this: God loved Adam and Eve just as He loves us. They were, after all, to be the parents of the whole human race. God is bound to have taught them the need for sacrifice in order to be saved...

- taught them what He was doing in sacrificing the animals, that He was clothing their sense of shame and guilt
- taught them that the sacrifice of the coming Savior was necessary to save them
- taught them that the serpent's (Satan's) bruising of the woman's seed referred to the Savior and the sacrifice He was to make for man and woman
- taught them that the crushing of the serpent's (Satan's) head was to be accomplished by the death of the Savior
- taught them that the Savior Himself was to give His life as their substitute, that He was to die for their sins (as their ransom and propitiation)
- taught them that it was by the blood of the sacrifice that they were to be reconciled to God

Some may argue that God did not reveal all this to Adam and Eve, that Scripture says nothing about it, that such in-depth revelation overlooks progressive revelation. In all honesty, such arguments may be true. But note these points:

First, Adam and Eve had been created perfect, which means perfect in the ability to reason, learn, grasp, and think things through. They had *just fallen* into sin, so sin could not have affected their reasoning ability all that much, not yet. It would take time, sin after sin, to take its toll upon their minds. True, their minds would become more and more depraved as they committed sin after sin. But such time had not yet passed for Adam and Eve. Some may argue that the mind and its reasoning ability was so totally corrupted by sin that Adam and Eve were unable to see what God was doing. This is most unlikely. This would make their minds and reasoning ability to be far less than what ours is today. The reasoning ability of the human mind is phenomenal despite sin and depravity. This fact is proven every day in the modern world through technology, science, and medicine. The point is this: Adam and Eve, even if they were left with nothing but their reasoning ability, could certainly grasp something of what God was doing. They were bound to realize that animals were being slaughtered and sacrificed in order for God to cover their shame and guilt. They were bound to reason *at least* this fact.

Second, God loved Adam and Eve. Why would He not discuss what He was doing with them?

Third, Adam and Eve were the parents of the whole human race. No one else existed. Whatever God wanted the human race to know, God had to teach Adam and Eve so they could in turn teach their children. One of the lessons God wanted man to know was this: how He, God, was to be approached. He was to be approached through sacrifice, the sacrifice of a life for a life, that of a substitute. Why would God not share this most basic of all truths—most basic of all needs that man has—with Adam and Eve?

The fact is, God did. Scripture shows us that God told Adam and Eve that He was to be approached through sacrifice. They taught their children how to approach God. This is seen in their son Abel's sacrifice and in the fact that God accepted his sacrifice.

> **"And Abel, he also brought of the firstlings of his flock and of the fat thereof. And the LORD had respect unto Abel and to his offering" (Ge.4:4).**

Fourth, Adam and Eve began life in a perfect world and knew perfect fellowship with God. In a perfect world God would share everything necessary with His people. Even after the first sin, God's love would certainly get man started off right. God would certainly share in detail how man was to worship and approach God, and that God was going to provide a Savior for man.

This is what this verse, Genesis 3:21, is teaching. God taught Adam and Eve that they were to approach Him through sacrifice, the shedding of blood. Then Adam and Eve taught their children. Not all the children listened and learned (Cain), just as all persons do not listen and learn today. Nevertheless, there is only one way to approach God, only one approach that God accepts:

⇒ the way of sacrifice
⇒ the way of His Son and the sacrifice of His dear Son's life for our life

Thought 1. Jesus Christ died for our sins, died in our place, in our stead, as our substitute. Jesus Christ took our sins upon Himself and bore the penalty and punishment of our sins, bore the judgment for us. Jesus Christ sacrificed His life for us. Therefore, we are able to stand before God *without sin, perfectly righteous*—all because

Christ has removed our sins from us. We are acceptable to God because we are counted sinless, and we are *counted sinless* because Jesus Christ took our sins off us and bore the punishment for us.

But note: this happens only when we trust—truly trust—Jesus Christ as our Savior, only when we trust Christ so much that we cast our whole lives upon Him in total commitment. It is then that God counts Christ as our substitute, then and only then that God counts our sins forgiven—as having been borne and paid for by Christ.

> **"For this is my blood of the new testament, which is shed for many for the remission of sins" (Mt.26:28).**

> **"For when we were yet without strength, in due time Christ died for the ungodly" (Ro.5:6).**

> **"Much more then, being now justified by his blood, we shall be saved from wrath through him" (Ro.5:9).**

> **"For I delivered unto you first of all that which I also received, how that Christ died for our sins according to the scriptures" (1 Co.15:3).**

> **"The next day John seeth Jesus coming unto him, and saith, Behold the Lamb of God, which taketh away the sin of the world" (Jn.1:29).**

> **"Who gave himself for our sins, that he might deliver us from this present evil world, according to the will of God and our Father" (Ga.1:4).**

> **"In whom we have redemption through his blood, the forgiveness of sins, according to the riches of his grace" (Ep.1:7).**

> **"Who gave himself for us, that he might redeem us from all iniquity, and purify unto himself a peculiar people, zealous of good works" (Tit.2:14).**

> **"How much more shall the blood of Christ, who through the eternal Spirit offered himself without spot to God, purge your conscience from dead works to serve the living God?" (He.9:14).**

> **"And almost all things are by the law purged with blood; and without shedding of blood is no remission" (He.9:22).**

> **"Forasmuch as ye know that ye were not redeemed with corruptible things, as silver and gold, from your vain conversation [behavior] received by tradition from your fathers; but with the precious blood of Christ, as of a lamb without blemish and without spot" (1 Pe.1:18-19).**

> **"Hereby perceive we the love of God, because he laid down his life for us: and we ought to lay down our lives for the brethren" (1 Jn.3:16).**

	L. The First Act of Deliverance or Salvation: Man Is Saved from Living Forever as a Sinner in a Fallen World, 3:22-24	for ever: 23 Therefore the LORD God sent him forth from the garden of Eden, to till the ground from whence he was taken.	3. God's deliverance or salvation a. God delivered man by driving him from the Garden of Eden
1. God's problem: Man had sinned; man knew not only good, but evil[DS1] 2. God's decision: Man must not be allowed to live forever as a sinner in a fallen world	22 And the LORD God said, Behold, the man is become as one of us, to know good and evil: and now, lest he put forth his hand, and take also of the tree of life, and eat, and live	24 So he drove out the man; and he placed at the east of the garden of Eden Cherubims, and a flaming sword which turned every way, to keep the way of the tree of life.	b. God delivered man by posting angelic beings, cherubim, to guard the entrance to the tree of life[DS2,3]

DIVISION II

ADAM, THE FIRST MAN (PART 1): THE BEGINNING OF MANKIND AND OF THE GODLY SEED—WHAT HAPPENED TO MAN AND THE EARTH, 2:4–3:24

L. The First Act of Deliverance or Salvation: Man Is Saved from Living Forever as a Sinner in a Fallen World, 3:22-24

(3:22-24) **Introduction**: God created man to bless him beyond all imagination (see outline and notes—Ge.2:15-17 for discussion). But man turned away from God and rejected Him. What was God to do? Was He to let His purpose for man be defeated? This was impossible—absolutely impossible—for He is God, and God's purposes can never be defeated. Therefore, God did exactly what He had told man He would do if man rebelled against Him:

⇒ God judged man (see outlines and notes—Ge.3:14-19 for discussion).
⇒ But God also put His purposes back on track. God worked out a way for man to still receive life and clothing, the clothing of righteousness (see outline and notes—Ge.3:20-21).

This we have already seen and studied. But now, God still has one more problem to handle. There still remains one more thing to do. God must deliver and save man from living forever as a sinner in a fallen world. This is the discussion of this great passage: *The First Act of Deliverance or Salvation: Man Is Saved from Living Forever as a Sinner in a Fallen World.*

1. God's problem: man had sinned; he knew not only good, but evil (v.22).
2. God's decision: man must not be allowed to live forever as a sinner in a fallen world (v.22).
3. God's deliverance or salvation (vv.23-24).

[1] (3:22) **Man—Sin—Evil**: God's problem was this: man had sinned; man knew not only good, but evil. Because of evil, catastrophic consequences were to fall upon man and his world. How to save man and his world from these catastrophic consequences—how to still fulfill His eternal purpose for man and the world—was the problem facing God. Now, what does Scripture mean when it says that man knows evil? It means at least two things.

a. To know evil means that man has *personally corrupted himself*. When God first created man, man was perfect, without any flaw whatsoever. In addition, man was given a perfect environment: man was placed in a perfect world, and even more than that, he was given *the Garden of Eden*, the most beautiful and bountiful paradise he could ever imagine. Man had all the fullness of life, and he was to live forever. He was in utopia, possessing everything—all the provision, security, joy, and happiness—he could ever want. And on top of this, he was given authority and dominion over all the world (see DEEPER STUDY # 3—Ge.1:28 for discussion). But even more than this, within Eden man had the very presence of God. Man talked and fellowshipped with God face to face. Eden was the very picture of heaven on earth, of what the new heavens and earth will be like. When God created man, He gave man everything *in perfection*. Man was perfect, and his environment was perfect. But man sinned. Man...

- turned away from God
- refused to follow God
- rejected God
- disobeyed God's commandment (Word)
- rebelled against God

This is what God means by evil. Evil is...

- turning away from God
- refusing to follow God
- rejecting God
- disobeying God's commandment (Word)
- rebelling against God

This was what Adam had done, turned away from God and taken of the forbidden fruit. Adam now knew evil.

⇒ Adam had walked away from God; he had chosen to be alienated from God, chosen to walk throughout life on his own.
⇒ Adam had refused to follow the perfect way of God; he had chosen to follow his own way in life, to do his own thing.

⇒ Adam had rejected the life of God which is eternal life; he had chosen to no longer live with God.
⇒ Adam had disobeyed God's commandment (Word); he had chosen not to be sinless and perfect.
⇒ Adam had rebelled against God; he had chosen not to live in the perfect world and presence of God.

Adam stood before God guilty and condemned. Adam now knew evil; Adam had acted against God. He had committed terrible evil against God.

Before Adam sinned, he knew nothing about evil, nothing whatsoever. But after he sinned, he knew evil. He personally corrupted himself.

b. To know evil means that man has *personally experienced evil*. Note exactly what Scripture says:

"Man is become as one of us, to know [personally know] good and evil" (v.22).

Man is said to know evil even as God knows evil. But there is a vast difference between God's knowledge of evil and man's knowledge of evil.

1) God knows evil because He sees evil as it lies spread out before Him. God does not know evil by experience. God does not think evil nor do evil. God knows evil only in the sense that He sees it as it happens, as it is committed by others. But how terrible this is. Just think of the pain that cuts God's heart when evil is done, when He is rejected, disobeyed, and turned against. Every thought and act of evil cuts God's heart and causes a wretched pain beyond anything we could ever know.

How much evil does God know about? Every evil thought and act upon earth. God even sees all the ramifications—every twist and turn—of every evil thought and act. God sees and knows...

• the first flash of an evil thought that crosses our minds
• the harboring of the evil thought
• the first arousal of evil desire or lust
• the decision to do evil
• the actual act of evil

Nothing is hid from God. God sees and knows all—every evil thought and act upon earth. This is how God knows evil, not by experience, but by seeing evil as it is spread out before Him. God sees evil as it happens, as others think and do evil. But this is not true with man.

2) Man knows evil by personal experience. Man thinks and does evil. Man harbors evil thoughts and man commits evil acts. Man has plunged himself into evil and learned what evil is by experience.

This was the great problem God faced. Man had sinned, and he was now imperfect and corrupt. God had created man to bless him beyond all imagination, but man had turned against and rejected God. What was God to do? Was He to let His purpose for man be defeated? He could not, for He was God, and God's purposes can never be defeated. Therefore, God fulfilled His Word: He judged man and then He provided the way of salvation and deliverance for man (see note—Ge.3:21, esp. pt.c.-d.. See note—Ge.3:15.)

This we have already seen and studied. But now, God still has one more problem to handle. There still remains one more thing to do. God must save and deliver man from living forever as a sinner in a fallen world.

> **"As it is written, There is none righteous, no, not one: there is none that understandeth, there is none that seeketh after God. They are all gone out of the way, they are together become unprofitable; there is none that doeth good, no, not one. Their throat is an open sepulchre; with their tongues they have used deceit; the poison of asps is under their lips: whose mouth is full of cursing and bitterness: their feet are swift to shed blood: destruction and misery are in their ways: and the way of peace have they not known: there is no fear of God before their eyes" (Ro.3:10-18).**
> **"For all have sinned, and come short of the glory of God" (Ro.3:23).**
> **"If we say that we have no sin, we deceive ourselves, and the truth is not in us" (1 Jn.1:8).**
> **"Every one of them is gone back: they are altogether become filthy; there is none that doeth good, no, not one" (Ps.53:3).**
> **"Who can say, I have made my heart clean, I am pure from my sin?" (Pr.20:9).**
> **"But we are all as an unclean thing, and all our righteousnesses are as filthy rags; and we all do fade as a leaf; and our iniquities, like the wind, have taken us away" (Is.64:6).**

DEEPER STUDY # 1
(3:22) **God—Trinity**: this note is discussed in DEEPER STUDY # 3 (Ge.3:24) to keep from breaking the reader's thought of the outline and its discussion.

---

2 (3:22) **Man—God—Mercy—World, Fallen:** God's decision was this: man must not be allowed to live forever as a sinner in a fallen world. Remember: the whole world was corrupted when Adam sinned (see note 1—Ge.3:17 for discussion). But Adam was still in paradise, still in the Garden of Eden, still in the perfect home God had created especially for man. Note the Scripture. God knew this fact: if He left Adam in the Garden, Adam could still eat the fruit from the *tree of life* and live forever (see note 4, *Tree of Life*—Ge.2:9 for discussion). But this would be the most tragic thing that could have happened to both Adam and God. Adam was sinful and corrupt. God just could not allow Adam to eat of the tree of life, not after having sinned: God could not allow sinful man and evil to continue on and on forever.

⇒ God could not allow man to live forever as *a sinful, corrupt being*; a being who would never again know the fullness of God's presence, love, grace, provision, care, security, joy, and peace; a being who would live under the curse of being judged, condemned, and punished forever and ever; a being who would never have the opportunity to be saved.

⇒ God could not allow Himself to be cursed, rejected, disobeyed, and often denied, not forever and ever, not by just any man who would choose to so react against God.

God had no choice. To save man, He made a heart-rending decision. God acted in mercy, both for Adam and for Himself: man must not be allowed to live forever as a sinner in a fallen and corrupt world. Just what God does is seen in the next note.

"And God saw that the wickedness of man was great in the earth, and that every imagination of the thoughts of his heart was only evil continually" (Ge.6:5. Note how this verse and history show how wise God's decision was; see Ro.3:10-18 included in the verses above under note 1, pt.b.)

3 (3:23-24) **Deliverance—Salvation**: God's deliverance or salvation was twofold.

a. God delivered man by driving him from the Garden of Eden. Note the double reference to God sending Adam out or expelling him from the Garden. The second reference states that God *drove* Adam out of the Garden (vv.23-24).

Remember, the Garden of Eden was paradise on earth, a picture of what the new heavens and earth will be when God recreates them. Within the Garden, man had everything—provision, security, joy, and fulfillment—all in perfection. Man talked face to face with God; walked and fellowshipped with God. Man worshipped, worked, and served God in perfection. This is, most likely, the reason God had to drive Adam from the Garden. Adam did not want to leave the presence of God nor the perfection of God's paradise. Adam knew that he was being...

- separated from God
- alienated from God
- removed from God's presence
- excluded from paradise

"But your iniquities have separated between you and your God, and your sins have hid his face from you, that he will not hear" (Is.59:2; see Ep.4:18).

Adam knew that his sin had come between him and God, and that he must bear the judgment of his sin. He knew this, but he had experienced paradise. Consequently, he did just what any of us would do: he struggled against leaving, against going out into the world. But God knew best. God loved Adam; therefore, God could not let Adam live forever as a sinful human being. Even if He had to force Adam out of the Garden, He would. And this God did. God forced Adam—drove him—out of the Garden. God banished Adam for at least two reasons.

1) God had to start all over with Adam: *put him on probation and under new terms.* Adam had failed the first probation, the first commandment and condition, established by God. God had told Adam that he would live forever unless he ate the forbidden fruit. If he ate the forbidden fruit—disobeyed this one commandment and condition—he would die. Adam ate; consequently, he had to die. God's Word had to be fulfilled, for He is God. As God, whatever He says must always be done. But as God, His purposes must also be done—always. His purposes can never be defeated. Therefore, God had to work things out for good, work them out so that His purposes for man could be fulfilled. But how? How could God now save and deliver man?

There was one way: give man another chance. God had to place man in a different environment and put him on another period of probation and give him new terms. This is what God did. God drove man out of the Garden of Eden—forced him to go out into the world, out into a new environment—and God put man on probation with new terms and conditions.

⇒ The new conditions focused upon *the promised seed* of the woman, the Savior of the world, that God had just promised Adam. Adam was now required to trust *the promised seed*, to focus upon the Savior for salvation. If Adam wished to be saved and restored to perfection—if he wished to be accepted by God and given the right to live in God's presence forever—Adam had to trust *the promised seed*, trust Him so much that he would commit his life totally to the Savior.

⇒ The new condition focused upon belief in and commitment to *the promised seed*, the Savior of the world. Belief and commitment was the new term and condition of the probation period. The decision was, once again, Adam's. Just as he was put on probation—given a decision to make—in the Garden of Eden (paradise), he was once again put on probation—given a decision to make—as he walked out in the new world.

This is the first reason God drove man out from the Garden: to give him another chance, another probation period, under new terms. (See DEEPER STUDY # 1, *Covenant*—Ge.2:15-17.)

2) God had to deliver and save Adam in such a way that Adam could be freed from sin, made righteous, and perfected forever. There was only one way to do this: put Adam out into the world and teach him to trust and focus upon *the promised seed* of the woman—the Savior of the world—the seed and Savior that God had already promised to Adam and the world. (See note 6—Ge.3:15 for more discussion.)

How would trusting the Savior free Adam from sin and make him righteous or perfect before God? Scripture tells us in just a few chapters ahead of this one, in Genesis 15:6. Also compare Ga.3:6.

"And he [Abraham] believed in the LORD; and he [God] counted it to him for righteousness" (Ge.15:6).
"Even as Abraham believed God, and it was accounted to him for righteousness" (Ga.3:6).

When Adam got out into the world and believed, really believed to the point of committing his life to the Savior, God's plan was to take Adam's belief and count it as righteousness. Adam was not righteous. Adam had already sinned. But God planned to take Adam's faith and count it as righteousness. God loved Adam this much, just as He loves us this much. If we love and honor the Savior, *God's very own Son*, enough to believe and commit our lives to Him, then God will do anything for us. If we will just honor, love, and trust His Son—the only Son God has—then God will take our faith and count it as righteousness. This was the only way Adam could be freed from sin, made righteous and perfected forever.

This was the second reason God drove man out of the Garden: to make it possible for Adam to be freed from sin and restored to perfection. God wanted Adam made righteous and perfected forever through faith in *the promised seed*, the coming Savior.

Thought 1. Adam and all the other Old testament believers looked ahead to *the promised seed*, the Savior of the world, whereas we look back to Him. They believed in the coming Savior; we believe in the Savior who has come. They believed in the promised Savior; we believe in the promises of the Savior.

Thought 2. God's great love for man is seen in what God did for Adam.
⇒ In justice, God could have put Adam in the grave right then and there, but in love God gave Adam another chance and put him on another probation under new rules.
⇒ In justice, God could have driven Adam into hell, but in love He only drove him out of the Garden into the world.
⇒ In justice, God could have left Adam to live forever as a sinner in this fallen world, but in love God provided a Savior who could save and restore Adam to perfection.

b. God delivered man by posting angelic beings, called cherubim, to guard the entrance to the tree of life (see DEEPER STUDY # 2, *Cherubim*—Ge.3:24 for discussion). There was the possibility that Adam and Eve might try to reenter the Garden some day in the future. They had failed to obey God before, and now, because of their sinful nature, they would be failing and disobeying God time and again. They might even try to reenter the Garden and do what they had done before: eat the forbidden fruit, which in this case was the tree of life. God, therefore, had to keep man away from the Garden as long as man was upon the earth. This God did by posting angelic beings to keep man out of the Garden. Adam would never try—not even dare—to enter the Garden with those magnificent and powerful beings guarding it.

There was another reason why God posted the angelic beings around the Garden. God had to teach man a much needed lesson: man's salvation—his freedom from sin and his perfection—could no longer be found in the Garden of Eden. Man could never again find his provision, security, joy, and happiness—his utopia, his heaven—here upon earth. He could only find salvation and perfection in *the promised seed*, the Savior of the world.

This was the second reason God posted the angelic cherubim to guard the Garden. Adam had to know this and he had to know it once and for all. His utopia was never again to be upon earth. His hope was to be in God's love and in God's love alone, a love so great...
• that God would send *the promised seed*, the Savior, to the world (see note 5—Ge.3:15 for discussion)
• that God would provide the clothing of righteousness for man (see note—Ge.3:21 for discussion)

> "For God so loved the world, that he gave his only begotten Son, that whosoever believeth in him should not perish, but have everlasting life" (Jn.3:16).
> "I am come that they might have life, and that they might have it more abundantly" (Jn.10:10).
> "Verily, verily, I say unto you, He that heareth my word, and believeth on him that sent me, hath everlasting life, and shall not come into condemnation; but is passed from death unto life" (Jn.5:24).
> "But God commendeth his love toward us, in that, while we were yet sinners, Christ died for us" (Ro.5:8).
> "For he hath made him to be sin for us, who knew no sin; that we might be made the righteousness of God in him" (2 Co.5:21).
> "But when the fulness of the time was come, God sent forth his Son, made of a woman, made under the law, to redeem them that were under the law, that we might receive the adoption of sons" (Ga.4:4-5).
> "But God, who is rich in mercy, for his great love wherewith he loved us, even when we were dead in sins, hath quickened us together with Christ, (by grace ye are saved)" (Ep.2:4-5).
> "Behold, what manner of love the Father hath bestowed upon us, that we should be called the sons of God: therefore the world knoweth us not, because it knew him not" (1 Jn.3:1).

DEEPER STUDY # 2
(3:24) **Cherubim**: the cherubim are said to be living creatures (Eze.1:5, 13-14, 19; Re.4:6-9). Just what they are—angelic beings or some other form of being—is unknown. They are mentioned some sixty-five times in Scripture. The *living creatures* and the seraphim seem to be the same being as the cherubim. They have many of the same characteristics or traits. In our study below we shall treat them as one. However, this is not certain: the cherubim, the living creatures and the seraphim, could be different races or classes of persons in the spiritual world or dimension of being. Note this:
⇒ Most of the references to the cherubim have to do with the ark of the covenant. Arising from both ends of the ark were two angelic beings called cherubim. They reached over and shadowed the mercy seat. The very presence of God was supposed to sit upon the lid or top of the ark between the glory of the two cherubim.

⇒ There are just a few major references to the *cherubim* and the *living creatures* in Scripture that describe them in detail: Is.6:1-3, 6; Eze.1:4-28; 10:1-22; Rev.4:6-9; 5:6, 11-14.

The Bible says the following about *the cherubim* and *the seraphim* and *the living creatures*: (See note—Re.4:6-9 for more discussion.)

1. They are in "the likeness of a man," yet they are vastly different from man. They have four faces and four or six wings and many other distinguishing features (see Eze.1:5-25; Rev.4:6-9).

2. Their function is several-fold.

a. They stand in the immediate presence of God and His glory. They surround His throne (Eze.1:25-28; Rev.4:6).

b. They, at least some of them, spend all their time praising God, never resting—neither during the day nor at night. Their praise is powerful in its description of God.

> "Holy, holy, holy LORD God Almighty, which was, and is, and is to come" (Re.4:8).
> "[They] give glory and honour and thanks to him that sat on the throne, who liveth for ever and ever" (Re.4:9).

c. They are always associated with God's most holy presence, His presence represented in the Holy of Holies within the tabernacle and upon the ark of the covenant (Ex.25:18; 26:1, 31; 36:8, 35; Ps.80:1, 99).

d. They seem to be mediators of God's presence in the world. They have something to do with the work of God's Spirit (Eze.1:20, 24; Ps.18:10).

e. They are associated with God in mercy (Ex.25:22; 37:9).

f. They are associated with God's judgment upon man (Ge.3:24).

DEEPER STUDY # 3

(3:24) **Trinity—God**: note that God says, "Man is become as one of us" (v.22). Note the expression, "as [like] one of us." Several questions need to be asked about who "*us*" is.

⇒ First, who is with God—who is it that man is about to become *like*?

⇒ Second, could God be talking to angels? If so, this would put angels on a par with God Himself. Such a levelling process that puts God upon the same level or in a class with angels is most unlikely. There is no being on a par with God, not on the same level nor in the same class as God. Thus, it is most unlikely that God is talking with angels.

⇒ Third, could this be a conversation between the persons of the Godhead, that is, the Trinity? We know from the experience of Christ that conversation does take place among the Trinity, that they discuss every major issue among themselves. This was certainly true of Christ, and it is the normal experience between persons. (See note 1—Ge.1:26.)

If this is not a conversation between the persons of the Godhead, then a questions arises. At what point in history is God going to begin to teach man about Himself (that is, the Trinity, His personhood)? In answering the question, this much is known.

1. Jesus Christ is the final revelation of God. When He was upon the earth, He revealed that there is a relationship between Himself as *God the Son* and *God the Father* (see Jn.8:18, 59; 10:27-39; 12:44-50; 17:1-26). And when He sent the Comforter, who is the Holy Spirit, into the world (Jn.7:37-39), this revealed that there is a relationship existing between *God the Son* and *God the Holy Spirit* and *God the Father*. Thus, Jesus Christ revealed that three distinct persons form the Godhead...

• that each exists co-equally as One in nature, perfection, and purpose

It is through Christ that man understands the truth of the Trinity. The question is, then, when did God begin to teach that *He was One*, but that *He existed in three persons*? Christ is the final revelation, but there was a span of time reaching back from Christ to a point when God first began to teach man about His personhood. Not that man could grasp in full understanding what God was revealing. Man could not, for in the grasping of all facts and truth, understanding comes by steps, progressively. Thus, the revelation of God's person and nature is bound to come progressively. But His person, just as with His nature, has to be mentioned at some point. There has to be a first time when He reveals His person, then a second time, then a third time, and so on. At what point was His person first mentioned or revealed?

2. A second fact is known. The Bible has already used the plural when referring to God: God said, "Let *us* make man in *our* image" (Ge.1:26). And then in this present passage, the plural is again used: "man is become as [like] one of *us*" (Ge.3:22). When was the plural with God first used?

Was it when Moses recorded these words? Or was Moses using some notes written by Adam or some successor? Or was he recording oral tradition? Or was he receiving direct revelation from the Spirit of God?

No one can know, not for sure. But as already stated, the revelation, the teaching of God's personhood, had to begin at some point in history. And, as with all facts and truth, it had to come progressively. Because of this, it would seem more reasonable to say that these words are a discussion between the Godhead instead of a conversation between God and angels or between God and some other being. It is just far more reasonable to say that the *progressive revelation and teaching* of God's person began from the first of creation with these discussions, with the use of the plural in these two passages. Whether they were first recorded by Moses or someone prior to Moses (Adam or a successor) is not that important. What we need to first understand is that God is discussing man's creation and expulsion from the Garden of Eden with the other two persons of the Godhead.

DIVISION III

ADAM, THE FIRST MAN (PART 2): THE BIRTH, DEVELOPMENT, AND CORRUPTION OF BOTH THE UNGODLY AND THE GODLY SEED (DESCENDANTS), 4:1–6:8

(4:1–6:8) **DIVISION OVERVIEW: Seed, Godly—Seed, Ungodly**: the book of *Genesis* is well written and well organized. It is written in an orderly, logical way, and it has an excellent outline to it.

⇒ Chapter one tells us about the creation of the universe, including the creation of man.

⇒ Chapter two gives us more detail about man and his world.

⇒ Chapter three tells us what happened to man and the earth. Chapter three reveals how man brought sin into the world and how he and his world had to be judged and condemned to corruption. But chapter three also reveals God's great promise of a Savior and of a godly seed of people who would survive and serve God down through the coming centuries.

Now, chapter four and five show how the seed (descendants) of the woman branch out into both *an ungodly and a godly line of people*. Some of the woman's seed will be godly people and some will be ungodly people. Chapter four and five discuss the children of Adam and Eve, the first man and woman upon earth. Their seed, their children and descendants, stand at the head of *the ungodly and the godly lines* of the human race.

⇒ Cain and his offspring represent *the ungodly line* of civilization and society.

⇒ Abel, who will be killed by Cain, and then Seth and his offspring represent *the godly line* of civilization and society. It is Abel who worships God as God dictated, and it is Seth and his seed who "call upon the name of the Lord" (Ge.4:26).

God made a most wonderful promise to Adam and Eve after they had sinned. He promised a seed—descendents, children—through whom *a godly line of people* was to be born, and He promised that *a Savior* would come through that line (Ge.3:15). Chapter four and five show us the beginning of God's promise being fulfilled. Chapter four and five give us *The Birth, Development, and Corruption of Both the Ungodly and the Godly Seed (Descendents) of the Human Race*. The fact to remember is this: from this point on, history—all of history—is a struggle to preserve *the godly line or seed* of the human race.

James Montgomery Boice, the excellent Presbyterian Expositor, gives a graphic description of how chapters four and five cover *the ungodly and godly lines* of humanity.

> *The fourth and fifth chapters of Genesis outline two cultures from the earliest years of earth's history: the culture of the godless and the culture of the godly....The two chapters together give a portrait of what Francis Schaeffer has termed "the two humanities."*
>
> *Or, since we are dealing with cultures as well as with individuals, 'the two cities'! This is the distinction invented by Saint Augustine as the basis for his monumental and highly influential work on the philosophy of history, entitled The City of God. According to Augustine, the history of the human race is the history of two groups of people, each having a distinct origin, development, characteristic, and destiny. He wrote that these are "two cities...formed by two loves: the earthly by the love of self, even to the contempt of God; the heavenly by the love of God; even to the contempt of self." In Augustine's work "city" means "society." The earthly society has as its highest expression the city cultures of Babylon and, in what was for Augustine more modern times, Rome. The other is the church, composed of God's elect. The former is destined to pass away. The latter is blessed by God and is to endure forever.*
>
> *The fourth and fifth chapters of Genesis discuss these two humanities, as we have already said. But so far as Genesis goes, the origin of the cities [civilizations, societies] is found one chapter earlier in the words of God to the serpent following the temptation and fall of Adam and Eve. God cursed the serpent, then gave this word both of decree and prophecy: 'I will put enmity between you and the woman, and between your offspring and hers; he will crush your head, and you will strike his heel.' Here are three sets of antagonists: 1) the serpent and the woman, 2) the descendants of the serpent and the descendants of the woman, and 3) Satan himself and the ultimate descendant of the woman, Jesus Christ. These are in conflict. But the victory of the godly seed is to be assured by the ultimate victory of Eve's specific descendant, Jesus.*[1]

---

[1] James Montgomery Boice. *Genesis*, Vol.1, p.215.

ADAM, THE FIRST MAN (PART 2): THE BIRTH, DEVELOPMENT, AND CORRUPTION OF BOTH THE UNGODLY AND THE GODLY SEED (DESCENDANTS), 4:1–6:8

		it came to pass, that Cain brought of the fruit of the ground an offering unto the LORD.	**worship of Cain & Abel**
	CHAPTER 4		a. Cain's false worship: Approached & offered produce—the works of his own hands—to God
	III. ADAM, THE FIRST MAN (PART 2): THE BIRTH, DEVELOPMENT, & CORRUPTION OF BOTH THE UNGODLY & THE GODLY SEED (DESCENDANTS), 4:1–6:8	4 And Abel, he also brought of the firstlings of his flock and of the fat thereof. And the LORD had respect unto Abel and to his offering:	b. Abel's true worship: Approached & offered a sacrifice—a substitute life—to God
	A. The First Children, Cain & Abel: False Vs. True Worship—the Beginning of False Worship, 4:1-7	5 But unto Cain and to his offering he had not respect. And Cain was very wroth, and his countenance fell.	4. Scene 4: God's response a. Accepted Abel & his offering b. Rejected Cain & his offering 5. Scene 5: Cain's reaction—very angry & downcast
1. Scene 1: The children's birth a. Cain's birth	And Adam knew Eve his wife; and she conceived, and bare Cain, and said, I have gotten a man from the LORD.	6 And the LORD said unto Cain, Why art thou wroth? and why is thy countenance fallen?	6 Scene 6: God's warning
b. Abel's birth **2. Scene 2: The work of Abel (a herdsman) & Cain (a farmer)**	2 And she again bare his brother Abel. And Abel was a keeper of sheep, but Cain was a tiller of the ground.	7 If thou doest well, shalt thou not be accepted? and if thou doest not well, sin lieth at the door. And unto thee shall be his desire, and thou	a. If you do right, you are accepted b. If you do not do right, sin lies at the door c. Sin desires you
3. Scene 3: The personal	3 And in process of time	shalt rule over him.	d. You must master sin

DIVISION III

ADAM, THE FIRST MAN (PART 2): THE BIRTH, DEVELOPMENT, AND CORRUPTION OF BOTH THE UNGODLY AND THE GODLY SEED (DESCENDANTS), 4:1–6:8

A. The First Children, Cain and Abel: False Versus True Worship—the Beginning of False Worship, 4:1-7

(4:1-7) **Introduction**: this is a significant passage of Scripture. The central lesson deals with true and false worship, true and false approaches to God. The lesson centers around the first two children born upon earth, Cain and Abel. Note how Scripture just covers the overall scenes of their lives. In one brief statement or description, whole periods of their lives are covered. Our minds thirst and reach out for more information, but the Holy Spirit has given us only this brief record. But note how much information is given when we closely observe each statement and description, and in some cases, the words.

This is, *The First Children, Cain and Abel: False Versus True Worship, the Beginning of False Worship.*

1. Scene 1: the children's birth. (vv.1-2).
2. Scene 2: the work of Abel (a herdsman) and Cain (a farmer) (v.2).
3. Scene 3: the personal worship of Cain and Abel (vv.3-4).
4. Scene 4: God's response (vv.4-5).
5. Scene 5: Cain's reaction—very angry and downcast (v.5).
6. Scene 6: God's warning (vv.6-7).

1 (4:1-2) **Cain—Abel—Parents—Faith—Life, Emptiness of—Vanity**: scene one is the children's birth.

a. There was the birth of Cain. Adam had sexual relations with his wife, Eve, and she became pregnant. Remember, there had never been a pregnancy or birth upon earth before. Adam and Eve had been created by the direct power of God's Word and breath. But not any more; hereafter, the human race was to be reproduced through the process of conception, pregnancy, and birth.

Just imagine the experience of Adam and Eve throughout the nine months, their surprise and joy…

* when Eve began to gain weight and her stomach began to enlarge
* when Eve began to feel movement within her and Adam began to feel the growing child *kick*

Today, the joy of expectant mothers and fathers is wonderful, but the joy of Adam and Eve must have been a joy beyond imagination. Just imagine being the father and mother of the first child ever born upon earth!

But, there was more to Adam and Eve's joy than just the pregnancy and birth of the first child. There was the hope of *the promised seed*, the Savior of the world. Remember:

⇒ God had promised that He would send the Savior through the seed of the woman. (See note 5—Ge.3:15 for discussion.)

⇒ Adam and Eve believed the promise of God. Their belief was so strong that Adam named the woman *Eve*, which means to give life or the mother of all living. (See note—Ge.3:20 for discussion.)

Adam and Eve were bound to be hoping, if not expecting, that this child would be their Savior, the One who was to restore them to perfection and make it possible for them to reenter the Garden of Eden, their paradise. What makes us say this? The name *Cain* (ganah, verb form). The Hebrew word means to acquire, get, or possess. When the child was born, Eve declared that her child was to be called Cain because she had acquired or gotten a man *from the Lord*. She thought the Lord had given her *the promised seed*, the very child who was to deliver the human race. Thus she wanted her son named *Cain* because her child *had been promised and was now given* by the Lord. (Note: James Montgomery Boice has an excellent discussion of this point. *Genesis, An Expositional Commentary*, Vol.1, p.199f.)

Thought 1. There are three great lessons for parents in this point.
1) Every parent should be as joyful and hopeful for their children as Adam and Eve were over their first child. But note: one's joy and hope can be turned into sorrow and tragedy by the child just as Adam and Eve's joy and hope were soon to be. Usually one thing makes the difference between a joyful or a sorrowful child: how the parent trains up the child.

> **"Train up a child in the way he should go: and when he is old, he will not depart from it" (Pr.22:6).**

2) Every parent needs—desperately needs—to believe in *the promised seed* of the world, the Savior, our Lord Jesus Christ.

> **"For God so loved the world, that he gave his only begotten Son, that whosoever believeth in him should not perish, but have everlasting life" (Jn.3:16).**
> **"Jesus said unto her, I am the resurrection, and the life: he that believeth in me, though he were dead, yet shall he live" (Jn.11:25).**
> **"Then said Jesus to them again, Peace be unto you: as my Father hath sent me, even so send I you" (Jn.20:21).**
> **"Whosoever believeth that Jesus is the Christ is born of God: and every one that loveth him that begat loveth him also that is begotten of him" (1 Jn.5:1).**
> **"That if thou shalt confess with thy mouth the Lord Jesus, and shalt believe in thine heart that God hath raised him from the dead, thou shalt be saved. For with the heart man believeth unto righteousness; and with the mouth confession is made unto salvation" (Ro.10:9-10).**

3) Every parent needs—desperately needs—to believe the Word of God and the promises of God.

> **"And now, brethren, I commend you to God, and to the word of his grace, which is able to build you up, and to give you an inheritance among all them which are sanctified" (Ac.20:32).**
> **"All scripture is given by inspiration of God, and is profitable for doctrine, for reproof, for correction, for instruction in righteousness" (2 Ti.3:16).**
> **"As newborn babes, desire the sincere milk of the word, that ye may grow thereby: if so be ye have tasted that the Lord is gracious" (1 Pe.2:2-3).**

b. There was the birth of *Abel* (hebhel). The Hebrew word means vanity, breath, temporary, meaningless, or empty. Why would Eve name her second son Abel, a name that meant empty or meaningless?
⇒ Had she already learned that Cain was not the promised seed or Savior? Had she become disillusioned by the fact? Was she now disheartened and downcast because she sensed that the promised Savior was not to come any time soon? Some commentators think this.
⇒ Was Eve just sensing the emptiness and meaninglessness of life itself? She and Adam were, most likely, having to work and work hard to cultivate enough land to provide food and to survive in a fallen and harsh environment. Some commentators think this.

Note the Scripture: Scripture does not say why Eve was sensing the vanity—emptiness, meaninglessness, and brevity—of life. But by naming the child Abel, Eve was saying that human existence is sometimes vanity upon vanity: life is sometimes empty and meaningless, and it is always temporary, ever so short, as brief as breath itself.

Thought 1. Man so often senses the vanity of life, life in all its emptiness, meaninglessness, and brevity.

> **"My days are swifter than a weaver's shuttle, and are spent without hope" (Jb.7:6).**
> **"Now my days are swifter than a post: they flee away, they see no good" (Jb.9:25).**
> **"Behold, thou hast made my days as an handbreadth; and mine age is as nothing before thee: verily every man at his best state is altogether vanity" (Ps.39:5).**
> **"Nevertheless man being in honour abideth not: he is like the beasts that perish" (Ps.49:12).**
> **"For when he dieth he shall carry nothing away: his glory shall not descend after him" (Ps.49:17).**
> **"For he remembered that they were but flesh; a wind that passeth away, and cometh not again" (Ps.78:39).**
> **"For he knoweth our frame; he remembereth that we are dust" (Ps.103:14).**
> **"Vanity of vanities, saith the Preacher, vanity of vanities; all is vanity" (Ec.1:2).**
> **"I said in mine heart, Go to now, I will prove thee with mirth, therefore enjoy pleasure; and, behold, this also is vanity" (Ec.2:1).**

"He that loveth silver shall not be satisfied with silver; nor he that loveth abundance with increase; this is also vanity" (Ec.5:10).

"All the labour of man is for his mouth, and yet the appetite is not filled" (Ec.6:7).

"Whereas ye know not what shall be on the morrow. For what is your life? It is even a vapour, that appeareth for a little time, and then vanisheth away" (Js.4:14).

"For all flesh is as grass, and all the glory of man as the flower of grass. The grass withereth, and the flower thereof falleth away" (1 Pe.1:24).

2 (4:2) **Cain—Abel—Labor**: scene two is the work of Abel and Cain. Abel was a herdsman and Cain a farmer. Note several facts.

First, their profession met the very basic needs of man: that of clothing and of food. Their chosen professions were honorable and contributed to meeting the needs of the family and society.

Second, they had learned their profession from their father. Remember, God Himself had shown Adam how to clothe his family with the skins of animals (Ge.3:21), and God had instructed Adam to till the ground (Ge.3:17-19, 23). As the father, he had apparently taught his sons to work diligently.

> **Thought 1.** Two great lessons are seen in the profession and work of the two sons.
> 1) Our profession—in fact, all professions—should always be for the good and betterment of man, to meet the very basic needs of man's life. We should never be engaged in any profession that damages, destroys, tears down, or hurts man or society.
> 2) Parents should always teach their children to work and to work diligently. And they should always teach their children to choose an honorable profession, never to work at anything that hurts or destroys life. (See the industries involved in alcohol, drugs, immorality, and crime.) Every child—every person—should always make whatever contribution he can to life and society. Everyone of us owes life and society this, just for the privilege of living in such a beautiful and wonderful universe. All the filth and crime of our cities and societies is due…
>   • to the dishonorable and destructive professions that some of us have chosen
>   • to our allowing some legitimate industries to pollute and destroy our environment and the quality of our lives
>   • to our not working diligently enough to do all we can for life and society

3 (4:3-4) **Worship—Offerings—Cain—Abel**: scene three is the worship of Cain and of Abel. Note: Scripture indicates that Cain and Abel approached God at a specific time and at a specific place for worship.
> ⇒ The specific time is indicated by the words "in the process [or course] of time" (v.3). The Hebrew means *at the end of the days*. What days? Scripture does not say. It could refer to the days of harvest, a very special time when Adam and his sons wanted to set aside a very special day of worship and offering to God.

However, it most likely refers to the end of the week, the seventh day of rest. Remember: God had already blessed the seventh day and set it apart as a day of rest and worship. (See note—Ge.2:3 for more discussion.)

But note this: it could also refer to the first time Cain and Abel worshiped on their own, apart from their parents. It may refer to the day when the two sons cut the apron strings—so to speak—and became men on their own and began to approach and worship God on their own. This may be the first time the two sons approached God independent of their parents.
> ⇒ The specific place is indicated by the fact that both Cain and Abel "brought" their offering to a *particular place* for worship. Where was that place? Again, Scripture does not say, and to guess is just that, a guess.

However, we would expect Adam to establish a place of worship. Adam's soul was just like our souls—except more so—restless, unfulfilled, and thirsty for fellowship with God. Adam had known perfect fellowship with God. In his fallen condition, he was bound to thirst deeply for God. He was bound to seek more and more for a restoration to the perfect fellowship he had once known. If knowing God in a personal way—if fellowship and communion with Him—is the summit of experiences, then Adam must have sought after God with a diligence seldom, if ever, matched. Having known God in perfection and having experienced perfect fellowship with God must have put an insatiable desire for God within Adam's heart.

Adam must have, therefore, established a very special place and a very special altar where he and his dear family sought after God and faithfully worshiped God. Where, then, was the place where Adam and his family worshiped? Again, Scripture does not say. But note this: it would be only logical and rational for Adam to worship God right at the entrance to the Garden of Eden, the very place where he had known face to face fellowship with God. Many commentators hold this position, thinking that God actually instructed Adam to build an altar and to worship Him at the entrance to the Garden where the cherubim stood guard. Note that God seems to still talk with Adam and his family face to face, probably from between the cherubim (Ge.4:6-7, 9-15). This fact plus the fact that the sons bring their offerings to a particular place for worship gives significant weight to the place of worship being at the entrance to the Garden. The Garden's entrance would certainly be the dearest and most meaningful spot to Adam's heart. And note two other things:
> ⇒ Adam would have been very careful how he *approached God*. He would want to please God to the utmost when he approached God, ever hoping to be restored to the perfect fellowship he had known. Therefore, when Adam entered the place of worship, he would approach God exactly as God had instructed: by the way of sacrifice. (See note—Ge.3:21.)

⇒ Adam would also have been very, very careful to teach his family how to approach and worship God. In fact, Adam would have shared time and again his own personal experiences with God, how wonderful face to face fellowship and communion with God is.

Now, to the major subject of these two verses and of this particular scene (v.3-4): the personal worship of Cain and Abel.

a. First, there was Cain's false worship: he approached God and offered produce—the works of his own hands—to God. Cain was a farmer, so he took what he had, produce, and he brought his produce as an offering to God. We can imagine that the produce was the very first of Cain's harvest and the very best produce he had.

b. Second, there was Abel's true worship: he approached God and offered a sacrifice—a substitute life—to God. Abel approached God by taking the first—the very best—of his flock and sacrificing the animal and offering it to God.

4 (4:4-5) **Worship—Offerings—Cain—Abel**: scene four: God's response to the worship of Cain and Abel. The Lord looked upon Abel with favor and accepted his offering, but He looked upon Cain with disfavor. He did not accept Cain's offering. Note several significant points.

a. God did not just accept and reject the offerings; He accepted and rejected the man as well.
⇒ Both Abel and his offering were accepted by God (v.4b).
⇒ Both Cain and his offering were rejected by God (v.5).

This is of critical importance: it was the offering that made the man either acceptable or unacceptable to God. Scripture is very clear about this. This is what this passage is all about—its major lesson—the worship of God, the false and true approach to God.

b. What was it that made Abel's offering acceptable? The New Testament tells us:

> **"By faith Abel offered unto God a more excellent sacrifice than Cain, by which he obtained witness that he was righteous, God testifying of his gifts: and by it he being dead yet speaketh" (He.11:4).**

What was the sacrifice of Abel? The sacrifice of an animal: its life, its blood. Why did Abel sacrifice an animal? Because his father, Adam, had taught him to approach God through the sacrifice of an animal. When Adam sinned, God killed an animal and clothed Adam with its skin. By this very act, God taught Adam...
• that sin causes death
• that an innocent substitute had to sacrificially die in order to clothe man's shame and guilt
• that thereafter man could approach God only if his shame and guilt were hid through the sacrificial death of an innocent substitute

This, of course, pointed to Christ, *the promised seed* and Savior of the world (see note 5—Ge.3:15; note 3:21 for more discussion). As pointed out above, Adam was bound to teach his family how to approach and worship God. This is what Abel is doing, approaching God just as his father had taught him. Abel had no other way—none whatsoever—to know that such a thing as killing an animal and offering it to God would be acceptable to God. Adam is bound to have taught him this approach to God.

Now, note the New Testament verse again: "By *faith* Abel offered to God a more excellent *sacrifice*...by which he obtained witness that he was *righteous*" (He.11:4).
⇒ Abel had *faith*—he believed—that God would accept him through the sacrifice of an innocent life.
⇒ God accepted Abel's approach and worship: he was counted *righteous* because he believed and approached God through the sacrifice of an innocent life.

Thought 1. Remember: the sacrifice pointed toward Christ, His sacrifice upon the cross for the sins of men. Abel might not have known the full revelation of Christ, but he believed that God accepted the sacrifice of the innocent life as a substitute for him. He believed, even as his father Adam believed, that God accepted the sacrifice...
• as bearing his sins for him
• as suffering the judgment of his sins for him, the judgment of death

> **"For the wages of sin is death; but the gift of God is eternal life through Jesus Christ our Lord" (Ro.6:23).**
> **"Who his own self bare our sins in his own body on the tree, that we, being dead to sins, should live unto righteousness: by whose stripes ye were healed" (1 Pe.2:24).**
> **"For Christ also hath once suffered for sins, the just for the unjust, that he might bring us to God, being put to death in the flesh, but quickened by the Spirit" (1 Pe.3:18).**

c. What was it that made Cain's offering unacceptable? Note what Cain did; note two facts about his offering:
⇒ Cain offered only produce to God, only what his own mind and hands had produced.
⇒ Cain did not offer what Abel offered: an animal sacrifice—a substitute life—to God. Cain did not approach God through the sacrifice of an innocent life.

Why? Why would Cain not approach God through the sacrifice of an innocent life? The answer is again found in the New Testament.

1) Cain did not do what Abel did: seek to be acceptable to God—seek the righteousness of God—through the sacrificial offering of an innocent life.

"By faith Abel offered to God a more excellent sacrifice...by which he obtained witness that he was righteous" (He.11:4).

"Not as Cain, who was of that wicked one, and slew his brother. And wherefore slew he him? Because his own works were evil, and his brother's righteous" (1 Jn.3:12).

2) Cain wanted to use a different way and approach to God. For some reason, he brought the fruit of his own hands to God. He wanted God to accept him because of his hard work and because he worshipped and gave offerings to God. Why did Cain approach God this way?

⇒ Was Cain reacting against the *bloody* sacrifice of animals as an approach to God? Scripture definitely says this. He just did not believe—not like Abel—that the sacrificial offering of an innocent life was the way to approach God (He.11:4). If he had, he would have offered a sacrifice to God.

⇒ Did Cain think that giving God the best of his own mind, work, and fruit was a much better way to approach God? That is, was Cain seeking to establish a different approach and way to God? This is exactly what Scripture says. Scripture says that Cain was a false teacher who sought to establish a false way to God. In fact, Scripture calls all false approaches and ways to God "the way of Cain" (Jude 11, see Jude 4).

Note what Scripture says:

"For there are certain men [false teachers] crept in unawares [quietly, secretly], who were before of old ordained to this condemnation, ungodly men, turning the grace of our God into lasciviousness, and denying the only Lord God, and our Lord Jesus Christ....Woe unto them! for they have gone in the way of Cain" (Jude 4, 11).

The point is this: Cain's worship was false. Cain was seeking God's acceptance...
- by his own way
- by his own approach
- by his own works
- by his own mind and ideas
- by some other approach than by the sacrifice of an innocent life.

This is the reason God rejected Cain's offering. Cain—just as Adam, Eve, Abel, and all of us—needed a Savior.

⇒ Cain needed the innocent (righteous) life that could bear his sin for him and stand before God as his righteousness.

⇒ Cain also needed the sacrifice of an innocent (righteous) life that could stand before God as his substitute in death.

⇒ Cain needed the faith; he needed to believe in God, that God would accept him if he approached God just as God had dictated: through the sacrifice of the innocent life. (See note—Ge.3:21 for more discussion.)

Thought 1. No person can earn, win, or merit salvation. No person can approach God through his own works, energy, efforts, fruits, ways, religion, ceremony, or ritual. The reason is clearly evident: no person is perfect: "We have all sinned and come short of the glory of God" (Ro.3:23). We have a sin problem and a death problem that has to be taken care of before we can ever be acceptable to God. God has taken care of this in the sacrifice of His Son for our sins. Jesus Christ took our sins upon Himself and died for them. This is what the sacrifice of the innocent life symbolized in the Old Testament. Abel believed God, believed that the death (the blood) of the sacrificial animal covered his sins. Therefore, God accepted him—accepted him because his sins were removed—by the blood of the animal.

"But God commendeth his love toward us, in that, while we were yet sinners, Christ died for us. Much more then, being now justified by his blood, we shall be saved from wrath through him" (Ro.5:8-9).

"Without shedding of blood is no remission" (He.9:22).

"Forasmuch as ye know that ye were not redeemed with corruptible things, as silver and gold, from your vain conversation [empty behavior and conduct] received by tradition from your fathers; but with the precious blood of Christ, as of a lamb without blemish and without spot" (1 Pe.1:18-19).

Thought 2. God accepts no person apart from Jesus Christ, *the promised seed* and Savior of the world. Before Christ came, the persons who truly believed in the promised Savior approached God through the sacrifice of an innocent life (an animal sacrifice). But since Christ has come, we who believe in Him—truly believe—know that He, Himself, is the great Lamb of God who was sacrificed for our sins.

The point is this: God has never accepted any person—Old Testament or New Testament, before Christ or after Christ—apart from the shedding of blood. The blood of the innocent life—the animal which pictured the coming Savior and His death—had to be shed for Old Testament believers. The blood of Christ Himself had to be shed for all persons through all the generations of human history.

"For when we were yet without strength, in due time Christ died for the ungodly" (Ro.5:6).

"The next day John seeth Jesus coming unto him, and saith, Behold the Lamb of God, which taketh away the sin of the world" (Jn.1:29).

"Purge out therefore the old leaven, that ye may be a new lump, as ye are unleavened. For even Christ our passover is sacrificed for us" (1 Co.5:7).

"For I delivered unto you first of all that which I also received, how that Christ died for our sins according to the scriptures" (1 Co.15:3).

"Who gave himself for our sins, that he might deliver us from this present evil world, according to the will of God and our Father" (Ga.1:4).

"And walk in love, as Christ also hath loved us, and hath given himself for us an offering and a sacrifice to God for a sweetsmelling savour" (Ep.5:2).

"How much more shall the blood of Christ, who through the eternal Spirit offered himself without spot to God, purge your conscience from dead works to serve the living God?" (He.9:14).

Thought 3. Note this: there have been two Scriptures thus far in Genesis that deal with the sacrifice of an animal(s). These two Scriptures are significant events in the early life of man's history as recorded in Genesis (Ge.3:21; 4:2-5). In both cases an animal was sacrificed.
⇒ In the first case, the animal's life was given up to clothe Adam and Eve, thereby symbolizing their need to be covered by God in righteousness through the sacrifice of another.
⇒ In the second case, the animal life was given up as an act of worship.

The clearest explanation as to why Abel offered an animal sacrifice and was approved by God is that God did institute salvation by animal sacrifice with Adam and Eve. Adam and Eve were bound to have taught their sons to approach God through animal sacrifice. But only Abel approached God properly. Cain, as so many down through history, rebelled and did not.

Thought 4. Some persons look upon the Old Testament sacrifice of animals as ugly, repulsive, and awful. They call such an approach to God a "bloody religion." They reject *the blood of Jesus Christ*—His death, His cross—as the major purpose for His life. They turn away from the sacrifice of His death to the teachings of His life. They claim to follow His teachings, to approach God by patterning their conduct, goodness, rituals, ceremonies, and religion after His teachings. They do just what Cain did, they offer God the best they are able to produce with their own hands and works.

Man just feels a little more humane, a little more civil, by denying "the blood of Christ" for the sins of the world. To reject what is sometimes called a "blood religion" makes a person feel more acceptable in a so-called *civilized society*. Two things need to be noted.
1) The cross should be viewed as repulsive. The cross is a symbol of sin and shame. Hanging upon the cross, God's *very own Son* bore our sins and the sins of the whole world (1 Jn.2:1-2). Sin and shame are always repulsive, and the fact that God's Son hung there *becoming sin for us* is abhorrent. Nothing could be any more distasteful than what actually happened.
2) The cross should be viewed as glorious. The cross is a symbol of life and of forgiven sins (1 Pe.2:20). Through the cross God gloriously reconciles man to Himself and to one another (see outline and notes—Ep.2:13-18). So much comes through the glorious work of the cross that Paul just exclaimed, "God forbid that I should glory, save in the cross of our Lord Jesus Christ" (Ga.6:14).

5 (4:5) **Cain—Anger:** scene five is Cain's reaction. He became angry—very angry—and downcast. The Hebrew is descriptive in picturing Cain's reaction: he burned with anger, ferocious anger, and his face and countenance fell and were downcast. Cain was furious, full of rage and malice, and his face showed it. He walked around looking downcast, deeply disappointed.

Cain was angry at God for not accepting and blessing his worship. He was angry because he could not approach and worship God as he wanted, because he was told that he was not acceptable to God if he did not worship God through the sacrifice of an innocent life. He should have been angry at himself, for his own unbelief and hypocrisy. Cain was the one at fault; he was the one who had disobeyed God and approached God in his own strength, with the works of his own hands. As soon as he felt his face and countenance fall, he should have fallen to his knees, begged for forgiveness, and repented of his unbelief and hypocrisy.

Cain was also angry with his brother, filled with envy and jealousy against his brother. Why? Because God had accepted and blessed the worship of Abel. Cain resented and despised Abel. He was furious because Abel was full of assurance and confidence, because Abel had done exactly what God had said, and God had richly blessed Abel. Again, Cain should have been angry at himself, repented, and begged God for forgiveness, but he refused and reacted instead.

"Cease from anger, and forsake wrath: fret not thyself in any wise to do evil" (Ps.37:8).

"He that is soon angry dealeth foolishly: and a man of wicked devices is hated" (Pr.14:17).

"He that is slow to anger is better than the mighty; and he that ruleth his spirit than he that taketh a city" (Pr.16:32).

"Make no friendship with an angry man; and with a furious man thou shalt not go" (Pr.22:24).

"Be not hasty in thy spirit to be angry: for anger resteth in the bosom of fools" (Ec.7:9).

"But I say unto you, That whosoever is angry with his brother without a cause shall be in danger of the judgment: and whosoever shall say to his brother, Raca, shall be in danger of the council: but whosoever shall say, Thou fool, shall be in danger of hell fire" (Mt.5:22).

"But now ye also put off all these; anger, wrath, malice, blasphemy, filthy communication out of your mouth" (Col.3:8).

6 (4:6-7) **Warning**: scene six is God's warning. This is a striking scene, a scene of God's love and compassion. Despite Cain's terrible sin of false worship, of unbelief and apostasy, God was willing to forgive Cain. In fact, God wanted Cain to repent and to approach God through sacrifice. God was not willing for Cain to perish, not without God first reaching out and trying to save Cain. God drives four points home to the heart of Cain.

a. If you do what is right, you will be accepted. Note that God asks several questions of Cain:
⇒ Why are you angry?
⇒ Why is your face and countenance downcast?

Note that God answers the questions Himself by asking Cain another question:
⇒ If you do what is right, will you not be accepted?

God used questions to stir Cain to think about right and wrong worship, about the right and wrong approach to God, about the right and wrong offering to secure God's approval. God longed for Cain to repent and to bring the right sacrifice, to approach God in the right way: by the sacrifice of an innocent life.

b. If you do not do what is right, then sin lies at the door. Doing right means approaching God properly, just like a person should. Abel's approach by animal sacrifice was doing right; therefore, his worship and approach to God was accepted. Cain's approach was not *doing right*; therefore, his offering was not accepted.

Cain did not do what was right; he did not approach and worship God as he should. Note: God calls this sin. Failing to approach and worship God as He dictates is sin. The picture of sin painted by the Hebrew is graphic: sin is like a wild beast crouching at the door of a person's house, ready to jump upon and devour the person.

But note: this is a particular sin, the sin of a false worship, of a false approach to God. It is this particular sin that is so fierce and ferocious.

Note this also: this is the first time the word *sin* (chattath) is mentioned in the Bible. It means to miss the mark just like an archer who misses his mark. Cain had missed the mark in his approach to God. He had approached and worshipped God, but his approach and worship had missed God.

c. Sin desires to have you. The sinful false worship—the sin of offering your own goodness and works, ritual and ceremony to God, the sin of personal goodness and righteousness—wants to enslave and devour you, to possess you. This particular sin, the sin of false worship and of a false approach to God, will lead to more and more sin. It will devour you and lead you into more and more self-righteousness and self-sufficiency.

d. You must master sin. You must approach and worship God as He dictates. You must *approach* God through sacrifice, and *depend* upon God for His presence and power to conquer and overcome sin.

> "There hath no temptation taken you but such as is common to man: but God is faithful, who will not suffer you to be tempted above that ye are able; but will with the temptation also make a way to escape, that ye may be able to bear it" (1 Co.10:13).
> "Now unto him that is able to do exceeding abundantly above all that we ask or think, according to the power that worketh in us" (Ep.3:20).

Note Cain's silence. No response is mentioned. Apparently, he never responded to God. He chose to continue on in his sin of false worship, of approaching God as he wished. He just continued to reject sacrifice as the only approach to God.

> "Jesus saith unto him, I am the way, the truth, and the life: no man cometh unto the Father, but by me" (Jn.14:6).
> "Jesus saith unto him, Have I been so long time with you, and yet hast thou not known me, Philip? he that hath seen me hath seen the Father; and how sayest thou then, Show us the Father?" (Jn.14:9).
> "For there is one God, and one mediator between God and men, the man Christ Jesus" (1 Ti.2:5).
> "For whatsoever is born of God overcometh the world: and this is the victory that overcometh the world, even our faith. Who is he that overcometh the world, but he that believeth that Jesus is the Son of God?" (1 Jn.5:4-5).

	B. The First Murder, Cain Kills Abel: The Undeniable Truth of Judgment—Sin Cannot Be Hid, 4:8-15	hand;	
1. There is the deception & murder: Cain lured Abel into a field, attacked and murdered him	8 And Cain talked with Abel his brother: and it came to pass, when they were in the field, that Cain rose up against Abel his brother, and slew him.	12 When thou tillest the ground, it shall not henceforth yield unto thee her strength; a fugitive and a vagabond shalt thou be in the earth.	b. The murderer experiences difficulty in his labor c. The murderer is always a restless, rootless soul, a wanderer upon earth
2. There is the confrontation with God a. God questioned Cain b. Cain denied responsibility for his brother c. God revealed an undeniable truth: Sin cannot be hid—the cry for justice is heard by God	9 And the LORD said unto Cain, Where is Abel thy brother? And he said, I know not: Am I my brother's keeper? 10 And he said, What hast thou done? the voice of thy brother's blood crieth unto me from the ground.	13 And Cain said unto the LORD, My punishment is greater than I can bear. 14 Behold, thou hast driven me out this day from the face of the earth; and from thy face shall I be hid; and I shall be a fugitive and a vagabond in the earth; and it shall come to pass, that every one that findeth me shall slay me.	**4. There is the reaction & complaint against God's judgment** a. The complaint against being alienated 1) From the fruitfulness of the earth 2) From God 3) From society b. The complaint against justice & revenge
3. There is the judgment of God a. The murderer bears the curse of sin in his soul	11 And now art thou cursed from the earth, which hath opened her mouth to receive thy brother's blood from thy	15 And the LORD said unto him, Therefore whosoever slayeth Cain, vengeance shall be taken on him sevenfold. And the LORD set a mark upon Cain, lest any finding him should kill him.	**5. There is the great mercy of God** a. God warns against revenge b. God assures Cain—gives him a sign

DIVISION III

ADAM, THE FIRST MAN (PART 2): THE BIRTH, DEVELOPMENT, AND CORRUPTION OF BOTH THE UNGODLY AND THE GODLY SEED (DESCENDANTS), 4:1–6:8

B. The First Murder, Cain Kills Abel: The Undeniable Truth of Judgment—Sin Cannot Be Hid, 4:8-15

(4:8-15) **Introduction**: this is the first murder upon earth. Cain commits a horrible sin: he murders his own brother, deliberately murders him. This is premeditated murder, murder in the first degree. But murder is not the only lesson of this passage. This passage deals with the undeniable truth of judgment, judgment both now while the sinner lives upon the earth and judgment to come. The great lesson of this passage is: *The First Murder, Cain Kills Abel: The Undeniable Truth of Judgment—Sin Cannot Be Hid.*

1. There is the deception and murder: Cain lured Abel into a field, attacked and murdered him (v.8).
2. There is the confrontation with God (vv.9-10).
3. There is the judgment of God (vv.11-12).
4. There is the reaction and complaint against judgment (vv.13-14).
5. There is the great mercy of God (v.15).

1 (4:8) **Cain—Murder—Seed, Ungodly**: there is the deception and murder: Cain lured Abel into a field, attacked and murdered him. Note several significant facts.

a. Cain had been angry, very angry, both at his brother and at God (v.8). He was angry because God had rejected him and his worship, but God had accepted Abel and his worship.

b. God had warned Cain that sin was crouching at his door (v.7). Sin was just like a wild beast, ready to lurch forward and consume him. And sin did. Cain allowed his bitterness and hostility against his brother and against God to fester and consume him. Cain plotted to kill his brother.

c. Cain is now seen deceiving Abel. This is the point of this verse: Cain talked his brother into going with him to some field, far away from where people could see and hear them. Cain pretended friendship, and disguised his true feelings of hostility. Abel had no idea what his brother was plotting. Cain deceived—deliberately and willfully deceived—his brother so he could carry out his murderous plot.

d. Note how often Abel is said to be Cain's "brother" throughout this passage (six times). This graphically shows how terrible Cain's sin was: it was his *very own brother*—the very brother who came from his own mother's womb—whom he plotted to kill and whom he eventually murdered.

e. The ungodly seed was now planted upon earth. Cain was the first man...
- who let sin consume him (Js.4:1-3).
- who became a permanent follower of "that old serpent, called the Devil" (Re.12:9; Jn.8:44).
- who launched the permanent seed of the serpent, the unbeliever and ungodly, upon earth (1 Jn.3:12. See note—Ge.4:16-24. Also see note, pt.2—Ge.3:15.)

Thought 1. Note the sins of Cain:
⇒ anger   ⇒ ignoring and rejecting God's warning and Word
⇒ deception   ⇒ choosing to follow the way of sin and of Satan
⇒ murder

Note carefully each of these sins and think about how many of us allow them to take hold of our lives. How many of us...

- become angry
- ignore and reject God's warning and Word
- deceive others
- choose to follow the way of sin and of Satan

When it comes to murder, we must always remember the words of Christ: when we allow anger to take root in our hearts, we are as guilty as a murderer, in danger of judgment and of hell fire (Mt.5:22).

We must heed the warning of God and His Word, lest we allow sin to grow within our hearts and we become consumed with sin. We must not walk in the way of Cain; we must not be a part of the ungodly seed, a follower of "that old serpent, called the Devil" (Re.12:9).

> "For the wages of sin is death; but the gift of God is eternal life through Jesus Christ our Lord" (Ro.6:23).
>
> "For to be carnally minded is death; but to be spiritually minded is life and peace" (Ro.8:6).
>
> "Then when lust hath conceived, it bringeth forth sin: and sin, when it is finished, bringeth forth death" (Js.1:15).
>
> "But the fearful, and unbelieving, and the abominable, and murderers, and whoremongers, and sorcerers, and idolaters, and all liars, shall have their part in the lake which burneth with fire and brimstone: which is the second death" (Re.21:8).
>
> "As righteousness tendeth to life: so he that pursueth evil pursueth it to his own death" (Pr.11:19).
>
> "The soul that sinneth, it shall die" (Eze.18:20).

Thought 2. This was the first murder upon earth. The lesson for us is clear: anger held within the heart is equal to murder in God's eyes.

> "But I say unto you, That whosoever is angry with his brother without a cause shall be in danger of the judgment: and whosoever shall say to his brother, Raca [a contemptible term of anger], shall be in danger of the council: but whosoever shall say, Thou fool [a cursing term of anger], shall be in danger of hell fire" (Mt.5:22).
>
> "Thou shalt not kill" (Ex.20:13).
>
> "For this, Thou shalt not commit adultery, Thou shalt not kill, Thou shalt not steal, Thou shalt not bear false witness, Thou shalt not covet; and if there be any other commandment, it is briefly comprehended in this saying, namely, Thou shalt love thy neighbor as thyself" (Ro.13:9).
>
> "But let none of you suffer as a murderer, or as a thief, or as an evildoer, or as a busybody in other men's matters" (1 Pe.4:15).
>
> "Not as Cain, who was of that wicked one, and slew his brother. And wherefore slew he him? Because his own works were evil, and his brother's righteous" (1 Jn.3:12).

2 (4:9-10) **Cain—Brotherhood—Heart—Murder:** there is the confrontation with God. Where did this confrontation take place? Scripture does not say. Perhaps it happened on the Sabbath when the family gathered together for worship and Abel's presence was missed. Remember: God apparently talked face to face with Adam's family during the early days of human history, probably from between the cherubim. (See note—Ge.4:3-4 for more discussion.) This fact, plus the fact that Cain feared retaliation, would indicate that others were present during the confrontation (see vv.14-15) and that they were informed of the secretive murder (see note—Ge.4:3-4 for discussion). Whatever the case, God confronted Cain and three significant things happened.

a. God questioned Cain: "Where is Abel your brother?" God was not asking for information; God knew exactly where Abel was. God sees and knows all things. God wanted Cain *to think* about his sin, about the terrible thing he had done, so that he would cry out for mercy. Cain was like so many of us after we have committed some terrible sin: we try to hide our sin and push it out of our minds. But this is never the thing to do, and Cain missed what every sinner needs: to face his sin and cry to God for forgiveness and mercy. Cain needed to change his ways before it was too late. He was soon to doom himself eternally unless he repented and cried out to God for mercy and forgiveness.

b. Cain denied responsibility for his brother.

"Cain, where is your brother?" God asked.

"I don't know. Am I my brother's keeper?" Cain replied.

Cain refused—absolutely refused—to take responsibility for his sin. Note how sin multiplies when we refuse to repent and face up to our sin. Cain committed sin after sin, built sin upon sin just like so many of us when we turn away from God.

1) Cain continued to rebel against God and he lied to God. He refused to face his sin and denied that he knew where Abel was. But he knew, and he knew that he had done a terrible wrong. Cain just wanted to live like he wanted, not like God demanded.

2) Cain *denied responsibility* for his brother. Cain sunk to the depths of selfishness and injustice. "Am I my brother's keeper?" Am I responsible for my brother?

⇒ For caring and looking after him?

⇒ For loving and watching over him?

⇒ For knowing where he is?

⇒ For knowing his condition, welfare, and circumstances?

Thought 1. What a lesson for us! How callous man has been toward his brother down through human history! How often we have ignored our brothers and sisters—our fellow human beings—when they have been in desperate need! The conditions, welfare, and circumstances of most brothers and sisters throughout the world are difficult: filled with hurt, pain, and suffering. Just think of all the hurting people in the world, all the...

- orphans
- widows and widowers
- prisoners
- broken-hearted

- backsliders
- diseased
- hungry
- poor

- divorced
- empty
- lonely
- suffering

- thirsty
- dying

The great tragedy is this: we deny that we know where they are. We deny responsibility for them. But, just as Cain lied, we are lying. Our communities and neighborhoods, our whole world, is full of hurting people, and we know it. God's voice still thunders forth: "Where is your brother? You are responsible! You are his brother, his keeper!"

3) Cain blinded his heart and mind against God more and more. He made himself think a most foolish thought: he could hide his sin from God.

"**He that covereth his sins shall not prosper: but whoso confesseth and forsaketh them shall have mercy**" (Pr.28:13).
"**Woe unto them that seek deep to hide their counsel from the LORD, and their works are in the dark, and they say, Who seeth us? and who knoweth us**" (Is.29:15).
"**Woe to the rebellious children, saith the LORD, that take counsel, but not of me; and that cover with a covering, but not of my spirit, that they may add sin to sin**" (Is.30:1).

4) Cain hardened his heart against God and refused to repent.

"**Happy is the man that feareth alway: but he that hardeneth his heart shall fall into mischief**" (Pr.28:14).
"**He, that being often reproved hardeneth his neck, shall suddenly be destroyed, and that without remedy**" (Pr.29:1).
"**But after thy hardness and impenitent heart treasurest up unto thyself wrath against the day of wrath and revelation of the righteous judgment of God**" (Ro.2:5).
"**But exhort one another daily, while it is called To day; lest any of you be hardened through the deceitfulness of sin**" (He.3:13).

c. God revealed an undeniable truth: sin cannot be hid; the cry for justice was and always will be heard by God. God asked, "What have you done? The voice of your brother's blood cries out to me from the ground" (v.10).
The picture is this: a terrible sin—a horrible injustice—had been committed against Abel. Abel wanted what we all want when we have been mistreated: correction of the mistreatment. Abel wanted justice executed. He had been murdered; his blood had been spilt upon the ground. Consequently, his blood cried for justice to be executed against the sin done against him. Note: God not only saw the sin of Cain, God heard the cry of Abel for justice.

Thought 1. Note this fact: Scripture says that Abel was a prophet and that his voice is still heard today. The point is this: his blood still cries out for justice against all who do evil against their brothers upon earth. Abel's blood still cries out against all the injustices against people, for all injustices to be corrected and rectified. His blood cries out for godly vengeance.

"**By faith Abel offered unto God a more excellent sacrifice than Cain, by which he obtained witness that he was righteous, God testifying of his gifts: and by it he being dead yet speaketh**" (He.11:4).
"**That the blood of all the prophets, which was shed from the foundation of the world, may be required of this generation; from the blood of Abel unto the blood of Zacharias, which perished between the altar and the temple: verily I say unto you, It shall be required of this generation**" (Lu.11:50-51).

But note: the blood of Christ proclaims a much greater message than the blood of Abel. Christ's blood proclaims redemption, even the forgiveness of sins, not vengeance.

"**And to Jesus the mediator of the new covenant, and to the blood of sprinkling, that speaketh better things than that of Abel**" (He.12:24).
"**In whom we have redemption through his blood, the forgiveness of sins, according to the riches of his grace**" (Ep.1:7).

3 (4:11-12) **Judgment—Cain:** God's judgment upon the murderer, Cain, was threefold. He was...

- to bear the curse of God in his soul
- to constantly experience difficulty in his labor
- to always be a restless soul, a wanderer upon earth

a. The murderer, Cain, was condemned to bear the curse of God within his soul. The soul of the murderer was to be affected—deeply disturbed and troubled—for the rest of his life. His soul was to bear the curse of God, to bear God's...

- displeasure
- dissatisfaction
- disappointment
- indignation
- wrath

The murderer's soul was to always sense disturbance and trouble, always sense being cursed. The horror of murder was never to leave the scene of the murderer. He was to always bear the curse of God, the curse of a disturbed and troubled soul, of God's displeasure, indignation, and wrath.

Thought 1. Scripture teaches two things about the curse of God upon sin.
1) Sin has put every person under the curse of God, the curse of a troubled and restless soul and of the wrath and indignation of God.

> **"For the wrath of God is revealed from heaven against all ungodliness and unrighteousness of men" (Ro.1:18).**
> **"For as many as are of the works of the law are under the curse: for it is written, Cursed is every one that continueth not in all things which are written in the book of the law to do them" (Ga.3:10).**
> **"Behold, I set before you this day a blessing and a curse; a blessing, if ye obey the commandments of the LORD your God, which I command you this day: and a curse, if ye will not obey the commandments of the LORD your God, but turn aside out of the way which I command you this day" (De.11:26-28).**
> **"Cursed be he that smiteth his neighbor secretly. And all the people shall say, cursed be he that taketh reward to slay an innocent person. And all the people shall say, Cursed be he that confirmeth not all the words of this law to do them" (De.27:24-26).**
> **"But it shall come to pass, if thou wilt not hearken unto the voice of the LORD thy God, to observe to do all his commandments and his statutes which I command thee this day; that all these curses shall come upon thee, and overtake thee: cursed shalt thou be in the city, and cursed shalt thou be in the field. Cursed shall be thy basket and thy store. Cursed shall be the fruit of thy body, and the fruit of thy land, the increase of thy kine [cattle], and the flocks of thy sheep. Cursed shalt thou be when thou comest in, and cursed shalt thou be when thou goest out" (De.28:15-19).**

2) Jesus Christ delivers us from the curse and wrath of God.

> **"Come unto me, all ye that labour and are heavy laden, and I will give you rest" (Mt.11:28).**
> **"Christ hath redeemed us from the curse of the law, being made a curse for us: for it is written, Cursed is every one that hangeth on a tree" (Ga.3:13).**
> **"Forasmuch then as the children are partakers of flesh and blood, he also himself likewise took part of the same; that through death he might destroy him that had the power of death, that is, the devil; and deliver them who through fear of death were all their lifetime subject to bondage" (He.2:14-15).**

b. The murderer, Cain, was to experience difficulty in his labor. He had spilt blood upon the ground, defiled the earth in the most horrible way imaginable. Consequently, he was to face problem after problem in securing his food and in meeting the other necessities of his life. No matter where he settled upon the earth, the earth was going to give him trouble. The earth would not yield abundant crops, not easily, not without great difficulty, strain, and toil. The murderer was to experience great difficulty in his life and labor, in securing the necessities of life: he was to know beyond most other people...

- pressure
- strain
- tension
- exhaustion
- emptiness
- sweat
- worry
- toil
- restlessness

Thought 1. The way of the murderer is very hard. No matter where he is upon earth, even if he works and has the security of a crime syndicate, the earth causes great difficulty for the murderer. He never knows freedom from restlessness and difficulty. He is cursed to know laborious pressure, strain, tension, sweat, worry, toil, exhaustion, restlessness, and emptiness in his life and labor, in meeting the most basic necessities of life.

But note this: the way of any sinner is hard, no matter what the sin is. All sin reaps terrible results and ends in death—eternal death—unless the sinner repents and turns to God.

> **"The wicked man travaileth with pain all his days, and the number of years is hidden to the oppressor" (Jb. 15:20).**
> **"Fools because of their transgression, and because of their iniquities, are afflicted" (Ps.107:17).**
> **"The way of transgressors is hard" (Pr.13:15).**
> **"Tribulation and anguish, upon every soul of man that doeth evil, of the Jew first, and also of the Gentile" (Ro.2:9).**
> **"Destruction and misery are in their ways [the ways of the sinner]: and the way of peace have they not known" (Ro.3:16-17).**

c. The murderer, Cain, was condemned to be a restless and rootless soul, a wanderer all the days of his life. Just like all murderers, Cain was condemned...

- to be unacceptable to most people
- to know the reproach and disgrace of people
- to fear being found out, no matter where he settled
- to be always looking over his shoulder

- to be restless, without peace or security
- to be rootless, often wandering and moving about
- to fear retaliation
- to fear justice

Thought 1. The sinner—the person who continues in sin, who never turns to God—is a restless and rootless soul, a wanderer upon earth. He is alienated and cut off from God, never fulfilling his purpose for being on earth. He never knows the secure rest and peace of God. He never knows the care, provision, protection, and love of God. He has nothing to look forward to except the justice of God. The sinner is a restless and rootless soul, a wanderer upon earth.

> "In the morning thou shalt say, Would God it were even! and at even thou shalt say, Would God it were morning! for the fear of thine heart wherewith thou shalt fear, and for the sight of thine eyes which thou shalt see" (De.28:67).
> "For all his days are sorrows, and his travail grief; yea, his heart taketh not rest in the night. This is also vanity" (Ec.2:23).
> "My heart panted, fearfulness affrighted me: the night of my pleasure hath he turned into fear unto me" (Is.21:4).
> "There is no peace, saith the LORD, unto the wicked" (Is.48:22).
> "But the wicked are like the troubled sea, when it cannot rest, whose waters cast up mire and dirt" (Is.57:20).
> "The way of peace they know not; and there is no judgment in their goings: they have made them crooked paths: whosoever goeth therein shall not know peace" (Is.59:8).
> "Our necks are under persecution: we labour, and have no rest" (Lam.5:5).
> "Destruction cometh; and they shall seek peace, and there shall be none" (Eze.7:25).

4 (4:13-14) **Judgment, Reaction Against—Justice**: note Cain's reaction and complaint against the judgment of God:

> "And Cain said unto the LORD, My punishment is greater than I can bear" (v.13).

This is not the response of a repentant soul; it is the complaint of a hardened heart against God. There is nothing in Cain's words to indicate repentance, that he is confessing and asking God to forgive his sin. He is reacting against the judgment of God, complaining that the judgment...

- is too great
- is too severe
- is unfair
- is abusive
- is too much for him or anyone else to bear
- is beyond—far outweighs—the sin he had committed

Note that Cain restates God's threefold judgment against him. He is emphasizing how great the punishment is:
"My punishment is greater than I can bear. Just look at the punishment you have pronounced upon me. You have alienated me...

- "cut me off from the fruitfulness of the earth, doomed me to struggle with great difficulty as I seek to meet the necessities of life.
- "cut me off from yourself, from your presence, care, and blessings as I walk throughout life.
- "cut me off from society, from ever being acceptable to them and from ever being at rest and having a permanent resting place."

Note also that Cain fears other men, that they might seek justice and not mercy. As stated, Cain is not deploring his sin; he is reacting and complaining about the judgment of God. He is accusing God of being unfair and too severe.

Thought 1. Note how typical this is of most people. Most people complain against the judgment of God. They do just what Cain did, seek to lighten or excuse their sin.
1) Most persons believe they will be acceptable to God, in the final analyses.

> "Wherefore doth a living man complain, a man for the punishment of his sins? Let us search and try our ways, and turn again to the LORD" (Lam.3:39-40).
> "And then will I profess unto them, I never knew you: depart from me, ye that work iniquity" (Mt.7:23).
> "And fear not them which kill the body, but are not able to kill the soul: but rather fear him which is able to destroy both soul and body in hell" (Mt.10:28).
> "Ye serpents, ye generation of vipers, how can ye escape the damnation of hell?" (Mt.23:33).
> "He that believeth on the Son hath everlasting life: and he that believeth not the Son shall not see life; but the wrath of God abideth on him" (Jn.3:36).
> "Marvel not at this: for the hour is coming, in the which all that are in the graves shall hear his voice, and shall come forth; they that have done good, unto the resurrection of life; and they that have done evil, unto the resurrection of damnation" (Jn.5:28-29).

"In flaming fire taking vengeance on them that know not God, and that obey not the gospel of our Lord Jesus Christ: who shall be punished with everlasting destruction from the presence of the Lord, and from the glory of his power" (2 Th.1:8-9).

"For if the word spoken by angels was stedfast, and every transgression and disobedience received a just recompense of reward; how shall we escape, if we neglect so great salvation; which at the first began to be spoken by the Lord, and was confirmed unto us by them that heard him" (He.2:2-3).

"The Lord knoweth how to deliver the godly out of temptations, and to reserve the unjust unto the day of judgment to be punished" (2 Pe.2:9).

"But the fearful, and unbelieving, and the abominable, and murderers, and whoremongers, and sorcerers, and idolaters, and all liars, shall have their part in the lake which burneth with fire and brimstone: which is the second death" (Re.21:8).

2) Few persons believe that God will ever judge them, not severely. The very idea that they are such great sinners that God would reject them is abhorrent to them. They rebel against such preaching and teaching.

3) Some persons even deny that God is going to judge the world. They say that a loving, caring God could never condemn a person forever, even if the person was Hitler or Stalin who slaughtered millions of people.

5 (4:15) **God, Mercy of**: there is the great mercy of God. Note the name used for God throughout this passage is LORD (Yahweh or Jehovah). This is the name used when there is a need to stress the redemption, faithfulness, grace, and mercy of God. It is the covenant of grace that God wants to build with every person upon earth. God is merciful, and He wanted Cain to cry out for His mercy and forgiveness. But as we have seen, Cain refused. He still wanted to go his own way and live his life like he wanted. He even complained about the judgment of God upon his murderous sin. But note what God did: He still acted in mercy. He still reached out to Cain.

First, God decreed that vengeance was not to be executed upon Cain. If anyone dared, then a sevenfold vengeance would fall upon the head of the avenger. The idea is that of a divine curse seven times worse than what Cain suffered; that of a complete and final judgment, perhaps of never having the chance of repentance.

Second, God set a mark upon Cain to assure him and to protect him. Was this a visible sign to keep vengeance-seekers from killing Cain or simply the assurance from God that no one would dare go against God's threat of a sevenfold judgment? Commentators are divided, and Scripture is not clear. However, men are seldom kept from doing what they want by the warnings of God, even the warning of eternal damnation. For this reason, the mark was probably a visible mark that reminded the people of Cain's day...

- that God definitely meant what He said: no person was to take vengeance upon Cain. God Himself would handle the judgment of Cain, the murderer.

Thought 1. God is merciful and gracious. As long as a person lives upon earth, there is hope for him. God will have mercy and forgive his sins, but the person must repent. The person must cry out to God for mercy and turn from his sin.

"But God, who is rich in mercy, for his great love wherewith he loved us, even when we were dead in sins, hath quickened [made us alive] us together with Christ, (by grace ye are saved)" (Ep.2:4-5).

"For by grace [by God's mercy] are ye saved through faith; and that not of yourselves: it is the gift of God: not of works, lest any man should boast" (Ep.2:8-9).

"Not by works of righteousness which we have done, but according to his mercy he saved us" (Tit.3:5).

"It is of the LORD's mercies that we are not consumed, because his compassions fail not" (Lam.3:22).

"And rend your heart, and not your garments, and turn unto the LORD your God: for he is gracious and merciful, slow to anger, and of great kindness, and repenteth him of the evil" (Joel 2:13).

"Who is a God like unto thee, that pardoneth iniquity, and passeth by the transgression...of his heritage? he retaineth not his anger for ever, because he delighteth in mercy" (Mi.7:18).

Thought 2. All vengeance must be left up to God. Scripture is clear about this.

"Dearly beloved, avenge not yourselves, but rather give place unto wrath: for it is written, Vengeance is mine; I will repay, saith the Lord" (Ro.12:19).

"And to you who are troubled rest with us, when the Lord Jesus shall be revealed from heaven with his mighty angels, in flaming fire taking vengeance on them that know not God, and that obey not the gospel of our Lord Jesus Christ" (2 Th.1:7-8).

"For we know him that hath said, Vengeance belongeth unto me, I will recompense, saith the Lord. And again, The Lord shall judge his people" (He.10:30).

"O LORD God, to whom vengeance belongeth; O God, to whom vengeance belongeth, show thyself" (Ps.94:1).

	C. The First Civilization & Society (Part 1): The Development of the First Ungodly Seed or Descendants, 4:16-24	the one was Adah, and the name of the other Zillah. 20 And Adah bare Jabal: he was the father of such as dwell in tents, and of such as have cattle. 21 And his brother's name was Jubal: he was the father of all such as handle the harp and organ.	6. A society of famous, wealthy, & gifted people a. Ranchers & tent-makers b. Musicians & inventors of musical instruments
1. A society that was secular & ungodly: Cain left God's presence	16 And Cain went out from the presence of the LORD, and dwelt in the land of Nod, on the east of Eden.	22 And Zillah, she also bare Tubalcain, an instructor of every artificer in brass and iron: and the sister of Tubalcain was Naamah.	c. Manufacturers & craftsmen d. Worshippers of beauty
2. A society that was rootless & restless: Cain dwelt in the land of Nod	17 And Cain knew his wife; and she conceived, and bare Enoch: and he builded a city, and called the name of the city, after the name of his son, Enoch.	23 And Lamech said unto his wives, Adah and Zillah, Hear my voice; ye wives of Lamech, hearken unto my speech: for I have slain a man to my wounding, and a young man to my hurt.	7. A society that sought revenge, that murdered, boasted in itself, felt self-sufficient, & was engulfed in lawlessness
3. A society of contractors & city-dwellers who honored & gloried in themselves	18 And unto Enoch was born Irad: and Irad begat Mehujael: and Mehujael begat Methusael: and Methusael begat Lamech.		
4. A society that continued to grow in its secular & ungodly heritage			
5. A society that worshipped the cult of beauty & sex	19 And Lamech took unto him two wives: the name of	24 If Cain shall be avenged sevenfold, truly Lamech seventy and sevenfold.	

DIVISION III

ADAM, THE FIRST MAN (PART 2): THE BIRTH, DEVELOPMENT, AND CORRUPTION OF BOTH THE UNGODLY AND THE GODLY SEED (DESCENDANTS), 4:1–6:8

C. The First Civilization and Society (Part 1): The Development of the First Ungodly Seed or Descendants, 4:16-24

(4:16-24) **Introduction**: remember, Chapters 4:1–6:8 are dealing with the ungodly and the godly seed (descendants) of early history. We have already studied how the ungodly and godly seed began:
  A. The First Children, Cain and Abel: False Vs. True Worship—the Beginning of False Worship, 4:1-7
  B. The First Murder, Cain Kills Abel: The Undeniable Truth of Judgment—Sin Cannot Be Hid, 4:8-15

Now, Scripture shows us how the ungodly line branched out and developed into an ungodly civilization and society. This is: *The First Civilization and Society (Part 1): The Development of the First Ungodly Seed or Descendants.*
  1. A society that was secular and ungodly: Cain left God's presence (v.16).
  2. A society that was rootless and restless: Cain dwelt in the land of Nod (v.16).
  3. A society of contractors and city-dwellers who honored and gloried in themselves (v.17).
  4. A society that continued to grow in its secular and ungodly heritage (v.18).
  5. A society that worshipped the cult of beauty and sex (v.19).
  6. A society of famous, wealthy, and gifted people (vv.20-22).
  7. A society that sought revenge, that murdered, boasted in itself, felt self-sufficient, and was engulfed in lawlessness (vv.23-24).

1 (4:16) **Civilization—Society—Cain—Secularism**: the ungodly seed or descendants developed a secular and ungodly society. Note the Scripture: "Cain went out from the presence of the Lord" (v.16).
Remember: God had confronted Cain about his sin in murdering his brother, Abel. God had pronounced the judgment, but at the same time God had reached out in mercy to Cain, longing for him to cry out for mercy and to repent (see outline and notes—Ge.4:8-15 for discussion). What was Cain's response? This was it:

"Cain went out from the presence of the Lord" (v.16).

In obstinacy and hardness of heart, Cain turned and walked away from the presence of God. But this means far more than just *walking out* of the presence of God. The very context of this passage shows that Cain was rejecting God Himself and all who stood for God. Cain was leaving, forsaking, and getting as far away as he could...
  • from the presence of God
  • from his godly parents, Adam and Eve, breaking their hearts even more
  • from the community and neighborhood of the godly (Adam and Eve had other children by this time, see Ge.5:4)
  • from the place and altar where God was worshipped
  • from the land where people were living godly lives

Cain chose to turn and walk away from both God and his godly family. He left and went into another country in order to live like he wanted, in order to be away from God and to do his own thing. He chose—deliberately chose—to live a secular and ungodly life, and to develop a secular and ungodly society. Cain separated himself from God, became alienated from God.

Cain got just what he wanted. This passage clearly shows that he gave birth to a secular, ungodly civilization and society. Cain is the father of the secular and ungodly civilizations and societies of the world. Cain was...

- the first of the ungodly seed or civilizations of Adam
- the first seed—the first human being—who deliberately chose to turn away from God *permanently*
- the first seed who chose to live a secular and ungodly life
- the first ungodly seed planted upon earth

Simply stated, Cain was the first person who let sin rule and reign his life, the first person who became a permanent follower of "that old serpent, called the Devil" (Re.12:9; Jn.8:44). Cain was the first person who launched the permanent seed of the serpent upon earth (1 Jn.3:12. See note, pt.2—Ge.3:15 for more discussion.) He began the first secular, ungodly society upon earth. He is the father of all the secular and ungodly civilizations and societies down through history.

> "They have rejected me, that I should not reign over them" (1 S.8:7).
> "But my people would not hearken to my voice; and Israel would none of me. So I gave them up unto their own hearts' lust: and they walked in their own counsels" (Ps.81:11-12).
> "I have called, and ye refused; I have stretched out my hand, and no man regarded; but ye have set at nought all my counsel, and would none of my reproof" (Pr.1:24-25).
> "His power and his wrath is against all them that forsake him" (Ezr. 8:22).
> "Thou hast forsaken me, saith the LORD, thou art gone backward: therefore will I stretch out my hand against thee, and destroy thee; I am weary with repenting" (Je.15:6).
> "For the invisible things of him from the creation of the world are clearly seen, being understood by the things that are made, even his eternal power and Godhead; so that they are without excuse: because that, when they knew God, they glorified him not as God, neither were thankful; but became vain in their imaginations, and their foolish heart was darkened. Professing themselves to be wise, they became fools....Who changed the truth of God into a lie, and worshipped and served the creature more than the Creator, who is blessed for ever" (Ro.1:20-22, 25).

2 **(4:16) Restlessness—Rootless—Civilization—Society—Cain**: the ungodly seed or descendants were a restless and rootless society. Cain "dwelt in the land of Nod" (v.16). The *land of Nod* (erets nodh) actually means the land of wanderings, restlessness, rootlessness, quaking, trembling, shaking. The idea is that of being restless and rootless, of wandering and moving all about as though the earth itself was shaking and shoving a person all over the place. Remember: Cain was the first to leave Adam's family and the godly community and to venture out into this land. Apparently, the land was later called "the land of Nod" because of Cain and his restless and rootless spirit. God had condemned Cain to be possessed with a restless and rootless spirit because of his ungodly behavior.

Thought 1. The person or society that turns away from God will always be restless and rootless. No person or society will know true peace until it turns to God. The reason is this: a person or society who lives only a secular life—who lives only for this world—has only what this world offers, and there is no escape from this world. Part of what this secular world offers is...

- restlessness and rootlessness
- brevity and shortness of life
- sickness and disease
- accident and suffering
- pain and hurt
- corruption and death

The secular world can offer some comfort, pleasure, money, position, recognition, honor, and security. But none of this is permanent; none of it arises beyond this earth. When one of the terrible tragedies of life strikes us, and sooner or later tragedy strikes every one of us, that is it. We are left only with what the secular world can give us. And the help of the secular world is limited, and it ends quickly. All the help of earth ends, and when it does, we are left without hope and help beyond this life. We are left without God—all because we as individuals and societies chose to live secular, ungodly lives.

The soul knows this, knows it down deep within. This is the reason the soul is always restless and rootless—never at peace and never settled—when it seeks only the secular life of this world. The things of this world can never satisfy the soul of man. The soul was made for God; therefore, the soul can never rest nor be rooted until it rests and is rooted in God.

> "In the morning thou shalt say, Would God it were even! and at even thou shalt say, Would God it were morning! for the fear of thine heart wherewith thou shalt fear, and for the sight of thine eyes which thou shalt see" (De.28:67).
> "For what hath man of all his labour, and of the vexation of his heart, wherein he hath laboured under the sun? For all his days are sorrows, and his travail grief; yea, his heart taketh not rest in the night. This is also vanity" (Ec.2:22-23).
> "There is no peace, saith the Lord, unto the wicked" (Is.48:22).

"But the wicked are like the troubled sea, when it cannot rest, whose waters cast up mire and dirt" (Is.57:20).

"The way of peace they know not; and there is no judgment in their goings: they have made them crooked paths; whosoever goeth therein shall not know peace" (Is.59:8).

"Our necks are under persecution: we labour, and have no rest" (Lam.5:5).

"Destruction cometh; and they shall seek peace, and there shall be none" (Eze.7:25).

3 (4:17) **Building—Construction—City—Cain**: the ungodly seed or descendants were contractors and city-dwellers who honored and gloried in themselves. Note several facts.

a. Cain had a wife. Who was she? His sister or half-sister or distant relative? Scripture is clear: Adam and Eve had other children. In fact Adam lived to be 930 years old (Ge.5:4-5). There must have been many children, and of course the children of each generation would have given birth to many other children. The potential population during Adam's life is staggering. James Montgomery Boice, the excellent Presbyterian expositor, points this out: if only one half of Adam's children lived, and if only half of the living got married, and if only half the married had children, then, even at the three half-rates, the population would still number more than a million at Adam's death.[1] (See Deeper Study # 2 for a chart on the godly seed or descendants of Adam—Ge.5:27-32.)

There was no danger of deformity or harmful genes due to intermarriage for two reasons:

⇒ This was the way God planned and purposed the human race to grow.

⇒ This was the very beginning of the human race. That is, Adam and his immediate family stood at the head of the stream of human life. The stream of human life—just like the stream of a river—was not polluted at the head or spring. It became polluted as it flowed downstream. The great Lutheran scholar H.C. Leupold states it well:

> *Cain's wife must have been his sister who followed him into exile; for Adam had sons and daughters according to 5:4....Marriage to a sister at this early stage of the development of the human race [cannot] be considered wrong or unnatural. If according to divine purpose the human race is to develop from one pair, then the marriage of brothers and sisters as well as of other close relatives will for a time be a necessity. Later on the nations may see fit to classify such unions as incestuous and seek to keep the human race from running its shoots back to the parent stem....But in the earlier history of mankind the union of those closely related was not abhorred. Abraham's wife was his half-sister (20:12); cf. also 24:4 and 28:2.*[2]

b. Cain and his wife had a son and named him Enoch (chanoch). The name means beginner, dedicated, or initiated. Apparently, Cain was hoping that his son would give him a new beginning—a new start—in life. But note: the new beginning was not with God, but apart from God. Cain was hoping and working for a new beginning within the secular world. He wanted a fresh start within the world, not with God.

c. Cain became a contractor and began to build a city. This, of course, was not a city like the modern cities of today. It was probably just a few houses enclosed within a wall. Apparently, as months and years passed, some other families had forsaken God and the godly line and they had joined Cain and his family in the land of Nod.

> **Thought 1.** Note how Cain is seeking to settle down, to build roots—a fixed residence—right here on earth. He should have been seeking heaven in order to settle the restlessness and rootlessness of his soul. There is nothing wrong with building a house on earth in which to live, but the first thing we should seek is a home in heaven. Only when we seek heaven will we find true rest and a permanent resting place.

> "But if from thence [from idolatry, from forsaking the Lord] thou shalt seek the Lord thy God, thou shalt find him, if thou seek him with all thy heart and with all thy soul" (De.4:29).

> "The Lord will give strength unto his people; the Lord will bless his people with peace" (Ps.29:11).

> "Depart from evil, and do good; seek peace, and pursue it" (Ps.34:14).

> "Seek the Lord, and his strength: seek his face evermore" (Ps.105:4).

> "Thou wilt keep him in perfect peace, whose mind is stayed on thee: because he trusteth in thee" (Is.26:3).

> "To whom he said, This is the rest wherewith ye may cause the weary to rest; and this is the refreshing: yet they would not hear" (Is.28:12).

> "O that thou hadst hearkened to my commandments! then had thy peace been as a river, and thy righteousness as the waves of the sea" (Is.48:18).

> "But seek ye first the kingdom of God, and his righteousness; and all these things shall be added unto you" (Mt.6:33).

> "Take my yoke upon you, and learn of me; for I am meek and lowly in heart: and ye shall find rest unto your souls" (Mt.11:29).

d. Cain gloried in his city and in his son. He named the city after his son, Enoch. He wanted the name of his son to be carried on forever. He was out to glorify the name and works of his family. He was now living only for the honor of this world, not for the honor of God.

---

[1] James Montgomery Boice. *Genesis,* Vol.1, p.211f.

[2] H.C. Leupold. *Genesis*, Vol.1, p.215f.

"Their inward thought is, that their houses shall continue for ever, and their dwelling places to all generations; they call their lands after their own names. Nevertheless man being in honour abideth not: he is like the beasts that perish" (Ps.49:11-12).

"For when he dieth he shall carry nothing away: his glory shall not descend after him" (Ps.49:17).

"Therefore hell hath enlarged herself, and opened her mouth without measure: and their glory, and their multitude, and their pomp, and he that rejoiceth, shall descend into it" (Is.5:14).

"As they were increased, so they sinned against me: therefore will I change their glory into shame" (Ho.4:7).

"How can ye believe, which receive honour one of another, and seek not the honour that cometh from God only?" (Jn.5:44).

"For all flesh is as grass, and all the glory of man as the flower of grass. The grass withereth, and the flower thereof falleth away" (1 Pe.1:24).

4 (4:18) **Heritage—Parents, Ungodly—Society**: the ungodly seed or descendants continued to grow in their secular heritage. Nothing is said about the generations mentioned here except for the last name, Lamech. Several points, however, can be made.

a. The ungodly seed and society continued to grow and develop upon earth. Secularism and ungodliness were branching out more and more, gaining a greater foothold with each passing generation.

b. The parents gave their children meaningful names. The great Pulpit Commentary gives the meaning of several different names as follows:
⇒ *Irad* meant townsman, citizen, the ornament of a city. He was, perhaps, a leader who brought honor to his hometown.
⇒ *Mehujael* meant smitten of God, the purified or formed of God. Note that the name of Mehujael ends in "el," which is the name of God, *El*ohim.
⇒ *Methusael* meant man of God. Note that his name ends with "el," the name for God as well.
⇒ *Lamech* meant strong youth, man of prayer or youth.

c. The names given the children suggest that the ungodly seed were religious, but their religion was only...
• a worldly religion
• a secular religion
• a humanistic, man-made religion

In the words of James Montgomery Boice,

> It is the kind of religion Cain chose by his aesthetically pleasing sacrifice. It is all too common today—a religion of beautiful liturgies, words, and music but without the promise of God's forgiveness of sin through the shed blood of Jesus Christ.[3]

It was the same false worship and religion that Cain had chosen and practiced that led to his tragic fall (see outline and notes—Ge.4:1-7).

"Having a form of godliness, but denying the power thereof: from such turn away" (2 Ti.3:5).

Matthew Henry says:

> They will assume the form of godliness...but they will not submit to the power of it, to take away their sin. Observe here:
> Men may be very bad and wicked...they may be lovers of themselves...yet have a form of godliness.
> A form of godliness is a very different thing from the power of it; men may have the one and be wholly destitute of the other....
> From such good Christians must withdraw themselves.[4]

5 (4:19) **Beauty—Immorality—Bigamy—Polygamy**: the ungodly seed or descendants worshipped the cult of beauty and sex. "Lamech took [married]...two wives" (v.19). He was the first bigamist upon earth, the very first person to practice polygamy. It took just seven generations for the ungodly to slap down God's ordained institution of marriage, one man for one wife. The ungodly seed ignored and rebelled against God and His commandment for purity of life and marriage (Ge.2:24; Mt.19:4-6, see Mal.2:14-15). In Lamech the passion of society to seek after the cult of beauty and sex was launched. This is suggested in the names of Lamech's two wives.
⇒ *Adah* means ornament, adorned, attractive, beauty, pleasure.
⇒ *Zillah* means the shady or shadow, probably referring to the beautiful color and shadow of her hair or skin.

Lamech was attracted by the beauty and pleasure of the flesh, so much so that he let his passion run loose. He wanted to have the presence and bodies of two attractive women at once. He asked each to become his wife and both agreed to become the wife of one man. He and his wives were consumed with the flesh: they gave themselves completely over to the

---

3   James Montgomery Boice. *Genesis*, Vol.1, p.212.
4   *Matthew Henry's Commentary*, Vol.5, p.844.

cult of beauty and immorality. They neither controlled their passion nor denied their immoral urges. They focused upon the body...

- the beauty and attractiveness of the flesh
- the passion and stimulation of the flesh
- the pleasure and sexual enjoyment of the flesh

Thought 1. The cult that worships beauty and sex has been in the world since the dawn of human history, but today, it is especially strong. Beauty and sex are so worshipped that they have become the dominant theme of advertisements throughout the industrialized world. Beauty and sex are used to sell everything from soap to cars. The cult is so worshipped and so acceptable, that most persons spend more time thinking about beauty and sex than they do in fellowship and prayer with God—far, far more time. In fact, the cult of beauty and sex has so gripped lives that within any given day most persons...

- spend more time in front of a mirror than they do with God
- spend more money on clothes, makeup (cosmetics), and beauty items than they do for God
- spend more time looking at clothes and dressing than they do with God
- spend more time in watching sexual scenes on television and in thinking, reading, and talking about sex than they do with God
- spend more time in desiring, wanting, and having sex than they do with God

A person, especially believers, should be as attractive as he or she can be, but not with the clothes and cosmetics that expose and attract attention to the flesh. *This is the key*: anything that exposes or attracts attention to our bodies—anything that causes thoughts within others to focus upon our bodies—is wrong. Our objective is to focus attention upon Christ. Christ is to be so dominant in our lives that people see Him in us—see a preciousness, a sweetness, a love, a caring, a meekness, a quietness, an inner strength of spirit—so much so that people are drawn to Him, not to our bodies, clothes, or makeup.

⇒ This is what must be practiced and lived by us all.
⇒ This is what must be taught to our children.
⇒ This is what must control the media we allow in our homes: television, films, and magazines.
⇒ This is what must dominate our lives: Christ and our testimony for Christ.

> **"In like manner also, that women adorn themselves in modest apparel, with shamefacedness and sobriety; not with broided hair, or gold, or pearls, or costly array; but (which becometh women professing godliness) with good works" (1 Ti.2:9-10).**
>
> **"[Your] adorning let it not be that outward adorning of plaiting the hair, and of wearing of gold, or of putting on of apparel; but let it be the hidden man of the heart, in that which is not corruptible, even the ornament of a meek and quiet spirit, which is in the sight of God of great price. For after this manner in the old time the holy women also, who trusted in God, adorned themselves, being in subjection unto their own husbands" (1 Pe.3:3-5).**
>
> **"Neither yield ye your members [body parts] as instruments of unrighteousness unto sin: but yield yourselves unto God, as those that are alive from the dead, and your members as instruments of righteousness unto God" (Ro.6:13).**
>
> **"Nevertheless man being in honour abideth not: he is like the beasts that perish. This their way is their folly: yet their posterity approve their sayings. Like sheep they are laid in the grave; death shall feed on them; and the upright shall have dominion over them in the morning; and their beauty shall consume in the grave from their dwelling" (Ps.49:12-14).**
>
> **"As a jewel of gold in a swine's snout, so is a fair woman which is without discretion" (Pr.11:22).**
>
> **"Favour is deceitful, and beauty is vain: but a woman that feareth the LORD, she shall be praised" (Pr.31:30).**
>
> **"Moreover the LORD saith, Because the daughters of Zion are haughty, and walk with stretched forth necks and wanton [seductive] eyes, walking and mincing as they go, and making a tinkling with their feet: therefore the Lord will smite with a scab the crown of the head of the daughters of Zion, and the LORD will discover their secret parts. In that day the Lord will take away the bravery of their tinkling ornaments about their feet, and their cauls, and their round tires like the moon, the chains, and the bracelets, and the mufflers, the bonnets, and the ornaments of the legs, and the headbands, and the tablets, and the earrings, the rings, and nose jewels, the changeable suits of apparel, and the mantles, and the wimples, and the crisping pins, the glasses, and the fine linen, and the hoods, and veils. And it shall come to pass, that instead of sweet smell there shall be stink; and instead of a girdle a rent; and instead of well set hair baldness; and instead of a stomacher a girding of sackcloth; and burning instead of beauty" (Is.3:16-24).**

6 (4:20-22) **Ungodly, The—Society—Culture—Music—Tentmaking—Ranch—Nomad—Metal Worker**: the ungodly seed or descendants were a society of famous, wealthy, and culturally gifted people. This is seen in the children of Lamech.

a. There was *Jabal*, the son born of Lamech's wife Adah. Scripture says that he was a rancher who raised livestock (miqueh). The Hebrew word seems to include more than mere cattle. It would include other livestock as well, such as camels and donkeys.[5]

---

5 H.C. Leupold. *Genesis*, Vol.1, p.220.

Jabal was also the discoverer of the nomadic tent. His need to constantly move the herds from pasture to pasture necessitated that he come up with some moveable housing for his own family and the families of his hired workers.

Note that Jabal was not only wealthy, but he became famous. He was known as the "father" of tentmakers and nomadic ranchers. He was the first to develop the livestock ranch and the idea of living in moveable tents while moving the stock from pasture to pasture.

b. There was *Jubal*, the second son of Lamech's wife Adah. Jubal was a musician who invented the harp (string instrument) and the flute (reed pipe) for music. Note that he invented the very first musical instruments upon earth: Jubal is the "father" of all string and pipe instruments. He was the first to develop the *cultured arts* for society.

c. There was *Tubal-cain*, who was Lamech's son by his other wife, Zillah. Tubal-cain was a metal-worker: he worked both with brass and iron. He was the first person ever known to take brass and iron and manufacture and craft all kinds of useful things. He most likely made such things as utensils, jewelry, decorative items, tools, and weapons.

d. There was *Naamah*, the sister of Tubal-cain. Why was a woman mentioned in the genealogy of Lamech when the names of women were seldom, if ever, listed in the roots of families? The name *Naamah* means beautiful, attractive, pleasant. Apparently, Naamah's beauty was so striking that she caught everyone's attention, so much so that she was well known down through the ages for her beauty.

Thought 1. Note a significant fact about the ungodly seed or descendants of society: there is nothing whatsoever, not even one word, mentioned about God in this coverage of the ungodly line of civilization and society. The only things discussed are the things of the world...
- the world's work and employment
- the world's wealth and possessions
- the world's culture and artistic interests
- the world's tools, decorative items, and weapons
- the world's fascination and lust for beauty and sex (the cult of beauty and sex)

All of these things—work, possessions, culture, art, tools or technology, beauty, and sex—are important, even necessary for society to survive and progress. But what about God? God is totally absent from *the ungodly line* of society. And the terrible tragedy is that God—the only living and true God—is still absent from the ungodly line of civilization and society. *The ungodly seed and descendants* march on forever building a society of people who seek to be famous, wealthy, powerful, and culturally gifted. But they build a people without God, a people without hope both in this life and in the life to come.

> "The man that wandereth out of the way of understanding shall remain in the congregation of the dead" (Pr.21:16).
> "For ye shall be as an oak whose leaf fadeth, and as a garden that hath no water" (Is.1:30).
> "Thus saith the LORD, What iniquity have your fathers found in me, that they are gone far from me, and have walked after vanity [emptiness], and are become vain?" (Je.2:5).
> "Therefore I said, Surely these are poor; they are foolish: for they know not the way of the LORD, nor the judgment of their God" (Je.5:4).
> "That at that time ye were without Christ, being aliens from the commonwealth of Israel, and strangers from the covenants of promise, having no hope, and without God in the world" (Ep.2:12).
> "So then because thou art lukewarm, and neither cold nor hot, I will spue thee out of my mouth. Because thou sayest, I am rich, and increased with goods, and have need of nothing; and knowest not that thou art wretched, and miserable, and poor, and blind, and naked" (Re.3:16-17).

[7] (4:23-24) **Murder—Self-Sufficiency—Boasting**: the ungodly seed or descendants developed a society that sought revenge, that murdered, boasted in itself, felt self-sufficient, and was engulfed in lawlessness.
Several facts need to be noted.

a. This is the first poetry, so far as we know, ever spoken upon earth. Note that it is a song of vengeance and of war, a song that has been entitled *Lamech's Sword Song*.[6]

b. The Hebrew can be translated as future or past...
- as something that Lamech would do if he were attacked by a man, or,
- as something Lamech had already done because he was attacked.

Commentators are divided over which way it should be translated, although most seem to understand it as an event that had actually happened.

c. The picture is that of Lamech taking into his hands a weapon (perhaps a sword-like weapon) that his son Tubal-cain had invented. Either one of two things happened:
⇒ Lamech waves the sword above his head in a warrior like manner, boasting that he could slay any man, old or young, who attacked him. Or...
⇒ Lamech took the sword and actually killed a young man for having injured him.

d. The point for us to see is the picture of society Lamech paints for us. Lamech and his ungodly forefathers had developed a society...

---

[6] H.C. Leupold. *Genesis*, Vol.1, p.222.

- that boasted in its own arm of strength
- that prided itself in its weapons of murder and war
- that sought revenge
- that declared its own self-sufficiency
- that denied and rebelled against any need for God
- that had become lawless and without true justice and morality

Note how boastful and self-reliant Lamech had become. In the fervor and excitement of the moment—with the power of the weapon he held in his hands—he remembered the curse of God upon his forefather, Cain. He remembered that God had promised to avenge Cain sevenfold against anyone who harmed Cain. Lamech cried out, if God could do that, then he, Lamech, with such a powerful weapon, could avenge himself seventy-seven times.

Lamech had reached the highest pitch (crescendo) of self-glory, pride, boasting, and self-sufficiency: he was declaring himself to be stronger and more powerful than God.

Thought 1. What a sad commentary on a society and civilization. Yet, the same commentary has been pronounced upon every civilization and society down through the centuries. History has had only one declaration: a declaration of human revenge, murder, boasting, self-sufficiency, and lawlessness.

⇒ In relation to revenge, God says this:

"Thou shalt not avenge, nor bear any grudge against the children of thy people, but thou shalt love thy neighbor as thyself: I am the LORD" (Le.19:18).

"Say not thou, I will recompense evil; but wait on the LORD, and he shall save thee" (Pr.20:22).

"Say not, I will do so to him as he hath done to me: I will render to the man according to his work" (Pr.24:29).

"But I say unto you, That ye resist not evil: but whosoever shall smite thee on thy right cheek, turn to him the other also" (Mt.5:39).

"Recompense to no man evil for evil. Provide things honest in the sight of all men" (Ro.12:17).

"Not rendering evil for evil, or railing for railing: but contrariwise blessing; knowing that ye are thereunto called, that ye should inherit a blessing" (1 Pe.3:9).

⇒ In relation to murder, God says this:

"Thou shalt not kill" (Ex.20:13).

"He saith unto him, Which? Jesus said, Thou shalt do no murder, Thou shalt not commit adultery, Thou shalt not steal, Thou shalt not bear false witness" (Mt.19:18).

"For this, Thou shalt not commit adultery, Thou shalt not kill, Thou shalt not steal, Thou shalt not bear false witness, Thou shalt not covet; and if there be any other commandment, it is briefly comprehended in this saying, namely, Thou shalt love thy neighbor as thyself" (Ro.13:9).

"But let none of you suffer as a murderer, or as a thief, or as an evildoer, or as a busybody in other men's matters" (1 Pe.4:15).

"Whosoever hateth his brother is a murderer: and ye know that no murderer hath eternal life abiding in him" (1 Jn.3:15).

⇒ In relation to boasting, God says this:

"For the wicked boasteth of his heart's desire, and blesseth the covetous, whom the LORD abhorreth" (Ps.10:3).

"They that trust in their wealth, and boast themselves in the multitude of their riches; none of them can by any means redeem his brother, nor give to God a ransom for him" (Ps.49:6-7).

"Be not wise in thine own eyes: fear the LORD, and depart from evil" (Pr.3:7).

"Whoso boasteth himself of a false gift is like clouds and wind without rain" (Pr.25:14).

"But now ye rejoice in your boastings: all such rejoicing is evil" (Js.4:16).

⇒ In relation to self-sufficiency, God says this:

"He that trusteth in his own heart is a fool: but whoso walketh wisely, he shall be delivered" (Pr.28:26).

"Therefore hear now this, thou that art given to pleasures, that dwellest carelessly, that sayest in thine heart, I am, and none else beside me" (Is.47:8).

"They have belied the LORD, and said, It is not he; neither shall evil come upon us; neither shall we see sword nor famine" (Je.5:12).

"The pride of thine heart hath deceived thee, thou that dwellest in the clefts of the rock, whose habitation is high; that saith in his heart, Who shall bring me down to the ground? (Ob.3).

"Ye have plowed wickedness, ye have reaped iniquity; ye have eaten the fruit of lies: because thou didst trust in thy way, in the multitude of thy mighty men" (Ho.10:13).

"Wherefore let him that thinketh he standeth take heed lest he fall" (1 Co.10:12).

⇒   In relation to lawlessness, God says this:

"For all have sinned, and come short of the glory of God" (Ro.3:23).

"Let not sin therefore reign in your mortal body, that ye should obey it in the lusts thereof" (Ro.6:12).

"Whosoever committeth sin transgresseth also the law: for sin is the transgression of the law" (1 Jn.3:4).

"All unrighteousness is sin" (1 Jn.5:17).

"And God saw that the wickedness of man was great in the earth, and that every imagination of the thoughts of his heart was only evil continually" (Ge.6:5).

"Every one of them is gone back: they are altogether become filthy; there is none that doeth good, no, not one" (Ps.53:3).

"Wash you, make you clean; put away the evil of your doings from before mine eyes; cease to do evil" (Is.1:16).

"Let the wicked forsake his way, and the unrighteous man his thoughts: and let him return unto the LORD, and he will have mercy upon him; and to our God, for he will abundantly pardon" (Is.55:7).

	D. The First Civilization & Society (Part 2): The Continuation of the Godly Seed or Descendants, 4:25-26
1. The godly line was set in place & appointed by God: Through Seth a. Adam & Eve have a son b. Eve names the son Seth: Acknowledges that God gave the son 2. The godly line recognized the weakness & mortality of man 3. The godly line confessed God & called upon God with a renewed spirit	25 And Adam knew his wife again; and she bare a son, and called his name Seth: For God, said she, hath appointed me another seed instead of Abel, whom Cain slew. 26 And to Seth, to him also there was born a son; and he called his name Enos: then began men to call upon the name of the LORD.

DIVISION III

ADAM, THE FIRST MAN (PART 2): THE BIRTH, DEVELOPMENT, AND CORRUPTION OF BOTH THE UNGODLY AND THE GODLY SEED (DESCENDANTS), 4:1–6:8

D. The First Civilization and Society (Part 2): The Continuation of the Godly Seed or Descendants, 4:25-26

(4:25-26) **Introduction**: the ungodly seed or descendants of Adam have just been pictured for us. Scripture has just shown how the ungodly seed of humanity began and grew at the beginning of human history, how they founded the ungodly civilizations and societies of the world. From the very beginning there was an ungodly line or branch of people upon earth, an ungodly line that still exists and will exist until Jesus Christ returns to earth and ends human history as it is known today.

Now in the present passage, Scripture shows us how the godly line continued upon earth. Adam, the first man upon earth, began the godly line. His son Abel lived a godly life, but he was killed by Cain, apparently before he was able to have children. Consequently, God had to give another son to Adam and Eve, another son through whom the godly seed or descendants would continue. This is the subject of the present passage. This passage shows us how God gave Adam and Eve another son...

- the son who was to carry on the godly line
- the son whose godly descendants were to give birth to the Savior, the single seed who was to save man from death and eternal judgment

This passage, along with the next passage (chapter five), pictures the birth and growth of the godly seed or descendants upon earth. This particular study is *The First Civilization and Society (Part 2): The Continuation of the Godly Seed or Descendants, of the Godly Civilization and Society upon Earth.*

1. The godly line was set in place and appointed by God: through Seth (v.25).
2. The godly line recognized the weakness and mortality of man (v.26).
3. The godly line confessed God and called upon God with a renewed spirit (v.26).

[1] (4:25) **Seth—Seed, Godly**: the godly line was set in place and appointed by God. Eve had suffered the loss of both her sons: Abel had been murdered, and Cain had forsaken God and the family to live a life of sin and ungodliness.

a. Adam and Eve desperately wanted another son to carry on the godly line, godly descendants through whom God's promise of a Savior could be fulfilled. Does this mean that Adam and Eve had no other sons who were godly, that there were no other people upon earth living godly lives? This is most unlikely. What it probably means is what it has always meant down through history: the particular seed—the person who was to be appointed and set in place by God to head up the godly line—had not yet been born. God had not yet chosen the child of Adam and Eve who was to continue the godly line that was to march down through the ages of human history.

Just picture Adam and Eve praying fervently—every day of their lives—for a son who would live a godly life and through whom God could send the Savior of the world.

When the son came, both Adam and Eve knew that God had answered their prayer. They knew their son was to be...

- the godly seed and descendent through whom the branch of godliness was to continue upon earth
- the godly seed and descendent through whom the Savior of the world was to come

This is the reason Eve named the baby boy *Seth*. The child had definitely been given by God. The name *Seth* (Sheth) means set, settled, placed, appointed. The idea is that Seth was set in place and appointed by God to head up the godly seed or descendants upon earth. Some commentators say that Seth also means substitute, that God was actually substituting Seth for the murdered Abel.[1,2]

---

[1] H.C. Leupold. *Genesis*, Vol.1, p.226.
[2] Herbert Lockyer. *All the Men of the Bible.* (Grand Rapids, MI: Zondervan Publishing House, 1958), p.297.

The point is this: the very name *Seth* shows how strongly Eve recognized God's hand in the birth of Seth. God was actively involved—His sovereignty and power were actively working—in the baby boy's birth.

⇒ God was faithful to His Word and promise.

⇒ God actually set in place and appointed Seth to continue the godly seed or line of descendants upon earth.

⇒ God actually substituted Seth for Abel, actually sent a substitute to continue the godly seed or descendants upon earth.

b. Note one other significant fact: there was a difference between Eve's attitude at Cain's birth and at Seth's birth. When Cain was born, Eve said:

"I have gotten [brought forth] a man from the Lord" (Ge.4:1).

The emphasis is upon *"I." "I* have gotten...." Eve recognized God's hand in the birth of her child, but she apparently felt somewhat *self-sufficient*, as though she and Adam had a great deal to do with fulfilling the promise of God for a godly seed and Savior. But Cain's ungodly ways taught Eve a strong lesson: she cannot bring about the godly seed and Savior within her own strength; in fact, she cannot even bring godliness to the earth within her own strength. Note how there was no self-sufficiency—no *"I"*—in Eve's statement at Seth's birth, not a trace of self-sufficiency. Trusting God totally, she declares:

"God...hath appointed me another seed instead of Abel, whom Cain slew" (v.25).

Eve had learned one of the great lessons of human history: *total* dependence upon God. No man and no woman, not even a combination of men and women...

• has the power to take the place of God and fulfill the promises of God for this earth.

• has the power to restore the *perfect life, knowledge, and fellowship* with God that Adam and Eve had known.

• has the power to provide a godly seed or descendants for the earth, especially the one seed who is to be the Savior of the world (Ge.3:15).

• has the power to provide the seed and Savior who can crush the head and power of the serpent, who can deliver man eternally from the power of "that old serpent, called the Devil" (Re.12:9; see Ge.3:15).

Only God can do these things. The promises of God are just that: promises, free gifts of God to be given by God and by God alone. Man has no part in saving himself. Adam and Eve could not earn, win, merit, or work for their salvation. God and God alone could save them. The promised Savior—their salvation—was to be a free gift, sent into the world by God alone and by His grace alone. Apparently, this was the great lesson Adam and Eve had learned between the birth of Cain and the birth of Seth: trust and total dependence in God.

> **Thought 1.** Total trust and dependence in God is the great lesson that every person must learn. No person will ever know the promises of God—not personally know them—unless he casts himself totally upon God. A person must totally trust God if he wants to be restored to the perfect life that Adam and Eve originally had with God. If a person wants to live forever—to triumph over sin, death, and hell—he must trust God. He must depend upon God for salvation. No person can save himself. A person does not even have the power to save himself from accidents, disease, and sickness, much less from sin and death. Any honest and thinking person knows this. Consequently, if a person is to be saved, he must totally depend upon God for salvation. This was the great lesson Adam and Eve had learned. They were able to do only what we do: look around and see all the sin, evil, corruption, accidents, diseases, sicknesses, and death upon earth. Between the birth of Cain and Seth, they saw it all and learned the great lesson of life: only God could provide salvation, only God could bring the Savior into the world.
>
> > **"For God so loved the world, that he gave his only begotten Son, that whosoever believeth in him should not perish, but have everlasting life. For God sent not his Son into the world to condemn the world; but that the world through him might be saved" (Jn.3:16-17).**
> > **"Verily, verily, I say unto you, He that heareth my word, and believeth on him that sent me, hath everlasting life, and shall not come into condemnation; but is passed from death unto life" (Jn.5:24).**
> > **"Being justified <u>freely</u> by his grace through the redemption that is in Christ Jesus" (Ro.3:24).**
> > **"For the wages of sin is death; but the gift of God is eternal life through Jesus Christ our Lord" (Ro.6:23).**
> > **"For by grace are ye saved through faith; and that not of yourselves: it is the gift of God: not of works, lest any man should boast" (Ep.2:8-9).**
> > **"Not by works of righteousness which we have done, but according to his mercy he saved us, by the washing of regeneration, and renewing of the Holy Ghost" (Tit.3:5).**
> > **"But the salvation of the righteous is of the LORD: he is their strength in the time of trouble" (Ps.37:39).**

☐2 (4:26) **Enoch—Man, Nature—Weakness—Mortality—Decay:** the godly line recognized the weakness and mortality of man. Seth had a son, and he named the son *Enoch* which means frail, mortal, weak, sickly. It means a "mortal, decaying man."[3] Why would Seth name his child Enoch?

---

3 *The Pulpit Commentary*, Vol.1, p.90.

⇒ Perhaps there was some frailty or sickly appearance about Enoch that made Seth grasp the mortality and weakness of human life.
⇒ Perhaps Seth was already gripped by the frailty and mortality of human life, and he expressed it by naming his child Enoch.

Whatever the case, Seth was very aware of the weakness of human nature, that man was mortal, subject to corruption and death. Seth was gripped with the fact that man...

• aged	• became sick	• was weak
• deteriorated	• had accidents	• was frail
• decayed	• suffered diseases	• was corruptible

Seth was conscious that man suffered all of this and so much more and that eventually man died. These thoughts were flooding his mind when he was considering what to name his son, apparently so much so that he named his son Enoch, the frail and mortal man.

Thought 1. Note this about Seth's view of man and of human nature. His view does not mean that Seth was discouraged and depressed over the nature of man, that he wallowed around in self-pity, moaning about...
• the pains, hurts, and frailties of the human body
• the diseases and accidents suffered
• the awful conditions and circumstances of life
• the terrible state of the world

Seth's view of human nature and of life was correct: he was merely facing the reality of life. Life—human nature, man himself, his body—is weak and frail, subject to all kinds of sicknesses and diseases, accidents and pains. Man's body does age and deteriorate, decay and die. Facing this fact is not to downgrade nor to minimize man and his ability. It is to face the reality of human life. Facing the reality of human frailty and mortality...
• makes us take care of our bodies more
• motivates us to work more quickly to get more done while there is still time
• drives us to do all we can to conquer the weaknesses and frailties of life through medicine and technology

Then, above all, facing the reality of human frailty and mortality causes us to seek after God. It causes us to depend upon God, to call upon Him to take care of us, to save us and give us life, both life abundant and life eternal, both now and forever.

"Remember, I beseech thee, that thou hast made me as the clay; and wilt thou bring me into dust again?" (Jb.10:9).
"What is man, that thou art mindful of him? and the son of man, that thou visitest him?" (Ps.8:4).
"Nevertheless man being in honour abideth not: he is like the beasts that perish" (Ps.49:12).
"For he remembered that they were but flesh; a wind that passeth away, and cometh not again" (Ps.78:39).
"What man is he that liveth, and shall not see death? shall he deliver his soul from the hand of the grave?" (Ps.89:48).
"For he knoweth our frame; he remembereth that we are dust. As for man, his days are as grass: as a flower of the field, so he flourisheth" (Ps.103:14-15).
"All go unto one place; all are of the dust, and all turn to dust again" (Ec.3:20).
"I, even I, am he that comforteth you: who art thou, that thou shouldest be afraid of a man that shall die, and of the son of man which shall be made as grass" (Is.51:12).
"But we are all as an unclean thing, and all our righteousnesses are as filthy rags; and we all do fade as a leaf; and our iniquities, like the wind, have taken us away" (Is.64:6).
"For all flesh is as grass, and all the glory of man as the flower of grass. The grass withereth, and the flower thereof falleth away" (1 Pe.1:24).
"But we have this treasure in earthen vessels, that the excellency of the power may be of God, and not of us" (2 Co.4:7).
"For we that are in this tabernacle do groan, being burdened: not for that we would be unclothed, but clothed upon, that mortality might be swallowed up of life" (2 Co.5:4).

Thought 2. Note the enormous difference between the godly as described above and the ungodly of this earth, between the godly such as Seth and the humanist or secularist such as Cain and his descendants.
1) Both the godly and the humanist see the frailty and mortality of life.
2) Both say that man should work diligently and do all he can to conquer the weaknesses and mortality of life, to do all he can through the development of medicine and technology. That is, every man—both the godly and ungodly—wants to be healthy, comfortable, secure, and to live as long as he can while he is upon earth.

But beyond these two points, the godly and the ungodly humanists or secularists differ. The humanist says that man lives only upon this earth and only for this life, that this life is all there is for man. He says there is no God and no Savior for man, not beyond this life. Man is perfectly sufficient to take care of himself. But note: this view of man is tragic, most tragic.

1) Humanism or secularism strips man of help beyond himself and other human beings. And down deep within his heart, every thinking and honest person knows this fact: he is frail and mortal. He will age and deteriorate, have accidents and diseases, get sick and die. No matter what help anyone gives in such situations, man's help is very limited. Man, with all his science and technology, can only *delay death*; he cannot stop it.
2) Humanism or secularism degrades man, minimizes man's worth and value. It makes man only an animal, only a beast of the earth, only a temporary creature who dies and returns to dust and remains dust. Humanism strips man of his eternal value and worth.
3) Humanism or secularism leads to lawlessness and injustice. If man is nothing more than an animal with no future life whatsoever, then taking advantage of a person or killing him has little meaning.
   ⇒ There is no eternal accountability, no fear of eternal judgment, of having to come face to face with God.
   ⇒ There is no image of God within man to value, no eternal life that makes man's life of eternal value.
   ⇒ There is no God to look after man's welfare, to meet man's needs nor to provide the necessities of life for man.

Thus every man is on his own, free to do and to take whatever is necessary to look after himself. The list could go on and on, but this is enough to show how radically the ungodly humanists or secularists differ from the godly of the earth. Humanism is helpless and hopeless...
- beyond man
- beyond this world
- beyond science, medicine, and technology

Tragically, everyone of these (man, the world, science, medicine, and technology) have their limitations and often fail. They fail while man—the mass of mankind—continues to walk upon earth without the help of God. They fail while God seeks after every living person upon earth, while God waits for man to awaken and face the reality that God is, that God exists. God longs for man to turn from his ungodly ways and to turn back to Him. God wants man to repent and to call upon Him, to do just what Seth and his descendants do in the next point: to confess and call upon God for salvation and help, both upon this earth and eternally.

"Take heed, brethren, lest there be in any of you an evil heart of unbelief, in departing from the living God" (He.3:12).
"But without faith it is impossible to please him: for he that cometh to God must believe that he is, and that he is a rewarder of them that diligently seek him" (He.11:6).
"That they should seek the Lord, if haply they might feel after him, and find him, though he be not far from every one of us" (Ac.17:27).
"Verily, verily, I say unto thee, We speak that we do know, and testify that we have seen; and ye receive not our witness" (Jn.3:11).
"He that believeth on him is not condemned: but he that believeth not is condemned already, because he hath not believed in the name of the only begotten Son of God" (Jn.3:18).
"He that believeth on the Son hath everlasting life: and he that believeth not the Son shall not see life; but the wrath of God abideth on him" (Jn.3:36).
"I said therefore unto you, that ye shall die in your sins: for if ye believe not that I am he, ye shall die in your sins" (Jn.8:24).
"Draw nigh to God, and he will draw nigh to you. Cleanse your hands, ye sinners; and purify your hearts, ye double minded" (Js.4:8).

3 (4:26) **Revival—Seed, Godly—Witnessing**: the godly line confessed God and called upon God with a renewed spirit. As discussed earlier, Adam and Eve knew what it was to walk and fellowship face to face with God. Adam had known the glory of a perfect body, a perfect environment, and a perfect fellowship and communion with God. Adam knew what it was to have God looking after him; he knew it perfectly. Once he had fallen—all throughout his life—he must have sought after God, longing for the presence and fellowship of God. Adam was bound to have done what so many of the godly do today: spent much time every day in the presence of God, praying, worshipping, praising, and honoring Him.

Note another fact as well: Adam was bound to do what any person would do who has experienced the strong and sweet fellowship of God: teach his children to give their hearts and lives to God and to worship Him. All the children may not respond; some may even react and turn away from God just as Cain did. But Adam must have taught his children the truth.

In light of Adam's commitment and worship of God, what does Scripture mean when it says, "then began men to call upon the name of the Lord" (v.26)? It means that Adam and the godly line—those who were truly following God—rededicated their lives to God with more fervor than ever before. They began to seek and to call upon the Lord more than ever. With renewed fervor and dedication, they...
- worshipped God more than ever, both publicly and privately
- confessed God more courageously than ever
- served God more diligently than ever
- bore and proclaimed the name of the Lord more than ever

What would cause such a revival among Adam and the godly seed? Three experiences:
⇒ A deeper sense of the frailty and mortality of human life. Adam had been living for 235 years and Seth for 105 years when Enoch was born. Remember: both must have witnessed suffering and death time and again. The earth was well populated by then. (See note 3—Ge.4:17 for more discussion.) Sensing the frailty and mortality of life drives the godly person to recommit his life to God.

⇒ The birth of Seth and then the birth of Seth's son would have caused a revival among Adam and the godly seed. Seeing the godly line actually being appointed and set in place by God—seeing it continue on for three generations—was enough to stir Adam and then Seth and then Enoch to recommit their lives to God and to lead all the godly descendants to worship and serve God with renewed fervor.

⇒ The worldliness of the ungodly seed of Cain and their rejection of God must have stirred the godly people to a renewed commitment to worship and proclaim God. This is always true of those who truly live godly lives and bear bold witness to God. Sin and evil—seeing the lost hurting, suffering, and dooming them-selves—always stir the godly to worship and witness more than ever.

Adam and the godly seed were witnesses to all three of these experiences. They experienced them first hand, and any one of them by itself was enough to stir a renewed commitment to God. But Adam and the godly seed had all three experiences. Just imagine the experience:

⇒ The ungodliness of Cain and his seed had always been before Adam's face ever since Cain had forsaken God and the family.

⇒ When Seth was born, Adam witnessed the mercy and power of God Himself as God appointed and set in place the godly seed and line.

⇒ Then when Seth had a son, the hour called for a dramatic recommitment of life. Adam knew beyond all question that God was fulfilling His glorious promise to give the godly seed to the world. And he knew that through that seed the Savior would be sent into the world, the Savior who would restore man to perfection, to the perfect world Adam had originally known.

Thought 1. The great need of the church and believers today is for revival, to confess God and to call upon God with renewed fervor.

"**This man was instructed in the way of the Lord; and being fervent in the spirit, he spake and taught diligently the things of the Lord**" (Ac.18:25).

"**I beseech you therefore, brethren, by the mercies of God, that ye present your bodies a living sacrifice, holy, acceptable unto God, which is your reasonable service. And be not conformed to this world: but be ye transformed by the renewing of your mind, that ye may prove what is that good, and acceptable, and perfect, will of God**" (Ro.12:1-2).

"**For which cause we faint not; but though our outward man perish, yet the inward man is renewed day by day**" (2 Co.4:16).

"**Wherefore I put thee in remembrance that thou stir up the gift of God, which is in thee by the putting on of my hands**" (2 Ti.1:6).

"**My son, give me thine heart, and let thine eyes observe my ways**" (Pr.23:26).

"**O come, let us worship and bow down: let us kneel before the LORD our maker**" (Ps.95:6).

"**Blessed are they that keep his testimonies, and that seek him with the whole heart**" (Ps.119:2).

"**But they that wait upon the LORD shall renew their strength; they shall mount up with wings as eagles; they shall run, and not be weary; and they shall walk, and not faint**" (Is.40:31).

"**And ye shall seek me, and find me, when ye shall search for me with all your heart**" (Je.29:13).

"**Therefore also now, saith the LORD, turn ye even to me with all your heart, and with fasting, and with weeping, and with mourning**" (Joel 2:12).

CHAPTER 5

E. The First Civilization & Society (Part 3): The Line of the Godly Seed or Descendants—Significant Events,[DS1] 5:1-32

1. **Event 1: God created man**
   a. Created man in His own likeness

   b. Created man, both male & female
   c. Blessed them
   d. Called them Adam, which means "man"
2. **Event 2: Adam had a son, born in his likeness & image**
3. **Event 3: God was faithful to His Word, to His promise**

4. **Event 4: Man died**

5. **Event 5: Godly parents taught their children about God, to follow Him, & to worship & live for Him**

This is the book of the generations of Adam. In the day that God created man, in the likeness of God made he him; 2 Male and female created he them; and blessed them, and called their name Adam, in the day when they were created. 3 And Adam lived an hundred and thirty years, and begat a son in his own likeness, after his image; and called his name Seth: 4 And the days of Adam after he had begotten Seth were eight hundred years: and he begat sons and daughters: 5 And all the days that Adam lived were nine hundred and thirty years: and he died. 6 And Seth lived an hundred and five years, and begat Enos: 7 And Seth lived after he begat Enos eight hundred and seven years, and begat sons and daughters: 8 And all the days of Seth were nine hundred and twelve years: and he died. 9 And Enos lived ninety years, and begat Cainan: 10 And Enos lived after he begat Cainan eight hundred and fifteen years, and begat sons and daughters: 11 And all the days of Enos were nine hundred and five years: and he died. 12 And Cainan lived seventy years, and begat Mahalaleel: 13 And Cainan lived after he begat Mahalaleel eight hundred and forty years, and begat sons and daughters: 14 And all the days of Cainan were nine hundred and ten years: and he died. 15 And Mahalaleel lived sixty and five years, and begat Jared: 16 And Mahalaleel lived af-

ter he begat Jared eight hundred and thirty years, and begat sons and daughters: 17 And all the days of Mahalaleel were eight hundred ninety and five years: and he died. 18 And Jared lived an hundred sixty and two years, and he begat Enoch: 19 And Jared lived after he begat Enoch eight hundred years, and begat sons and daughters: 20 And all the days of Jared were nine hundred and sixty and two years: and he died. 21 And Enoch lived sixty and five years, and begat Methuselah: 22 And Enoch walked with God after he begat Methuselah three hundred years, and begat sons and daughters: 23 And all the days of Enoch were three hundred sixty and five years: 24 And Enoch walked with God: and he was not; for God took him. 25 And Methuselah lived an hundred eighty and seven years, and begat Lamech: 26 And Methuselah lived after he begat Lamech seven hundred eighty and two years, and begat sons and daughters: 27 And all the days of Methuselah were nine hundred sixty and nine years: and he died. 28 And Lamech lived an hundred eighty and two years, and begat a son: 29 And he called his name Noah, saying, This same shall comfort us concerning our work and toil of our hands, because of the ground which the LORD hath cursed. 30 And Lamech lived after he begat Noah five hundred ninety and five years, and begat sons and daughters: 31 And all the days of Lamech were seven hundred seventy and seven years: and he died. 32 And Noah was five hundred years old: and Noah begat Shem, Ham, and Japheth.

6. **Event 6: One godly man, Enoch, dedicated his life totally to God**
   a. He walked with God

   b. He was translated, taken into God's presence without dying
7. **Event 7: One man, Methuselah, lived longer than anyone else, lived longer as a testimony to God's grace & judgment to come**

8. **Event 8: Godly men believed in the coming rest & comfort promised by God[DS2]**

   a. Lamech is exhausted with the struggle & toil of life

   b. Lamech names his son Noah: Believes in the coming comfort & rest

DIVISION III

ADAM, THE FIRST MAN (PART 2): THE BIRTH, DEVELOPMENT, AND CORRUPTION OF BOTH THE UNGODLY AND THE GODLY SEED (DESCENDANTS), 4:1–6:8

E. The First Civilization and Society (Part 3): The Line of the Godly Seed or Descendants—Significant Events, 5:1-32

(5:1-32) **Introduction—Genealogy**: this is the first godly genealogy listed in the Bible, the first roots of the earth's godly heritage. How do we know this? Several facts show us.

⇒ The first man upon earth, Adam, who was a godly man, is listed in this genealogy; but the second man, Cain, is not listed. Why? Because Cain was an ungodly man.

⇒ The son of Adam who is listed is Seth (v.3), and the son of Seth who is listed is Enos (v.6). These sons were the godly descendants of Adam, the seed that God had appointed and set in place and through whom God had promised to send the Savior.

⇒ The author of Genesis is very aware of the seed promised by God. He has already mentioned the seed (Genesis 3:15), and he knows about God's promise to Abraham, that Abraham was to bear the seed through whom the Savior would come. The writer knows that this line of godly persons will ultimately run up to Abraham, and that God will then reaffirm His promise of the godly seed and Savior to Abraham. The author is going to be writing about God's promise to Abraham in just a few chapters.

What the author is doing in this genealogy is this: he is listing the genealogy of the godly seed or descendants. He is showing how God appointed and set in place the godly line of people through whom He could fulfill His promise, His promise…

• that the woman's seed would always have a godly line of people
• that the woman's seed—the godly line or descendants—would eventually bear one descendent who would be the Savior of the world (See note—Ge.3:15 for more discussion)

Several facts need to be noted about the godly genealogy before actually studying it.

First, this is the genealogy of Adam, of the godly line that descended from Adam. It does not list all the godly descendants of Adam. The genealogy takes each generation and lists only one descendent, the one descendent who formed the line through whom *the promised seed*, the Savior of the world, was to come.

Second, many of the godly descendants were contemporaries. They had the godly influence of each other, at least those who lived close by one another.

Third, this is not a list of all the godly people upon earth. It is a list of only the godly line through whom the promised seed, the Savior, was to come. There were other godly persons upon earth, at least up until Noah's time. Each of the descendants mentioned in the godly genealogy are said to have had other sons and daughters (vv.4, 7, 10, 13, 16, 19, 22, 26, 30).

Fourth, note exactly what is said: "This is the book [sepher] of the generations [descendants, offspring] of Adam" (v.1). The Hebrew word for *book* (sepher) means any size document ranging from a one page divorce document to a large book. What document, then, is this?

⇒ Is the author referring to some document or book that had been written from the earliest of times, when man was first upon earth? A document or book that the author is using to gather information about the early history and genealogy of man upon earth? Or…

⇒ Is the author referring to the genealogy he is about to write?

We cannot say, not for sure; but the latter is unlikely, for this is the only Old Testament genealogy that begins this way, that is, by adding the word *book* to it. In fact, there is only one other genealogy that begins this way, and it is in the New Testament, "The book of the generation of Jesus Christ" (Mt.1:1).

Note where these two unique genealogies are placed in the Bible: in the first book of the Old Testament, and in the first book of the New Testament. Without question, Matthew had some book or document that listed the genealogy of Jesus Christ, and he was copying the genealogy and including it in his own writing, The Gospel of Matthew. Therefore, he is saying so and giving credit to the fact. Most likely, this is exactly what the author of Genesis was doing: being honest and giving credit to another document. Apparently, he also had a book or document that listed the genealogy of the godly seed who lived before the flood. The great *Pulpit Commentary* says this:

> If…the original compiler of this ancient document was Noah…no one would be more likely or better qualified than he to preserve some memorial of the last race of which he and his family were the sole survivors, it [gives additional proof] of the intelligence and culture of the [age].[1]

Now, to our study of the genealogy. This is, *The First Civilization and Society (Part 3): The Line of the Godly Seed or Descendants—Significant Events*. (Note: because of the length of this study, a person may wish to divide it into two or three messages or lessons. If so, Enoch is a good place to make the division because of the length of his study. See note 6—Ge.5:21-24.)

1. Event 1: God created man (vv.1-2).
2. Event 2: Adam had a son, born in his likeness and image (v.3).
3. Event 3: God was faithful to His Word, to His promise (vv.3-5).
4. Event 4: Man died (v.5).

---

[1] *The Pulpit Commentary*, Vol.1, p.93.

5. Event 5: Godly parents taught their children about God, to follow Him and to worship and live for Him (vv.6-20).
6. Event 6: One godly man, Enoch, dedicated his life totally to God (vv.21-24).
7 Event 7: One man, Methuselah, lived longer than anyone else, lived longer as a testimony to God's grace and judgment to come (vv.25-26).
8. Event 8: Godly men believed in the coming rest and comfort promised by God (vv.27-32).

DEEPER STUDY # 1
(5:1-32) **Genealogy, Chart of**: to keep from breaking the thought of this study, the chart is being placed as DEEPER STUDY # 2—Ge.5:27-32.

---

1 (5:1-2) **Creation—Man**: the first significant event, God created man. Man did not just appear by chance; he did not just evolve through some freak accident of nature; he did not come from some random evolutionary process. There was plan and purpose behind man's appearance upon earth, the plan and purpose of God. Man is the climactic creation of God. Man is the creature that God planned and purposed eternally—long, long before the earth was ever founded. God and God alone created man. Note four facts about God's creation of man. (See outline and notes—Ge.1:26-31; 2:7 for more discussion.)

a. God made man in the likeness of God; He created man with the highest dignity and nature possible. This means that man was created just like God...
- in perfection
- in holiness
- in love
- in spirit

(See DEEPER STUDY # 2—Ge.1:26 for more discussion.)

b. God created both male and female, He created them...
- to love, comfort, and help each other
- to carry on the human race. God appointed Adam and Eve to be the head of the human race, to stand as the first man and woman upon earth (See outline and notes—Ge.2:18-25 for more discussion.)
- to work and subdue the earth (See notes—Ge.1:28; 2:19-20 for more discussion.)

c. God blessed the man and woman, gave them His glorious benediction (see note 3—Ge.1:28 for discussion).
d. God called both the male and female "Adam." The word "Adam" means *man earth*, *red earth*. God gave this name to the male and female so they would have a constant reminder...
- that they had come from the humblest origin, from dust as well as from His Godly hand
- that He is God, the only living and true Intelligence and Power, who alone could take dirt and create life

Note: the fact that God Himself named Adam and Eve was not given in the earlier account of man's creation. This is new information. God created man, both male and female, in His own likeness and blessed them with every imaginable blessing. Man was created perfect: he had everything necessary to live both in perfection and for eternity. This is the first significant event to note in the godly genealogy.

2 (5:3) **Depravity—Man, Nature—Adam—Seth**: the second significant event, Adam had a son born in his own likeness, in his own image. There is a deliberate contrast between the statements...
- that "God created Adam in His likeness" (Ge.5:1)
- that "Adam begat a son in his own likeness" (Ge.5:3)

The point is this: Seth was a being just like Adam, in the image of Adam, and not in the perfect image of God, at least not in the perfect image that man had when God first created Adam. Right after God created Adam, Adam sinned; he fell. Adam experienced what it was to be "hid" (Ge.3:8-10) and "cut off" (Ge.3:23-24) from God. He was to die (Ge.2:17; 3:19; 5:5; see DEEPER STUDY # 1—He.9:27). He had corrupted the perfect nature that God had originally given him. Simply stated...
- Adam experienced the transformation from a perfect and innocent human nature to a fallen human nature

Whatever is involved in a *fallen human nature*, Seth was born "in his father's likeness, in his father's image." Seth too possessed a fallen human nature. He too was corruptible and doomed to die. (See notes—Ge.2:16-17; DEEPER STUDY # 3—Mt.1:16; note—Ro.5:12-21.)

Now, what is involved in a fallen human nature? In contrast to God's image, the nature God first gave Adam, there are at least five things involved in a fallen human nature. (See DEEPER STUDY # 2—Ge.1:26 for more discussion.)

a. A perfect human nature would be absolutely perfect, without any flaw or defect whatsoever. But a fallen human nature is the exact opposite. A fallen human nature is full of defects and flaws. A fallen human nature...
- has an imperfect body and mind
- is subject to sickness, disease, and accident
- has a limited capacity to learn
- experiences pain and suffering
- senses alienation, loneliness, and emptiness
- sheds tears of sadness, sorrow, and grief
- is sinful, corruptible, and dies

b. A perfect human nature would be holy: sinless, righteous, pure, and godly. But a fallen human nature is the exact opposite. A fallen human nature is unholy and wicked. A fallen human nature is...

- sinful
- unrighteous
- impure
- immoral
- ungodly

c. A perfect human nature would be love: always devoted, loyal, cherishing, loving, merciful, gracious, and compassionate. But a fallen human nature is the exact opposite. A fallen human nature is...

- often selfish
- often undevoted and disloyal
- often unloving and ungracious
- often unmerciful and lacking in compassion

d. A perfect human nature would have the spirit of immortality, the power to live forever. But a fallen human nature is the exact opposite: it has the spirit of death. A fallen human nature dies; it returns to the dust of the earth. (See Deeper Study # 3—Ge.2:17; Deeper Study # 1—He.9:27.)

e. A perfect human nature would be in perfect union with God: it would worship, fellowship, and serve God in an unbroken consciousness of His presence. But a fallen human nature would be the exact opposite. It is alienated and separated from God. It follows its own will and desires and does its own thing. It creates gods of its own and worships and follows the gods created by its own mind and imagination. A fallen human nature desperately needs to be reconciled with God. (See Ac.17:29; Ro.1:21-23; Ga.4:8.)

The point is this: when Adam and Eve sinned, they experienced the transformation from a perfect, innocent human nature to a fallen human nature. Consequently, when they had children, the children were born *in their likeness, in their image*. The children were born with the same fallen human nature.

Thought 1. Arthur Pink states the point of human depravity well:

> *By sin Adam lost the image of God and became corrupt in his nature and a fallen parent could do no more than beget a fallen child. Seth was begotten in the likeness of a sinful father! Since Noah was the direct descendent of Seth and is the father of us all, and since he was able to transmit to us only that which he had, himself, received from Seth, we have here the doctrine of universal depravity. Every man living in the world today is, through Noah and his three sons, a descendent of Seth, hence it is...here taken at the beginning of [Scripture] to trace the spring back to its fountain head, and show how all are, by nature, the fallen offspring of a fallen parent—that we have all been begotten in the image and likeness of a corrupt and sinful father.*[2]

"Wherefore, as by one man sin entered into the world, and death by sin; and so death passed upon all men, for that all have sinned" (Ro.5:12).
"For since by man came death" (1 Co.15:21).
"Thy first father hath sinned" (Is.43:27).
"For the wages of sin is death; but the gift of God is eternal life through Jesus Christ our Lord" (Ro.6:23).

3 (5:3-5) **God, Faithfulness of—Promises, Fulfilled**: the third significant event, God was faithful to His Word, to His promise. God had promised a godly seed and Savior to the world, that there would always be a godly people upon earth and through this people—the godly seed—He would send one very special seed, the Savior of the world.
Note the Scripture (v.3):

"And Adam lived an hundred and thirty years, and begat a son in his own likeness, after his image; and called his name Seth" (v.3).

God fulfilled His promise: God gave Adam a son, Seth, who was to become the first son of the godly line (see note 1—Ge.4:25 for more discussion). Above all else, it is this that the godly genealogy teaches: the faithfulness of God. Note how God faithfully causes one godly son after another to be born, how God carries the godly line from generation to generation (vv.3-32). Each godly father had other children, both sons and daughters (vv.4, 7, 10, 13, 16, 19, 22, 26, 30). But only one son could be the godly line through whom the Savior was to come. How was that son to be chosen? By God or by man?

⇒ Since the fathers were godly men, could they ever determine who should be in the godly line? Think of all the temptations within the world, all the increasing lawlessness and wickedness, how far short man really is, even the godly. How could any human being conceivably choose which child was to carry on the godly line?

⇒ If the fathers had chosen the godly line, they would have corrupted and doomed it. Despite their godliness in following God and in being part of the godly line, they were still imperfect, still full of flaws and defects. If they had chosen the godly line, they would have doomed it and the Savior could have never come.

⇒ The godly seed and Savior had been promised by God; therefore, God alone knew how He wanted the godly line to develop. God alone could make the choice. It was His promise—His Word, His purpose—to send the Savior into the world through the godly seed of the woman. And God was faithful, faithful to the ultimate degree. This is what this genealogy is all about: God's faithfulness in fulfilling His promise to send the Savior to

---

2 Arthur Pink. *Gleanings in Genesis*, p.74.

the world. The very first forefathers of the Savior are here listed: Adam, Seth, and all the other men who were chosen to be the first of the godly seed.

Thought 1. God is faithful to the ultimate degree. He will do for us what He did for Adam and the godly line: prove to be faithful. God will keep us safe and secure. He will deliver us from all evil and give us an abundant entrance into the everlasting kingdom of our Lord and Savior, Jesus Christ. All we have to do is repent and turn our lives completely over to Him: follow Him and give all we are and have to Him and His great cause of world missions.

"God is faithful, by whom ye were called unto the fellowship of his Son Jesus Christ our Lord" (1 Co.1:9).

"Being confident of this very thing, that he which hath begun a good work in you will perform it until the day of Jesus Christ" (Ph.1:6).

"...I know whom I have believed, and am persuaded that he is able to keep that which I have committed unto him against that day" (2 Ti.1:12).

"Who are kept by the power of God through faith unto salvation ready to be revealed in the last time" (1 Pe.1:5).

"Now unto him that is able to keep you from falling, and to present you faultless before the presence of his glory with exceeding joy, to the only wise God our Saviour, be glory and majesty, dominion and power, both now and ever" (Jude 24-25).

"Because thou hast kept the word of my patience, I also will keep thee from the hour of temptation, which shall come upon all the world, to try them that dwell upon the earth" (Re.3:10).

"And, behold, I am with thee, and will keep thee in all places whither thou goest, and will bring thee again into this land; for I will not leave thee, until I have done that which I have spoken to thee of" (Ge.28:15).

"Know therefore that the LORD thy God, he is God, the faithful God, which keepeth covenant and mercy with them that love him and keep his commandments to a thousand generations" (De.7:9).

"O love the lord, all ye his saints: for the lord preserveth the faithful" (Ps.31:23).

"For the lord loveth judgment, and forsaketh not his saints; they are preserved for ever" (Ps.37:28).

"I will sing of the mercies of the LORD for ever: with my mouth will I make known thy faithfulness to all generations" (Ps.89:1).

"The lord will perfect that which concerneth me: thy mercy, O LORD, endureth for ever: forsake not the works of thine own hands" (Ps.138:8).

4 (5:5) **Death—Adam**: the fourth significant event, man died. Note the Scripture:

"Adam lived...nine hundred and thirty years: and he died" (v.5).

Remember: Adam had been created perfect. God's purpose was for man to live forever without ever having to die. But God had warned Adam: he would die if he ate the forbidden fruit, that is, if he...
- chose to turn away from God
- chose to walk his own way in life
- disobeyed God
- rebelled against God

Tragically, this was exactly what Adam did. He turned away from God and rebelled against God. He disobeyed God and walked his own way. Adam did his own thing: he ate the forbidden fruit. From that point—from that very moment of sin—Adam became mortal, subject to corruption, aging, deterioration, and decay. Adam was afflicted with the seed of corruption, with the process of dying, day by day and degree by degree, and eventually he moved more and more toward that inevitable day of death. His body was doomed to die and return to dust.

This is the report of Scripture; this is one of the lessons of this godly genealogy. Note: the reign of death over man is seen eight times in this chapter alone (vv.5, 8, 11, 14, 17, 20, 27, 31).

Thought 1. Gloriously, the love and power of God is seen in this one fact: no person has to die. No person has to ever taste or experience death. Jesus Christ has tasted and experienced death for us. Jesus Christ has died for us. He has already paid the penalty and judgment of sin for us. If we commit our lives to Him—totally commit them—we will never die. When the moment comes for us to leave this world, quicker than the eye can blink (11/100 of a second), God will transfer us right into His presence. One moment we will be in this world; the next moment we will be in the glorious presence of God. We will never lose consciousness of being alive; never know what the experience of death is.

"For God so loved the world, that he gave his only begotten Son, that whosoever believeth in him should not perish, but have everlasting life" (Jn.3:16).

"He that believeth on the Son hath everlasting life: and he that believeth not the Son shall not see life; but the wrath of God abideth on him" (Jn.3:36).

"Verily, verily, I say unto you, He that heareth my word, and believeth on him that sent me, hath everlasting life, and shall not come into condemnation; but is passed from death unto life" (Jn.5:24).

"For the wages of sin is death; but the gift of God is eternal life [beginning right now] through Jesus Christ our Lord" (Ro.6:23).

"For he that soweth to his flesh shall of the flesh reap corruption; but he that soweth to the Spirit shall of the Spirit reap life everlasting" (Ga.6:8).

"And the Lord shall deliver me from every evil work, and will preserve [transfer] me unto his heavenly kingdom: to whom be glory for ever and ever" (2 Ti.4:18).

5 (5:6-20) **Parents—Teaching—Children—Family**: the fifth significant event, the godly parents taught their children about God, to follow Him and to worship and live for Him. Three significant facts in this godly genealogy leap out at us:
  ⇒ All the persons listed here were believers; they followed God and worshipped and lived for Him. They believed in God and they believed God's Word, His promise to send the godly seed, the Savior, into the world.
  ⇒ All the persons listed here covered many generations of people, but they were all from one family. This line of believers—these godly followers of God—were all from the same family, and their godly line was never broken down through the years. These godly parents taught their children about God, to follow, worship, and live for Him.
  ⇒ Some of the children listened to the witness of their parents, but not all. Cain had the same godly parents, Adam and Eve, as Seth; but Cain rejected his parents and rebelled against God. Apparently, many of the children, when they became adults, rejected God and followed after the way of Cain and ungodliness. We know this because of the large population upon the earth at this time. (See note—Ge.4:17 for more discussion.) The children's rejection of God must have broken the hearts of their parents, just as it does the hearts of parents today. Nevertheless, the parents did not become discouraged, nor begin to question and blame God. They remained faithful and continued to teach the Word and promises of God to their children and grandchildren.

Thought 1. Two great lessons can be gleaned from the godly parents of antiquity.
1) We must teach our children about God...
   • to follow Him and to worship and live for Him.
   • to believe His Word and promises, in particular the promise of the godly seed that has been fulfilled in Christ, the Savior of the world.

> "Now to Abraham and his seed were the promises made. He saith not, And to seeds, as of many; but as of one, And to thy seed, which is Christ" (Ga.3:16).
> "And if ye be Christ's, then are ye Abraham's seed, and heirs according to the promise" (Ga.3:29).
> "For God so loved the world, that he gave his only begotten Son, that whosoever believeth in him should not perish, but have everlasting life" (Jn.3:16).
> "Verily, verily, I say unto you, He that heareth my word, and believeth on him that sent me, hath everlasting life, and shall not come into condemnation; but is passed from death unto life" (Jn.5:24).
> "Therefore it is of faith, that it might be by grace; to the end the promise might be sure to all the seed; not to that only which is of the law, but to that also which is of the faith of Abraham; who is the father of us all" (Ro.4:16).

2) We must not be discouraged or blame God when some of our children rebel and reject God. We must remain faithful and continue to teach the truth of Christ and His Word, no matter what some children may do. In fact, we must teach the truth with more fervor than ever before, never backing off. And we must pray fervently; we must intercede in prayer, never letting up. We must take more time than ever before for intercessory prayer, getting alone before God and crying out to Him for our children and loved ones. God promises to hear prayer, intercessory prayer, prayer that comes boldly before Him and wrestles with Him for help.
   ⇒ We must teach our children, teach them ever so diligently.

> "Only take heed to thyself, and keep thy soul diligently, lest thou forget the things which thine eyes have seen, and lest they depart from thy heart all the days of thy life: but teach them thy sons, and thy sons' sons" (De.4:9).
> "And thou shalt teach them [God's commandments] diligently unto thy children, and shalt talk of them when thou sittest in thine house, and when thou walkest by the way, and when thou liest down, and when thou risest up" (De.6:7).
> "And that their children, which have not known any thing, may hear, and learn to fear the LORD your God, as long as ye live in the land" (De.31:13).
> "Train up a child in the way he should go: and when he is old, he will not depart from it" (Pr.22:6).
> "Whom shall he teach knowledge? and whom shall he make to understand doctrine? them that are weaned from the milk, and drawn from the breasts" (Is.28:9).
> "So when they had dined, Jesus saith to Simon Peter, Simon, son of Jonas, lovest thou me more than these? He saith unto him, Yea, Lord; thou knowest that I love thee. He saith unto him, Feed my lambs" (Jn.21:15).

"That they may teach the young women to be sober, to love their husbands, to love their children" (Tit.2:4).

⇒ We must pray for our children, intercede and wrestle in prayer for them.

"Ask, and it shall be given you; seek, and ye shall find; knock, and it shall be opened unto you" (Mt.7:7).
"And all things, whatsoever ye shall ask in prayer, believing, ye shall receive" (Mt.21:22).
"And he spake a parable unto them to this end, that men ought always to pray, and not to faint" (Lu.18:1).
"If ye abide in me, and my words abide in you, ye shall ask what ye will, and it shall be done unto you" (Jn.15:7).
"Hitherto have ye asked nothing in my name: ask, and ye shall receive, that your joy may be full" (Jn.16:24).
"He shall call upon me, and I will answer him: I will be with him in trouble; I will deliver him, and honour him" (Ps.91:15).
"And it shall come to pass, that before they call, I will answer; and while they are yet speaking, I will hear" (Is.65:24).

6 (5:21-24) **Enoch—Walk, Spiritual—Dedication—Commitment—Seeking, After God**: the sixth significant event, one godly man, Enoch, dedicated his life totally to God. Even the name Enoch (Chanokh) means dedicated. It could also mean initiator and teacher. Apparently, Enoch did three significant things:
⇒ He *totally dedicated and committed* his life to God—again, *totally*.
⇒ He initiated or began a *deeper kind* of walk and life with God, a *deeper kind* of communion and fellowship with God.
⇒ He taught men the life and walk of total commitment to God, of unbroken communion and fellowship with God.

Enoch was a most unusual person, a person who surrendered and yielded his life completely to God, who gave up all to follow God. He apparently lived a life of total *self-control* and *self-denial*. But he was not perfect, for he was but a mere man. He was as all other men are, sinful and mortal. Nevertheless, Enoch gave his life so completely to God—so totally—that he had a very, very special relationship with God.

Interestingly, more is said about Enoch in the New Testament than in the Old Testament. There are five passages of Scripture that deal with him. Two of these are in other genealogies that just list his name with no comment (1 Chr.1:3; Lu.3:37). But the other three passages tell us a great deal about Enoch.

"And Enoch lived sixty and five years, and begat Methuselah: and Enoch walked with God after he begat Methuselah three hundred years, and begat sons and daughters: and all the days of Enoch were three hundred sixty and five years: and Enoch walked with God: and he was not; for God took him" (Ge.5:21-24).
"By faith Enoch was translated that he should not see death; and was not found, because God had translated him: for before his translation he had this testimony, that he pleased God. But without faith it is impossible to please him: for he that cometh to God must believe that he is, and that he is a rewarder of them that diligently seek him" (He.11:5-6).
"And Enoch also, the seventh from Adam, prophesied of these, saying, Behold, the Lord cometh with ten thousands of his saints, to execute judgement upon all, and to convince all that are ungodly among them of all their ungodly deeds which they have ungodly committed, and of all their hard speeches which ungodly sinners have spoken against him" (Jude 14-15).

The Genesis passage gives us the outline of Enoch's life. Two very significant things are said about him. (The following study on Enoch's life is given in a broader outline because of the importance Scripture places upon his life.)

a. ENOCH WALKED WITH GOD (vv.21-24a)

Scripture declares twice that "Enoch walked with God" (vv.22, 24). Walking means forward movement, steady progress. Enoch did not walk a little and then stop or turn aside, backsliding. He was not fluctuating up and down. Enoch was genuine through and through; he was steadfast and persevering. He walked with God consistently, growing and growing more and more. What does it mean "to walk with God"? The life of Enoch shows us.

1) To *walk with God* means that Enoch had a conversion experience. Enoch was born to sinful parents in a sinful world just like all other persons. From all indications Enoch had been living a sinful, wicked life, running around with the ungodly crowd of his day. But something happened in his life that changed him, that caused him to confess and repent of his sin—something so convicting that it aroused him to turn back to God. Something happened that stirred him to begin to live a life of self-control and self-denial. What was it?

Scripture says this: "Enoch walked with God *after* he begat Methuselah" (v.22). Note the word *after*. Scripture seems to be saying that it was after his son's birth that Enoch began to walk with God. Apparently, the birth of his first son struck Enoch, struck him with a deep, intense sense of responsibility for the child. Enoch was convicted...
• of his sinful, ungodly life
• of his duty to provide a godly home for his son and any other children who might come

- of his duty to lead his son to trust and follow God and to believe God's Word and promise to send the Savior into the world

What did Enoch do when God convicted him of these things? He did exactly what every sinful and ungodly father should do: he began to "walk with God" (v.22). Enoch repented, changed his life, and turned back to God. He turned away from sin and began to live for God. He began to live a life of self-denial and self-control. The next point clearly shows this.

"Verily I say unto you, Except ye be converted, and become as little children, ye shall not enter into the kingdom of heaven" (Mt.18:3).
"I tell you, Nay: but, except ye repent, ye shall all likewise perish" (Lu.13:3).
"Then Peter said unto them, Repent, and be baptized every one of you in the name of Jesus Christ for the remission of sins, and ye shall receive the gift of the Holy Ghost" (Ac.2:38).
"Repent ye therefore, and be converted, that your sins may be blotted out, when the times of refreshing shall come from the presence of the Lord" (Ac.3:19).
"Repent therefore of this thy wickedness, and pray God, if perhaps the thought of thine heart may be forgiven thee" (Ac.8:22).
"And the times of this ignorance God winked at; but now commandeth all men every where to repent" (Ac.17:30).
"If my people, which are called by my name, shall humble themselves, and pray, and seek my face, and turn from their wicked ways; then will I hear from heaven, and will forgive their sin, and will heal their land" (2 Chr.7:14).
"Let the wicked forsake his way, and the unrighteous man his thoughts: and let him return unto the Lord, and he will have mercy upon him; and to our God, for he will abundantly pardon" (Is.55:7).
"Cast away from you all your transgressions, whereby ye have transgressed; and make you a new heart and a new spirit: for why will ye die [eternally]?" (Eze.18:31).

2) To *walk with God* means to believe God and to be diligent in seeking after God's promises. The passage in the book of *Hebrews* shows this:

"By faith Enoch...pleased God. But without faith it is impossible to please him: for he that cometh to God must believe that he is, and that he is a rewarder of them that diligently seek him" (He.11:5-6).

Note what Enoch believed and what we must believe:
⇒ Enoch believed that God is, that He truly exists, that He is the only living and true God, the true Creator and Sustainer of the universe, the Lord and Master of life. Enoch knew what we must know: if God is, if God truly exists, then we owe our lives to Him. We must walk with God—follow, worship, fellowship, and serve Him—with all our hearts.
⇒ Enoch believed that God rewards those who diligently seek after Him. This refers to the great rewards or promises of the Savior. Enoch believed the promises of God, that God would give a godly line of people to the world and through that godly line, He would send the Savior to the world. Enoch believed in the promise of the Savior, the Savior who would deliver the godly from all the corruption of sin, death, and judgment to come. How do we know that Enoch believed all this about the Savior? Because of the reference in Jude 14-15 which will be discussed in point five below.

3) To *walk with God* means to develop an unbroken communion and fellowship with God. The phrase means to *walk about* with God, *to live* with God, to have the most intimate fellowship and communion with God.[3] Enoch did what we should do: he sought after an unbroken fellowship and communion with God.
⇒ Enoch sought to keep his mind and thoughts upon God and upon the things that are true and profitable.

"Finally, brethren, whatsoever things are true, whatsoever things are honest, whatsoever things are just, whatsoever things are pure, whatsoever things are lovely, whatsoever things are of good report; if there be any virtue, and if there be any praise, think on these things" (Ph.4:8).

⇒ Enoch sought to cast down every imagination and to captivate every thought for God.

"Casting down imaginations, and every high thing that exalteth itself against the knowledge of God, and bringing into captivity every thought to the obedience of Christ" (2 Co.10:5).

⇒ Enoch sought to keep his mind upon God.

"Thou wilt keep him in perfect peace, whose mind is stayed on thee: because he trusteth in thee" (Is.26:3).

---

3 H.C. Leupold. *Genesis*, Vol.1, p.241.

⇒ Enoch sought to pray always, to walk and live in a spirit of prayer, all day long.

> "And he spake a parable unto them to this end, that men ought always to pray, and not to faint" (Lu.18:1).
> "Praying always with all prayer and supplication in the Spirit, and watching thereunto with all perseverance and supplication for all saints" (Ep.6:18).
> "Continue in prayer, and watch in the same with thanksgiving" (Col.4:2).
> "Pray without ceasing" (1 Th.5:17).

4) To "walk with God" means to live a holy and godly life, a life of separation, a life that is completely different from the sinful lives of others. This does not mean a monastic life, a life that withdraws from the world. It means that Enoch began to live a life of self-control...
- that Enoch quit doing things that were sinful, wicked, evil, and ungodly
- that Enoch started doing thing that were pure, righteous, good, and godly

We know this from the fact that Enoch "walked with God" (vv.22, 24). He walked just like God and lived just like God. He lived a holy and godly life. But we also know that Enoch lived a holy and godly life from Jude. Jude tells us that Enoch stood against and preached against the ungodliness of his day (Jude 14-15). This is seen in the next point.

5) To "walk with God" means to bear a strong witness and testimony for God. Again, the Jude passage shows us this fact about Enoch:

> "And Enoch also, the seventh from Adam, prophesied of these, saying, Behold, the Lord cometh with ten thousands of his saints, to execute judgement upon all, and to convince all that are ungodly among them of all their ungodly deeds which they have ungodly committed, and of all their hard speeches which ungodly sinners have spoken against him" (Jude 14-15).

Enoch was a preacher, a preacher of righteousness. Note what his message was.

a) First, the Lord is coming with ten thousands of His saints—with all the believers who have died up to that time in history. The Lord is coming to judge the world, to execute judgment upon "all," upon everyone who has ever lived in the world.

This is a clear reference to the coming again of Jesus Christ in judgment and this is the first reference to His coming again in Scripture. How did Enoch know about the coming of God in judgment? Did God reveal the fact in a special revelation as He was to do to future prophets? Or did God reveal the truth to Adam earlier, and then Adam taught the truth to his children and grandchildren? We do not know. But we must remember that Enoch knew and believed the promise of God concerning the coming Savior. He knew that God was going to send the Savior to deliver the godly from the corruption of sin, death, and judgment to come. And here in Jude, he somehow knew that the Savior was also coming in judgment.

b) Second, Enoch preached against the ungodly lives people were living. He was a strong and forceful witness. Note how often he uses the word ungodly: four times. He declares that the Lord is coming to convict...
- *all* the ungodly
- of *all* their ungodly deeds
- that they did in an *ungodly way*
- because they were *ungodly sinners*

Remember: most of Enoch's audience were cousins of his, not too many generations removed from him. This shows just how strong and forceful a preacher Enoch was. It makes us wonder how many people tried to get him to tone down his message, the truth of judgment, and to concentrate on the love and care of God?

Note one other fact in the Jude reference. This was an ungodly age, an age when few people were following God and living righteous lives. This will be clearly seen in the next outline and passage of Scripture (Ge.6:1-8).

Thought 1. Was Enoch's day more ungodly than our day? The thinking and honest person has to confess that it was not much more, if any more, ungodly. Just think how wild ungodliness is running today, the awful rampage of evil in the world...

• lying	• alcohol	• hatred
• stealing	• immorality	• demonism
• killing	• greed	• witchcraft
• murder	• assaults	• materialism
• lawlessness	• injury	• secularism
• drugs	• anger	• denial or questioning of God

Thought 2. How many of us preach as strongly and forcefully as Enoch did? The love and mercy of God must, of course, always be preached and taught. But so must the coming again and judgment of God. How many people are lost because we have not warned them of coming judgment?

> "And then shall appear the sign of the Son of man in heaven: and then shall all the tribes of the earth mourn, and they shall see the Son of man coming in the clouds of heaven with power and great glory" (Mt.24:30).
> "Whom we preach, warning every man, and teaching every man in all wisdom; that we may present every man perfect in Christ Jesus" (Col.1:28).

"Now we exhort you, brethren, warn them that are unruly, comfort the feebleminded, support the weak, be patient toward all men" (1 Th.5:14).

"And to you who are troubled rest with us, when the Lord Jesus shall be revealed from heaven with his mighty angels, in flaming fire taking vengeance on them that know not God, and that obey not the gospel of our Lord Jesus Christ: who shall be punished with everlasting destruction from the presence of the Lord, and from the glory of his power" (2 Th.1:7-9).

"Preach the word; be instant in season, out of season; reprove, rebuke, exhort with all longsuffering and doctrine" (2 Ti.4:2).

"These things speak, and exhort, and rebuke with all authority. Let no man despise thee" (Tit.2:15).

"And as it is appointed unto men once to die, but after this the judgment" (He.9:27).

"The Lord knoweth how to deliver the godly out of temptations, and to reserve the unjust unto the day of judgment to be punished" (2 Pe.2:9).

"Behold, he cometh with clouds; and every eye shall see him, and they also which pierced him: and all kindreds of the earth shall wail because of him" (Re.1:7).

"Cry aloud, spare not, lift up thy voice like a trumpet, and show my people their transgression" (Is.58:1).

"When I say unto the wicked, Thou shalt surely die; and thou givest him not warning, nor speakest to warn the wicked from his wicked way, to save his life; the same wicked man shall die in his iniquity; but his blood will I require at thine hand" (Eze.3:18).

"Nevertheless, if thou warn the wicked of his way to turn from it; if he do not turn from his way, he shall die in his iniquity; but thou hast delivered thy soul" (Eze.33:9).

Thought 3. Note what Scripture has to say about the believer's walk.
1) Noah walked with God.

"Noah was a just man and perfect in his generations, and Noah walked with God" (Ge.6:9).

2) Abraham was required to walk before God.

"And when Abram was ninety years old and nine, the LORD appeared to Abram, and said unto him, I am the Almighty God; walk before me, and be thou perfect" (Ge.17:1).

3) We are all required to walk with God.

"He hath showed thee, O man, what is good; and what doth the LORD require of thee, but to do justly, and to love mercy, and to walk humbly with thy God?" (Mi.6:8).

4) We are to walk before God.

"I will walk before the LORD in the land of the living" (Ps.116:9).

5) We are to walk after God.

"Ye shall walk after the LORD your God, and fear him, and keep his commandments, and obey his voice, and ye shall serve him, and cleave unto him" (De.13:4).

6) We are to follow God and walk in love.

"Be ye therefore followers of God, as dear children; and walk in love, as Christ also hath loved us, and hath given himself for us an offering and a sacrifice to God for a sweetsmelling savour" (Ep.5:1-2).

7) We are to walk in Christ.

"As ye have therefore received Christ Jesus the Lord, so walk ye in him" (Col.2:6).

8) We are to walk by faith, not by sight.

"For we walk by faith, not by sight" (2 Co.5:7).

9) We are to walk in light.

"But if we walk in the light, as he is in the light, we have fellowship one with another, and the blood of Jesus Christ his Son cleanseth us from all sin" (1 Jn.1:7).

10) We are to walk in truth.

"For thy lovingkindness is before mine eyes: and I have walked in thy truth" (Ps.26:3).

"Teach me thy way, O LORD; I will walk in thy truth: unite my heart to fear thy name" (Ps.27:11, see 2 Jn.4; 3 Jn.3).

11) We are to walk in newness of life.

"Therefore we are buried with him by baptism into death: that like as Christ was raised up from the dead by the glory of the Father, even so we also should walk in newness of life" (Ro.6:4).

12) We are to walk in the Spirit.

"This I say then, Walk in the Spirit, and ye shall not fulfil the lust of the flesh" (Ga.5:16).

13) We are to walk worthy of our calling and vocation.

"I therefore, the prisoner of the Lord, beseech you that ye walk worthy of the vocation where-with ye are called" (Ep.4:1).

14) We are to walk carefully.

"See then that ye walk circumspectly, not as fools, but as wise" (Ep.5:15).

15) We are to pray for God to keep us from stumbling and falling that we may walk before Him.

"For thou hast delivered my soul from death: wilt not thou deliver my feet from falling, that I may walk before God in the light of the living?" (Ps.56:13).

16) We are to walk as Christ walked.

"He that saith he abideth in him ought himself also so to walk, even as he walked" (1 Jn.2:6).

17) We shall walk with Christ in heaven and be clothed in white (purity, perfection).

"Thou hast a few names even in Sardis which have not defiled their garments; and they shall walk with me in white: for they are worthy" (Re.3:4).

Thought 4. Note that Enoch had a large family of both sons and daughters (v.22). A person can "walk with God"—have a close fellowship and communion with God—and be a strong minister and still be married.

b. ENOCH WAS TRANSLATED—TAKEN—INTO GOD'S PRESENCE WITHOUT DYING (v.24)

Note what Scripture says: "He was not" (enennu) or "He was no more" (NIV) or "He was seen no more" (NEB). Scripture simply means that Enoch was translated—transferred from earth to heaven, to be with God. Enoch was transferred right into the presence of God without ever dying. The New Testament clearly tells us this:

"By faith Enoch was translated that he should not see death; and was not found, because God had translated him [taken him up]: for before his translation he had this testimony, that he pleased God" (He.11:5).

B.H. Carroll has an excellent description of Enoch's experience, of what the word "translated" means:

God translated him. This is an old Latin word, an irregular verb, and it simply means carried over or carried across. God carried him across. Across what? Across death. Death is the river that divides this world from the world to come, and here was a man that never did go through that river at all. When he got there God carried him across. God transferred him; translated him; God picked him up and carried him over and put him on the other shore.[4]

Now, why did God translate Enoch so that he would not experience death? Why did God not let him die like other men? There are at least four reasons.

1) God translated Enoch because Enoch walked so closely with God, because Enoch lived a life of complete surrender, of complete control and self-denial. Note what Scripture says:

"Enoch walked with God: and he was not; for God took him" (v.24).

Enoch's "walking with God" is closely tied to God taking him on home to heaven. That is, the very reason for God taking Enoch on home to heaven was because Enoch walked so closely with God. Enoch had apparently gained an unbroken consciousness of God's presence, an unbroken fellowship and communion with God.
⇒ Enoch's "walk with God" had become so intimate and intense,
⇒ and Enoch longed so much for face to face fellowship with God...

...that God just could not leave him upon earth any longer.

---

4 Quoted by Arthur W. Pink. *Gleanings in Genesis*, p.79.

Thought 1. "He did not live like the rest, so he did not die like the rest"[5]

2) God translated Enoch to demonstrate and symbolize His power to execute judgment. Enoch's generation was ungodly, and he preached a strong, aggressive message to his ungodly generation (Jude 14-15). But despite their ungodliness, God loved the people. He wanted them saved. By giving them a living demonstration of His power...

- He proved that He really exists
- He proved His power to judge the ungodly. If He could translate a person, He had the power to condemn and judge a person
- He stirred some to repent and follow God

The ungodly could hardly miss the warning.

3) God translated Enoch to demonstrate and symbolize the promise of eternal life. Enoch believed God's promise of the godly seed, that God was going to send the Savior into the world. He believed that the Savior was going to save man from sin, death, and judgment, and that He was going to restore man to the perfection and eternal life Adam had known. Enoch's translation demonstrated that eternal life is a reality. Man can live forever with God.

Note this: Enoch's translation also symbolizes the resurrection of believers at the return of Christ. Enoch's translation is a picture of what God is going to do for the believer: raise him up and take him to heaven.

"For God so loved the world, that he gave his only begotten Son, that whosoever believeth in him should not perish, but have everlasting life" (Jn.3:16).

"And he that reapeth receiveth wages, and gathereth fruit unto life eternal: that both he that soweth and he that reapeth may rejoice together" (Jn.4:36).

"Verily, verily, I say unto you, He that heareth my word, and believeth on him that sent me, hath everlasting life, and shall not come into condemnation; but is passed from death unto life" (Jn.5:24).

"But these are written, that ye might believe that Jesus is the Christ, the Son of God; and that believing ye might have life through his name" (Jn.20:31).

"For he that soweth to his flesh shall of the flesh reap corruption; but he that soweth to the Spirit shall of the Spirit reap life everlasting" (Ga.6:8).

"These things have I written unto you that believe on the name of the Son of God; that ye may know that ye have eternal life, and that ye may believe on the name of the Son of God" (1 Jn.5:13).

4) God translated Enoch to be an encouragement to other believers, both in his ungodly day and ours. God proved His promise and power to give eternal life. Enoch should stir us to press on, to believe God more strongly than ever before and to stand fast.

"Therefore, my beloved brethren, be ye stedfast, unmovable, always abounding in the work of the Lord, forasmuch as ye know that your labour is not in vain in the Lord" (1 Co.15:58).

"And let us not be weary in well doing: for in due season we shall reap, if we faint not" (Ga.6:9).

"Stand fast in one spirit, with one mind striving together for the faith of the gospel" (Ph.1:27).

"Wherefore seeing we also are compassed about with so great a cloud of witnesses, let us lay aside every weight, and the sin which doth so easily beset us, and let us run with patience [endurance] the race that is set before us" (He.12:1).

"But none of these things move me, neither count I my life dear unto myself, so that I might finish my course with joy, and the ministry, which I have received of the Lord Jesus, to testify the gospel of the grace of God" (Ac.20:24).

7 (5:25-26) **Methuselah:** the seventh significant event, one man, Methuselah, lived longer than anyone else, lived longer as a testimony to God's grace and judgment to come. The name *Methuselah* means man of the weapon or javelin or of the spear (H.C. Leupold, Derek Kidner, Victor Hamilton). Or it can mean...

- "When he is gone it will come."
- "When he is dead, it shall come"[6]
- "[When] he dies [there will be] a sending forth"[7]
- "When he dies there shall be [a]...sending forth of waters"[8]

Just which of the two meanings is correct cannot be known with absolute certainty. But in searching the Scriptures and in looking back upon Enoch's life and the events of his day, it makes far more sense to think that Methuselah's name means "when he dies it shall come."

⇒ Enoch's apparent conversion took place when Methuselah was born (v.22). Apparently, his life changed and changed radically. Why? Could it be that God gave him a special revelation of the coming judgment unless he and his fellow citizens repented?

⇒ Methuselah's name can mean and is actually said by some scholars to mean, "When he dies, it shall come" (see Arthur Pink. *Gleanings in Genesis*, p.76).

---

5 *Matthew Henry's Commentary*, Vol.1, p.49.
6 Donald Grey Barnhouse. *Genesis*, p.45.
7 *Matthew Henry's Commentary*, Vol.1, p.50.
8 John Gill. *Gill's Commentary*, Vol.1. (Grand Rapids, MI: Baker Book House, 1980), p.35.

⇒ Enoch was a godly man—very godly—the kind of man to whom God would choose to reveal the coming judgment. If God was going to choose a person to whom He could reveal the coming judgment of world destruction, it would be someone who "walked with God," someone who walked ever so closely and intimately with God. This was Enoch, the very father who named Methuselah.

⇒ Enoch preached strongly and aggressively against the ungodliness of his day. Most of the godly would have, of course, borne testimony against man's sin and of God's great forgiveness and love. But from the indication of Scripture, Enoch was much stronger and more aggressive in his preaching against the ungodly living of people. Why? Could God have given him a special revelation of coming judgment unless people repented of their sin?

When these facts are considered, the weight of the facts points to Methuselah's name meaning "when he dies, it shall come."

Apparently, God gave Enoch a revelation of the coming judgment upon earth, the coming judgment that lay right over the horizon, right before the people. Therefore, one of two things happened:

⇒ God told Enoch to name the child Methuselah, or...

⇒ Enoch acted on his own and declared the fact in the name of his son.

Whatever the case, Methuselah's very name stood as a testimony to the people of his day and time: "When he dies, it—the judgment of God—will come upon earth." And it did. Methuselah died in the year 1656, the very year the flood came upon earth. (See DEEPER STUDY # 2—Ge.5:27-32 for chart.) This fact also points to the meaning of Methuselah's name. He lived longer than anyone else upon earth (969 years), and he bore testimony longer than anyone else:

⇒ the testimony of God's wonderful grace in blessing the godly line and people while upon earth.

⇒ the testimony of God's coming judgment unless men repent of their ungodliness.

Thought 1. Enoch was not the only prophet to whom God has revealed the fact of judgment upon sin. God has revealed the coming judgment to New Testament prophets as well. If we—the generations since Christ has come—do not repent, God's judgment upon the world is coming a second time.

⇒ Jesus Christ declared that judgment is coming.

"When the Son of man shall come in his glory, and all the holy angels with him, then shall he sit upon the throne of his glory: and before him shall be gathered all nations: and he shall separate them one from another, as a shepherd divideth his sheep from the goats" (Mt.25:31-32).

⇒ The writer to the Hebrews declared that judgment is coming.

"And as it is appointed unto men once to die, but after this the judgment" (He.9:27).

⇒ Peter declared that judgment is coming.

"The Lord knoweth how to deliver the godly out of temptations, and to reserve the unjust unto the day of judgment to be punished" (2 Pe.2:9).

"But the day of the Lord will come as a thief in the night; in the which the heavens shall pass away with a great noise, and the elements shall melt with fervent heat, the earth also and the works that are therein shall be burned up. Seeing then that all these things shall be dissolved, what manner of persons ought ye to be in all holy conversation and godliness, looking for and hasting unto the coming of the day of God, wherein the heavens being on fire shall be dissolved, and the elements shall melt with fervent heat? Nevertheless we, according to his promise, look for new heavens and a new earth, wherein dwelleth righteousness" (2 Pe.3:10-13).

⇒ Jude declared the very same message as Enoch.

"And Enoch also, the seventh from Adam, prophesied of these, saying, Behold, the Lord cometh with ten thousands of his saints, to execute judgement upon all, and to convince all that are ungodly among them of all their ungodly deeds which they have ungodly committed, and of all their hard speeches which ungodly sinners have spoken against him" (Jude 14-15).

8 (5:27-32) **Noah—Rest—Comfort**: the eighth significant event, godly men believed in the coming rest and comfort promised by God. This is seen in the name Lamech gave his son, Noah. Noah means *comfort* or *rest*. Note what Lamech said when Noah was born.

"And he called his name Noah, saying, This same shall comfort us concerning our work and toil of our hands, because of the ground which the LORD hath cursed" (v.29).

Apparently, for some reason Lamech was weary, bone weary. He was tired and exhausted from having to struggle to earn a living day by day. The pressure, tension, and toil was bearing heavily upon his mind, so heavily that his thoughts ran back to God's curse upon the earth. In thinking about the curse, he also thought about the Savior—*the promised seed*—God had promised and the glorious perfection He would bring to man and the earth, the perfection that Adam had originally known. This is probably the reason Lamech named his son Noah, which means comfort and rest. Lamech was expressing his faith in God's glorious promise to send the Savior, *the promised seed*, to restore man and the earth to perfection, to perfect comfort and rest.

Noah brought comfort to the human race in at least four ways.

a. Noah preserved the human race through the flood.

b. Noah preserved the godly line through the flood.

c. Noah preserved the hope for the promised Savior. This he did by preserving the godly line, for the godly are the ones who believe and look for the Savior (Tit.2:12).

d. Noah preserved the hope for the deliverance of the earth which God had cursed. Again, this he did by preserving the godly line; it is for their sake that God shall deliver the earth from the curse (Re.21:1-5).

Thought 1. What a dynamic example of faith Lamech is: believing the promises of God despite being exhausted day by day, exhausted from having to face the struggle of difficult toil and labor hour by hour just to earn a livelihood. No matter the toil or exhaustion, no matter our circumstances in having to earn a living day by day, we must learn to trust the promises of God.

"But seek ye first the kingdom of God, and his righteousness; and all these things [necessities of life] shall be added unto you" (Mt.6:33).

"Casting all your care upon him; for he careth for you" (1 Pe.5:7).

"Thou preparest a table before me in the presence of mine enemies: thou anointest my head with oil; my cup runneth over" (Ps.23:5).

"Oh how great is thy goodness, which thou hast laid up for them that fear thee; which thou hast wrought for them that trust in thee before the sons of men!" (Ps.31:19).

"For thou hast been a strength to the poor, a strength to the needy in his distress, a refuge from the storm, a shadow from the heat, when the blast of the terrible ones is as a storm against the wall" (Is.25:4).

DEEPER STUDY # 2

(5:27-32) **Genealogy—Christ**: note that many of the godly line were living at the same time. For example, Lamech, the father of Noah, knew Adam.

⇒ Lamech was born in the year of 874.

⇒ Adam did not die until the year of 930.

But note: when the flood came (1656), all of the godly line had died except Noah.

THE GODLY SEED OR DESCENDANTS AND LINE

	WAS BORN IN THE YEAR	DIED IN THE YEAR		TOTAL YEARS OF LIFE
Adam	1	930		930
Seth	130	1042		912
Enosh	235	1140		905
Cainan	325	1235		910
Mahalaleel	395	1290		895
Jared	460	1422		962
Enoch	622	987		365
Methuselah	687		1656	969
Lamech	874	1651		777
Noah	1056	2006		950
THE GREAT FLOOD			1656	

236

			upon earth
	CHAPTER 6	God came in unto the daughters of men, and they bare children to them, the same became mighty men which were of old, men of renown.	
	F. The First Civilization & Society (Part 4): The Corruption of the Godly Line—Co-mingling with the Ungodly Line, *DS1* **6:1-8**	5 And God saw that the wickedness of man was great in the earth, and that every imagination of the thoughts of his heart was only evil continually.	**4. Fact 4: God saw man's wickedness** a. The wickedness was great b. Every imagination & thought was evil
1. Fact 1: The godly ignored God, becoming worldly & immoral a. The human race began to multiply b. The godly fed their minds on sex c. The godly ignored & rebelled against God	And it came to pass, when men began to multiply on the face of the earth, and daughters were born unto them, 2 That the sons of God saw the daughters of men that they were fair; and they took them wives of all which they chose.	6 And it repented the LORD that he had made man on the earth, and it grieved him at his heart. 7 And the LORD said, I will destroy man whom I have created from the face of the earth; both man, and beast, and the creeping thing, and the fowls of the air; for it repenteth me that I have made them.	**5. Fact 5: God grieved over man & condemned man** a. God regretted He ever made man b. God judged & condemned man to be destroyed—wiped off the face of the earth—both man & land animals
2. Fact 2: God became disturbed & warned man a. God would withdraw His Spirit b. God's grace was limited: Judgment was coming **3. Fact 3: Man became lawless as well as immoral in developing the first society**	3 And the LORD said, My spirit shall not always strive with man, for that he also is flesh: yet his days shall be an hundred and twenty years. 4 There were giants in the earth in those days; and also after that, when the sons of	8 But Noah found grace in the eyes of the LORD.	**6. Fact 6: God remembered His grace & saved Noah**

DIVISION III

ADAM, THE FIRST MAN (PART 2): THE BIRTH, DEVELOPMENT, AND CORRUPTION OF BOTH THE UNGODLY AND THE GODLY SEED (DESCENDANTS), 4:1–6:8

F. The First Civilization and Society (Part 4): The Corruption of the Godly Line—Co-mingling with the Ungodly Line, 6:1-8

(6:1-8) **Introduction**: remember, in chapter four we saw the birth, growth, and corruption of the ungodly line of people upon earth (Ge.4:1-24). Then we saw the descendants of Adam who continued the godly line of people upon earth (Ge.4:25-5:32). In the first civilization and society, two streams of people were developing upon earth…

- the godly stream (line) who worshipped and served God
- the ungodly stream (line) who neglected and denied God and who lived unrighteous lives

Civilization and society were developing along two streams—two lines of people—the godly and the ungodly. The godly walked with God; the ungodly walked after the flesh and the things of this world. (See outline and notes—Ge.4:1-24; Ge.5:1-32 for more discussion.)

Now, this passage covers the corruption of the godly line. Believers, those who followed God, married unbelievers, those who neglected and denied God and lived unrighteous lives. The result was the same as it has always been down through history: the ungodly pulled the godly down, leading them into a life of sin and wickedness. We shall soon see that the godly line became corrupted, so corrupted that God had to destroy the whole human race.

This is *The First Civilization and Society (Part 4): The Corruption of the Godly Line—Co-mingling with the Ungodly of the Earth*.

1. Fact 1: the godly ignored God, becoming worldly and immoral (vv.1-2).
2. Fact 2: God became disturbed and warned man (v.3).
3. Fact 3: man became lawless as well as immoral in developing the first society upon earth (v.4).
4. Fact 4: God saw man's wickedness (v.5).
5. Fact 5: God grieved over man and condemned man (vv.6-7).
6. Fact 6: God remembered His grace and saved Noah (v.8).

DEEPER STUDY # 1

(6:1-8) **Sons of God**: there are two major interpretations of this passage. The two positions need to be looked at before studying the passage. The interpretations focus upon the term "sons of God." Who are they?

1. Some interpreters (for example, Donald Gray Barnhouse, James Montgomery Boice, and Arthur W. Pink) say the "sons of God" are angels. Five major reasons are usually given.
   a. The term *sons of God* definitely refers to angels in Job (Jb.1:6; 2:1; 38:7).
   b. Giants (nephilim) were born as a result of the union between the sons of God and the women (v.4). This position often says that this union was the historical basis for ancient mythology that talks about half-human, half-divine beings upon earth, that the myths would be embellished, but they would be stirred by faint memories of giant people before the flood. (See Homer and other ancient writers.)

    c. Angels may appear in bodily form to men, for example, when the angels appeared to Lot (Ge.19:1-5).

    d. Three passages in the New Testament, according to the interpreters of this position, seem to refer to this passage in Genesis (1 Pe.3:18-20; 2 Pe.2:4; Jude 6-7).

    e. Jewish writers (Philo, Josephus, and the author of the apocryphal book of *I Enoch*) definitely say this is a reference to angels.

2. Other interpreters (for example, Matthew Henry, H.C. Leupold, Keil and Delitzsch, *The Pulpit Commentary*, Chrysostom, Augustine, Calvin, and Luther) say "the sons of God" refers to believers, the true followers of God, the godly line or descendants of Seth. Ten reasons are usually given.

    a. The *sons of God* must be believers, for it is the only way to understand the sequence of thought in the early chapters of Genesis. The early chapters are dealing with the godly line of Adam and Seth and with the ungodly line of Cain, two streams of the human race moving in opposite directions, one godly and the other ungodly.

    b. The term "sons of God" definitely refers to believers throughout Scripture.

      ⇒ In De. 32:5 Israel is called "His children" (Hebrew, God's sons).

      ⇒ In Ps. 73:15 the godly are called "the generation of God's children" (Hebrew, God's sons).

      ⇒ In Ps.80:17 Israel is called the son whom God had made strong.

      ⇒ In Ho.1:10 Israel is called the "sons of the living God" (Hebrew, bene el chay).

      H.C. Leupold states the case as strongly as it can be stated:

> But who are these "sons of God"? Without a shadow of doubt, the Sethites—the ones just described in chapter five as having in their midst men who walked with God, like Enoch (v.22), men who looked to higher comfort in the midst of life's miseries, like Lamech (v.29), men who publicly worshipped God and confessed His name (4:26). Such men merit to be called the "sons of God" (bene elohim), a title applied to true followers of God elsewhere in the Old Testament Scriptures. When the psalmist refers to such (Ps.73:15) as "the generation of thy children," he uses the same word 'sons,' describing them as belonging to God. De. 32:5 uses the same word "sons" ("children," A.V.) in reference to Israel. Ho.1:10 is, if anything, a still stronger passage, saying specifically to Israel, "Ye are sons of the living God" (He. bene el chay). Ps.80:17 also belongs here.[1]

    c. The words and context of this very passage tell us that the "sons of God" were men. When the "sons of God" committed this terrible sin...

      • God said, "My spirit shall not always strive with *man*" (v.3).

      • "God saw that the wickedness of *man* was great" (v.5).

      • "It repented the Lord that He had made *man*" (v.6).

      • "The Lord said, I will destroy *man*" (v.7).

      Every verse deals with man; no verse—not even one reference—uses the word angel. The whole context deals with man, godly man, how he became corrupt, so corrupted that God was going to be forced to destroy man from off the face of the earth unless he repented.

    d. Again, note the context: if the male sinners were angels marrying human women, why are the men of the godly line being judged? There is no record in Genesis up to this point that the godly line of Seth had become grossly corrupted. Why then are men now being condemned and judged if the sinners of this passage were angels and ungodly women? Should not the ungodly women and angels be the ones judged? Satan, the leader of the fallen angels, was judged earlier (Ge.3:14). If the "sons of God" are angels, why are the angels not the ones being judged here? The point is clear: the "sons of God" refer to the godly of the earth. The godly began to intermarry with the ungodly line and to corrupt themselves with the worldly ways of the ungodly.

    e. Jesus Christ Himself interpreted this passage for us. Note exactly what He said:

> **"But as the days of Noe were, so shall also the coming of the Son of man be. For as in the days that were before the flood they were eating and drinking, marrying and giving in marriage, until the day that Noe entered into the ark" (Mt.24:37-38).**
>
> **"And as it was in the days of Noe, so shall it be also in the days of the Son of man. They did eat, they drank, they married wives, they were given in marriage, until the day that Noe entered into the ark, and the flood came, and destroyed them all" (Lu.17:26-27).**

      Who does "they" refer to? To the people—all the people, both the godly and the ungodly—upon the earth during the days of Noah. Christ is referring to people, not to angels. Christ is telling us exactly what happened to the civilization and society of that day. Men and women, both the godly and the ungodly, were marrying and remarrying and living worldly, ungodly lives.

    f. Jesus Christ said that angels do not marry.

> **"For in the resurrection they neither marry, nor are given in marriage, but are as the angels of God in heaven" (Mt.22:30).**

      Note the statement of Genesis: the "sons of God...took them wives" (v.2). H.C. Leupold points out that this is definitely referring to sexual and adulterous relationships, but it is also referring to marriage, for this is the standard way for the Hebrew to express marriage.[2]

---

[1] H.C. Leupold. *Genesis*, Vol.1, pp.250-251.

[2] Ibid., p.253.

g. Scripture tells us that intermarriage between the godly and the ungodly was strictly forbidden among the godly in the earliest days of history, long before the law was ever recorded.
⇒ The law of Moses, which was to be written after the flood, was to forbid intermarriage.

> **"Neither shalt thou make marriages with them [the ungodly line]; thy daughter thou shalt not give unto his son, nor his daughter shalt thou take unto thy son. For they will turn away thy son from following me, that they may serve other gods: so will the anger of the LORD be kindled against you, and destroy thee suddenly" (De.7:3-4).**

⇒ But long before the law against intermarriage was ever adopted on a national basis, Isaac and Rebekah were deeply concerned lest Jacob marry an ungodly person. This definitely lends strong Scriptural support to the law existing among the godly line of believers, existing from the very earliest days of history.

> **"And Rebekah said to Isaac, I am weary of my life because of the daughters of Heth: if Jacob take a wife of the daughters of Heth, such as these which are of the daughters of the land, what good shall my life do me?" (Ge.27:46).**
> **"And Isaac called Jacob, and blessed him, and charged him, and said unto him, Thou shalt not take a wife of the daughters of Canaan" (Ge.28:1).**

h. There is no Scripture any place to indicate...
• that angels are sexual beings
• that angels have ever had sexual relations with men or women
• that angels are physical beings with human bodies, nor that they are both physical and spiritual beings. In fact, Scripture declares the very opposite, that angels are spiritual beings (He.1:14; see Mt.8:16; 10:1; Mk.1:27; 3:11; Ac.5:16; 8:7).

i. The New Testament passages that are sometimes said to refer to this passage are not referring to this Genesis passage, not at all. The New Testament passages are referring to the original fall of the angels, to the time when they followed Satan in his rebellion against God (see outline and DEEPER STUDY # 1—1 Pe.3:19-20; note—2 Pe.2:3-9, esp. v.4; Jude 5-7).
j. The thought of angels marrying and having sex with earthly women...
"Is...monstrous...and mythical."[3]
"Defies the normalities of experience."[4]
"Introduces the mythological element as well as polytheism into the Scriptures and makes the Bible a record of strange and fantastic tales and contradicts the [Scripture]."[5]

1 (6:1-2) **Seed, Godly—Immorality—Worldliness**: the first fact—the godly ignored God, becoming worldly and immoral. Three things are suggested in these two verses.
a. The human race began to multiply upon earth. This, of course, refers to both the godly and ungodly families upon earth. But note: when the ungodly increase, so do sin and evil. More and more children were being born into ungodly families, families that stressed the outward and worldly rather than the inward and spiritual.
This meant a terrible thing, for the ungodly always outnumber the godly. There are always more people who follow their own way in life than those who follow God. Consequently, sin and evil were increasing at a far more rapid rate than righteousness and godliness. Eventually, the godly were bound to be contaminated and corrupted unless they guarded and attached themselves ever so closely to God. This will be seen in the next point (point two). For now, the point to see is this: when the ungodly increase, so do sin and evil. The more sinners increase upon earth, the more sin there will be upon earth. This was exactly what was happening in the early stages of man's history. The population was increasing ever so rapidly and so were sin and evil. Sin and evil were increasing at a far greater pace than was righteousness and godliness.

> **Thought 1.** The more sinners congregate and get together, the more sin grows. This is clearly seen...
> • when people flock to large population centers and ignore God.
> • when people get together for parties and forget God, wearing clothing that exposes their bodies and dancing with enticing movements and drinking to loosen their inhibitions. Note how much more likely people are to sin when they are in a group of worldly people than when they are all alone. They are much more bold in sinning within a group. It is far easier to sin if someone else is doing it, no matter what it is: sexual immorality, stealing, assaulting, killing.

> **"When the wicked are multiplied, transgression increaseth: but the righteous shall see their fall" (Pr.29:16).**

b. The godly became worldly and immoral, and they fed their minds upon sex (v.2). They did not control nor deny their immoral sexual urges. This is the picture being painted in verse two. The godly men began to look at the women of the world, at those who did not follow God. Note what they began to notice: that the women were fair, beautiful, and shapely. They focused their thoughts upon their beautiful faces and shapely bodies, and they desired them. They looked at

---

3 *The Pulpit Commentary*, Vol.1, p.102.
4 Derek Kidner. *Genesis*, p.84.
5 H.C. Leupold. *Genesis*, Vol.1, pp.252-253.

the outward, physical appearance and forgot the inward, spiritual beauty. They did not control their eyes nor their thoughts. The result was tragic: they co-mingled with the ungodly and did all that co-mingling involves: dating, partying, playing around, touching, caressing, kissing, fondling; and they engaged in illicit sex. They looked and saw, and fed their minds upon the worldly and immoral and they engaged in sexual immorality. They completely ignored God and went about doing their own thing, satisfying the lusts of their flesh. They refused to control and deny their carnal lusts.

⇒ Verse six tells us how enslaved man became to the passion of lust.

"Every imagination of the thoughts of his heart was only evil continually" (Ge.6:5).

⇒ Compare these verses.

"For out of the heart proceed evil thoughts, murders, adulteries, fornications, thefts, false witness, blasphemies" (Mt.15:19).
"Because that, when they knew God, they glorified him not as God, neither were thankful; but became vain in their imaginations, and their foolish heart was darkened" (Ro.1:21).
"Among whom [the worldly] also we all had our conversation [behavior, conduct] in times past in the lusts of our flesh, fulfilling the desires of the flesh and of the mind; and were by nature the children of wrath, even as others" (Ep.2:3).
"Unto the pure all things are pure: but unto them that are defiled and unbelieving is nothing pure; but even their mind and conscience is defiled" (Tit.1:15).
"The thoughts of the wicked are an abomination to the LORD" (Pr.15:26).
"For as he thinketh in his heart, so is he: Eat and drink, saith he to thee; but his heart is not with thee" (Pr.23:7).

c. The godly ignored and rebelled against God. They married the ungodly. They married "all which they chose." Jesus Christ tells us they were marrying and remarrying, marrying time and again.

"But as the days of Noe were, so shall also the coming of the Son of man be. For as in the days that were before the flood they were eating and drinking, marrying and giving in marriage, until the day that Noe entered into the ark" (Mt.24:37-38).
"And as it was in the days of Noe, so shall it be also in the days of the Son of man. They did eat, they drank, they married wives, they were given in marriage, until the day that Noe entered into the ark, and the flood came, and destroyed them all" (Lu.17:26-27).

Lust was running wild, and note: this was lust among the *godly line of believers*. The picture is that believers were turning away from God and beginning to live like the world. They were drinking and living immoral and impure lives, marrying, divorcing, and remarrying time and again, remarrying whomever they wished. God's will and demand for purity and godliness—for a distinctive line of godly believers—was totally forgotten. The human race was losing its godly line of believers: practically everyone was living an ungodly and immoral life, doing his own thing, living like he wished. Hardly any person followed God; hardly any person lived a separated, godly life. The godly line of believers—the godly seed of Seth—was corrupted, almost wiped out and completely erased from the earth. As we shall see in note 6, there was only a handful of godly people still on earth, only Noah and his immediate family.

The great 18th century Bible commentator John Gill shares the account of several Arabic writers on this passage. The picture painted is graphic:

Immediately after the death of Adam the family of Seth was separated from the family of Cain; Seth took his sons and their wives to a high mountain (Hermon), on the top of which Adam was buried, and Cain and all his sons lived in the valley beneath, where Abel was slain; and they on the mountain obtained a name for holiness and purity...they, their wives and their children, went by the common name of the sons of God...these were adjured, by Seth and by succeeding patriarchs, by no means to go down, from the mountain and join the Cainites; but notwithstanding in the times of Jared some did go down...and after that others, and at this time it became general; and being taken with the beauty of the daughters of Cain and his posterity, they did as follows: and they took them wives of all that they chose...they intermarried with them, which the Cainites might not be averse unto; they took to them wives as they fancied, which were pleasing to the flesh, without regard to their moral and civil character, and without the advice and consent of their parents, and without consulting God and his will in the matter...they took women as they pleased, and were to their liking and committed fornication, to which the Cainites were addicted; for they spent their time in singing and dancing, and in uncleanness, whereby the posterity of Seth or sons of God were allured to come down and join them, and commit fornication with them.[6]

The name of this patriarch [Jared] signifies descending; and, according to the Arabic writers, he had his name from the posterity of Seth, descending from the holy mountain in his time; for upon a noise being heard on the mountain, about a hundred men went down to the sons of Cain contrary to the prohibition...of Jared, and mixed themselves with the daughters of Cain, which brought on the apostasy; when Jared was near his end he called to him Enoch, Methuselah, Lamech, Noah, and their children, and said unto them, ye know what some have done, that they have gone down from the mountain, and have had conversation [immoral behavior] with the

---

6 John Gill. *Gill's Commentary*, Vol.1, p.37.

daughters of Cain, and have defiled themselves; take care of your purity, and do not descend from the holy mountain; after which he blessed them and having appointed Enoch his successor, he died.[7]

Thought 1. The believer—true godly believer—must live a life of separation and holiness. This does not mean that we are to withdraw from the world and live monastic lives. We are *in the world*, but we are not to be *of the world*. We live among the unbelievers of the world, but we are not to participate in their ungodly behavior…

- drinking
- partying
- telling off-colored jokes
- committing immoral acts

- being greedy and covetousness
- divorcing and remarrying
- deceiving and lying
- being unjust

Believers are to be separated from the world and its ungodly behavior, separated in the sense of being committed to God and His righteousness.

"**Be ye not unequally yoked together with unbelievers: for what fellowship hath righteousness with unrighteousness? and what communion hath light with darkness?**" (2 Co.6:14).

"**Wherefore come out from among them, and be ye separate, saith the Lord, and touch not the unclean thing; and I will receive you, and will be a Father unto you, and ye shall be my sons and daughters, saith the Lord Almighty**" (2 Co.6:17-18).

"**I beseech you therefore, brethren, by the mercies of God, that ye present your bodies a living sacrifice, holy, acceptable unto God, which is your reasonable service. And be not conformed to this world: but be ye transformed by the renewing of your mind, that ye may prove what is that good, and acceptable, and perfect, will of God**" (Ro.12:1-2).

"**And have no fellowship with the unfruitful works of darkness, but rather reprove them**" (Ep.5:11).

"**If ye were of the world, the world would love his own: but because ye are not of the world, but I have chosen you out of the world**" (Jn.15:19).

"**Now we command you, brethren, in the name of our Lord Jesus Christ, that ye withdraw yourselves from every brother that walketh disorderly, and not after the tradition which he received of us**" (2 Th.3:6).

2 (6:3) **Conviction—Holy Spirit—Sin**: the second fact—God became disturbed and warned man. Remember, there was great preaching going on during these days:

⇒ Adam lived for 930 years. He no doubt proclaimed the truth of God: the perfection of the original creation, his own sin and fall, the promised Savior, and the absolute necessity of obedience and sacrifice in approaching God. Adam taught, preached, and warned his children and grandchildren and their descendants for 930 years.

⇒ Enoch also preached and warned the world of their ungodly deeds and of the coming judgment of God upon all ungodliness (Jude 14, 15).

⇒ Methuselah's very name stood as a reminder of coming judgment. He was also most likely a preacher (see note—Ge.5:25-26).

⇒ Noah was a preacher of righteousness, warning the people up to the very end (2 Pe.2:5).

These are just the preachers we know about; there were probably others. But, in the final analysis, the witness and warning of the preachers was to no avail, not for the mass of mankind. Most people refused to heed the warning of God through the preachers. The people marched right on in their sinful and ungodly ways. The result: God became disturbed, very disturbed, and He warned man. God gave man two warnings.

a. God would withdraw His Spirit: His Spirit would not always strive with man, not forever. The preachers were warning the people, and the Spirit of God was doing just what He does with people today: convicting them of sin and of coming judgment. But the people were resisting and quenching the convictions of the Spirit. They were not listening to the voice of God struggling within their hearts. They wanted to live like they wanted, to do their own thing.

Note the statement that man is "flesh" or *mortal* and *corrupt* (v.3). This means that man was no longer just a sinner, but he…

- had given himself over to the flesh completely and fully
- had abandoned himself, become enslaved to the flesh
- had sunk to the level of living only for the flesh
- had begun to live only for the things of the flesh and of the world

The result: man was about to reach the point of no return, to reach the point where he would be so enslaved to sin and the flesh that he would never repent and turn back to God.

Consequently, God had no choice. God had to give man a final warning: if man did not repent, God would withdraw His Spirit. God's Spirit would no longer strive and struggle with the soul of man. God would withdraw His Spirit and let judgment fall upon the ungodliness and unrighteousness of men.

Thought 1. H.C. Leupold gives the following as the reason why God was threatening to withdraw His Spirit from man.

---

[7] John Gill. *Gill's Commentary*, Vol.1, p.34.

> *Men...no longer cared about having their homes [the] centers of godly instruction where divine truth prevailed, being taught by father and by mother...instead [they] chose any woman whatsoever, as the fancy of the moment moved them, to rear their offspring. At that point God determines that He will let His Spirit no longer do His work of reproving and restraining (yadhon), because man has degenerated. Man is no longer simply sinful, as he has been right along since the Fall; the race has also as a whole practically sunk to the level of being "flesh" (basar), just plain, ordinary, weak and sinful stock, abandoned to a life of sin. Man has forfeited all hope of further efforts of God's grace.*[8]

> **"And grieve not the Holy Spirit of God, whereby ye are sealed unto the day of redemption" (Ep.4:30).**
> **"Quench not the Spirit" (1 Th.5:19).**
> **"Of how much sorer punishment, suppose ye, shall he be thought worthy, who hath trodden under foot the Son of God, and hath counted the blood of the covenant, wherewith he was sanctified, an unholy thing, and hath done despite unto the Spirit of grace?" (He.10:29).**
> **"Cast me not away from thy presence; and take not thy holy spirit from me" (Ps.51:11).**
> **"But they rebelled, and vexed his holy Spirit: therefore he was turned to be their enemy, and he fought against them" (Is.63:10).**
> **"But the spirit of the LORD departed from Saul, and an evil spirit from the LORD troubled him" (1 S.16:14).**
> **"But they refused to hearken, and pulled away the shoulder, and stopped their ears, that they should not hear" (Zec.7:11).**

b. God's grace was limited: judgment was coming. God gave man one hundred and twenty years to repent. God warned man, apparently through Noah: His grace would flow upon the earth for 120 years more, then judgment would fall unless man repented. God would give man one last chance.

> **"Knowing this first, that there shall come in the last days scoffers, walking after their own lusts, and saying, Where is the promise of his coming? for since the fathers fell asleep, all things continue as they were from the beginning of the creation....But, beloved, be not ignorant of this one thing, that one day is with the Lord as a thousand years, and a thousand years as one day" (2 Pe.3:3-4, 8-9).**
> **"Which sometime were disobedient, when once the longsuffering of God waited in the days of Noah, while the ark was a preparing, wherein few, that is, eight souls were saved by water" (1 Pe.3:20).**
> **"For my name's sake will I defer mine anger, and for my praise will I refrain for thee, that I cut thee not off" (Is.48:9).**

---

3 (6:4) **Lawlessness—Sin—Robbery—Thieves—Attackers—Civilization—Society**: the third fact—man became lawless as well as immoral in developing the first society upon earth. The word *giants* (nephilim) means "fallers, apostates from true religion"; "falling on men with violence"; "strong and robust in body, and leaders of others."[9] H.C. Leupold says that the word "giants" is probably based upon the Hebrew root *naphal*, meaning to fall upon and attack. The word, therefore, refers both to the strong of the earth such as the leaders and the powerful, and to the attackers, robbers, and bandits of the earth..[10] Simply stated...

- the earth had become a place where sex, immorality, and the flesh were focused upon (see note—Ge.6:1-2 for more discussion).
- the earth had become a place where the powerful and the strong ruled and dominated.
- the earth had become lawless, full of attackers, robbers, and bandits. The earth was filled with violence.
- the earth had become a place where the powerful and immoral and even the lawless were the famous of the earth, the very people who were well known and idolized. The powerful, strong, and immoral were the heros of the day, the people most admired and esteemed.

Thought 1. Think how much our society is like the first society of earth.
⇒ Think of the cult of beauty and sex, the emphasis upon sex and the flesh today, how sex and the flesh dominate the media, advertisements, and the very thoughts and minds of people.
⇒ Think how the strong, powerful, unjust, and immoral rule today; how money, wealth, position, and might control the lives of people all over the world.
⇒ Think how lawless so many societies have become, full of attackers, robbers, and bandits. Think how lawless and uncontrolled people become even when some natural disaster has stricken an area and the local residents are suffering. We live in a day of lawlessness and violence.
⇒ Think how the powerful and immoral and even some of the lawless have become the famous of the earth, the idols of society. The person may be the most immoral person imaginable—have had several husbands or wives, be a heavy drinker, adulterer, and drug user—but if he or she holds some high position, has money, or is featured in films or sports, the person is built up in the media, made famous and idolized by many.
⇒ Think how many film stars, athletes, and leaders within the world live immoral and unjust lives; yet they are the giants, the famous and the idols of the earth. Even some believers—carnal believers—hold them in the highest esteem.

---

[8] H.C. Leupold. *Genesis*, Vol.1, p.255.
[9] William Wilson. *Wilson's Old Testament Word Studies*, p.185.
[10] H.C. Leupold. *Genesis*, Vol.1, p.258.

Thought 2. The lawlessness and immorality of man is spelled out in Scripture, clearly spelled out. This is the true condition of society and civilization. Just think of the newscasts that come across our screens and the headlines that dominate the front pages of our newspapers every day. The following is God's indictment against man, against the lawless and immoral society man has developed:

> **"As it is written, There is none righteous, no, not one: there is none that understandeth, there is none that seeketh after God. They are all gone out of the way, they are together become unprofitable; there is none that doeth good, no, not one. Their throat is an open sepulchre; with their tongues they have used deceit; the poison of asps is under their lips: whose mouth is full of cursing and bitterness: their feet are swift to shed blood: destruction and misery are in their ways: and the way of peace have they not known: there is no fear of God before their eyes"** (Ro.3:10-18; see Ro.1:18-32).

> **"Now the works of the flesh are manifest, which are these; Adultery, fornication, uncleanness, lasciviousness, idolatry, witchcraft, hatred, variance, emulations, wrath, strife, seditions, heresies, envyings, murders, drunkenness, revellings, and such like: of the which I tell you before, as I have also told you in time past, that they which do such things shall not inherit the kingdom of God"** (Ga.5:19-21).

> **"This know also, that in the last days perilous times shall come. For men shall be lovers of their own selves, covetous, boasters, proud, blasphemers, disobedient to parents, unthankful, unholy, without natural affection, trucebreakers, false accusers, incontinent, fierce, despisers of those that are good, traitors, heady, highminded, lovers of pleasures more than lovers of God; having a form of godliness, but denying the power thereof: from such turn away"** (2 Ti.3:1-5).

4 (6:5) **Depravity—Sin—Wickedness—Man—Heart—Thoughts—Imaginations**: the fourth fact—God saw man's wickedness upon the earth.

a. God saw that man's wickedness was great upon the earth. By great is meant that man's wickedness *multiplied*. Man committed more and more sin, more and more acts of wickedness. Society was not getting better, not becoming more and more righteous and godly; society was becoming more lawless and crime-ridden. Lawlessness and crime, immorality and corruption were increasing more and more every year, not decreasing. The wickedness of man had swept the earth—swept every place where man was. (How much like today!)

But *great wickedness* does not only mean that sin multiplied, it also means that sin became more *extreme and terrible*. Sin became…

- more mean and vile
- more immoral and perverse
- more destructive and terrifying
- more evil and devilish
- more fleshly and carnal

- more lustful and sensual
- more obscene and flagrant
- more filthy and foul
- more gross and heinous

Since Adam's fall into sin, man had become exceedingly sinful and more and more bold in his sin. Man was now committing *great wickedness* upon the earth, and God saw man's great wickedness. But God saw something else about man as well.

b. God saw that every imagination and thought of man was evil—evil continually—evil all the time. In other words, God saw that man was depraved, totally depraved.

What does Scripture mean by this? Does it mean that man never does anything that is good? No! For we know that man does many things that are good. Man often shows mercy and compassion, and he often works to build up the good of society. Total depravity means at least three things.

⇒ Man has a sinful nature; therefore, he fails and sins. Man cannot keep from sinning and doing wicked things. No matter how much man tries not to fail and sin, he will still find himself failing and sinning ever so often.

⇒ Man is short of perfection; therefore, man comes short in everything he does. Man can do nothing perfectly, not with absolute perfection.

⇒ Man has a corrupt nature; therefore, he contaminates, pollutes, sours, spoils, and hurts whatever he does or touches.

The excellent expositor James Montgomery Boice says this:

> *When we say that men and women are "totally depraved" (a good theological term for "only evil all the time"), we do not mean to say that they never do anything that we would call good or that they never have aspirations in the direction of real good. We mean rather that even their best is always spoiled by their essentially sinful nature.*[11]

Now, to the point. In God's eyes, man's heart was evil, and note: it was *only evil*; that is, it was corrupted and contaminated and short of perfection. Anything short of perfection is evil: it stands opposed to God and His perfection.

In addition, the very imaginations and thoughts of man were continually evil. Man's mind was flooded with thoughts and imaginations that were…

- self-centered and self-seeking
- self-exalting and prideful
- covetous and full of greed
- condemning and judgmental

- bitter and hateful
- despiteful and vengeful
- violent and destructive
- sexual and immoral

---

[11] James Montgomery Boice. *Genesis*, Vol.1, p.252.

- negative and attacking
- suspicious and unbelieving
- lustful and sensual
- fleshly and obscene

On and on the list could go, covering the unending flow of evil thoughts and imaginations that flash across man's mind every day of his life. The mind is never still, never without thought, most likely thousands of thoughts within every twenty-four hour period. How many of the thousands of thoughts are negative and evil within a day? How many are short of perfection? Tens? Hundreds? Only God knows. But this much we know: our minds are bombarded with negative and evil thoughts every day of our lives. They constantly attack us and we cannot stop them. This does not mean that we never think good thoughts. We do, and we know this. But we also know—if we think about it and are honest—that evil and negative thoughts often flood across our minds. This is what God saw: He saw the thoughts and imaginations of man, that they were evil continually.

Note one other fact as well: a man's heart controls the kind of thoughts he has. If his heart is set on good things, he will think more good thoughts than he does evil and negative thoughts. He will never be completely free of the negative thoughts, for he has a sinful nature. But, as stated, he will think more good thoughts than evil thoughts. What a man must do is make sure his heart is good, that it follows after God and is focused upon God and the things of God. But this was the very problem of the first civilization and society upon earth: the people rejected God. They ignored, neglected, denied, and rebelled against God. Their hearts—their very thoughts and imaginations—were set on the things of the flesh and of the world. They wanted their fleshly desires satisfied and they wanted to get all the possessions and positions of this world they could. Again, this is what God saw: He saw the thoughts and imaginations of men, that they were given over to evil, continually given over to fleshly desires and covetousness.

> **"For they [wise words, God's Word] are life unto those that find them, and health to all their flesh" (Pr.4:22).**
>
> **"But those things which proceed out of the mouth come forth from the heart; and they defile the man. For out of the heart proceed evil thoughts, murders, adulteries, fornications, thefts, false witness, blasphemies: these are the things which defile a man" (Mt.15:18-20).**
>
> **"A good man out of the good treasure of his heart bringeth forth that which is good; and an evil man out of the evil treasure of his heart bringeth forth that which is evil: for of the abundance of the heart his mouth speaketh" (Lu.6:45).**

Thought 1. The condition of the human heart is tragic. Jesus Christ had much to say about the evil nature of man. Note how forceful and revealing His statements are. (This thought is taken from a message presented by Roger R. Nicole as given by James Montgomery Boice.)

⇒ Man is just like the salt that has lost its savor (Mt.5:13).
⇒ Man is just like a corrupt tree that produces corrupt fruit (Mt.7:17).
⇒ Man is evil (Lu.11:13).
⇒ Man is an "evil and adulterous generation," a wicked generation (Mt.12:39, 45).
⇒ Man has a heart that produces evil thoughts, adulteries, fornications, murders, thefts, covetousness, wickedness, deceit, an evil eye, blasphemy, pride, foolishness—a host of evil things (Mk.7:21-23).
⇒ Man has a hard heart, so hard that God has had to grant some permissive commandments in dealing with man (Mt.19:8).
⇒ Man is not good; in fact, there is none good but God (Mk.10:18).
⇒ Man, even the most ethical, religious, and upper class, can be compared to wicked servants (Mt.21:33-41).
⇒ Man is at best a hypocrite, even the most ethical and religious of men (Mt.23:2-39).
⇒ Man is depraved and passes on his depravity from birth to birth: "That which is born of the flesh is flesh" (Jn.3:6).
⇒ Man is unwilling to respond to Christ and His offer of eternal life: "Ye will not come to me that ye might have life" (Jn.5:40).
⇒ Man does not have the love of God in him (Jn.5:42).
⇒ Man rejects God's Son, Jesus Christ, and refuses to receive Him (Jn.5:43).
⇒ Man does not believe the Holy Scriptures, God's very own Word to man (Jn.5:47).
⇒ Man's works within the world are evil (Jn.7:7).
⇒ No man keeps the law (Jn.7:19).
⇒ Man shall die in his sins (Jn.8:21).
⇒ Man is from beneath, not from above (Jn.8:23).
⇒ Man's father is not God, but the devil, who is a murderer and a liar (Jn.8:38, 44).
⇒ Man is not of God, not of the nature of God (Jn.8:47).
⇒ Man is not of the sheep of God's Son, not a follower of Christ (Jn.10:26).
⇒ Man hates Christ and hates His Father (Jn.15:23-25).
⇒ Man is blind and he is leading the blind (Mt.15:14).
⇒ Man is condemned already because he does not believe God's Son (Jn.3:18).
⇒ Man loves darkness because his deeds are evil (Jn.3:19).
⇒ Man can be freed from darkness only if he follows Christ (Jn.8:12).
⇒ Man cannot see nor enter the kingdom of God unless he is born again (Jn.3:3, 5).
⇒ Man is so sinful that he must pray daily for God to forgive his sins (Mt.6:12).
⇒ Man is so diseased by sin that he must confess his condition before the physician (God) can heal him (Mt.9:12).
⇒ Man is deeply burdened and heavy laden (Mt.11:28).[12]

---

[12] Roger R. Nicole as given by James Montgomery Boice. *Genesis,* Vol.1, pp.253-254.

5 (6:6-7) **Judgment—God—Man**: the fifth fact—God grieves over man and condemns man. Two significant facts need to be noted.

a. God regrets that He ever made man. The Hebrew word for *grieved* or *repented* (yinnahem) means to pant, groan, lament, or grieve because of the misery of others or of oneself (*The Pulpit Commentary*, Vol.1, p.104). In this case, God grieved over man, that He had ever made man. How could God ever regret that He had made man?

⇒ Because man was bringing sin into the universe, multiplying the misery, pain, destruction, devastation, injury, and death that sin causes for man and the universe.

⇒ Because man's wickedness was cutting the heart of God and grieving Him just like a disobedient child cuts and grieves the heart of his father. God's heart was broken over the misery and pain man was causing by his wickedness.

⇒ Because man was arousing the holiness and wrath of God against sin. God is love and His love reaches out to man. But God is also holy and His holiness has to act even as His love acts. God's holiness has to strike out against injustices and immoralities—against all wickedness—in order to protect the name of God. God has to protect His name, that He is truly God, the Just One and the Loving One, the Sovereign Lord of the universe who is perfect in love and justice. Being perfect, God has to correct all the injustices and wrongs of the earth. Consequently, He had to judge and condemn man for his wickedness. This grieved God to the depths of His heart—so much so that He wished He had not made man.

⇒ Because man was condemning himself, cutting himself off and separating himself from God forever, dooming himself to spend eternity in hell apart from God. This was not the purpose for which God had made man, thus God regretted that He had ever made man.

In the words of Matthew Henry:

> *Here is…God's resentment of man's wickedness. He did not see it as an unconcerned spectator, but as one injured and affronted by it; he saw it as a tender father sees the folly and stubbornness of a rebellious and disobedient child, which not only angers him, but grieves him, and makes him wish he had been written childless.*[13]

Thought 1. Matthew Henry also points out these facts.

⇒ God is *pressed* by the sins of man

"Behold, I am pressed under you, as a cart is pressed that is full of sheaves" (Am. 2:13).

⇒ God is *wearied* by man's sins.

"Thou hast wearied me with thine iniquities" (Is.43:24).

⇒ God is broken by man's sins.

"I am broken with their whorish heart, which hath departed from me, and with their eyes, which go a whoring after their idols: and they shall loathe themselves for the evils which they committed in all their abominations" (Eze.6:9).

⇒ God is grieved by man's sins.

"Forty years long was I grieved with this generation, and said, It is a people that do err in their heart, and they have not known my ways" (Ps.95:10).

⇒ God is grieved to the depths of His heart with man's sins.[14]

"And it repented the LORD that he had made man on the earth, and it grieved him at his heart" (Ge.6:6).

b. God judged and condemned man to be destroyed—wiped off the face of the earth—both man and land animals. The Hebrew word for destroy is descriptive: it means…

• to blot out as a writer blots out words he wants removed
• to wipe off as dust is wiped off furniture

God determined to blot out man, to wipe him off the face of the earth. But remember why:

1) The great wickedness of man had multiplied and become extreme and terrible, so much so that man and his wickedness was no longer bearable (Ge.6:5).

2) Man was God's creature, the most noble and dignified creature ever created, but man abused God's love and purpose in creating him. Man rebelled against God: he rejected God's love and purpose in creation. Man chose to reject, ignore, neglect, and deny God, his Creator. We must always remember the business of creation, the self-evident truths:

⇒ When something is created, it must fulfill its purpose or else it is thrown aside as useless and destroyed.

⇒ If man does not serve God—fulfill God's purpose for creating him—then God has no choice: God has to destroy man, for man is useless to the purpose of God.

⇒ Man cannot expect God to excuse him when man neglects, ignores, denies, and rejects God. Being a creature of God does not excuse the wickedness and rebellion of the creature.

⇒ If the creature (man) rejects the love and grace of God, then he must face the justice of God.

---

13 *Matthew Henry's Commentary*, Vol.1, p.53.
14 Ibid., p.53.

Note that all land creatures were also to be destroyed with man. Why? Because the earth and animals were created for man: they existed for man. Therefore, when man was destroyed, they were also destroyed. They were not destroyed willingly, but by reason of man, because of his wickedness. (How much like today! How many animals and species of animals are killed because of man's pollution and sport—all out of greed and pride.)

"Shall not the Judge of all the earth do right?" (Ge.18:25).

"I the LORD search the heart, I try the reins, even to give every man according to his ways, and according to the fruit of his doings" (Je.17:10).

"He cometh to judge the earth: he shall judge the world with righteousness, and the people with his truth" (Ps.96:13).

"I said in mine heart, God shall judge the righteous and the wicked: for there is a time there for every purpose and for every work" (Ec.3:17).

"For the Son of man shall come in the glory of his Father with his angels; and then he shall reward every man according to his works" (Mt.16:27).

"And as it is appointed unto men once to die, but after this the judgment" (He.9:27).

"The Lord knoweth how to deliver the godly out of temptations, and to reserve the unjust unto the day of judgment to be punished" (2 Pe.2:9).

"And Enoch also, the seventh from Adam, prophesied of these [false teachers], saying, Behold, the Lord cometh with ten thousands of his saints, to execute judgment upon all, and to convince all that are ungodly among them of all their ungodly deeds which they have ungodly committed, and of all their hard speeches which ungodly sinners have spoken against him" (Jude 14-15).

"And I saw the dead, small and great, stand before God; and the books were opened: and another book was opened, which is the book of life: and the dead were judged out of those things which were written in the books, according to their works" (Re.20:12).

6 (6:8) **Grace—Salvation—Seed, Godly**: the sixth fact—God remembered His grace; He preserved Noah. God could not forget or violate His promise. God had just pronounced His judgment upon the terrible wickedness of men: man was to be wiped off the face of the earth. But God had promised from the beginning—promised to Adam and Eve—*a godly seed of believers* through whom a Savior would come and deliver man from the sin and death of this earth. The Savior was to restore man to his original world of perfection and to live face-to-face in fellowship with God. If God was going to destroy the earth, who would carry on the godly line of believers so that the Savior could be born? Who would God save through the destruction of the world in order to carry on the godly line?

There was one man who would remain true to God up until the day of his death. That man was Noah. "Noah found grace in the eyes of the Lord" (v.8). What does this mean? It means that Noah believed God's promise concerning the godly seed, the coming Savior. Noah believed that God was going to preserve a godly people and send the Savior through that people. Therefore, God showered His grace and His favor upon Noah. God had mercy upon Noah and chose Noah to be the person to be saved through the coming judgment. Noah's *faith in the promise of God—his faith in the coming Savior—saved him*. Noah was saved "by grace through faith" in the coming Savior (Ep.2:8-9). "Noah found grace in the eyes of the Lord" because he believed God, believed God's promise of salvation through *the promised seed*, the coming Savior.

Note: this is the first time *grace* or *favor* is mentioned in the Bible.

Thought 1. Every person is saved just like Noah was: by the grace of God through faith in *the promised seed*, the Savior, the Lord Jesus Christ.

"For by grace are ye saved through faith; and that not of yourselves: it is the gift of God: not of works, lest any man should boast" (Ep.2:8-9).

"For God so loved the world, that he gave his only begotten Son, that whosoever believeth in him should not perish, but have everlasting life" (Jn.3:16).

"But we believe that through the grace of the Lord Jesus Christ we shall be saved" (Ac.15:11).

"Being justified freely by his grace through the redemption that is in Christ Jesus" (Ro.3:24).

"For the grace of God that bringeth salvation hath appeared to all men" (Tit.2:11).

"Not by works of righteousness which we have done, but according to his mercy he saved us, by the washing of regeneration, and renewing of the Holy Ghost; which he shed on us abundantly through Jesus Christ our Savior; that being justified by his grace, we should be made heirs according to the hope of eternal life" (Tit.3:5-7).

DIVISION IV

NOAH: THE MAN CHOSEN TO PRESERVE MANKIND AND THE GODLY SEED THROUGH WORLD DESTRUCTION (THE FLOOD), 6:9–9:29

(6:9–9:29) **DIVISION OVERVIEW: Noah—Seed, Godly**: this Scripture begins a new section of *Genesis*. It covers the generation of Noah: this is the record, the history, the story of Noah.

Remember how wicked man had become. Man had made the earth a cesspool of immorality and a society of lawlessness and violence (see Ge.6:1-2, 4-5, 11). Man was living to fulfill the desires and lusts of his flesh, living for the cult of beauty and sex, living for money, possessions, position, power, recognition, and honor. Man had forgotten God altogether and was living only for himself and self-gratification. Man was not fulfilling his purpose for being upon the earth. In fact, man was working against the very purpose for which God had created him. Man was destroying both the earth and himself. He was standing opposed to God and to everything God stood for and had purposed for the earth. God had no choice; God had to destroy man, to wipe man off the face of the earth.

But what about God's promise? God had promised that there would always be a *godly line* of people upon the earth, a godly line through whom He could send the Savior to the world. How could God destroy man and the earth and still fulfill His promise? There was only one way: God had to choose one man and his family and save them through the destruction of the earth. This is what this section of Scripture is all about: this is the history of Noah. Noah and his family were the people chosen by God to survive the destruction of the earth, the people chosen to preserve mankind and the *godly line* of believers through world destruction.

This section of Scripture is the record of the great flood that covered the earth, the account of God's judgment upon man—all because of his great wickedness, his terrible, gross wickedness. But this is also the story of a courageous man, perhaps the most courageous man who has ever lived. This is the story of a man who stood toe to toe with the rest of the world, who stood faithful to God when everyone else—all of humanity—turned against God. Imagine standing all alone against the whole world. This was Noah. Noah stood for God when everyone else forsook and denied God and went their own way in life, rejecting the way of God.

Again, this is the generation—the history and story—of *Noah: The Man Chosen to Preserve Mankind and the Godly Seed Through World Destruction (The Flood)* (Ge.6:9-9:29).

NOAH: THE MAN CHOSEN TO PRESERVE MANKIND AND THE GODLY SEED THROUGH WORLD DESTRUCTION (THE FLOOD), 6:9–9:29

A. Noah and the Rest of Mankind: A Great Contrast of Character—Why God Destroyed the Earth, 6:9-12

B. Noah and the Ark: God's Great Demand for Faith—What Noah Had to Believe, 6:13-22

C. Noah and the Last Week: God's Great Invitation and Noah's Great Obedience, 7:1-9

D. Noah and the Flood: God's Great Judgment of the Earth, 7:10-24

E. Noah and God: God's Great Preservation (Salvation) of Life, 8:1-14

F. Noah and the Great Day: God Sent Noah Forth into the World to Begin a New Life, 8:15-22

G. Noah and the New Beginning (Part 1): God Established a New World Order for Man, 9:1-7

H. Noah and the New Beginning (Part 2): God Established a New Covenant with Man—The Noahic Covenant, 9:8-17

I. Noah and the Human Race: The Future of the Human Race Foretold, 9:18-29

		man and perfect in his generations, and Noah walked with God.	b. He was perfect or blameless
	IV. NOAH: THE MAN CHOSEN TO PRESERVE MANKIND & THE GODLY SEED THROUGH WORLD DESTRUCTION (THE FLOOD), 6:9–9:29		c. He walked with God
			d. He reared a godly family
		10 And Noah begat three sons, Shem, Ham, and Japheth.	
	A. Noah & the Rest of Mankind: A Great Contrast of Character—Why God Destroyed the Earth, 6:9-12	11 The earth also was corrupt before God, and the earth was filled with violence.	2. The character of mankind
			a. Man was corrupt
			b. Man had filled the earth with violence
		12 And God looked upon the earth, and, behold, it was corrupt; for all flesh had corrupted his way upon the earth.	c. Man was seen by God
			d. Man had corrupted his way upon earth
1. The character of Noah a. He was just or righteous	9 These are the generations of Noah: Noah was a just		

DIVISION IV

NOAH: THE MAN CHOSEN TO PRESERVE MANKIND AND THE GODLY SEED THROUGH WORLD DESTRUCTION (THE FLOOD), 6:9–9:29

A. Noah and the Rest of Mankind: A Great Contrast of Character—Why God Destroyed the Earth, 6:9-12

(6:9-12) **Introduction**: note the great contrast between Noah and the rest of the earth.
⇒ Noah was just and perfect and he walked with God.
⇒ The rest of the earth was corrupt and violent, so much so that the earth was "filled with violence" (v.11). All the people—not just most, but all—had corrupted their way upon the earth (v.12).

This is why God destroyed the earth and why Noah and his family alone were saved. This is the message of this descriptive passage: *Noah and the Rest of Mankind: A Great Contrast of Character—Why God Destroyed the Earth.*
1. The character of Noah (vv.9-10).
   a. He was just or righteous.
   b. He was perfect or blameless.
   c. He walked with God.
   d. He reared a godly family.
2. The character of mankind (vv.11-12).
   a. Man was corrupt.
   b. Man had filled the earth with violence.
   c. Man was seen by God.
   d. Man had corrupted his way upon earth.

1 (6:9-10) **Noah—Just—Righteous—Perfect—Walk, Spiritual—Family**: the character of Noah was very distinctive: he was a distinguished and noble man. Noah rose head and shoulders above the people of his day, not in their eyes, but in God's eyes. The people of Noah's day, no doubt, despised and persecuted him. Noah's life and preaching bothered them just like the life and preaching of any godly person bothers the ungodly who surround him (see 2 Pe.2:5). The ungodly did not live righteous and pure lives; consequently, they did not want to be around Noah nor around his preaching. The righteousness and purity of his life and words pricked their consciences and convicted their hearts. It reminded them that they were wicked, living immoral and lawless lives. In their eyes, Noah was a fanatic, perhaps bordering on insanity. In such an ungodly environment, people would be mocking and making him the subject of their jokes. Some persons would even try to stop him and hush him up, some through gentle persuasion, others by threats. But Scripture is clear: Noah endured all the persecution; he remained faithful and loyal to God, courageously so. Scripture gives four strong traits of Noah's character.
a. Noah was *just or righteous* (tsaddiq). The Hebrew word means two things.
   1) To be *just or righteous* means to be justified before God, to be counted righteous by God. How is a person justified or counted righteous by God? Scripture is always clear about this: by really believing in the promised Savior, the Lord Jesus Christ. Noah believed the promise of God: he believed that God would send *the promised seed,* the Savior, into the world to save those who truly follow God.
   Note: this is the first time the word "just" or "righteous" is used in the Bible. Others before Noah were just or righteous, but this is the first time the word is used by Scripture. Remember also that the word *grace* was first used in referring to Noah. Noah is the person with whom both words, *grace* and *righteous,* are first used:
   ⇒ "Noah found grace in the eyes of the Lord" (v.8).
   ⇒ "Noah was a just [or righteous] man" (v.9).

As stated earlier, Noah's faith in the promise of God—his faith in the coming Savior—saved him. Noah was saved "by grace through faith" in the coming Savior (Ep.2:8-9). "Noah found grace in the eyes of the Lord"

248

because he believed God, believed God's promise of salvation through the coming Savior. Noah believed God, believed God's promise; therefore...

- God took Noah's belief and counted it as righteousness, counted it as his justification
- God took Noah's faith and counted it as his acceptance and approval before God

> **"By faith Noah, being warned of God of things not seen as yet, moved with fear, prepared an ark to the saving of his house; by the which he condemned the world, and became heir of the righteousness which is by faith" (He.11:7).**
> **"And he believed in the LORD; and he counted it to him for righteousness" (Ge.15:6).**
> **"Therefore being justified by faith, we have peace with God through our Lord Jesus Christ" (Ro.5:1).**
> **"Even as Abraham believed God, and it was accounted to him for righteousness" (Ga.3:6).**
> **"For by grace are ye saved through faith; and that not of yourselves: it is the gift of God: not of works, lest any man should boast" (Ep.2:8-9).**

2) To be *just or righteous* also means to live a righteous life and to treat others in a fair and just way. It means to be upright, honest, and virtuous; to be right in relation to the law (*The Pulpit Commentary*, Vol.1, pp.107-108). To be *just or righteous* means to obey God's law, to do what God says, to keep God's commandments, to live a righteous, pure, clean, and moral life; to be just and fair to others; to never cheat, steal, lie, or deceive others. Noah lived a just and righteous life, both before God and man.

> **Thought 1.** It is not enough to claim that we are saved, justified, and accepted by God. It is not enough to believe that God accepts us, that He would never reject and condemn us—not in the final analysis. Too many of us believe this, and we are wrong. Why? How can we say this? Because we must not only profess God, we must also live lives that are *just* and *righteous* before God and man. We must live what we profess. If we profess to follow God and do not keep His commandments, we lie. We are not just nor righteous. We have a false profession; we are hypocrites.

> > **"For I say unto you, That except your righteousness shall exceed the righteousness of the scribes and Pharisees, ye shall in no case enter into the kingdom of heaven" (Mt.5:20).**
> > **"Awake to righteousness, and sin not; for some have not the knowledge of God: I speak this to your shame" (1 Co.15:34).**
> > **"And this I pray, that your love may abound yet more and more in knowledge and in all judgment; that ye may approve things that are excellent; that ye may be sincere and without offence till the day of Christ; being filled with the fruits of righteousness, which are by Jesus Christ, unto the glory and praise of God" (Ph.1:9-11).**
> > **"Break off thy sins by righteousness, and thine iniquities by showing mercy to the poor; if it may be a lengthening of thy tranquility" (Da.4:27).**
> > **"Sow to yourselves in righteousness, reap in mercy; break up your fallow ground: for it is time to seek the LORD, till he come and rain righteousness upon you" (Ho.10:12).**

b. Noah was perfect or blameless among his generation of people (v.9). The Hebrew word for *perfect* or *blameless* (tamim) does not mean sinless perfection. It means to be without blemish, blameless before others; to be moral, a person of purity and integrity, of honesty; to be whole, complete, and sound in all of life, a person with a pure and strong self-image.

⇒ Noah was a complete believer, a whole, sound believer. He was just what he should be in every area of life. He did not come up short in any area of life. He was everything that God wanted in a person.
⇒ Noah was without blemish, blameless before others. When others looked at Noah, they saw a moral, pure person and a man of integrity, honesty, and truthfulness. The world saw a person who lived just what he professed.

> **Thought 1.** Imagine being everything that God wants a person to be! Are you? Am I? Are we complete and mature believers—complete and mature in every area of life? Are we blameless in the eyes of God and of the world? Persons of morality and integrity? Or, do we have blemishes?

> > **"That ye may be blameless and harmless, the sons of God, without rebuke, in the midst of a crooked and perverse nation, among whom ye shine as lights in the world" (Ph.2:15).**
> > **"In the body of his flesh through death, to present you holy and unblameable and unreproveable in his sight: if ye continue in the faith grounded and settled, and be not moved away from the hope of the gospel, which ye have heard, and which was preached to every creature which is under heaven; whereof I Paul am made a minister" (Col.1:22-23).**
> > **"And the Lord make you to increase and abound in love one toward another, and toward all men, even as we do toward you: to the end he may stablish your hearts unblameable in holiness before God, even our Father, at the coming of our Lord Jesus Christ with all his saints" (1 Th.3:12-13).**
> > **"And the very God of peace sanctify you wholly; and I pray God your whole spirit and soul and body be preserved blameless unto the coming of our Lord Jesus Christ" (1 Th.5:23).**
> > **"Wherefore, beloved, seeing that ye look for such things, be diligent that ye may be found of him in peace, without spot, and blameless" (2 Pe.3:14).**

c. Noah *walked with God* (v.9). This is the second time a person is said to have walked with God. Enoch was the first; Noah is the second (see note—Ge.5:21-24 for discussion).

d. Noah reared a godly family (v.10). Why is Noah's bearing three sons being repeated here (see Ge.5:32)? To stress that Noah's godly life had an influence upon his family. The point is this:

⇒ Noah was godly (v.9).
⇒ Noah had three sons whom he reared in the ways of God (v.10).

This is clearly seen in what follows: God saved the whole family of Noah (Ge.6:18; 7:1, 7, 14; 8:16, 18). The whole family were apparently believers. The whole family was chosen by God to preserve the human race.

Note this: when Noah was born, five of his grandfathers and great grandfathers were still living, and they were all godly men. (See DEEPER STUDY # 2, *Chart*—Ge.5:27-32 for more discussion.)

- Enosh
- Cainan
- Mahalaleel
- Jared
- Methuselah
- Lamech, Noah's father

The godly influence, preaching, and teaching of these men were bound to have a great impact upon Noah. He had a strong heritage in the ways of the Lord. It was only natural that Noah rear his children to trust and follow God.

Remember also, Noah was "a preacher of righteousness" (2 Pe.2:5). His family heard him preach time and again: they saw and heard him proclaim the righteousness and judgment of God to the ungodly of their day. As with any genuine minister, Noah taught the truth of God to his family as well as to the people of the earth.

> **Thought 1.** Noah sets a dynamic example for us in the rearing of our children. We must rear them to know God and to follow after God with all of their hearts.
>
> > "**Only take heed to thyself, and keep thy soul diligently, lest thou forget the things which thine eyes have seen, and lest they depart from thy heart all the days of thy life: but teach them thy sons, and thy sons' sons**" **(De.4:9).**
> >
> > "**And these words, which I command thee this day, shall be in thine heart: and thou shalt teach them diligently unto thy children, and shalt talk of them when thou sittest in thine house, and when thou walkest by the way, and when thou liest down, and when thou risest up**" **(De.6:6-7).**
> >
> > "**Train up a child in the way he should go: and when he is old, he will not depart from it**" **(Pr.22:6).**
> >
> > "**Whom shall he teach knowledge? and whom shall he make to understand doctrine? them that are weaned from the milk, and drawn from the breasts**" **(Is.28:9).**
> >
> > "**And, ye fathers, provoke not your children to wrath: but bring them up in the nurture and admonition of the Lord**" **(Ep.6:4).**
> >
> > "**One that ruleth well his own house, having his children in subjection with all gravity**" **(1 Ti.3:4).**
> >
> > "**That they may teach the young women to be sober, to love their husbands, to love their children**" **(Tit.2:4).**

2 (6:11-12) **Earth—Man—Sin—Violence—Corruption:** the character of mankind was terrible and tragic. The picture is that of the whole earth sitting there "before God" (v.11), and God looks upon the earth and sees a terrible scene: the whole earth is corrupt and filled with violence. All flesh—all mankind—had corrupted their way before God. No one was living a holy and godly life. Note that the word "earth" means *mankind*. Man had become so earthly—he had defiled the earth so much—that he could be referred to as the earth:

⇒ "The earth...was corrupt" (v.11).
⇒ "The earth was filled with violence" (v.11).
⇒ "God looked upon the earth" (v.12).
⇒ "It [the earth] was corrupt" (v.12).

Remember: man had received the earth as a gift from God, but now man had abused and defiled his heritage.

What an indictment against man! To be so earthly, so unheavenly, that he would abuse and defile his heritage. Imagine! He had defiled the earth so much that he himself could be called *the earth*. Man's wickedness had spread so much that it now swept over the whole earth. Wherever man was, the earth was defiled and corrupted. Four things are said about mankind's character during this period of early history.

a. Mankind was corrupt before God. This refers back to what was covered earlier: mankind became worldly and immoral and fed their minds upon the cult of beauty and sex (see note 1—Ge.6:1-2 for discussion).

b. Mankind filled the earth with violence, with senseless attacks and killings. They became lawless as well as immoral (see note—Ge.6:4 for discussion).

c. Mankind was seen by God. God saw all of the corruption and violence of man. Nothing was hid from his eyes. He knew that man had gone too far and now needed to be judged and wiped off the face of the earth (see note 4, pt.a.—Ge.6:5; 6:6-7 for discussion).

d. All mankind had corrupted their way upon earth (v.12). When God first created man, He laid before man *the way of godliness and of life*, both abundant and eternal life. But note what happened: mankind corrupted its way. They forsook the way of God and went their own way in life. They chose the way of corruption, the way...

- of pain and suffering in birth
- of birth defects and imperfections
- of stumbling about and falling into evil

- of accident and injury
- of sickness and disease
- of selfishness and greed
- of earthly position and honor that is ever so temporary
- of aging and dying

On and on the list could go. But note this: there were not just a few persons who corrupted their way upon earth, not just a few communities and cities of people. The whole earth, all mankind, corrupted their way. Every person was living an immoral and lawless life. Everyone was selfish and greedy, wanting more and more of the possessions and fleshly stimulations of this world. Everyone had turned away from God and was seeking after his own desires and pleasures.

Thought 1. Sin is universal. We all stand guilty before God. We have all forsaken the way of God and followed our own way of life.

"Help, LORD; for the godly man ceaseth; for the faithful fail from among the children of men" (Ps.12:1).
"Every one of them is gone back: they are altogether become filthy; there is none that doeth good, no, not one" (Ps.53:3).
"Who can say, I have made my heart clean, I am pure from my sin?" (Pr.20:9).
"All we like sheep have gone astray; we have turned every one to his own way; and the LORD hath laid on him the iniquity of us all" (Is.53:6).
"But we are all as an unclean thing, and all our righteousnesses are as filthy rags; and we all do fade as a leaf; and our iniquities, like the wind have taken us away" (Is.64:6).
"For all have sinned, and come short of the glory of God" (Ro.3:23).
"This know also, that in the last days perilous times shall come. For men shall be lovers of their own selves, covetous, boasters, proud, blasphemers, disobedient to parents, unthankful, unholy, without natural affection, trucebreakers, false accusers, incontinent, fierce, despisers of those that are good, traitors, heady, highminded, lovers of pleasures more than lovers of God; having a form of godliness, but denying the power thereof: from such turn away" (2 Ti.3:1-5).

	B. Noah & the Ark: God's Great Demand for Faith—What Noah Had to Believe, 6:13-22	do bring a flood of waters upon the earth, to destroy all flesh, wherein is the breath of life, from under heaven; and every thing that is in the earth shall die.	destruction—a flood of water

1. Belief 1: God's Word—God was going to destroy both man & the earth
  a. Destroy all the people & the earth itself
  b. The reason: Man had filled the earth with violence
	13 And God said unto Noah, The end of all flesh is come before me; for the earth is filled with violence through them; and behold, I will destroy them with the earth.	18 But with thee will I establish my covenant; and thou shalt come into the ark, thou, and thy sons, and thy wife, and thy sons' wives with thee.	4. Belief 4: God's promise of personal salvation
			  a. Eternally through a covenant
			  b. Immediately through the ark

2. Belief 2: God's command—build an ark in the middle of nowhere^{DS1}
  a. Its material: Cypress
  b. Its separate rooms
  c. Its waterproofing, v.14
  d. Its huge size & boxlike shape
	14 Make thee an ark of gopher wood; rooms shalt thou make in the ark, and shalt pitch it within and without with pitch.
	15 And this is the fashion which thou shalt make it of: The length of the ark shall be three hundred cubits, the breadth of it fifty cubits, and the height of it thirty cubits.
		19 And of every living thing of all flesh, two of every sort shalt thou bring into the ark, to keep them alive with thee; they shall be male and female.
		20 Of fowls after their kind, and of cattle after their kind, of every creeping thing of the earth after his kind, two of every sort shall come unto thee, to keep them alive.
			5. Belief 5: God's commission, the awesome task of saving two of every living animal upon earth
			  a. To bring them into the ark
			  b. To make sure one is male & one female

e. Its window: Served as ventilation & a lighting system
  f. Its door
 	
  g. Its height: Was three decks or stories high
	16 A window shalt thou make to the ark, and in a cubit shalt thou finish it above; and the door of the ark shalt thou set in the side thereof; with lower, second, and third stories shalt thou make it.	21 And take thou unto thee of all food that is eaten, and thou shalt gather it to thee; and it shall be for food for thee, and for them.
		22 Thus did Noah; according to all that God commanded him, so did he.
			c. To store enough food to feed all the animals & his own family

3. Belief 3: God's means of	17 And, behold, I, even I,	manded him, so did he.	6. Belief 6: God's way of salvation, a salvation that demands obedience

DIVISION IV

NOAH: THE MAN CHOSEN TO PRESERVE MANKIND AND THE GODLY SEED THROUGH WORLD DESTRUCTION (THE FLOOD), 6:9–9:29

B. Noah and the Ark: God's Great Demand for Faith—What Noah Had to Believe, 6:13-22

(6:13-22) **Introduction**: Noah lived in troublesome times, probably the most troublesome times in human history. Man had become corrupt and wicked: there was not a godly person left upon earth. Imagine! Only Noah and his dear family still believed and followed God.

The Bible says that Noah had *great faith*, so great that he is listed in the *The Bible's Great Hall of Fame* (see Heb.11:7). Just what Noah believed is discussed here in this passage of Scripture (Ge.6:13-22). The things God called upon Noah to believe are unbelievable, yet Noah did just that: he believed God. He believed what God said, accepted God's Word, and did what God commanded. This is the subject of this great passage of Scripture: *Noah and the Ark: God's Great Demand for Faith—What Noah Had to Believe.*

(Remember: Noah was apparently 480 years old when God confronted him and told him to build the ark (see note—Ge.7:5-9; see 6:13; 5:32, see 7:6).

1. Belief 1: God's Word—God was going to destroy both man and the earth (v.13).
2. Belief 2: God's command—build an ark in the middle of nowhere (vv.14-16).
3. Belief 3: God's means of destruction—a flood of water (v.17).
4. Belief 4: God's promise of personal salvation (v.18).
5. Belief 5: God's commission, the awesome task of saving two of every living animal upon earth (vv.19-21).
6. Belief 6: God's way of salvation, a salvation that demands obedience (v.22).

1 (6:13) **Judgment—Belief—God's Word**: first, Noah had to believe God's Word, that God was going to destroy both man and the earth. God said two things about the coming judgment.

a. God revealed that He was going to put an end to all people. He was going to destroy all mankind, both them and the earth. Picture God confronting and revealing this fact of judgment to Noah. Lying there in prayer, prostrate before God, Noah must have been stricken with utter terror. The picture of no life and no earth—total destruction—was bound to be a terrifying thought. Note the end of the verse where God reemphasized that judgment was coming: Noah must listen and heed the fact. Noah must prepare and do exactly what God said, for God—beyond all question—was going to destroy both mankind and the earth.

b. God revealed why He was going to destroy man: because man had filled the earth with violence (v.13). By violence is meant all the forms of sin and corruption that violate God and man. The first society and civilization upon earth were corrupt and filled with violence (Ge.6:1-7, 11-12). Not just most persons, but every person, had forsaken God and corrupted his way upon earth. Ungodliness was running wild: people were engaging in all forms of immoral and sexual misbehavior. They were living selfish lives, seeking and coveting more and more of this world and its possessions and pleasures. Lawlessness and violence were sweeping the earth: robbery, theft, assaults, and senseless killings were happening daily within every community.

> **"God looked upon the earth, and behold, it was corrupt; for all flesh [all mankind, every living person] had corrupted his way upon the earth" (v.12).**

Man was not taking care of the earth nor himself. He was not offering himself and the earth as a sacrifice to God, not following God nor praising and worshipping God. Man was not fulfilling his purpose for being upon earth. Contrariwise, he was corrupting himself and the earth, doing the very opposite of what God had purposed.

God had no choice: He had promised that *a godly line of believers* would always be upon earth, *a godly line* through whom He could send the Savior to the world. Therefore, man had to be wiped off the earth and a new beginning had to be made. But how? How could God wipe mankind off the earth and still fulfill His promise to save man? There was only one way: by choosing one man and his family and saving them through the destruction of the earth. That man was Noah.

Remember what we have already learned about Noah in the former passage of Scripture:
⇒ Noah was a godly man, a man who walked with God (v.9).
⇒ Noah and his family were the only godly people left upon earth.

Imagine being the only godly person upon earth! Standing all alone in one's confession of God, in worshipping and witnessing for God. Imagine not knowing another godly person upon earth, not a single person who worships and lives for God. Noah was a man of faith, a great man of faith. The first thing Noah had to believe was this: judgment was coming. God was going to destroy both man and the earth.

> **"And as it is appointed unto men once to die, but after this the judgment" (He.9:27).**
> **"The Lord knoweth how to deliver the godly out of temptations, and to reserve the unjust unto the day of judgment to be punished" (2 Pe.2:9).**
> **"He cometh to judge the earth: he shall judge the world with righteousness, and the people with his truth" (Ps.96:13).**

> **Thought 1.** There was a reason why God could wait no longer, why God had to go ahead and destroy the earth: there was only one godly family left. There was the possibility that this family could become influenced by the world and its ways and turn away from God, or that the worldly of the earth would react and kill Noah and his family because of his witness for God against their ungodly lives. Consequently God had to destroy the earth and save the family. God needed Noah and his family to carry on the godly line and to fulfill His promise to send the Savior to the world.

> **"The Lord is not slack concerning his promise, as some men count slackness; but is longsuffering to us-ward, not willing that any should perish, but that all should come to repentance" (2 Pe.3:9).**

2 (6:14-16) **Ark, The—Faith:** second, Noah had to believe God's command to build an ark in the middle of nowhere. Visualize one man building a boat the size of one and one half football fields—about 150 yards long—on the outskirts of some city out in the middle of nowhere. There was no seaport anyplace close by, no boat ramp by which the boat could slide down into the water, no way conceivable to ever get the huge boat into the water. Imagine what the neighbors and community would think and be saying about the man: "Strange, eccentric, queer, a fanatic," to say the least.

This was Noah. God's call to Noah was one of the most difficult calls ever issued a person. God had a great mission for Noah to carry out, but Noah would have to trust God completely and fully.
⇒ Noah would have to believe God's Word explicitly—accept exactly what God said.
⇒ Noah would have to obey God's Word, do every single thing that God said.

Simply stated, Noah would have to cast himself wholly upon God and His Word. If Noah did what God said, the world would think him strange, would ridicule and mock him. The world would not understand his behavior, why he was so fanatical about God and so against the pleasures and things of the world. Noah would have few, if any, friends throughout the world, except his own family. And even some of his family would most likely not understand him. Just think of the accusations and ridicule Noah suffered while he was building the boat and preaching the coming judgment and righteousness of God (2 Pe.2:5).

Was Noah willing to pay the price? Willing to give his life up totally to God, to obey and follow God's Word explicitly? Willing to do everything God said? Willing to carry out every single command?

Here is what God told Noah to do, and remember, this was the ancient world we are talking about. There were no modern ship building factories and no major seaports in the ancient world. God told Noah to build an ark, a huge structure. The specifications were exact and detailed.

a. The material was to be *gopher wood.* What kind of wood was this? We are not sure, but most Biblical scholars believe it was probably cypress, an evergreen tree which is very adaptable to ship building and is long-lasting when water-soaked. Some forms of cypress even grow in swamps.

b. The ark was to have some separate rooms, that is, cabins or areas, positioned off to the side (v.14). These, of course, would provide separate areas for the animals and food and provide living quarters for Noah and his family.

c. The ark was to be waterproofed by sealing the boards—both inside and outside—with pitch. This must have been some type of tar or asphalt material.

d. The ark was to be of enormous size. The exact measurement of a cubit or foot in that day is not known. But if we even take the smallest length of 18 inches for a cubit, the size of the ark would be equal to a modern ocean liner:

⇒ 150 yards long
⇒ 25 yards wide
⇒ 15 yards high

Note that the dimensions are box-shaped: the ark was a huge box-like structure built only to float, not maneuver, through the water.

e. The ark was to have an opening (tsohar, skylight) for ventilation and light. The opening was to be within 18 inches of the top; that is, the opening was to run all the way around the ark. (This is the meaning of the Hebrew according to H.C. Leupold.[1] The ark also had one or more hatch or drop-like windows (Ge.8:6). Note how adequately God provided for light and ventilation in the ark, both a skylight and windows. These, of course, would have been openings with wood partitions that could be either lifted up and braced or swung open on some kind of hinge.

f. The ark was to have only one door.

g. The ark was to have three decks, to be three stories high.

These were God's instructions to Noah: he was to build a huge ark—a mammoth box-like structure—in the middle of nowhere, in a place where there was no seaport. Again, was Noah willing to pay the price? Was he willing to believe God's Word, God's instructions? Imagine Noah prostrate on his face before God receiving these instructions. He was bound to be shocked at such an unbelievable command, stricken with all kinds of questions, amazed at receiving such incredible instructions from God. God, of course, knew all about Noah's emotional shock, all about the questions rambling through Noah's mind. And God knew how to meet Noah's need and how to answer the questions. Just what God had to say to Noah will be seen in the remaining notes of this passage. But for now, the point to see is the great faith that was being demanded of Noah, that Noah was being asked...

- to believe the unbelievable
- to do the incredible
- to accept God's Word at face value
- to obey God by standing up for God and His Word, by standing against the ridicule and mockery of the world

Thought 1. Several lessons can be learned from the command of God to build the ark.

1) We must believe God—accept His Word—no matter how incredible it may seem. We may be as Noah was bound to be—questioning and not understanding—but we must *trust and obey* God and His Word, all of His instructions to us.

2) The Hebrew word for *pitch* (kopher) is the same word for *atonement*. It means to *cover*. The picture is this:

⇒ The pitch sealed the ark and made it secure from the destruction and judgment that was to fall upon the earth. In this the pitch is a type or picture of Christ. The blood of Christ seals the believer against the destruction and judgment that every person has to face in the future. Christ bore the judgment of sin for us; He has paid the atonement—the sacrifice—for our sins.

"**For the life of the flesh is in the blood: and I have given it to you upon the altar to make an atonement for your souls: for it is the blood that maketh an atonement for the soul**" (Le.17:11).

"**And not only so, but we also joy in God through our Lord Jesus Christ, by whom we have now received the atonement**" (Ro.5:11).

3) The one door into the ark pictures this: there is only one way to God, only one door that leads to the safety and security of God's salvation. That way and that door is Jesus Christ, God's very own Son.

"**I am the door: by me if any man enter in, he shall be saved, and shall go in and out, and find pasture**" (Jn.10:9).

"**Jesus saith unto him, I am the way, the truth, and the life: no man cometh unto the Father, but by me**" (Jn.14:6).

"**Neither is there salvation in any other: for there is none other name under heaven given among men, whereby we must be saved**" (Ac.4:12).

"**By whom also we have access by faith into this grace wherein we stand, and rejoice in hope of the glory of God**" (Ro.5:2).

DEEPER STUDY # 1

(6:14-16) **Ark, The**: the ark was a box-like structure of enormous size. It was huge, built only to float, not to maneuver through the water. (See sketch on page 259.)

James Montgomery Boice says this about the ark:

---

[1] H.C. Leupold, *Genesis*, Vol.1, pp.271-272.

Several things can be said about these measurements to begin with. First, if this was the size of the ark, it was of great proportions, greater than the size of any ancient sailing vessel. In fact, it was not until 1858 that a vessel of greater length was constructed: the Great Eastern (692 by 83 by 30 feet). Second, it can be shown through simulated tests in water that a box-like structure of the ark's dimensions is exceedingly stable, indeed, almost impossible to capsize. Whatever our judgment about the carrying capacity of the ark, therefore, there is an obvious presumption in favor of the design having come from God. For how would Noah or anyone else at that time know how to construct such a large seaworthy craft except by revelation?

What about the "millions and millions" of species? There is some difficulty in determining what is meant by the biblical word "kind," as in "two of every kind of bird, of every kind of animal and of every kind of creature that moves along the ground" (v.20). If this corresponds to our modern classification of "family," the maximum number of families represented on the ark would be about seven hundred. But suppose the word actually corresponds to our word "species"? In that case, the number would be much higher—but not beyond the ark's capacity.

Tim LaHaye and John Morris in their book, The Ark on Ararat, cite the following table of the number of animal species put forward by Ernst Mayr, one of America's leading taxonomists.

Mammals	3,700
Birds	8,600
Reptiles	6,300
Amphibians	2,500
Fishes	20,600
Tunicates, etc.	1,325
Echinoderms	6,000
Arthropods	838,000
Mollusks	107,250
Worms, etc.	39,340
Coelenterates, etc.	5,380
Sponges	4,800
Protozoans	28,400
Total Animals	*1,072,300*

That is a large number, of course, but not all these species had to be on the ark. Obviously the fish did not. Nor did the tunicates, echinoderms, mollusks, coelenterates, sponges, protozoans, most arthropods, and most worms. Simple subtraction brings the previously large number down to approximately 35,000 or 70,000 individual animals, one male and one female. Moreover, although we usually think of large animals when we think of the ark (elephants, hippopotamuses, giraffes), most land animals are in fact quite small. The average size is less than that of a sheep. Since 240 sheep fit comfortably in an average size two-deck railroad car and since the volume of the ark would have been equal to 569 such cars, calculations show that the animals to be saved would have fit into approximately 50 percent of the ark's carrying capacity, leaving room for people, food, water, and whatever other provisions may have been necessary.

As LaHaye and Morris note, "Such simple calculations are certainly not beyond the abilities of the scoffers. What does seem to be beyond them is the willingness to try to see if the biblical story is feasible."[2,3]

3 (6:17) **Judgment—Flood, World**: third, Noah had to believe God's means of destruction, that God was going to bring a flood of waters upon the earth. Remember: Noah was probably prostrate, flat on his face before God. He was bound to be in a state of shock as God told him to build a huge ark in the middle of nowhere. Now terror struck his heart. God declared that He was going to destroy every living creature upon earth, both man and animal. Note that three things are stressed about the coming judgment.

a. God Himself was going to launch and execute the judgment. Note the stress in the Hebrew: "*I, even I* do bring a flood of waters upon the earth" (v.17). It was God Himself—Elohim, the Mighty God, the Sovereign Lord of the universe—who was going to cause the waters to burst forth and destroy man.

b. The flood and judgment were definitely coming, coming beyond all question. Again, this is seen in God's emphasis: "*I, even I*" will do it. It is not a matter...

- of wondering if judgment is coming
- of questioning if judgment is coming
- of perhaps judgment is coming

The judgment of every living thing *is* coming. "*I, even I*"—God Himself—is going to execute the judgment.

c. All flesh—every living soul—upon the earth shall be destroyed and die. Genesis 7:22 says that this refers to the people and animals upon *dry land*, not to the fish and water animals. Water, of course, does not destroy these, although some water creatures would have been destroyed by the pressure of the water shooting up from the subterranean caverns when the crust of the earth broke open. (See note—Ge.7:10-12 for more discussion.)

Thought 1. We must all face the judgment of God and give an account for how we have lived upon earth. Judgment is sure: judgment is coming and cannot be escaped. How can we be so sure of this? Because it is God Himself who has spoken and declared that judgment is coming. We must listen and heed the declaration of His Word.

---

2   Tim F. LaHaye and John D. Morris. *The Ark on Ararat*. (Nashville and New York: Thomas Nelson, 1976), p.237.
3   James Montgomery Boice. *Genesis*, Vol.1, pp. 262-263.

"For the Son of man shall come in the glory of his Father with his angels; and then he shall reward every man according to his works" (Mt.16:27).

"When the Son of man shall come in his glory, and all the holy angels with him, then shall he sit upon the throne of his glory: and before him shall be gathered all nations: and he shall separate them one from another, as a shepherd divideth his sheep from the goats: and he shall set the sheep on his right hand, but the goats on the left. Then shall the King say unto them on his right hand. Come, ye blessed of my Father, inherit the kingdom prepared for you from the foundation of the world....Then shall he say also unto them on the left hand, Depart from me, ye cursed, into everlasting fire, prepared for the devil and his angels....And these shall go away into everlasting punishment: but the righteous into life eternal" (Mt.25:31-34, 41, 46).

"And to you who are troubled rest with us, when the Lord Jesus shall be revealed from heaven with his mighty angels, in flaming fire taking vengeance on them that know not God, and that obey not the gospel of our Lord Jesus Christ: who shall be punished with everlasting destruction from the presence of the Lord, and from the glory of his power" (2 Th.1:7-9).

"And as it is appointed unto men once to die, but after this the judgment" (He.9:27).

"The Lord knoweth how to deliver the godly out of temptations, and to reserve the unjust unto the day of judgment to be punished" (2 Pe.2:9).

"But the heavens and the earth, which are now, by the same word are kept in store, reserved unto fire against the day of judgment and perdition of ungodly men. But, beloved, be not ignorant of this one thing, that one day is with the Lord as a thousand years, and a thousand years as one day. The Lord is not slack concerning his promise, as some men count slackness; but is longsuffering to us-ward, not willing that any should perish, but that all should come to repentance. But the day of the Lord will come as a thief in the night; in the which the heavens shall pass away with a great noise, and the elements shall melt with fervent heat, the earth also and the works that are therein shall be burned up" (2 Pe.3:7-10).

"And Enoch also, the seventh from Adam, prophesied of these, saying, Behold, the Lord cometh with ten thousands of his saints, to execute judgment upon all, and to convince all that are ungodly among them of all their ungodly deeds which they have ungodly committed, and of all their hard speeches which ungodly sinners have spoken against him" (Jude 14-15).

"And I saw a great white throne, and him that sat on it, from whose face the earth and the heaven fled away; and there was found no place for them. And I saw the dead, small and great, stand before God; and the books were opened: and another book was opened, which is the book of life: and the dead were judged out of those things which were written in the books, according to their works. And the sea gave up the dead which were in it; and death and hell delivered up the dead which were in them: and they were judged every man according to their works. And death and hell were cast into the lake of fire. This is the second death. And whosoever was not found written in the book of life was cast into the lake of fire" (Re.20:11-15).

"He cometh to judge the earth: he shall judge the world with righteousness, and the people with his truth" (Ps.96:13).

"I the LORD search the heart, I try the reins, even to give every man according to his ways, and according to the fruit of his doings" (Je.17:10).

"I said in mine heart, God shall judge the righteous and the wicked" (Ec.3:17).

4 (6:18) **Salvation—Promise—Faith—Comfort**: fourth, Noah had to believe God's promise of personal salvation, that God was going to save him and his dear family. Noah was bound to be shaken to the core and stricken with terror. Imagine his emotions: he had just been told that the whole earth was to be destroyed, all life, both human and animal; and it was to happen soon, during his lifetime. His home, his community, his city, his world—all the earth, his neighbors, his friends, his relatives—all were to be destroyed. There was to be nothing whatsoever left upon earth. The earth with all life was to be destroyed. The images flashing across Noah's mind must have been terrorizing. (Note: the images of so terrorizing a judgment are most likely what made Noah such a fearless preacher of righteousness and judgment. He saw that judgment was coming. He believed God and His Word.)

God knew Noah's thoughts and emotions; therefore, God knew that Noah needed to be comforted and assured. Noah needed the promise of God, that God would save him and his dear family. But remember: Noah had to believe God's promise.

Now, note that God promised and established His covenant with Noah. God told Noah that the covenant was now his—personally his—to carry on. What covenant? There was only one covenant in existence that fits into the context of the coming judgment to destroy the earth: the covenant of *the promised seed*, the Savior of the world, that God had promised to send to save the world. (See note 5—Ge.3:15 for more discussion. Also see Ge.9:11 where God enlarges His covenant with Noah.)

Noah knew this fact: *the promised seed*, the Savior, was coming to restore believers to the perfect paradise Adam had known. Remember, Adam was still living when Noah's father, Lamech, was born. In fact, Lamech was 56 years old when Adam died (see DEEPER STUDY # 2—Ge.5:27-32). As pointed out earlier, Adam was bound to have shared his glorious experience with God in the Garden of Eden with his descendants. Any of us would have done the same with all who were willing to listen. The godly line of believers would have, of course, listened to Adam. Adam would have also taught—to the point of indoctrination—the great promise and great covenant of God. The Adamic covenant was the promise of being saved eternally, of having the tempter, that old serpent, the devil, destroyed (see Rev.12:9). The covenant was the promise that evil would be completely destroyed and righteousness fully restored to earth, perfectly restored.

Noah, therefore, knew that God was choosing him to carry on the godly line through whom *the promised seed* and Savior would come.

Noah was able to rest in the glorious promise of God: God would save him through the flood and eternally through the coming seed and Savior of the world. *The promised seed* and Savior was to come through his very loins. God was establishing His covenant, the covenant of *the promised seed*, with Noah. But again, Noah had to believe and trust the promise of God.

> "But the salvation of the righteous is of the LORD: he is their strength in the time of trouble" (Ps.37:39).
>
> "Behold, God is my salvation; I will trust, and not be afraid: for the LORD JEHOVAH is my strength and my song; he also is become my salvation" (Is.12:2).
>
> "And it shall be said in that day, Lo, this is our God; we have waited for him, and he will save us: this is the LORD; we have waited for him, we will be glad and rejoice in his salvation" (Is.25:9).
>
> "The LORD thy God in the midst of thee is mighty; he will save, he will rejoice over thee with joy; he will rest in his love, he will joy over thee with singing" (Zep.3:17).
>
> "For God so loved the world, that he gave his only begotten Son, that whosoever believeth in him should not perish, but have everlasting life" (Jn.3:16).
>
> "And it shall come to pass, that whosoever shall call on the name of the Lord shall be saved" (Ac.2:21).
>
> "For the wages of sin is death; but the gift of God is eternal life through Jesus Christ our Lord" (Ro.6:23).
>
> "That if thou shalt confess with thy mouth the Lord Jesus, and shalt believe in thine heart that God hath raised him from the dead, thou shalt be saved. For with the heart man believeth unto righteousness; and with the mouth confession is made unto salvation" (Ro.10:9-10).
>
> "For whosoever shall call upon the name of the Lord shall be saved" (Ro.10:13).

Note: God tells Noah who is to enter the ark. God is very specific. He spells out exactly who is to be saved: only Noah and his immediate family.

Note also, this is the first time the word *covenant* is used in Scripture. However, this is not the first covenant God established with man (see DEEPER STUDY # 1—Ge.2:15-17 for the first covenant; note 5—Ge.3:15 for more discussion).

5 (6:19-21) **Faith—Commission**: fifth, Noah had to believe God's commission, the awesome task of saving two of every living animal upon earth. Imagine the weight and pressure—the heavy sense of responsibility—that must have swept across Noah's mind and settled in his heart when God began to give Noah this awesome task:

⇒ to capture two of every living creature upon earth.
⇒ to bring them all into the ark.
⇒ to make sure one is a male and one a female.
⇒ to store enough food and water to feed them all, enough food to last one whole year (see DEEPER STUDY # 1—Ge.8:6-14).
⇒ to keep them alive within the ark.

The very idea of saving two of every species of animal must have overwhelmed Noah. God was commissioning him to reach out and save the creatures of the world. The task was an awesome weight to put upon a man's shoulders. This God knew, but note the help God promised. The animals would come to Noah to be saved (v.20). What does this mean? Did the animals sense the coming storm and disaster, as animals often do? Or did God act upon the animals and cause them to approach the ark?

Scripture does not say, but both methods of gathering the animals are probably true. Noah would unquestionably need God's help to complete such an awesome task.

Thought 1. Noah's great commission is a picture of the great commission given us. God has given every believer the charge to reach out and save mankind from the coming judgment. We must go forth and proclaim Christ, the Savior of the world. We must do all we can to proclaim the Savior to all people everywhere.

> "Go ye therefore, and teach all nations, baptizing them in the name of the Father, and of the Son, and of the Holy Ghost: teaching them to observe all things whatsoever I have commanded you: and, lo, I am with you alway, even unto the end of the world" (Mt.28:19-20).
>
> "And he said unto them, Go ye into all the world, and preach the gospel to every creature" (Mk.16:15).
>
> "But ye shall receive power, after that the Holy Ghost is come upon you: and ye shall be witnesses unto me both in Jerusalem, and in all Judaea, and in Samaria, and unto the uttermost part of the earth" (Ac.1:8).

6 (6:22) **Obedience**: sixth, Noah had to believe the way of salvation, that he had to obey God to be saved. This is a phenomenal verse: Noah believed God and all that God said. Noah believed these facts:

⇒ God was going to destroy the whole earth.
⇒ God had spoken to him personally, spoken and instructed him to build and enter the ark of safety (vv.14-16).
⇒ God was going to save him and his dear family.

How do we know that Noah believed these facts? Because he obeyed God and built the ark. He did all that God commanded him to do—*all*. Noah knew that the only way he could ever be saved was to obey God, to do exactly what God had said. If he rejected God and disobeyed the Word of God, Noah knew he would perish along with all those who denied and rejected God. Thus Noah believed God: he accepted everything that God said and did exactly what God commanded.

Thought 1. The greatness of Noah's belief can be seen in this: many people do not even believe that the great flood took place, that Noah ever built an ark. Despite all the incredible evidence that points toward the flood and toward Noah's ark, they still choose to walk in their denial of God and His Holy Word.

Noah's great faith is seen in this: he had no evidence. He had nothing but the sheer Word of God, yet he acted upon God's Word. He believed everything that God said, and did all that God commanded. What a great example for us to follow!

"Not every one that saith unto me, Lord, Lord, shall enter into the kingdom of heaven; but he that doeth the will of my Father which is in heaven" (Mt.7:21).

"If ye keep my commandments, ye shall abide in my love; even as I have kept my Father's commandments, and abide in his love" (Jn.15:10).

"Let no man deceive you with vain words: for because of these things cometh the wrath of God upon the children of disobedience" (Ep.5:6).

"And to you who are troubled rest with us, when the Lord Jesus shall be revealed from heaven with his mighty angels, in flaming fire taking vengeance on them that know not God, and that obey not the gospel of our Lord Jesus Christ" (2 Th.1:7-8).

"And being made perfect, he became the author of eternal salvation unto all them that obey him" (He.5:9).

"Blessed are they that do his commandments, that they may have right to the tree of life, and may enter in through the gates into the city" (Re.22:14).

"O that there were such an heart in them, that they would fear me, and keep all my commandments always, that it might be well with them, and with their children for ever!" (De.5:29).

"This book of the law shall not depart out of thy mouth; but thou shalt meditate therein day and night, that thou mayest observe to do according to all that is written therein: for then thou shalt make thy way prosperous, and then thou shalt have good success" (Jos.1:8).

THE ARK

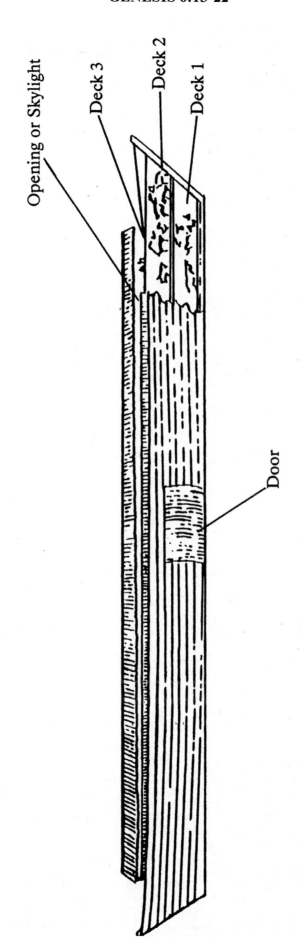

Opening or Skylight

Deck 3

Deck 2

Deck 1

Door

Estimated Size:

- ∧ Length: 300 cubits or 150 yards
- ∧ ∧ Width: 50 cubits or 25 yards
- ∧ 30 cubits or 15 yards

	CHAPTER 7	forty nights; and every living substance that I have made will I destroy from off the face of the earth.	days to repent
	C. Noah & the Last Week: God's Great Invitation & Noah's Great Obedience, 7:1-9		2) The judgment: A flood of water 3) The destruction: All life wiped out
1. The great invitation of God: To enter the ark	And the LORD said unto Noah, Come thou and all thy house into the ark; for thee have I seen righteous before me in this generation.	5 And Noah did according unto all that the LORD commanded him.	**3. The great obedience of Noah** a. He did all that God commanded
2. The great reasons for God's invitation a. Because Noah was righteous before God b. Because the animal life of the earth had to be saved 1) Seven of the clean animals for worship & food 2) Two of all animals to preserve life	2 Of every clean beast thou shalt take to thee by sevens, the male and his female: and of beasts that are not clean by two, the male and his female. 3 Of fowls also of the air by sevens, the male and the female; to keep seed alive upon the face of all the earth.	6 And Noah was six hundred years old when the flood of waters was upon the earth. 7 And Noah went in, and his sons, and his wife, and his sons' wives with him, into the ark, because of the waters of the flood. 8 Of clean beasts, and of beasts that are not clean, and of fowls, and of every thing that creepeth upon the earth,	b. He went into the ark & took only those commanded by God c. He followed God's instructions to save the animals: Just as God had commanded him
c. Because judgment was imminent, at hand 1) God's grace: Seven more	4 For yet seven days, and I will cause it to rain upon the earth forty days and	9 There went in two and two unto Noah into the ark, the male and the female, as God had commanded Noah.	

DIVISION IV

NOAH: THE MAN CHOSEN TO PRESERVE MANKIND AND THE GODLY SEED THROUGH WORLD DESTRUCTION (THE FLOOD), 6:9–9:29

C. Noah and the Last Week: God's Great Invitation and Noah's Great Obedience, 7:1-9

(7:1-9) **Introduction**: there is a great gap of time between chapter six and seven, probably a gap of 120 years. Chapter six ended with God telling Noah to build the ark; chapter seven begins with God telling Noah to enter the ark (see note—Ge.7:5-9. See Ge.6:3, see 6:13-14; 7:1). Imagine! Noah had been building the ark for 120 years. For 120 years Noah had been preaching the coming judgment of God while building this monstrous box-like structure. Again, imagine the neighbors, community, and public at large. Think of their curiosity, and how strange they thought Noah was, this man who was building this boat-like structure out in the middle of dry land—all because he thought God was going to judge the sins of man by sending a flood of waters upon the earth. Sometimes the unbelief and the jokes, ridicule, mockery, and persecution must have been almost unbearable. But Noah was faithful and enduring to the Lord and to the great call God had given him, faithful to the end.

Noah preached, and he finished the ark despite all the trials and abuse of the people. This he did in the midst of a godless society, a society that had turned completely away from God. There was not a person—not a single person—who followed God and lived like God said to live. Noah and his family alone followed God and obeyed His Word. Now, God reappeared to Noah and gave him additional instructions.

Note: these are the last seven days—the events of the last week—right before the rain began. This is the great subject of this passage: *Noah and the Last Week: God's Great Invitation to Noah and Noah's Great Obedience.*

1. The great invitation of God: to enter the ark (v.1).
2. The great reasons for God's invitation (vv.1-4).
3. The great obedience of Noah (vv.5-9).

1 (7:1) **Ark—Invitation—Come—Justification—Righteousness—Parents**: there was the great invitation of God. God spoke to Noah and told him to "come—enter into the ark." These words must have been both comforting and terrifying to Noah. Comforting because Noah knew that he was now to be vindicated and delivered from all the trials of this evil world and from the abuse of the ungodly. Terrified because he knew that the earth and every living thing upon it was now to be destroyed. Just picture the thoughts that were bound to be flashing across Noah's mind: every friend, relative, neighbor, and person upon earth was to be destroyed, wiped off the face of the earth; every animal, house, building, tree, shrub—all the earth and everything upon it was to be destroyed.

⇒ What was the earth to look like?
⇒ What was it going to be like to be the only living family upon earth to survive, only one of eight souls?
⇒ What was it going to be like living locked up in the ark for so long a time?
⇒ What was it going to be like facing a storm so ferocious that it was going to flood the whole earth?

The emotions and thoughts that Noah was experiencing would surge through the body of any person who was about to go through such an experience as Noah was. But Noah had God and His comforting presence, and God knows how to comfort and carry His followers through frightening and terrifying experiences, even the experience of death itself. Note how God comforted and assured Noah.

a. God said, "Come—enter into the ark." The Hebrew word is *come, enter*. These were tender words, like the words of a father who calls out to his children to come into the house when he sees a storm or night approaching.[1] God was assuring Noah...

- that He was within the ark as well as outside the ark
- that He would be with Noah no matter where Noah went
- that He would look after Noah within the ark as well as without the ark

Thought 1. Several pictures can be gleaned from this great invitation from God to Noah.

1) There is the picture of Christ, of the safety and security from judgment which man can find in Christ. Noah found safety and security from judgment by entering the ark. We can find safety and security from the coming judgment by entering Christ, that is...
   - by placing our lives into His hands
   - by approaching Christ and following Him into the safety of God's presence
   - by approaching the safety and security of God's presence through Christ
   - by approaching God through Christ

2) There is the picture of the great *"come invitations"* of God's Word. God invites people time and time again to *"come."*

> "And the LORD said unto Noah, Come thou and all thy house into the ark; for thee have I seen righteous before me in this generation" (Ge.7:1).
> "Come now, and let us reason together, saith the LORD: Though your sins be as scarlet, they shall be as white as snow; though they be red like crimson, they shall be as wool" (Is.1:18).
> "Ho, every one that thirsteth, come ye to the waters, and he that hath no money; come ye, buy, and eat; yea, come, buy wine and milk without money and without price" (Is.55:1).
> "Come unto me, all ye that labour and are heavy laden, and I will give you rest" (Mt.11:28).
> "Again, he sent forth other servants, saying, Tell them which are bidden, Behold, I have prepared my dinner: my oxen and my fatlings are killed, and all things are ready: come unto the marriage" (Mt.22:4).
> "And sent his servant at supper time to say to them that were bidden, Come; for all things are now ready" (Lu.14:17).
> "And the Spirit and the bride say, Come. And let him that heareth say, Come. And let him that is athirst come. And whosoever will, let him take the water of life freely" (Re.22:17).

b. God told Noah that his whole family was to enter the ark. This was bound to help ease the heart of Noah, for those whom he loved the most—his immediate family—were to be saved along with him. Does this mean that Noah's sons and their wives were followers of God? Probably, for Noah was a godly man, and as a godly man, his duty was to lead and instruct his children to follow God. Year after year of living with and being taught by a godly father like Noah was bound to make an impact upon the three boys and eventually upon their wives. The very fact that God would choose them to be saved and the fact that they entered the ark point to their being true believers, true followers of the only living and true God. It is doubtful they would have entered the ark if they had not believed.

Thought 1. Noah's godly example before his children shows us the critical importance of godly parents. Remember: there were no other godly people upon earth, not a single person followed God. There was only Noah and his wife and three sons. Imagine what it was like being the only young person who followed God, the only young person who lived righteously and godly, who obeyed one's parents, who stood against the crowd and did not curse, drink, cheat, or go too far sexually. These were Noah's sons. They apparently followed God and stood right beside their father in living and preaching righteousness to their ungodly generation. What a lesson for the fathers of the world: to live godly lives before their children and to teach their children to follow God, to follow Him above all else.

> "And thou shalt teach them [God's commandments] diligently unto thy children, and shalt talk of them when thou sittest in thine house, and when thou walkest by the way, and when thou liest down, and when thou risest up" (De.6:7).
> "Train up a child in the way he should go: and when he is old, he will not depart from it" (Pr.22:6).
> "Whom shall he teach knowledge? and whom shall he make to understand doctrine? them that are weaned from the milk, and drawn from the breasts" (Is.28:9).
> "And, ye fathers, provoke not your children to wrath: but bring them up in the nurture and admonition of the Lord" (Ep.6:4).

---

[1] *Matthew Henry's Commentary*, Vol.1, p.58.

Thought 2. Righteousness is an absolute essential for a person to enter God's presence. God invites no unrighteous person—allows no unrighteous person—to enter and live in the safety of His presence. A person must approach God through the righteousness of Jesus Christ—must *take on*, clothe himself in, the righteousness of Jesus Christ—to be acceptable to God. A person must become righteous in Jesus Christ to be invited to enter the ark of God's security from the judgment to come.

> "For he hath made him to be sin for us, who knew no sin; that we might be made the righteousness of God in him" (2 Co.5:21).
> "But of him are ye in Christ Jesus, who of God is made unto us wisdom, and righteousness, and sanctification, and redemption" (1 Co.1:30).
> "And by him all that believe are justified from all things, from which ye could not be justified by the law of Moses" (Ac.13:39).
> "Therefore being justified by faith, we have peace with God through our Lord Jesus Christ" (Ro.5:1).

2 (7:1-4) **Invitation—Righteousness—Judgment**: there were the great reasons for God's invitation to enter the ark of safety and security.

a. God invited Noah to enter the ark because Noah was righteous before God (v.1). Noah believed God, believed what God said, and did what God said. Believing and obeying God always pleases God. It pleases Him just like it pleases us when people believe us and follow our advice and counsel. Noah pleased God; therefore, God wanted to save Noah. God wanted to look after Noah, and God wanted to use Noah in His great purpose for the earth. This is the reason Noah was saved and used by God to carry on the human race: he was righteous before God. Noah simply believed God and did what God said. (See note, pt.1—Ge.6:9-10 for more discussion.)

b. Noah was to save the animal life of the earth (vv.2-3). Note that seven of all clean animals were to be saved and two of the unclean animals. Originally, some 120 years before, when God first told Noah about the coming flood, God said that Noah would be saving two of every animal. Why the switch to seven animals now? Because it is now time for the details to be spelled out. When God instructed Noah 120 years before, only general instructions concerning the animals were needed. Now, in entering the ark, the details are needed: some clean animals would be needed for sacrifice and worship; therefore, more were naturally needed. Also, the clean animals would provide food for Noah and his family (see Ge.9:3).

Note the clearly stated purpose for two of every kind of animal, both a male and a female: to reproduce offspring and to keep their kind alive upon the earth (v.3b).

c. Noah and his family were invited into the ark because judgment was imminent (v.4).

1) God gave man a final chance to repent, a last act of grace. God gave Noah seven days to make final preparations and to continue preaching to the lost of his generation. Just imagine the fervor of his preaching as he proclaimed that the judgment of God was to fall within seven days. Imagine the scene as he did just what every true preacher would do: preach day by day and count down the days one by one: seven, six, five, four, three, two, one—only one more day—and then, at last, this is the day of climactic judgment.

> "By faith Noah, being warned of God of things not seen as yet, moved with fear, prepared an ark to the saving of his house; by the which he condemned the world, and became heir of the righteousness which is by faith" (He.11:7).

God gave the earth one final week—a whole week of grace, even telling them when the judgment was to fall—yet the people still disbelieved. They still rejected God and refused to repent. The people just did not believe that God was going to judge them and destroy the earth and begin all over again.

2) God spelled out the judgment that was to fall upon the earth: there was to be a deluge of rain never seen before. A flood of rain was to fall upon the earth for forty days and forty nights.

Thought 1. Throughout history God has used the number forty to symbolize a great period of trial that ends in great victory and triumph over evil.[2]

⇒ Israel wandered about in the wilderness for forty years before entering the promised land (Nu.14:33).
⇒ The spies who were sent to scout out Canaan before Israel entered the land stayed and scouted out the land for forty days (Nu.13:25).
⇒ Moses was in the mountain receiving the law of God for forty days and nights (Ex.24:18).
⇒ Elijah fasted for forty days and nights (1 K.19:8).
⇒ Nineveh was given forty days to repent (Jonah 3:4).
⇒ Jesus Christ fasted for forty days before He faced the onslaught of the devil's temptations (Mt.4:2).
⇒ Jesus Christ was on earth for forty days after His resurrection and phenomenal ascension into heaven (Ac.1:3).

3) God Himself pronounced the terrible destruction of the judgment: He was going to destroy every living creature He had made. In the Hebrew God literally said that He was going *to wipe or blot out* every living creature from the face of the earth.

---

2 *The Pulpit Commentary*, Vol.1, p.114.
   H.C. Leupold. *Genesis*, Vol.1, p.291.

Thought 1. We marvel at the unbelief of people in Noah's day. But they were no different from the people of our day. Look at the unbelief of our world. Few believe; most disbelieve. In fact, many people even deny that the great flood ever took place. Many persons do not believe that God ever destroyed the earth. But they are wrong. God did. And the great tragedy is this: God is going to be forced to destroy the earth again. People are still rejecting God, even cursing and denying Him. Just think of the times throughout the day when God's name is cursed. Think of the people who deny and reject God. Just think how few people we know who really believe and follow God, who really live for Him. This is the reason God declares that judgment is to once again fall upon the earth. In fact, God declares that both the earth and the heavens—the whole universe—will soon be judged and destroyed. But this time, it will be final. God is going to stop human history as it now exists: sinful, evil, and imperfect. God declares that He is going to remake the earth and the heavens, recreate them in perfection. He declares that He is going to populate them with angelic beings and with those people who have believed and followed Him down through the ages. Note how clearly God declares this:

"Knowing this first, that there shall come in the last days scoffers, walking after their own lusts, and saying, Where is the promise of his coming? for since the fathers fell asleep, all things continue as they were from the beginning of the creation. For this they willingly are ignorant of, that by the word of God the heavens were of old, and the earth standing out of the water and in the water: whereby the world that then was, being overflowed with water, perished: but the heavens and the earth, which are now, by the same word are kept in store, reserved unto fire against the day of judgment and perdition of ungodly men. But, beloved, be not ignorant of this one thing, that one day is with the Lord as a thousand years, and a thousand years as one day. The Lord is not slack concerning his promise, as some men count slackness; but is longsuffering to us-ward, not willing that any should perish, but that all should come to repentance. But the day of the Lord will come as a thief in the night; in the which the heavens shall pass away with a great noise, and the elements shall melt with fervent heat, the earth also and the works that are therein shall be burned up. Seeing then that all these things shall be dissolved, what manner of persons ought ye to be in all holy conversation and godliness. Looking for and hasting unto the coming of the day of God, wherein the heavens being on fire shall be dissolved, and the elements shall melt with fervent heat? Nevertheless we, according to his promise, look for new heavens and a new earth, wherein dwelleth righteousness" (2 Pe.3:3-13).

"And I saw a new heaven and a new earth: for the first heaven and the first earth were passed away; and there was no more sea. And I John saw the holy city, new Jerusalem, coming down from God out of heaven, prepared as a bride adorned for her husband. And I heard a great voice out of heaven saying, Behold, the tabernacle of God is with men, and he will dwell with them, and they shall be his people, and God himself shall be with them, and be their God. And God shall wipe away all tears from their eyes; and there shall be no more death, neither sorrow, nor crying, neither shall there be any more pain: for the former things are passed away. And he that sat upon the throne said, Behold, I make all things new. And he said unto me, Write: for these words are true and faithful. And he said unto me, It is done. I am Alpha and Omega, the beginning and the end. I will give unto him that is athirst of the fountain of the water of life freely. He that overcometh shall inherit all things; and I will be his God, and he shall be my son. But the fearful, and unbelieving, and the abominable, and murderers, and whoremongers, and sorcerers, and idolaters, and all liars, shall have their part in the lake which burneth with fire and brimstone: which is the second death" (Re.21:1-8).

"For verily I say unto you, Till heaven and earth pass, one jot or one tittle shall in no wise pass from the law, till all be fulfilled" (Mt.5:18).

"Heaven and earth shall pass away, but my words shall not pass away" (Mt.24:35).

"Of old hast thou laid the foundation of the earth: and the heavens are the work of thy hands. They shall perish, but thou shalt endure: yea, all of them shall wax old like a garment; as a vesture shalt thou change them, and they shall be changed: but thou art the same, and thy years shall have no end" (Ps.102:25-27).

"And all the host of heaven shall be dissolved, and the heavens shall be rolled together as a scroll: and all their host shall fall down, as the leaf falleth off from the vine, and as a falling fig from the fig tree" (Is.34:4).

"Lift up your eyes to the heavens, and look upon the earth beneath: for the heavens shall vanish away like smoke, and the earth shall wax old like a garment, and they that dwell therein shall die in like manner: but my salvation shall be for ever, and my righteousness shall not be abolished" (Is.51:6).

"For, behold, I create new heavens and a new earth: and the former shall not be remembered, nor come into mind" (Is.65:17).

"For as the new heavens and the new earth, which I will make, shall remain before me, saith the LORD, so shall your seed and your name remain" (Is.66:22).

3 (7:5-9) **Obedience:** there was the great obedience of Noah. The stress of these verses is the explicit obedience of Noah: he did exactly what God said to do.

Note: it had not yet begun to rain. Noah was still acting by faith. All he had was what we have: God's Word and the warning of judgment to come. He had nothing else other than God's Word. He had built the ark with nothing other than God's Word to go on, and now, he enters the ark with nothing but God's Word to go on. Not a drop of rain had yet fallen; nothing had yet happened to indicate that judgment was about to fall upon the earth. God alone had spoken to Noah, and Noah had acted on God's Word alone. Three facts are clearly stated in these verses.

a. Noah was 600 hundred years old when he entered the ark and the flood of water began (vv.5-6). Compare Ge.6:3, 13 and note that Noah spent 120 years building the ark. This means that Noah was 480 years old when God first told him to build the ark and prepare for the coming judgment. Just think of the great faith and obedience of Noah: he did the most strange and unbelievable thing imaginable. He built a huge box-like structure out in the middle of nowhere, and all the while he preached the righteousness and coming judgment of God. The ark was about 450 feet long. Noah did this—worked at building the ark and at preaching—for 120 years, all in obedience to the Word of God. All he had to go on was the Word and warning of God. Again, just think of the great faith and obedience of Noah: 120 years doing the strange and unbelievable, all based solely upon the Word of God.

b. Noah went into the ark and took only those whom God had said were to enter (v.7). Only Noah and his family, which included his wife and his three sons and their wives, were allowed to enter the ark—only eight persons altogether. Think how difficult this was: isolating himself and his family from the rest of mankind, thinking—yea, knowing within his heart—that he and his family were to be the only survivors left from the coming holocaust, the only survivors upon the whole earth.

⇒ Just imagine the emotions—the effect upon you—if you knew that only eight people had survived a worldwide holocaust and you were one of the survivors.

The apprehension, fear, sense of loneliness and of the unknown must have been almost unbearable. But Noah acted, and his action was based solely upon the Word of God. God had said to enter the ark with his family, and he obeyed. He did exactly what God said to do. Note why: to escape the flood of waters, the coming judgment (v.7b).

c. Noah followed God's instructions to save the animals (vv.8-9). He took two, a male and a female, of all animals (v.9). Note that Noah's great obedience is restated: he did exactly as God commanded. He disobeyed in nothing. He obeyed God completely and fully. He followed the Word of God, did exactly what God said to do. As Scripture says: "[God] saved Noah the eighth person, a preacher of righteousness, bringing in the flood upon the world of the ungodly" (2 Pe.2:5).

"Now therefore, if ye will obey my voice indeed, and keep my covenant, then ye shall be a peculiar treasure unto me above all people: for all the earth is mine" (Ex.19:5).

"O that there were such an heart in them, that they would fear me, and keep all my commandments always, that it might be well with them, and with their children for ever!" (De.5:29).

"Not every one that saith unto me, Lord, Lord, shall enter into the kingdom of heaven; but he that doeth the will of my Father which is in heaven" (Mt.7:21).

"If ye keep my commandments, ye shall abide in my love; even as I have kept my Father's commandments, and abide in his love" (Jn.15:10).

"Then Peter and the other apostles answered and said, We ought to obey God rather than men" (Ac.5:29).

"And being made perfect, he became the author of eternal salvation unto all them that obey him" (He.5:9).

"Blessed are they that do his commandments, that they may have right to the tree of life, and may enter in through the gates into the city" (Re.22:14).

	D. Noah & the Flood: God's Great Judgment of the Earth, 7:10-24	shut him in. 17 And the flood was forty days upon the earth; and the waters increased, and bare up the ark, and it was lift up above the earth.	3. The great fulfillment of God's Word in judgment a. God flooded water upon the earth for 40 days, but bore up the ark
1. The great power of God in judgment	10 And it came to pass after seven days, that the waters of the flood were upon the earth. 11 In the six hundredth year of Noah's life, in the second month, the seventeenth day of the month, the same day were all the fountains of the great deep broken up, and the windows of heaven were opened. 12 And the rain was upon the earth forty days and forty nights.	18 And the waters prevailed, and were increased greatly upon the earth; and the ark went upon the face of the waters. 19 And the waters prevailed exceedingly upon the earth; and all the high hills, that were under the whole heaven, were covered. 20 Fifteen cubits upward did the waters prevail; and the mountains were covered.	1) The waters increased greatly, but the ark floated 2) The waters mightily rose more & more until all the mountains were covered 3) The waters mightily rose to a height of 20 feet
a. God's power had the traumatic day fixed b. God's power violently broke up the earth's crust & burst loose all the earth's subterranean waters c. God's power opened up the floodgates of heaven: A violent, torrential downpour for 40 days & nights			
2. The great salvation of God in judgment a. Noah & his family went into the ark	13 In the selfsame day entered Noah, and Shem, and Ham, and Japheth, the sons of Noah, and Noah's wife, and the three wives of his sons with them, into the ark; 14 They, and every beast after his kind, and all the cattle after their kind, and every creeping thing that creepeth upon the earth after his kind, and every fowl after his kind, every bird of every sort. 15 And they went in unto Noah into the ark, two and two of all flesh, wherein is the breath of life. 16 And they that went in, went in male and female of all flesh, as God had commanded him: and the LORD	21 And all flesh died that moved upon the earth, both of fowl, and of cattle, and of beast, and of every creeping thing that creepeth upon the earth, and every man: 22 All in whose nostrils was the breath of life, of all that was in the dry land, died. 23 And every living substance was destroyed which was upon the face of the ground, both man, and cattle, and the creeping things, and the fowl of the heaven; and they were destroyed from the earth: and Noah only remained alive, and they that were with him in the ark. 24 And the waters prevailed upon the earth an hundred and fifty days.	b. God destroyed all life 1) All flesh perished, both animal & man 2) Every living thing upon dry land perished 3) Every living thing upon the ground was wiped out c. God saved Noah & all those in the ark with him **4. The great time that the water flooded the earth in judgment**
b. Every animal went into the ark 1) Each kind or species of animal 2) The animals went two by two to Noah 3) One male & one female went in c. God Himself shut the door to the ark			

DIVISION IV

NOAH: THE MAN CHOSEN TO PRESERVE MANKIND AND THE GODLY SEED THROUGH WORLD DESTRUCTION (THE FLOOD), 6:9–9:29

D. Noah and the Flood: God's Great Judgment of the Earth, 7:10-24

(7:10-24) **Introduction**: this is the record of the great flood that swept over and covered the earth in Noah's day. God sent the flood upon the earth as a judgment upon man's immorality, lawlessness, and violence. Man had become so sinful and evil—so immoral, so lawless, so violent—there was not a godly person left upon earth. No one truly followed God except Noah and his dear family.

The Bible is not the only book that reports the flood. It is a surprise to most people when they hear that most cultures have traditions about a worldwide flood that swept the earth. In fact, there are hundreds of flood traditions around the world. They differ, of course. This is expected because of the passage of time and local customs and languages. Nevertheless, this very fact—that hundreds of cultures and peoples have these stories—is evidence that the stories have all come from one original source. They have come from a source that existed not just centuries but millenniums ago, come from the very survivors of the flood. (Tim LaHaye and John Morris have done excellent research on the flood and the traditions of the flood in their book, *The Ark on Ararat.* Also see James Montgomery Boice. *Genesis,* Vol.1, pp.285-287.)

The point of this tragic passage is not only to record the great flood and judgment of the past, but to lead us to ponder the final judgment and salvation yet to come. This is the study of *Noah and the Flood: God's Great Judgment of the Earth.*
1. The great power of God in judgment (vv.10-12).
2. The great salvation of God in judgment (vv.13-16).
3. The great fulfillment of God's Word in judgment (vv.17-23).
4. The great time that the water flooded the earth in judgment (v.24).

1 (7:10-12) **Judgment**: there was the great power of God in judgment. Note three significant points about the power of God to judge the earth.

a. God's power had the traumatic day fixed in history. The day of judgment had been predestined. One week before the flood, God had told Noah that he had seven days to prepare, that seven days from then He would send a terrifying flood of water to wipe man from the face of the earth (Ge.7:4).

Now, on the seventh day, the terrifying flood waters began to pour forth. The event was so significant—so important, so momentous—that it must never be forgotten. The time has been recorded forever. The judgment of God fell; the devastating flood waters began to pour forth...

- in the 600th year of Noah's life
- on the 17th day of the second month

Thought 1. The day of our judgment, the day when we are to stand before God in judgment, is also fixed in history. The day for our judgment is already predetermined. No person knows when the day will be: one hundred years from now? Five years? One year? Tomorrow? Later today? Only God knows. Christ clearly said this:

> "But of that day and that hour knoweth no man, no, not the angels which are in heaven, neither the Son, but the Father. Take ye heed, watch and pray: for ye know not when the time is" (Mk.13:32-33).
> "Watch therefore, for ye know neither the day nor the hour wherein the Son of man cometh" (Mt.25:13).
> "Watch therefore: for ye know not what hour your Lord doth come" (Mt.24:42).
> "The lord of that servant shall come in a day when he looketh not for him, and in an hour that he is not aware of, and shall cut him asunder, and appoint him his portion with the hypocrites: there shall be weeping and gnashing of teeth" (Mt.24:50-51).
> "Be ye therefore ready also: for the Son of man cometh at an hour when ye think not" (Lu.12:40).
> "The lord of that servant will come in a day when he looketh not for him, and at an hour when he is not aware, and will cut him in sunder, and will appoint him his portion with the unbelievers" (Lu.12:46).

b. God's power violently broke up the earth's crust and burst loose all the earth's subterranean waters. Earthquakes must have taken place all over the earth. Note exactly what Scripture says...

- "All the fountains of the great deep [were] broken up" (v.11)

The idea is that all the waters underneath the earth's crust—all the caverns, springs, rivers, lakes, and perhaps seas of water—were *violently broken up*. The crust of the earth cracked under the violence of quake after quake and the waters burst loose and shot forth from under the crust of the earth. The picture is this: the subterranean water from beneath the earth and the water from the great oceans were violently discharged by quake after quake and hurled from their beds, churning and surging forth in huge, gigantic tidal waves. It would have been the raging and surging of the water that destroyed all those who tried to escape in other boats and ships of the day.

⇒ Leupold says: "The 'great deep' must be subterranean water of which there is still much and of which there may have been more in early days. It seems to be an established fact that 'outbursts of subterranean water are a frequent accompaniment of seismic disturbances [earthquakes] in the alluvial districts of great rivers....There must have been *vast upheavals* on every hand, for these fountains of the great deep 'were broken open.'"[1]

⇒ Leupold says again: "Note should be taken of the tremendous geological possibilities that lie behind the breaking open of the fountains of the great deep. The vastness of these eruptions must be in proportion to the actual depth of the Flood....The Flood was of astounding power and magnitude....Such eruptions from subterranean sources must have caused a rush of waters upon the earth comparable to the highest tidal wave. Such waves in turn must have been capable of producing effects of almost incalculable magnitude. So, then, the effects caused by the waters of the great deep (1:2), as they surged about on the earth in process of formation, together with the effects brought about by this great Flood, seem to us an entirely adequate explanation for geological formations of every kind, as they are now to be observed."[2]

⇒ The great *Pulpit Commentary* says: "The earth and other obstructions were broken up, and so a passage opened for the fountains [or subterranean waters]...this denotes violent changes in the depths of the sea, or in the action of the earth."[3]

⇒ Derek Kidner says: "A vast upheaval of the sea-bed" took place.[4]

c. God's power opened up the floodgates of heaven: a violent torrential downpour fell from the sky. Heavy rains—torrential downpours never witnessed before nor since—fell upon the earth. The torrential downpours continued, without any break whatsoever, for forty days and forty nights.

Note this: the torrential rain apparently stopped after forty days, but the waters flooded the earth for 150 days (Ge.8:2-3). This is significant, in particular when considering the core and surface of the earth. The breaking up of the earth's crust and the violent quaking of the earth's surface, and the churning and surging of the waters continued for 150 days, even

---

[1] H.C. Leupold. *Genesis*, Vol.1, pp.295-296.
[2] Ibid., p.296.
[3] *The Pulpit Commentary*, Vol.1, p.117.
[4] Derek Kidner. *Genesis*, p.91.

over the highest mountain peaks. It would continue for almost a year over the rest of the earth. This kind of violent, quaking movement, and erosion of the earth's core and land masses would drastically affect the shape and geological formations of the earth. The surface and inner core of the earth was apparently so changed that it was like a new earth. Absolutely nothing—no mountain, no valley, no body of water, no island, no continent, no land mass—could possibly be the same after so violent a quaking and flooding of the earth.

⇒ Just imagine the force required to break up all the subterranean waters around the world, the enormous quaking of the earth's core required to burst loose and shoot forth all the underground water under the earth's crust.

⇒ Just imagine the change throughout the earth's crust as the torrential rain fell for forty days and nights without stopping: all the erosion and washing away of mountains, all the valleys that filled up with the sediment from higher ground.

Just imagine the change within the earth's core and over the earth's surface as the force of the subterranean waters burst forth and as the force of the torrential rains flooded the earth. Imagine how drastic a change must have taken place...

• as mountains and hills eroded and literally washed away from the onslaught of the rushing water
• as valleys and crevices were filled up with the soil and debris from the higher elevations
• as quakes shifted and shot up mounds of dirt and hills and, most likely, even mountains

Again, nothing could ever be the same, not after such a violent quaking and forceful burst of water shot forth both from beneath the earth and from above the earth. Most if not all of the earth—both the core and the surface, both the rock formations and mineral deposits—was changed forever. As stated, two sources of water had changed it:

⇒ All the subterranean water had been broken up and shot forth by quake after quake—broken up by the power of God Himself.

⇒ Torrential downpours had fallen upon the earth—the very floodgates of the sky had been opened by God Himself.

> **"Behold, he withholdeth the waters, and they dry up: also he sendeth them out, and they overturn the earth" (Jb. 12:15).**

Thought 1. Think of the shifting and changing of the earth's core and surface that must have taken place under the violence of the surging and raging of the flood. The appearance—the geological change—of the earth must have been so drastically changed that the earth was totally different from what it had been, just like a brand new earth, both within its core and without on its surface.

But that was not all: verse twenty-four tells us that the waters flooded the earth for 150 days. The waters—the worldwide oceans—actually rose and surged and raged to their highest peak for 150 days. (Note: the aftershocks of such massive earthquakes that were necessary to burst loose the subterranean waters would continue on for days and months. This probably means that the core of the earth was also undergoing eruptions for 150 days. The impact of this violence upon the earth—upon the geological and fossil formations—would be tremendous.)

Any person who has ever worked around the pressure and force of water knows that it drastically changes its environment. The pressure and force of the great flood, the worldwide torrential rain and bursting loose of the earth's crust and shooting forth of all the subterranean waters—the awesome judgment of God—was bound to drastically change the earth forever thereafter, both its core and surface. This was the awesome judgment of God upon the earth in Noah's day. (See note—Ge.7:24 for more discussion. Also see DEEPER STUDY # 9, point B, Introduction to the Seven Days of Creation, Ge.1:1-2:3 for more discussion.)

---

2 (7:13-16) **Ark, The—Salvation:** there was the great salvation of God even in the midst of judgment: the ark of safety.

These verses tell us who went into the ark. Note that this information is given three times: in verses 1-4, 7-9, and now on the very day when the flood broke loose (vv.13-16). Why is this information—who entered the ark—stressed so much by Scripture?

There is one primary reason: it stresses the salvation of God, the eternal mercy and grace of God. Even in the midst of judgment—even as judgment fell—God was merciful. God was saving some, and here is a list of who they were:

⇒ Noah
⇒ Shem, Ham, and Japheth, Noah's three sons.
⇒ Noah's wife and the wives of his three sons.
⇒ The animals: at least two, a male and a female, of every kind of animal.

It was these that God had mercy upon and saved in the ark. Noah believed and followed God and taught his family to seek after God, and it was these—Noah and his dear family—who were the only people upon earth following God. Noah had lived in the midst of a lawless and immoral society, but he had stood firm for God and bore strong testimony to the righteousness and judgment of God. Therefore, God had mercy upon Noah and his dear family. God saved them and two of every kind of animal, saved them through the terrifying judgment, saved them through the ark of safety and security.

Note this: the Lord Himself shut the door to the ark. The idea is that God sealed the door to protect Noah from a leaking boat. There is a possibility that God was also protecting him from the violence of the people who might attack the ark and try to gain entrance. However, it is doubtful that any person had time to do anything with the torrential downpour that began to fall and with the violent wall of water that shot up from the subterranean caverns, rivers, lakes, and ocean beds. When God broke up the heavens and earth's crust with quake after quake, the people were bound to panic and have little if any time to do anything before the crushing waters swept them away to their death.

The point is this: Noah was now in the ark. Noah was in the ark of safety and security from the storm of coming judgment. The ark was Noah's vessel of refuge, the place appointed by God to save Noah and his family from the terrifying judgment that was about to fall upon the earth.

> **Thought 1.** The ark was a type or picture of Jesus Christ. Jesus Christ is the believer's refuge from judgment, the terrifying judgment of hell and eternal separation from God. Note how clearly the ark symbolizes what Christ does for us.

THE ARK	JESUS CHRIST
God Himself purposed and planned the ark, even to the most minute details (Ge.6:14-16).	God Himself purposed and planned the coming of Christ to save man, even before the foundation of the earth (Ep.1:3-4; 2 Ti.1:9-10; Tit.1:2; 1 Pe.1:2).
There was only one door to the ark (Ge.6:16).	Jesus Christ is the only door—the only way—to enter the presence of God (Jn.10:7, 9; 14:6; 1 Ti.2:5-6; 1 Jn.2:1).
God gave the provision for light within the ark. One window—an opening, a skylight—ran all the way around the ark. It ran within eighteen inches of the top (Ge.6:16).	God has given the provision of light to the world: Jesus Christ is the light of the world (Is.9:2; Jn.1:4; 8:12; 12:35; Ep.5:14; Re.21:23).
Some kind of pitch, probably some form of tar or asphalt, covered and sealed the ark. The Hebrew word for *pitch* (kopher) is the same word for atonement, which means to cover (Ge.6:14).	The blood of Jesus Christ covers the sins of the believer, cleanses and seals the believer before God (Ro.5:9; 5:11; Ep.1:7; He.9:14; 1 Pe.1:18-19; 1 Jn.1:7b; Re.1:5b).
God Himself gave the great invitation to come and enter the ark (Ge.7:1).	God Himself invites man to come and enter the ark—the safety and security—of His Son, the Lord Jesus Christ (Is.1:18; Jn.3:16-17; Mt.11:28; 22:2-4; Re.22:17).
The ark was a vessel of refuge, the place of safety and security from the torrential judgment about to fall upon the earth (Ge.6:17-18; 7:10-24).	Jesus Christ is the believer's refuge, the believer's safety and security from the coming judgment of hell and eternal separation from God (Jn.3:16; 5:24; Ro.5:9-10; Ro.6:23; He.7:25; 2 Pe.2:9).
The ark saved Noah and his family through the waters of judgment (Ge.7:10-24).	Jesus Christ saves the believer through the waters of judgment. The waters of baptism symbolize the saving work of Christ for the true believer. Peter used the ark and the waters of the flood to illustrate this point (1 Pe.3:20-21).
God called Noah to separate from the world—from its wickedness, evil and doom—by entering the ark (Ge.7:1).	God now calls people to live a life of separation from evil through Christ (Jn.15:19; 2 Co.5:17; 6:14-15, 17-18; 2 Th.3:6).
The ark was the salvation of both Noah and his family (Ge.6:18; 7:1, 7, 13, 23).	Jesus Christ is the hope of salvation for all families (Ac.16:30-31; see Ac.16:15).
The ark was secured—the door was closed—by God Himself (Ge.7:16b).	God Himself secures the believer through His Son, the Lord Jesus Christ. The believer has perfect security—God sees to it—through His Son the Lord Jesus Christ (Jn.10:28-29; Ph.1:6; 2 Ti.1:12b; 1 Pe.1:3-5; Jude 24-25).
God kept the door of mercy—the door of the ark—opened right up until the end. But when it was time for judgment the door was shut. There had been a time for grace, but there was also a time for judgment (Ge.7:16b, see 2 Pe.2:5).	God has his ministers and followers all over the world preaching the gospel of salvation. God has the door of mercy opened today, but the end is soon coming when the door will be shut and judgment will fall (Lu.13:24-27; Mt.25:1-13).

3 (7:17-23) **Judgment:** there was the great fulfillment of God's Word in judgment. This is the point of these verses, to show that God means exactly what He says, and He will do exactly what He says. When He warns us against sin and judgment, He means it. He will judge us if we reject, curse, and deny Him—if we do not live for Him. God fulfilled His Word; He did exactly what He said in the days of Noah.

a. God flooded water upon the earth for forty days, both the raging, surging water from underneath the crust of the earth and the torrential rains from the sky (vv.17-20). This is exactly what God had said He would do:

"And, behold, I, even I, do bring a flood of waters upon the earth" (Ge.6:17a).
"[After] seven days, I will cause it to rain upon the earth forty days and forty nights" (Ge.7:4).

God fulfilled His Word, did exactly what He had said: He flooded the earth for forty days and forty nights (v.17). The greatness of this act of God—of the flood—is beyond comprehension. It is an act of unparalleled magnitude, an enormous act, an act of immense power, strength and might, an act that God alone could do, the Sovereign Lord and Creator of the universe. Note how the magnitude and might of the waters are described:

⇒ The water increased. The Hebrew says, grew greatly and mounted up. The waters prevailed, that is, rose more and more, increased greatly, grew mightily, and mounted up upon the earth (v.18).

⇒ The waters prevailed exceedingly upon the earth; that is, rose and mounted up more and more and grew mightily over the earth, grew so mightily that "all the high mountains" were covered, all the mountains that were under the whole sky (v.19).

⇒ The waters rose and mounted up to a height of twenty feet (fifteen cubits) above the mountains. The ark was 45 feet high, so the water had to rise twenty feet in order to keep the ark from running aground upon some mountain peak. Again, the stress is the surety of God's Word and warning: God always means what He says, and He will fulfill His Word and do exactly what He says. He warned man against judgment if man continued in sin and rejection. Man continued; consequently, God had no choice. He had to judge man and flood the earth for forty days (v.20).

Note that the ark floated upon the water. It was not destroyed.

> **Thought 1.** God judges man because of man's selfishness and corruption, his self-sufficiency and rejection of God, his immorality and evil thoughts, his lawlessness and violence.
>
> **"And it came to pass, when men began to multiply on the face of the earth, and daughters were born unto them, that the sons of God saw the daughters of men that they were fair; and they took them wives of all which they chose. And the LORD said, My spirit shall not always strive with man, for that he also is flesh: yet his days shall be an hundred and twenty years" (Ge.6:1-3).**
>
> **"And God saw that the wickedness of man was great in the earth, and that every imagination of the thoughts of his heart was only evil continually. And it repented the LORD that he had made man on the earth, and it grieved him at his heart. And the LORD said, I will destroy man whom I have created from the face of the earth; both man, and beast, and the creeping thing, and the fowls of the air; for it repenteth me that I have made them" (Ge.6:5-7).**
>
> **"The earth also was corrupt before God, and the earth was filled with violence. And God looked upon the earth, and, behold, it was corrupt; for all flesh had corrupted his way upon the earth. And God said unto Noah, The end of all flesh is come before me; for the earth is filled with violence through them; and, behold, I will destroy them with the earth" (Ge.6:11-13).**
>
> **"And, behold, I, even I, do bring a flood of waters upon the earth, to destroy all flesh, wherein is the breath of life, from under heaven; and every thing that is in the earth shall die" (Ge.6:17).**

b. God destroyed all life (vv.21-23a). This is a tragic scene, yet it is a righteous or just act by God. God had no choice: He had warned man, warned him time and again, but man refused to heed God's warnings.

Despite God's warnings, man continued to curse, reject, deny, and rebel against God. Man continued to live immoral and lawless lives, filling the earth with violence. The tragedy of man's terrible evil and the justice of God are so significant that the judgment is repeated three times.

⇒ All flesh perished, every living thing that moved upon the earth, both animal and man (v.21).

⇒ Every living thing upon dry land, every living thing that had the breath of life in its nostrils, perished (v.22).

⇒ Every living thing upon the face of the ground was *wiped out*, both man and animal (v.23).

Remember what the Lord Jesus Christ said about the people of Noah's day and of Lot's day: that the last generation upon earth would be just like their day. The people of Noah's day were living selfish, indulgent, and materialistic lives right up until the end. They were eating, partying, drinking, marrying, and divorcing time and again, buying and selling, planting and building. This they were doing, not heeding the warning of judgment against sin.

> **"As it was in the days of Noe, so shall it be also in the days of the Son of man. They did eat, they drank, they married wives, they were given in marriage, until the day that Noe entered into the ark, and the flood came, and destroyed them all. Likewise also as it was in the days of Lot; they did eat, they drank, they bought, they sold, they planted, they builded; but the same day that Lot went out of Sodom it rained fire and brimstone from heaven, and destroyed them all. Even thus shall it be in the day when the Son of man is revealed" (Lu.17:26-30).**

The people of Noah's day were drowning long before the flood came upon the earth, drowning in...

- immorality and pleasure
- divorce and remarriage
- violence and lawlessness
- drunkenness and drugs
- partying and sensuality
- possessions and money
- buying and selling
- property and building

They rejected God, even denied and rebelled against Him, even cursed and swore against His name. They wanted nothing to do with God, and they had nothing to do with God. They rejected God even up until the very day that the flood waters burst loose. No wonder they had to face the judgment of God; no wonder God broke loose and burst forth seas and the subterranean caverns, rivers, and beds of water under the crust of the earth; no wonder God sent torrential rains never seen before nor since upon the earth; no wonder God swept them all away in the raging, surging bursts of water upon the earth. They were an immoral, self-centered, indulgent, lawless, violent, evil, and sinful people. God had warned the people, and now He was fulfilling His Word. He was doing exactly what He had to do: judging the people.

> **"Know ye not that the unrighteous shall not inherit the kingdom of God? Be not deceived: neither fornicators, nor idolaters, nor adulterers, nor effeminate [homosexuals], nor abusers of themselves with mankind. Nor thieves, nor covetous, nor drunkards, nor revilers, nor extortioners, shall inherit the kingdom of God" (1 Co.6:9-10; see Ge.6:1-2, 5, 11-13).**
>
> **"Now the works of the flesh are manifest, which are these; Adultery, fornication, uncleanness, lasciviousness, idolatry, witchcraft, hatred, variance, emulations, wrath, strife, seditions, heresies, envyings, murders, drunkenness, revellings, and such like: of the which I tell you before, as I have also told you in time past, that they which do such things shall not inherit the kingdom of God" (Ga.5:19-21).**
>
> **"But the fearful, and unbelieving, and the abominable, and murderers, and whoremongers, and sorcerers, and idolaters, and all liars, shall have their part in the lake which burneth with fire and brimstone: which is the second death" (Re.21:8).**

c. God saved Noah and all those in the ark with him (v.23b). This, too, was the fulfillment of God's Word. God had promised to save Noah.

> **"But with thee will I establish my covenant; and thou shalt come into the ark, thou, and thy sons, and thy wife, and thy sons' wives with thee. And of every living thing of all flesh" (Ge.6:18-19a).**
>
> **"And the LORD said unto Noah, Come thou and all thy house into the ark; for thee have I seen righteous before me in this generation. Of every clean beast thou shalt take to thee by sevens, the male and his female: and of beasts that are not clean by two, the male and his female" (Ge.7:1-2).**

Picture the scene: Noah is sitting there in the ark while thousands outside are being swept away by onrushing floods and bursts of water, screaming out in fright and terror, but their voices could not be heard because of the roar from the onrushing waters. There was no one to save them, not now. They had waited too late. But there sat Noah and his family in the ark, safe and secure, saved from the terrifying, but just, judgment of God.

Noah is a living example of the mercy of God. He and he alone had believed and followed God. He and he alone had obeyed and based his life upon the Word of God and the warning of God. Therefore, God saved Noah and his dear family, saved them through the terrifying judgment.

Thought 1. God will save any person who believes and follows Him, any person who fully obeys and bases his life upon His Word and His warnings.

> **"For God so loved the world, that he gave his only begotten Son, that whosoever believeth in him should not perish, but have everlasting life" (Jn.3:16).**
>
> **"Verily, verily, I say unto you, He that heareth my word, and believeth on him that sent me, hath everlasting life, and shall not come into condemnation; but is passed from death unto life" (Jn.5:24).**
>
> **"And it shall come to pass, that whosoever shall call on the name of the Lord shall be saved" (Ac.2:21).**
>
> **"For whosoever shall call upon the name of the Lord shall be saved" (Ro.10:13).**
>
> **"For the grace of God that bringeth salvation hath appeared to all men, teaching us that, denying ungodliness and worldly lusts, we should live soberly, righteously, and godly, in this present world; looking for that blessed hope, and the glorious appearing of the great God and our Savior Jesus Christ" (Tit.2:11-13).**
>
> **"Knowing this first, that there shall come in the last days scoffers, walking after their own lusts, and saying, Where is the promise of his coming? for since the fathers fell asleep, all things continue as they were from the beginning of the creation. For this they willingly are ignorant of, that by the word of God the heavens were of old, and the earth standing out of the water and in the water: whereby the world that then was, being overflowed with water, perished: but the heavens and the earth, which are now, by the same word are kept in store, reserved unto fire against the day of judgment and perdition of ungodly men. But, beloved, be not ignorant of this one thing, that one day is with the Lord as a thousand years, and a thousand years as one day. The Lord is not slack concerning his promise, as some men count slackness; but is longsuffering to us-ward, not willing that any should perish, but that all should come to repentance. But the day of the Lord will come as a thief in the night; in the which the heavens shall pass away with a great noise, and the elements shall melt with fervent heat, the earth also and the works that are therein shall be burned up. Seeing then that all these things shall be dissolved, what manner of persons ought ye to be in all holy conversation and godliness. Looking for and hasting unto the coming of the day of God, wherein the heavens being on fire shall be dissolved, and the elements shall melt with fervent heat? Nevertheless we, according to his promise, look for new heavens and a new earth, wherein dwelleth righteousness" (2 Pe.3:3-13).**

270

"Behold, God is my salvation; I will trust, and not be afraid: for the Lord Jehovah is my strength and my song; he also is become my salvation" (Is.12:2).

4 (7:24) **Flood, The—Judgment**: there was the great time that the waters flooded the earth in judgment, 150 days. This means that the waters stayed at their full height or peak (elevation) for 150 days. (See note, pt.d.—Ge.8:1-5 for more discussion.) Just imagine these facts:

⇒ *All* the high mountains under the whole heaven were covered. This is a Hebrew superlative, that is, Scripture is declaring that the whole earth was flooded, not just a part of the earth. The flood was a universal flood. Again, the word *all* is a Hebrew superlative.[5]

⇒ The water rose twenty feet above the mountains.

⇒ The water flooded the earth at its full peak for 150 days.

The point is this: only God could do such a thing. No matter how much scientific proof is ever gathered for the flood—and the scientific proof is great—the flood was caused by God. All the explainable and unexplainable features of the flood were caused and worked out by God. For example:

⇒ One theory says that before the flood a canopy of clouds and fog always hung above the earth. The clouds and fog filtered the rays of the sun and delayed aging and decay as we know them today. Those who hold this position say this is the reason people lived so long and why grape juice or wine did not ferment until after the flood (see Ge.9:20).

⇒ Another theory says that God tilted the earth on its axis to its present 23 1/2 degrees. This caused violent quakes and eruptions of the earth's crust and oceans. It is also said to account for the change in seasons and climate after the flood.

Again, whatever happened, God was behind it all. He was the Person who caused and worked out both what we can explain and cannot explain. The flood was the judgment of God upon an immoral, lawless, and violent world. (See notes—Ge.6:1-8; pt.b.,c.—7:10-12 for more discussion.)

Thought 1. The flood took place too long ago for us—both scientists and theologians—to be able to work out all the details. Where we cannot work out the details, God expects us to believe His Word. We should continue to investigate the details and discover the facts, yes; but first and foremost, we should believe God and believe His Word while we seek the answers to our questions. As we all know, despite our great intelligence and resourcefulness, we are far more ignorant of past history and of the universe than we are knowledgeable.

---

5 H.C. Leupold. *Genesis*, Vol.1, pp.301-302.

1. Scene 1: God remembered & moved in behalf of Noah & the animals
  a. God caused a wind to pass over the earth
 	
  b. God stopped the subterranean waters
  c. God stopped the torrential rain
 	
  d. God caused the waters to begin to recede
 	
  e. God rested the ark upon the mountains of Ararat
 	
  f. God gave Noah & his dear family sight of the mountaintops
 	
2. Scene 2: Noah's great patience & faith[DS1]
  a. Noah—in faith—waited patiently forty days
    1) He opened the hatch
    2) He sent forth a raven that remained outside & flew back & forth
	CHAPTER 8
	
	E. Noah & God: God's Great Preservation (Salvation) of Life, 8:1-14
	
	And God remembered Noah, and every living thing, and all the cattle that was with him in the ark: and God made a wind to pass over the earth, and the waters assuaged;
	2 The fountains also of the deep and the windows of heaven were stopped, and the rain from heaven was restrained;
	3 And the waters returned from off the earth continually: and after the end of the hundred and fifty days the waters were abated.
	4 And the ark rested in the seventh month, on the seventeenth day of the month, upon the mountains of Ararat.
	5 And the waters decreased continually until the tenth month: in the tenth month, on the first day of the month, were the tops of the mountains seen.
	6 And it came to pass at the end of forty days, that Noah opened the window of the ark which he had made:
	7 And he sent forth a raven, which went forth to and fro, until the waters were dried up
		from off the earth.
		8 Also he sent forth a dove from him, to see if the waters were abated from off the face of the ground;
		9 But the dove found no rest for the sole of her foot, and she returned unto him into the ark, for the waters were on the face of the whole earth: then he put forth his hand, and took her, and pulled her in unto him into the ark.
		10 And he stayed yet other seven days; and again he sent forth the dove out of the ark;
		11 And the dove came in to him in the evening; and, lo, in her mouth was an olive leaf plucked off: so Noah knew that the waters were abated from off the earth.
		12 And he stayed yet other seven days; and sent forth the dove; which returned not again unto him any more.
		13 And it came to pass in the six hundredth and first year, in the first month, the first day of the month, the waters were dried up from off the earth: and Noah removed the covering of the ark, and looked, and, behold, the face of the ground was dry.
		14 And in the second month, on the seven and twentieth day of the month, was the earth dried.
			b. Noah—in faith—patiently waited seven more days
			    1) He sent forth a dove
			
			    2) The dove found no resting place & returned to Noah in the ark
			    3) Noah tenderly reached out his hand & took the dove to himself into the ark
			
			  c. Noah—in faith—patiently waited seven more days
			    1) He sent the dove again
			    2) The dove did not return until evening, returning with a fresh olive branch
			    3) Noah knew the waters had receded
			
			  d. Noah—in faith—patiently waited seven more days: Sent the dove & it did not return
			
			  e. Noah—in faith—patiently waited twenty-nine more days, until the first month of the year, day one
			    1) He removed the covering of the ark
			    2) He saw the ground was drying out
			
			  f. Noah—in faith—patiently waited 57 more days, waited until the earth was completely dry (2nd month, day 27)

DIVISION IV

NOAH: THE MAN CHOSEN TO PRESERVE MANKIND AND THE GODLY SEED THROUGH WORLD DESTRUCTION (THE FLOOD), 6:9–9:29

E. Noah and God: God's Great Preservation (Salvation) of Life, 8:1-14

(8:1-14) Introduction: imagine the feelings and emotions of Noah and his dear family, the restlessness that must have gripped their minds and hearts. Is it even possible to imagine what they experienced?

⇒ Imagine being caught in the heaviest torrential rain to ever strike the earth, a rain so heavy that you could not see your hand in front of your face. Imagine a torrential downpour that heavy falling for forty days and forty nights upon the earth.

⇒ Imagine being caught in the middle of quake after quake—quakes so violent that all the subterranean waters broke loose and shot up from the caverns, rivers, lakes, and springs that lie underneath the crust of the earth.

The forty days of the erupting earth and torrential rain must have been a terrifying time, a time so terrifying that the small band of survivors often fell to their knees, individually and jointly. Their hearts must have cried out continually for the mercy of God as they went about their daily duties of survival and of taking care of the animals. After the violent storm and eruptions of the earth for forty days, everything apparently quieted down to some degree, although the water still rose and still churned and raged on for a total of 150 days (Ge.7:24).

Noah and his dear family had plenty of work to do. Picture them caring for, feeding, and cleaning up after the animals and after themselves. But keep this in mind: they were enclosed in a box-like structure, three stories high and 150 yards long, the length of one and one half football fields. They had to take care of the animals and themselves for 150 days, floating within the shell of the ark. They were bound to feel...

- cooped up
- restless
- shut in
- confined
- almost imprisoned

Here and there—sometimes—nerves were bound to become edgy and words sharp. Emotions were bound to be ruffled and feelings were bound to be hurt. The little band of survivors were believers, but they were human beings, sinful human beings who had been saved only by God's mercy and grace. They were, therefore, just like us, subject to such human emotions and feelings. There must have also been times when they wondered, "How much longer will the flood last? How much longer will we be cooped up? How much longer before God will deliver us and let us step on the earth again? And, what will it be like: no one left—no man, no woman, no child, no animal—just us, our family, the eight of us?" Imagine the thoughts that crossed their minds and the conversation between them as they sat around together after a long and hard day's work. Imagine the questions, apprehension, anxiety, fear, and perhaps even trembling. Just four men and four women left upon earth. Can we imagine their feelings, emotions, and conversations? Is is possible?

Now, note the great message of this passage, for God saved this courageous family. God saved these eight souls who had been so courageous in following and worshipping God in the midst of an immoral and lawless society. This is the Scripture that covers *Noah and God: God's Great Preservation and Salvation of Life.*

1. Scene 1: God remembered and moved in behalf of Noah and the animals (vv.1-5).
2. Scene 2: Noah's great patience and faith (vv.6-14).

1 (8:1-5) **Flood, The—God, Mercy—Ark, The—Ararat, Mount of**: there was the first scene: God remembered and moved in behalf of Noah and the animals. God never forgot Noah. God is *Elohim*, the Almighty God, the Lord and Majesty of the universe who created and sustains all things. Consequently, God has perfect intelligence and memory. He never forgets. When Scripture says that God remembered Noah and the animals, it means that God cared for His creation, cared for the people and animals He had created. God remembered and thought upon them; He loved them and He was *now ready to act in their behalf*. His mind had now reached the point when His love and care was to be demonstrated: action was now to be taken; something was now to be done for them. God was not going to leave them in their predicament. God remembered them; He was now going to deliver them and save them.

Again, God never forgot Noah; He never forgets anything. But it had been 150 days since God had spoken to Noah; 150 days since God had instructed him. It was almost like God had forgotten Noah, for one hundred and fifty days is a long time. Imagine being cooped up in a box-like structure—the ark, a house, anyplace—for 150 days. Did Noah feel forsaken, as though God had forgotten him? He was the leader of the small band of survivors, the only eight people left upon earth. Was Noah feeling the pressure, being questioned by them, feeling the responsibility, feeling all alone, wondering why God did not meet him and give some direction? Any or all of this is possible, and most likely the feelings and thoughts did arise at various times during the 150 days. But now, God remembered Noah: it was time to act...

- to show concern and to have mercy
- to preserve and save life, both the life of man and of the animals

Therefore, God remembered Noah and the animals: He had mercy and compassion for them. How? God did six significant things for Noah.

a. God caused a wind to pass over the earth. Wind is "air in motion."[1] This particular wind, just like all else with the flood, was a very special wind stirred up by God to help recede the water from the earth.

⇒ Was a hot sultry wind to help increase the evaporation of the water quicker than usual?
⇒ Was it a strong wind to help move some of the water to its proper channels and beds?
⇒ Was it a wind to simply help dry the earth?
⇒ Was it a wind to help drive away and dissolve the massive clouds that hung over the earth?

We are not told. All Scripture says is that the wind was the work of God, a special wind created by God Himself to help recede the waters.

b. God stopped the subterranean water from pouring forth upon the earth. He closed up the caverns, rivers, and lakes lying right underneath the earth's crust. God was demonstrating His mercy to man by stopping the surging forth of subterranean water upon earth.

c. God stopped the torrential rain (v.2). The Hebrew word *yikkale* is emphatic: it means that the torrential rain was stopped; it ended. The rain no longer fell upon the earth. In mercy, God stopped the water from building up upon the earth any longer.

d. God caused the waters to begin to recede. Note when: after 150 days (v.3). The waters remained at their peak for 150 days. Genesis 7:24 makes this clear. Now after 150 days the waters began to recede.[2] The commentator Victor Hamilton gives a clear translation of verse three:

The waters returned from off the earth: they began to withdraw at the end of a hundred and fifty days (v.3).[3]

e. God rested the ark upon some peak in the mountains of Ararat (v.4). What peak? What particular mountain did the ark settle upon? Scripture does not say; it uses the plural: *the mountains of Ararat*. This is the mountain range found...

- in the present nation of Armenia or eastern Turkey
- in the ancient Assyrian kingdom of *Urartu*

The highest peak in the mountain range is Mt. Ararat itself which towers some 17,000 feet high. Note that the exact date is given when the ark rested upon the mountain peak: on the 17th day of the 7th month.

---

1 *Funk & Wagnalls Standard Desk Dictionary*, Vol.2. (Lippincott & Crowell Publishers, 1980), p.327.
2 H.C. Leupold. *Genesis*, Vol.1, pp.306, 310-311.
3 Victor Hamilton. *The Book of Genesis,* Vol.1, p.299.

f. At last, God gave Noah and his dear family sight of the mountaintops (v.5). The Hebrew points out that the waters were decreasing rapidly, miraculously.[4] God, in His mercy toward man, was at work. He was causing the water to recede so that Noah and his dear family could be saved and repopulate the earth. It was now the first day of the 10th month, two and a half months after the ark had first rested upon some mountain peak. Imagine their joy when they first felt the ark rest upon dry land, and now imagine their joy as they are able to look out some hatch or trap-like window. What they see causes their hearts to leap with joy, for they see the peaks of surrounding mountains. They know as never before that God is merciful, that He is receding the water and saving them. This small band of believers must have done exactly what any believer would have done: praised God and rejoiced in Him for His great salvation.

Thought 1. Note that the exact time is given when the ark brought the passengers to safety. Christian believers are told that "when the fulness of the time was come, God sent forth His son...to redeem them...." (Ga.4:4-5). There was and is a preparation—a set time—for God's people to be brought to safety. (See note—Ge.8:6-14.) As the points of this note show, God remembers His people; God remembers every living thing. What He demands is faith and patience in Him as He carries us through the trials of this life and our coming departure from this earth.

"Casting all your care upon him; for he careth for you" (1 Pe.5:7).
"Let not your heart be troubled: ye believe in God, believe also in me. In my Father's house are many mansions: if it were not so, I would have told you. I go to prepare a place for you" (Jn.14:1-2).
"But when the fulness of the time was come, God sent forth his Son, made of a woman, made under the law, to redeem them that were under the law, that we might receive the adoption of sons. And because ye are sons, God hath sent forth the Spirit of his Son into your hearts, crying, Abba, Father" (Ga.4:4-6).
"For ye have not received the spirit of bondage again to fear; but ye have received the Spirit of adoption, whereby we cry, Abba, Father. The Spirit itself beareth witness with our spirit, that we are the children of God: and if children, then heirs; heirs of God, and joint-heirs with Christ; if so be that we suffer with him, that we may be also glorified together" (Ro.8:15-17).

Thought 2. God delivers His people through the trials of this life. Sometimes the journey may be long and hard, even as Noah's was. But God still delivers us through all the sufferings of life, if we just trust Him as Noah did. This is the reason Scripture tells us to joy and rejoice through the trials of life: God delivers and saves us.

"Rejoice in the Lord always: again I say, Rejoice" (Ph.4:4).
"Beloved, think it not strange concerning the fiery trial which is to try you, as though some strange thing happened unto you: but rejoice, inasmuch as ye are partakers of Christ's sufferings; that, when his glory shall be revealed, ye may be glad also with exceeding joy" (1 Pe.4:12-13).
"My brethren, count it all joy when ye fall into divers temptations" (Js.1:2).
"Although the fig tree shall not blossom, neither shall fruit be in the vines; the labour of the olive shall fail, and the fields shall yield no meat; the flock shall be cut off from the fold, and there shall be no herd in the stalls: yet I will rejoice in the LORD, I will joy in the God of my salvation" (Hab.3:17-18).
"And they departed from the presence of the council, rejoicing that they were counted worthy to suffer shame for his name" (Ac.5:41).
"And when they had laid many stripes upon them, they cast them into prison, charging the jailor to keep them safely....And at midnight Paul and Silas prayed, and sang praises unto God: and the prisoners heard them" (Ac.16:23, 25).
"As sorrowful, yet alway rejoicing; as poor, yet making many rich; as having nothing, and yet possessing all things" (2 Co.6:10).
"For ye had compassion of me in my bonds, and took joyfully the spoiling of your goods, knowing in yourselves that ye have in heaven a better and an enduring substance" (He.10:34).

Thought 3. God can control nature, the rain, winds, and storms of the earth. He can control all the trials inflicted upon us by nature or man when it is His will to do so, when it fulfills His purposes.
⇒ Think of this: how many storms—how many devastating acts of nature and of evil men—would have never happened if we had prayed like we should, prayed much and prayed faithfully?
⇒ Ask this question: if we truly sought God and walked with God as Noah did (see Ge.6:9), would God move in behalf of the earth and of mankind more often? Would He save us more often from the devastating storms and evils of life?

"Ye have not, because ye ask not" (Js.4:2).
"Ask, and it shall be given you; seek, and ye shall find; knock, and it shall be opened unto you" (Mt.7:7).
"And all things, whatsoever ye shall ask in prayer, believing, ye shall receive" (Mt.21:22).
"If ye abide in me, and my words abide in you, ye shall ask what ye will, and it shall be done unto you" (Jn.15:7).

---

4 H.C. Leupold. *Genesis*, Vol.1, p.312.

"Now unto him that is able to do exceeding abundantly above all that we ask or think, according to the power that worketh in us" (Ep.3:20).

"O thou that hearest prayer, unto thee shall all flesh come" (Ps.65:2).

"If my people, which are called by my name, shall humble themselves, and pray, and seek my face, and turn from their wicked ways; then will I hear from heaven, and will forgive their sin, and will heal their land" (2 Chr.7:14).

"When thou passest through the waters, I will be with thee; and through the rivers, they shall not overflow thee: when thou walkest through the fire, thou shalt not be burned; neither shall the flame kindle upon thee" (Is.43:2).

"And it shall come to pass, that before they call, I will answer; and while they are yet speaking, I will hear" (Is.65:24).

"Call unto me, and I will answer thee, and show thee great and mighty things, which thou knowest not" (Je.33:3).

---

2 (8:6-14) **Patience—Faith—Trust—Noah—Salvation—Deliverance**: there was the second scene: Noah's great faith and patience before God. His faith and patience are clearly seen in the six events pointed out in the outline:

a. Note the great faith and patience of Noah.

1) Noah—in faith—patiently waited forty days after seeing the mountaintops before sending the raven out to search for dry land (v.6).

2) Noah—in faith—patiently waited seven more days before sending a dove out to search for dry land. The time frame of seven days is not actually given in verse 8, but note verse 10. The Hebrew says that Noah waited "*another* seven days" and "*again*" sent forth the dove. This points back to a seven day waiting period for sending each of the birds out (v.8).

3) Noah—in faith—patiently waited seven more days before sending the dove out again (v.10).

4) Noah—in faith—patiently waited seven more days before sending the dove out again (v.12).

5) Noah—in faith—patiently waited twenty-nine more days before removing the covering of the ark (v.13).

6) Noah—in faith—patiently waited fifty-seven more days until the earth was completely dry (v.14).

Noah's great faith and patience in God is unquestionable. This is the stress of these nine verses. Noah was trusting God and patiently waiting for God to dry out the earth so that he and his dear family could leave the ark and begin their new life upon the earth.

Imagine how difficult it was for them to keep waiting and waiting! They had been inside of the ark for almost a year, never even allowed to go out on the deck. They were bound to feel cooped up and confined, caged and shut in, almost imprisoned. And now, the water was receding: they could see the water level dropping and exposing more and more of the mountains and land every day. How excited they must have been! The urge to throw open the door and to step out on dry ground must have gnawed and gnawed at them. Yet how fearful they must have been, for they had no idea what lay ahead! The judgment of God had fallen and destroyed all life upon earth, both man and beast—all life except the few people and animals left upon the ark. What would life be like with no other people upon earth? What were they to expect—what kind of relationship with God—from now on? What would God now expect from them? So far as we know, God had not given Noah any new message or revelation since He had locked Noah into the ark. Excitement and a desire to get out of the ark were bound to fill their hearts, yes; but an apprehension, uneasiness, anxiety, and fear were also bound to be attacking their thoughts and emotions.

But through it all—through all the mental anguish and emotional uneasiness—Noah trusted God and waited patiently upon God.

Thought 1. What a dynamic example for us, a dynamic example of faith in God and of patience with God! No matter what confronts us, the apprehension, uneasiness, and fear could never match what Noah suffered. Yet, through it all he trusted and patiently waited upon God. May God grant to us the same faith and patience that Noah demonstrated.

"In your patience possess ye your souls" (Lu.21:19).

"Rejoicing in hope; patient in tribulation; continuing instant in prayer" (Ro.12:12).

"For ye have need of patience, that, after ye have done the will of God, ye might receive the promise" (He.10:36).

"Knowing this, that the trying of your faith worketh patience. But let patience have her perfect work, that ye may be perfect and entire, wanting nothing. If any of you lack wisdom, let him ask of God, that giveth to all men liberally, and upbraideth not [does not find fault]; and it shall be given him" (Js.1:3-5).

"Be patient therefore, brethren, unto the coming of the Lord. Behold, the husbandman waiteth for the precious fruit of the earth, and hath long patience for it, until he receive the early and latter rain. Be ye also patient; stablish your hearts: for the coming of the Lord draweth nigh" (Js.5:7-8).

"Oh how great is thy goodness, which thou hast laid up for them that fear thee; which thou hast wrought for them that trust in thee before the sons of men!" (Ps.31:19).

"The LORD redeemeth the soul of his servants: and none of them that trust in him shall be desolate" (Ps.34:22).

"Commit thy way unto the LORD; trust also in him; and he shall bring it to pass" (Ps.37:5).

"Trust in the LORD with all thine heart; and lean not unto thine own understanding" (Pr.3:5).

"Thou wilt keep him in perfect peace, whose mind is stayed on thee: because he trusteth in thee. Trust ye in the LORD for ever: for in the LORD JEHOVAH is everlasting strength" (Is.26:3-4).

"Who is among you that feareth the LORD, that obeyeth the voice of his servant, that walketh in darkness, and hath no light? let him trust in the name of the LORD, and stay upon his God" (Is.50:10).

Thought 2. Note how Noah did not become impatient and run ahead of God. He did not rush the will of God. It was God's will for him to leave the ark, but when? What Noah needed was faith and patience in God...

- faith that God would clearly show him when to leave the ark
- the patience to seek after God and to wait until God did show him

This Noah did, and this we must do. We must have faith and patience that God will clearly show us His will and show us when to act.

b. Note that Noah waited seven days each time he sent the birds out to search for dry land (vv.7, 8, 10, 12). This definitely points toward the Sabbath, the fact that Noah sent the birds out on the day already sanctified by God, the day of worship. Noah sent the birds out in *hope, great hope in God*. No better day could be chosen to send them forth than the day of worship. To have chosen the Sabbath day, the day of prayer and worship, was only natural. We—every genuine believer who had experienced what Noah had experienced—would have done the very same thing: sent forth the birds in hope, prayer, and worship on the very special day God had set aside for the worship of God. (See note—Ge.2:3 for more discussion.)

Thought 1. The significance Noah placed upon the day of worship should speak to us. How often we neglect the day of worship, the very day God Himself set apart for us to concentrate upon Him, to rest and seek Him.

"And God blessed the seventh day, and sanctified it [set it apart]: because that in it he had rested from all his work which God created and made" (Ge.2:3).

"Remember the sabbath day, to keep it holy" (Ex.20:8).

"Six days thou shalt work, but on the seventh day thou shalt rest: in earing time and in harvest thou shalt rest" (Ex.34:21).

"Blessed is the man that doeth this, and the son of man that layeth hold on it; that keepeth the sabbath from polluting it, and keepeth his hand from doing any evil" (Is.56:2).

"If thou turn away thy foot from the sabbath, from doing thy pleasure on my holy day; and call the sabbath a delight, the holy of the LORD, honourable; and shalt honour him, not doing thine own ways, nor finding thine own pleasure, nor speaking thine own words: then shalt thou delight thyself in the LORD; and I will cause thee to ride upon the high places of the earth, and feed thee with the heritage of Jacob thy father: for the mouth of the LORD hath spoken it" (Is.58:13-14).

"And upon the first day of the week, when the disciples came together to break bread, Paul preached unto them, ready to depart on the morrow; and continued his speech until midnight" (Ac.20:7).

"Upon the first day of the week let every one of you lay by him in store, as God hath prospered him, that there be no gatherings when I come" (1 Co.16:2).

c. Note several small details about the six events of this passage.
1) Noah probably sent a raven out because it was a scavenger and could find food floating or lying about more easily than most other birds. Note the raven did not return to the inside of the ark, but flew back and forth, probably resting on top of the ark. Noah and the passengers probably heard the cawing of the bird as it roosted on the ark.
2) The dove is a bird that stays closer to the ground than most other birds. This is probably the reason Noah sent out a dove in search of dry ground. If the bird stayed out, Noah would know that the water had receded enough to expose some of the low lying land.
3) Note the tenderness of Noah and the dove. When the dove returned, Noah put his hand out the hatch and the dove flew in and lit upon his hand (v.9). A man who is tender toward animals is usually a tender man.
4) Note that the dove did not return until the evening hours on its second journey. As the late afternoon and early evening hours wore on, how expectant and hopeful the passengers must have been! They thought the dove was not returning! The water had receded enough for the land to begin drying out and the dove could now remain outside the ark. It would not be long now! They would soon be able to disembark and settle upon earth!

What an increase of joy and expectancy must have surged through their hearts when the bird returned with the evidence: a fresh olive leaf plucked from a tree (the Hebrew says that the leaf was a fresh or new leaf). The survivors now knew beyond a doubt that God had saved them. There was peace between God and the survivors of faith. Those who truly believed and followed God had been saved from the judgment upon an evil world.

Thought 1. James Montgomery Boice points out that this experience was so moving that the picture of a dove carrying an olive branch is the sign of peace even today.[5]

5) When the dove did not return on its third trip, the survivors knew beyond all question that the water had receded and the earth would now be drying out rather quickly.

---

5   James Montgomery Boice. *Genesis,* Vol.1, p.298.

6) Twenty-nine days later Noah removed a portion of the top of the ark, looked out, and saw that the water had completely receded. The earth was drying out.

7) It was 57 days later before the earth was completely dried out (see DEEPER STUDY # 1—Ge.8:6-14 for a chart on "The Time of the Flood").

DEEPER STUDY # 1

(8:6-14) **Flood, The**: the chart below is based upon the following facts. The calendar in Noah's day seems to be made up of 12 months of 30 days each.

⇒ It is said to be 150 days that the waters remained at their peak (Ge.7:24).

⇒ It is said to be 150 days—probably a period of 5 months (30 days each)—between the beginning of the flood to the time the ark settled on Mt. Ararat (Ge.8:4).

Both of these references seem to point to a period of five months of thirty days each. The following chart is based upon twelve months of thirty days each. This means that Noah and the other survivors were in the ark for...

- one year and 10 days according to the calendar year of Noah's day
- one year and 5 days according to today's solar year

THE TIME OF THE FLOOD

	Month	Day	Total Days	Scripture
Flood begins. The rain and subterranean waters break loose.	2	17		7:11
Flood continues for 40 days.			40	7:12
Flood prevails for a total of 150 days.			150	7:24
Ark settles on Mt. Ararat on the same day the waters begin to recede (150 days after the flood began).	7	17	150	8:4
Mountaintops are seen 73 days later.	10	1	223	8:5
Raven sent after 40 days.			263	8:6-7
Dove sent after 7 days.			270	8:8, see 8:10
Dove sent after 7 more days and returned with a tree branch.			277	8:10
Dove sent after 7 more days and did not return.			284	8:12
Earth's surface is seen to be drying 29 days later.	1	1	313	8:13
Earth's surface is dried 57 days later.	2	27	370	8:14

	F. Noah & the Great Day: God Sent Noah Forth into the World to Begin a New Life, 8:15-22	ing thing, and every fowl, and whatsoever creepeth upon the earth, after their kinds, went forth out of the ark.	out of the ark, each according to its kind or species
1. Scene 1: God's long-awaited instructions a. First, to leave the ark & take his family	15 And God spake unto Noah, saying, 16 Go forth of the ark, thou, and thy wife, and thy sons, and thy sons' wives with thee.	20 And Noah builded an altar unto the LORD; and took of every clean beast, and of every clean fowl, and offered burnt offerings on the altar.	3. Scene 3: Noah's first act—he set up a place for worship a. He built an altar b. He offered a sacrifice, a burnt offering, to God^{DS1}
b. Second, to bring out all the animals so they could breed & replenish the earth	17 Bring forth with thee every living thing that is with thee, of all flesh, both of fowl, and of cattle, and of every creeping thing that creepeth upon the earth; that they may breed abundantly in the earth, and be fruitful, and multiply upon the earth.	21 And the LORD smelled a sweet savour; and the LORD said in his heart, I will not again curse the ground any more for man's sake; for the imagination of man's heart is evil from his youth; neither will I again smite any more every thing living, as I have done.	4. Scene 4: God's great pleasure with Noah's sacrifice & God's great promises to Noah & the human race a. To never again curse the earth with a universal flood b. To never again destroy all life with a universal flood
2. Scene 2: Noah's strict obedience a. He led his family out of the ark b. He then led the animals	18 And Noah went forth, and his sons, and his wife, and his sons' wives with him: 19 Every beast, every creep-	22 While the earth remaineth, seedtime and harvest, and cold and heat, and summer and winter, and day and night shall not cease.	c. To guarantee the times & seasons of the earth

DIVISION IV

NOAH: THE MAN CHOSEN TO PRESERVE MANKIND AND THE GODLY SEED THROUGH WORLD DESTRUCTION (THE FLOOD), 6:9–9:29

F. Noah and the Great Day: God Sent Noah Forth into the World to Begin a New Life, 8:15-22

(8:15-22) **Introduction**: remember the feelings and emotions of Noah and his dear family. They and the animals had been upon the ark for a year and ten days. Just imagine what they had experienced as God judged the earth for its lawlessness, immorality, and violence:

⇒ the convulsive upheaval of the earth as the subterranean waters broke loose from their underground caverns.
⇒ the torrential downpour of rain for 40 consecutive days and nights.
⇒ the covering of the whole earth with water.
⇒ every living person and animal being drowned—all except the few survivors upon the ark.

They had experienced the living reality of God's judgment, that God means exactly what He says when He warns men against sin: against lawlessness, immorality, and violence. As stated, they had been inside the ark which was floating around for a whole year and ten days, aware of the awesome judgment and power of God. The little band of survivors was bound to sense some apprehension, uneasiness, awe, and fear before God, for they had witnessed God's awesome judgment. In addition, having been stranded inside the ark for 370 days, they were bound to feel confined, cooped up, caged, shut in, and almost imprisoned. The urge to just burst out and touch dry land must have gripped them from time to time.

Just imagine the excitement that gripped the survivors...

• when they felt the ark strike Mt. Ararat and settle upon it (Ge.8:5)
• when they looked out and saw the mountain tops for the first time in over 200 days (Ge.8:5)
• when the raven was sent out to search for dry land and did not return (Ge.8:6-7)
• when the dove was sent out and brought back an olive branch and then sent out again and did not return (Ge.8:10, 12)
• when they removed part of the top of the ark, stepped out, and looked at the ground below and saw that it was drying out (Ge.8:13)
• as they waited 57 more days for the earth to dry out completely (Ge.8:14)

Excitement must have flooded their hearts as they experienced each of these events. They knew that the day when they could step out upon dry ground was soon arriving. They knew that they could soon leave the ark and settle once again upon the earth. This is the subject of this great passage: *Noah and the Great Day: God Sent Noah Forth into the World to Begin a New Life.*

1. Scene 1: God's long-awaited instructions (vv.15-17).
2. Scene 2: Noah's strict obedience (vv.18-19).
3. Scene 3: Noah's first act—he set up a place for worship (v.20).
4. Scene 4: God's great pleasure with Noah's sacrifice and God's great promises to Noah and the human race (vv.21-22).

1 (8:15-17) **God, Faithfulness of**: there was the first scene: God's long-awaited faithfulness and command. God spoke to Noah. God had not given any new instructions to Noah since the day He had told Noah to enter the ark (Ge.7:1f).

That had been over a year before. God had promised to save Noah through the awful judgment that was to come upon the earth (Ge.6:17-18). God was faithful. His faithfulness had been proven throughout the deluge of water that had flooded the earth; He had saved Noah through the judgment. Now, God's faithfulness was to be proven in the new instructions He was about to give. Noah's salvation was about to be completed.

Note the instructions of God.

a. Go forth from the ark, you and your dear family (v.16). This was the final step of deliverance from the judgment of God. Noah was now to step out of the ark onto the earth. Imagine the apprehension and fear, the thoughts and wondering about what lay outside. The earth had been utterly devastated and wasted by the deluge of water. But note the stress and force of God's instructions: "Go forth from the ark—do it now, immediately. Don't fear to the point that you hesitate or delay. Your day of deliverance and salvation has arrived. Go forth now."

b. Second, God says, "Bring forth all the animals, so they can reproduce and multiply upon the earth" (v.17).

Noah and the survivors of God's awesome judgment were now to build a new life upon earth. God had been faithful to His Word and to His promise. He had judged the lawlessness, immorality, and violence of men; but in mercy, He had saved those He had promised to save, those who truly believed and followed Him.

Thought 1. God did not forsake Noah and his dear family. There may have been times over the long days of the terrifying judgment when they feared what would happen to them. But God was faithful: the day came when He completed their long awaited salvation and deliverance. What a lesson for us! We should never despair, never allow a trial or temptation to overcome us. God will always deliver us if we will only trust and patiently wait upon God. Our redemption—our glorious salvation—draws near. God is faithful; He is going to complete our salvation and deliverance from this sinful world and the terrifying judgment to come. God is going to complete our redemption.

"Being confident of this very thing, that he which hath begun a good work in you will perform it until the day of Jesus Christ" (Ph.1:6).

"But the Lord is faithful, who shall stablish you, and keep you from evil" (2 Th.3:3).

"I know whom I have believed, and am persuaded that he is able to keep that which I have committed unto him against that day" (2 Ti.1:12).

"Blessed be the God and Father of our Lord Jesus Christ, which according to his abundant mercy hath begotten us again unto a lively hope by the resurrection of Jesus Christ from the dead, to an inheritance incorruptible, and undefiled, and that fadeth not away, reserved in heaven for you, who are kept by the power of God through faith unto salvation ready to be revealed in the last time" (1 Pe.1:3-5).

"Now unto him that is able to keep you from falling, and to present you faultless before the presence of his glory with exceeding joy" (Jude 24).

"Behold, he that keepeth Israel shall neither slumber nor sleep" (Ps.121:4).

Thought 2. It had been over a year since God had met and spoken to Noah. There may have been times when he felt God was too far off, out of reach, or not concerned enough; times when he felt God had forgotten all about him. But note: God had not forgotten. He knew all about Noah and the survivors, and He knows all about us. God is not far off in outer space someplace, unconcerned with us. God knows every trial and temptation we face, and He cares for us. God promises to look after us if we will only trust Him and live for Him.

"Blessed are they which do hunger and thirst after righteousness: for they shall be filled" (Mt.5:6).

"But seek ye first the kingdom of God, and his righteousness; and all these things shall be added unto you" (Mt.6:33).

"Casting all your care upon him; for he careth for you" (1 Pe.5:7).

"Trust in the LORD with all thine heart; and lean not unto thine own understanding. In all thy ways acknowledge him, and he shall direct thy paths" (Pr.3:5-6).

"The fear of man bringeth a snare: but whoso putteth his trust in the LORD shall be safe" (Pr.29:25).

"Oh how great is thy goodness, which thou hast laid up for them that fear thee; which thou hast wrought for them that trust in thee before the sons of men!" (Ps.31:19).

"Many sorrows shall be to the wicked: but he that trusteth in the LORD, mercy shall compass him about" (Ps.32:10).

"The LORD redeemeth the soul of his servants: and none of them that trust in him shall be desolate" (Ps.34:22).

"Trust in the LORD, and do good; so shalt thou dwell in the land, and verily thou shalt be fed" (Ps.37:3).

"Commit thy way unto the LORD; trust also in him; and he shall bring it to pass" (Ps.37:5).

"It is better to trust in the LORD than to put confidence in man" (Ps.118:8).

"Thou wilt keep him in perfect peace, whose mind is stayed on thee: because he trusteth in thee. Trust ye in the LORD for ever: for in the LORD JEHOVAH is everlasting strength" (Is.26:3-4).

2 (8:18-19) **Obedience**: there was the second scene: Noah's strict obedience to God. Noah went out of the ark just as God had instructed him. The impact of such a moment could never be described, not adequately, not fully. But let us imagine the scene as best we can. The earth had been devastated by an enormous flood, a flood so great that it had covered even the highest mountain peaks. The vegetation of the earth—the forests, trees, bushes, fruits, and grasses of the earth—most had been uprooted and destroyed. Only seed remained, seed that had been left scattered all over the earth as the waters had receded into the lakes, rivers, caverns, and sea beds of the earth.

The earth was no longer filled with the lush green of the forests and the beautiful colors of shrubs and flowers. The earth was no longer filled with fruit-bearing trees, bushes, and vegetables. The earth Noah stepped out upon was mostly barren land, barren with debris scattered all over its surface. Uprooted trees and vegetation were lying everywhere. And remember: all the people and animals had drowned as well. Bones were probably scattered here and there among the debris. Most of the carcasses, if not all, would have decayed or been eaten by the sea creatures over the year of the flood. Only the bones would be lying among the debris. Keep in mind also that most of the bones would have been buried from the convulsions that had taken place in the subterranean crust of the earth and from the erosion caused by the rushing waters as they flowed and settled into the beds of the earth.

The point is this: when Noah stepped out from the ark upon the earth, he stepped upon a devastated earth. He confronted...

- the stark reality of sin, how terrible it is, how awful the results are
- the stark reality of the judgment of God, how terrible it is, how awful the wrath of God is
- the stark reality of God's love and salvation, of how God will save a person who truly believes and follows Him. Noah knew this, for he had believed and followed God, and there he stood having just been saved through the terrifying judgment of God

When Noah stepped out of the ark onto the earth, he was bound to be gripped...

- with a renewed reverence and respect for God, and a renewed fear and awe of God
- with a renewed commitment and determination to obey and serve God as never before

Note how clearly this is seen in the Scripture: "Noah went forth" out of the ark. The impact is that he *immediately went out*; he *immediately obeyed God*. He was not leaving the ark because he could no longer take the feelings of being confined and cooped up, could no longer bear the urge to be free from the enclosed quarters of the ark. Noah went out only because God had instructed him to leave the ark and only because God had *then and there* instructed him to leave. Noah knew that God was depending upon him.

⇒ Noah knew that the great purpose of God for the earth and for the human race was resting upon his shoulders, upon his strict obedience to God.

This is the reason Noah obeyed God, obeyed Him in the most strict sense. This is the reason Noah had waited so patiently upon God's instructions before leaving the ark, waited despite all his feelings of confinement. This is the reason Noah did exactly what God said despite whatever fears he was experiencing. He had no idea what lay outside the ark and no idea what lay ahead for him and his small family as they faced each day all alone upon the earth. But God had spoken and given His instructions; therefore, Noah obeyed God immediately. He left the ark and launched out to start a new life, to begin the human race and civilization all over again.

Thought 1. When God speaks and shows us His will, we must obey and obey immediately. We must do exactly what God says, even if we do not know what lies ahead. We must do the will of God despite the questions and unknowns that may lie ahead of us.

"**Thus did Noah; according to all that God commanded him, so did he**" (Ge.6:22).
"**Now therefore, if ye will obey my voice indeed, and keep my covenant, then ye shall be a peculiar treasure unto me above all people: for all the earth is mine**" (Ex.19:5).
"**This day the LORD thy God hath commanded thee to do these statutes and judgments: thou shalt therefore keep and do them with all thine heart, and with all thy soul**" (De.26:16).
"**This book of the law shall not depart out of thy mouth; but thou shalt meditate therein day and night, that thou mayest observe to do according to all that is written therein: for then thou shalt make thy way prosperous, and then thou shalt have good success**" (Jos.1:8).
"**And Samuel said, Hath the LORD as great delight in burnt offerings and sacrifices, as in obeying the voice of the LORD? Behold, to obey is better than sacrifice**" (1 S.15:22).
"**Not every one that saith unto me, Lord, Lord, shall enter into the kingdom of heaven; but he that doeth the will of my Father which is in heaven**" (Mt.7:21).
"**Then Peter and the other apostles answered and said, We ought to obey God rather than men**" (Ac.5:29).
"**Though he [Jesus Christ] were a Son, yet learned he obedience by the things which he suffered**" (He.5:8).

3 (8:20) **Worship—Altar—Burnt Offering**: there was the third scene: Noah's first act was to set up a place for worship. Note the point made by Scripture.

⇒ Noah's first concern was not to build a house. This would have been the first concern of many people who had gone through a torrential rain like Noah and the survivors. They would have wanted shelter just in case bad weather set in again.

⇒ Noah's first concern was not to celebrate with a party. This would have been the first thing many people would have done when they had been shut up in a small building for 370 days. Their hearts would be so filled with joy over their release that they would want to share their joy and release with friends in a party of celebration.

⇒ Noah's first concern was not to map out plans for survival in a devastated and barren world. This would have been the first urge of many survivors cast upon a devastated earth.

But not Noah. Noah's first concern was not for himself nor for his family, but for God.

a. The very first thing Noah did was establish a place for worship: he built an altar, established a place where he and his dear family could worship God as they settled and became adjusted to their new life.

Note: this is the first time the word *altar* is mentioned in the Bible. But this was not the first time an offering was made. Offerings were made to God from the very beginning of human history:

⇒ The first sacrifice of an animal was made by God Himself, made in order to clothe the very first man and woman upon earth, Adam and Eve. (See note—Ge.3:21 for more discussion.)

⇒ The second sacrifice and offering was offered by Cain and Abel, the first two sons of Adam and Eve, offered in worship to God. (See notes—Ge.4:3-4; 4:4-5 for more discussion.)

Remember: Noah's father, Lamech, was 56 years old when Adam died. Adam would have unquestionably taught his children and grandchildren God's will concerning altars, sacrifice, and worship—just how God was to be approached and how man was to become acceptable to God. (See DEEPER STUDY # 2—Ge.5:27-32 for a chart on the genealogy of the godly seed or descendents of early man.) The godly seed or line of believers have always had their set places to worship God, and they have always worshipped God. To think otherwise is foolish. In the Old Testament, the godly line of believers worshipped God primarily at altars and approached God through the sacrifice or the shed blood of animals. In the New Testament, the godly line of believers worship God primarily in church and approach God through the sacrifice or shed blood of Christ.

Any person, no matter what generation, who truly knows and loves God personally, worships God. God is first and foremost in his life. This was true with Noah. This is what Noah is doing: establishing the place for worship—building an altar—where he and his dear family can worship God while they go about getting settled and adjusted in their new life. The earth is devastated and barren. More than ever, they needed their altar, their worship center, where they could meet God and worship Him on a regular basis.

Thought 1. What a dynamic example for us!
⇒ How much we need the church, to meet God there, to be faithful in our worship of Him in church.

"Not forsaking the assembling of ourselves together, as the manner of some is; but exhorting one another: and so much the more, as ye see the day approaching" (He.10:25).

⇒ How much we need prayer and worship closets, places that are special to us, places where we can meet and worship God on a daily basis. Most true believers have special places for prayer and worship, places that are very dear to them. Our need is to use them more and more, to seek after God and to pray and worship God more and more within our prayer closets.

"But thou, when thou prayest, enter into thy closet, and when thou hast shut thy door, pray to thy Father which is in secret; and thy Father which seeth in secret shall reward thee openly" (Mt.6:6).
"And he came out, and went, as he was wont [accustomed], to the mount of Olives; and his disciples also followed him. And when he was at the place, he said unto them, Pray that ye enter not into temptation. And he was withdrawn from them about a stone's cast, and kneeled down, and prayed" (Lu.22:39-41).
"On the morrow, as they went on their journey, and drew nigh unto the city, Peter went up upon the housetop to pray about the sixth hour [probably his custom to pray on the housetop wherever he was]" (Ac.10:9).
"And Moses and Aaron went from the presence of the assembly unto the door of the tabernacle of the congregation, and they fell upon their faces: and the glory of the LORD appeared unto them" (Nu.20:6).
"Now when Daniel knew that the writing was signed, he went into his house; and his windows being open in his chamber toward Jerusalem, he kneeled upon his knees three times a day, and prayed, and gave thanks before his God, as he did aforetime" (Da.6:10).
"And Cornelius said, Four days ago I was fasting until this hour; and at the ninth hour I prayed in my house, and, behold, a man stood before me in bright clothing" (Ac.10:30).

b. Once Noah had built the altar, he worshipped God. He offered a sacrifice, a burnt offering, to God. It was only natural that Noah's mind and heart were upon God. Noah loved God, for God had saved him. God had brought him through the terrible judgment that had fallen upon the earth. Noah knew God personally and intimately, and his heart was just flowing upward to God in praise and thanksgiving for God's great deliverance. Noah was bound to be longing for God's presence...

• longing to approach and worship God
• longing to praise God for Himself and for His deliverance
• longing to ask God for continued forgiveness, forgiveness for his weaknesses, failures, and sin—all of which were bound to happen because of his human nature
• longing to make a renewed commitment, a rededication of his life to God
• longing to ask God for His continued guidance, provision, and protection

This is exactly what the burnt offering is in Scripture. It was an offering that a person offered when he wanted…
- to thank and praise God
- to make a renewed commitment
- to ask and petition God for something

Note how great the sacrifice was that Noah made: he did not offer and sacrifice just one animal; he sacrificed one of every clean animal in the ark, one of every kind or species of animal. He sacrificed dozens of animals. Why? Scripture does not say, but it was probably due to the fear, reverence, and awe of God that flooded Noah's heart and mind. He had just gone through the most terrifying demonstration of God's awesome power and judgment. Noah would want what any of us would want in similar circumstances: to show God our utter trust and respect for Him and His awesome power.

How long did it take to offer one of every kind of animal? How many hours? Days? Scripture does not say, but Noah probably gave as much to God as any person has ever given. There were only seven of every clean animal left on earth, yet Noah offered one of each kind.

Thought 1. Note three significant lessons for us.
1) God has saved us, all true believers. He has delivered us from the terrible judgment that is to fall upon all the ungodly and evil of this earth. Our salvation is the first thing for which we should thank God.

> "Notwithstanding in this rejoice not, that the spirits are subject unto you; but rather rejoice, because your names are written in heaven" (Lu.10:20).
> "But when the fulness of the time was come, God sent forth his Son, made of a woman, made under the law, to redeem them that were under the law, that we might receive the adoption of sons. And because ye are sons, God hath sent forth the Spirit of his Son into your hearts, crying, Abba, Father" (Ga.4:4-6).
> "For ye have not received the spirit of bondage again to fear; but ye have received the Spirit of adoption, whereby we cry, Abba, Father" (Ro.8:15).

2) We must make the worship of God the center of our lives. We must seek and worship God first and always.

> "Give unto the LORD the glory due unto his name: bring an offering, and come before him: worship the LORD in the beauty of holiness" (1 Chr.16:29).
> "LORD, I have loved the habitation of thy house, and the place where thine honour dwelleth" (Ps.26:8).
> "One thing have I desired of the LORD, that will I seek after; that I may dwell in the house of the LORD all the days of my life, to behold the beauty of the LORD, and to inquire in his temple" (Ps.27:4).
> "Blessed are they that dwell in thy house: they will be still praising thee" (Ps.84:4).
> "For a day in thy courts is better than a thousand. I had rather be a doorkeeper in the house of my God, than to dwell in the tents of wickedness" (Ps.84:10).
> "O come, let us worship and bow down: let us kneel before the LORD our maker" (Ps.95:6).
> "O worship the LORD in the beauty of holiness: fear before him, all the earth" (Ps.96:9).
> "I was glad when they said unto me, Let us go into the house of the LORD" (Ps.122:1).
> "Then saith Jesus unto him, Get thee hence, Satan: for it is written, Thou shalt worship the Lord thy God, and him only shalt thou serve" (Mt.4:10).
> "And were continually in the temple, praising and blessing God" (Lu.24:53).
> "Not forsaking the assembling of ourselves together, as the manner of some is; but exhorting one another: and so much the more, as ye see the day approaching" (He.10:25).
> "Saying with a loud voice, Fear God, and give glory to him; for the hour of his judgment is come: and worship him that made heaven, and earth, and the sea, and the fountains of waters" (Re.14:7).

3) Noah made a great sacrifice, giving one of every kind of animal. We must follow His example: we must make a great sacrifice to God—give all we are and have to Him.

> "And he said to them all, If any man will come after me, let him deny himself, and take up his cross daily, and follow me" (Lu.9:23).
> "I beseech you therefore, brethren, by the mercies of God, that ye present your bodies a living sacrifice, holy, acceptable unto God, which is your reasonable service. And be not conformed to this world: but be ye transformed by the renewing of your mind, that ye may prove what is that good, and acceptable, and perfect, will of God" (Ro.12:1-2).
> "Then Peter began to say unto him, Lo, we have left all, and have followed thee" (Mk.10:28).
> "So likewise, whosoever he be of you that forsaketh not all that he hath, he cannot be my disciple" (Lu.14:33).
> "Lay not up for yourselves treasures upon earth, where moth and rust doth corrupt, and where thieves break through and steal: but lay up for yourselves treasures in heaven, where neither moth nor rust doth corrupt, and where thieves do not break through nor steal: for where your treasure is, there will your heart be also" (Mt.6:19-21).

DEEPER STUDY # 1

(8:20) **Altar—Worship—Burnt Offering**: throughout the Old Testament we often read where a person builds an altar and offers a sacrifice, that is, *a burnt offering to God*. What does this mean? What was the person doing? In the simplest of terms, he was doing what we do when we approach God: he was either approaching and worshipping God or else seeking something from God. Man approaches God for at least five reasons or purposes:

⇒ to worship God
⇒ to thank and praise God
⇒ to ask forgiveness for sins
⇒ to recommit or rededicate his life
⇒ to petition God, that is, ask God for something

These facts in particular should be noted about the burnt offering.
1. Four animals were used in animal sacrifices. The rich sacrificed the larger animals and the poor the small birds.

⇒ a bullock or an ox (Le.1:5)
⇒ a sheep or lamb (Le.1:10)
⇒ a goat (Le.1:10)
⇒ a pigeon or turtledove (Le.1:14)

2. The burnt offering was a freewill offering. The person approached God of his own free will; he simply wanted to come to God. God did not force him to come; God never forces any person to enter His presence. The person approaches God because he chooses to come to God.

> **"If his offering be a burnt sacrifice of the herd, let him offer a male without blemish: he shall offer it of his own *voluntary will* at the door of the tabernacle of the congregation before the LORD" (Le.1:3).**
> **"Ye shall offer at *your own will* a male without blemish, of the beeves [cattle], of the sheep, or of the goats" (Le.22:19).**

3. The animal offered and sacrificed was to always be a clean animal, an animal that was completely free from blemishes, diseases, injuries, or defects of any kind.

> **"Ye shall offer at your own will a male without blemish, of the beeves [cattle], of the sheep, or of the goats. But whatsoever hath a blemish, that shall ye not offer: for it shall not be acceptable for you. And whosoever offereth a sacrifice of peace offerings unto the LORD to accomplish his vow, or a freewill offering in beeves or sheep, it shall be perfect to be accepted; there shall be no blemish therein. Blind, or broken, or maimed, or having a wen [running sore], or scurvy, or scabbed, ye shall not offer these unto the LORD, not make an offering by fire of them upon the altar unto the LORD" (Le.22:19-22).**

4. The animal was sacrificed—its life was given up and its blood shed—as a substitute or ransom for the person's sins. The picture was this:

a. The person put his hand upon the head of the animal. This symbolized that in faith—truly believing—the person was identifying with the sacrifice of the animal...

• symbolizing that his sins were being transferred to the animal
• symbolizing that he was being freed from the penalty of sin
• symbolizing that through the sacrifice, the animal was bearing his sins, bearing the penalty, judgment, and punishment for his sins

The animal was pictured as dying for the person, as the person's substitute or ransom (redemption). The animal symbolized *propitiation*, the covering and sacrifice for the person's sins. (See note—1 Jn.2:1-2 for more discussion.)

> **"And he shall put his hand upon the head of the burnt offering; and it shall be accepted for him to make atonement [cleansing, redemption, ransom, expiation, reconciliation] for him" (Le.1:4).**
> **"And Moses said unto Aaron, Go unto the altar, and offer thy sin offering, and thy burnt offering, and make an atonement for thyself, and for the people: and offer the offering of the people, and make an atonement for them; as the LORD commanded" (Le.9:7).**
> **"And the priest shall offer the burnt offering and the meat offering upon the altar: and the priest shall make an atonement for him, and he shall be clean" (Le.14:20).**

b. This, of course, pointed to Jesus Christ, who was to be sacrificed for our sins upon the cross. Jesus Christ died for us, bore the penalty, judgment, and punishment for our sins. Jesus Christ died as our substitute before God, as the propitiation—the covering and sacrifice—for our sins.

> **"The next day John seeth Jesus coming unto him, and saith, Behold the Lamb of God, which taketh away the sin of the world" (Jn.1:29).**
> **"But God commendeth his love toward us, in that, while we were yet sinners, Christ died for us" (Ro.5:8).**

"Purge out therefore the old leaven, that ye may be a new lump, as ye are unleavened. For even Christ our passover is sacrificed for us" (1 Co.5:7).

"For he hath made him to be sin for us, who knew no sin; that we might be made the righteousness of God in him" (2 Co.5:21).

"And walk in love, as Christ also hath loved us, and hath given himself for us an offering and a sacrifice to God for a sweetsmelling savour" (Ep.5:2).

"Who gave himself for us, that he might redeem us from all iniquity, and purify unto himself a peculiar people, zealous of good works" (Tit.2:14).

"Neither by the blood of goats and calves, but by his own blood he entered in once into the holy place, having obtained eternal redemption for us. For if the blood of bulls and of goats, and the ashes of an heifer sprinkling the unclean, sanctifieth to the purifying of the flesh: how much more shall the blood of Christ, who through the eternal Spirit offered himself without spot to God, purge your conscience from dead works to serve the living God" (He.9:12-14).

"So Christ was once offered to bear the sins of many; and unto them that look for him shall he appear the second time without sin unto salvation" (He.9:28).

"Forasmuch as ye know that ye were not redeemed with corruptible things, as silver and gold, from your vain conversation received by tradition from your fathers; but with the precious blood of Christ, as of a lamb without blemish and without spot" (1 Pe.1:18-19).

"Who his own self bare our sins in his own body on the tree, that we, being dead to sins, should live unto righteousness: by whose stripes ye were healed" (1 Pe.2:24).

"But if we walk in the light, as he is in the light, we have fellowship one with another, and the blood of Jesus Christ his Son cleanseth us from all sin" (1 Jn.1:7).

"And they sung a new song, saying, Thou art worthy to take the book, and to open the seals thereof: for thou wast slain, and hast redeemed us to God by thy blood out of every kindred, and tongue, and people, and nation" (Re.5:9).

5. The animal was then burned upon the altar. The fire of the burnt offering symbolized the holiness and wrath of God...

- that was judging and consuming the sin being borne by the animal
- that was purifying that which was impure

The fire pointed to Jesus Christ bearing the wrath of God's holiness of us. Jesus Christ bore the reaction of God's holiness against sin, bore God's wrath against sin for us.

"But God commendeth his love toward us, in that, while we were yet sinners, Christ died for us. Much more then, being now justified by his blood, we shall be saved from wrath through him" (Ro.5:8-9).

"And he went a little farther, and fell on his face, and prayed, saying, O my Father, if it be possible, let this cup pass from me [the cup of God's wrath against sin]: nevertheless not as I will, but as thou wilt" (Mt.26:39. See DEEPER STUDY # 4, Cup—Mt.26:39 for discussion.)

6. The smell that arose from the burning meat was a pleasing, satisfying aroma. This symbolized that the sacrifice pleased and satisfied God. The sacrifice satisfied God's holiness and made the person acceptable to God. The person, of course, had to be sincere in approaching God, believing with all of his heart that God accepted the sacrifice as a substitute for his sins.

"The priest shall burn all on the altar, to be a burnt sacrifice, an offering made by fire, of a sweet savour [aroma] unto the LORD" (Le.1:9).

This points to the death of Jesus Christ pleasing God. God is satisfied—perfectly satisfied—with the blood of Jesus Christ being shed for man. God accepts the death of Jesus Christ as man's payment and judgment for sin. God now accepts us when we come to Him through the death of Christ, accepts us because we approach Him through...

- the perfect payment for sin
- the payment made by the perfect Son of God
- the death of the Lord Jesus Christ

"And walk in love, as Christ also hath loved us, and hath given himself for us an offering and a sacrifice to God for a sweetsmelling savour [pleasing, satisfying aroma]" (Ep.5:2).

"Therefore doth my Father love me, because I lay down my life, that I might take it again. No man taketh it from me, but I lay it down of myself. I have power to lay it down, and I have power to take it again. This commandment have I received of my Father" (Jn.10:17-18).

"Who his own self bare our sins in his own body on the tree, that we, being dead to sins, should live unto righteousness: by whose stripes ye were healed" (1 Pe.2:24).

---

4 (8:21-22) **Covenant**: there was the fourth scene: God's great pleasure with Noah's sacrifice and God's great promises to Noah and the human race. God saw Noah as he stepped out of the ark upon the earth, saw his fear and apprehension. God saw the horror of Noah when he looked around upon the devastated and barren earth, covered with scattered debris everywhere. God saw the questions flooding Noah's mind, wondering if God would launch the judgment and flooding again, for he and his dear family were still of Adam's race, still sinful and sure to sin in the future. As stated, God

saw the fear and apprehension, the questioning and wondering of Noah's heart and mind. But God also saw Noah's worship...
- God saw Noah's fear of God, the reverence and awe before God that flooded Noah's heart
- God saw Noah's sense of being a sinful creature, of being short of God's glory
- God saw Noah's recommitment and rededication of life
- God saw Noah's great sacrifice, the sacrifice of dozens of animals—all in faith—his trusting God to accept the animals' sacrifice in behalf of himself and his dear family

God was bound to be pleased with Noah, pleased with his faith and sincerity of heart, pleased with the great offering and sacrifice he was making. Note how Scripture describes God's response: the Lord smelled the pleasing, soothing aroma of Noah's great sacrifice. That is, God was pleased, greatly pleased—His holiness and wrath against sinful man were soothed, propitiated, satisfied—with the sacrificial offering made by Noah. But note this: it was not the sacrifice of the animal that pleased and soothed God. We must always remember this when dealing with animal sacrifice in the Old Testament. What pleased God was what the sacrifice symbolized or pointed to: the sacrifice of Jesus Christ upon the cross. God saw beyond the animal sacrifice to the death of His Son, the Lord Jesus Christ, for the sins of the world. Jesus Christ—the offering and sacrifice of His life—is the propitiation (the satisfaction and covering) for our sins. The animal sacrifice only pointed to Jesus Christ.

> **"My little children, these things write I unto you, that ye sin not. And if any man sin, we have an advocate with the Father, Jesus Christ the righteous: and he is the propitiation for our sins: and not for ours only, but also for the sins of the whole world" (1 Jn.2:1-2).**
> **"For all have sinned, and come short of the glory of God; being justified freely by his grace through the redemption that is in Christ Jesus: whom God hath set forth to be a propitiation through faith in his blood, to declare his righteousness for the remission of sins that are past, through the forbearance of God; to declare, I say, at this time his righteousness: that he might be just, and the justifier of him which believeth in Jesus" (Ro.3:23-26).**

The point is this: God was so pleased with Noah's great offering that He purposed within Himself to do three great things for Noah and the human race. Note that God was *not speaking* and giving these promises to Noah, not at this point. Rather, God was *thinking* these things within His own heart. Noah's great offering—the offering of so many sacrifices at one time by one man, the sacrifice of one of every kind of clean animal—stirred God to do three great things for man. (But remember: God was looking beyond the great sacrifice of Noah to the symbol of the sacrifice, that of the great sacrifice of His Son, the Lord Jesus Christ. It was the future death of Christ that was enabling [making it possible for] God to make these great promises to Noah and mankind.)

a. God promised to never again curse the earth with a flood despite man's depravity and sinfulness (v.21). This is the way this verse should read: even though man is sinful—despite his depravity—God will never again curse the earth with a worldwide flood. Why? Because of the great offering made by Noah which symbolized the great sacrifice of His Son, the Lord Jesus Christ.

Derek Kidner states it well:

> The Lord's resolve not to renew the judgment is based on the accepted sacrifice [of Christ]....The real propitiation, in the mind of God, was the sacrifice of Jesus.[1]

> **"And, having made peace through the blood of his [Christ's] cross, by him to reconcile all things unto himself; by him, I say, whether they be things in earth, or things in heaven. And you, that were sometime alienated and enemies in your mind by wicked works, yet now hath he reconciled. In the body of his flesh through death, to present you holy and unblameable and unreproveable in his sight" (Col.1:20-22).**

Note that man's terrible depravity and sinfulness is again stated (v.21b; see Ge.6:5). Note also that the earth had been cursed after Adam's sin (see Ge.3:17) and again during the flood. But God has now promised that He will never again send a universal flood upon the earth as a judgment upon sin. The earth will never again be destroyed, not until the end time when it will be remade into a perfect earth (see 2 Pe.3:3-13; Ro.8:19-22).

b. God purposed to never again destroy life upon earth with a universal flood, neither man nor animal (v.21). Note: this refers only to a worldwide flood, not to local calamities and judgments upon countries, cities, or people (see Sodom and Gomorrah, local earthquakes, floods, and other disasters).

c. God purposed to guarantee the times and seasons of the earth until the end of the world (v.22). This probably points to environmental havoc during the days of the flood. The environment—times and seasons—must have been convulsively disrupted. But with this promise of God, a universal devastation of the times and seasons would never again fall upon the earth—not as a judgment from God—not until the end of the world.

Note: this promise is guaranteed only as long as the earth remains. There is to be an end to the earth. Scripture declares that God is going to destroy and remake the whole universe. God is going to create a new heavens and earth, a perfect heavens and earth, and repopulate the universe with those who believe and follow Him (see 2 Pe.3:3-13; Rev.21:1f).

Thought 1. Noah believed God, that He would accept him and his family through the sacrifice of the animals. We must believe God, that He will accept us through the sacrifice of Christ upon the cross. It is the aroma of Christ's sacrifice, His death alone, that pleases God and makes us acceptable to Him.

---

[1] Derek Kidner. *Genesis*, p.93.

"The next day John seeth Jesus coming unto him, and saith, Behold the Lamb of God, which taketh away the sin of the world" (Jn.1:29).

"For when we were yet without strength, in due time Christ died for the ungodly" (Ro.5:6).

"For I delivered unto you first of all that which I also received, how that Christ died for our sins according to the scriptures" (1 Co.15:3).

"Who gave himself for our sins, that he might deliver us from this present evil world, according to the will of God and our Father" (Ga.1:4).

"And walk in love, as Christ also hath loved us, and hath given himself for us an offering and a sacrifice to God for a sweetsmelling savour" (Ep.5:2).

"And, having made peace through the blood of his cross, by him to reconcile all things unto himself; by him, I say, whether they be things in earth, or things in heaven. And you, that were sometime alienated and enemies in your mind by wicked works, yet now hath he reconciled. In the body of his flesh through death, to present you holy and unblameable and unreproveable in his sight" (Col.1:20-22).

"Forasmuch as ye know that ye were not redeemed with corruptible things, as silver and gold, from your vain conversation [conduct] received by tradition from your fathers; but with the precious blood of Christ, as of a lamb without blemish and without spot" (1 Pe.1:18-19).

"Hereby perceive we the love of God, because he laid down his life for us: and we ought to lay down our lives for the brethren" (1 Jn.3:16).

"Unto him that loved us, and washed us from our sins in his own blood" (Re.1:5).

1. The blessing of God upon man **2. The mission of man: To re-populate the earth** **3. The supremacy of man** a. Over the earth: No longer ex-ists in an absolute sense b. Over the animals: Now gained through fear, not af-fection **4. The provision of food for man** a. Can eat all living animals b. Can eat all vegetation	**CHAPTER 9** **G. Noah & the New Begin-ning (Part 1): God Estab-lished a New World Order for Man, 9:1-7** And God blessed Noah and his sons, and said unto them, Be fruitful, and multiply, and replenish the earth. 2 And the fear of you and the dread of you shall be upon every beast of the earth, and upon all the fishes of the sea; into your hand are they delivered. 3 Every moving thing that liveth shall be meat for you; even as the green herb	have I given you all things. 4 But flesh with the life thereof, which is the blood thereof, shall ye not eat. 5 And surely your blood of your lives will I require; at the hand of every beast will I require it, and at the hand of man; at the hand of every man's brother will I require the life of man. 6 Whoso sheddeth man's blood, by man shall his blood be shed: for in the image of God made he man. 7 And you, be ye fruitful, and multiply; bring forth abundantly in the earth, and multiply therein.	c. One exception: Cannot eat an animal with its life—its blood—still in it **5. The establishment of govern-ment for man** **6. The protection of life for man** a. The law governing animals which kill people: To be exe-cuted b. The law governing murderers 1) Punishment by God 2) Execution by men c. The reason 1) Man's value: Is made in God's image 2) Man's purpose: To re-populate the earth in order to fulfill the purpose of God

DIVISION IV

NOAH: THE MAN CHOSEN TO PRESERVE MANKIND AND THE GODLY SEED THROUGH WORLD DESTRUCTION (THE FLOOD), 6:9–9:29

G. Noah and the New Beginning (Part 1): God Established a New World Order for Man, 9:1-7

(9:1-7) **Introduction**: remember Noah's emotional state, his state of mind, as God began to speak to him and his sons.

⇒ Noah had witnessed the terrifying judgment of God upon the whole earth: the volcanic eruption of the subterra-nean waters and the torrential downpour of a worldwide storm that lasted for forty days and nights.

⇒ Noah had been cooped up in the ark for 370 days knowing that he and his dear family—only eight souls—were the only living survivors left upon earth.

⇒ Noah had just stepped out upon some peak in the mountains of Ararat and what he saw was horrifying: the utter devastation of the earth; a barren earth with debris scattered all over its surface; here and there bones that had not been buried by the erosion from the receding waters; and then, most likely, he saw water still rushing and receding from the valleys below.

⇒ Noah had been so gripped by the power and judgment of God—so stricken with reverence and fear for God—that he immediately turned to God in worship. The very first thing he did after disembarking was to build an al-tar and offer a sacrifice to God. But he did not sacrifice one animal: he sacrificed dozens of animals, one of every kind or species of animal. Noah was so thankful to God for saving him and so fearful of God's awesome power and terrifying judgment—so appreciative and so fearful—that he just lifted up his heart to God time and again. Noah did just what genuine believers have often done: he recommitted his life to God, and he begged God to forgive his sins and to accept the praise of his heart for so great a deliverance and salvation. There was one difference, however, between Noah's worship and all of us who have succeeded him: Noah was driven to worship God because he had been an eyewitness of the awesome power and terrifying judgment of God. He was stricken with an intense fear and reverence for God unparalleled in human history.

This was Noah's emotional state, his state of mind. He and his dear family—only eight souls—were the only survivors upon earth. And the earth was barren, totally devastated. He had no idea what lay ahead; the future was uncertain. He felt what any of us would have felt: insecure, restless, unsure, hesitant, wondering, questioning what to do.

As stated, what Noah did was turn to God. He cast himself totally upon God and offered the largest sacrifice ever made to God. Noah wanted God to know that he was totally dependent upon Him—that he trusted God explicitly to instruct and guide him as he made a new beginning upon earth.

This God did. God knew Noah's needs, knew his state of mind, his fear and uncertainty; but God also knew Noah's dependence and trust upon God. Therefore, God met Noah, instructed and guided Noah. This is the great subject of this passage: *Noah and the New Beginning (Part 1): God Established a New World Order for Man.*

1. The blessing of God upon man (v.1).
2. The mission of man: to repopulate the earth (v.1).
3. The supremacy of man (v.2).
4. The provision of food for man (vv.3-4).
5. The establishment of government for man (v.5).
6. The protection of life for man (vv.5-7).

1 (9:1) **Blessing**: the new world order established the blessing of God upon man. Remember, Noah and his small family—only eight persons—were the only people left upon earth. They stood as the representatives of the whole human race.

Noah was a second Adam, the head of the human race just as Adam had been the head at creation. Thus, whatever God established with Noah applied to the whole human race. Note the first thing God did:

"God blessed Noah and his sons" (v.1).

In blessing Noah, God was giving the same blessing to all persons who were to be born in the future, to all the descendents of the human race. *To bless* means...
- to bestow a gift upon a person
- to confer something upon a person: some benefit, pleasure, delight, or bliss[1]
- to extend good will and good intentions toward a person[2]
- to act in love toward a person; to grant mercy and grace—abundantly

This means a most wonderful thing: God was pouring out—abundantly pouring out—upon Noah and the human race...
- His mercy and grace
- His good will and intentions
- His pleasure and joy
- His great gifts

We are all enormously blessed with the mercy and grace of God, with His good will and great gifts. What are the gifts? The first gift is just this: the great blessing of God. He established His blessing upon us—upon the whole human race—when He blessed Noah and his sons. The specific blessings are spelled out in the next four notes.

> **Thought 1.** The great problem is this: too many of us do not receive the great mercy and grace of God. Too many of us walk through life without God—ignoring, neglecting, even denying Him—never allowing God to have mercy and bestow His grace upon us. We never allow God to bless us, to look after and care for us. The great need of man today is to receive the mercy and grace of God, the blessings of God, which He has poured out upon the earth through His Son, the Lord Jesus Christ.
>
> > "But seek ye first the kingdom of God, and his righteousness; and all these things [housing, clothing, food] shall be added unto you" (Mt.6:33).
> > "But God, who is rich in mercy, for his great love wherewith he loved us, even when we were dead in sins, hath quickened us together [made us alive, eternally alive] with Christ, (by grace ye are saved;)....For by grace are ye saved through faith; and that not of yourselves: it is the gift of God: not of works, lest any man should boast" (Ep.2:4-5, 8-9).
> > "Not by works of righteousness which we have done, but according to his mercy he saved us, by the washing of regeneration, and renewing of the Holy Ghost; which he shed on us abundantly through Jesus Christ our Saviour; that being justified by his grace, we should be made heirs according to the hope of eternal life" (Tit.3:5-7).
> > "Casting all your care upon him; for he careth for you" (1 Pe.5:7).
> > "Blessed be the Lord, who daily loadeth us with benefits, even the God of our salvation" (Ps.68:19).
> > "Fear thou not; for I am with thee: be not dismayed; for I am thy God: I will strengthen thee; yea, I will help thee; yea, I will uphold thee with the right hand of my righteousness" (Is.41:10).

2 (9:1) **Man, Purpose—Mission, of Man**: the new world order established the mission of man.

"Be fruitful, and multiply, and replenish the earth" (v.1).

The human race had been decimated, completely wiped out except for eight people: Noah and his small family (1 Pe.3:20). The earth had to be repopulated. Without people, God's great purpose for the universe and man could never be fulfilled. Therefore, God gave man the great mission of repopulating the earth. Noah and his sons and all succeeding generations were to reproduce and fill the earth with human beings. This was the very same mission God had given to Adam and Eve. There are five great reasons why God re-established the mission of reproduction for man.

a. Reproduction establishes the closest bond and union possible between husband and wife—a relationship of love, care, trust, and loyalty. God wanted Noah and his wife and his three sons and their wives to walk, work, and worship hand in hand as they journeyed through life together. The relationship established and built by husband and wife was to serve as the basis for all other relationships upon earth and within the societies and nations of earth. All groups—whether societies or nations—were to walk and work together in love, care, trust, and loyalty.

b. Reproduction establishes the family. Reproduction institutes the rule and principle of one man and one woman for each other. There was to be no separation or divorce—no split families, no children without a father or mother—when God first created man and woman and established the new world order with Noah and his sons.

c. Reproduction builds a much stronger love, trust, and loyalty within man and woman. Love, trust, and loyalty are weakened and destroyed when intimate relationships are carried on with other persons. When love, trust, and loyalty are weakened within the strongest bond known to man, that of the family, they are weakened in all the other relationships of life: at work, at play, and with one's country.

d. Reproduction teaches man that all people are of one blood, from one source. Therefore, all people—all races and nations—are to live in peace and unity, working together to subdue the earth. There was to be no prejudice, discrimination,

---

1 William Wilson. *Wilson's Old Testament Word Studies*, p.42.
2 *Matthew Henry's Commentary*, Vol.1, p.69.

violence, greed, selfishness, or war upon earth—not originally, not when God first created man. And within the new world order, it is still God's wish that men live in love and peace, without prejudice, discrimination, violence, greed, selfishness, or war.

e. Reproduction teaches that man is as important as woman and woman as man, that all succeeding generations of men and women are to be as highly esteemed as the first man and woman were. There is to be no abuse and no enslavement of women or men in God's creation. Both are involved in the mission of God for the earth.

> **"And he answered and said unto them, Have ye not read, that he which made them at the beginning made them male and female, and said, For this cause shall a man leave father and mother, and shall cleave to his wife: and they twain shall be one flesh? Wherefore they are no more twain, but one flesh. What therefore God hath joined together, let no man put asunder" (Mt.19:4-6).**

Thought 1. Donald Grey Barnhouse makes an interesting point. He says that man's mission to be fruitful "does not refer, merely, to the reproduction of the species, but to fruitfulness in every good work before God (Colossians 1:10). Man is not here on earth to live according to his whim, but to live in accordance with God's plan."[3]

> **"That ye might walk worthy of the Lord unto all pleasing, being fruitful in every good work, and increasing in the knowledge of God" (Col.1:10).**

3 (9:2) **Man, Purpose; Supremacy—Science—Animals**: the new world order established the supremacy of man upon earth. Note two significant facts.

a. Man's supremacy over the earth—the great mission of man to *subdue* the earth—no longer exists, not in a perfect, absolute sense. Note that this Scripture does not mention that man is to subdue the earth. God's new world order says nothing about man gaining supremacy over the earth. But this was not true with Adam. When God created Adam and Eve, He told them to *subdue the earth* (Ge.1:28). This meant that man...

- was to rule over and master the earth
- was to look after and care for the earth
- was to investigate, research, and discover the earth's resources
- was to develop and use the earth's resources
- was to manage and supervise the earth with all its provision and resources

But when Adam sinned, man's ability to subdue the earth was marred and weakened—greatly so. Sin corrupted man, weakened his ability to subdue and manage the earth. Since man's fall into sin, the earth and man are in a rage of violence and suffering...

- Nature runs wild with natural disaster after natural disaster: hurricanes, typhoons, cyclones, tornadoes, floods, volcanic eruptions, earthquakes, dangerous lightning, violent storms, locust plagues, famines, and on and on. Nature constantly runs wild.
- Man runs wild with violent act after violent act: child abuse, wife abuse, husband abuse, parent abuse, rape, assaults, maiming, murder, war, robbery, cheating, stealing, lying, assassination, terrorist acts, arson, and on and on.
- The earth is full of disease, pestilence, and accidents—all causing suffering and destroying life and huge sections of the earth and its resources.

The point is this: the earth—that is, its nature—is far from being under the control of man. It used to be when God first created man, but not now, not since man's rebellion against God, not since man's terrible fall into sin. Sin has marred and weakened man's rule and sovereignty over the earth.

Does this mean that man should not seek to subdue the earth? No! For man's mind and ability have not been totally destroyed, only corrupted and weakened. Man still has the ability to explore, invent, and develop the science and technology to tackle problems. Man...

- can develop technology to control some elements of the earth
- can develop laws to control man's behavior
- can develop self-improvement training and counseling to help personal development and production

But man will never be able to totally subdue the earth and himself; never be able to create a perfect environment and nature that is completely free from destruction, corruption, devastation, aging, tragedy, decay, deterioration, and death.

Is there no hope, then, that a perfect earth can ever be achieved? Yes! But not by man. Man's rule and sovereignty over the earth has been forfeited by sin. Scripture declares that the earth and the evil of man's nature will be conquered and overcome, but by God, not by man. God has promised to restore man's sovereignty over the earth, in fact, over the whole universe. How? Through Jesus Christ. Jesus Christ has secured the right to rule and reign over the earth. He is going to return to the earth, establish His government, and restore man to his original position of dominion and sovereignty—right along with Himself.

This is the reason God's new world order says nothing about man subduing the earth: he can't, not perfectly, not in an absolute sense. Man no longer rules supremely over the earth, not since he sinned and rebelled against God. Only God can gain supremacy over the earth since sin. Only God can conquer the sin and corruption of the earth and restore perfection to the earth. Only God can regain and restore the supremacy of a perfect earth to man. And this He is doing through His Son, the Lord Jesus Christ. The mission of subduing the earth is now in the hands of God's Son, not man. But man is to work at subduing and controlling all he can—under Christ and for the glory of Christ. (See note—He.2:6-8 for more discussion.)

---

[3] Donald Grey Barnhouse. *Genesis*, p.61.

"And the Lord said, Who then is that faithful and wise steward, whom his lord shall make ruler over his household, to give them their portion of meat in due season? Blessed is that servant, whom his lord when he cometh shall find so doing. Of a truth I say unto you, that he will make him ruler over all that he hath" (Lu.12:42-44).

"The Spirit itself beareth witness with our spirit, that we are the children of God: and if children, then heirs; heirs of God, and joint-heirs with Christ; if so be that we suffer with him, that we may be also glorified together" (Ro.8:16-17).

"For the creature [creation] was made subject to vanity, not willingly, but by reason of him who hath subjected the same in hope, because the creature itself also shall be delivered from the bondage of corruption into the glorious liberty of the children of God. For we know that the whole creation groaneth and travaileth in pain together until now. And not only they, but ourselves also, which have the firstfruits of the Spirit, even we ourselves groan within ourselves, waiting for the adoption, to wit, the redemption of our body" (Ro.8:20-23).

"Do ye not know that the saints shall judge [oversee, manage, rule] the world? and if the world shall be judged by you, are ye unworthy to judge the smallest matters? Know ye not that we shall judge angels? how much more things that pertain to this life?" (1 Co.6:2-3).

"If we suffer, we shall also reign with him: if we deny him, he also will deny us" (2 Ti.2:12).

"But one in a certain place testified, saying, What is man, that thou art mindful of him? or the son of man, that thou visitest him? Thou madest him a little lower than the angels; thou crownedst him with glory and honour, and didst set him over the works of thy hands: thou hast put all things in subjection under his feet. For in that he put all in subjection under him, he left nothing that is not put under him. But now we see not yet all things put under him. But we see Jesus, who was made a little lower than the angels for the suffering of death, crowned with glory and honour; that he by the grace of God should taste death for every man" (He.2:6-9).

"But the day of the Lord will come as a thief in the night; in the which the heavens shall pass away with a great noise, and the elements shall melt with fervent heat, the earth also and the works that are therein shall be burned up. Seeing then that all these things shall be dissolved, what manner of persons ought ye to be in all holy conversation and godliness, looking for and hasting unto the coming of the day of God, wherein the heavens being on fire shall be dissolved, and the elements shall melt with fervent heat? Nevertheless we, according to his promise, look for new heavens and a new earth, wherein dwelleth righteousness" (2 Pe.3:10-13).

"And hast made us unto our God kings and priests: and we shall reign on the earth" (Re.5:10).

"And I saw a new heaven and a new earth: for the first heaven and the first earth were passed away; and there was no more sea....And God shall wipe away all tears from their eyes; and there shall be no more death, neither sorrow, nor crying, neither shall there be any more pain: for the former things are passed away" (Re.21:1, 4).

"And there shall be no more curse: but the throne of God and of the Lamb shall be in it; and his servants shall serve him: and they shall see his face; and his name shall be in their foreheads. And there shall be no night there; and they need no candle, neither light of the sun; for the Lord God giveth them light: and they shall reign for ever and ever" (Re.22:3-5).

b. Man's supremacy over the animals does still exist in the new world order. But the fall of man into sin has radically altered the relationship between animal and man. When God created Adam and Eve, He gave them dominion over the animals. Dominion means to rule over, to master, to control, to manage, to look after and care for. Originally, when God first created the animals and man, there was apparently no savagery among animals. Neither man nor animal ate other animals (Ge.1:30, see 9:3). Man and animal lived side by side in peace and harmony and, apparently, with some affection for each other—at least among the higher order of animals. But man was the ruler, the dominating force, the leader among all the creatures of the earth.

But note what has happened since the fall and corruption of man and the world. Animals live in a world of savagery, having to struggle for food and fight for survival against other animals. And not only this, but as stated, the relationship between the animals and man has been tragically corrupted by the fall of man. Man would probably have been devoured and done away with long ago by the animal world if not for one thing: in the new world order God put an *instinctive fear* of man within animals. There is a natural instinct within animals to shrink and draw back from man. Fallen man does have dominion and supremacy over the animal world in the new world order, but it is based upon new terms: fear and terror, not harmony and affection. Man now rules the animal world by fear, not by affection.

Matthew Henry states it well:

> The horse and ox patiently submit to the bridle and yoke, and the sheep is dumb both before the shearer and before the butcher; for the fear and dread of man are upon them....Those creatures that are any way hurtful to us are restrained...though now and then man may be hurt by some of them, they do not combine together to rise up in rebellion against man....What is it that keeps wolves out of our towns, and lions out of our streets, and confines them to the wilderness, but this fear and dread?[4]

Thought 1. A new day is coming when the original harmony and affection between animals and man will be restored. God promises a new age and a new day, a new earth and a new world, when perfection and peace shall reign upon the earth. The lamb will lie down with the lion. A renovated earth, a new heavens and earth, is coming.

---

4 *Matthew Henry's Commentary*, Vol.1, p.69.

"The wolf also shall dwell with the lamb, and the leopard shall lie down with the kid; and the calf and the young lion and the fatling together; and a little child shall lead them. And the cow and the bear shall feed; their young ones shall lie down together: and the lion shall eat straw like the ox. And the sucking child shall play on the hole of the asp, and the weaned child shall put his hand on the cockatrice' den. They shall not hurt nor destroy in all my holy mountain: for the earth shall be full of the knowledge of the LORD, as the waters cover the sea" (Is.11:6-9).

"The wolf and the lamb shall feed together, and the lion shall eat straw like the bullock: and dust shall be the serpent's meat. They shall not hurt nor destroy in all my holy mountain, saith the LORD" (Is.65:25).

"And in that day will I make a covenant for them with the beasts of the field, and with the fowls of heaven, and with the creeping things of the ground: and I will break the bow and the sword and the battle out of the earth, and will make them to lie down safely" (Ho.2:18).

4 (9:3-4) **Food—Vegetation—Animals, Eating**: the new world order established the provision of food for man.

a. Man was given the right to eat the flesh of living animals. When man fell into sin and when the earth suffered the devastation of the flood, the environment and vegetation of the earth apparently suffered terribly.

⇒ The ability of the environment to provide the very best atmosphere and nutrients for man's strength and life was apparently weakened. Man would no longer live as long as he had before the flood. Sin and the flood drastically altered man's environment, food supply, strength, and life span. The earth could no longer have the environment nor produce the nutrients—the quality of food—that it once had.

⇒ The ability of the earth to produce an overabundance of food was bound to have also been limited. The earth was no longer perfect: there was a limit to what the earth would now produce and supply. In addition to its limited supply capabilities, the earth would now suffer natural disasters that would destroy vegetation and food supplies, natural disaster such as flooding, storms, famines, heat waves, dry spells, and a host of other disorders within nature.

This was probably the reason God enlarged man's food supply—within the new world order—to include animals. Man had been exclusively a vegetarian when he was first created (see note—Ge.1:29-30 for more discussion). But now, perhaps for the reason above, and perhaps for other reasons, God allows man to eat the flesh of all animals that live and move, animals such as fish, birds, cattle, and pigs.

Note: later on in history, a distinction would be made between clean and unclean animals for religious and ceremonial purposes, especially among the Jews. But under the new world order, for the purpose of food, man was given the right to use whatever animal he needed for food.

"For every creature of God is good, and nothing to be refused, if it be received with thanksgiving" (1 Ti.4:4).

b. Man was given the right to continue eating whatever vegetation he desired (v.3). (See note—Ge.1:29-30 for more discussion.)

c. God has set one exception to eating animals: man is not to eat an animal with its life—its blood—still in it. Live animals are not to be eaten, nor dead animals with their blood still in them. There are several good reasons for this restriction.

⇒ It prevents disease.

⇒ It prevents savagery, cruelty to animals.

⇒ It teaches a connection between life and the blood.

⇒ It reminds man of the blood of the atonement, the blood of the sacrifice, that is necessary for man to be accepted by God. This was definitely one of the reasons why God gave this instruction. This is clearly seen by the reference to the life of the animal being in the blood.

"For the life of the flesh is in the blood: and I have given it to you upon the altar to make an atonement for your souls: for it is the blood that maketh an atonement for the soul" (Le.17:11; see Le.17:14).

Thought 1. Every time we eat meat, we should think of the blood that was poured out to provide life for us, that is, the nourishment that we might live and not die from starvation. This thought, of course, points toward Jesus Christ, who died for us—shed His blood—that we might *live forever*.

"For this is my blood of the new testament, which is shed for many for the remission of sins" (Mt.26:28).

"Much more then, being now justified by his blood, we shall be saved from wrath through him" (Ro.5:9).

"In whom we have redemption through his blood, the forgiveness of sins, according to the riches of his grace" (Ep.1:7).

"Neither by the blood of goats and calves, but by his own blood he entered in once into the holy place, having obtained eternal redemption for us. For if the blood of bulls and of goats, and the ashes of an heifer sprinkling the unclean, sanctifieth to the purifying of the flesh: how much more shall the blood of Christ, who through the eternal Spirit offered himself without spot to God, purge your conscience from dead works to serve the living God?" (He.9:12-14).

"Forasmuch as ye know that ye were not redeemed with corruptible things, as silver and gold, from your vain conversation received by tradition from your fathers; but with the precious blood of Christ, as of a lamb without blemish and without spot" (1 Pe.1:18-19).

"But if we walk in the light, as he is in the light, we have fellowship one with another, and the blood of Jesus Christ his Son cleanseth us from all sin" (1 Jn.1:7).
"Unto him that loved us, and washed us from our sins in his own blood" (Re.1:5).

5 (9:5) **Government—Law—Judicial System**: the new world order established government for man. Note what God is doing in these verses: He is establishing the law that is to protect the life of man. He is setting up the death penalty as the most basic law of the new world order. Life is the greatest possession a man has. If his life—the greatest possession he has—is to be protected, then all of his possessions are to be protected, for they are of less value. When God says that man's greatest possession is to be protected, his life, God is automatically including man's lesser possessions such as property, justice, and liberty. The greater includes the lesser: the life of man includes his liberty and the justice due him. His life involves all that he is and has. The law of protection involves the *whole* man: his life, and all that is included in his life. This is the reason God spells out the law governing murder, the taking of a man's life. If man's life is to be protected, then everything that involves his life is to be protected. Men are to develop and establish laws to protect all the possessions and the liberty and justice of a person.

The point is this: God is establishing government—laying the seed for government—in this passage. Noah and his sons and the succeeding generations of people were, no doubt, expected to take this most basic law and build both society and government upon it.

Note that both law and government were established by God: law and government are both divine institutions. Therefore, both the law and government are to be obeyed.
⇒ Leupold says this:

> By this word [Scripture] government is instituted, this basis institution for the welfare of man. For if man receives power over other men's lives under certain circumstances [to execute the death penalty upon murderers], then...power over the lesser things is naturally included, such as power over property to the extent of being able to demand various types of work and service as need may arise. Government, then, being grounded on this word, is not by human contract, or by surrender of certain powers, or by encroachment of priestcraft. It is a divine institution.[5]

⇒ James Montgomery Boice says:

> Government is...divinely established. That is, the authority of the state is from God and must be obeyed, save in those areas where from time to time it opposes itself to the greater authority which is God's.[6]

⇒ Scripture says:

> **"Let every soul be subject unto the higher powers. For there is no power but of God: the powers that be are ordained of God. Whosoever therefore resisteth the power, resisteth the ordinance of God: and they that resist shall receive to themselves damnation. For rulers are not a terror to good works, but to the evil. Wilt thou then not be afraid of the power? do that which is good, and thou shalt have praise of the same: for he is the minister of God to thee for good. But if thou do that which is evil, be afraid; for he beareth not the sword in vain: for he is the minister of God, a revenger to execute wrath upon him that doeth evil. Wherefore ye must needs be subject, not only for wrath, but also for conscience sake" (Ro.13:1-5).**

⇒ James Montgomery Boice again says:

> There are two errors that people tend to make in regard to human government.
> ⇒ One is disregard for the state. It is a refusal to recognize its authority, expressed in a scorn of public leaders and a flaunting of perfectly valid laws. This is what Paul is primarily dealing with in Romans.
> ⇒ The other error is to regard the state more highly than we ought, believing that the government will solve our problems. This is the characteristic error of American democracy, particularly at the present time.[7]

6 (9:5-7) **Government—Murder—Life, Protection of**: the new world order established the protection of life for man. This is a sinful, evil world; therefore, the passions of men must be controlled. Within society, passions are controlled and held in check by law. God knows this; therefore, God established the law protecting man's life. God instituted the death penalty for the new world order. Note three significant points.

a. The law governing animals. Animals are important to the earth and to man, to the environment and to nature, but they were created *for man*. Man is the summit of God's creation, the primary being who is to carry out God's purpose for the universe.

Therefore, if an animal attacks and kills a person, the animal is to be put to death. Justice is to be executed upon the animal. Savage attacks by animals upon people are not to be allowed.

b. The law governing murderers. Willful murderers are to face two judgments. Note exactly what Scripture says about capital punishment.

5 H.C. Leupold. *Genesis*, Vol.1, p.333.
6 James Montgomery Boice. *Genesis*, Vol.1, p.307.
7 Ibid., p.307.

1) God Himself will punish murderers (v.5c). The Hebrew says:

> *At the hand of every man's brother I will demand the life of man.*[8]

Matthew Henry says:

> *The righteous God will certainly [execute justice] for blood, though men cannot or do not. One time or other, in this world or in the next, he will both discover concealed murders, which are hidden from man's eye, and punish avowed and justified murders, which are too great for man's hand.*[9]

2) Men are to execute justice upon murderers. Willful murderers are to be punished by judges and jurors of men (v.6).

"Whoever sheds man's blood, by man shall his blood be shed" (v.6).

Again, Matthew Henry has an excellent comment:

> *By man shall his blood be shed, that is, by the magistrate, or whoever is appointed or allowed to be the avenger of blood. There are those who are ministers of God for this purpose, to be a protection to the innocent, by being a terror to the malicious and evil-doers, and they must not bear the sword in vain, Rom.xiii. 4 [13:4]....Wilful murder ought always to be punished with death. It is a sin which the Lord would not pardon in a prince (2 Kings xxiv. 3, 4 [24:3-4]), and which therefore a prince should not pardon in a subject.*[10]

c. There are two strong reasons why murder is to be punished.
   1) Man's value: man is of the highest value; he is made in the very image of God. This means a most significant thing:
      ⇒ A person is to bear the image of God upon earth. He is to let God live within him, within his body, let God live and move and have His being within him. The person is to think, speak, and behave—let God think, speak, and behave within him—just like God would if God were walking within his body. The person is to bear and to live out the image of God upon earth.
      ⇒ Now, to kill a person is to remove the image of God from the earth. It is just like removing God from the earth. Imagine a world without God, without His presence, love, care, concern, knowledge, and strength. To kill a person removes the person from the earth. All that he is, all that he was and could contribute to the earth and society, and all of his love, care, concern, knowledge, strength, and contributions are removed from the earth. When a person is murdered, a part of God's very own image is removed from the earth. In a sense, when a person is murdered and taken from the earth, there is less of God's image upon the earth. All that the person could have contributed to society and the earth is lost forever.

   Murder is a serious offense to God, the most serious. Man is created in the very image of God. Therefore, if man is murdered, justice is to be executed. The murderer is to be put to death. The death penalty is to be enacted.
   2) Man's purpose also necessitates that a murderer be punished. Man's basic purpose upon earth is to repopulate the earth, to continue producing people to fellowship with God, to worship and serve God. This does not mean that man is to overpopulate the earth, only that he is to keep it populated. If the savagery of men eliminated the human race, there would be no human beings left to fellowship with God, to worship or serve God. Thus, the primary purpose of man is to continue the human race, to continue producing and leading people to God. Note that the murderer acts against the great purpose of man: murder destroys human life, eliminates a person's fellowship, worship, and service of God upon earth. This is the reason the murderer must be executed: he must not be allowed to take other lives, to destroy God's purpose for man, that of fellowshipping with God and of producing other followers of God.

> **"Whoso sheddeth man's blood, by man shall his blood be shed: for in the image of God made he man" (Ge.9:6).**
> **"Thou shalt not kill" (Ex.20:13).**
> **"He that smiteth a man, so that he die, shall be surely put to death" (Ex.21:12).**
> **"And he that killeth any man shall surely be put to death" (Le.24:17).**
> **"And if he smite him with an instrument of iron, so that he die, he is a murderer: the murderer shall surely be put to death....Moreover ye shall take no satisfaction for the life of a murderer, which is guilty of death: but he shall be surely put to death" (Nu.35:16, 31).**
> **"Thou shalt not kill" (Ro.13:9).**
> **"But let none of you suffer as a murderer" (1 Pe.4:15).**
> **"Whosoever hateth his brother is a murderer: and ye know that no murderer hath eternal life abiding in him" (1 Jn.3:15).**

Thought 1. The matter of determining life and death is given to man only in an official or governmental capacity. A man does not have the personal right to take another man's life. God made this clear in the Ten Commandments: "Thou shall not kill" (Ex.20:13). But God did give Noah the official or governmental right to execute justice.

---

8 *The Interlinear Bible*, Vol.1. Translated by Jay P. Green, Sr. (Grand Rapids, MI: Baker Book House, 1976), p.20.
9 *Matthew Henry's Commentary*, Vol.1, p.70.
10 Ibid., p.70.

	H. Noah & the New Beginning (Part 2): God Established a New Covenant with Man—the Noahic Covenant, 9:8-17	and every living creature that is with you, for perpetual generations:	generations
1. The author of the covenant		13 I do set my bow in the cloud, and it shall be for a token of a covenant between me and the earth.	b. It is a sign set by God Himself
2. The recipients of the covenant	8 And God spake unto Noah, and to his sons with him saying,		1) Set in the clouds
a. Noah & his sons	9 And I, behold, I establish my covenant with you, and with your seed after you;	14 And it shall come to pass, when I bring a cloud over the earth, that the bow shall be seen in the cloud:	2) Set to be a sign
b. Noah & his seed or descendents, v.9			c. It is a sign to provoke remembrance
c. Every living creature upon earth	10 And with every living creature that is with you, of the fowl, of the cattle, and of every beast of the earth with you; from all that go out of the ark, to every beast of the earth.	15 And I will remember my covenant, which is between me and you and every living creature of all flesh; and the waters shall no more become a flood to destroy all flesh.	1) Remembrance of the covenant of God
			2) Remembrance of the flood & its judgment
3. The covenant itself	11 And I will establish my covenant with you; neither shall all flesh be cut off any more by the waters of a flood; neither shall there any more be a flood to destroy the earth.	16 And the bow shall be in the cloud; and I will look upon it, that I may remember the everlasting covenant between God and every living creature of all flesh that is upon the earth.	d. It is a sign to provoke remembrance that the covenant is everlasting
a. Is God's personal covenant already existing: "My covenant"			
b. Is the promise to never again destroy the earth with a universal flood			
c. Is a new world order	12 And God said, This is the token of the covenant which I make between me and you	17 And God said unto Noah, This is the token of the covenant, which I have established between me and all flesh that is upon the earth.	**5. The assurance of the covenant: God & His Word**
4. The sign of the covenant: The rainbow			
a. It is a sign given to all			

DIVISION IV

NOAH: THE MAN CHOSEN TO PRESERVE MANKIND AND THE GODLY SEED THROUGH WORLD DESTRUCTION (THE FLOOD), 6:9–9:29

H. Noah and the New Beginning (Part 2): God Established a New Covenant with Man—the Noahic Covenant, 9:8-17

(9:8-17) **Introduction**: the flood was the most horrible of tragedies. Every living thing upon earth was wiped out except one small family—eight persons—and a boat load of animals. The trauma of witnessing such a scene must have been one of the most terrifying experiences possible.

⇒ Imagine the trauma of living through a torrential rain that lasted 40 days and 40 nights—never a break in the rain—a rain so heavy and thick that a person could not see his hand in front of his face.

⇒ Imagine the trauma of experiencing all the subterranean waters breaking loose from volcanic eruption after volcanic eruption, all the subterranean waters lying right underneath the crust of the earth bursting loose, shooting upward, and rushing madly about flooding the earth (Ge.7:11).

⇒ Imagine the trauma as the fact gradually dawned upon Noah and his dear family: their family was the only surviving family upon earth. All others had perished because they had cursed God, rejected and rebelled against Him, and refused to follow and obey Him.

⇒ Imagine the trauma of living upon the boat for a whole year, of having a whole year to think about righteousness, sin, death, and the judgment of God.

⇒ Imagine the trauma of knowing that you are a sinner and that God judges sin, judges sin beyond any question. Noah knew this. How then could he know that God would not rise up and judge him and his dear family when they sinned in the future, judge them as He had just done all other sinners? The trauma of such attacking thoughts must have stricken the survivors with terror.

Left only to themselves, Noah and the survivors would have been terrified; they would have lived in constant fear and terror. But they were not left to themselves: God was with them. God loved Noah and his dear family, loved them because they had trusted Him and were true followers of God.

⇒ God cared about them, about their needs. God knew about their apprehension and fear, knew about the uneasiness, uncertainty, and insecurity that often attacked their hearts.

⇒ God knew that Noah and his dear family needed one thing above all else: assurance—the assurance that the terrifying tragedy of the flood would never again take place. They needed to know, beyond a shadow of a doubt, that they and their seed would survive and replenish the earth. This assurance is just what God gives. This is the great subject of this passage: *Noah and the New Beginning (Part 2): God Established a New Covenant with Man.*

1. The author of the covenant (v.8).
2. The recipients of the covenant (vv.9-10).
3. The covenant itself (v.11).
4. The sign of the covenant: the rainbow (vv.12-16).
5. The assurance of the covenant: God and His Word (vv.17).

1 (9:8) **Covenant**: note the author of the covenant. The author is God and God alone. Usually a covenant is an agreement between two parties. Each party agrees to do something; thereby a covenant of behavior is established between them. But not in this case, not in the Noahic covenant. In this covenant—the Noahic covenant—the promise of God will be fulfilled no matter what Noah and the rest of mankind do. This is what might be called...

- a one way covenant
- an unconditional covenant
- a covenant of promise
- a covenant of grace

Neither Noah nor any other person has to do anything in order to receive this promise of God. The Noahic covenant is an unconditional covenant, a covenant of promise, a covenant of grace, a covenant that is established and set up by God no matter how man behaves. God and God alone established the Noahic covenant. Note how clearly this is brought out:

⇒ "behold, I establish my covenant" (v.9).
⇒ "I will establish my covenant" (v.11).
⇒ "The covenant which I make" (v.12).
⇒ "I will remember my covenant" (v.15).
⇒ "The covenant, which I have established" (v.17).

(See DEEPER STUDY # 1, *Covenant*—Gen.2:15-17 for more discussion.)

Again, this covenant—the Noahic covenant—is established by God and by God alone. No man had anything to do with setting up this covenant or promise of God.

2 (9:9-10) **Covenant, Noahic**: note the recipients of the covenant. God gave this promise, this covenant...

- to Noah and his sons
- to their seed or descendants. (Remember, the word *seed* is the Biblical term for descendant and refers to all the descendants of Noah. This means that the Noahic covenant was given to the whole human race, for Noah stood at the head of the human race, as the father of all who were yet to be born upon the earth. All the seed—all of the human race—are traced back to Noah. But also remember this most important fact: when the word *seed* is used in connection with the promises or covenants of God, it is singular and refers primarily to the promised Savior or Messiah of the world, the Lord Jesus Christ Himself. Scripture itself tells us this [see Ga.3:16])
- to all animals

This is a most wonderful fact: it means that the Noahic covenant is given to every living being upon earth, both man and animal. It means that we who live today—all of us—are the recipients of the Noahic covenant. These great promises of God are given to us and to all our children, even those who are yet to be born. These great promises are even given to the animals of the earth. What are the promises? What is the Noahic covenant established by God with us and the earth? This is the discussion of the next point.

3 (9:11) **Covenant, Noahic—Flood, The Great—Promises**: note the covenant itself. There were at least two, perhaps three, parts to the covenant.

a. The covenant was God's own personal covenant, a covenant that already existed, that God had already established with man. This is seen in three facts.

1) God called the covenant "My covenant." The words "my covenant" point to a covenant that already existed, that had already been established.[1]

2) Note the word *established* (qum). The Hebrew word can mean *to fulfill, to carry out, to continue,* or *to keep.*[2] God could be saying that He was fulfilling and carrying out His own personal covenant, the covenant already established with man.

Now, to what covenant was God referring? There was only one major covenant existing prior to Noah: the covenant of *the promised seed* which had first been given to Adam.

Keep in mind the terrifying experience Noah had been through and his great need for assurance, his great need to feel safe and secure. God was now giving Noah great assurance, assuring Noah that he was counted godly and acceptable to God. In addition, God was reminding Noah of the earlier promise He had made, that Noah was to be a direct descendent of *the promised seed*, that he and his seed were to be the godly line through whom the Savior of the world was to come. (See note—Ge.6:18 for more discussion.)

3) There is a third fact that points to *the promised seed* being a part of God's covenant with Noah. Standing there, Noah was the only living father upon earth. All other fathers had been destroyed in the flood. Noah stood as the father—the head—of the whole human race, as the father of all succeeding generations. It is almost impossible, if not totally impossible, to think that God would not cover His great promise with Noah, the promise or covenant

---

[1] *The Pulpit Commentary*, Vol.1, p.143.
[2] Victor Hamilton. *The Book of Genesis*, p.316.

of *the promised seed*, of the coming Savior to the world. God loves man too much—loved Noah too much—not to give the only surviving man upon earth the great assurance of salvation, the great hope of the coming Savior. God had given the assurance of *the promised seed* to Adam right after Adam had experienced his terrifying fall into sin. Why not now give the same assurance to Noah right after his terrifying experience?

The evidence of the verse points strongly to God doing just this. When God said, "I will establish [fulfill, continue, and carry out]—*my covenant* with you," He was most likely talking about the covenant of *the promised seed*. When Noah heard these words, his heart must have been flooded with great peace and security, for he knew...

- that he was acceptable to God
- that God was looking after and caring for him in a very special way
- that God had chosen him for a great purpose, that of bearing *the promised seed*, the line through whom the Savior of the world would come

b. The covenant was also the promise to never again destroy the earth with a universal flood. The great Pulpit Commentary says this is but an enlargement of the covenant of *the promised seed* (the Adamic covenant). The covenant with Noah assures the continuation of the earth and of man so that God can fulfill His covenant of *the promised seed*.[3] The promise of the seed necessitated a safe earth for the survival and continuation of the human race. People had to survive upon earth for God to fulfill His covenant with Adam and Eve, the promise to send the Savior to the world.

Note that this part of the covenant with Noah said two things:
⇒ Never again will *all flesh*—all life—be destroyed by a universal flood.
⇒ Never again will *the earth* itself be destroyed by a universal flood.

Noah could ask for no greater assurance, no greater safety and security than this. As has been seen in the Introduction, Noah needed great assurance, for the flood had been a terrifying experience for him and his dear family (see Introduction note—Ge.9:8-17). God knew that they needed assurance to feel safe and secure as they marched forth into the new world. Noah needed to feel perfectly safe and secure...

- in order to function as a normal human being, emotionally stable and settled
- in order to fulfill the will and purpose of God for man and the earth
- in order to carry on life to the fullest

God knew that Noah needed this kind of assurance, this kind of emotional security. This is the very reason God established this great covenant with Noah:
⇒ a covenant that promised never again to destroy the earth with a universal flood.
⇒ a covenant that was to fulfill and continue God's own personal covenant with man, the great promise of *the promised seed,* the Savior of the world.

Thought 1. Remember, this covenant was given to the whole human race, to us all. We can have the same assurance, the same emotional safety and security that Noah experienced.

1) We can have assurance, feel safe and secure, that the earth will never again be judged and destroyed by a universal flood nor by any other worldwide disaster. Natural disasters will happen on a local basis: people and property will be destroyed here and there by floods, tornados, hurricanes, earthquakes, famine, and other natural disasters. But a universal flood—a worldwide natural disaster—will never again wipe out every living soul upon earth, not until the end time, the final judgment of the earth. People will be upon the earth as long as the earth stands.

2) We can have assurance, feel safe and secure, that *the promised seed* has come. Jesus Christ is the Savior of the world. Jesus Christ will do for us what He did for Noah: save us both now and eternally, save us from sin and death. But, just as a drowning man has to call and then reach up for someone to save him, so we have to call and reach up for the Lord. We have to call upon the Lord to save us; we have to take the hand of the Savior and follow Him in order to be saved. *The promised seed*, the Lord Jesus Christ, does not automatically save us. We choose whether or not to be saved; we choose whether or not to let Him save us. We can have assurance, feel safe and secure, if we call upon Him and let Him save us.

"Come unto me, all ye that labour and are heavy laden, and I will give you rest" (Mt.11:28).
"For God sent not his Son into the world to condemn the world; but that the world through him might be saved. He that believeth on him is not condemned: but he that believeth not is condemned already, because he hath not believed in the name of the only begotten Son of God" (Jn.3:17-18).
"But these are written, that ye might believe that Jesus is the Christ, the Son of God; and that believing ye might have life through his name" (Jn.20:31).
"And it shall come to pass, that whosoever shall call on the name of the Lord shall be saved" (Acts 2:21).
"For whosoever shall call upon the name of the Lord shall be saved" (Ro.10:13).
"Give thanks unto the LORD, call upon his name, make known his deeds among the people" (1 Chron.16:8).
"And it shall come to pass, that whosoever shall call on the name of the LORD shall be delivered" (Joel 2:32).

---

3 *The Pulpit Commentary*, Vol.1, p.143.

3) We can have assurance, feel safe and secure, against the terrible day of judgment to come, the judgment of the end time. We can know that we have eternal life, that we shall never die, but that we shall live with God forever and ever.

> "For God so loved the world, that he gave his only begotten Son, that whosoever believeth in him should not perish, but have everlasting life" (Jn.3:16).
> "For God sent not his Son into the world to condemn the world; but that the world through him might be saved" (Jn.3:17).
> "He that believeth on the Son hath everlasting life: and he that believeth not the Son shall not see life; but the wrath of God abideth on him" (Jn.3:36).
> "Verily, verily, I say unto you, He that heareth my word, and believeth on him that sent me, hath everlasting life, and shall not come into condemnation; but is passed from death unto life" (Jn.5:24).
> "He that loveth his life shall lose it; and he that hateth his life in this world shall keep it unto life eternal" (Jn.12:25).
> "And this is the record, that God hath given to us eternal life, and this life is in his Son. He that hath the Son hath life; and he that hath not the Son of God hath not life" (1 Jn.5:11-12).
> "These things have I written unto you that believe on the name of the Son of God; that ye may know that ye have eternal life, and that ye may believe on the name of the Son of God" (1 Jn.5:13).

c. The covenant might also include the points covered in the New World Order established by God in the former outline (see outline and notes—Ge.9:1-7). Many commentators do include the provisions covered there in the Noahic covenant.
⇒ The regulation of seasons (Ge.8:22 see Ge.9:11).
⇒ The mission of man: to repopulate the earth (Ge.9:1, 7).
⇒ The supremacy of man: to rule over the earth (Ge.9:2).
⇒ The provision of food for man (Ge.9:3-4).
⇒ The establishment of human government and of capital punishment (vv.5-7).

In summary, note that God's covenant covers only a universal flood, not a local flood here and there upon earth. There have been and still will be local floods that destroy both lives and property so long as we live in a corruptible world where nature sometimes runs wild.

Note also that the Noahic covenant stands as strong evidence against all local flood theories. The local flood theories hold that *The Great Flood* was a local flood that covered only Noah's local community or some larger but limited area. But note this: the covenant spelled out in verse eleven deals with a universal flood or else it is meaningless. How could the covenant be a promise that there would never again be a local flood to destroy the earth? There have been many local floods and many lives and properties destroyed by local floods down through history. As stated, the covenant itself gives evidence—strong evidence—that *The Great Flood* was just that, a great flood, a universal flood that wrecked the whole earth.

4 (9:12-16) **Covenant, Noahic—Rainbow—Promises**: note the sign of the covenant, the rainbow.

a. The rainbow is a sign given to all generations. It was not just a sign given to Noah and his family; it was a sign given to all of us, to all generations of people.

b. The rainbow is a sign set in the clouds by God Himself, set there for the purpose of being a sign of His great covenant with Noah and mankind.

1) Note that the rainbow is set in the clouds by God Himself. God Himself created the laws of nature that caused the rainbow to form. Picture a thunderstorm, the kind that usually comes in late afternoon in most lands. Imagine its thunderous roar and flashing lightning, the apprehension—sometimes fear—that strikes most hearts because of its dangerous winds and lightning. The rainbow appears after the storm when the rays of sunlight break through the clouds and the most beautiful colors are reflected in the breaking clouds, colors that form a bow across the sky.

The rainbow is a sign—a promise—set in the clouds by God Himself. The laws of nature that cause the rainbow to form were established and set in motion by God.

But, when did the rainbow first appear? After the flood or before the flood? Did *The Great Flood* cause violent changes in the atmosphere and cloud formations of the earth?
⇒ If so, then the rainbow most likely appeared first in the days of Noah.
⇒ If not, then the rainbow most likely already existed, and God simply pointed to it and made it a sign. God would simply be giving it a new meaning, a new significance, in the eyes of man.

2) Note that the rainbow is a sign that God will never again destroy the earth with a universal flood, a sign given to all generations (v.12). The fact that God gave a sign to back up his covenant shows just how terrorized Noah was. Again, just imagine having witnessed the destruction of the whole earth by a torrential rain and the volcanic eruption of all the subterranean waters of the earth. Imagine your thoughts of God, of sin, and of judgment—how you would cry out for mercy—as you float around upon the waters in a barge-like boat for a whole year. Then imagine standing upon the earth alone, with no one except your own small family of eight persons. All of your friends and neighbors—all of your fellow human beings and all animals—were drowned and gone. Only you and

your small family survived. Terror, fear, apprehension, wondering, and questioning would fill your soul and being. This was Noah. This was the reason he needed assurance from God. Noah was just what we would have been, literally terrorized. He needed to be reassured time and again by God that he would not suffer the judgment of God, never again, not like he had just witnessed.

This is what God was doing with the rainbow: giving Noah a double assurance of safety and security. God had just given him the assurance of His covenant of promise; now God, in mercy, gave Noah a double assurance, a sign that he nor his seed (descendents) would ever again experience the judgment of God in a universal flood. This is what the rainbow is all about: it is a sign of assurance, of safety and security, that never again will God judge the earth with a universal flood. Never again will all men be wiped off the face of the earth by a natural disaster such as the great and terrifying flood. The rainbow is God's sign—His assurance—that the earth as a whole will never again be destroyed, not until the end time. Between now and the end of the world, large masses of people will continue upon the earth and will still have time to repent and turn to *the promised seed* of God, the Savior of the world. This is what the rainbow signifies: God's mercy upon man and the earth, God's mercy upon the corruptible earth and all the generations of sinful men.

c. The rainbow is a sign to provoke remembrance of the covenant and of the flood and its judgment by God. Note that God says He always remembers His covenant when the rainbow appears in the sky. God never forgets His covenant, but when the rainbow appears, He especially remembers the terrifying judgment of the flood and the great covenant He has made with man.

The point is this: we too should remember, but we often fail. Too often, when the rainbow appears, we just admire and point out its beauty and quickly move back to whatever we were doing. This, however, is not the purpose for which God gave the rainbow. God gave the rainbow for a sign...

- that we would remember and think upon the terrible judgment that fell upon the earth
- that we would remember His great covenant, that never again would He judge the earth with a torrential flood
- that we would remember the great mercy of God to sinful man, that He will save us if we will repent and turn to *the promised seed* and Savior, the Lord Jesus Christ

d. The rainbow is a sign to provoke remembrance that the covenant is everlasting (v.16). God will always remember this one thing:

⇒ as long as the earth stands, all living creatures are safe from having to face a worldwide judgment from God. Life upon earth will never be wiped out, not completely, not fully, not by a flood nor by any other natural disaster. The species of both animal and man will continue to live upon the earth until God is ready to end human history and bring all men into final judgment.

The point is this: God remembers His covenant, that it is everlasting. The rainbow is a sign that He remembers.

Thought 1. We too should remember the terrifying judgment of God, in particular this fact: we can escape the final judgment of God as long as we are still living and turn to *the promised seed*, the Savior of the world, the Lord Jesus Christ.

"Let the wicked forsake his way, and the unrighteous man his thoughts: and let him return unto the LORD, and he will have mercy upon him; and to our God, for he will abundantly pardon" (Is.55:7).

"But if the wicked will turn from all his sins that he hath committed, and keep all my statutes, and do that which is lawful and right, he shall surely live, he shall not die" (Eze.18:21).

"Therefore also now, saith the LORD, turn ye even to me with all your heart, and with fasting, and with weeping, and with mourning" (Joel 2:12).

"And saying, Repent ye: for the kingdom of heaven is at hand" (Mt.3:2).

"And he came into all the country about Jordan, preaching the baptism of repentance for the remission of sins" (Lu.3:3).

"Then Peter said unto them, Repent, and be baptized every one of you in the name of Jesus Christ for the remission of sins, and ye shall receive the gift of the Holy Ghost" (Ac.2:38).

"Repent ye therefore, and be converted, that your sins may be blotted out, when the times of refreshing shall come from the presence of the Lord" (Ac.3:19).

"Repent therefore of this thy wickedness, and pray God, if perhaps the thought of thine heart may be forgiven thee" (Ac.8:22).

5 (9:17) **Assurance—Word of God**: note the assurance of the covenant: God and His Word. This is the purpose of this verse: to give Noah and us absolute assurance—perfect safety and security—that His covenant is true. Note the words, "God said." The covenant is assured...

- by God Himself
- by God's Word

No greater assurance could stand behind a covenant. God's promise that He would establish (fulfill, continue, and carry out) His covenant upon earth is assured.

⇒ God has already sent *the promised seed* and Savior to earth, the Lord Jesus Christ.
⇒ God has not judged and destroyed the earth with a universal flood, not since Noah's day, and He never will.

In fact, no universal judgment will fall upon the earth that will destroy all life, not until the final end and judgment of the universe. That day is coming, but until then, any person living upon the earth has the opportunity of repenting and turning to *the promised seed* and Savior of the world, the Lord Jesus Christ.

This great covenant, the Noahic covenant, is assured. It shall stand fast until the end of the world. Both God and His Word give us this assurance.

> "For verily I say unto you, Till heaven and earth pass, one jot or one tittle shall in no wise pass from the law [God's Word], till all be fulfilled" (Mt.5:18).

> "Heaven and earth shall pass away, but my words shall not pass away" (Mt.24:35).

> "For ever, O LORD, thy word is settled in heaven" (Ps.119:89).

> "The grass withereth, the flower fadeth: but the word of our God shall stand for ever" (Is.40:8).

> "But the word of the Lord endureth for ever. And this is the word which by the gospel is preached unto you" (1 Pt.1:25).

I. **Noah & the Human Race: The Future of the Human Race Foretold, 9:18-29**

1. **The branches of the human race are given**
   a. Three branches: Shem, Ham (the father of Canaan), & Japheth
   b. These three branches produced the races that populated earth
2. **The sin & failure of the human race was continued**
   a. The sins of Noah: Drunkenness,[DS1] sensuality, & disobedience to God
   b. The sins of Ham
      1) Dishonored his father
      2) Scorned his father
      3) Turned away from his father's faith
      4) Is clearly seen by the stark

18 And the sons of Noah, that went forth of the ark, were Shem, and Ham, and Japheth: and Ham is the father of Canaan.
19 These are the three sons of Noah: and of them was the whole earth overspread.
20 And Noah began to be an husbandman, and he planted a vineyard:
21 And he drank of the wine, and was drunken; and he was uncovered within his tent.
22 And Ham, the father of Canaan, saw the nakedness of his father, and told his two brethren without.
23 And Shem and Japheth took a garment, and laid it upon both their shoulders, and went backward, and covered the nakedness of their father; and their faces were backward, and they saw not their father's nakedness.
24 And Noah awoke from his wine, and knew what his younger son had done unto him.
25 And he said, Cursed be Canaan; a servant of servants shall he be unto his brethren.
26 And he said, Blessed be the LORD God of Shem; and Canaan shall be his servant.
27 God shall enlarge Japheth, and he shall dwell in the tents of Shem; and Canaan shall be his servant.
28 And Noah lived after the flood three hundred and fifty years.
29 And all the days of Noah were nine hundred and fifty years: and he died.

contrast of his brothers' behavior: Their honor & respect for their father

3. **The future of the human race was predicted**

   a. Canaan: The father of an enslaved people

   b. Shem: The father of a people whose God is to be blessed

   c. Japheth: The father of the largest nations—will enjoy the tents, the blessings, of Shem

4. **The death of the human race was demonstrated**

DIVISION IV

NOAH: THE MAN CHOSEN TO PRESERVE MANKIND AND THE GODLY SEED THROUGH WORLD DESTRUCTION (THE FLOOD), 6:9–9:29

I.   Noah and the Human Race: The Future of the Human Race Foretold, 9:18-29

(9:18-29) **Introduction**: this event of Scripture took place years after *The Great Flood*, probably several decades later. We know this because Canaan, the son of Ham, had already been born. When Noah and his three sons disembarked from the ark, the sons had no children. Canaan was the fourth son of Ham (Ge.10:6), and he is already old enough to have apparently chosen to live an ungodly life. He was probably an adult, for it is unlikely a child would be cursed for irresponsible behavior (a child is usually corrected and taught, not cursed) (v.25). All this points to this prophecy of the human race taking place during the later years of Noah's life.

Noah stood at the head of the human race. He had produced the branches that were to bring forth all the races of the earth. This is the captivating subject of this passage: *Noah and the Human Race: The Future of the Human Race Foretold*.

1. The branches of the human race are given (vv.18-19).
2. The sin and failure of the human race was continued (vv.20-23).
3. The future of the human race was predicted (vv.24-27).
4. The death of the human race was demonstrated (vv.28-29).

[1] (9:18-19) **Race, Human—Mankind—History—Population—Forefathers—Humanity**: the branches of the human race are given. Noah had three sons:
   ⇒ Shem
   ⇒ Ham
   ⇒ Japheth

These three sons stand at the head of the three main branches of the human race. All the races and people of the earth can be traced back to one of these three branches. The races of the earth can look back at these three branches and find the very beginning of their…
   • racial heritage
   • roots
   • heredity
   • ancestry
   • history

Note how clearly this is stated: the three branches produced the races that *populated and spread out* over the whole earth (v.19). Shem, Ham, and Japheth gave rise to everyone who lives today, to all the races and people of the earth. After *The Great Flood*, the earth was repopulated by these three sons of Noah, sons who formed the three great branches of the human race.

Thought 1. This means that the human race—all people and all nations—have come from one source. All races are tied and bound together by a common ancestor. The unity of the human race is a fact; the universal brotherhood of man is a living reality. There should be no prejudice, discrimination, or classes among us. We are all brothers and sisters, bound together by a common ancestor. We are, therefore, to love one another, to practice brotherly love.

> "Thou shalt love thy neighbor as thyself" (Mt.22:39).
> "This is my commandment, That ye love one another, as I have loved you" (Jn.15:12).
> "Let love be without dissimulation [hypocrisy]. Abhor that which is evil; cleave to that which is good" (Ro.12:9).
> "See that ye love one another with a pure heart fervently" (1 Pe.1:22).

2 (9:20-23) **Noah—Ham—Sin—Drunkenness—Immodesty—Sensuality—Mockery—Ridicule—Eye, Sins of—Honor—Respect**: the sin and failure of the human race was continued. This is seen both in the sin of Noah and in the sin of his youngest son, Ham.

a. First, there was the sin of Noah (vv.20-21). After the flood, one the very first things Noah and his sons had to do was plant food for their families. Thus they became farmers. At some point through the years, Noah planted a vineyard. Now, note the simple and straightforward description of Noah's sin: he drank too much of the wine...

- and became intoxicated or drunk
- and uncovered himself—stripped himself naked—within his tent

This is the first time wine and drunkenness are specifically mentioned in Scripture. Was this the first time wine had ever become fermented and intoxicating, or did wine exist before and Scripture has just not mentioned it before now? Did Noah know what he was doing—getting drunk—or was he caught completely off guard by some grape juice that had become fermented?

⇒ Remember the ungodly people before the flood, their wicked and immoral lives? It is most unlikely that wine and drunkenness were not a part of their sin and shame, and if so, Noah would have known about the danger of fermented wine.

⇒ The Scripture actually says that Noah drank of "the wine," not just "wine," but "the wine." By using the definite article ("the") Scripture indicates that Noah knew what he was doing. He knew what fermented wine was, that it made a person drunk.

⇒ The straightforward manner in which the story is told strongly points to the sin and guilt of Noah. This is the very point of the story: to show that Noah sinned and his son looked upon his sin and mocked him instead of helping him. Consequently, Noah pronounced a curse upon the son.

There is little, if any, doubt that Noah was guilty of sin, guilty of deliberate and willful sin. He knew exactly what he was doing, that wine ("the wine") would make him drunk. Several facts about Noah's sin leap out at us.

1) Noah sinned and failed despite his having been a godly man. Before the flood, Noah was a righteous man who had lived a just and blameless life before the people of his generation. Noah had walked with God (Ge.6:9). The New Testament even says that Noah was "a preacher of righteousness" (2 Pe.2:5). But now, after the flood, Noah committed a tragic and serious sin.

Thought 1. No person is above sin, not even a servant of God. Anyone can fall into sin, some serious and tragic sin. No matter who the person is—no matter how godly he has been and how high a position he may hold—he is still a sinful and depraved creature, and he can still fall and commit some serious sin. Noah, the great man of God, sinned, and so can we. (Note: we are not talking about sinning in general, but some serious and tragic sin. We all sin, for we are all short of God's glory—totally depraved. But none of us have to fall and commit serious sin, the kind of sin that causes damage to the lives of others and to the name of Christ.

> "Every one of them is gone back: they are altogether become filthy; there is none that doeth good, no, not one" (Ps.53:3).
> "Who can say, I have made my heart clean, I am pure from my sin?" (Pr.20:9).
> "All we like sheep have gone astray; we have turned every one to his own way; and the LORD hath laid on him the iniquity of us all" (Is.53:6).
> "But we are all as an unclean thing, and all our righteousnesses are as filthy rags; and we all do fade as a leaf; and our iniquities, like the wind, have taken us away" (Is.64:6).
> "For all have sinned, and come short of the glory of God" (Ro.3:23).
> "If we say that we have no sin, we deceive ourselves, and the truth is not in us" (1 Jn.1:8).

2) Noah's sin resulted in severe and terrible consequences.
⇒ Noah's youngest son, Ham, sinned and received a divine curse (vv.24-25).
⇒ Nothing more is written about Noah, except his death. It is as though Noah's life bore no more good after his sin.

Thought 1. The consequences of sin are always terrible. Scripture declares this fact:

> "As righteousness tendeth to life: so he that pursueth evil pursueth it to his own death" (Pr.11:19).
> "But your iniquities have separated between you and your God, And your sins have hid his face from you, that he will not hear" (Is.59:2).
> "But we are all as an unclean thing, and all our righteousnesses are as filthy rags; and we all do fade as a leaf; and our iniquities, like the wind, have taken us away" (Is.64:6).
> "Therefore thus saith the LORD, Behold, I will bring evil upon them, which they shall not be able to escape; and though they shall cry unto me, I will not hearken unto them" (Je.11:11).
> "The soul that sinneth, it shall die" (Eze.18:4).
> "Wherefore, as by one man sin entered into the world, and death by sin; and so death passed upon all men, for that all have sinned" (Ro.5:12).
> "For the wages of sin is death; but the gift of God is eternal life through Jesus Christ our Lord" (Ro.6:23).
> "How shall we escape, if we neglect so great salvation; which at the first began to be spoken by the Lord, and was confirmed unto us by them that heard him" (He.2:3).

3) Noah failed in his old age after having walked with God for years. The flood happened when Noah was 600 years old; thus, he had walked with God for the greater part of his life. This sin apparently happened in the last one or two hundred years of his life, for he lived after the flood for 350 years.

    The point is this: in the latter years of his life, Noah let up and did not guard his spiritual life like he should. Consequently, he sinned and failed late in life.

    Thought 1. Sinning in one's old age has also happened to some other godly men.
  ⇒ Moses sinned in the latter years of his life by disobeying God, and was not allowed to enter the promised land because of his disobedience (Nu.20:7-13).
  ⇒ David sinned in the latter years of his life by committing adultery with Bathsheba and having her husband killed (2 S.11:1-27).

4) Noah apparently fell into sin because he neglected his prayer and worship time with God and because he failed to keep a watchful eye against temptation. Very frankly, Noah gave in to a simple temptation. Noah was not a drunkard, not a habitual drinker, or else Scripture would have told us. Noah's flesh was not craving drink; to become drunk was a new thing for him. If he had been spiritually strong—living before God in prayer and worship—he would not have caved in to a temptation that aroused little craving from his flesh. Noah fell into this tragic sin simply because his heart and mind were not upon God. It is unlikely that he was even thinking about God during the days surrounding his fall. His neglect of daily prayer and worship must have been going on for days.

> "Also day by day, from the first day unto the last day, he read in the book of the law of God" (Ne.8:18).
> "Seek the LORD and his strength, seek his face continually" (1 Chr.16:11).
> "So will I sing praise unto thy name for ever, that I may daily perform my vows" (Ps.61:8).
> "Mine eye mourneth by reason of affliction: LORD, I have called daily upon thee, I have stretched out my hands unto thee" (Ps.88:9).
> "Blessed is the man that heareth me, watching daily at my gates, waiting at the posts of my doors" (Pr.8:34).
> "Watch and pray, that ye enter not into temptation: the spirit indeed is willing, but the flesh is weak" (Mt.26:41).
> "And he said to them all, If any man will come after me, let him deny himself, and take up his cross daily, and follow me" (Lu.9:23).
> "And he spake a parable unto them to this end, that men ought always to pray, and not to faint" (Lu.18:1).
> "Praying always with all prayer and supplication in the Spirit, and watching thereunto with all perseverance and supplication for all saints" (Ep.6:18).
> "Pray without ceasing" (1 Th.5:17).
> "Study to show thyself approved unto God, a workman that needeth not to be ashamed, rightly dividing the word of truth" (2 Ti.2:15).

5) Noah's sin was the terrible sin of drunkenness (see DEEPER STUDY # 1—Ge.9:21 for discussion).
6) Noah's sin was also the terrible sin of sensuality, immodesty, and immorality. The Hebrew word for *uncovered* shows this; it is reflexive action: Noah "*uncovered [yithgal] himself.*" It was, apparently, a deliberate uncovering. Noah was drunk and he stripped himself naked within his tent. All restraints were gone, all modesty, decency, respect, honor, dignity, and morality. Noah had foolishly let down his guard and become drunk. He had let loose, and just as drink usually affects the urges of the flesh, his flesh became activated. His sensual and sexual urges were running loose. Noah stripped himself naked. Why?
⇒ To display his body before himself, perhaps feeling proud of his manliness?
⇒ To lie stripped to attract his wife in case she walked into the tent?
⇒ To have sex with his wife or to react against his wife because she had refused his advances toward her?

On and on we could guess as to why Noah stripped himself naked, but Scripture just does not say. All it says is that Noah did get drunk, and he uncovered himself, stripped himself naked within his tent. He deliberately allowed the sensual, immodest, and immoral urges of his flesh to run wild.

Thought 1. Scripture tells us how drink causes the sensual and immoral urges of the flesh to run wild.

"Thou shalt be drunken, and shalt make thyself naked" (Lam.4:21).

"Woe unto him that giveth his neighbor drink, that puttest thy bottle to him, and makest him drunken also, that thou mayest look on their nakedness! Thou art filled with shame for glory: drink thou also, and let thy foreskin be uncovered: the cup of the LORD's right hand shall be turned unto thee, and shameful spewing shall be on thy glory" (Hab.2:15-16).

"And they made their father [Lot] drink wine that night: and the firstborn [daughter] went in, and lay with her father; and he perceived not when she lay down, nor when she arose" (Ge.19:33).

"On the seventh day, when the heart of the king was merry with wine, he commanded Mehuman, Biztha, Harbona, Bigtha, and Abagtha, Zethar, and Carcas, the seven chamberlains that served in the presence of Ahasuerus the king, to bring Vashti the queen before the king with the crown royal, to show the people and the princes her beauty: for she was fair to look on" (Est.1:10-11).

7) Noah's sin was, however, far more than drunkenness and immorality. Noah's root sin was disobedience to God. Noah just neglected and ignored God. As pointed out above (pt.d), Noah had failed in his daily prayer and worship and failed to stand watch against temptation. He had been neglecting and ignoring God, disobeying God day by day. Consequently, it was but a short step to some serious disobedience, to falling and committing some tragic sin of disobedience.

Thought 1. Disobedience is a very serious sin to God.

"But if ye will not obey the voice of the LORD, but rebel against the commandment of the LORD, then shall the hand of the LORD be against you, as it was against your fathers" (1 S.12:15).

"Not every one that saith unto me, Lord, Lord, shall enter into the kingdom of heaven; but he that doeth the will of my Father which is in heaven. Many will say to me in that day, Lord, Lord, have we not prophesied in thy name? and in thy name have cast out devils? and in thy name done many wonderful works? And then will I profess unto them, I never knew you: depart from me, ye that work iniquity" (Mt.7:21-23).

"Let no man deceive you with vain words: for because of these things cometh the wrath of God upon the children of disobedience" (Ep.5:6).

"And to you who are troubled rest with us, when the Lord Jesus shall be revealed from heaven with his mighty angels, in flaming fire taking vengeance on them that know not God, and that obey not the gospel of our Lord Jesus Christ" (2 Th.1:7-8).

"For if the word spoken by angels was stedfast, and every transgression and disobedience received a just recompense of reward; how shall we escape, if we neglect so great salvation; which at the first began to be spoken by the Lord, and was confirmed unto us by them that heard him" (He.2:2-3).

b. Second, there was the sin of Ham (vv.22-23). Note several things.
1) Did Ham commit some sexual sin with his drunken father? Some commentators think so.
   ⇒ v. 22 says that Ham "*saw* the nakedness of his father." The Hebrew means more than just looking at his father; it means that he saw with pleasure, joy, and satisfaction. Does this imply more than just looking with pleasure at his father? Does *just looking* merit such a terrible curse as was pronounced upon the younger son of Ham (v.25)?
   ⇒ v. 24 says that Noah found out "what his younger son *had done* to him." This might refer to some physical act or sexual sin, but it could simply refer to Ham dishonoring and mocking Noah (v.22).
   ⇒ In other Scriptures *to uncover the nakedness* of someone means to commit some sexual sin (Le.18:6-9; 20:11, 17-21; Eze.16:36-37). In Le.20:17 the word "see" is used instead of "uncover." The word "see" means to have sexual relations.[1]

"And if a man shall take his sister, his father's daughter, or his mother's daughter, and see her nakedness, and she see his nakedness; it is a wicked thing; and they shall be cut off in the sight of their people: he hath uncovered his sister's nakedness; he shall bear his iniquity" (Le.20:17).

In this passage the word "see" has the same force that the word "know" often has throughout Scripture. For example, "Adam *knew* Eve...and she conceived" (Ge.4:1). Both words—"see" and "know"—sometimes mean to *see* and *know* in the most intimate sense; to have sexual relations.

---

[1] Victor Hamilton. *The Book of Genesis*, p.322.

These facts definitely point to some sexual sin being involved. But other commentators think not. And, note this: Scripture does not specifically say that a sexual sin was committed, unless the word "saw" means sexual relations as it does in Le.20:17 above.

Ham committed at least three serious and tragic sins (four, if a person holds that he committed a sexual sin). These are covered in points 2), 3), and 4) below.

2) Ham tragically dishonored his father. This is seen not only in the act of Ham, but in the word "saw." The Hebrew means to gaze upon, to look upon intently, to look upon with pleasure, to look upon with satisfaction.[2] Ham saw his father naked and deliberately stood there looking upon him. Why? Because he was receiving some kind of satisfaction from it. He was pleased to see his father in such a state of drunkenness, shame, and dishonor. For some reason, Ham felt ill will toward his father. Consequently...

- he refused to throw a covering over his father. He just let him lie there in his shameful nakedness
- he took great satisfaction and pleasure in seeing his father shame himself

Simply stated, Ham dishonored his father. He showed the utmost disrespect and spite for him.

3) Ham scorned, ridiculed, and showed contempt for his father. Ham went right out and told his brothers about his father's drunkenness and nakedness. The word for *told* (wayyaggedh) means that he told them with delight.[3] He actually got joy and satisfaction in telling them. He was able to ridicule and mock his father's behavior, to show scorn and contempt in the hope that his brothers might feel ill will toward their father as well.

Thought 1. Dishonoring parents has always been a serious sin in the eyes of God.

> "If a man have a stubborn and rebellious son, which will not obey the voice of his father, or the voice of his mother, and that, when they have chastened him, will not hearken unto them....And they shall say unto the elders of his city, This our son is stubborn and rebellious, he will not obey our voice; he is a glutton, and a drunkard. And all the men of his city shall stone him with stones, that he die: so shalt thou put evil away from among you; and all Israel shall hear, and fear" (De.21:18, 20-21).
>
> "Cursed be he that setteth light by his father or his mother" (De.27:16).
>
> "A wise son maketh a glad father: but a foolish man despiseth his mother" (Pr.15:20).
>
> "And he that smiteth his father, or his mother, shall be surely put to death" (Ex.21:15).
>
> "For every one that curseth his father or his mother shall be surely put to death: he hath cursed his father or his mother; his blood shall be upon him" (Le.20:9).
>
> "For God commanded, saying, Honour thy father and mother: and, He that curseth father or mother, let him die the death" (Mt.15:4).

Thought 2. Disobedience to parents is a common problem within society.

> "This know also, that in the last days perilous times shall come. For men shall be lovers of their own selves, covetous, boasters, proud, blasphemers, disobedient to parents, unthankful, unholy" (2 Ti.3:1-2).
>
> "There is a generation that curseth their father, and doth not bless their mother" (Pr.30:11).
>
> "For the son dishonoureth the father, the daughter riseth up against her mother, the daughter in law against her mother in law; a man's enemies are the men of his own house" (Mi.7:6).

Thought 3. Ham scorns and ridicules his father, Noah. Note that Noah is:
⇒ his father
⇒ an aged man
⇒ a minister of righteousness

Too often, the young scorn and ridicule each of these. God says this about honoring each:
⇒ honoring the father

> "My son, hear the instruction of thy father, and forsake not the law of thy mother" (Pr.1:8).
>
> "My son, keep thy father's commandment, and forsake not the law of thy mother" (Pr.6:20).
>
> "Hearken unto thy father that begat thee, and despise not thy mother when she is old" (Pr.23:22).
>
> "Children, obey your parents in the Lord: for this is right" (Ep.6:1).

⇒ honoring old age

> "Thou shalt rise up before the hoary [aged] head, and honour the face of the old man, and fear thy God: I am the LORD" (Le.19:32).

---

2 H.C. Leupold. *Genesis*, Vol.1, p.346.
3 Ibid., p.346.

"Rebuke not an elder, but entreat him as a father; and the younger men as brethren" (1 Ti.5:1).

"Likewise, ye younger, submit yourselves unto the elder. Yea, all of you be subject one to another, and be clothed with humility: for God resisteth the proud, and giveth grace to the humble. Humble yourselves therefore under the mighty hand of God, that he may exalt you in due time" (1 Pe.5:5-6).

⇒ honoring ministers

"Remember them which have the rule over you [ministers], who have spoken unto you the word of God: whose faith follow, considering the end of their conversation [behavior]" (He.13:7).

"And we beseech you, brethren, to know them which labour among you [ministers], and are over you in the Lord, and admonish you; and to esteem them very highly in love for their work's sake. And be at peace among yourselves" (1 Th.5:12-13).

4) Ham apparently had turned away from the faith of his father. Basically—in the core of his being—Noah was a very godly man, despite his serious and tragic fall at this point in his life. Noah had been chosen and used by God in a great way, and he was a true preacher of righteousness (2 Pe.2:5). Ham, if his heart had been right with God, could not have shown such dishonor and scorn toward such a godly man as Noah, no matter how far the godly man had fallen. In fact, no true believer can show dishonor and scorn toward any person, no matter how terrible a sinner the person may be. True believers just do not dishonor, ridicule, and scorn other persons. This could be the chief reason why Ham felt so much ill will toward his father: he felt dissatisfied and unfulfilled because he had rejected both the God and the preaching of his father.

"He therefore that despiseth, despiseth not man, but God, who hath also given unto us his holy Spirit" (1 Th.4:8).

The sin of Ham was serious and tragic. Just how serious is seen in two facts. First, Shem and Japheth showed the greatest respect and honor for their father. They controlled themselves and did not join in the mockery of their father. They took some garment, walked backwards into the tent to the bed of their father, and covered their father's nakedness. They walked backwards so they would not see their father's nakedness. What a contrast to the behavior of Ham. Their act—the very way they went about covering their father—stands in stark contrast to Ham's behavior. Their respect and honor show how terrible Ham's dishonor toward their father was.

Second, the curse placed upon Ham shows how serious Ham's sins were. This is the discussion of the next few verses (vv.24-27, note 5).

DEEPER STUDY # 1

(9:21) **Drunkenness**: to be drunk means to be intoxicated with drink or drugs (Lu.21:34; Ro.13:13; Ga.5:21; see Pr.20:1; Is.28:7; Eze.23:32; 39:19). Drunkenness is a work of the flesh and it often leads to other sins of the flesh: partying, loose behavior, immodest clothing, exposure of the body, sexual thoughts, immorality, wicked or evil and unjust behavior or violence and physical abuse, notions of grandeur, strength or power. The Bible says several things about drunkenness.

1. Drunkenness leads to prostitution and takes away a person's heart, mind, and understanding.

"For they shall eat, and not have enough: they shall commit whoredom [prostitution], and shall not increase: because they have left off to take heed to the LORD. Whoredom and wine and new wine take away the heart" (Ho.4:10-11).

"Look not thou upon the wine when it is red, when it giveth his color in the cup, when it moveth itself aright. At the last it biteth like a serpent, and stingeth like an adder. Thine eyes shall behold strange women, and thine heart shall utter perverse things" (Pr.23:31-33).

2. Drunkenness leads to immoral behavior.

"And they made their father [Lot] drink wine that night: and the firstborn [daughter] went in, and lay with her father; and he perceived not when she lay down, nor when she arose" (Ge.19:33).

"On the seventh day, when the heart of the king was merry with wine, he commanded Mehuman, Biztha, Harbona, Bigtha, and Abagtha, Zethar, and Carcas, the seven chamberlains that served in the presence of Ahasuerus the king, to bring Vashti the queen before the king with the crown royal, to show the people and the princes her beauty: for she was fair to look on" (Est.1:10-11).

"Woe unto him that giveth his neighbor drink, that puttest thy bottle to him, and makest him drunken also, that thou mayest look on their nakedness!" (Hab.2:15).

3. Drunkenness usually takes place secretly, under the cover of darkness.

"For they that sleep sleep in the night; and they that be drunken are drunken in the night" (1 Th.5:7).

4. Drunkenness leads to much trouble and sorrow.

> "Who hath woe? who hath sorrow? who hath contentions? who hath babbling? who hath wounds without cause? who hath redness of eyes? They that tarry long at the wine; they that go to seek mixed wine" (Pr.23:29-30).
> "Woe unto them that rise up early in the morning, that they may follow strong drink; that continue until night, till wine inflame them!" (Is.5:11).

5. Drunkenness leads to other forms of misbehavior and sin.

> "And not many days after the younger son gathered all together, and took his journey into a far country, and there wasted his substance with riotous living" (Lu.15:13).
> "And be not drunk with wine, wherein is excess; but be filled with the Spirit" (Ep.5:18).

6. Drunkenness leads to poverty.

> "He that loveth pleasure shall be a poor man: he that loveth wine and oil shall not be rich" (Pr.21:17).
> "Be not among winebibbers; among riotous eaters of flesh: for the drunkard and the glutton shall come to poverty: and drowsiness shall clothe a man with rags" (Pr.23:20-21).

7. Drunkenness causes leaders to forget the law, to stumble in judgment, and to act unjustly.

> "It is not for kings, O Lemuel, it is not for kings to drink wine; nor for princes strong drink: lest they drink, and forget the law, and pervert the judgment of any of the afflicted" (Pr.31:4-5).
> "But they also have erred through wine, and through strong drink are out of the way; the priest and the prophet have erred through strong drink, they are swallowed up of wine, they are out of the way through strong drink; they err in vision, they stumble in judgment" (Is.28:7).
> "Belshazzar the king made a great feast to a thousand of his lords, and drank wine before the thousand. Belshazzar, whiles he tasted the wine, commanded to bring the golden and silver vessels which his father Nebuchadnezzar had taken out of the temple which was in Jerusalem; that the king, and his princes, his wives, and his concubines, might drink therein" (Da.5:1-2; see v.3-31).

8. Drunkenness makes it impossible to grasp the fleeting opportunities of time.

> "Redeeming the time, because the days are evil. Wherefore be ye not unwise, but understanding what the will of the Lord is. And be not drunk with wine" (Ep.5:16-18).

9. Drunkenness is not wise.

> "Wine is a mocker, strong drink is raging: and whosoever is deceived thereby is not wise" (Pr.20:1).

10. Drunkenness is not to be a part of the believer's life.

> "Let us walk honestly, as in the day; not in rioting and drunkenness, not in chambering and wantonness, not in strife and envying" (Ro.13:13).
> "And be not drunk with wine, wherein is excess; but be filled with the Spirit" (Ep.5:18).
> "Ye are all the children of light, and the children of the day: we are not of the night, nor of darkness. Therefore let us not sleep, as do others; but let us watch and be sober. For they that sleep sleep in the night; and they that be drunken are drunken in the night. But let us, who are of the day, be sober, putting on the breastplate of faith and love; and for an helmet, the hope of salvation" (1 Th.5:5-8).

11. Drunkenness is addictive.

> "Look not thou upon the wine when it is red, when it giveth his color in the cup, when it moveth itself aright. At the last it biteth like a serpent, and stingeth like an adder. Thine eyes shall behold strange women, and thine heart shall utter perverse things. Yea, thou shalt be as he that lieth down in the midst of the sea, or as he that lieth upon the top of a mast. They have stricken me, shalt thou say, and I was not sick; they have beaten me, and I felt it not: when shall I awake? I will seek it yet again" (Pr.23:31-35).
> "Blessed art thou, O land, when thy king is the son of nobles, and thy princes eat in due season, for strength, and not for drunkenness!" (Ec.10:17).
> "Come ye, say they, I will fetch wine, and we will fill ourselves with strong drink; and to morrow shall be as this day, and much more abundant" (Is.56:12).

12. Drunkenness excludes a person from the kingdom of God.

> "Nor thieves, nor covetous, nor drunkards, nor revilers, nor extortioners, shall inherit the kingdom of God" (1 Co.6:10).

> "Envyings, murders, drunkenness, revellings, and such like: of the which I tell you before, as I have also told you in time past, that they which do such things shall not inherit the kingdom of God" (Ga.5:21).

13. Drunkenness results in judgment.

> "And take heed to yourselves, lest at any time your hearts be overcharged with surfeiting, and drunkenness, and cares of this life, and so that day [of judgment] come upon you unawares" (Lu.21:34).
>
> "Woe to the crown of pride, to the drunkards of Ephraim, whose glorious beauty is a fading flower, which are on the head of the fat valleys of them that are overcome with wine! Behold, the Lord hath a mighty and strong one, which as a tempest of hail and a destroying storm, as a flood of mighty waters overflowing, shall cast down to the earth with the hand. The crown of pride, the drunkards of Ephraim, shall be trodden under feet" (Is.28:1-3).
>
> "Woe unto him that giveth his neighbor drink, that puttest thy bottle to him, and makest him drunken also, that thou mayest look on their nakedness! Thou art filled with shame for glory: drink thou also, and let thy foreskin be uncovered: the cup of the LORD'S right hand shall be turned unto thee, and shameful spewing shall be on thy glory" (Hab.2:15-16).
>
> "For while they be folden together as thorns, and while they are drunken as drunkards, they shall be devoured as stubble fully dry" (Na.1:10).

3 (9:24-27) **Canaan—Shem—Japheth—Race, Human—History—Prophecy**: the future of the human race was predicted. When Noah awoke from his drunken stupor, he noticed something different, perhaps the way the covering was thrown over him. Apparently, he asked his sons about the matter, and the older sons told him what had happened. Noah's heart, as any godly father's heart would be, was broken...
- broken because of what he had done to God
- broken because his sin had led his son to commit a most grievous sin

But more than Noah's heart being broken, God's heart was broken, broken because His servant had fallen into sin and tragically affected his testimony and family so much. God convicted Noah, and Noah repented. How do we know this? Because God moved upon Noah with the *spirit of prophecy* and led Noah to predict the future of the human race. Remember, Noah's three sons stood at the head of the three branches of the human race. The three sons—the three branches of the human race—now became the focus of Scripture (Ge.9:24-11:32). God is leading Noah *to reveal* the future of the three branches of the human race. It is critical to know this: Noah is not reacting against Ham in this passage, for Noah stands as guilty as his son, if not more guilty, because of his call and position as a minister of righteousness. What is happening is due to God: God is using Noah and the terrible incident *to predict* the future of the human race. God wants to use the prediction...
- as a guide to show the utter necessity of following God instead of the ways of the world
- as a warning against sin and shame as they walk throughout life

a. There was the prediction about the youngest son of Ham, Canaan: he was predicted to be the father of an enslaved people. Note several significant facts.
1) Why is Ham's son, Canaan, predicted to be the father of a cursed people instead of Ham? That is, why was Canaan cursed and not Ham himself? All kinds of reasons have been suggested by various commentators, but the truth seems to lie in the following.

   First, Canaan was already walking in the footsteps of his father, living a sensual life and denying the faith of the God of Noah.

   Scripture definitely teaches that a man sows what he reaps (Ga.6:7) and that the sins of the fathers are passed on down through generation after generation (Ex.20:5). Life demonstrates this truth time and again. Unfortunately, a father sins and falls. Although he might regret his sin and even repent, his son still follows in his sinful footsteps and never repents.

   The influence of parents upon their children is undeniable. Their influence is great, almost incomprehensible. For example, we know today how influential parents are through their genes and behavior: every child...
- inherits the genes of their parents
- follows the behavior of their parents—to a large extent

   This does not mean that a child cannot break the behavioral pattern of a bad parent; he can. He can choose to act differently, to behave properly, to live a good and moral life. But most do not; most continue on in the kind of immoral life their parents lived.

   Apparently, Canaan followed a sinful path in life, following in the footsteps of his father, Ham. Noah observed his evil, and under the inspiration of God's Spirit, Noah *prophetically* uttered the course of Canaan's life. In addition, Noah saw that the impact of a father's influence upon his son was to be demonstrated time and again down through history in the seed of Canaan.

   Second, the very name *Canaan* means the submissive one. It comes from the Hebrew meaning to stoop, submit, bend, subjugate. Why would Ham give his baby son such a name? Ham had to be thinking of obedience, of the submission a son owed to his father. Was Ham a tyrannical—perhaps abusive—father? The great Old

Testament commentators Keil and Delitzsch think so: *"The father, when he gave him this name, thought only of submission to his own commands."*[4]

2) Why was Canaan alone cursed and not the other sons of Ham? First, some commentators say this: that all the sons of Ham were not to be enslaved and dominated by other nations down through history. Therefore, the prediction of being a cursed people did not apply to them; it applied only to Canaan and his seed or descendants. The other sons of Ham were just to be insignificant in their influence down through history; therefore, there is not a prediction of either a blessing or curse upon them. Second, other commentators hold to the position taken by Keil and Delitzsch:
⇒ That the curse predicted falls primarily upon Canaan and his seed or descendants.
⇒ That the curse is also predicted for Ham and his other sons.

How can this be, when Scripture does not specifically say so? By implication. The proof is this:
⇒ Ham and his sons *are not included in the blessings* pronounced upon the other sons.
⇒ They must, therefore, be included *in the curse* pronounced upon Canaan and his seed.

God is predicting through Noah the future of the human race, of the three branches that are to spread out and cover the earth. If Ham's other sons are not included in the curse predicted upon Canaan, then three quarters of Ham's branch is not covered; a good portion of the human race is omitted. This would not make sense when the very prophecy is focusing upon the future of the human race as a whole. Therefore, Ham himself and his other three sons must be included in the prediction made about Canaan, or else the prophecy is incomplete.

Keil and Delitzsch add this: *And history confirms [this] supposition*:
⇒ *The Canaanites were partly exterminated, and partly subjected to the lowest form of slavery, by the Israelites, who belonged to the family of Shem; and those who still remained were reduced by Solomon to the same condition (1 Kings ix. 20, 21).*
⇒ *The Phoenicians, along with the Carthaginians and the Egyptians, who all belonged to the family of Canaan, were subjected by the Japhetic Persians, Macedonians, and Romans.*
⇒ *The remainder of the Hamitic tribes either shared the same fate, or still sigh, like the negroes, for example, and other African tribes, beneath the yoke of the most crushing slavery.*[5]

Now, having said all this, note what the verse says: "A *slave of slaves* shall he be to his brothers." This term "slave of slaves" most likely refers to his other three brothers. They were to be enslaved, but he (Canaan's descendants) was to be a slave of slaves, the lowest of slaves. He was even to be enslaved by his enslaved brothers.

3) The prediction about the Canaanites was this: he was to be "a servant of servants" (v.25). The phrase means the lowest of servants or slaves. The Canaanites were the people who occupied Palestine or the land of Canaan when Israel set out from Egyptian slavery to conquer the land of Palestine. They were primarily conquered by the Jews under the leadership of Joshua (Jos.9:22-27; see 9:1-21) and of Solomon (1 K.9:20-21).

4) James Montgomery Boice makes a statement that is worthy of quote, a statement that shows the deep-seated prejudice of the human heart and how far men will go in stretching and abusing the Scriptures:

> *We are going to see in the next chapter that this curse was pronounced on the ancient peoples of the Near East, most of whom were later conquered by the Jews under Joshua. But notice this: they were not the Negro races. In an earlier generation prejudiced minds used this text to justify their enslaving of Africa's black populations, but this is without any biblical basis and is a proof rather of the expositors' sin. Not until the middle of the nineteenth century, when the slave trade was at its height, did anyone ever imagine that Ham was the father of the black races or that there was a curse on them.*[6]

b. There was the prediction about Shem: he was to be the father of a people whose God is to be blessed (v.26). Note that God is blessed here, not Shem, not directly. Shem's blessing is all wrapped up in God Himself. Two things are meant by this blessing:
⇒ The knowledge of God—of the only true and living God, of the true religion—was to come through Shem and his descendants. Abraham was to be part of the seed, a descendent of Shem, and through Abraham the nation of Israel was to be born.
⇒ *The promised seed*, the Savior of the world, was to come through the line of Shem.

Thus, the God of Shem is to be blessed because He is going to choose the line of Shem...
• to proclaim the only living and true God to the world
• to bear *the promised seed*, the Savior of the world

One other thing is said about Shem: he is to rule over Canaan. Canaan is to be the servant of Shem. As pointed out above, the Jews did conquer and enslave the Canaanites (pt.a.3) above).

c. There was the prediction about Japheth (v.27). Three things are forseen and predicted by God through Noah.

---

4 Keil and Delitzsch. *Commentary on the Old Testament*, Vol.1, pp.157-158.
5 Ibid., p.158.
6 James Montgomery Boice. *Genesis*, Vol.1, pp.321-322.

1) Japheth will be enlarged by God; that is, his territory and prosperity will be enlarged. The descendants of Japheth were to be the great Indo-European nations of the earth. This will be seen in Chapter 10. The largest portion of land and wealth would be held by the great Gentile nations of the earth, the descendants of Japheth.
2) Japheth shall live in the tents of Shem. This refers to sharing in the spiritual blessings of Shem:
   ⇒ the belief in God, the only living and true God
   ⇒ the belief in *the promised seed*, the Savior of the world

   Not every descendent or person within the Gentile nations—in fact, not many when compared to the whole population—believe in God and Christ. But all have the opportunity to live in the tents of Shem, in the spiritual blessings of *the promised seed*, of the Lord Jesus Christ Himself.
3) Japheth, too, was to rule over Canaan. Some of the descendants of Japheth were to conquer and enslave some of the descendants of Ham.

4 (9:28-29) **Death—Noah**: the death of the human race was demonstrated. Think what a great and courageous man Noah was:
   ⇒ He was the man who stood against the world as a testimony to the only living and true God, who stood when everyone else—*everyone*—forsook God.
   ⇒ He was the man who obeyed God and built a huge barge-like boat out in the middle of nowhere, all the while preaching that a terrifying judgment was coming unless people repented and turned back to God.
   ⇒ He was the man whom Scripture declares was righteous and perfect and walked with God (Ge.6:9).

Yet Noah died. At age 950, he died. The point is this: if such a godly man as Noah died, then we all have to die. The death of Noah stands as a demonstration of the grip sin has upon the human race. We shall all die. This is the reason we must turn to the God of Noah and to *the promised seed*, the Savior of the world. The Lord Jesus Christ is our only hope of conquering death and of living eternally with God.

> **"For God so loved the world, that he gave his only begotten Son, that whosoever believeth in him should not perish, but have everlasting life"** (Jn.3:16).
> **"He that believeth on him is not condemned: but he that believeth not is condemned already, because he hath not believed in the name of the only begotten Son of God"** (Jn.3:18).
> **"He that believeth on the Son hath everlasting life: and he that believeth not the Son shall not see life; but the wrath of God abideth on him"** (Jn.3:36).
> **"Verily, verily, I say unto you, He that heareth my word, and believeth on him that sent me, hath everlasting life, and shall not come into condemnation; but is passed from death unto life"** (Jn.5:24).
> **"And as it is appointed unto men once to die, but after this the judgment"** (He.9:27).
> **"Wherefore, as by one man sin entered into the world, and death by sin; and so death passed upon all men, for that all have sinned"** (Ro.5:12).

DIVISION V

NOAH'S SONS: THE THREE BRANCHES CHOSEN TO REPOPULATE AND TO SCATTER OVER THE EARTH, 10:1–11:9

(10:1–11:9) **DIVISION OVERVIEW: Race, Human**: this begins a new section of *Genesis*, a most interesting section. It shows how the human race *repopulated and scattered* over the face of the earth. After the Great Flood, Noah stood at the head of the human race, and his sons stood at the head of the three branches that were to repopulate the earth. This is the major subject of this important section of Scripture: *Noah's Sons: The Three Branches Chosen to Repopulate and to Scatter over the Earth*, Ge.10:1–11:9.

NOAH'S SONS: THE THREE BRANCHES CHOSEN TO REPOPULATE AND TO SCATTER OVER THE EARTH, 10:1–11:9

A. The Growth of the Human Race and the Birth of Nations, 10:1-32
B. The Scattering of the Human Race Over the Earth: The People's Tragic Mistake and Sin—the Secular City and False Worship (The Tower of Babel), 11:1-9

CHAPTER 10

V. NOAH'S SONS: THE THREE BRANCHES CHOSEN TO REPOPULATE & TO SCATTER OVER THE EARTH, 10:1–11:9

A. The Growth of the Human Race & The Birth of Nations,[DS1] 10:1-32

1. The origin & unity of the human race: There were three branches from one man, Noah

Now these are the generations of the sons of Noah, Shem, Ham, and Japheth: and unto them were sons born after the flood.

2. The branch of Japheth: The Indo-Europeans

a. The sons of Japheth

2 The sons of Japheth; Gomer, and Magog, and Madai, and Javan, and Tubal, and Meshech, and Tiras.

b. The descendants of Gomer

3 And the sons of Gomer; Ashkenaz, and Riphath, and Togarmah.

c. The descendants of Javan

4 And the sons of Javan; Elishah, and Tarshish, Kittim, and Dodanim.
5 By these were the isles of the Gentiles divided in their land; every one after his tongue, after their families, in their nations.

3. The branch of Ham: The Orientals, Africans, & Canaanites

a. The sons of Ham
b. The descendants of Cush

6 And the sons of Ham; Cush, and Mizraim, and Phut, and Canaan.
7 And the sons of Cush; Seba, and Havilah, and Sabtah, and Raamah, and Sabtechah: and the sons of Raamah; Sheba, and Dedan.

c. The rise of the first world tyrant: Nimrod[DS2]

8 And Cush begat Nimrod: he began to be a mighty one in the earth.
9 He was a mighty hunter before the LORD: wherefore it is said, Even as Nimrod the mighty hunter before the LORD.

d. The rise of the first world empires
   1) The great Babylonian Empire
   2) The great Assyrian Empire

10 And the beginning of his kingdom was Babel, and Erech, and Accad, and Calneh, in the land of Shinar.
11 Out of that land went forth Asshur, and builded Nineveh, and the city of Rehoboth, and Calah,
12 And Resen between Nineveh and Calah: the same is a great city.

e. The descendants of Mizraim

13 And Mizraim begat Ludim, and Anamim, and Lehabim, and Naphtuhim,
14 And Pathrusim, and Casluhim, (out of whom came Philistim,) and Caphtorim.
15 And Canaan begat Sidon his firstborn, and Heth,
16 And the Jebusite, and the Amorite, and the Girgasite,
17 And the Hivite, and the Arkite, and the Sinite,
18 And the Arvadite, and the Zemarite, and the Hamathite: and afterward were the families of the Canaanites spread abroad.
19 And the border of the Canaanites was from Sidon, as thou comest to Gerar, unto Gaza; as thou goest, unto Sodom, and Gomorrah, and Admah, and Zeboim, even unto Lasha.
20 These are the sons of Ham, after their families, after their tongues, in their countries, and in their nations.
21 Unto Shem also, the father of all the children of Eber, the brother of Japheth the elder, even to him were children born.
22 The children of Shem; Elam, and Asshur, and Arphaxad, and Lud, and Aram.
23 And the children of Aram; Uz, and Hul, and Gether, and Mash.
24 And Arphaxad begat Salah; and Salah begat Eber.
25 And unto Eber were born two sons: the name of one was Peleg; for in his days was the earth divided; and his brother's name was Joktan.
26 And Joktan begat Almodad, and Sheleph, and Hazarmaveth, and Jerah,
27 And Hadoram, and Uzal, and Diklah,
28 And Obal, and Abimael, and Sheba,
29 And Ophir, and Havilah, and Jobab: all these were the sons of Joktan.
30 And their dwelling was from Mesha, as thou goest unto Sephar a mount of the east.
31 These are the sons of Shem, after their families, after their tongues, in their lands, after their nations.
32 These are the families of the sons of Noah, after their generations, in their nations: and by these were the nations divided in the earth after the flood.

f. The descendants of Canaan
   1) The descendants listed

   2) The borders of the Canaanites

4. The branch of Shem: The Middle Eastern people, the line of "the promised seed"

a. The sons of Shem

b. The descendants of Aram

c. The descendants of Arphaxad
   1) His son Salah
   2) His grandson Eber
   3) His great grandson Peleg: Lived when the earth was divided
   4) His great grandson Joktan
d. The descendants of Joktan

e. The borders of the Shemites

f. Conclusion: The branches of Shem, Japheth, and Ham—all the branches of the human race—are connected. They all come from one root, one source: Noah[DS3]

DIVISION V

NOAH'S SONS: THE THREE BRANCHES CHOSEN TO REPOPULATE AND TO SCATTER OVER THE EARTH, 10:1–11:9

A. The Growth of the Human Race and the Birth of Nations, 10:1-32

(10:1-32) **Introduction**: chapter ten of Genesis is, by far, the earliest *Table of Nations* known to man, the earliest ethnological table. It is the historical record of the human race; it tells us where the nations and people of the earth originated. It gives us the roots of the human race, the birth of the nations of the earth. This chapter of Genesis—this table of nations—stands alone in the world of literature. It is unmatched; nothing even remotely compares to it. Note several facts.

1. The exact number of descendants or social groups given is sometimes debated. The number ranges from sixty-eight to seventy-one. For example, the *NIV Study Bible* says there were 70, but H.C. Leupold lists 69.

2. The classification used in the table makes it hard for us to always know who is meant.

⇒ Sometimes individuals are named. For example, v.8 says that "Cush begat Nimrod." Both men definitely represent persons.

⇒ Sometimes we do not know if individuals or whole groups of people or families are named. For example, v.13 mentions Ludim, Anamim, Lehabim, and Naphtuhim. These were definitely groups or families of people, but is the founder of the family being named or the family group?

⇒ Sometimes whole tribes of people are being named, but we do not know if the ancestor of the tribe had the same name. For example, v.16 lists the Jebusites: did they come from an ancestor named Jebu?

3. Some of the three branches settled in the same areas of the world. For example, some of the descendants of Ham, the sons of Cush, settled in Arabia (v.7); but some of the descendants of Shem—Joktan and Sheba—also settled in Arabia (vv.26-28).

4. Throughout chapter ten the family branch of some descendants is developed and others are omitted. There is a great lesson here for nations and for individuals. Moses omitted the records of some for three possible reasons.

⇒ The families had not achieved nor contributed enough to be in the mainstream of life.

⇒ The families had not shown enough initiative and care in preserving records.

⇒ The families did not believe enough in *the promise of the seed*, the Savior of the world, to preserve the records of the promise as it related to their heritage.

5. The accuracy of the table of nations is indisputable. The omission of some branches shows the honesty of the author. He did not include the development of the branches because he did not know them: he had no record of them. If his purpose had been to gain fame or to create some great record of the development of the nations, he would have written a complete table of nations in order to impress the readers.

The great Lutheran theologian H.C. Leupold says this:

> *No nation of antiquity has anything to offer that presents an actual parallel to this Table of Nations. Babylonian and Egyptian lists that seem to parallel this are merely a record of nations conquered in war. Consequently, the spirit that prompted the making of such lists is the very opposite of the spirit that the Biblical list breathes.*[1]

6. The Table of Nations has at least two great religious purposes.

a. It shows that all nations and all people have come from one source, from a common ancestor, Noah. This means...

• that the unity of the human race is a fact: a living reality, an historical truth
• that the common link of *brotherhood* binds the human race together, all nations and all people
• that there is no place for prejudice and discrimination among the human races of the earth

The human race stands together as brothers and sisters, bound together by a common ancestor. Consequently, we are to love one another; we are to live together in *brotherly love*.

> **"Thou shalt love thy neighbor as thyself" (Mt.22:39).**
> **"This is my commandment, That ye love one another, as I have loved you" (Jn.15:12).**
> **"Let love be without dissimulation [hypocrisy]. Abhor that which is evil; cleave to that which is good" (Ro.12:9).**
> **"See that ye love one another with a pure heart fervently" (1 Pe.1:22).**

b. The Table of Nations shows how the nations of the world are related to God's chosen race, the race chosen to bear the Savior of the world (the branch of Shem). It shows how the nations of the earth came from the same godly source—same godly ancestor (Noah)—who was himself part of the chosen race. This hints at a glorious truth: the nations of the world are tied to the chosen race; they will, therefore, be touched by the Savior of the world. The promise of the Savior's coming is for the nations of the earth as well as for the chosen race.

---

[1] H.C. Leupold. *Genesis*, Vol.1, p.358.

"For God so loved the world, that he gave his only begotten Son, that whosoever believeth in him should not perish, but have everlasting life" (Jn.3:16).

"And he is the propitiation for our sins: and not for ours only, but also for the sins of the whole world" (1 Jn.2:2).

"For there is no difference between the Jew and the Greek: for the same Lord over all is rich unto all that call upon him. For whosoever shall call upon the name of the Lord shall be saved" (Ro.10:12-13).

"For I am not ashamed of the gospel of Christ: for it is the power of God unto salvation to every one that believeth; to the Jew first, and also to the Greek" (Ro.1:16).

Now, to the discussion of the Scripture itself. The subject of this important Scripture, Chapter Ten, is *The Growth of the Human Race and the Birth of Nations*.

1. The origin and unity of the human race: there were three branches from one man, Noah (v.1).
2. The branch of Japheth: the Indo-Europeans (vv.2-5).
3. The branch of Ham: the Orientals, Africans, and Canaanites (vv.6-20).
4. The branch of Shem: the Middle Eastern people, the line of *the promised seed* (vv.21-32).

Note: the following authors have excellent details on the descendants that spread out over the earth:
- ❖ James Montgomery Boice. *Genesis, An Expositional Commentary*, Vol.1. Grand Rapids, MI: Zondervan Publishing House, 1938.
- ❖ Victor Hamilton. *The Book of Genesis,* Vol.1, Grand Rapids, MI: Eerdmans Publishing Co., 1990.
- ❖ Keil and Delitzsch. *Commentary on the Old Testament*, Vol.1. Grand Rapids, MI: Eerdmans Publishing Co., n.d.
- ❖ H.C. Leupold. *Genesis*, Vol.1. Grand Rapids, MI: Baker Book House, 1942.
- ❖ *NIV Study Bible*. Grand Rapids, MI: Zondervan Bible Publishers, 1985.
- ❖ *The Pulpit Commentary*, Vol.1, ed. by HDM Spence and Joseph S. Exell. Grand Rapids, MI: Eerdmans Publishing Co., 1950.

DEEPER STUDY # 1
(10:1-32) **Map—Ancient World—Race, Human**: a map of the ancient world and of the Table of Nations is given in DEEPER STUDY # 3, Ge.10:31-32.

---

1 (10:1) **Race, Human—Mankind, Unity of; Origin of—Noah**: the origin and unity of the human race: there were three branches from one godly man, Noah. (See note—Ge.9:18-19. Also see Introduction, pt.6a —Ge.10:1-32 for discussion.)

2 (10:2-5) **Japheth—Race, Human—Mankind—Indo-Europeans**: the branch of Japheth: the Indo-Europeans. The descendants of Japheth spread out and populated...
- the area of India and the surrounding territories
- the European continent

Japheth had seven sons, but the descendants of only two are given. To make it easier to grasp the growth of the human race, two things are being done:
- ⇒ A chart on each family branch is given.
- ⇒ Each son is immediately discussed with his descendants. Note that Scripture lists the sons and then the descendants. As stated, we are discussing the descendants right along with the son in order to give the full picture of that branch of the human race.

a. *Japheth*: there were seven sons or branches of Japheth (v.2).

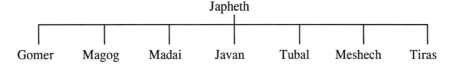

Now, quickly glance at the Scripture: note that v.3 lists three grandsons by Gomer and v.4 lists four grandsons by Javan. These are the only grandsons of Japheth listed; no descendants are given for five of the sons. Remember what was pointed out in the introduction to this passage: this shows the accuracy of this Table of Nations. The author was not interested in fame nor in creating some fabulous record of the development of nations. If that had been his purpose, he would have fabricated a complete family tree of the nations of the earth in order to impress the readers (see Introduction, pt.5—Ge.10:1-32).

  1) *Gomer*: see point b. below.
  2) *Magog*: no descendants are listed for the second of Japheth's sons. *Magog* gave rise to the ancient Scythians and Tartars who lived above (north of) the Black Sea. They later migrated and settled much of modern day Russia. The people of Magog will have a major role to play during the final days of world history (Eze., chapters 38–39. See outline and notes—Re.20:7-10.)

3) *Madai*: no descendants are given for the third son of Japheth. The *Madai* are the ancient people of Media who later spread out into Persia. Somewhat later some of them moved down into India (see 2 K.17:6; 18:11; Is.13:17; 21:2). The wise men (Magoi) who visited Jesus as a young baby were from Media (Mt.2:2).

4) *Javan*: see point c. below.

5) *Tubal*: no descendants are listed for this son of Japheth. The *Tubal* are the people who settled in eastern Asia Minor around Turkey. They later moved farther north and east settling down in territory now known as the Russian states. Tubal is often associated in Scripture with Meshech. Both people are to be involved in the events of the end time.

> **"Son of man, set thy face against Gog, the land of Magog, the chief prince of Meshech and Tubal, and prophesy against him, and say, Thus saith the LORD GOD; Behold, I am against thee, O Gog, the chief prince of Meshech and Tubal" (Eze.38:2-3; see chapters 38-39).**

6) *Meshech*: no descendants are given for this son of Japheth. These people were called *Mosochi* who settled in the lands of Turkey and later migrated north into the Russian states. They founded the city of Moscow (note the similarity between Moscow and Mosochi). Again, Meshech and Tubal are often connected together in Scripture. Meshech will also be a major factor in the close of human history (see Eze.38:2-3).

> **"Son of man, set thy face against Gog, the land of Magog, the chief prince of Meshech and Tubal, and prophesy against him, and say, Thus saith the LORD GOD; Behold, I am against thee, O Gog, the chief prince of Meshech and Tubal" (Eze.38:2-3; see chapters 38-39).**

7) *Tiras*: no descendants are given for the seventh son of Japheth. These people were the ancestors of either the Thracians (mentioned in some Egyptian literature) or perhaps the Etruscans. These were people of Italy.

Thought 1. History has shown that the descendants of Japheth failed God in at least three areas of life.
1) They failed to hold fast to the knowledge of God—to know Him personally—as they scattered over the earth.

> **"For the invisible things of him from the creation of the world are clearly seen, being understood by the things that are made, even his eternal power and Godhead; so that they are without excuse: because that, when they knew God, they glorified him not as God, neither were thankful; but became vain in their imaginations, and their foolish heart was darkened. Professing themselves to be wise, they became fools. And changed the glory of the uncorruptible God into an image made like to corruptible man, and to birds, and fourfooted beasts, and creeping things" (Ro.1:20-23).**

2) They failed to follow after God—to walk after Him—as they scattered over the earth.

> **"I am the Almighty God; walk before me, and be thou perfect" (Ge.17:1).**
> **"I will walk before the LORD in the land of the living" (Ps.116:9).**
> **"See then that ye walk circumspectly, not as fools, but as wise" (Ep.5:15).**
> **"But if we walk in the light, as he is in the light, we have fellowship one with another, and the blood of Jesus Christ his Son cleanseth us from all sin" (1 Jn.1:7).**
> **"He that saith he abideth in him ought himself also so to walk, even as he walked" (1 Jn.2:6).**

3) They failed to teach their descendants (their children) about God.

> **"And these words, which I command thee this day, shall be in thine heart: and thou shalt teach them diligently unto thy children, and shalt talk of them when thou sittest in thine house, and when thou walkest by the way, and when thou liest down, and when thou risest up" (De.6:6-7).**
> **"Train up a child in the way he should go: and when he is old, he will not depart from it" (Pr.22:6).**

Thought 2. James Montgomery Boice has an excellent thought on the future of the descendants of Japheth, the Indo-Europeans of the earth:

> *God enlarged the territory of Japheth to include the whole of Europe and even parts of Asia. Moreover, if the expansion of the races proceeded as anthropologists and others today believe—from northeastern Russia across the Bering Strait into Alaska and from there down into the North American and South American continents—this family of nations eventually possessed most of this world's territory. But at what cost! Apart from those Indo-Europeans who remembered their roots and delighted to take refuge in the descendants of Shem, the Messiah, this block of people has gained the whole world at the loss of its soul. It will not find its soul save in Him who created it originally.*
>
> *The sons of Japheth should have mastered four great truths: that there is one God to which their roots bear record, that all the peoples of the earth are one people, that truth is one, and that there is only one salvation. But we have not remembered this. Abandoning the true God, we have made other gods 'like mortal man and birds and animals and reptiles,' as Paul says in Romans (1:22). Having lost our*

knowledge of the one God, we have also lost our awareness that the peoples of the earth are one people. Therefore, we have exalted ourselves and have tried to exploit those we consider to be inferior. We have abandoned belief in one truth and so seek truth in a plurality of forms. Most tragic of all, we have lost sight of God's promise of a deliverer, which goes all the way back to God's words to our first parents in Eden on the occasion of the Fall.

In his commentary Calvin bemoans those who 'voluntarily become forgetful of the grace and salvation of God," pushing "memory of the deluge" far into the past and little remembering 'by what means or for what end they had been preserved.' Many of these are with us today. If you are one, learn from this Table of Nations. Turn from your rebellion against the true God and come to Him in Jesus where alone He may be found."[2]

b. *Gomer*: the descendants of Gomer, the first son of Japheth (v.3).

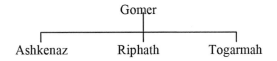

The descendants of Gomer are identified as the Cimmerians. They spread north and west of the Black Sea, settling such areas as Ancient Galatia, Phyrgia, Bithynia, and the upper region of the Euphrates River in Armenia. These descendants eventually spread westward into Europe and became known as...

- the Gauls of France
- the Celtics of Briton
- the Galacia of Spain
- the Germans
- the Welsh
- the Irish

The people of Gomer will join the forces that stand against God in the end time. They are to be destroyed by God Himself.

> **"Thus saith the Lord GOD; Behold, I am against thee, O Gog, the chief prince of Meshech and Tubal....And I will turn thee back, and...all of them handling swords....Persia, Ethiopia, and Libya with them; all of them with shield and helmet: Gomer, and all his bands" (Eze.38:3-6).**

1) *Ashkenaz*: a people who probably settled north of the Euphrates River within the territory of modern Armenia, probably around the area of Ararat (see Je.51:27). Later, some of the descendants spread out into Germany.
2) *Riphath* or *Diphath*: it is uncertain where these people settled, but they are listed in the genealogy of 1 Chr.1:6. They are most likely the ancient Paphalagonians. Some commentators think they eventually spread out to the farthest regions of Europe and that their name gave rise to the name *Europe*.
3) *Togarmah*: these people settled above the Euphrates River, within the border of Armenia and Turkey. Later, they most likely migrated into Germany. The army of Togarmah also joins the armies of Gog in the great battle of the last days.

> **"Thus saith the LORD GOD; Behold, I am against thee, O Gog, the chief prince of Meshech and Tubal....And I will turn thee back, and...all of them handling swords....Persia, Ethiopia, and Libya with them; all of them with shield and helmet: Gomer, and all his bands; the house of Togarmah of the north quarters, and all his bands" (Eze.38:3-6).**

c. *Javan*: the descendants of Javan, the fourth son of Japheth (vv.4-5).

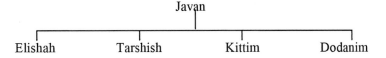

The descendants of Javan are the Greek people of the world. They were the ancient Ionians who settled along the northern and western coast of the Mediterranean Sea. Note what verse 5 says: it was these ancient Greeks or Ionians who moved out, explored, and settled various lands and territories, each with its own language.

The people of Greece developed one of the greatest societies upon earth. They will play a major role when God ends human history.

> **"Behold, I will make thee know what shall be in the last end of the indignation: for at the time appointed the end shall be. The ram which thou sawest having two horns are the kings of Media and Persia. And the rough goat is the king of Grecia: and the great horn that is between his eyes is the first king. Now that being broken, whereas four stood up for it, four kingdoms shall stand up out of the nation, but not in his power. And in the latter time of their kingdom, when the transgressors are come to**

---

the full, a king of fierce countenance, and understanding dark sentences, shall stand up. And his power shall be mighty, but not by his own power: and he shall destroy wonderfully, and shall prosper, and practice, and shall destroy the mighty and the holy people" (Da.8:19-24. See Deeper Study # 1—Rev.13:2 for more discussion.)

1) *Elishah*: these people were either the settlers of Alashia, the island of Cyprus, or of Sicily and southern Italy (NIV). They were merchants of the very finest blue and purple clothing (Eze.27:7).
2) *Tarshish*: these people lived on the ocean. But who were they? Where were they located? Most commentators say on the coast of Spain. Remember this: Tarshish was the seaport city to which Jonah was fleeing when he was running away from the call of God.

> "Now the word of the LORD came unto Jonah the son of Amittai, saying, Arise, go to Nineveh, that great city, and cry against it; for their wickedness is come up before me. But Jonah rose up to flee unto Tarshish from the presence of the LORD, and went down to Joppa; and he found a ship going to Tarshish; so he paid the fare thereof, and went down into it, to go with them unto Tarshish from the presence of the LORD" (Jona.1:1-3).

3) *Kittim*: these people migrated to the island of Cyprus in the Mediterranean Sea (see Num 24:24; Je.2:10; Eze.27:6).
4) *Dodanim*: these people settled on the Mediterranean island of Rhodes (1 Chr.1:7).

3 (10:6-20) **Ham—Race, Human—Mankind**: the branch of Ham: the Oriental, African, and Canaanite people. The descendants of Ham spread out and populated ancient Asia or the far east and Africa, such places as...
- Arabia
- Ethiopia
- Egypt
- Canaan
- the Oriental nations
- the African nations
- Iran
- Iraq

James Montgomery Boice says this about the three branches of the human race:

> *The distribution of the Indo-European people was eastward into certain parts of Persia and India, and westward and northward into Europe and points beyond. The descendants of Shem...tended to stay in the area of the Middle East. This leaves, by a simple process of elimination, the south (Africa) and the far east (all oriental countries) to have been settled by Ham and his descendants.*[3]

a. *Ham*: there were four sons or branches of Ham. Note that the descendants of three sons are given: Cush (vv.7-12); Mizraim (vv.13-14); and Canaan (vv.15-20).

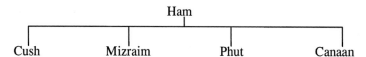

	Ham		
Cush	Mizraim	Phut	Canaan

1) *Cush*: see point b. below.
2) *Mizraim*: see point e. below.
3) *Phut* or *Put*: these descendants settled in Africa either in Libya or else in the land that is now called Somalia (Eze.27:10). They were later enslaved by the Syrians (Na.3:9).
4) *Canaan*: see point f. below.

b. *Cush*: the descendants of Cush, the first son of Ham (v.6).

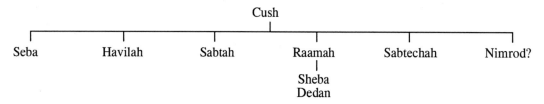

Note the chart: Cush had five sons. Nimrod was a descendent of Cush, but we do not know what branch or line he came from (vv.8-12). This is the reason for the question mark beside his name.

---

3 James Montgomery Boice. *Genesis,* Vol.1, p.329.

The name *Cush* means *Ethiopia* in the Bible; thus, the descendants of Cush settled in Ethiopia which is in Africa. But again, note the reference to Nimrod (vv.8-12). At some point in history the family of Cush split and one group moved eastward over into Arabia and the Middle East area of Babylon in Iraq. Apparently some, if not all, of the Cushites eventually migrated into the lands of the far East, developing the Oriental nations of the earth. All seven of the sons listed here seem to have been located in Arabia, probably migrating there from Ethiopia.

Thought 1. Ethiopia is of special interest to us as believers because of the Ethiopian eunuch who was led to Christ by Philip. The Ethiopian eunuch was the first convert of Ethiopia (Ac.8:26-40).

c. The rise of the first tyrant, Nimrod (vv.8-9). The Cush who begat Nimrod may be a different Cush from the Cush of verse 6. Because of the interest and length of points 3-4, they are being discussed in a separate note. (See Deeper Study # 2, pt.1—Ge.10:8-12.)

d. The rise of the first world empires. (See Deeper Study # 2, pt.2—Ge.10:8-12.)

e. *Mizraim*: the descendants of Mizraim, the second son of Ham (vv.13-14).

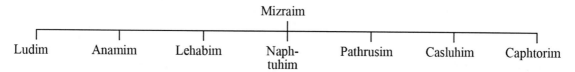

Mizraim: Ludim, Anamim, Lehabim, Naphtuhim, Pathrusim, Casluhim, Caphtorim

The Hebrew name Mizraim means Egypt, which was and is located in northern Africa. The Egyptians have always been one of the most influential people down through history because they were one of the most advanced civilizations in the early history of man. Here is their beginning, their origin, the ancestors of their race. They came from Mizraim, one of the sons of Ham, who was the youngest son of Noah.

Please note: the actual location of most of these people is unknown. The best research points to the following:

1) *Ludim* or *Lud*: the Lydians, possibly located just west of Canaan in Asia Minor (see Is.66:19; Je.46:9; Eze.27:10; 30:5).

2) *Anamim*: these Canaanites are probably the people of Cyrene who settled west of Egypt. Remember, the man who carried the cross of Christ was Simon of Cyrene (Mt.27:32).

3) *Lehabim* or *Lubim*: the Libyans who settled west of Egypt in northern Africa (see 2 Chr.12:3; Je.46:9; Eze.30:5; Na.3:9).

4) *Naphtuhim*: probably the people who migrated to Middle Egypt and were later known as the people of Memphis.

5) *Pathrusim*: the descendants of southern Egypt, the people of Pathros.

6) *Casluhim*: these people are unknown, but since northern and southern Egypt have just been mentioned as being settled by other descendants, they most likely settled in northern Egypt around the Delta area.

Note that the Philistines, who were to be the bitter enemies of Israel, are said to have come from the Casluhim people. However, Amos 9:7 and Je.47:4 say they came from the island of Caphtor, which is Crete. What happened was probably this: sometime later in history some of the Cretians or Caphtorians sailed down to northern Egypt, and the Philistine people arose from the Egyptian strain of Cretians or Caphtorians. As stated, the Philistines were to be the bitter enemies of Israel. They were one of the fiercest oppressors of Israel during the time of Saul, David, and Sampson (see 1 S.17:1f).

7) Caphtorim: the people who settled on the island of Crete. Remember, the island was to be evangelized by Paul, and the church was to be pastored by Titus. Much later Paul was to say to Titus:

"For this cause left I thee in Crete, that thou shouldest set in order the things that are wanting, and ordain elders in every city, as I had appointed them" (Tit.1:5).

f. *Canaan*: the descendants of Canaan, the fourth son of Ham (vv.15-20).

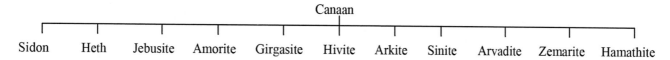

Canaan: Sidon, Heth, Jebusite, Amorite, Girgasite, Hivite, Arkite, Sinite, Arvadite, Zemarite, Hamathite

The Canaanites settled in the land of Canaan, that was later to become known as Palestine. Note four significant facts about the Canaanites.

First, the Canaanites were an ungodly and unrighteous people, an utterly immoral and unjust society. The two well known cities of Sodom and Gomorrah were Canaanite cities. Note what Scripture says about these ancient people:

⇒ God had to judge Sodom by raining fire down upon the city because of its corruption.

"And they called unto Lot, and said unto him, Where are the men which came in to thee this night? bring them out unto us; that we may know them [illicit sex]....And when the morning arose, then the angels hastened Lot, saying, Arise, take thy wife, and thy two daughters, which are here; lest thou be consumed in the iniquity of the city" (Ge.19:5, 15).

"And the LORD spake unto Moses, saying, Speak unto the children of Israel, and say unto them, I am the LORD your God. After the doings of the land of Egypt, wherein ye dwelt, shall ye not do: and after the doings of the land of Canaan, whither I bring you, shall ye not do: neither shall ye walk in their ordinances....None of you shall approach to any that is near of kin to him, to uncover their nakedness: I am the LORD. The nakedness of thy father, or the nakedness of thy mother, shalt thou not uncover: she is thy mother; thou shalt not uncover her nakedness. The nakedness of thy father's wife shalt thou not uncover: it is thy father's nakedness. The nakedness of thy sister, the daughter of thy father, or daughter of thy mother, whether she be born at home, or born abroad, even their nakedness thou shalt not uncover. The nakedness of thy son's daughter, or of thy daughter's daughter, even their nakedness thou shalt not uncover: for theirs is thine own nakedness....Neither shalt thou lie with any beast to defile thyself therewith: neither shall any woman stand before a beast to lie down thereto: it is confusion. Defile not ye yourselves in any of these things: for in all these the nations are defiled which I cast out before you: and the land is defiled: therefore I do visit the iniquity thereof upon it, and the land itself vomiteth out her inhabitants. Ye shall therefore keep my statutes and my judgments, and shall not commit any of these abominations; neither any of your own nation, nor any stranger that sojourneth among you: (for all these abominations have the men of the land done, which were before you, and the land is defiled;) that the land spue not you out also, when ye defile it, as it spued out the nations that were before you. For whosoever shall commit any of these abominations, even the souls that commit them shall be cut off from among their people. Therefore shall ye keep mine ordinance, that ye commit not any one of these abominable customs, which were committed before you, and that ye defile not yourselves therein: I am the LORD your God" (Le.18:1-3, 6-10, 23-30).

Second, the future of the Canaanites had been foretold in the prophecy by Noah. They were to be a conquered and enslaved people (see note—Ge.9:24-27 for more discussion).

Third, the Canaanites were the people who occupied Palestine or the land of Canaan when Israel set out from Egyptian slavery to conquer the land. They were primarily conquered by Israel under Joshua (see Jos.9:22-27; see 9:1-21) and Solomon (1 K.9:20-21).

Fourth, the land of Canaan was to become "The Land of Promise" or "The Promised Land" to the Jews.

"And the LORD appeared unto Abram, and said, Unto thy seed will I give this land: and there builded he an altar unto the LORD, who appeared unto him" (Ge.12:7).

"In the same day the LORD made a covenant with Abram, saying, Unto thy seed have I given this land, from the river of Egypt unto the great river, the river Euphrates" (Ge.15:18).

"And I will give unto thee, and to thy seed after thee, the land wherein thou art a stranger, all the land of Canaan, for an everlasting possession; and I will be their God" (Ge.17:8).

"And Joseph said unto his brethren, I die: and God will surely visit you, and bring you out of this land unto the land which he sware to Abraham, to Isaac, and to Jacob" (Ge.50:24).

1) The descendants of Canaan. Keep in mind that Canaan himself was the youngest son of Ham, and that Ham was the son of Noah. Noah was the godly grandfather of Canaan. But Canaan apparently paid little attention to his grandfather's godly testimony. From all indications, he ignored or forsook God just as his father, Ham, had done. (See note, pt.2—Ge.9:20-23 for more discussion.) The descendants of Canaan were these:

a) *Sidon*: this area was to become a great commercial city that sat on the Mediterranean Sea just north of Canaan. It was a Phoenecian city. Later on in history it was to be eclipsed by the city of Tyre, which was to be founded just twenty miles south of Sidon (1 K.5:6; 1 Chr.22:4; Eze.27:8).

"Be still, ye inhabitants of the isle; thou whom the merchants of Zidon, that pass over the sea, have replenished....Be thou ashamed, O Zidon: for the sea hath spoken, even the strength of the sea, saying, I travail not, nor bring forth children, neither do I nourish up young men, nor bring up virgins" (Is.23:2, 4).

b) *Heth*: the ancestor of the Hittite people. They originally appear in Asia Minor and eventually built a great empire that ruled throughout western Asia. They ruled most of Canaan during Abraham's time.

"And Abraham stood up from before his dead [wife], and spake unto the sons of Heth, saying, I am a stranger and a sojourner with you: give me a possession of a buryingplace with you, that I may bury my dead [wife] out of my sight" (Ge.23:3-4).

c) *Jebusite*: the people who settled the area of Jerusalem. They were the citizens of Jerusalem when David conquered the city.

"And the king [David] and his men went to Jerusalem unto the Jebusites, the inhabitants of the land: which spake unto David, saying, Except thou take away the blind and the lame, thou shalt not come in hither: thinking, David cannot come in hither. Nevertheless David took the strong hold of Zion: the same is the city of David" (2 S.5:6-7).

d) *Amorite*: the people who settled mostly in the Judean mountains of Palestine. However, they became so numerous and spread so far over the land that the Canaanites were sometimes called the Amorites. They first appeared during the time of Abraham.

> "In the same day the LORD made a covenant with Abram, saying, Unto thy seed have I given this land, from the river of Egypt unto the great river, the river Euphrates: the Kenites, and the Kenizzites, and the Kadmonites, and the Hittites, and the Perizzites, and the Rephaims, and the Amorites, and the Canaanites, and the Girgashites, and the Jebusites" (Ge.15:18-21).

Note that Joshua defeated the Amorites.

> "Therefore the five kings of the Amorites, the king of Jerusalem, the king of Hebron, the king of Jarmuth, the king of Lachish, the king of Eglon, gathered themselves together, and went up, they and all their hosts, and encamped before Gibeon, and made war against it. And the men of Gibeon sent unto Joshua to the camp to Gilgal, saying, Slack not thy hand from thy servants; come up to us quickly, and save us, and help us: for all the kings of the Amorites that dwell in the mountains are gathered together against us. So Joshua ascended from Gilgal, he, and all the people of war with him, and all the mighty men of valor" (Jos.10:5-7).

e) *Girgashite*: the actual location of these people is unknown. They too are in the list of nations whose territory was promised to Abraham (Ge.15:18-21). Joshua fought against these people.

> "And ye went over Jordan, and came unto Jericho: and the men of Jericho fought against you, the Amorites, and the Perizzites, and the Canaanites, and the Hittites, and the Girgashites, the Hivites, and the Jebusites; and I delivered them into your hand" (Jos.24:11).

f) *Hivite*: the name means "villagers" or "settlers in cities".[4] They lived in Shechem (Ge.34:2), Gibeon (Jos.9:7), and at Mt. Hermon (Jos.11:3).

g) *Arkite and Sinite*: these people were Phoenecians who settled to the north of Tripolis, just below Lebanon (1 Chr.1:15-16).

h) *Arvadite*: the Phoenecian settlers of the island city Arvad, which sits right off the coast above Palestine or Canaan. It is only about 100 miles north of Beruit (Eze.27:8, 11).

i) *Zemarite*: probably the settlers of Simyra or Tsumra in the same vicinity as the other Phoenician cities above.

j) *Hamathite*: these people settled the northernmost territory of Palestine or Canaan. They were the founders of the Hamath, a large city that sat on the Orantes River (Nu.13:21; 34:8; 1 K.8:65).

2) The territory of Canaan is clearly spelled out (v.18b-20). They spread out...
   - from Sidon in the north,
   - to Gerer in the south,
   - over to the southern area of the Dead Sea where four cities were located: Sodom and Gomorrah and Admah and Zeboim. The territory of the Canaanites even went beyond these cities over to Lasha, which is an unknown city that apparently sat somewhere along the coast of the Dead Sea.

DEEPER STUDY # 2

(10:8-12) **Nimrod—Dictators—Tyrants—Leaders, World**: the rise of the first tyrant or world dictator, Nimrod. This passage is a break in the Table of Nations. It discusses the first world dictator, the first tyrant who set out to build the first empire upon earth. Scripture gives two significant points about him.

1. Nimrod was the first tyrant or world dictator to arise upon the scene of human history (vv.8-9). The name *Nimrod* (Marad) means to rebel, to revolt. Note that the word *mighty* is used three times in referring to Nimrod:
   ⇒ He became a mighty one, a mighty warrior on earth (v.8).
   ⇒ He was a mighty hunter before the Lord (v.9).
   ⇒ He was such a powerful ruler that people created a phrase or expression to describe him: "Nimrod a mighty hunter before the Lord" (v.9).

The word *hunter* (gibbor tsayidh, v.9) means to hunt animals, but it can also mean to hunt people in order to enslave them. The word *mighty* means warrior or tyrant, one who prevails and is victorious, gaining dominion over other people.[5] The phrase *before the Lord* (v.9) means *in the sight of the Lord* or "openly before the Lord."

The point is this: Nimrod rebelled and revolted against the ruling authorities of his day, both man and God.

a. Nimrod sought to *rule over people*, to control as many people and lands as he could (see vv.10-12). He sought to enslave people, attacking them as though they were mere animals for the hunt. The picture is that he hunted people by force, violence, and tyranny, that he oppressed people and enslaved them to his will and purposes.

b. Nimrod *rebelled against God*. This is seen...
   - in his building a secular and godless empire.
   - in his enslaving people in order to build an empire, the empire of Babylon, an empire based upon slavery (vv.10-12).
   - in his trying to build a tower of religion, a worldwide religion of false worship, the Tower of Babel. (See outline and notes—Ge.11:1-9; 11:3-4.)

---

4 *The Pulpit Commentary*, Vol.1, p.160.
5 William Wilson. *Wilson's Old Testament Word Studies*, p.275.

The Jewish historian Josephus says that Nimrod led the people away from God by encouraging them to put their security and happiness in the state or government.

> He persuaded them not to ascribe it [their security and happiness] to God, as if it was through his means [the building of the state or government] they were happy....He also gradually changed the government into tyranny—seeing no other way of turning men from the fear of God, but to bring them into a constant dependence upon his power [the power of the state].[6]

Remember this fact: it was Nimrod who mobilized the people to build the secular city and empire of Babylon and the Tower of Babel—all in defiance of God (Ge.11:1-9). Nimrod was the first world dictator, the first world tyrant, who set out to build a worldwide empire.

Thought 1. Nimrod ignored the brotherhood of the human race. He forgot his roots and the heritage of the human race. He forgot that all people have come from one source, one origin, one man: Noah. And most tragic of all, he forgot that Noah was godly: he ignored the God of Noah. The result was catastrophic: he mistreated people. He used people as mere animals to feed his lusts for power and pleasure. He enslaved them to do his bidding, to build his empire. How like so many persons today who forget the brotherhood of men. So many misuse and oppress others...
- in business, to build their own little empires
- in seeking pleasure
- in seeking money and wealth
- in seeking position
- in seeking fame
- in seeking power

> "Also thou shalt not oppress a stranger" (Ex.23:9).
> "Thou shalt not oppress an hired servant that is poor and needy, whether he be of thy brethren, or of thy strangers that are in thy land within thy gates" (De.24:14).
> "For the oppression of the poor, for the sighing of the needy, now will I arise, saith the LORD; I will set him in safety from him that puffeth at him" (Ps.12:5).
> "Withhold not good from them to whom it is due, when it is in the power of thine hand to do it" (Pr.3:27).
> "He that oppresseth the poor reproacheth his Maker: but he that honoureth him hath mercy on the poor" (Pr.14:31).
> "If thou seest the oppression of the poor, and violent perverting of judgment and justice in a province, marvel not at the matter: for he that is higher than the highest regardeth; and there be higher than they" (Ec.5:8).
> "Thou shalt love thy neighbor as thyself" (Mt.22:39).
> "Let love be without dissimulation [hypocrisy]. Abhor that which is evil; cleave to that which is good. Be kindly affectioned one to another with brotherly love; in honour preferring one another" (Ro.12:9-10).
> "And be ye kind one to another, tenderhearted, forgiving one another, even as God for Christ's sake hath forgiven you" (Ep.4:32).

2. Nimrod set out to build the first worldwide empire (vv.10-12). This is the beginning of world empires, the very first empire to sweep a section of the world and rule over multitudes of people. But note, this empire of Nimrod's was not out to serve people, not out to establish and guarantee...
- true services for people
- true happiness and security for people
- true law and order for people

Nimrod's empire was out to stir revolt and subject people to the whims of a power-crazed dictator. His empire was to be a secular empire, an empire that eliminated God—the only living and true God—from the face of the earth. His empire included the following:
a. The great Babylonian Empire.
⇒ *Babel* or *Babylon*: this was the beginning of Nimrod's empire (v.10). Genesis 11:2-4 tells us what happened. After the great flood, most if not all of the people still lived around Ararat where Noah and his small family had settled (Ge.8:4f). Apparently, Nimrod had gathered around him a small armed force that was able to conquer the other rulers among the people. Nimrod then mobilized the people to leave Ararat and move to Shinar or the area of Babylon. There they were to build a city that would serve as the capital of the empire he was building for the people and the generations yet to be born to them. (See outline and notes—Ge.11:1-9; 11:3-4.) Note this: from this point on Babylon becomes a godless city and stands opposed to God's people. Scripture looks upon Babylon as a godless empire, a godless system, and a godless religion (see Jos.7:21; Is.13:1f; 47:1f; Dan.4:30). It is eventually to be utterly destroyed (see notes—Re.18:1-24).
⇒ *Erech*: a city lying over 100 miles southeast of Babylon and southwest of modern Baghdad in Iraq. The ancient name for the city was Uruk; the modern name is Warka.
⇒ *Accad* or *Akkad*: a city that was in northern Babylonia located on the Euphrates River.

---

6 Flavius Josephus. *Josephus Complete Works.* Translated by William Whiston. (Grand Rapids, MI: Kregel, 1960), Ant. 1. 4:2.

⇒ *Calneh*: the location is unknown, but it was bound to be someplace within striking distance of Babylon.

b. The great Assyrian Empire (v.11). Note: this verse should read, "From that land [Babylon] he went forth into Assyria...." (v.11, NASV).

Nimrod struck out from the region of Babylon and marched against the land of Assyria, all for the purpose of adding to his empire. Within Assyria he founded four more great cities.

⇒ *Nineveh*: the city was built on the Tigris River, the upper Tigris, on the east side. It sat across the river from the present-day city of Mosul. Remember what God said to Jonah about Nineveh:

"Arise, go to Nineveh, that great city, and cry against it; for their wickedness is come up before me" (Jona.1:2).

⇒ *Rehoboth, Calah*, and *Resen*: all three cities are thought to have been suburbs of Nineveh, smaller population centers that were either built to handle the overflow of the great city, Nineveh, or else to give a front line defense for Nineveh against any future attacking conquerors.

---

4 (10:21-32) **Shem—Race, Human—Mankind**: the branch of Shem: the Middle East descendants, the line of *the promised seed*. Note three facts before actually looking at the descendants of Sham.

First, note the name of Eber (v.21). He was the great grandson of Shem (see chart below). Eber was the father of the Hebrews. The very name *Hebrew* was taken from the Hebrew word *Eber*. Abraham and the children of Israel were to come from the line of Eber: it was his descendants who were to be the chosen line through whom *the promised seed*, the Savior of the world, was to come.

Second, note that Shem is said to be the older brother of Japheth. Remember also that Ham is said to be the youngest brother (Ge.9:24). Why, then, if Shem is the oldest son of Noah, are Shem's descendants listed last in "The Table of Nations"? For emphasis and continuity. From this point on, the focus of the Bible is to be upon the descendants of Shem, the chosen line of Israel and the coming Messiah or Savior of the world. Thus, it is only natural to list the line of Shem last so that the connection can be shown between Shem and the rest of the Bible.

Remember the prophecy of Noah about Shem: he was to be the father of a people whose God—the only living and true God—was to be blessed. Shem's descendants were to reach out to the world and lead all people to worship and bless God. (See note, pt.2—Ge.9:24-27 for more discussion.)

Third, the ancient Shemites or Semites scattered all over the Middle East, and so far as we know, they did not migrate beyond the Middle East. Shem is the ancestor of the Arabs, Arameans or Syrians, and Hebrews.

a. There were five sons or branches of Shem (v.22).

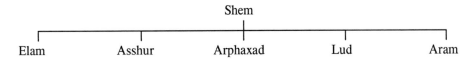

Shem — Elam, Asshur, Arphaxad, Lud, Aram

1) *Elam*: settled east of Mesopotamia beyond the Tigris River. Mesopotamia is the name for the land between the Euphrates and Tigris Rivers. The Elamites actually covered an area that reached from the Red Sea to the Persian Gulf. They later united with Media and formed the great Persian Empire.

The Elamites first appeared in the time of Abraham. They joined forces with several other kingdoms and conquered Sodom and Gomorrah and in the process took Lot, the nephew of Abraham, captive. Abraham pursued the Elamites, defeated them, and freed Lot (Ge.14:1-16).

2) *Asshur*: these people were the Assyrians who settled in northern Mesopotamia along the region of the upper Tigris River. Assyria was one of the kingdoms Nimrod settled. Nineveh was the great capital he built there. (See DEEPER STUDY # 2, pt.2b—Ge.10:8-12 for more discussion.)

3) *Arphaxad*: see point c. below.

4) *Lud*: the Lydians of Asia Minor.

5) *Aram*: see point b. below.

b. *Aram*: there were four descendants of Aram (v.23).

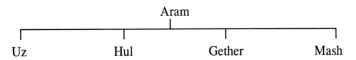

Aram — Uz, Hul, Gether, Mash

The land of Aram was northeast of Palestine. It stretched from the Jordan River over into part of what is known as Armenia today. It was the land known as Syria.

1) *Uz*: probably a part of the Arabian desert. The actual location is unknown. Of interest is the fact that it was the homeland of Job.

"There was a man in the land of Uz, whose name was Job; and that man was perfect and upright, and one that feared God, and eschewed evil" (Jb. 1:1).

2) *Hul and Gether*: nothing is known except that they were Aramean or Syrian territories.

3) *Mash*: either covered southern Armenia or else it was the modern Lebanon.

c. *Arphaxad*: the descendants of Arphaxad (vv.24-25).

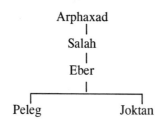

Arphaxad
|
Salah
|
Eber
|
Peleg   Joktan

1) *Arphaxad and Salah*: nothing is known about Arphaxad or his son Salah except that they were ancestors of Abraham and the chosen line. (See outline and notes—Ge.11:10-26 for discussion. See Ge.46:12; Nu.26:20; 1 Chr.2:3; 4:21-23.)

2) *Eber*: we have already seen that *Eber* is the name for *Hebrew*. (See the beginning of this note, First fact—Ge.10:21-32.)

3) *Peleg*: this son's name mean's *division* or to *divide*. Note the statement made about him: "during his life the earth was divided." What does this mean? Commentators have suggested the following explanations:

⇒ It refers to the families of the earth dividing up the land into districts or territories, probably due to overpopulation and the need to move farther and farther apart from one another. The division was either led by Peleg or else took place in his lifetime.

⇒ It refers to some catastrophic volcanic eruption that divided the earth into continents and islands. The earth is thought to have been one huge land mass. This huge volcanic eruption is thought to have taken place during Peleg's life, right after the Tower of Babel judgment when God scattered and separated the human races over the earth (Ge.11:1-9).

⇒ It refers to the great scattering and division of the human race after the Tower of Babel. It was there that God confused their language and caused them to separate and divide from each other. This view has Scriptural support in the scattering of the people at the Tower of Babel (Ge.11:1-9).

4) *Joktan*: see point d. below.

d. *Joktan*: there were thirteen descendants of Joktan (vv.26-29). They were all Arabian people.

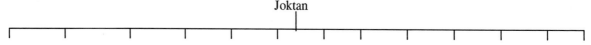

Joktan

Almodad   Sheleph   Hazarmaveth   Jerah   Hadoram   Uzal   Diklah   Obal   Abimael   Sheba   Ophir   Havilah   Jobab

1) *Almodad*: settled in south Arabia, possibly in the area of Al-murad.
2) *Sheleph*: the area of Yeman, probably around Salaf or Sulaf.
3) *Hazarmaveth*: an area in south Arabia around Hadramaut.
4) *Jerah*: unknown, but perhaps close to a fortress known as Jerakh.[7]
5) *Hadoram*: most likely in Yemen someplace.
6) *Uzal*: probably the name of the ancient capital of Yemen.
7) *Diklah*: the name means date-palm, thus it was probably a region where the fruit was plentiful. Perhaps around the modern Dakalah in Yemen.
8) *Obal and Abimael*: unknown other than being in Arabia, most likely south Arabia.
9) *Sheba*: probably the Sabeans, a people who settled southwest Arabia.
10) *Ophir*: unknown, but perhaps in southern Arabia on the Persian Gulf. Solomon's ships used the port of Ophir for shipping cargo (1 K.9:28; 1 Chr.29:3-4; 2 Chr.8:17-18; 9:10; Jb.22:24; 28:16; Ps.45:9).
11) *Havilah*: settled on the border of Arabia just north of Yemen (Ge.2:11-12; 25:16-18; 1 S.15:7).
12) *Jobab*: thought to be associated with the area of Jahaibab which is located close to modern Mecca.[8]

e. The borders of the Shemites (v.30): their territory stretched from Mesha in the north toward Sephar, over to the eastern hills or mountains. Just where these were located is unknown. All we know is that the boundary was within southern Arabia.

f. The conclusion is this: the branches of Shem, of Japheth, and of Ham—all the branches of the human race—are connected; they all come from one source: Noah (vv.31-32).

Thought 1. We can draw at least two great lessons from the Shemite branch of the human race.

1) The Shemitic races of the world came from the same origin as the other races of the world. We are all from the same source; we all have the same roots: Noah and his three sons. Consequently...

• The Shemitic races—the Arabs and the Hebrews—should not exalt themselves above other people. They are not superior human beings, neither by race nor by religion. They are not favorites of God. God has no favorites, shows no partiality to any race or person upon earth.

---

7   James Montgomery Boice. *Genesis,* Vol.1, p.337.
8   Victor Hamilton. *The Book of Genesis,* Vol.1, p.346.

"Then Peter opened his mouth, and said, Of a truth I perceive that God is no respecter of persons: but in every nation he that feareth him, and worketh righteousness, is accepted with him" (Ac.10:34-35).

"And [God] hath made of one blood all nations of men for to dwell on all the face of the earth, and hath determined the times before appointed, and the bounds of their habitation" (Ac.17:26).

"For there is no respect of persons with God" (Ro.2:11).

"For there is no difference between the Jew and the Greek: for the same Lord over all is rich unto all that call upon him. For whosoever shall call upon the name of the Lord shall be saved" (Ro.10:12-13).

- The Shemitic races—the Arabs and the Jews—are not to be discriminated against. Just as they are not superior human beings, neither are they inferior human beings. All the racial hatred of people against the Jews and Arabs is wrong, dead wrong. They are one with the rest of us, with all human races. Therefore, they are to be treated as brothers in brotherly love.

2) The line of Shem (through the Hebrews) was to become the chosen line through whom God was to send *the promised seed*, the Savior to the world. God chose the Jewish nation, Israel, to proclaim the glorious news that there is only one true and living God, and that there is only one Messiah and Savior for the world, *the promised seed*, the Lord Jesus Christ Himself. But Israel failed. Instead of sharing the news, they hoarded the news. They kept the message of the only living and true God and of His promise to send the Savior to themselves. They refused to be God's missionary force to the world.

The point is this: we—the true followers of Christ—must not fail as did Israel. We must not hoard the message; we must share it. We must go forth with diligence and proclaim the glorious news that God has sent *the promised seed* to the world, sent Him in the person of the Lord Jesus Christ.

"Go ye therefore, and teach all nations, baptizing them in the name of the Father, and of the Son, and of the Holy Ghost: teaching them to observe all things whatsoever I have commanded you: and, lo, I am with you always, even unto the end of the world" (Mt.28:19-20).

"And he said unto them, Go ye into all the world, and preach the gospel to every creature" (Mk.16:15).

"But ye shall receive power, after that the Holy Ghost is come upon you: and ye shall be witnesses unto me both in Jerusalem, and in all Judaea, and in Samaria, and unto the uttermost part of the earth" (Ac.1:8).

"Go, stand and speak in the temple to the people all the words of this life" (Ac.5:20).

"And the things that thou hast heard of me among many witnesses, the same commit thou to faithful men, who shall be able to teach others also" (2 Ti.2:2).

DEEPER STUDY # 3
(10:31-32) **Map—Ancient World—Race, Human**: see next page, page 324.

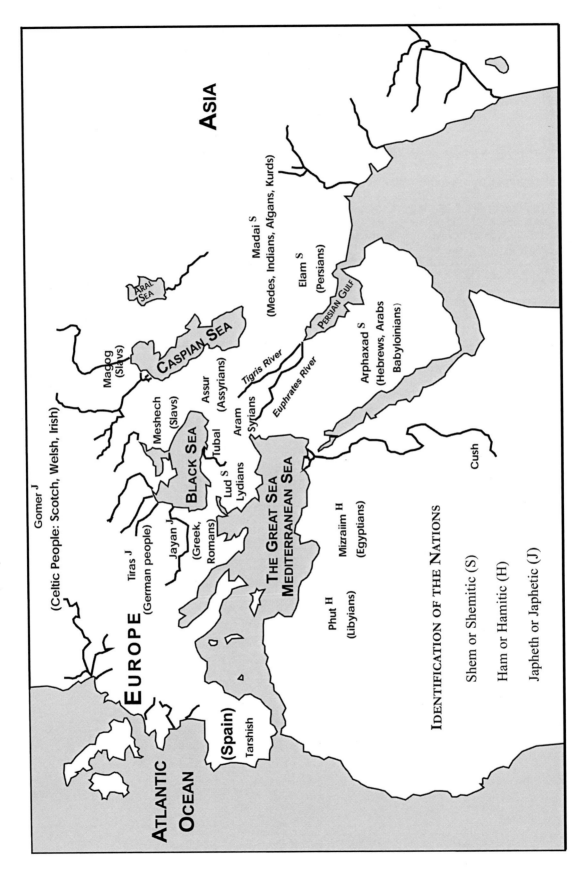

CHAPTER 11

B. The Scattering of the Human Race Over the Earth: The People's Tragic Mistake & Sin—the Secular City & False Worship (the Tower of Babel), 11:1-9

And the whole earth was of one language, and of one speech.

2 And it came to pass, as they journeyed from the east, that they found a plain in the land of Shinar; and they dwelt there.

3 And they said one to another, Go to, let us make brick, and burn them thoroughly. And they had brick for stone, and slime had they for mortar.

4 And they said, Go to, let us build us a city and a tower, whose top may reach unto heaven; and let us make us a name, lest we be scattered abroad upon the face if the

face of the whole earth.

5 And the LORD came down to see the city and the tower, which the children of men builded.

6 And the LORD said, Behold, the people is one, and they have all one language; and this they begin to do: and now nothing will be restrained from them, which they have imagined to do.

7 Go to, let us go down, and there confound their language, that they may not understand one another's speech.

8 So the LORD scattered them abroad from thence upon the face of all the earth: and they left off to build the city.

9 Therefore is the name of it called Babel; because the LORD did there confound the language of all the earth: and from thence did the LORD scatter them abroad upon the face of the earth.

1. Two major facts about the early human race
   a. They had one language
   b. They moved or migrated in mass—as a whole civilization—for some reason: To the land of Shinar

2. The tragic mistake & sin of the human race: Building a secular city & false worship center
   a. Their excitement & commitment to the project
   b. Their secular purpose: To gain fame
   c. Their worldly purpose: To gain security apart from God
   d. Their religious purpose: To reach heaven by themselves[DSI]

3. The intervention of God to restrain man's godless purpose
   a. God saw the secular city & false religion
      1) He saw their unity, single-minded purpose
      2) He saw their one language
      3) He saw their great capability
      4) He saw the pride of their imagination
   b. God pronounced His verdict: To restrain man's evil purposes by confusing man's language
   c. God restrained man's evil purpose
      1) Scattered them
      2) Stopped their secular empire & religion

4. The eternal memorial to God's power
   a. The very name of Babel or Babylon
   b. The different languages & nationalities of the world

DIVISION V

NOAH'S SONS: THE THREE BRANCHES CHOSEN TO REPOPULATE AND TO SCATTER OVER THE EARTH, 10:1–11:9

B. The Scattering of the Human Race Over the Earth: The People's Tragic Mistake and Sin the Secular City and False Worship (the Tower of Babel), 11:1-9

(11:1-9) **Introduction**: this event—the building of the great city of Babylon and of the Tower of Babel—apparently took place during the days of Peleg and of Nimrod. Remember:
   ⇒ The earth was divided in the days of Peleg, the fifth generation from Noah (Ge.10:25).
   ⇒ Nimrod set out to build Babylon, the secular empire (Ge.10:8-12).

What happened was probably this: after the great flood, Noah and his small family settled down in the area of Ararat. During the five generations the families grew and grew to such a point that they could have numbered 30,000 or more.[1] Whatever the true number, the population was rather large by Peleg's day.

In so far as Nimrod is concerned, what happened was probably what has happened time and again down through history—thousands of times—whether in small bands of people or in world empires. Nimrod arose, rallied a band of armed men around him, revolted against the authorities, and took control of the government and people—all by force. We saw this in our earlier discussion of Nimrod (see note—Ge.10:8-12).

Then something happened: for some reason, Nimrod wanted to move his kingdom and people from the area of Ararat eastward. Why?
   ⇒ Perhaps famine.
   ⇒ Perhaps the land of Shinar was extremely fertile in that day.[2]
   ⇒ Perhaps to just expand his empire.

Based on the description of Nimrod (Ge.10:8-12), he was most likely out to expand his empire, to simply rule over more land. If so, he would have left a small society of people behind to hold claim to the area of Ararat for his empire. This would have been necessary for his empire to continue in power down through the centuries.

Whatever the reason, two facts strongly point to the movement or migration of the people under Nimrod's leadership.
   ⇒ Nimrod founded the city of Babylon.

   "And the beginning of his kingdom was Babel, and Erech, and Accad, and Calneh, in the land of Shinar" (Ge.10:10).

---
1 Keil and Delitzsch. *Commentary on the Old Testament*, Vol.1, p.176.
2 H.C. Leupold. *Genesis*, Vol.1, p.384.

⇒ The present passage says that the people journeyed eastward and settled in a plain in the land of Shinar (v.2). Babylon is in the land of Shinar as Ge.10:10 says.

This seems to be the background of what is happening in the present passage. This is a most interesting study: *The Scattering of the Human Race: The People's Tragic Mistake and Sin—The Secular City and False Worship (the Tower of Babel).*
1. Two major facts about the early human race (vv.1-2).
2. The tragic mistake and sin of the human race: building a secular city and false worship center (vv.3-4).
3. The intervention of God to restrain man's godless purpose (vv.5-8).
4. The eternal memorial to God's power (v.9).

1 (11:1-2) **Race, Human—Language**: two major facts about the early human race.

a. The whole earth had one language and one speech. *The whole earth* refers to Noah and his descendents, to his small family who had survived the great flood and to the people born through their families. Since they had all come from Noah, it was only natural that there would be one language upon earth. All the people were bound to speak the same language. Note the distinction between *one language* and *one speech.*

In the Hebrew *one speech* means one vocabulary, the same meaning for the same things. Their concepts and thoughts were the same, were expressed by the same word.

The point being made is this: it was their common language that enabled the people...

- to communicate
- to share together
- to help one another
- to work together
- to play together
- to learn together

Simply stated, their common language did for them what our language does for us: enabled them to live and work together. It enabled them to advance as a society and civilization.

b. The people moved or migrated in mass—as a whole civilization, at least most of them—for some reason (see note 1—Ge.11:1-9 for discussion).

2 (11:3-4) **Babel, Tower of—Babylon—City, Secular—Civilization, Secular—Religion, False—Worship, False**: the tragic mistake and sin of the human race. After reaching Shinar, the area of Babylon in Iraq, the people settled down and began to establish a new civilization and society. At some point, Nimrod and his counselors realized they needed to do something to hold the people and empire together. Thus, they challenged the people with the vision of building a great city and a great religious center in the form of a gigantic tower. The city and religious center no doubt were to be the capital of the great empire and religion Nimrod set out to build across the world.

Now, note this: Nimrod did just what every great leader has to do: he challenged the people to follow him. The problem with Nimrod's challenge was that he was a godless tyrant, a godless dictator. This is seen in the following points.

a. The people were excited—very excited—about the building project (vv.3-4). They gave their whole-hearted support. This is seen in their attitude about the project:
⇒ "Come, let us make brick" (v.3, NASB).
⇒ "Come, let us build for ourselves a city" (v.4, NASB).

Note also that they suggested burning the bricks thoroughly, that is, to dry kiln them and to seal them together with a mortar-like substance. They wanted to use the very best building materials available, to make the city and religious center as permanent as possible.

The point to see is this: the people were behind the project one hundred percent. Their loyalty and lives belonged to Nimrod, to do the bidding of the state and government. He had them in the palm of his hands; he had the people united in the cause of holding the people together and building a worldwide empire.

b. The people had a secular purpose for building the city and religious tower: they were out to gain fame, to make a name for themselves (v.4). As we saw in an earlier passage, Nimrod wanted to lead the people to build a great empire (see DEEPER STUDY # 2—Ge.10:8-12 for more discussion). Babylon was to be the capital of that empire.

Now, note this: there is nothing wrong with building a great nation and people. Every leader and every people should desire to be strong. But they should be strong in order to meet the needs of the people, including their need to worship and serve God. They should be strong in order to build a healthy and strong society, not to make a name for themselves. This was the tragic mistake of the human race: they undertook the building projects to gain...

- fame
- recognition
- reputation
- honor
- glory

They were out to build a memorial to their name, to boost their own ego and pride. They themselves wanted to boast in their abilities and power, and they wanted succeeding generations to boast in them as the empire grew down through the ages.

Thought 1. Note how the people were setting themselves up—setting man up—as the god of history. Man was building a secular world completely devoid of the only living and true God. Man was rebelling against God—excluding, ignoring, and eliminating God entirely from the earth and human history.

Note another fact: nothing is said about God nor about service to the people, nothing whatsoever. Glance at vv.3-4 again; note how egotistical, self-sufficient, and godless the ambition of the people was. God and ministry were completely left out. The purpose of the people was totally secular. They were acting independently of God, totally eliminating God from their plans and lives. They were building the secular city and religion, a godless empire, and a man-made religion, all as a memorial to their names and generation.

c. The people had a worldly purpose for building the city and great tower. They were out to gain security, to protect themselves, but without God. Note what Scripture says: they sought...

- to keep everyone together
- to keep from being scattered all over the face of the earth
- to keep everyone within one great empire.

They knew what any of us would have known: the population was going to grow and people were going to move out farther and farther from one another. As they did, conflicts of interest would arise, and factions would grow, and skirmishes and wars would break out. The solution to this was a unified people: keep everyone within the same empire, under one rule, one state, one government. This was probably the reason Nimrod went all about building city after city and keeping the population under his control and within his empire (Ge.10:10-11).

Now, note this: there is nothing wrong with security and unity among people. These are noble ambitions. In fact, security and unity are needs that we desperately need both as individuals and nations. The wrong is this:

⇒ leaving God out of our search for security and unity.
⇒ denying God's part in security and unity.
⇒ seeking security and unity only from a worldly and humanistic basis, as though man himself can secure and unify people.
⇒ ignoring man's first and deepest need: the need to know beyond any question that he is secure and united (reconciled) with God; that he is never going to die, but rather live forever and ever with God.

Thought 1. It is God—the only living and true God—that gives man the foundation of security and a unified spirit with others. God is the basis upon which all security and unity must be built; in fact, man can never be perfectly secure and unified until he bases his life and security upon God. Nations and people will continue to be insecure and divided until they begin with God, begin with the security and reconciliation that He gives. Once a person has been truly reconciled to God, he loves God and he loves all the people of God. Again, God is the basis of security and unity, the only true basis upon which man can build an earthly and national security and unity.

This was the tragic mistake of the human race: they undertook the building of an empire apart from God. They sought security and unity from a worldly basis, not from God.

Note another fact as well: the people were disobeying God and rebelling against Him by not scattering over the whole earth and subduing it. God had told Adam and Eve and then Noah and his sons to populate the earth and to gain dominion over it (Ge.1:28; 9:1). Of course, as the people moved out upon the earth, God wanted the people to base their security and unity upon Him. But, as is seen above, this was not what they did. They sought to build an empire without God.

Thought 1. Matthew Henry says this:

> They [sought to] unite in one glorious empire...to build this city and tower, to be the metropolis of the their kingdom and the centre of their unity. It is probable that...ambitious Nimrod was in all this. He...aimed at universal monarchy...under pretence of uniting for their common safety, he contrives to keep them in one body, that, having them all under his eye, he might not fail to have them under his power.[3]

d. The people had a religious purpose for building the city and great tower: they were out to reach heaven by themselves, through their own efforts. Note several significant facts.

1) There is no mention of God in the people's plans; no mention whatsoever of the only living and true God, of the sovereign LORD and Majesty of the universe, of the Creator and Sustainer of all things. Quickly glance at v.3-4 and note how self and only self is stressed, man and only man. Man was going to build the city (empire) and great tower and man was going to build them *by himself* and *for himself*. God—the only living and true God—was forgotten, completely ignored and neglected.

2) The purpose for building the great tower was the same as for the city: to gain a name for themselves (v.4). They were out to build a worldwide religion and to make Babylon the center of that religion. They were seeking to be the religious center of the world down through the centuries, to be recognized and honored as the religious center of the empire. Again, note that God's name has no part in their purpose, only *their names*. They were building to honor their names, the names of their empire and generation, not God's name.

3) This was definitely a religious center, a great tower. (See DEEPER STUDY # 1—Ge.11:4 for a picture of the tower.) The tower was what is called in the Middle East a temple-tower, a *ziggurat*. The great temple-towers or *ziggurats* were built as *staircases to heaven*. The *NIV Study Bible* gives the names of several *ziggurats* to illustrate the point:

⇒ "The House of the Seven Guides of Heaven and Earth" (at Borsippa).
⇒ "The House of the Foundation—Platform of Heaven and Earth" (at Babylon).
⇒ "The House of the Mountain of the Universe" (at Asshur).[4]

---

3 *Matthew Henry's Commentary*, Vol.1, p.79.
4 *NIV Study Bible*, note on Ge.11:4, p.23.

The point is this: the great tower was being built as a symbol that the people were building a stairway to heaven, building a stairway up to God. The people were building…

- a religion, a man-made religion, up to God
- a stairway, a man-made stairway, up to God
- a path, a man-made path, up to God
- a way, a man-made way, up to God

The great tower was only a symbol. The people knew they could never build a temple literally up into heaven. If the people had been ignorant, thinking they could actually reach into heaven with a tower, they would not have built on the plain of Babylon which lies almost at sea level. They would have built the tower on a mountain. As stated, the tower was…

- to be a symbol of their worldwide religion, the religion that was to help hold the empire and people together
- to be a symbol of their name, a name that stood for religion, for building a stairway that reached up into heaven
- to be a symbol of their own works, the great effort they put into building a stairway of religion that reached up into heaven

This was the tragic mistake of the human race: they undertook to build a great tower in reaching up to God, a religion of works and self-effort. They thought themselves capable of reaching God on their own, thought they were good enough and righteous enough to reach God by their own works and efforts.

Thought 1. This is the same tragic mistake made by most people today. Most people still try to reach God…

- by their own works and efforts
- by their own goodness and morality
- by following their own man-made steps to God

Most people still try to build a stairway of works and goodness up to God. But, all human works and efforts to reach God are doomed to failure. There are two reasons why.

1) God is perfect and any person who is going to enter heaven and live with Him must be perfect. But no person is perfect. We have all sinned and come short of God's glory, of His perfection. Therefore, no matter how many stairways we build up to God—no matter how good we may be—we are not perfect. Therefore, we cannot reach heaven and enter God's presence. If we are ever going to be good enough to enter heaven, God has to remake us and perfect us. But before that, He has to take care of our sin and death problems. This is the glorious gospel. God has taken care of all this through Jesus Christ our Lord, taken care of…

- the sin problem through the *righteousness* of Jesus Christ
- the death problem through the *death* of Jesus Christ

God perfects us through Jesus Christ. When we truly believe in Jesus Christ, God takes our belief and counts it as the righteousness and death of Jesus Christ. God *counts us*…

- as *righteous* in Jesus Christ
- as *having died* in Jesus Christ

Therefore, the punishment for our sins has been borne by the death of Jesus Christ. We stand righteous, sinless, and perfect before God *through Christ*. We enter heaven and are acceptable to God—counted perfect—through Christ and Christ alone.

> "And he [Abraham] believed in the LORD; and he counted it to him for righteousness" (Ge.15:6).
> "For what saith the scripture? Abraham believed God, and it was counted unto him for righteousness" (Ro.4:3).
> "But he was wounded for our transgressions, he was bruised for our iniquities: the chastisement of our peace was upon him; and with his stripes we are healed" (Is.53:5).
> "For all have sinned, and come short of the glory of God; being justified [counted righteous] freely by his grace through the redemption that is in Christ Jesus" (Ro.3:23-24).
> "But God commendeth his love toward us, in that, while we were yet sinners, Christ died for us" (Ro.5:8).
> "Who gave himself for our sins, that he might deliver us from this present evil world, according to the will of God and our Father" (Ga.1:4).
> "Knowing that a man is not justified [counted righteous] by the works of the law, but by the faith of Jesus Christ, even we have believed in Jesus Christ, that we might be justified by the faith of Christ, and not by the works of the law: for by the works of the law shall no flesh be justified" (Ga.2:16).
> "And be found in him, not having mine own righteousness, which is of the law, but that which is through the faith of Christ, the righteousness which is of God by faith" (Ph.3:9).
> "Much more then, being now justified by his blood, we shall be saved from wrath through him" (Ro.5:9).
> "For he that is dead [counted dead, justified] is freed from sin" (Ro.6:7).
> "Who his own self bare our sins in his own body on the tree, that we, being dead to sins, should live unto righteousness: by whose stripes ye were healed" (1 Pe.2:24).

"For Christ also hath once suffered for sins, the just for the unjust, that he might bring us to God, being put to death in the flesh, but quickened by the Spirit" (1 Pe.3:18).

"And ye know that he was manifested to take away our sins; and in him is no sin" (1 Jn.3:5).

2) No person can personally penetrate heaven and enter the presence of God, not by his own works and efforts. We should know this, for we are physical beings in the material dimension and world, and God is a spiritual being in the spiritual and heavenly dimension. The physical world cannot penetrate the spiritual world. For example, what person among us has ever gone up into heaven? No one! Jesus asked the same question, and He said "No man" (Jn.3:13). If a person is going to ever enter heaven and live with God, God has to come to earth and show us how to reach heaven. This He has done in the Lord Jesus Christ. As shown in point one above, we reach heaven through the Lord Jesus Christ. This is exactly what Christ tells us.

"And no man hath ascended up to heaven, but he that came down from heaven, even the Son of man which is in heaven. And as Moses lifted up the serpent in the wilderness, even so must the Son of man be lifted up: that whosoever believeth in him should not perish, but have eternal life. For God so loved the world, that he gave his only begotten Son, that whosoever believeth in him should not perish, but have everlasting life. For God sent not his Son into the world to condemn the world; but that the world through him might be saved. He that believeth on him is not condemned: but he that believeth not is condemned already, because he hath not believed in the name of the only begotten Son of God" (Jn.3:13-18).

"Jesus saith unto him, I am the way, the truth, and the life: no man cometh unto the Father, but by me" (Jn.14:6).

4) This was the beginning of false religion after The Great Flood. Babylon was the place where false religion was born upon earth; Babylon is the *Mother of False Religion*. This is exactly what Scripture declares in the last book of the Bible. Note that the first book of the Bible reveals that Babylon gave birth to false religion, and the last book of the Bible declares that Babylon is the *Mother of False Religion*.

"MYSTERY, BABYLON THE GREAT, THE MOTHER OF HARLOTS AND ABOMINATIONS OF THE EARTH" (Re.17:5).

No matter what the religion is, if its emphasis is upon works and human goodness, it comes up short and fails to reach God. The religion may go by the name of...
- astrology
- humanism
- secularism
- any one of the major religions of the earth

But, it makes a tragic mistake and sins before God if it teaches that people can build a stairway to God, that people can work and become good enough for God to accept them. This was the tragic mistake made by the people at the Tower of Babel. This was the beginning of all false religion upon earth. (See note—Col.2:8 for more discussion.)

James Montgomery Boice says:

The citizens of Babylon had rejected the knowledge of the true God. Therefore, we should expect the creation of a false religion as part of their dubious cultural achievements. Again, the Bible speaks of "mystery Babylon," that is, of the reality symbolized by the earthly city, saying that it is "the mother of prostitutes and of the abominations of the earth" (Re.17:5). This refers, as do the ideas of prostitution and abomination throughout the Bible, to false religion.

There is evidence that this was the case historically. Morris notes, "The essential identity of the various gods and goddesses of Rome, Greece, India, Egypt, and other nations with the original pantheon of the Babylonians is well established. [In fact], Nimrod himself was apparently later deified as the chief god ("Merodach" or "Marduk") of Babylon.[5]

"Regard not them that have familiar spirits [mediums], neither seek after wizards [spiritists], to be defiled by them: I am the LORD your God" (Le.19:31).

"There shall not be found among you any one that maketh his son or his daughter to pass through the fire, or that useth divination, or an observer of times [sorcery], or an enchanter [interprets omens], or a witch [witchery], or a charmer [casts spells], or a consulter with familiar spirits [mediums], or a wizard [spiritist], or a necromancer [one who calls up the dead]. For all that do these things are an abomination unto the LORD" (De.18:10-12).

5   James Montgomery Boice. *Genesis,* Vol.1, p.341. The reference to Morris is to Henry M. Morris. *The Genesis Record: A Scientific and Devotional Commentary on the Book of Beginnings.* (Grand Rapids, MI: Baker Book House, 1976), pp.17-18.

Some commentators believe that this was the birth of astrology upon earth, that a zodiac actually sat on the top story of the great tower. (See note—Col.2:8 for more discussion.)
⇒ Donald Grey Barnhouse says this:

> *The tower was a ziggurat on top of which was a zodiac by which the priests hoped to get knowledge from the stars. It was an open, defiant turning to Satan and the beginning of devil worship. This is why the Bible everywhere pronounces a curse on those who consult the sun, the moon, and the stars of heaven.*[6]

⇒ James Montgomery Boice says:

> *It [the great tower] had a representation of the heavens (a Zodiac) upon it....Astrology, which focuses on a study of the zodiac, originated in Babylon. Turn to any book on astrology and you will find that it was the Chaldeans (another name for the inhabitants of Babylon) who first developed the zodiac by dividing the sky into sections and giving meanings to each on the basis of the stars that are found there. A person's destiny is said to be determined by whatever section or 'sign' he is born under. From Babylon, astrology passed to the empire of ancient Egypt where it mingled with the native animism and polytheism of the Nile. The pyramids were constructed with certain mathematical relationships to the stars. The Sphinx has astrological significance. It has the head of a woman, symbolizing Virgo, the virgin, and the body of a lion, symbolizing Leo. Virgo is the first sign of the zodiac, Leo the last. So the Sphinx (which incidentally means 'joining' in Greek) is the meeting point of the zodiac, indicating that the Egyptian priests believed the starting point of the earth in relation to the zodiac lay in Egypt, on the banks of the Nile.*
>
> *By the time the Jews left Egypt for Canaan, astrology had infected the population there. Hence, some of the strictest warnings in the Bible against astrology date from this period (Le.19:31; Deut.18). Still later, astrology entered the religious life of Rome.*
>
> *The interesting thing about these biblical denunciations of astrology is that astrology is identified with demonism or Satanism in the sense that Satan and his hosts were actually being worshiped in the guise of the signs or planets. This is the reason for the Bible's stern denunciation of these practices.*[7]

"If there arise among you a prophet, or a dreamer of dreams, and giveth thee a sign or a wonder, and the sign or the wonder come to pass, whereof he spake unto thee, saying, Let us go after other gods, which thou hast not known, and let us serve them; thou shalt not hearken unto the words of that prophet, or that dreamer of dreams: for the LORD your God proveth you, to know whether ye love the LORD your God with all your heart and with all your soul" (De.13:1-3).

"But the prophet, which shall presume to speak a word in my name, which I have not commanded him to speak, or that shall speak in the name of other gods, even that prophet shall die. And if thou say in thine heart, How shall we know the word which the LORD hath not spoken? When a prophet speaketh in the name of the LORD, if the thing follow not, nor come to pass, that is the thing which the LORD hath not spoken, but the prophet hath spoken it presumptuously: thou shalt not be afraid of him" (De.18:20-22).

"Stand now with thine enchantments, and with the multitude of thy sorceries, wherein thou hast laboured from thy youth; if so be thou shalt be able to profit, if so be thou mayest prevail. Thou art wearied in the multitude of thy counsels. Let now the astrologers, the stargazers, the monthly prognosticators [those who foretell signs], stand up, and save thee from these things that shall come upon thee. Behold, they shall be as stubble; the fire shall burn them; they shall not deliver themselves from the power of the flame: there shall not be a coal to warm at, nor fire to sit before it. Thus shall they be unto thee with whom thou hast laboured, even thy merchants, from thy youth: they shall wander every one to his quarter; none shall save thee" (Is.47:12-15).

"Hear ye the word which the LORD speaketh unto you, O house of Israel: thus saith the LORD, Learn not the way of the heathen, and be not dismayed at the signs of heaven [astrology]; for the heathen are dismayed at them" (Je.10:1-2; see Da.1:18-20; 2:27-28).

DEEPER STUDY # 1

(11:4) Babel, Tower of: the Tower of Babel was a religious center, a temple-tower, what is called a ziggurat in the Middle East. They were built as staircases to heaven. (See note, pt.4,c—Ge.11:3-4 for more discussion.) The temple-towers of Babylon were gigantic structures of several stories that rose upward in the sky hundreds of feet above the ground. They were shaped somewhat like a pyramid with a shrine on the top. A walkway or stairs on the outside led up to each receding story above. The Tower of Babel would have looked something like this: see picture next page.

---

6 Donald Grey Barnhouse. *Genesis*, p.71.
7 James Montgomery Boice. *Genesis*, Vol.1, pp.341-342.

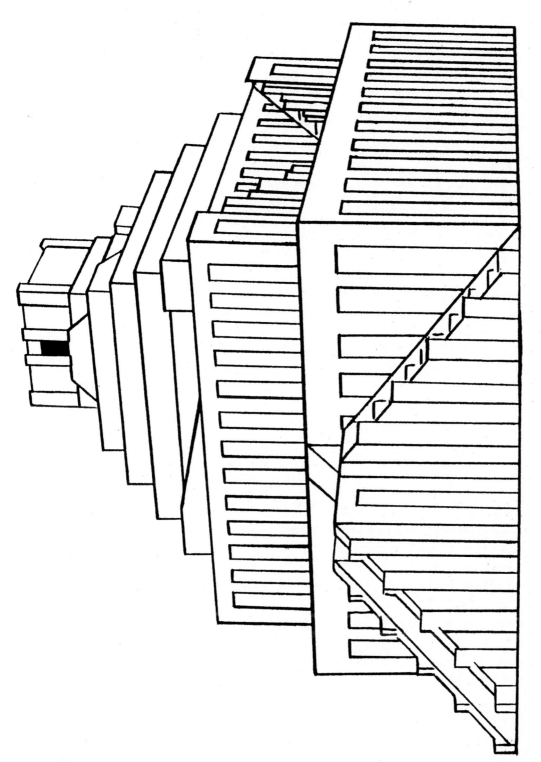

TOWER OF BABEL

A Babylonian Ziggurat: most known ziggurats measured approximately 1000–1200 feet around the base.)

3 (11:5-8) **Judgment—Anthropomorphic:** the intervention of God to restrain man's godless purpose. Note three significant facts.

a. God saw the secular city and false religion the people were building (v.5). When Scripture says that God "came down to see the city," this is what is called *anthropomorphic* language. This simply means that human traits are ascribed to God. God already knew about the secular city and great tower. Scripture is just using descriptive language to give us a clearer and more interesting picture of what happened. What really happened was this: God saw the godless purposes of the people, so He came down to earth in *judicial action* to judge them.

Throughout history God has often allowed the evil purposes of men to continue, to take their course. (See Hitler, Stalin, and others who have sought to build world empires, enslaving and slaughtering millions to achieve their ends.) But not this time, not when Nimrod had united the whole human race to build a one-world empire and religion. Why? Four reasons are given by Scripture.

1) God saw the unity, the single-minded purpose of the people (v.6). They were as one people, as one body, set on a single purpose, and that purpose was godless.

2) God saw the one language of the people (v.6). They were able to communicate and understand one another without any problem. They had the same concepts, thoughts, and mind processes that enabled them to plan and to execute their plans both efficiently and effectively. And, again, their plans and actions were secular and godless.

3) God saw that the people had great capability (v.6). If they were left on their own—left as one people with one language—they would succeed in building a godless empire and tower of religion.

4) God saw the pride of their imagination and the evil of their purpose (v.6). He knew all about their rebellion and godless purpose in building the secular city and religious tower. God knew their imaginations—how prideful and egotistical man was—that man wanted...

- to gain fame
- to gain recognition
- to gain power
- to gain wealth
- to be honored
- to be his own person
- to govern his own life
- to do what he wanted

God knew man's imaginations—how prideful and egotistical man was—that man did not want to admit...
- that he needed help
- that he could not build the right kind of society and world by himself
- that he is sinful and depraved and cannot bring utopia—the glorious empire—to earth through his own efforts

These are the reasons why God intervened in the building of the city of Babylon and the great religious Tower of Babel. God knew the godless purpose of man, that man was building a city and empire and a man-made religion that was to be godless, to exclude God entirely—the only true and living God—from the earth.

b. God pronounced His verdict: to restrain man's evil purpose by confusing man's language (v.7). Language is learned, and as it is learned, the mind develops an ability to arrange and organize its thoughts in a certain way. That is, the minds of the human races differ: minds differ as to the way they organize and arrange material and thoughts. Just how the mind organizes and arranges thoughts is determined to a large degree by the language a person learns.

The point is this: when God confused the language of the people, their minds—their world of concepts and thoughts—were bound to be affected as well as their languages. There was a total lack of communication and understanding as to the thoughts, concepts, and meaning of the other languages. The people simply could not understand one another. There was apparently only an understanding among various family groups.

c. God restrained man's evil purpose (v.8). Note what Scripture says: God scattered the people over the face of the whole earth. He had confused their language; they could not understand one another. Consequently, they slowly—probably over weeks and months—drifted apart and developed communities and cities of their own. The history of the various families is recorded in *The Table of Nations* of Chapter 10.

The point is this: God stopped the people's secular empire and false religion, stopped them by confusing their language and scattering them over the face of the earth.

Note this: God was having mercy upon man by stopping man's evil purposes. We know this because of the name of God that is used throughout this passage, the name *Jehovah* or *Yahweh* (vv.5-9). This is the redemptive name of God (see note—Ge.2:4 for discussion). God was stopping man from building a worldwide godless empire in order to pave the way for man's salvation. If a worldwide empire was allowed to rule the world—a godless empire—then God would not be able to raise up a people through whom He could send *the promised seed*, the Savior of the world. Thus, in confusing the language and scattering the people over the earth...

- God was stopping man's godless purpose, but God was also preparing to save man by raising up a godly people

> **"He disappointeth the devices of the crafty, so that their hands cannot perform their enterprise" (Jb.5:12).**
> **"He leadeth counsellors away spoiled, and maketh the judges fools" (Jb.12:17).**
> **"Therefore their inhabitants were of small power, they were dismayed and confounded: they were as the grass of the field, and as the green herb, as the grass on the housetops, and as corn blasted before it be grown up" (Is.37:27).**
> **"It is he that sitteth upon the circle of the earth, and the inhabitants thereof are as grasshoppers; that stretcheth out the heavens as a curtain, and spreadeth them out as a tent to dwell in: that bringeth the princes to nothing; he maketh the judges of the earth as vanity" (Is.40:22-23).**
> **"Behold, all they that were incensed against thee shall be ashamed and confounded: they shall be as nothing; and they that strive with thee shall perish" (Is.41:11).**

"Thus saith the Lord, thy redeemer, and he that formed thee from the womb, I am the Lord that maketh all things; that stretcheth forth the heavens alone; that spreadeth abroad the earth by myself; that frustrateth the tokens of the liars, and maketh diviners mad; that turneth wise men backward, and maketh their knowledge foolish" (Is.44:24-25).

"Verily thou art a God that hidest thyself, O God of Israel, the Saviour. They shall be ashamed, and also confounded, all of them: they shall go to confusion together that are makers of idols. But Israel [all true believers] shall be saved in the Lord with an everlasting salvation: ye shall not be ashamed nor confounded world without end" (Is.45:15-17).

"But the Lord is with me as a mighty terrible one: therefore my persecutors shall stumble, and they shall not prevail: they shall be greatly ashamed; for they shall not prosper: their everlasting confusion shall never be forgotten. But, O Lord of hosts, that triest the righteous, and seest the reins and the heart, let me see thy vengeance on them: for unto thee have I opened my cause. Sing unto the Lord, praise ye the Lord: for he hath delivered the soul of the poor from the hand of evildoers" (Je.20:11-13).

4 (11:9) **Babylon—Babel, Tower of—God, Power**: the eternal memorial to God's power. The very name *Babel or Babylon* means confusion. The name was given to the city and tower because God confused the languages of men there. Later on, the people of the area changed the meaning to *the gate of God* (Victor Hamilton. *The Book of Genesis*, p.357). But no matter what meaning man tries to give to the name of Babel, it stands as a memorial to God's great power. When we hear the name Babel or Babylon or hear a different language from our own, we should always think of the enormous power of God, of just what He did at Babel.

⇒ Both Babylon and the different languages and nationalities of the earth stand as an eternal memorial to God's great power.

Thought 1. God expects us to remember Him at every turn of life. It is our duty to remember and acknowledge Him.

"When I remember thee upon my bed, and meditate on thee in the night watches" (Ps.63:6).

"In all thy ways acknowledge him, and he shall direct thy paths" (Pr.3:6).

"Remember now thy Creator in the days of thy youth, while the evil days come not, nor the years draw nigh, when thou shalt say, I have no pleasure in them" (Ec.12:1).

"When my soul fainted within me I remembered the Lord: and my prayer came in unto thee, into thine holy temple" (Jona.2:7).

DIVISION VI

SHEM, NOAH'S SON: THE SON CHOSEN TO CARRY ON THE GODLY SEED, 11:10-32

(11:10-31) **DIVISION OVERVIEW: Man, History of—Failure, of Man—History**: remember what had just happened. Man had attempted to build the secular city and a tower of false religion. Man had just tried to eliminate God—the only true and living God—from his life, from both society and religion. Man had just built...

- Babylon, the secular city, the city without God
- the Tower of Babel, the secular religion and false worship—all created by man's own imaginations, his thoughts of what religion should be

Man had just failed God again, failed to follow and worship God as the Creator and Savior of life. Man had just proven his sinfulness and depravity once again. This was but another terrible failure of man, another repeat of what has happened ever since God has created man.

At this point in our study of Genesis, it would be wise to look at man's terrible failures down through history. The Bible teaches that there have been or else will be eight terrible periods of failure by man, eight times that God's heart has been tragically grieved and cut to the core, eight times that God has had or else will have to step in and miraculously save man.

⇒ First, God created Adam, but Adam turned away from God, so far away that he would not return to God on his own. God had to seek after Adam to save him (Ge. Chapters 1-3).

⇒ Second, the son of Adam, Cain, dishonored God and cut the heart of God by presenting a false worship to God and by murdering his brother Abel, who was the chosen line of *the promised seed* (Ge. Chapter 4). But God chose another son of Adam, Seth, to be the ancestor of *the promised seed*.

⇒ Third, down through the generations, the godly line of Seth began to fellowship and intermarry with the ungodly line, so much so that the godly line became as corrupt as the ungodly. Eventually, there was only one godly man left on earth, Noah. The whole human race had become so unrighteous and ungodly that God had to judge and destroy them all through a worldwide flood. But God intervened and saved one man and his small family to preserve the godly line and the human race (Ge. Chapters 5-6).

⇒ Fourth, as stated above, the human race had attempted to build the secular city and tower of religion, a city and religion that would be *totally void of God*, that would be a memorial to the name of man and his enormous ability and technology. Man had become so focused upon the earth that he had become totally secular and humanistic, having nothing to do with God, not with the true and living God. He wanted religion only in so far as it served the state and allowed the passions and urges of man to be fulfilled. Man's personal relationship with God and man's duty to God was completely lost in man's pursuit of the secular society and the pleasures of the flesh. God had no choice but to stop and judge man. This He did by confusing the languages of men and causing them to scatter over the earth (Ge. Chapter 11).

⇒ Fifth, after God scattered the human race over the earth, He gave them generation after generation to repent and to follow and worship Him. But they still refused. In fact, the godly line once again polluted itself and became so corrupted that they began to worship idols (Jos.24:2,15). This will be seen in the discussion of the present passage. The spiritual decline of man, even those of the godly line, was so great that God had to change His method of dealing with man. God moved away from dealing with the human race as a whole and chose one man, Abraham, and through him created a whole new race of people. It was through the descendents of Abraham, a whole new race of people (the Jews or Israel), that God was to fulfill His promise to send *the promised seed* into the world. (See outline and notes—Ge.11:10-32; 12:1-9 for more discussion.)

⇒ Sixth, man still failed: the Jews or Israel failed to worship and serve God *in spirit and in truth*. They became a very self-righteous and prejudicial people, even in the true religion. They hoarded the truth instead of carrying and sharing the truth with the world. They refused to be the missionary force for God to the world. And most tragic of all, when God sent *the promised seed* to the world—the Messiah and Savior, the Lord Jesus Christ— they killed Him. They refused to accept Him and had Him murdered upon the cross. But God's eternal purpose for saving man was now accomplished: the way for man to be saved from sin, death, and judgment to come was now completed by the death and resurrection of His Son, the Lord Jesus Christ. Therefore, God turned away from depending upon one nation to proclaim the truth to the world and turned to every person. Today God offers eternal salvation and challenges every human being of all nations to follow and worship Him through His Son, the Lord Jesus Christ. Jesus Christ is *the promised seed*, the Savior, who was sent into the world to save the human race and every person who will call upon Him and follow Him (*Exodus - Jude*).

⇒ Seventh, the Bible tells us that the human race will again fail. Man will again seek to build a secular world and religion. This will take place at the end of what is called *the church age* or at the beginning of *the great tribulation period* that is coming upon the earth. But God will again intervene, judge man, and usher in what the Bible calls *the millennium*. The millennium will be a period of one thousand years when Satan will be bound and Christ will return to the earth to rule over the nations and the human race (the book of *Revelation*; 2 Th. Chapter 2; Mt.24:15; Da.9:24-27; 11:31; 12:11).

⇒ Eighth, at the end of the millennium man will once again be tested. God will have given man the ultimate utopia of life, the rule and reign of His own Son upon the earth. Therefore, to determine who is genuine in following His Son, God will test man by setting Satan loose—by allowing Satan to once again tempt man. Tragically, man will again attempt to build the secular state, a state complete devoid of God. But this time—after having given man the greatest society possible through the reign of His Son—God will have had enough of man's rebellion, denial, cursing, and rejection. God will end human history, judge man at the final judgment, and recreate a new heavens and earth for all those who have followed him throughout all of human history (*Revelation*, Chapters 20-22).

The point is this: God has given the human race opportunity after opportunity, generation after generation, to follow and serve Him, but man as a whole has refused. Man has rebelled against God: denied, cursed, ignored, neglected, and rejected Him. And, as we have seen in the early chapters of Genesis, the awful tragedy is this: in each instance man has turned so far away from God that there has hardly been a godly person left upon earth. This has happened four times in the early history of man (*Genesis*, Chapters 1–11:9).

SHEM, NOAH'S SON: THE SON CHOSEN TO CARRY ON THE GODLY SEED, 11:10-32

A. The Preservation of the Promised Seed (Part 1), 11:10-26
B. The Preservation of the Promised Seed (Part 2): The Beginning of a Great Life (Abram), 11:27-32

	VI. SHEM, NOAH'S SON: THE SON CHOSEN TO CARRY ON THE GODLY SEED, 11:10-32	thirty years, and begat Peleg: 17 And Eber lived after he begat Peleg four hundred and thirty years, and begat sons and daughters. 18 And Peleg lived thirty years, and begat Reu: 19 And Peleg lived after he begat Reu two hundred and nine years, and begat sons and daughters.	
	A. The Preservation of the Promised Seed (Part 1), 11:10-26		
1. Fact 1: A particular son of Noah, Shem, was chosen to continue *the promised seed*	10 These are the generations of Shem: Shem was an hundred years old, and begat Arphaxad two years after the flood: 11 And Shem lived after he begat Arphaxad five hundred years, and begat sons and daughters.	20 And Reu lived two and thirty years, and begat Serug: 21 And Reu lived after he begat Serug two hundred and seven years, and begat sons and daughters. 22 And Serug lived thirty years, and begat Nahor:	
2. Fact 2: The genealogies of the Bible list descendants, not necessarily sons	12 And Arphaxad lived five and thirty years, and begat Salah: 13 And Arphaxad lived after he begat Salah four hundred and three years, and begat sons and daughters. 14 And Salah lived thirty years, and begat Eber: 15 And Salah lived after he begat Ever four hundred and three years, and begat sons and daughters. 16 And Eber lived four and	23 And Serug lived after he begat Nahor two hundred years, and begat sons and daughters. 24 And Nahor lived nine and twenty years, and begat Terah: 25 And Nahor lived after he begat Terah an hundred and nineteen years, and begat sons and daughters. 26 And Terah lived seventy years, and begat Abram, Nahor, and Haran.	3. Fact 3: No personal information is given on any of the fathers listed in this genealogy 4. Fact 4: The genealogies of the Bible sometimes list the most important son or ancestor first, not necessarily the son born first: Compare Abraham

DIVISION VI

SHEM, NOAH'S SON: THE SON CHOSEN TO CARRY ON THE GODLY SEED, 11:10-32

A. The Preservation of the Promised Seed (Part 1), 11:10-26

(11:10-26) **Introduction**: in the present passage man failed God again. There was a spiritual decline even in the godly line, a decline so great that God changed His method of dealing with man. God moved away from dealing with the human race as a whole and chose one man (Abraham) and created a whole new race of people through him, a people through whom He could send *the promised seed* into the world. This passage deals with *Shem, Noah's Son, the Son Chosen to Carry on the Godly Seed: The Preservation of the Promised Seed (Part 1)*.

1. Fact 1: a particular son of Noah, Shem, was chosen to continue *the promised seed* (vv.10-11)
2. Fact 2: the genealogies of the Bible list descendants, not necessarily sons (vv.12-22)
3. Fact 3: no personal information is given on any of the fathers listed in this genealogy (v.23).
4. Fact 4: the genealogies of the Bible sometimes list the most important son or ancestor first, not necessarily the son born first: compare Abraham (vv.24-26).

[1] (11:10-11) **Seed, Promised—Shem**: a particular son of Noah was chosen to continue *the promised seed*: Shem. Note two facts abut the genealogy of Shem.

a. Noah had predicted that Shem and his descendants would be the chosen line for *the promised seed*. The prophecy had been simple, stating only that *the Lord God of Shem was to be blessed* (Ge.9:26). Note that God was the one to be blessed, not Shem and his descendants, not directly. The name of God was to be blessed *through Shem and his descendants*, through what God was going to do through them. What was God going to do through them?

⇒ Provide the line through which *the promised Savior* was to come.
⇒ Provide the line through which the knowledge of God was to be kept before the minds of men.

The God of Shem was to be blessed because the line of Shem was to give the Savior and the knowledge of God to the world.

b. Note that Shem and his descendants were only providing the line or descendants—only being the channel—through which the two great things were to be done. Nothing whatsoever is said about Shem or his immediate descendants blessing God, only that their God would be blessed. As will be seen, Shem and his immediate descendants, the descendants in this genealogy, declined spiritually, significantly so. By the time the last father in the genealogy is mentioned, Terah, the whole godly line had become corrupted. Terah and his family had become worshippers of idols.

> **"And Joshua said unto all the people, Thus saith the LORD God of Israel, Your fathers dwelt on the other side of the flood in old time, even Terah, the father of Abraham, and the father of Nachor: and they served other gods....And if it seem evil unto you to serve the LORD, choose you this day whom ye will serve; whether the gods which your fathers served that were on the other side of the flood, or the gods of the Amorites, in whose land ye dwell: but as for me and my house, we will serve the LORD"** (Jos.24:2, 15).

Apparently, man did just what he had done before the flood, corrupted the whole human race, even the godly line.

2 (11:12-22) **Genealogy—Seed, Promised**: the genealogies of the Bible list descendants, not necessarily sons.

a. First, note the genealogy of Shem.

	Was Born in the Year	Died in the Year after Creation	Total Years
THE GREAT FLOOD 1656			
Noah	1056	2006	950
Shem	1558	2158	600
Arphaxad	1658	2096	438
Salah	1693	2126	433
Eber	1723	2187	464
Peleg	1757	1996	239
Reu	1787	2026	239
Serug	1819	2049	230
Nahor	1849	1997	148
Terah	1878	2083	205
Terah's oldest son (?)		1948	
Abraham (?)		2008	

b. Second, note the reference to *begat* or *fathered* throughout the genealogy (vv.10-26). These often refer to descendants way down the line of a person and not to an immediate child. This means that a genealogy...
- may have gaps, whole generations of people not listed
- may cover much longer periods—many more years and generations, even centuries—than the genealogy seems to indicate

An example of this exists in this genealogy. Luke tells us that the son of Arphaxad who was in the promised line is not listed here: Cainan. Arphaxad fathered Cainan and Cainan fathered Salah (Lu.3:36). Note the names of Arphaxad and Salah above: Luke says that Cainan is to be placed right between them, that Cainan was the son or a descendent of Arphaxad. This shows us that there is at least one other generation that belongs in this genealogy. Perhaps there are more; we actually have no way to tell.

3 (11:23) **Genealogy—Depravity—Excuse, No**: no personal information is given on any of the godly line listed in this genealogy. Why? Glance at the verses and note that the only facts given are that each person lived to a certain age and fathered a certain descendent (vv.10-26).

We know some of Shem's history, the first father in the genealogy; and we know some of the history of the last father listed, Terah. But we know nothing about any of the fathers between the first and last persons listed. As asked, Why? Why is no personal information given on these fathers of the godly line? Had all the godly line been affected by the secularism and man-made religions of their day, so affected that every single one of them had lost their testimony for God, so affected that...
- not a single person followed God?
- not a single person contributed anything for God that was significant enough to mention?
- not a single person rejected the secularism and religious idols of the day?

Apparently, this was the case. No one on earth was living a pure and godly life; no one was living totally for God. Note two facts:

a. The idol worship of Terah and his family, who were of the godly line, points toward the ungodliness and unrighteousness of the day. A terrible spiritual decline took place among the whole human race, including the godly line through whom *the promised seed* was to come.

Scripture tells us this: this period of human history and the condition of the human race during this period was the worst of times.
⇒ In Isaiah, God challenges Israel to remember these days, to remember that even Abraham, who was their father, had himself been chosen from the very *pit of sin and unrighteousness*.

"Hearken to me, ye that follow after righteousness, ye that seek the LORD: look unto the rock whence ye are hewn, and to the hole of the pit whence ye are digged. Look unto Abraham your father, and unto Sarah that bare you: for I called him [out of that pit] alone, and blessed him, and increased him" (Is.51:1-2).

⇒ Joshua challenged the people by referring to these days.

"And Joshua said unto all the people, Thus saith the LORD God of Israel, Your fathers dwelt on the other side of the flood in old time, even Terah, the father of Abraham, and the father of Nachor: and they served other gods. And I took your father Abraham from the other side of the flood" (Jos.24:2-3).

"And if it seem evil unto you to serve the LORD, choose you this day whom ye will serve; whether the gods which your fathers [Terah and his family] served that were on the other side of the flood, or the gods of the Amorites, in whose land ye dwell: but as for me and my house, we will serve the LORD" (Jos.24:15).

⇒ Paul apparently referred to these days and applied them to both his and our day:

"When they knew God, they glorified him not as God, neither were thankful; but became vain in their imaginations, and their foolish heart was darkened. Professing themselves to be wise, they became fools, and changed the glory of the uncorruptible God into an image made like to corruptible man, and to birds, and fourfooted beasts, and creeping things. Wherefore God also gave them up to uncleanness through the lusts of their own hearts, to dishonour their own bodies between themselves: who changed the truth of God into a lie, and worshipped and served the creature more than the Creator, who is blessed for ever. Amen. For this cause God gave them up unto vile affections: for even their women did change the natural use into that which is against nature: and likewise also the men, leaving the natural use of the woman, burned in their lust one toward another; men with men working that which is unseemly, and receiving in themselves that recompense of their error which was meet. And even as they did not like to retain God in their knowledge, God gave them over to a reprobate mind, to do those things which are not convenient; being filled with all unrighteousness, fornication, wickedness, covetousness, maliciousness; full of envy, murder, debate, deceit, malignity; whisperers, backbiters, haters of God, despiteful, proud, boasters, inventors of evil things, disobedient to parents, without understanding, covenantbreakers, without natural affection, implacable, unmerciful: who knowing the judgment of God, that they which commit such things are worthy of death, not only do the same, but have pleasure in them that do them" (Ro.1:21-32).

b. The human race, including the godly line, was without excuse. They all had a strong witness for decade after decade. Glance at the chart of the genealogy and note how long the descendants had the witness of Noah and Shem.
⇒ Noah lived 350 years after the flood which was about the year 2006.
⇒ Shem lived unto the year 2158.

But note this: if Noah was living during the life of so many of the godly line, why were more of them not influenced by him? Remember three facts.
1) Noah was only one man and one man can only preach and teach so much, and he can only reach out to so many people. People can, and in fact most do, reject the gospel of God.
2) Man's heart is corrupt: gripped by selfishness, greed, and the passion for pleasure, wealth, fame, and power—all to the neglect of others. Despite the desperate needs of others—their hunger and starvation, their sickness and disease, their homelessness and poverty, their suffering and dying...
   • man steals and hoards from them
   • man neglects and ignores them
   • man abuses and kills them

The behavior of man throughout history is a living testimony to this terrible and tragic truth. The heart of man is corrupt. No matter how much Noah and Shem cried for righteousness, those who lived for this world rejected their cry. And, as stated, even those of *the promised line* were apparently caught up in the secularism of the day. *The Tower of Babel* outline and notes shows the tragic godlessness of this particular period of man's history. (See notes—Ge.11:1-9 for discussion.)
3) Remember also the possibility of gaps in the genealogy. The generations from Shem to Abraham could number many more than are listed here (see note—Ge.11:12 for more discussion).

Thought 1. Note two lessons:
1) We must guard against the influence of secularism and man-made religion. Even the godly can be caught up in the attraction and approval of this world and its religion of self-righteousness and self-exaltation.

"This know also, that in the last days perilous times shall come. For men shall be lovers of their own selves, covetous, boasters, proud, blasphemers, disobedient to parents, unthankful, unholy" (2 Ti.3:1-2).

"And God looked upon the earth, and, behold, it was corrupt; for all flesh had corrupted his way upon the earth" (Ge.6:12).

"Help, LORD; for the godly man ceaseth; for the faithful fail from among the children of men" (Ps.12:1).

"The fool hath said in his heart, There is no God. They are corrupt, they have done abominable works, there is none that doeth good" (Ps.14:1).

"The good man is perished out of the earth: and there is none upright among men: they all lie in wait for blood; they hunt every man his brother with a net" (Mi.7:2).

2) God warns us both as a society and as individuals: He will give us up to our passions. He gave Shem's age up, and He warns us that He will give us up to our passions as well. We will reap what we sow.

"Wherefore God also gave them up to uncleanness through the lusts of their own hearts, to dishonor their own bodies between themselves: who changed the truth of God into a lie, and worshipped and served the creature more than the Creator, who is blessed for ever. Amen. For this cause God gave them up unto vile affections: for even their women did change the natural use into that which is against nature: and likewise also the men, leaving the natural use of the woman, burned in their lust one toward another; men with men working that which is unseemly, and receiving in themselves that recompense of their error which was meet. And even as they did not like to retain God in their knowledge, God gave them over to a reprobate mind, to do those things which are not convenient" (Ro.1:24-28).

"Be not deceived; God is not mocked: for whatsoever a man soweth, that shall he also reap. For he that soweth to his flesh shall of the flesh reap corruption; but he that soweth to the Spirit shall of the Spirit reap life everlasting" (Ga.6:7-8).

"For with what judgment ye judge, ye shall be judged: and with what measure ye mete, it shall be measured to you again" (Mt.7:2).

---

4 (11:24-26) **Genealogy—Abram—Abraham**: the genealogies of the Bible sometimes list the most important son or ancestor first, not necessarily the son born first. This is what was done with Noah's sons: Shem, Ham, and Japheth. Japheth was actually the first son of Noah, but Shem is listed first because he was the most important son, the line of *the promised seed* (see Ge.5:32, 7:13; etc.)

Another example is our present passage of Scripture. In Ge.10:26 Abraham is said to have been the first son born to Terah. But we know that he is listed first because of his importance: he was first in importance, not first in birth. The following facts tell us this:
⇒ Ge.12:4 says that Abraham left Haran when he was 75 years old.
⇒ Acts 7:4 says that when he left Haran, his father Terah was dead.

Now, if Abraham was actually the first son of Terah, he was born when Terah was 70 (as v.26 says), and he lived only until Abraham was 75; thus, he lived to be only 145 years old. But note: the present passage says that Terah lived to be 205 years old. Most likely, Abraham was born when Terah was 130 years old. This is the reason for the question mark beside Terah's oldest son and Abraham. Whether or not Abraham was born in the year of 2008, of course, depends upon how many gaps are in the genealogy (see note—Ge.11:12-22 for discussion).

The point is this: the genealogies of the Bible sometimes list the most important son first, not necessarily the first born.

		of Haran, the father of Milcah, and the father of Iscah.	
1. Fact 1: Terah had three sons	**B. The Preservation of the Promised Seed (Part 2): The Beginning of a Great Life (Abram), 11:27-32**	30 But Sarai was barren; she had no child.	**4. Fact 4: Abram's importance: He married & fathered no children but he pursued God's promise**
2. Fact 2: Haran's importance a. He fathered Lot	27 Now these are the generations of Terah: Terah begat Abram, Nahor, and Haran; and Haran begat Lot.	31 And Terah took Abram his son, and Lot the son of Haran his son's son, and Sarai his daughter in law, his	a. He was led by God to leave Ur, a land of idolatry
b. He died in the presence of his father in Ur of the Chaldees	28 And Haran died before his father Terah in the land of his nativity, in Ur of the Chaldees.	son Abram's wife; and they went forth with them from Ur of the Chaldees, to go into the land of Canaan; and they came unto Haran, and dwelt	b. He was led by God to journey to Canaan, "the promised land"
3. Fact 3: Nahor's importance: He married & fathered children but he did not pursue God's promise	29 And Abram and Nahor took them wives: the name of Abram's wife was Sarai; and the name of Nahor's wife, Milcah, the daughter	there. 32 And the days of Terah were two hundred and five years: and Terah died in Haran.	c. He had to pursue the promise alone: His father died

DIVISION VI

SHEM, NOAH'S SON: THE SON CHOSEN TO CARRY ON THE GODLY SEED, 11:10-32

B. The Preservation of the Promised Seed (Part 2): The Beginning of a Great Life (Abram), 11:27-32

(11:27-32) **Introduction**: this is a significant passage of Scripture, significant in this sense: it launches the great call and life of Abraham. This is also a transitional passage of Scripture, transitional in this sense: it launches the movement of God from dealing with the human race as a whole to dealing with one man (Abram or Abraham) and his descendants, the race of people who were to be born to him, the Jews or Israel.

Remember, the human race had corrupted itself again. Everyone, including the promised line...

- was following after the world and its secularism: its pleasures, possessions, fame, honor, and power
- was following after the man-conceived religions of the world, the idols and gods created by the ideas and imaginations of men

Even Terah, the father of Abram, had become an idol worshipper (Jos.24:2). From all that we can tell from Scripture, no one was following the true and living God.

Once again, if the godly line was to be saved—if *the promised seed* was to be sent into the world—God Himself would have to intervene and move upon the scene of world history, intervene out of pure mercy and grace. God would have to overcome His grief and hurt over man's sin and act completely on His own—have to reach down upon earth and choose a man, not because the man deserved or merited it, but because God loved man and wanted to save him (God's unmerited grace). God would have to choose a man and present to him *the promised seed* and *the promised land* (heaven), and challenge him to follow God.

This is exactly what God did. God reached down and chose Abram and offered the promises to him, if he would only follow God. This is the discussion of this great passage: *The Preservation of the Promised Seed: The Beginning of a Great Life.*

1. Fact 1: Terah had three sons (v.27).
2. Fact 2: Haran's importance (vv.27-28).
3. Fact 3: Nahor's importance: he married and fathered children but he did not pursue God's promise (v.29).
4. Fact 4: Abram's importance: he married and fathered no children but he pursued God's promise (vv.29-32).

1 (11:27) **Terah—Seed, Godly**: the first fact concerns Terah: Terah had three sons...

- Abram
- Nahor
- Haran

This passage of Scripture concerns these three sons, the importance of their lives. It also shows us the influence of a father upon his children. Remember, Terah was of *the promised line*, the line of people God had chosen to bear *the promised seed*, the Savior of the world. Of all the people upon earth, those who were in *the promised line* should have lived godly lives. They should have followed God and been dynamic testimonies before an ungodly world. In fact, this was one of the primary reasons God had chosen them: to be dynamic witnesses of the only living and true God. But many of *the promised line* failed to follow God; many walked after the ways of the world and lived carnal and secular lives, seeking after the pleasures and possessions of the earth. And many others even became idolaters, following after and worshipping the man-made gods of man's imagination. Tragically, this was true of Terah, the father of Abram, and the tragic impact of his ungodly life upon his three sons is seen in the rest of this study.

2 (11:27-28) **Haran—Lot—Ur of the Chaldees—Terah—Parents—Fathers, Influence of**: the second fact concerns Haran's importance. Two significant facts are given about Haran.

a. Haran was the father of Lot. Why mention this fact? Who was Lot? He was the nephew of Abram who moved with Abram into the land of Canaan (see Ge.11:27-32; 12:4-5). Lot believed in and trusted God. Scripture clearly says that Lot was counted *just* or *righteous* by God.

> **"And delivered just Lot, vexed with the filthy conversation of the wicked: (for that righteous man dwelling among them, in seeing and hearing, vexed his righteous soul from day to day with their unlawful deeds)" (2 Pe.2:7-8).**

However, Lot lived a selfish and carnal life.
⇒ He chose to live among the ungodly of the earth instead of living among godly believers (Ge.13:5-13).
⇒ He offered his daughters to a mob of sex-crazed men in order to save himself and some guests (Ge.19:4-11).
⇒ He was such a poor example before his two daughters that they got him drunk in order to lie with him in an attempt to bear children (Ge.10:30-38).

The point is this: Haran fathered Lot, and Lot lived a carnal and worldly life before his children, and they in turn lived a carnal and worldly life. This is the first significant fact about Haran: he fathered Lot, fathered a carnal and worldly son. But why? What was there about Haran that influenced Lot to live a worldly and carnal life? Part of the answer is found in the next point.
b. Haran died in the presence of his father, Terah, in Ur of the Chaldees. This was the original home of Terah and his family, Ur of the Chaldees. The city was located about 120-140 miles south of Babylon, right above the Persian Gulf, in the land known as southern Mesopotamia. Ur was a great city. Archeology has discovered the remains of the city, and excavations show that it was...
• a city of culture and education, with the latest mathematical tables, dictionaries, and student study books
• a city of architecture with the very finest buildings and housing
• a city of idolatry with a large temple built for the worship of the moon god "Ur"

Note that the very name of the city was taken from the *moon god, Ur.*
Now, note what Scripture says in Joshua:

> **"And Joshua said unto all the people, Thus saith the LORD God of Israel, Your fathers dwelt on the other side of the flood in old time, even Terah, the father of Abraham, and the father of Nachor: and they served other gods" (Jos.24:2; see 24:15).**

Terah, the father of Haran, worshipped idols. And note the reference to "fathers," and the plural "they."
⇒ The fathers of Terah worshipped idols.
⇒ Terah worshipped idols.
⇒ The three sons of Terah also worshipped idols.

Haran and the other two sons of Terah were born and bred in a family that had worshipped idols for several generations, born and bred in a home that worshipped false gods.

The point is this: the father's influence upon his children was enormous. One generation after another was following in the ungodly steps of the fathers who went before.
⇒ Lot lived a carnal and worldly life because his father, Haran, had lived an idolatrous life.
⇒ Haran lived an idolatrous life because his father, Terah, had. And on and on the story goes.

Note: Scripture says that Haran, who was an adult and had fathered several children, died in the presence of Terah. We might wonder how Terah felt watching his son die when he had been an idol-worshipper, how he felt knowing that he himself had led his son into false worship?

Thought 1. Three strong lessons can be drawn from the facts given about Haran.
1) A parent can have an evil influence upon his children.

> **"And [Ahaziah] he did evil in the sight of the LORD, and walked in the way of his father, and in the way of his mother" (1 K.22:52).**
> **"He [Ahaziah] also walked in the ways of the house of Ahab: for his mother was his counsellor to do wickedly" (2 Chr.22:3).**
> **"And the LORD saith, Because they [Israel, the people] have forsaken my law which I set before them, and have not obeyed my voice, neither walked therein; but have walked after the imagination of their own heart, and after Baalim, which their fathers taught them" (Je.9:13-14).**
> **"But I said unto their children in the wilderness, Walk ye not in the statutes of your fathers, neither observe their judgments, nor defile yourselves with their idols: I am the LORD your God; walk in my statutes, and keep my judgments, and do them" (Eze.20:18-19).**
> **"They have despised the law of the LORD, and have not kept his commandments, and their lies caused them to err, after the which their fathers have walked" (Am. 2:4).**
> **"And she [the daughter], being before instructed of her mother [Herodias], said, Give me here John Baptist's head in a charger" (Mt.14:8).**

2) A parent can have a good influence upon his children.

> "And if thou [Solomon] wilt walk before me, as David thy father walked, in integrity of heart, and in uprightness, to do according to all that I have commanded thee, and wilt keep my statutes and my judgments" (1 K.9:4).
> "And the LORD was with Jehoshaphat, because he walked in the first ways of his father David, and sought not unto Baalim" (2 Chr.17:3).
> "And he [Uzziah] did that which was right in the sight of the LORD, according to all that his father Amaziah did" (2 Chr.26:4).
> "When I call to remembrance the unfeigned faith that is in thee [Timothy], which dwelt first in thy grandmother Lois, and thy mother Eunice; and I am persuaded that in thee also" (2 Ti.1:5).

3) God commands all parents to set a godly example before their children.

> "And thou shalt teach them [commandments] diligently unto thy children, and shalt talk of them when thou sittest in thine house, and when thou walkest by the way, and when thou liest down, and when thou risest up" (De.6:7).
> "Train up a child in the way he should go: and when he is old, he will not depart from it" (Pr.22:6).
> "And, ye fathers, provoke not your children to wrath: but bring them up in the nurture and admonition of the Lord" (Ep.6:4).

3 (11:29) **Nahor—Promises, of God—Seed, The Promised—Unbelief**: the third fact concerns Nahor's importance. The outline point states his importance well: he married and fathered children but he did not pursue God's promise, neither *the promised seed* (the Savior) nor *the promised land* of Canaan (heaven). How do we know this?
⇒ Verse 31 tells us: Nahor did not journey with Abram and Terah to seek *the promised land* of Canaan.
⇒ Ge.31:53 tells us that Nahor worshipped and followed idols, that his god was a different god than the God of Abraham, Isaac, and Jacob.

> "The God of Abraham, and the God of Nahor, the God of their father, judge betwixt us. And Jacob sware by the fear [the God] of his father Isaac" (Ge.31:53).

⇒ Ge.31:19, 32 tells us that the whole family of Nahor worshipped idols. Genesis 31 tells the story about Jacob fleeing from Nahor's son, Laban, out of fear for his life. Unknown to Jacob, Rachel, his wife, had stolen Laban's idols. Laban was her father. But note: as pointed out, Laban was the son of Nahor. The worship of idols—false gods—had been passed on down through the generations by Nahor.

When God's call came to Abram, for him to take his family out of the idolatry of Ur and travel to *the promised land* of Canaan, Nahor refused.
⇒ He rejected Abram's witness to God as the only living and true God.
⇒ He rejected Abram's testimony about *the promised seed* and *the promised land* of Canaan.

Nahor chose to stay in Ur of the Chaldees and to seek the pleasures and possessions of the world. He chose the gods of this earth—the gods of man's imaginations—rather than the true and living God who had revealed Himself to Abram. God had called Abram and his family to repent and to begin to seek after *the promised seed* and *the promised land*. God's call to Abram will be seen in the next note, but for now the thing to see is Nahor's importance, whose importance is *negative* and stands as a lesson and warning to us all. Nahor refused to believe and to pursue God's promise, God's *promised seed* and God's *promised land*.

Thought 1. Nahor's significance is prominent in a *negative* way. He did not build his life upon the great promises of God; therefore, Nahor is not considered a great man. Nahor stands as a warning to us:
1) We must not reject God's *promised seed*, the Lord Jesus Christ.
⇒ To reject means that we will miss out on eternal salvation.

> "He came unto his own, and his own received him not. But as many as received him, to them gave he power to become the sons of God, even to them that believe on his name" (Jn.1:11-12).
> "For God so loved the world, that he gave his only begotten Son, that whosoever believeth in him should not perish, but have everlasting life. For God sent not his Son into the world to condemn the world; but that the world through him might be saved. He that believeth on him is not condemned: but he that believeth not is condemned already, because he hath not believed in the name of the only begotten Son of God" (Jn.3:16-18).

⇒ To reject means that we shall face the judgment and wrath of God.

> "He that believeth on the Son hath everlasting life: and he that believeth not the Son shall not see life; but the wrath of God abideth on him" (Jn.3:36).
> "I said therefore unto you, that ye shall die in your sins: for if ye believe not that I am he, ye shall die in your sins" (Jn.8:24).
> "And if any man hear my words, and believe not, I judge him not: for I came not to judge the world, but to save the world. He that rejecteth me, and receiveth not my words, hath one

that judgeth him: the word that I have spoken, the same shall judge him in the last day" (Jn.12:47-48).

2) We must not reject God's *promised land*. Canaan is a symbol or type and picture of *the promised land of heaven* that is promised to us all (see He.11:10, 16).

"But lay up for yourselves treasures in heaven, where neither moth nor rust doth corrupt, and where thieves do not break through nor steal" (Mt.6:20).

"Notwithstanding in this rejoice not, that the spirits are subject unto you; but rather rejoice, because your names are written in heaven" (Lu.10:20).

"In my Father's house are many mansions: if it were not so, I would have told you. I go to prepare a place for you. And if I go and prepare a place for you, I will come again, and receive you unto myself; that where I am, there ye may be also" (Jn.14:2-3).

"But he, being full of the Holy Ghost, looked up stedfastly into heaven, and saw the glory of God, and Jesus standing on the right hand of God, and said, Behold, I see the heavens opened, and the Son of man standing on the right hand of God" (Ac.7:55-56).

"For we know that if our earthly house of this tabernacle were dissolved, we have a building of God, an house not made with hands, eternal in the heavens" (2 Co.5:1).

"For our conversation [citizenship] is in heaven; from whence also we look for the Saviour, the Lord Jesus Christ: who shall change our vile body, that it may be fashioned like unto his glorious body, according to the working whereby he is able even to subdue all things unto himself" (Ph.3:20-21).

"The hope which is laid up for you in heaven, whereof ye heard before in the word of the truth of the gospel" (Col.1:5).

"For Christ is not entered into the holy places made with hands, which are the figures of the true; but into heaven itself, now to appear in the presence of God for us" (He.9:24).

"For he [Abraham] looked for a city which hath foundations, whose builder and maker is God" (He.11:10).

"But now they desire a better country, that is, an heavenly: wherefore God is not ashamed to be called their God: for he hath prepared for them a city" (He.11:16).

"Blessed be the God and Father of our Lord Jesus Christ, which according to his abundant mercy hath begotten us again unto a lively [living] hope by the resurrection of Jesus Christ from the dead, to an inheritance incorruptible, and undefiled, and that fadeth not away, reserved in heaven for you" (1 Pe.1:3-4).

"[Christ] who is gone into heaven, and is on the right hand of God; angels and authorities and powers being made subject unto him" (1 Pe.3:22).

Thought 2. Note one other significant fact about Nahor: he married his niece, the daughter of his brother, Haran. She bore Rebecca, who was to become the wife of Isaac.

[4] (11:29-32) **Abram—Promises, of God—Seed, The Promised—Land, The Promised**: the fourth fact concerns Abram's importance. His importance is in stark contrast with his brother Nahor. Remember:
⇒ Nahor married and *fathered children* but he did not pursue God's promise.
⇒ Abram married and *fathered no children* but he pursued God's promise. What promise? God's promise that He would send *the promised seed* to the earth and give *the promised land* to those who followed Him as the only living and true God.

Note verse 30: Sarah was barren; she had no children. From the very first, Abram demonstrated *great faith, enormous faith, strong faith*. He had no child, yet he believed God's promise: he believed that God would give him a son, and through that son *the promised seed* would come who would bless all the nations of the earth. Abram had no child, yet he believed God's promise of *the promised seed*, that he himself had been chosen to be *the promised line* of God's people, *the promised line* through whom the Savior of the world was to come.

How do we know that this is what Abram believed? From Scripture.
a. Note what Scripture says in Acts 7:2-3.

"And he [Stephen] said, Men, brethren, and fathers, hearken; The God of glory appeared unto our father Abraham, when he was in Mesopotamia, before he dwelt in Charran [Haran], and said unto him, Get thee out of thy country, and from thy kindred, and come into the land which I shall show thee" (Ac.7:2-3).

Stephen declared that God appeared to Abram while he was still in Ur, before he left for Haran. Abram was still in Ur of the Chaldees when God first gave him the promise of *the promised land*.
b. Note what Scripture says in Genesis 15:7.

"And he [the Lord] said unto him, I am the LORD that brought thee out of Ur of the Chaldees, to give thee this land to inherit it" (Ge.15:7).

Scripture definitely says that God called and led Abram from Ur of the Chaldees, led him to seek after *the promised land*. But this is not all: note what else God said to Abram in this passage, Genesis 15:3-7.

"And Abram said, Behold, to me thou [God] hast given no seed: and, lo, one born in my house is mine heir. And, behold, the word of the LORD came unto him, saying, This shall not be thine heir [Eliezer of Damascus]; but he that shall come forth out of thine own bowels shall be thine heir. And he brought him forth abroad, and said, Look now toward heaven, and tell the stars, if thou be able to number them: and he said unto him, So shall thy seed be. And he believed in the LORD; and he counted it to him for righteousness. And he said unto him, I am the LORD that brought thee out of Ur of the Chaldees, to give thee this land to inherit it" (Ge.15:3-7).

Scripture says that the promise of God to Abram included both *the promised seed* and *land*.
c. Note what Scripture says in Nehemiah 9:7-8.

"Thou art the LORD the God, who didst choose Abram, and broughtest him forth out of Ur of the Chaldees, and gavest him the name of Abraham; and foundest his heart faithful before thee, and madest a covenant with him to give the land of the Canaanites, the Hittites, the Amorites, and the Perizzites, and the Jebusites, and the Girgashites, to give it, I say, to his seed, and hast performed thy words; for thou art righteous" (Ne.9:7-8).

Again, the promise of God to Abram included *the promised land* and *the promised seed*.
d. Note what Scripture says in Genesis 12:1-3.

"Now the LORD had said unto Abram, Get thee out of thy country, and from thy kindred, and from thy father's house, unto a land that I will show thee: and I will make of thee a great nation, and I will bless thee, and make thy name great; and thou shalt be a blessing: and I will bless them that bless thee, and curse him that curseth thee: and in thee [in your seed] shall all families of the earth be blessed" (Ge.12:1-3).

Scripture again says that the promise of God to Abram included both *the promised land* and *the promised seed*.
e. Now, note the present passage, Genesis 11:31, where Terah is said to have taken his family to Canaan, *the promised land*. Terah is named first because he was the father, but we know from the Scriptures above that God had called Abram to leave Ur and journey to *the promised land*. Thus what was happening was that Abram was journeying to *the promised land*: and he took his father, wife, and nephew Lot with him. Undoubtedly, he encouraged his brother Nahor as well to believe God's promise and journey with him.
The point is this: Abram and the family left Ur of the Chaldees and journeyed to Canaan because God had confronted him, demanded his repentance, and given him the two great promises of God...

* *the promised land* of Canaan (heaven)
* *the promised seed*, the seed of a great nation of descendants and the seed of one descendent in particular, the Savior, the Lord Jesus Christ

These two great promises were bound to stir great assurance and security within the heart of Abram, the great assurance and security of God Himself.
Note that Abram traveled about 600 miles to Haran and for some unknown reason, remained there. While there, Terah died. We shall see in the next Scripture, Genesis 12, that after Terah's death, while still in Haran, God appeared to Abram a second time. But for now, the point to note is Abram's great faith in God's promises and his great obedience in *diligently seeking* after God and *the promised land*. Keep in mind that Abram is one of the greatest men who has ever lived. This is the beginning of his journey to greatness. Abram built his life upon the greatness of God's two great promises: the promises of *the promised land* and of *the promised seed*.

Thought 1. Every person should do exactly what Abram did: begin the journey to a great life. A great life is begun by seeking two fundamental things, the same two things that Abram sought.
1) We must seek *the promised seed*, the Lord Jesus Christ.

"Look unto me, and be ye saved, all the ends of the earth: for I am God, and there is none else" (Is.45:22).
"Seek ye the LORD while he may be found, call ye upon him while he is near" (Is.55:6).
"And ye shall seek me, and find me, when ye shall search for me with all your heart" (Je.29:13).
"For every one that asketh receiveth; and he that seeketh findeth; and to him that knocketh it shall be opened" (Lu.11:10).
"If I do not the works of my Father, believe me not" (Jn.10:37).
"That they should seek the Lord, if haply they might feel after him, and find him, though he be not far from every one of us" (Ac.17:27).
"For whosoever shall call upon the name of the Lord shall be saved" (Ro.10:13).

2) We must seek *the promised land*, heaven.

"By faith Abraham, when he was called to go out into a place which he should after receive for an inheritance, obeyed; and he went out, not knowing whither he went. By faith he sojourned in the land of promise, as in a strange country, dwelling in tabernacles with Isaac and Jacob, the heirs with him of the same promise: for he looked [sought after] a city which hath foundations, whose builder and maker is God" (He.11:8-10).

"These all died in faith, not having received the promises, but having seen them afar off, and were persuaded of them, and embraced them, and confessed that they were strangers and pilgrims on the earth. For they that say such things declare plainly that they seek a country" (He.11:13-14).

"But now they desire a better country, that is, an heavenly: wherefore God is not ashamed to be called their God: for he hath prepared for them a city" (He.11:16).

"But without faith it is impossible to please him: for he that cometh to God must believe that he is, and that he is a rewarder of them that diligently seek him" (He.11:6).

"Blessed are they that do his commandments, that they may have right to the tree of life, and may enter in through the gates into the city [heaven]" (Re.22:14).

GENESIS
OUTLINE & SUBJECT INDEX

REMEMBER: When you look up a subject and turn to the Scripture reference, you have not only the Scripture, but also an outline and a discussion (commentary) of the Scripture and subject.

This is one of the GREAT VALUES of *The Preacher's Outline & Sermon Bible®*. Once you have all the volumes, you will not only have what all other Bible indexes give you, that is, a list of all the subjects and their Scripture references, BUT in addition you will have...

- An outline of every Scripture and subject in the Bible
- A discussion (commentary) on every Scripture and subject
- Every subject supported by other Scriptures or cross references

DISCOVER THE GREAT VALUE for yourself. Quickly glance below to the subject of **ABASE**. Note that the topical outline of the subject is immediately ready for study, teaching, or preaching.

> **ABASE - ABASED**
> Caused by.
> Approaching God in the wrong way. 4:3-4; 4:4-5

Turn to the reference. Glance at the Scripture and outline of the Scripture, then read the commentary. You will immediately see the GREAT VALUE of the INDEX of *The Preacher's Outline & Sermon Bible®*.

OUTLINE & SUBJECT INDEX

ABASE - ABASED
Caused by.
Approaching God in the wrong way. 4:3-4; 4:4-5
Seeking a secular society & religion. 11:1-9, see 10:8-12
False worship. 4:3-4; 4:4-5

ABEL, ADAM'S SON
Discussed. 4:1-2
Fate of. Murdered by his brother, Cain. 4:8
Meaning of his name. 4:1-2
Second child upon the earth. 4:1-2

ABIDE - ABIDING (See **WALK, SPIRITUAL**)

ABIMAEL
Descendant of Joktan. 10:21-32

ABRAHAM - ABRAM
Call of. By God's grace & God's grace alone. 11:27-32
Faith of.
A pursuing faith, a faith that pursued God's promises. 11:29-32
What Abraham believed. 11:29-32
Family of.
Discussed. 11:27-32
Father was Terah. 11:27-32
Seed of.
Was Christ. 11:29-32
Was nations of people. 11:29-32
Testimony of.
Pursued God's promises: the promised seed & the promised land. 11:29-32
Witnessed to his family. 11:29

ABUNDANCE - ABUNDANT (See **BLESSINGS**)

ABUSE (See **PERSECUTION**)

ACCAD or AKKAD, CITY OF
Founded by Nimrod. 10:8-12

ACCEPTABLE - ACCEPTANCE
How one becomes **a**. to God.
By approaching God correctly. 3:21; 4:3-4; 4:4-5; 8:20
By true worship. 4:3-4; 4:4-5; 8:20

ACCESS
How man draws near God.
By being totally dedicated to God; by walking with God. 5:21-24; 6:9-10
By faith in the promised seed, the Savior. 6:8
By living a godly life. 6:9-10, see 6:8
By the blood of the sacrifice. 3:21; 4:3-4; 4:4-5; 8:20, DS#1

ACCOUNTABLE - ACCOUNTABILITY
Why people are accountable.
Because of false worship. 4:3-4; 4:4-5
Because of approaching God wrongly. 4:3-4; 4:4-5
Because of immorality. 6:1-2, see 6:6-7
Because of lawlessness & violence. 6:4, see 6:6-7; 6:11-12, see 6:13
Because of building a secular state & man-made religion. 11:1-9, see 10:8-12

ADAH
Meaning. 4:19

ADAM (See **MAN, Creation of**)
And men. Head of the human race. 5:1-32; 5:1-2
Covenant between God & Adam. Discussed. 2:15-17; 3:15
Creation of. 1:26-31; 2:7
Clothed in the light—the glory and righteousness—of God. 1:26; 3:7; 3:21
Discussed. 1:26-31; 2:7
Example of.
Faith. 3:20
Hope in the promised seed, the Savior of the world. 4:1-2
Fact.
Recognized the frailty & mortality of man. 4:26

Taught his family, his children, to work & to worship God. 4:1-7; 4:2; 4:3-4
Fall of.
Affected the earth, but the earth is to be restored. 2:15
Counteracted by Christ. 2:15 (Thgt. 1)
Origin - Source.
Adam's deliberate sin. 3:6
Sin & rebellion against God. 1:26 DS#2; 1:28, DS#3
Results.
Experienced evil as well as good. 3:22
Three judgments upon. 3:17-19
Genealogy of.
Chart. 5:1-32
Eight significant events. 5:1-32
History of. Discussed. 2:4-6:8
Nature of.
Created innocent, perfect. 2:16-17; 2:25
Eight significant traits seen in Adam. 2:15-17 (Note 3)
Moral & just. 2:16-17
Provision for. Life, clothing & righteousness. 3:20-21
Purpose. Threefold. 2:15-17
Test of. Discussed. 2:16-17
Vs. Christ. Chart. Contrast between Garden of Eden & Garden of Gethsemane. 2:10
Why Adam was judged. Three reasons. 3:17-19

ADULTERY - ADULTERESS (See **IMMORALITY**)
Caused by.
Cult of beauty & sex. 4:19; 6:1-2
Looking & lusting. 6:1-2
Results in.
Bigamy. 4:19
Judgment. 6:6-7; 6:13

ADVERSARY
Man vs. God. The visible struggle against God. pp.7-9
Satan vs. God. The invisible struggle against God. pp.9-10

ASTROLOGY (See **SORCERY**)
Fact. Is empty, meaningless. 1:16-18
Origin. Babylon. Discussed. 11:3-4
(Pt.4,d)

ASTRONOMY
Science of. Says the universe is billions
of years old. 1:1–2:3, DS#9

ATHEISTS - ATHEISM
Disproven by creation. 1:1 (Note 2)

ATMOSPHERE
Creation of. Discussed. 1:6-8

ATONEMENT (See **PROPITIATION;
SACRIFICIAL SYSTEM**)

ATTRACTIVE - ATTRACTIVENESS
Discussed. Cult of beauty & sex. 4:19;
6:1-2

ATTRIBUTES (See **GOD**)

AUTHORITY (See **POWER**)

AVAILABLE - AVAILABILITY
(See **ACCESS; APPROACH -
APPROACHABLE**)

AVENGE - AVENGING (See
REVENGE)

AWE (See **FEAR; REVERENCE**)

BABEL, TOWER OF
Destruction of. Stands as a memorial to
God's power. 11:9
Discussed. 11:1-9; 11:4
Picture of. 11:4

BABYLON, CITY OF
Founded by Nimrod. 10:8-12
Origin - Founding of. Discussed. 11:1-9

BACKBITERS - BACKBITING
Caused by. Sin & failure. 9:20-23

BACKSLIDING (See **APOSTASY**)
Caused by.
Disobedience. 3:1-6
Drunkenness. 9:20-23
Hostility against parents. 9:20-23
Influence of others. 3:6; 11:27-28
Influence of parents. 11:27-28; 11:29;
11:29-32
Lust of the flesh. 3:1-6; 6:1-2
Worldliness. 11:27-28
Examples.
Adam & Eve. 3:1-6
Ham. 9:20-23
Lot. 11:27-28
Noah. 9:20-23
Terah. 11:29-32

BARA
Hebrew word for create. 1:1, DS#9; 1:20

BARRIERS (See **DISCRIMINATION;
DIVISION; PREJUDICE**)

BEAUTY
Discussed. Cult of **b**. & sex. 4:19; 6:1-2

BEGAT
Meaning. 11:12-22

BEGINNING, IN THE
Meaning. 1:1 (Note 1)

BEGUILE (See **DECEIVE**)

BELIEVE - BELIEVING - BELIEFS
(See **FAITH; OBEDIENCE; TRUST**)
Duty. Must **b**. God & His Word. 5:21-
24; 6:22
Essential - Importance of **b**.
To be saved. 4:25; 4:26
To receive the promises of God. 4:25;
11:29-32
Example of great **b**.
Enoch. 5:21-24
Noah. 6:22

BELIEVER - BELIEVERS
Discussed. Sin & corruption of. Cause of.
6:1-2; 6:4; 6:5; 6:11-12
Duty.
In relation to God.
To approach God through the blood
of sacrifice. 3:21; 4:3-4; 4:4-5
To believe God & His Word.
Abraham. 11:29-32
Enoch. 5:21-24
Noah. 6:22; 7:5-9
To obey God. 6:22; 7:5-9
To pursue God's promises.
11:29-32
To walk with God. 5:21-24; 6:9-10
In relation to oneself.
Not to cover one's guilt & shame.
3:7
To control oneself. (See **SELF-
CONTROL**)
To deny oneself. (See **SELF-
DENIAL**)
To flee temptation. 3:2
To live a righteous & blameless life.
6:9-10
In relation to others.
To teach one's children to live for
God. 3:21 (Pt.4); 4:3-4; 4:4-5;
4:26; 5:6-20; 7:1
To witness to one's brother. 11:29
Names - Titles. Sons of God. 6:1-8

BENEVOLENCE (See **GIVE - GIVING;
MINISTRY; SERVICE**)

BETRAYAL (See **APOSTASY; BACK-
SLIDING; DENIAL**)

BIBLE
Archeology. Verifies the facts of the Bi-
ble. p.7
Contents. p.1
Inspiration & Authority. pp.2-7
Lives changed by. p.3
Meaning. p.1
Opposition against. p.3
Origin. pp.1-2
Prophecy of. Fulfilled. pp.6-7
Story of. pp.6-11
God & Man & Satan: The Struggle of
Redemption & Salvation. pp.10-11
God & Man: The Visible Struggle.
pp.7-9
God & Satan: The Invisible Struggle.
pp.9-10
Translations. p.2
Unbelief in. p.3
Unity of. p.4

BIGAMY - BIGAMIST
First **b**. upon earth. Lamech. 4:19

BIGOTRY (See **DISCRIMINATION;
PREJUDICE**)

BIRDS
Of Noah. Raven & dove sent out to
search for dry land. 8:6-14

BIRTH, NEW (See **BORN AGAIN; NEW
CREATION**)

BITTER - BITTERNESS
Caused by.
Anger at a person's worship & reli-
gion. 4:5, see 4:4-5
Jealousy & envy of the godly person's
assurance & confidence. 4:5, see
4:4-5
Parents' failure & sin. 9:20-23
Results.
Cursed. 9:24-27, esp.25
Judgment. 4:11-12
Mockery, ridiculing, scorning. 9:20-23
Murder. 4:8

BLAMELESS
Meaning. 6:9-10

BLAMING OTHERS
Caused by. Sin. 3:10-13

BLESS - BLESSINGS
B. of God.
Listed. 1:28 (Note 3)
Meaning. 9:1
Upon mankind. 9:1-7

BOASTING - BOASTERS
Caused by.
Glorying in man. 4:23-24
Self-sufficiency. 4:23-24

BORN AGAIN (See **NEW CREATION;
NEW LIFE; REGENERATION**)
Essential - Necessity. Reasons why one
must be born again. 1:26, DS#2
Source - How one is born again.
By believing & pursuing God's prom-
ises of salvation. 11:29-32
By God's Word & power. Revealed in
creation. Intro. 1:1–2:3, DS#3; 1:26,
DS#2
By the grace of God. (See **GRACE**)

BREATH OF GOD
Given to man. 1:27; 1:28; 2:7 (Note 2)

BRING FORTH
Meaning. 1:24

BROTHER - BROTHERHOOD (See
EQUALITY OF MAN)
Basis of.
Creation. 1:28 (Note 4)
Common ancestor. 10:1-32 (Intro.)
The image of God. 1:27
Destruction of **b**. Caused by.
Blaming others for one's own failure.
3:10-13
Denying responsibility. 4:9-10
Refusing to follow God with a brother.
11:29

BUILD - BUILDERS - BUILDING (See **CONSTRUCTION**)
Evil builders. Built a secular city & religion. 11:3-4
Great building projects. Great cities.
Accad. 10:8-12
Babylon. 10:8-12; 11:1-9
Calah. 10:8-12
Calneh. 10:8-12
Enoch. 4:17
Erech. 10:8-12
Nineveh. 10:8-12
Rehobeth. 10:8-12
Resin. 10:8-12
Wise builders. Build in obedience to God's leadership (the ark). 6:14-16

BURDEN - BURDENED (See **PRESSURE**)

BURNT OFFERING
Discussed. 8:20
Purpose of. 8:20

CAIN, ADAM'S SON
Built the first city. 4:17
Discussed. 4:1-7
First child upon the earth. 4:1-2
Meaning. 4:1-2
First murderer upon the earth. Murdered his brother, Abel. 4:8-15

CALAH, CITY OF
Founded. By Nimrod. 10:8-12

CALNEH, CITY OF
Founded. By Nimrod. 10:8-12

CANAAN
Descendants of. Discussed. 10:6-20
History of. Settled by Canaan, a son of Ham. 10:6-20, pt.6
Prophecy concerning. To be an enslaved branch of the human race. 9:24-27
Son of Ham. 9:18; 9:22; 10:6-20
Symbol of. Heaven. 1:7 (Thgt.4); 11:29; 11:29-32

CANAANITES
Origin. Listed in the Table of Nations. 10:6-20

CAPHTORIM
Descendant of Mizraim. 10:6-20

CAPITAL PUNISHMENT
Established - Instituted. When first established. 9:5

CARE - CARING
C. of God.
Revealed in creation. Intro. 1:1–2:3, DS#4
Stirs God to save man. (See **SALVATION**)
Stirs God to seek after man. 3:8; 3:9

CARNAL (See **COVETOUSNESS; FLESH - FLESHLY; LUST**)
Caused by.
Co-mingling & intermarrying with the worldly. 6:1-8
Seeking beauty & sex. 4:19; 6:1-2; 6:5
Worldliness. 11:27-28

CASLUHIM
Descendant of Mizraim. 10:6-20

CAST
An act of judgment - Who & what is to be cast out. Those who sin. 3:23-24

CAUSE (See **PURPOSE**)

CENSOR - CENSORING (See **BLAME; CRITICISM; JUDGING OTHERS**)

CEREMONY - CEREMONIAL LAW (See **RELIGION; SACRIFICIAL SYSTEM**)
Fact.
Abel had an altar for sacrifice & worship. 4:3-4; 4:4-5
Noah built an alter for worship. 8:20

CHARACTER
Of believers. (See **BELIEVER**, Duty)
Of unbelievers. (See **UNBELIEVER; Who Unbelievers Are**)

CHARGE
First c. given to man. 2:15-17

CHARITY - CHARITABLENESS (See **GIVE - GIVING; MINISTERING; SERVICE**)

CHARTS (See **TABLES**)
Of Adam. 5:1-32
Of the human race. 10:1-32, DS#3
Of the nations of antiquity. 10:1-32, DS#3
Of Noah. 10:1-32, DS#3; 11:12-22
Of Shem. 11:12-22
Of the godly seed. 5:1-32; 11:12-22
Of the ungodly seed. 4:16-24

CHASTISEMENT (See **DISCIPLINE, GODLY**)

CHEER - CHEERFULNESS (See **JOY; REJOICING**)

CHERUBIM
Discussed. 3:24

CHILDBEARING
Pain of. Is a result of woman's sin. 3:16
Results.
Brings joy. 4:1-2
Causes one to remember the weakness & mortality of man. 4:26
Stirs one to remember God. 4:25

CHILDREN - CHILDLIKENESS (See **FAMILY; PARENTS**)
Dangers - Failures. Facing c. (See **FAMILY**)
Discussed.
First children upon earth, Cain & Abel. 4:1-7
The experience of the first birth upon earth. 4:1-2
Duties toward - Treatment of. To teach c. about God. 5:6-20; 7:1; 11:27-28
Fact. Inherit the nature of their parents. 5:3
Godly example of. Noah's sons. Were the only godly c. upon earth. 7:1

CHILDREN OF GOD (See **BELIEVERS**)

CHOSEN, THE (See **ELECT, THE; PREDESTINATION**)
Who the c. are.
Abraham. 11:29-32
Noah. 6:9-10; 6:18; 9:8-17
Seth. 4:25-26
The promised seed. 3:15

CHRISTIAN - CHRISTIANS (See **BELIEVERS**)

CHRISTIAN LIBERTY (See **LIBERTY, CHRISTIAN; FREE WILL**)

CHRISTOLOGY - CHRISTOLOGICAL
Fact. Genesis has a c. or Christ-centered purpose. p.19

CHRONOLOGY
Of the New Testament. pp.15-16
Of the Old Testament. pp.13-14

CHURCH
Worship. Example for believers. Noah. 8:20

CHURCH DISCIPLINE (See **DISCIPLINE**)

CITIZENSHIP (See **GOVERNMENT**)

CITIZENSHIP, HEAVENLY (See **HEAVEN**)

CITY - CITIES
Father of c. Cain. 4:17
Founded.
Accad. 10:8-12
Babylon. 10:8-12; 11:1-9
Calah. 10:8-12
Calneh. 10:8-12
Enoch. 4:17
Erech. 10:8-12
Nineveh. 10:8-12
Rehoboth. 10:8-12
Resen. 10:8-12
Origin. Of the first secular city. 4:16; 11:1-9

CIVILIZATION (See **SOCIETY**)
Described as.
Restless. Development of restlessness within society. 4:16
Rootless. Development of rootlessness within society. 4:16
Discussed. Corruption of c. 6:1-8
Fact. Developed along two streams of people, the godly & the ungodly. 4:1-6:8; 6:1-8
Secular c. Discussed. Development of the secular society. 4:16; 6:1-8
Ungodly c.
Discussed. 4:16-24; 6:1-8
First ungodly c. 4:16-24

CLAMOR
Example of. Confusion of tongues at Babel. 11:5-8; 11:9

CLEAVE - CLEAVING
In marriage. 2:22-24

CLOSED-MINDEDNESS (See **HARD - HARDNESS OF HEART; STUBBORN**)

CLOTHE - CLOTHING, SPIRITUAL
Duty. To **c.** oneself, to put on righteousness. 3:21

CLOTHING (See **DRESS - DRESSING**)
Discussed. Cult of beauty & sex. 4:19
Fact. Many dress to attract attention. 6:1-2

CLOUD
Fact. Prehistoric earth was covered with a heavy mist of thick clouds & fog. 2:6, see 1:9-10

CO-EXISTENCE (See **TRINITY**)

COME
The great **c.** invitations of God's Word. 7:1

COMFORT - COMFORTED (See **PEACE; REST, SPIRITUAL**)
Spiritual **c.** Hope for. By early man. 5:27-32 (Note 8)

COMFORTER, THE (See **HOLY SPIRIT**)

COMMANDMENT - COMMANDMENTS
Duty.
Not to eat the forbidden fruit. 2:16-17; see 3:11
To "come—enter into the ark" of God's safety. 7:1; see 7:13-16
To establish government to protect the rights of people. 9:5
To protect the life of man. 9:5-7
First **c.** given to man: not to eat the forbidden fruit. 2:16-17
Subjects of the **c.**
Foods to eat. 9:3-4
Government, establishment of. 9:5
Murder. 9:5-7
Protection of life. 9:5-7
World order. 9:1-7

COMMISSION (See **WITNESSING**)
Great **c.**
Symbol - Type - Picture of.
Abraham & the **c.** given him. 11:29-32
Noah & the **c.** given him. 6:19-21

COMMIT - COMMITMENT (See **DEDICATION; OBEDIENCE**)
Call to **c.**
To prepare to escape the coming judgment. 6:13-22
To pursue God's promises. 11:29-32
Kinds of.
Carnal **c.** 9:20-23; 11:23
Total **c.** Enoch. 5:21-24

COMMUNE - COMMUNION (See **DEVOTION; FELLOWSHIP; PRAYER**)
Example of. Enoch. Strong, intimate **c.** with God. 5:21-24

COMPASSION (See **MERCY**)

COMPLACENT - COMPLACENCY
Caused by.
Failing to keep a watchful eye against temptation. 3:1; 9:20-23
Listening to temptation instead of fleeing & rebuking the tempter. 3:6

Neglect of daily devotions, prayer, & worship. 9:20-23
Not controlling one's thoughts. 3:1 (Note 2)
Results.
Drunkenness. 9:20-23
Listening to temptation & giving in. 3:17-19, see 3:6
Misleading others. 3:6; 9:20-23; 11:27; 11:27-28; 11:29
Worldliness. 11:27; 11:27-28; 11:29

COMPLAIN - COMPLAINING
Against God.
Because of judgment. 4:13-14
Caused by.
Guilt & blaming others. 3:10-13
Setting a bad example. 9:20-23
Characteristic - Trait. Of guilty persons. 3:10-13; 4:13-14; 9:20-23

COMPROMISE
Results.
Bigamy. 4:19; 6:1-2
Destruction. 6:11-12; 6:13
Evil imaginations & thoughts. 6:5
Guilt & shame. 3:7
Immorality, lawlessness, & violence. 6:1-2; 6:11-12
Leads others astray. 3:6
Sin - Temptation of.
Co-mingling with the ungodly. 6:1-2
Eve led Adam to sin. 3:6
Follows the cult of beauty & sex. 4:19; 6:1-2

CONCEAL - CONCEALMENT
Of sin. Discussed. 3:8; 4:9-10

CONCEIT - CONCEITED (See **PRIDE**)

CONCERN - CONCERNED (See **CARE - CARING; MERCY**)

CONDEMN - CONDEMNATION (See **JUDGMENT**)

CONFESS - CONFESSING - CONFESSION (See **PROFESSION, SPIRITUAL; SALVATION; WORSHIP**)

CONFORM - CONFORMED - CONFORMITY (See **COMPROMISE; WORLDLINESS**)

CONSCIENCE
Duty. To heed the convictions of **c.** & of God's Spirit. 6:3
Function - Purpose - Work.
To arouse man to make great sacrifices to God. 8:20 (Note 3, pt.2)
To convict man of sin. 6:3
To open one's eyes to sin. 3:7

CONSECRATION (See **COMMITMENT; DEDICATION**)

CONSISTENCY (See **COMMITMENT; DEDICATION**)

CONSOLATION (See **COMFORT; PEACE**)

CONSTANCY (See **ENDURANCE; PERSEVERANCE; STEDFASTNESS**)

CONSTRUCTION (See **BUILDING**)
Father of **c.** Cain. 4:17

CONTEMPT (See **BITTER - BITTERNESS; DESPISE**)

CONTENT - CONTENTMENT (See **JOY; PEACE**)

CONTENTION - CONTENTIOUS (See **ARGUE; BLAME; CRITICISM; DIVISION**)
Caused by.
False worship. 4:3-4; 4:4-5; 4:8
Seeking revenge & boasting. 4:23-24
Sin & blaming others. 3:10-13

CONTINENTS
Creation of. Discussed. 1:9-10

CONTRARY (See **ARGUE; CRITICISM; DIVISION**)

CONTROVERSY (See **ARGUE; CONTENTION; CRITICISM; DIVISION**)

CONVERSION - CONVERTED (See **RENEW - RENEWAL; REPENTANCE**)
How a person is **c.**
By God's grace, pure grace (Abraham). 11:27-32
By putting on the righteousness of God. 3:21
By responding to God's call. 3:8; 3:9
By thinking upon a child's birth (Enoch). 5:21-24
By turning to God & following the promises of God. 11:29-32

CONVICT - CONVICTION (See **CONSCIENCE; REPENTANCE**)
Essential. Must be **c.** of sin. 3:9
Fact. God's Spirit will not always strive, convict man. 6:3
Source of.
God's love & call. 3:9
God's mercy. 4:15
God's questioning. 4:9-10
God's warning. 4:6-7

COOPERATION (See **BROTHERHOOD; UNITY**)

CORRUPT - CORRUPTION
Caused by. Man & his wickedness. 6:1-8; 6:11-12
Everything has the seed of **c.** within it. 1:1 (Note 1. Thgt.3)

COUNSEL, GOD'S (See **PURPOSE**, Of God)
Fact.
God discussed the creation of man within the Godhead. 1:26 (Note 1)
God discussed the fall of man within the Godhead. 3:22, DS#1

COUNTERFEIT (See **HYPOCRISY; PROFESSION, FALSE**)

COURAGE
Example. Noah. 8:1-14; 8:15-22; 8:18-19; 9:1-7; 9:8-17

DECEIT - DECEIVE - DECEPTION
(See **LIE**)
Who & what **d.**
Angry persons. 4:8
Satan. 3:6

DECISION
Duty - essential.
Must be converted when God calls.
11:29-32
Must obey God when He calls. 6:22
Must turn to God when He seeks &
calls. 3:9
Rejected.
By Cain. 4:6-7; 4:15
By Nahor. 11:29

DEDAN
Descendant of Cush. 10:6-20

DEDICATE - DEDICATION (See
COMMITMENT)
Total **d.** Enoch. 5:21-24

DEFILE - DEFILEMENT (See **IMMO-
RALITY; SIN**)
Cause of **d.**
Cult of beauty & sex. 4:19; 6:1-2
Immorality, lawlessness, & violence.
6:1-8, esp. 6:7; 6:11-12; 6:13

DEGRADATION, SPIRITUAL (See **SIN**)

DELIVER - DELIVERANCE (See **SAL-
VATION**)
Fact. Is a set time for deliverance. 8:1-5
From what.
Saved from living forever as a sinner.
Adam. 3:22-24
Trials, all trials. 8:1-5; 8:15-17
How a person can be delivered.
By God. Delivered Noah. 8:1-14;
8:15-22
By the seeking Savior. 3:9

DELUGE (See **FLOOD, THE GREAT**)

DEMONS (See **SATAN**)

DENIAL, SELF (See **SELF-DENIAL**)

DENY - DENIAL (See **APOSTASY;
BACKSLIDING; UNBELIEF**)

DENYING SELF (See **SELF-DENIAL**)

DEPRAVED - DEPRAVITY
Caused by.
Man giving himself over to anger.
4:6-7; 4:8
Man giving himself over to the flesh.
6:1-2; 6:5
Discussed.
Early man. Corrupted himself. 6:1-2;
6:5; 11:24-25
Early society. 6:1-2; 6:5; 11:10-31
Eight periods of history when man ut-
terly fails & God has to step in &
save man. 11:10-26
Five things involved in **d.** 5:3
The heart. 6:5
View of. Jesus Christ. 6:5

DESERTION (See **APOSTASY; BACK-
SLIDING; UNBELIEF**)

DESIRE (See **LUST**)
Bad & evil **d.**
For illicit sex. 6:1-2
For the forbidden pleasure. 3:1-6
To approach God in one's own way.
4:3-4
To think immoral thoughts. 6:5

DESPAIR (See **DISAPPOINTMENT;
HOPELESSNESS**)

DESPISE - DESPISING - DESPITE (See
BITTER; CONTEMPT)
Caused by. Sin & disapproval by God.
4:3-4; 4:5
Results.
Dishonoring parents. 9:20-23
Murder. 4:8

DESPONDENCY (See **DISAPPOINT-
MENT; HOPELESSNESS**)

DESTINY (See **DEATH; ETERNAL
LIFE; JUDGMENT; WARNING**)

**DESTITUTE - DESTITUTION,
SPIRITUAL** (See **SIN**)

DESTROY - DESTRUCTION (See
JUDGMENT)
Who is **d.**
The immoral, lawless, & violent.
6:1-8, esp. 6:7; 6:11-12; 6:13
Those with evil imaginations &
thoughts. 6:5; 6:6-7

DETEST - DETESTABLE (See **BIT-
TERNESS - HATRED**)

DEVIL (See **SATAN**)

DEVOTION - DEVOTIONS (See
COMMITMENT; MEDITATE)
Example of. Enoch. Total **d.** 5:21-24
Kinds of. Total **d.** 5:21-24; 6:22

DICTATOR
First **d.** Nimrod. 10:8-12

DIETARY LAWS (See **COMMAND-
MENTS**)

DIFFICULTIES (See **PROBLEMS;
TRIALS; TEMPTATIONS**)

DIKLAH
Descendant of Joktan. 10:21-32

DILIGENCE - DILIGENTLY (See
**ENDURANCE; PERSEVERANCE;
STEDFASTNESS**)
Duty.
To be **d.** in following God. 5:21-24
To be **d.** in obeying God's command-
ments. 6:22; 7:5-9, esp. 9
To be **d.** in pursuing God's promises.
11:29-32
To be **d.** in worshipping & sacrificing
to God. 8:20; 9:1-7

DISAPPOINTMENT (See **SIN**, Results)
Caused by.
A secular society. 11:1-9
A secular, man-made religion. 11:1-9
Children dishonoring their parents.
4:8; 9:20-23; 9:24-27

False worship. 4:3-4; 4:4-5
Sins of children. 4:8; 9:20-23; 9:24-27
Sins of parents. 9:20-23; 11:27-28

DISCIPLINE, GODLY (See
JUDGMENT)
Why God **d.**
Because of drunkenness. 9:18-29
Because of false worship. 4:1-7
Because of immorality, lawlessness, &
violence. 6:1-8
Because of secularism & false, worldly
religion. 11:1-9
Because of sin. 3:1-6

DISCIPLINE, PHYSICAL (See
COMMITMENT; DEDICATION)

DISCORD (See **ARGUMENT;
CONTENTION; DIVISION; STRIFE**)

DISCOURAGEMENT (See **SIN**, Results;
HOPELESSNESS; SORROW)

DISCRIMINATION (See **PREJUDICE**)
Duty.
To be no **d.** against other races. 1:28
(Note 4); 9:18-19; 10:1-32 (Pt.6);
10:1
To be no **d.** against women. 1:27;
2:18-25

DISHONOR (See **SHAME**)
Of family. Example. Cain **d.** his family.
4:16, see 4:1-7; 4:8-15
Of parents. Example. Ham **d.** his father,
Noah. 9:20-23

DISOBEDIENCE (See **BACKSLIDING;
SIN**)
Caused by.
Following a bad example. 9:20-23;
9:24-27; 11:27-28; 11:29; 11:29-32
Influence of others. 3:6
Neglecting devotions & worship.
9:20-23
Temptation. 3:1-6
Consequence of. Five consequences. 3:7-
13
Example of.
Adam & Eve. 3:1-6
Noah. 9:20-23
Judgment of. Upon man & woman. 3:16;
3:17-19

DISSATISFACTION (See **SIN**, Results;
HOPELESSNESS; SORROW)
Caused by.
Cult of beauty & sex. 4:19; 6:1-2
False worship. 4:3-4
Lust for power & fame. 10:10-12;
11:1-9

DISTRUST (See **UNBELIEF**)

**DIVINE JUDGMENT THEORY OF
CREATION**
Discussed. 1:2 (Note 4)

DIVISION - DISSENSION (See **ARGU-
MENTS; DISCRIMINATION**)
Caused by.
Choosing the world over God. 11:29;
see 11:29-32
Drunkenness. 9:20-23
Sin. 3:10-13

Results.
Blaming others. 3:10-13
Hostility & mockery. 9:20-23

DOCTRINE
Fact.
Genesis has a **d**. purpose. p.19
Genesis pictures & illustrates most of the N.T. **d**. p.21

DOCTRINE, FALSE (See **TEACHING, FALSE**)

DODANIM
Descendant of Javan. 10:2-5

DOMINION
Meaning. 1:28; 9:2

DOUBLE-MINDED (See **HALF-HEARTED; INCONSISTENCY; INDECISION**)

DOUBT - DOUBTING (See **UNBELIEF**)
What is questioned & **d**.
God's existence. Six beliefs of man refuted. 1:1 (Note 2)
Word of God & judgment. 3:3

DOVE
Bird sent out by Noah to search for dry land. 8:6-14

DRESS - DRESSING (See **CLOTHING**)
Discussed. Cult of beauty & sex. 4:19
Fact. Many dress to attract attention. 6:1-2

DRINK - DRINKING (See **DRUNKEN-NESS**)
Symbol of. **D**. Christ, the living water. 1:9 (Thgt.3); 1:10 (Thgt.4)

DRUGS (See **DRUNKENNESS**)

DRUNKENNESS (See **DRUGS**)
Discussed. 9:21
Example of. Noah. 9:20-23

DULL - DULLNESS, SPIRITUAL (See **COMPLACENCY; HARD - HARD-NESS**)
Caused by.
Bad parental influence. 9:20-23; 9:24-27; 11:27-28; 11:29; 11:29-32
Drunkenness. 9:20-23
False worship. 4:1-7
Listening to the tempter's voice. 3:1-6
Sin & anger. 4:1-7

DUTY (See The Subject Desired, Duty of)

DYING TO SELF (See **SELF-DENIAL**)

EARTH (See **UNIVERSE**)
Age of. Seven days of creation. Intro. 1:1-2:3, DS#9
Creation of. (See **CREATION**)
Two theories. The Unshaped or Undeveloped **E**. & the Gap Theory. 1:2 (Note 9)
Destruction of. First destruction.
By the Great Flood. 7:10-24
Experience of, by Noah. 8:1-14
Utterly devastated. 8:18-19
Discussed.
A new world order established. 9:1-7

Regulation of day & night, seasons & years. 1:14-19
Duty toward.
To serve God by looking after the earth. 2:15
To subdue & have dominion over. 1:28; 9:2
Facts.
Corrupted & filled with violence by man. 6:1-2; 6:4; 6:5; 6:11-12; 6:13
Size of **e**., solar system, & heavenly bodies. 1:1 (Note 3)
Was destroyed by a flood of waters. 6:17; 7:10-24
Prehistoric - Primeval **e**.
First picture of. 2:4-6
How the **e**. became imperfect. By Adam's sin. 3:17
Judgment of.
Cursed because of Adam's sin. 3:17
Destroyed because of lawlessness & immorality. 6:1-6; 6:11-12; 6:13-22
Minute world of. 1:1 (Note 3)
Nations & countries of. Birth & growth of. 10:1-32
Origin of sin & evil within the **e**.
Adam & Eve's sin. 3:1-6; 3:17
Satan's fall. 1:2, DS#4
Population of. During Adam's life. One million plus. 4:17
Prehistoric Primeval earth. Described. 1:2; 1:3-5; 1:6-8; 1:9-10; 1:11-13; 1:14-19; 1:20-23; 1:24-25; 1:26-31; 2:4-6
Present state of the **e**. Affected by the fall of man & sin. 1:29-30; 3:17; 9:2
The new **e**. Will be recreated into a perfect **e**. Intro. 1:1-2:3, DS#5; 1:2 (Note 4, Thgt.2); 3:17

EAT - EATING (See **FOOD**)

EBER
Descendant of Shem & Salah. 10:21-32
Name of. Means "Hebrew." 10:21-32

EDEN, GARDEN OF (See **UTOPIA; PARADISE, EARTHLY**)
Discussed. 2:8-14
Fact.
Man was driven out of Eden. 3:23-24
Met man's three basic needs. 2:9
Was a real historical place. Significance of. 2:8
False views of. Two false views. 2:8
Vs. the Garden of Gethsemane. 2:10

EFFEMINATE (See **HOMOSEXUALITY**)

EGYPT
Symbol of. World & worldliness. 1:7 (Thgt.4)

ELAM
Descendant of Shem. 10:21-32

ELDERLY
Example of failing, sinning in old age. Noah. 9:20-23

ELECT - ELECTION (See **CHOSEN; PREDESTINATION**)

ELISHAH
Descendant of. Japheth & Javan. 10:2-5

ELOHIM
Name - Title of God. Meaning. 1:1, DS#2

EMBARRASS - EMBARRASSMENT (See **DISHONOR; GUILT; SHAME**)
Duty. Not to **e**. one's parents. 9:20-23

EMOTIONS (See **INSECURITY**)
In facing the terrible judgment of God. Noah. 8:1-14; 8:15-22; 8:18-19; 9:1-7; 9:8-17

EMPIRE
First **e**. Founded by Nimrod. 10:8-12

EMPLOYMENT (See **LABOR; SERVICE; WORK**)
Duty. To subdue & control the earth. 1:28; 2:15; 9:2
Of early man. 4:16-24
Farmer. 4:2
Herdsman. 4:2
Manufacturers & craftsmen. 4:20-22
Metal workers. 4:20-22
Musicians & inventors. 4:20-22
Ranchers & tentmakers. 4:20-22

ENCOURAGE - ENCOURAGEMENT
How God **e**.
By delivering through terrible trials. 8:15-17
By giving a child to a childless couple. 4:25
By His blessings. (See **BLESSINGS**)
By His care. (See **CARE**, Of God)
By His grace. (See **GRACE**)
By His great covenants with man. (See **COVENANTS**)
By seeking the sinner. 3:8
By the clothing of righteousness. 3:21
By the promise of salvation. 6:18; 9:11
By the promised land (heaven). 11:29-32
By the promised seed (Jesus Christ). 3:15; 11:29-32

ENDURE - ENDURANCE (See **FAITHFULNESS; PERSEVERANCE**)
Duty.
To **e**. in following after God. 5:21-24; 7:1-9
To **e**. in following after the promised seed (Christ) & the promised land (heaven). 11:29-32
To **e**. in pursuing God's promises despite the impossible. 11:29-32
To **e**. in witnessing for God despite trials. 7:5-9
Example of. Noah. 7:5-9; 8:1-14; 8:15-22; 9:1-7

ENEMIES
Caused by.
A spirit of revenge. 4:23-24
False worship & anger. 4:1-7, see 4:8

ENOCH, CITY OF
Founded by Cain. Named after his son. 4:17

ENOCH, GODLY
Discussed. 5:21-24
Fact. Was translated without ever dying. 5:21-24

ENOCH, SON OF CAIN
Birth of. 4:17

ENOSH, SON OF SETH
Continued the godly seed upon earth.
4:25-26
Meaning of name. 4:26

ENSLAVEMENT, SPIRITUAL
By what.
Cult of beauty & sex. 4:19; 6:1-2
False worship & religion. 4:3-4;
11:1-9
Idolatry. 11:23; 11:29-32
Immorality, lawlessness, & violence.
6:1-8; 6:13
Lust for power. 10:10-12
Secularism. 10:10-12; 11:1-9
Worldliness & carnality. 6:1-2; 11:27;
11:27-28; 11:29-32

ENTICE - ENTICEMENT
What it is that e.
Cult of beauty & sex. 4:19; 6:1-2
Forbidden fruit. 3:1-6

ENTROPY
Law of Thermodynamics. Evidence against
evolution. Intro. 1:1–2:3, DS#9

ENVIRONMENT
Duty toward e. Must protect. 1:12-13
Present state. Affected by the fall of man
& sin. 1:29-30; 3:17; 9:2

ENVY
Evil of. Leads to murder. 4:1-7, see 4:8

EQUALITY OF MAN (See **BROTHER-HOOD**)
Basis of.
Common ancestor. 10:1-32 (Intro.)
Creation. 1:28 (Note 4)
Image of God. 1:27

ERECH, CITY OF
Founded by Nimrod. 10:8-12

ESCAPE
Fact. Cannot e. from God's presence.
1:8 (Thgt.1)

ESTEEM (See **HONOR, Of Self;
GLORYING IN SELF; PRIDE;
SELF-ESTEEM**)

ETERNAL LIFE
Fact. God created man to live forever.
2:16-17 (Note 3)
Results. Assurance. 9:11
Source - How to secure.
By dedicating one's life totally to
God. 5:21-24
By the grace of God. 6:8
By the Tree of Life. 2:9 (Note 4)
Through the promised seed.
3:15; 3:23-24; 6:18; 9:11;
11:29-32

ETHIOPIA
Founded by. Descendants of Ham &
Cush. 10:6-20
Mentioned in relation to the Garden of
Eden. 2:10-14

EUPHRATES RIVER
Mentioned in relation to the Garden of
Eden. 2:10-14

EUROPE - EUROPEANS
Origin of. 10:2-5

EVE, THE FIRST WOMAN (See
WOMAN, Creation of)
Creation of. Discussed. 1:26-31; 1:27;
2:18-25
Judgment upon. Threefold judgment.
3:16
Name. Meaning. 3:20
Provision for. Life, clothing, & right-
eousness. 3:20-21
Sin of. Was deceived. 3:6
Temptation of. Discussed. 3:1-6

EVIL (See **SIN**)
Origin - Source.
Adam. 3:22
How e. began within the universe &
upon earth. 3:1
Man's sin & rebellion against God.
3:1-6; 3:6
Satan's fall. 1:2, DS#4

EVIL ASSOCIATIONS (See **SEPARA-TION**)
Results.
Leads others to sin. 3:6
Sin grows. 6:1-2

EVIL DESIRE (See **DESIRE**, Bad & Evil;
Lust)

EVIL SPEAKING (See **TONGUE**)

EVIL SPIRITS (See **SATAN**)

EVIL WORKS - EVIL DEEDS (See **SINS**)

EVOLUTION
Discussed. Intro. 1:1–2:3, DS#9; 1:25

EXALT - EXALTATION
Results.
Immorality. 4:19
Murder. 4:23-24
Selfish & evil e. Comes from - caused by.
Boasting. 4:23-24
Lust for power. 10:10-12; 11:1-9

EXAMINE - EXAMINATION (See
TEST - TESTING)
Fact. God tests man. 2:16-17

EXAMPLE (See **TESTIMONY**)

EXCUSE, NO
Fact.
Early man was without e. for not living
a godly life. 11:23
The godly seed was without e. for not
living godly lives. 11:23
Man is without e. 1:1 (Note 3, pt.4, Thgt.1)

EXCUSES
E. for not confessing sin. 3:10-13

EXPOSURE - EXPOSED
Of sin & sinners.
God sees & knows. 4:9-10
God sees all sin, even man's thoughts
& imaginations. 6:5
One cannot hide from God. 3:8

EYE
Sins of.
Looking & lusting. 3:6
Looking at nakedness. 9:20-23

FAITH
Duty.
To believe God & His Word. 5:21-24;
6:22; 11:29-32
To believe God's way of salvation
(Noah). 6:22
To believe in salvation by the blood of
the sacrifice. 3:21
To believe in *the promised land.* 11:29-32
To believe in the promised seed & the
promised land (Abraham). 11:29-32
To believe in *the promised seed.* 3:15;
5:21-24; 6:18; 11:29-32
Example of.
Abraham. What Abraham believed.
11:29-32
Adam.
Believed in salvation by the blood
of the sacrifice. 3:20
Believed in the promised seed. 3:15
Noah.
Great **f.** & patience before God.
8:6-14
The unbelievable things he had to
believe. 6:13-22
Forsaking - Departing from. (See
APOSTASY; BACKSLIDING)

FAITHFUL - FAITHFULNESS
Duty.
To be **f.** in obeying God's command-
ments. 6:22; 7:5-9, esp. 9
To be **f.** in pursuing God's promises.
11:29-32
To be **f.** in teaching children. (See
**CHILDREN; FAMILY; TEACH-
ING**)
To be **f.** in walking with God. 5:21-24
To be **f.** in worshipping & sacrificing
to God. 8:20; 9:1-7
Of God.
In delivering Noah through judgment.
8:1-14; 8:15-17
To His promise to send the godly seed.
5:3-4

FAITHLESSNESS (See **DOUBT;
UNBELIEF; UNFAITHFULNESS**)
Sin of.
Not believing God enough to forsake
the world. 11:29
Not believing God's way of salvation.
4:3-4; 4:4-5

FALL OF MAN (See **MAN**, Fall of)

FALLING AWAY - FALL, SPIRITUAL
(See **APOSTASY; BACKSLIDING**)

FALSEHOOD (See **DECEPTION;
HYPOCRISY**)

FAME - FAMOUS
Discussed.
The first craftsman & metal worker.
4:20-22
The first musician & inventor of musi-
cal instruments. 4:20-22
The first rancher & tent-maker. 4:20-22
Sins involving. Seeking to make a name
for oneself. 11:3-4

GENTILES
Birth of Gentile nations. 10:1-32
Prophecy about.
    To be the largest nations. 9:24-27
    To share in the promised seed. 9:24-27

GENTLE - GENTLENESS
Of man toward animals. 8:6-14 (pt.3)

GEOLOGY
Ages of. Discussed. Were the seven days of creation literal or geological ages? Intro. 1:1–2:3, DS#9
Geological change within the earth. Caused by. The great flood. Intro. 1:1–2:3, DS#9; 7:10-12; 7:24
Science of. Says the universe is billions of years old. Intro. 1:1–2:3, DS#9

GETHER
Descendant of Shem & Aram. 10:21-32

GETHSEMANE
Vs. the Garden of Eden. 2:10

GIANTS
Meaning. 6:4

GIHON RIVER
Mentioned in relation to the Garden of Eden. 2:10-14

GIRGASITE
Descendant of. Canaan. 10:6-20

GIVE - GIVING (See **SELF-DENIAL**)
Duty. To sacrifice to the ultimate. 8:20

GLORY
Fact. First man, Adam, was clothed with the glory of God. 1:26, DS#2; 3:7; 3:21

GLORY OF GOD
Fact. Man is short of God's **g**. 3:7
Nature. Includes at least five qualities. 1:26, DS#2

GLORY OF MAN
Fact.
    Is short of God's glory. 3:7; 3:21
    Was clothed in the glory of God initially. 1:26, DS#2; 3:7; 3:21
    Was lost due to sin. 3:7; 3:21

GLORYING IN MAN (See **BOASTING; PRIDE; SELF-SUFFICIENCY**)
Caused by.
    Achievements. 4:17
    Cult of beauty & sex. 4:19; 6:1-2
    Defeating enemies. 4:23-24
    Feeling strong & self-sufficient. 4:23-24; 6:4
    Possessing weapons. 4:23-24
Results.
    A secular society & man-made religion. 11:3-4
    Dictatorship. 10:8-12
    False worship. 4:3-4; 4:4-5
    Murder. 4:23-24; 4:8
    Seeking to make a name for oneself. 4:17; 11:3-4

GOD
Care for man. (See **CARE - CARING**)
Creator. (See **CREATION**)
Deliverance of. (See **DELIVERANCE**) 8:1-14
Described. (See **GOD**, Names - Titles)
    As the seeking Savior. 3:9
Existence of.
    Revealed in creation. Intro. 1:1–2:3, DS#1-9, esp. 2)
    Was in the beginning. 1:1 (Note 1)
Faithfulness of. (See **FAITHFULNESS, Of God**) 8:1-14; 8:15-17
Foreordination of. (See **FOREORDI-NATION**)
Goodness of. (See **GOODNESS, Of God**)
Holy - Holiness of. (See **HOLY - HO-LINESS, Of God**)
Knowledge of. Is omniscient.
    Knows a man's thoughts & imaginations. 6:5
    Revealed in creation. Intro. 1:1–2:3, DS#4
    Sees & knows all. No sin can be hid. 3:8; 3:9; 4:9-10
Love of.
    Is the seeking Savior. 3:9
    Revealed in creation. Intro. 1:1–2:3, DS#1
Mercy of. (See **MERCY, Of God**)
Misconceptions of.
    Seems distant, removed, far away. Noah's experience. 8:15-17
    Six misconceptions. Refuted. 1:1 (Note 2)
Names - Titles.
    Almighty God (Elohim). 1:1, DS#2
    Elohim, Almighty God, the Strong & Mighty One. 1:1
    In Genesis. p.21
    LORD God (Jehovah or Yahweh Elohim) 2:4
    Seeking Savior. 3:9
Nature - Attributes - What God is like.
    Almighty God. 1:1, DS#2
    Discussed. A chart on what creation reveals about God. Intro. 1:1–2:3, DS#7
    Is a God of form, fullness, completeness, fulfillment, satisfaction. Intro. 1:1–2:3, DS#8
    Is good. Revealed in creation. Intro. 1:1–2:3, DS#5
    Is gracious. Revealed in creation. Intro. 1:1–2:3, DS#5
    Is intelligent. Revealed in creation. Intro. 1:1–2:3, DS#4
    Is light. 1:3 (Thgt.2).
    Is love. Revealed in creation. Intro. 1:1–2:3, DS#1,5,6
    Is orderly. Revealed in creation. Intro. 1:1–2:3, DS#5,6
    Is personal & revealing. 2:4
    Is redeeming. 2:4
    Is self-existent & eternal. 1:1
    Is self-sufficient. 1:1
    Is the Triune God (See **TRINITY**)
Power of.
    Can control nature. 8:1-5; 7:10-24
    Is omnipotent. Revealed in creation. Intro. 1:1–2:3, DS#3
    Is the Almighty God. 1:1, DS#2
Predestination of. (See **FOREORDINA-TION; PREDESTINATION**)

Sins against. (See **SINS**)
Trinity. (See **TRINITY, THE**)
Who struggles & fights against.
    Man: the visible struggle against God. pp.7-9
    Satan: the invisible struggle against God. pp.9-10

GODLESS - GODLESSNESS (See **UNGODLY**)

GODLY - GODLINESS (See **HOLINESS**)

GODS, FALSE (See **IDOLS - IDOLATRY**)
Fact.
    Is only the creation of man. 11:3-4
    Is only the notion, idea, & imagination of man. 4:4-5; 11:3-4

GOMER
Descendant of. Japheth. 10:2-5
Descendants. Discussed. 10:2-5

GOOD - GOODNESS
Of God.
    Caused God to create man. Intro. 1:1–2:3, DS#5,6,7; 2:15
    Questioning & doubting. Root of temptation & sin. 3:2; 3:3
    Revealed in creation. Intro. 1:1–2:3, DS#5

GOOD WORKS (See **MINISTERING; SERVICE; WORKS, GOOD**)

GOVERNMENT
Establishment of. Institution of. When first established. 9:5
Secular. First secular government. 11:3-4, see 4:17
Source of. God. 9:5

GRACE
Danger - Sin against.
    Hiding from God's seeking **g**. 3:9; 3:10-13
    Refusing to heed God's **g**. & warning. 3:6-7; 6:3; 6:6-7
Of God.
    Caused God to create man. Intro. 1:1–2:3, DS#5,6,7; 2:15
    First use of the word "grace" in Scripture: refers to Noah. 6:8; 6:9-10
    Fulfilled His promises & saved man by His **g**. alone. 4:25
    Kept the godly line & promised seed alive despite man's sin. 4:25; 5:3-4; 6:8; 6:18; 9:11; 11:10-31; 11:27-32
    Questioning & doubting. Root of temptation & sin. 3:3; 3:4
    Revealed in creation. Intro. 1:1–2:3, DS#5
    Seeks man despite man's sin & hiding. 3:6-7; 3:9; 3:10-13
    Warns & delays judgment. 4:15; 6:3; 6:6-7
    Wills to shower His **g**. & goodness upon man. Intro. 1:1–2:3, DS#6,7; 2:15

GRATITUDE (See **THANKFUL**)
Example. Noah: Great **g**. for deliverance from judgment. 8:20

GREAT - GREATNESS (See POWER)
Seeking worldly **g**.
By boasting in one's strength & power. 4:23-24
By building projects. 4:17; 10:8-12; 11:3-4
By building an empire. 11:3-4
By enslaving & ruling over people. 10:8-12
By founding a religion or religious movement. 11:3-4
By self-honor. 4:17

GREAT COMMISSION (See COMMISSION)

GREED (See COVET; LUST)

GRIEF (See DISAPPOINTMENT; HEAVINESS; SORROW)
Of God.
Caused by.
Disobedience & man fleeing from God. 3:10-13
Sin: immorality, lawlessness, violence. 6:3; 6:6-7
Over man hiding from God. 3:8; 3:9
Over man. Man grieved God's Spirit. 6:3
Over man's constant failure (eight terrible periods of failure). 11:10-31
Over man's evil thoughts & imaginations. 6:6-7, see 6:5
Over man's idolatry. 11:27-32
Over man's immorality, lawlessness, & violence. 6:6-7

GRIPE - GRIPING (See COMPLAINING)

GROWTH, SPIRITUAL
Essential. Must dedicate one's life totally to God. 5:21-24
Source - How one grows.
By being righteous & blameless. 6:8
By believing in God's promises. 6:8; 6:29-32
By making a great sacrifice to God. 8:20
By obeying God. 6:22; 7:5-9; 8:18-19
By pursuing God's promises. 11:29-32
By walking with God—consistently. 5:21-24; 6:9
Four strong traits. 6:9-10

GRUMBLE - GRUMBLING (See COMPLAINING; TONGUE)

GUILT (See SHAME)
Origin - Source of. Sin - turning away from God. 3:7

HADORAM
Descendants of Shem & Joktan. 10:21-32

HALF-HEARTEDNESS - HALF-HEARTED (See INCONSISTENT; INDECISION)
Results.
Causing others to sin (Noah & his son, Ham). 9:20-23
Following others into sin (Adam & Eve). 3:6
Leading others into idolatry. 11:27; 11:27-28
Leading others to reject God. 11:29

HAM
Ancestor of. Such places as: Arabia, Ethiopia, Egypt, Canaan, Oriental nations, African nations, Iran, Iraq, etc. 10:6-20
Prophecy concerning. To be the father of a cursed people, an enslaved people upon earth. 9:24-27
Sin of. Against Noah, his father. Fourfold sin. 9:20-23
Son of Noah. One of the three main branches of the human race. 9:18-19; 10:6-20

HAMATHITE
Descendants of Canaan. 10:6-20

HAPPY - HAPPINESS
Source - Stirred by.
A new born baby. 4:1-2
The expectation of the promised seed, the Savior. 4:1-2

HARAN
Brother of Abraham. Apparently lived an idolatrous life. 11:27-28

HARD - HARDENED - HARDNESS OF HEART (See INDIFFERENCE; UNBELIEF)
Caused by.
Continuing to sin. 6:5
Rejecting God's correction. 4:6-7; 4:9-10
Rejecting the conviction of God's Spirit. 6:3
Rejecting the witness of a believer. 11:29
Worldliness. 6:1-8; 11:27-28; 11:29
Result.
Anger. 4:4-5; 4:6-7
Bearing ungodly children. 4:16-24
Complaining. 4:13-14
Evil imaginations & thoughts. 6:5
False worship. 4:3-4
Judgment. 4:11-12; 6:6-7; 6:13
Result.
Leaving God's presence. 4:16
Murder. 4:8; 4:23-24

HATE - HATRED
Results - Effects.
Being cursed. 9:24-27, esp. 25
Judgment. 4:11-12
Mocking, ridiculing, scorning. 9:20-23
Murder. 4:8; 4:23-24
Who is hated.
Enemies. 4:23-24
Parents. 9:20-23
The godly. Cain hated Abel. 4:1-7

HAUGHTY - HAUGHTINESS (See BOASTING; PRIDE)

HAVILAH
Descendants of Cush. 10:6-20
Mentioned in relation to the Garden of Eden. 2:11-14

HAZARMAVETH
Descendants of Joktan. 10:21-32

HEART (See HARD - HARDNESS)
Depravity of. (See DEPRAVITY)
Fact. Is evil in God's eyes. 6:5

HEAVEN
Fact.
Enoch was translated into **h**. without ever dying. 5:21-24
No person can penetrate **h**., the spiritual world. 11:3-4 (pt.4)
Seek - Seeking. By building a stairway of works to heaven. Tower of Babel. 11:3-4
Symbol - Type of. Land of Canaan. 11:29 (Thgt.1); 11:29-32

HEAVENLY BEINGS (See ANGELS; SATAN; GOD; Etc.)

HEAVENLY BODIES
Facts about. Size of. Galaxies, sun, universe. 1:1 (Note 3); 1:14-15
Meaning. Are three **h**. 1:8
New **h**. Will be recreated into a perfect **h**. Intro. 1:1–2:3, DS#5; 1:2 (Note 4; Thgt.2); 3:17

HEAVY - HEAVINESS
Caused by.
False worship. 4:5 (Note 5)
Having to struggle for survival & food. 3:17
Murder. 4:14

HEBREW
Comes from the name of *Eber*, a descendant of Shem. 10:21-32

HERITAGE
Ungodly. Development of upon earth. 4:18

HETH
Descendants of Canaan. 10:6-20

HIDE - HIDING - HID
From God. Caused by. Sin. 3:8

HISTORY
Discussed. Eight periods of history when man utterly failed & God has to step in & save man. 11:10-31
Of man. Origin of. Three main branches. 9:18-19; 10:1-11:9
Pivotal points of. 1:26-31; 2:7; 2:16-17 (Note 3& DS#6,7; 3:1-6; 3:7-13; 3:19
Adam. 5:3, see 1:26-31; 2:7; 2:16-17 (Note 3 & DS#6,7; 3:1-6; 3:7-13; 3:19
Prophecy concerning. Future foretold. 9:18-29; 9:24-27

HIVITE
Descendants of Canaan. 10:6-20

HOLY - HOLINESS
Duty. To live a life of separation & holiness. 6:1-2 (Thgt.1)
Fact. Man does not live a **h**. or godly life. 6:11-12
Of God. Described as light. 1:3 (Thgt.2)

HOLY SPIRIT
Fact. Will not always strive with man. 6:3
Work of.
In relation to creation.
Discussed the creation of man within the Godhead. 1:26 (Note 1)
Involved in creation. 1:2
In relation to man. Discussed the fall of man within the Godhead. 3:22

HOME (See **FAMILY; MARRIAGE**)
Need for a **h**. Reasons for a **h**. 2:8

HOMELESS - HOMELESSNESS
Caused by.
Mocking & dishonoring parents. 3:20-23, see 3:24-28, esp. 3:25
Sin. 4:11-12, see 4:8-15

HOMOSEXUALITY
Example of. A son with his father. 9:20-23

HONOR - HONORED (See **DISHONOR; WORSHIP**)
Duty. To **h**. one's parents. 9:20-23
Example. **H**. of parents. Two sons **h**; one son dishonors. 9:20-23
Of God. (See **REVERENCE; WORSHIP**)
Of self.
Seeking **h**. & fame for one's name & family. 4:17
Seeking **h**. & fame for one's society & religion. 10:8-12; 11:3-4

HOPE (See **INHERITANCE, SPIRITUAL**)
Basis of - For what.
Righteousness. God's provision of. 3:21
The promised land, heaven. 11:27-31
The promised seed, the Savior. 3:15; 4:25; 5:3-4; 5:21-24; 6:8; 6:18; 9:11; 11:10-31; 11:27-31
Source of.
God's grace. (See **GRACE, Of God**)
God's promise. (See **HOPE, Basis of**)

HOPELESS - HOPELESSNESS (See **DISAPPOINTMENT**)
Caused by.
Secular, man-made religion. 11:1-9
Seeking a secular society. 11:1-9
Sensing the brevity of life. 4:1-2 (pt.2)

HUL
Descendant of Shem & Aram. 10:21-32

HUMAN RACE (See **RACE, HUMAN**)

HUMANISM
Disproven by creation. 1:1, DS#2
Error of - Weaknesses of. Discussed. 4:26, DS#2
Vs. the godly. 4:26, DS#2

HUMILIATION (See **SHAME**)

HUNGER, SPIRITUAL
Aroused - Stirred by.
A deep sense of the weakness & brevity of life. 4:26
God's two great promises. 11:29-32
Knowing all about God's judgment. 8:20

HUSBAND (See **CHILDREN; FAMILY; MAN**)

HYPOCRISY - HYPOCRITE (See **DECEPTION**)
Characteristics - Traits of.
False worship (Cain). 4:3-4; 4:4-5
Worldliness & carnality (Lot). 11:27-28

IDOLS - IDOLATRY (See **GODS, FALSE; SORCERY**)
Error of. Is secular & humanistic, denying the true God. 1:1 (Note 2); 11:3-4
Example of.
Terah, Abraham's father & family. 11:23; 11:27-32
Tower of Babel. 11:3-4
Nature.
Are not gods—only notions, ideas, imaginations of men. 4:4-5; 11:3-4
Is false worship. 4:3-4; 4:4-5; 11:3-4; 11:23; 11:27-32

IGNORE - IGNORING (See **NEGLECT**)
What is **i**.
God. 4:16; 11:10-31
God's warning. 2:16-17, see 3:1-6; 3:17-19
Responsibility for one's brother. 4:9-10
The convictions of God's Spirit. 6:3
The Promised Seed (Christ) & the promised land (heaven). 11:29
The right approach to God. 4:3-4

IMAGE OF GOD
Man. Was created in the **i**. of God. 1:26; 1:27; 2:7; 5:1-2

IMAGE, SELF (See **SELF-IMAGE; SELF-ESTEEM**)

IMAGINATIONS
Evil **i**. Creates false gods. (See **IDOLATRY**)
Fact. Are evil. 6:5

IMMODESTY
Example of. Noah stripping naked. 9:20-23

IMMORALITY
Caused by.
Co-mingling with the immoral & ungodly. 6:1-2; 6:4
Looking & lusting. 6:1-2
The cult of beauty & sex. 4:19; 6:1-2
Discussed.
First polygamy upon earth. 4:19
Example of.
Early society. 6:1-2
Ham. 9:20-23
Lamech. 4:19
Noah. 9:20-23
Results.
Bigamy. 4:19
Judgment & destruction. 6:1-2; 6:4; 6:5; 6:11-12

IMMORTALITY (See **ETERNAL LIFE; HEAVEN**)

IMPARTIAL (See **DISCRIMINATION; PREJUDICE**)

IMPENITENCE (See **HARD - HARDNESS; REBELLION; STUBBORN**)

IMPERFECTION (See **PERFECTION; SIN; UNBELIEF**)

IMPURITY (See **ADULTERY; IMMORALITY**)

IN THE BEGINNING
Meaning. 1:1 (Note 1)

INCONSISTENCY - INCONSISTENT (See **FICKLENESS; HALF-HEARTED; WAVERING**)
Example.
Lot. 11:27-28
Noah. 9:20-23
How people are **i**.
Failing God & sinning in old age. 9:20-23
Living among the worldly. 11:27-28

INDECENT - INDECENCY (See **SHAME**)
Caused by.
Drunkenness. 9:20-23
Looking & lusting. 6:1-2

INDECISION - INDECISIVENESS (See **HALF-HEARTED**)
Example of. Lot & his worldliness. 11:27-28
Results. Makes a person worldly & carnal. 11:27-28

INDEPENDENCE (See **PURPOSE, Of Man; SELF-SUFFICIENCY**)

INDIFFERENCE (See **HARDNESS; UNBELIEF**)

INDIGNATION (See **ANGER; WRATH**)

INDO-EUROPEANS
Origin. 10:2-5

INDULGENCE (See **COVET; GREED; IMMORALITY; LUST**)

INFLUENCE
Evil **i**. (See **STUMBLINGBLOCK**)
Good **i**. (See **TESTIMONY**)

INGRATITUDE
Trait of men.
Is seen in failing God despite all the blessings of God. 3:22-24; 9:20-23
Is seen in rejecting God despite the grace of God. 4:13-14; 4:16

INHERITANCE, SPIRITUAL (See **HOPE; REWARD**)
What the inheritance is.
The promised seed, the Savior. 3:15; 6:18; 9:11; 11:10-31; 11:27-31
The promised land. 11:10-31; 11:27-31

INIQUITY (See **SIN**)

INJURY (See **MURDER; PERSECUTION**)

INJUSTICE (See **JUST - JUSTICE**)
Results. Causes great suffering in the world. 4:9-10

INSECURITY (See **EMOTIONS; SECURITY**)
Caused by.
Fear of God. 9:8-17
Judgment of God. 4:13-14; 8:1-14
Natural devastation & destruction. 8:1-14
Unknown, The. 8:15-22; 9:1-7

INSTABILITY (See **INCONSISTENCY; WAVERING**)

INSTRUCT - INSTRUCTION (See **TEACHING**)

INTELLIGENCE
Of God. Is Supreme, omniscient. Intro. 1:1–2:3, DS#4

INTERCESSION (See **PRAYER**)

INTOXICATION (See **DRUNKENNESS**)

INVITATION (See **CALL; COME; DECISION**)
Extended by God. To Noah. To enter the ark of safety & security. Type of Christ. 7:1; 7:13-16
Kinds of. Great "come i." of God. 7:1

IRAD, SON OF ENOCH
Meaning. 4:18

IRRESPONSIBLE - IRRESPONSIBIL-ITY (See **INCONSISTENCY; SIN**)
Caused by. Denying one's duty to his brother. 4:9-10
Results.
Anger & murder. 4:3-4; 4:4-5; 4:8; 4:23-24
Drunkenness. 9:20-23
Failing God in old age. 9:20-23
Immorality. 4:19; 6:1-2
Worldliness & carnality. 11:27-28

ISRAEL
Chosen by God. Five purposes. Intro. Purpose, p.19

JABAL
First rancher & tent-maker. 4:20-22

JAPHETH
Descendants of.
Sin & failure of. Threefold. 10:2-5 (Thgt.1)
Were Indo-Europeans. Discussed. 10:2-5
Prophecy concerning. To be the father of the great Gentile nations of the earth. 9:24-27
Son of Noah. One of the three main branches of the human race. 9:18-19; 10:1; 10:2-5

JAVAN
Descendant of Japheth. Discussed. 10:2-5

JEALOUSY (See **ENVY**)
Results. Murder. 4:8

JEHOVAH
Name - title of God. Meaning. 2:4 (Note 2); 2:7

JEBUSITE
Descendants of Canaan. 10:6-20

JERAH
Descendant of Shem & Joktan. 10:21-32

JESUS CHRIST
Cross.
Is repulsive & attractive. 4:4-5 (Pt.3, Thgt.4)
Judged & condemned Satan. 3:15 (Note 5)

Death. Symbolized by. The blood & sacrifice of animals. 3:21; 8:20
Names - Titles - Identity. Promised Seed, The. 3:15; 3:23-24
Return. Proclaimed by Enoch. 5:21-24 (Pt.I, 5)
Work of.
His work in destroying Satan & evil spirits. To defeat Satan totally. 3:15
His work as the Promised Seed & Savior.
Believed in by Adam & Eve. 3:23-24
Believed in by the godly line. 5:6-32
Believed in by Enoch. 5:21-24
Believed in by Noah. 6:18; 9:11
Believed in by Abraham. 11:10-31; 11:27-31

JEWS (See **HEBREW**)

JOBAB
Descendant of Shem & Joktan. 10:21-32

JOKTAN
Descendant of Shem & Eber. 10:21-32

JOY
Source - Stirred by.
A new born baby. 4:1-2
Marriage. Coming together for the first time. 2:22-24
Salvation & deliverance. From judgment. 8:15-22
The expectation of the promised seed, the Savior. 4:1-2

JUBAL
First musician & musical instrument inventor. 4:20-22

JUDGING OTHERS (See **BLAME; CRITICISM; DIVISION**)
Caused by. Sin. 3:10-13

JUDGMENT (See **DAMNED**)
First j. upon sin. Discussed. 3:14-15; 3:16; 3:17-19
How God judges. Three ways. 4:11-12
Misconceptions of - Reactions against.
Complain & murmur against. 4:13-14
Doubting & questioning. Leads to temptation & sin. 3:3
Of man.
By the Great flood. Reasons why. 6:1-2; 6:4; 6:5; 6:11-12; 6:13; 7:10-24
In the future. Predicted. 5:21-24 (pt.I, 5); 6:17 (Thgt.1)
Last chance given to the people of Noah's day. 7:1-4
Of the earth.
By the great flood.
Devastated the earth. 7:10-12
Discussed. 7:10-24
Foretold by God. 6:13; 6:17; 7:1-4, esp. 7:4
Never to be repeated. 9:11; 9:12-16
Prediction of j. given to Noah by God. 6:13; 6:17; 7:1-4, esp. 4
Reasons why. 6:5; 6:6-7; 6:13
Two sources of water: subterranean waters burst forth & torrential rains. 7:10-12
Will not occur until the end time. 9:11; 9:12-16
Surety of.

All who turn away from God will face judgment. 3:9
Because God will execute j. 4:9-10
Because of God's Word. He always fulfills His Word. 7:17-24
Upon early man.
Reason why. 6:6-7; 6:13
Upon Adam & Eve. 3:16; 3:17
Upon the human race in Noah's day. The Great flood. 7:10-12
Upon the human race. At the Tower of Babel. 11:5-8
Upon Satan. Discussed. 3:14-15
When will God judge.
Time is fixed. 7:10-12
Time was fixed in the Great flood of Noah's day. 7:10-12
Who executes.
God. 3:14-15; 3:16; 3:17-19; 4:11-12
Jesus Christ. 3:15
Who is to be judged.
Murderers. 4:9-10; 4:11-12
Satan. 3:14-15; 3:15
Sinners. 4:11-12
The immoral. 6:1-2, see 6:6-7
The lawless. 6:5, see 6:6-7
The ungodly. 5:21-24 (pt.I, 5)
The violent. 6:5, see 6:6-7; 6:13
Those who turn away from God. 3:9
Why God judges.
Because a person dishonors his parents. 9:20-23, see 9:24-27
Because of sin & disobedience. 3:16; 3:17-19
Because of false religion & secularism. 11:5-8, see 11:3-4
Because of wickedness & violence. 4:8; 6:6-7; 6:13

JUDGMENT THEORY OF CREATION, DIVINE
Discussed. 1:2, DS#4

JUDICIAL SYSTEM
Established - Institution of.
Source of. God. 9:5
When first established. 9:5

JUST - JUSTICE
First use in Scripture. Refers to Noah. 6:9-10
Meaning. 6:9-10
Misconception - Error of.
Doubting & questioning. Leads to sin. 3:3
React & complain against. 4:13-14
Surety. God will execute j. 4:9-10

JUSTIFICATION - JUSTIFY
First use in Scripture. Refers to Noah. 6:9-10
Meaning. 6:9-10

KEEP - KEEPING (See **OBEDIENCE**)

KEPT - KEEPING POWER OF GOD (See **SECURITY**)

KILL - KILLING (See **MURDER**)

KIND - KINDNESS (See **CARE - CARING; MINISTERING**)
Of God. (See **GRACE**)
Brings man & woman together. 2:22-24

KINGDOM
First k. Founded by Nimrod. 10:8-12

Death of. Died at age 950. 9:28-29
Discussed.
Feelings & emotional state after the
flood. 9:1-7; 9:8-17
Feelings & emotional state during the
flood. 8:1-14
Head of the human race. 9:18-19;
9:24-27; 10:1
History of. 6:9-9:29
Family of. A godly family. 6:9-10; 7:1-4
Heritage - roots. A direct descendant of
the godly line. 5:27-32; 6:18; 9:11
Listed in God's Great Hall of Fame.
6:13-22
Obedience of. Believed & obeyed God's
Word explicitly. 6:22; 7:5-9; 8:18-19
Sons of. Were the three ancestors of the
human race. 9:18-19; 10:1, see 10:1-32

NOAH'S FLOOD (See **FLOOD, THE GREAT**)

NOBLE
Example of **n.** persons.
Enoch. 5:21-24
Noah. 6:9-10

OATH - OATHS
Of God. (See **COVENANTS**)
To Adam. 3:15
To Noah. 6:18; 9:8-17

OBAL
Descendant of Shem & Joktan. 10:21-32

OBEY - OBEDIENCE (See **COMMIT-MENT; FAITHFULNESS**)
Basis of. Belief in God's Word. 6:22;
7:5-9
Duty. To obey God, trusting His Word &
instructions. 6:22; 7:5-9; 8:18-19
Example of. Noah. 6:22; 7:5-9; 8:18-19
Results. Salvation. 6:22; 7:13-16; 7:17-23

OBSTINATE - OBSTINACY (See **HARD - HARDNESS OF HEART; UNBELIEF**)

OCCULT (See **ASTROLOGY; SOR-CERY**)

OFFEND - OFFENDING (See **STUM-BLING BLOCK**)

OFFERING - OFFERINGS (See **SACRI-FICE - SACRIFICIAL SYSTEM**)
Duty. Must make the right **o.** to God.
4:3-4
Kinds of **o.** Burnt **o.** Discussed. 8:20

OLD AGE (See **ELDERLY**)

OLD TESTAMENT
Believers of. Looked forward to Christ.
3:23-24 (Thgt.1)
Christ in every book. pp.10-11
Chronology of. pp.13-14
Difference between O.T. believers &
N.T. believers. 4:4-5 (Pt.3, Thgt.2)

OMISSION (See **IGNORE - IGNORING; NEGLECT - NEGLECTING**)

OMNIPOTENCE (See **GOD**, Power of)

OMNISCIENCE (See **GOD**, Knowledge of)

ONENESS (See **BROTHERHOOD; FELLOWSHIP; EQUALITY OF MAN**)

OPHIR
Descendant of Shem & Joktan. 10:21-32

OPPOSE - OPPOSITION
Against God. By a godless society. 4:23-24; 10:8-12; 11:3-4
Against the Bible. Discussed. p.3

ORDER
Of God. Revealed in creation. Intro. 1:1–2:3, DS#5

ORIENT - ORIENTALS
Origin of. Listed in the table of nations.
10:6-20

OUTER SPACE (See **HEAVENLY BODIES; SPACE, OUTER**)

OUTWARD APPEARANCE (See **APPEARANCE, OUTWARD; DRESS**)

OVER-CONFIDENCE (See **SELF-SUFFICIENCY**)

PAIN
Suffering of.
Result of woman's sin. 3:16
Woman suffers more **p.** than man.
3:16

PANTHEISM
Disproven by creation. 1:1 (Note 2)

PARADISE, EARTHLY (See **EDEN, GARDEN OF; UTOPIA**)
Discussed. 2:18-15
Lost **p.** 3:1-6, see 3:7-13; 3:16; 3:17-19;
3:22

PARDON (See **FORGIVENESS**)

PARENTS (See **FAMILY & Related Subjects**)
Duty. To teach children about God. 5:6-20; 7:1; 11:27-28
Godly. Example. Noah. Importance of
godly **p.** 7:1
Influenced by children. Abraham upon
his father. 11:29-32
Irresponsible or evil **p.** Influence of
worldliness.
Of Haran upon Lot. 11:27-28
Of Terah upon Haran. 11:27-28
Of Terah upon Nahor. 11:29
Sins against. Dishonoring **p.** 9:20-23

PARTIALITY (See **DISCRIMINATION; FAVORITISM; PREJUDICE**)

PARTYING (See **SOCIAL FUNCTIONS**)
Caused by.
Looking & desiring sex. 6:1-2
The cult of beauty & sex. 6:1-2
Results.
Adulterous & immoral relationships.
6:1-2, see 4:19
Being enslaved & worshipping beauty
& sex. 6:1-2, see 4:19
Worldliness & immorality. 6:1-2

PASSION - PASSIONS (See **LUST**)

PATHRUSIM
Descendant of Ham & Mizraim. 10:6-20

PATIENCE (See **ENDURANCE; PER-SEVERANCE; STEDFASTNESS**)
Example of. Noah. Great **p.** & faith.
8:6-14

PEACE (See **RECONCILIATION**)
Lack of.
Caused by. Sin. 3:9
Depravity. 5:3
Source - How one secures peace. By
trusting the promised seed, Jesus Christ.
3:15 (Note 5)

PELEG
Descendant of Shem & Eber. 10:21-32

PENALTY
Of sin. Is death. 2:16-17; 2:17; 3:6; 3:19;
5:3; 5:5

PENITENCE (See **CONFESSION; FORGIVENESS; REPENTANCE; SALVATION**)

PERDITION (See **DESTRUCTION; JUDGMENT**)

PERFECT - PERFECTION
Source - How one is **p.**
By the promised seed. 3:15 (Note 5)
By the righteousness of God. 3:23-24
Discussed. Man's fall from **p.** 3:7-13
Fact. Man is short of **p.**, depraved. 5:3
Meaning. 6:9-10
Of the first man. Discussed. 1:26, DS#2;
3:7

PERISH - PERISHING (See **DEATH; DESTRUCTION; JUDGMENT**)
Who is to **p.**
All who are born into this world. 5:3
(Note 2); 5:5
The immoral, lawless, & violent. 6:1-8, esp. 6:7; 6:11-12; 6:13
Those who take the forbidden fruit.
2:16-17, see 3:19
Those with evil imaginations. 6:5;
6:6-7

PERJURY (See **LYING**)

PERMISSIVE - PERMISSIVENESS (See **IMMORALITY; PARENTS, Irrespon-sible or evil**)

PERSECUTION - PERSECUTORS
By whom.
False worshippers, the wicked. 4:8,
see 4:1-7
Those who oppose the Bible. p.3
Who is **p.**
Those who follow the Bible. p.3
True worshippers. 4:8, see 4:1-7

PERSEVERE - PERSEVERANCE - PERSISTENCE (See **ENDURANCE**)
Duty.
To **p.** in following after God. 5:21-24;
7:1-9
To **p.** in preaching despite opposition.
7:1-9; 7:5-9

To **p**. in pursuing the godly seed (Christ) & the promised land (heaven). 11:29-32
Example of. Noah. 7:5-9; 8:1-14; 8:15-22; 9:1-7; 9:8-17

PERSUADE - PERSUASION
Eve persuaded Adam to sin. 3:6
Evil **p**. (See **STUMBLINGBLOCK**)

PHILISTINES
History of. 10:14

PHILOSOPHY - PHILOSOPHERS (See **REASON - REASONING**)
Worldly - Secular **p**. Vs. God.
Attempts to build a secular world apart from God. 10:8-12; 11:3-4
Six **p**. refuted. 1:1 (Note 2)

PHUT OR PUT
Descendant of Ham. 10:6-20

PHYSICAL
Weakness of. Cannot penetrate the spiritual. 11:3-4 (Pt.4)

PHYSICAL WORLD & DIMENSION (See **CORRUPTION**)
Is corruptible, wasting away. 1:1 (Pt.2, Thgt.3); 1:10 (Thgt.4); 3:17
Weakness of. Cannot penetrate the spiritual. 11:3-4 (Pt.4)

PISON RIVER
Mentioned in relation to the Garden of Eden. 2:10-14

PLANT LIFE - VEGETATION
Creation of. Discussed. 1:11-13
Purpose of. Major functions of. 1:12-13

PLEASURE - PLEASURE SEEKERS (See **WORLDLY - WORLDLINESS**)
Caused by.
Following the cult of beauty & sex. 4:19; 6:1-2
Listening to temptation. 3:1-6
Looking & lusting. 6:1-2; 3:6
Results.
Death. 3:19, see 2:15-17
Drunkenness. 9:20-23
Immorality & adultery. 4:19; 6:1-2
Leads others to sin & fall. 3:6; 9:20-23

POETRY
First poem spoken upon earth. Known as *Lamech's Sword Song*. 4:23-24

POLLUTION (See **ENVIRONMENT**)

POLYGAMY - POLYGAMIST
First **p**. upon earth. Lamech. 4:19

POLYTHEISM
Disproven by creation. 1:1 (Note 2)

POPULATION
Of the earth. During Adam's life. One million plus. 4:17
Origin - Source. Three major branches. 9:18-19; 10:1

POSITION
Seeking **p**. Was a trait of early man. 6:4

POVERTY, SPIRITUAL (See **SIN**)

POWER - POWERFUL
Of God. (See **GOD**, Power of)
Seeking worldly power.
To build a secular government & religion. 10:8-12; 11:1-9
To build a secular, worldwide religion. 11:3-4
To build a worldwide empire. 10:8-12; 11:1-9
Was a trait of early society. 6:4; 10:8-12; 11:3-4

PRAISE (See **PRAYER; THANKSGIVING; WORSHIP**)
Duty.
To **p**. God for animal life. 1:21; 1:24; 1:27
To **p**. God for both water & land. 1:10
To **p**. God for creation. 1:1 (Note 3)
To **p**. God for plant life & vegetation. 1:11-13
To **p**. God for the air. 1:6
To **p**. God for the heavens. 1:8, see 1:1 (Note 3)

PRAYER
Duty. To pray always, gaining an unbroken fellowship with God. Enoch. 5:21-24
Example of. Enoch. 5:21-24
Hindrances - Failure in **p**. Results in backsliding. 9:20-23

PREACH - PREACHING
Duty.
To **p**. a strong message. 5:21-24
To **p**. no matter the ridicule & mockery of people. 7:1-9; 7:5-9

PREDESTINATION (See **CHOSEN; FOREKNOWLEDGE**)
Of God. Revealed in creation. Intro. 1:1–2:3, DS#6

PREJUDICE (See **DISCRIMINATION**)
Duty. To hold no **p**. against other people. 1:28 (Note 4); 9:18-19; 10:1-32; 10:1 (Pt.6)
Evil & sin of. Twisting Scripture to support **p**. 9:24-27 (Pt.1)

PREPARE - PREPARATION (See **COMMITMENT; DEDICATION; SELF-DENIAL**)
Essential. To **p**. for coming judgment. 6:13-22

PRESSURE
Caused by.
Facing natural disasters & destruction. 8:1-14
Facing the judgment of God. 4:13-14; 8:1-14; 9:8-17
Facing the unknown. 8:15-22; 9:1-7

PRESUME - PRESUMPTION
Sin of.
Offering a false worship to God. 4:3-4
Professing God, but living a worldly life. 11:27-28

PRETEND - PRETENSION (See **HYPOCRISY; PROFESSION, FALSE**)

PRIDE (See **BOASTING; GLORYING IN MAN; SELF-SUFFICIENCY**)
Caused by.
Achievements. 4:17; 10:8-12; 11:3-4
Defeating enemies. 4:23-24

Feeling strong & self-sufficient. 4:23-24; 6:4
Glorying in man. 4:23-24
Possessing weapons. 4:23-24
Seeking a name for oneself. 11:3-4
Self-sufficiency. 4:23-24
Results.
A secular society & man-made religion. 11:3-4
Dictatorship. 10:8-12
False worship. 4:3-4; 4:4-5
Murder. 4:23-24; 4:8
Seeking to make a name for oneself. 4:17; 11:3-4
Warning against.
Conceit, self-sufficiency, & spiritual **p**. 3:6 (Note 6)
Verses. 3:6 (Note 6)

PRINCE OF THIS WORLD (See **SATAN**)

PRINCIPALITIES (See **ANGELS; EVIL SPIRITS; SATAN**)

PRIVILEGE (See **BLESSINGS**)

PROBATION (See **COVENANT**)
Adamic **p**.
Adam was put on **p**. & given new terms after the fall. 3:23-24
Adam's first **p**. 2:15-17
Adam's second **p**. 3:23-24

PROBLEMS (See **TRIALS**)

PROCRASTINATION (See **EXCUSES; SLOTHFULNESS**)

PROFESSION (See **LABOR; WORK, SECULAR**)
First **p**. upon earth, farmer & herdsman. 4:2

PROFESSION, FALSE - PROFESSION ONLY (See **HYPOCRISY; IDOLATRY; WORSHIP, False Approach**)
Error - Misconceptions of.
Worships God, but is a false worship. 4:3-4; 4:4-5; 11:3-4; 11:23; 11:27-32
Professes, but lives an immoral & lawless life. 6:1-2
Fact. Is only the notions, ideas, & imaginations of men. 4:4-5; 11:3-4

PROFESSION, SPIRITUAL OR RELIGIOUS (See **CONFESSION; WORSHIP**)
Essential **p**.
A faith that obeys God. 6:22; 6:5-9
A life that is totally dedicated to God, that actually walks with God. 5:21-24
A strong faith that pursues God's promises. 11:29-32
A true worship. 3:3-4; 3:4-5; 8:20

PROMINENCE (See **FAME; HONOR; PRIDE**)

PROMISE - PROMISES
Of God.
Fulfilled by the mercy & grace of God alone. 4:25; 11:27-32
Listed.
The godly Seed. 3:15; 4:1-6:8; 4:25; 5:3-4; 6:8; 6:18; 9:11; 11:10-31; 11:27-32
The promised land. 11:27-32; 11:29-32

Rejected by Nahor, Abraham's brother. 11:29

The Promised Seed. (See **SEED, THE PROMISED**)

To never again destroy the earth with a universal flood. 9:11; 9:11-16; 9:17

Surety of. Will always be fulfilled by God. 3:15

To whom God makes **p.**

To those who live godly lives in an ungodly world. 6:1-8, see 6:18; 9:11

To those who pursue God's promises. 11:29-32

To those who walk with God. 5:21-24; 6:9-10, see 6:18; 9:11

PROMISED LAND (See **LAND, THE PROMISED**)

PROMISED SEED (See **LINE, THE PROMISED; SEED, THE PROMISED**)

PROOF - PROOFS

Of what.

Creation. pp.25-44; 1:1–2:3

God's existence. pp.25-44; 1:1–2:3

The Bible, its inspiration & authority. pp.2-7

PROPHECY

Concerning - Of what.

The earth's first destruction. Given to Noah by God. 6:13; 6:17; 7:1-4

The earth: to never again destroy the earth until the end time. 9:11; 9:11-16; 9:17

The human race. Future foretold. 9:24-27

The promised land. (See **LAND, THE PROMISED**)

The promised seed. (See **PROMISED SEED, THE**)

PROPITIATION (See **RECONCILIATION; REDEMPTION**)

Meaning.

Of Old Testament **p.** 3:21; 8:20

Symbolized - Typed. In animal sacrifice. Burnt offering. 8:20

Source of.

Animal sacrifice. 3:21; 8:20

Jesus Christ. Died as our **p.** 3:21; 8:20

PROUD (See **PRIDE**)

PROVE - PROVED (See **PROFESSION, SPIRITUAL; PROOFS**)

PROVIDENCE (See **GOD**, Nature)

PROVISION, DIVINE

List of **p.**

Life. 3:20

Necessities. Clothing. 3:21

Righteousness. 3:21

Source. God. 3:20-21

PROVOKED (See **ANGER**)

PUNISHMENT (See **DAMNED; JUDGMENT**)

PURITY (See **MORALITY; IMMORALITY; RIGHTEOUSNESS**)

PURPOSE

Of creation. Seen in the very fact that God exists. 1:1 (Note 3)

Of God. Revealed in creation. Intro. 1:1–2:3, DS# 6

Of man.

Discussed. 2:15-17; 9:1-7

Fourfold **p.** upon earth. 9:1-7

Revealed in creation. Intro. 1:1–2:3, DS#5,6,7

Threefold **p.** for being created. 1:28 (Note 4)

To allow God to shower his goodness & grace upon man. Intro. 1:1–2:3, DS#5,6,7; 2:15

To work & subdue the earth. Discussed. 1:28, DS#3; 9:2

PUT ON - SPIRITUAL CLOTHING

Duty: to put on the righteousness of God. 3:21

Source. God & His righteousness. 3:21

QUARREL (See **ARGUMENT; CONTENTION; DIVISION; STRIFE**)

QUENCH - QUENCHING

Duty. Not to **q.** the Spirit's conviction within one's heart. 6:3

QUESTION - QUESTIONING

About God.

Man is without excuse in **q.** God. 1:1 (Pt.4)

Six beliefs that deny God's existence. 1:1 (Note 2)

Fact. Man is an inquisitive creature, always asking **q.** 1:1–2:3

QUICKEN - QUICKENING (See **CONVERSION; RENEWAL**)

QUIET TIME (See **DEVOTION - DEVOTIONS; WORSHIP**)

RAAMAH

Descendant of Ham & Cush. 10:6-20

RACE, HUMAN (See **MAN**)

Corruption of.

Between Noah & Abraham. 11:10-26; 11:27-32

In the days of Adam. 4:16-24

In the days of Noah. 6:1-8

Discussed.

Corrupted. Always corrupts itself. 11:10-26; 11:23

Eight periods of history when man utterly fails & God has to stop in & save man. 11:10-31

Scattering of the human race over the earth. 11:1-9

Diversity of races. Stands as a memorial to God's power. 11:9

Fact. Is saved & delivered by the mercy & grace of God alone. 4:25; 5:3-4; 6:8; 6:18; 9:11; 11:10-31; 11:27-32

Growth of. Table of nations. 10:1-32

Origin.

Adam. Head of the human race. 4:1-6:8; 4:1-2; 5:3

Noah. Head of the human race. 9:18-19; 10:1; 10:32

Of races upon earth. 10:1-32; 11:1-9

Three major branches of: sons of Noah. 9:18-19

Prophecy about. Future foretold. 9:24-27

RAGE (See **ANGER; WRATH**)

Example of.

A boasting, revengeful **r.** 4:23-24

A murderous **r.** 4:8

RAILING - RAILER (See **ARGUING; MOCKERY; SCOLDING**)

RAINBOW

Discussed. 9:12-16

Purpose: to be a sign of God's covenant with man. 9:12-16

What man is to think about when he sees the **r.** 9:12-16

RANSOM (See **REDEEM - REDEMPTION**)

Meaning. Of Old Testament sacrifice. 3:21; 8:20

Source - How a person is **r.**

By approaching God through the blood of the sacrifice. 4:3-4; 4:4-5

By Jesus Christ. Died as our **r.** 3:21; 8:20

By O.T. animal sacrifice. 3:21; 8:20

Symbolized - Typed. In animal sacrifice. Burnt offering. 8:20

RASH - RASHNESS (See **RECKLESS**)

RATIONALISM - RATIONALIST (See **PHILOSOPHY; REASON - REASONING**)

RAVEN

Bird sent out by Noah to search for dry land. 8:6-14

REAL - REALITY (See **TRUTH**)

REAP - REAPING (See **WITNESSING**)

REASON - REASONING (See **PHILOSOPHY**)

Proves.

God's existence. Intro. 1:1–2:3, DS#1-9; 1:1-2

The Bible, its inspiration & authority. pp.2-7

REBELLION (seditions) (See **REJECTION; UNBELIEF**)

Against God. Characteristic - Trait.

Of murderers. 4:8; 4:23-24

Of secular & ungodly societies. 4:16; 10:8-12; 11:3-4

Of secular, man-made religion. 4:4-5; 11:34

Of the disobedient & sinners. 3:6

Of the immoral. 4:19

Of the prideful & self-sufficient. 4:23-24; 11:3-4

Of the unrepentant. 4:16

Of those who seek revenge. 4:23-24

REBUKE - REBUKED

By God.

R. the devil. 3:14-15

R. the false worshipper. 4:4-5; 4:6-7; 6:5-8, see 6:2-3
R. the immoral. 6:6-7, see 6:1-2; 6:3
R. the murderer. 4:9-10
R. the secularist. 6:5-8, see 6:2-3
R. the sinner. 3:10-13; 3:16; 3:17-19
R. the violent. 6:11-12; 6:13; 6:17, see 6:4
R. those who build secular, man-made religions. 6:5-8, see 6:2-3

RECEIVE - RECEIVED (See **OBEDIENCE**)
Duty.
To **r.** the call of God.
To enter the ark of safety, the Lord Jesus Christ. 7:1, see 7:13-16
To repentance. 3:9
To **r.** the instructions of God.
About how to escape death. 2:16-17; 2:17
About how to escape the coming judgment. 6:13-22
To **r.** the promises of God.
The covenant of God. 2:15-17; 9:11
The promised seed & the promised land. 11:27-32; 11:29-32

RECKLESS - RECKLESSNESS
In relation to God.
Approaching God in the wrong way. 4:3-4; 4:4-5
Building a secular society. 4:16-24; 11:1-9
Building a secular, man-made religion. 11:1-9
Co-mingling with & marrying the ungodly. 6:1-2
Denying one's responsibility for others. 4:9-10
Dishonoring one's parents. 9:20-23, see 9:24-27
Disobeying the commandments of God. 2:16-17, see 3:1-6; 3:19
Filling one's mind with immoral & lawless imaginations. 6:5
Following the cult of beauty & sex. 4:19; 6:1-2
Ignoring God's warning. 4:6-7
Ignoring the convictions of God's Spirit. 6:3
Leaving God's presence. 4:16
Living a lawless & violent life. 6:4; 6:11-12; 6:13
Murdering people. 4:8; 4:23-24
Not heeding the message of preachers. 6:14-16; 7:1-9; 7:10-24
Rejecting the promised seed (Jesus Christ) & the promised land (heaven). 11:29

RECOGNITION (See **PRIDE; SELF-RIGHTEOUSNESS; SELF-SEEKING**)
Sins involving. Seeking to be recognized. 4:17; 11:3-4

RECOMPENSE (See **RETALIATION; REVENGE**)

RECONCILE - RECONCILIATION (See **ALIENATION; JUSTIFICATION; REDEMPTION; SALVATION**)
How one is **r.**
By the blood of the sacrifice. 3:21; 8:20, DS#1

By the promised seed, the Savior. 3:15 (Note 5)
By the seeking Lord. 3:9, see 3:8

RECREATION
Questionable **r.**
Drinking (drunkenness) & drugs. 9:20-23
Worldly, immoral social gatherings. 6:1-2

RECREATION THEORY OF CREATION
Discussed. 1:2, DS#4

REDEEM - REDEMPTION (See **PROPITIATION; RANSOM; RECONCILIATION**)
Purpose - Results.
To clothe one in the righteousness of God. 3:21
To cover one's sins under the blood of the sacrifice. 3:21; 8:20, DS#1
To make one acceptable to God. 4:3-4; 4:4-5
To reconcile one to God. 3:21
Source of **r.**
By approaching God through the blood of the sacrifice. 4:3-4; 4:4-5
By the blood of the sacrifice. 3:21; 8:20, DS#1
The promised seed, the Savior. 3:15 (Note 5)

REFORMATION (See **REGENERATION**)

REFUSE - REFUSING (See **REJECT - REJECTION**)

REGENERATION (See **BORN AGAIN; NEW CREATION**)
Source - How one receives.
By believing & pursuing the promises of salvation. 11:29-32
By God's power. Revealed in creation. Intro. 1:1–2:3, DS#1
By God's Word. Revealed in creation. Intro. 1:1–2:3, DS#1
By the seeking Lord. 3:9
By the Spirit of God. 1:6 (Thgt 4)

REHOBOTH, CITY OF
Founded by Nimrod. 10:8-12

REJECT - REJECTED - REJECTION (See **REBELLION; UNBELIEF**)
Duty.
Not to reject God's warnings, but to do well. 4:6-7
Not to reject the promised seed (Christ) & the promised land (heaven). 11:29
What it is that man **r.**
God's warnings. (See **WARN - WARNINGS**)
That He will withdraw His Spirit. 6:3
That judgment is coming. 6:6-7; 6:13, see 6:11-12; 6:17
That sin results in death. 2:16-17; 3:1-6; see 3:19; 5:3
Salvation by the blood of the sacrifice. 3:21; 4:3-4; 4:4-5; see 8:20
The approach demanded by God. 4:3-4; 4:4-5

The convictions of God's Spirit. 6:3
The promised seed (Jesus Christ). 11:29
The promised land (heaven). 11:29
True worship. 4:3-4; 4:4-5; 11:2-3

REJOICE - REJOICING (See **JOY**)

RELATIONSHIPS (See **BROTHERHOOD**)
Disturbed - Broken **r.** Caused by.
Blaming others. 3:10-13
Dishonoring one's parents. 9:20-23
Forsaking God & one's godly family. 4:16
Rejecting the witness of a loved one. 11:29
Sin. 3:10-13

RELIGION (See **TEACHING, FALSE**)
False approaches to **r.**
Astrology. 1:16-18; 11:3-4 (Pt.4,d)
Good works. 4:3-4; 4:4-5
Self-righteousness. 4:3-4; 4:4-5
Of the ancient world. Idolatrous. 11:2-3; 11:10-11; 11:23; 11:27-28
Origin of false **r.**
Astrology. 11:3-4 (Pt.4,d)
Early temple towers. Tower of Babel. 11:3-4
The first man-made **r.** 4:3-4; 4:4-5; 11:1-9
The first secular **r.** 11:3-4
The first worldwide false **r.** 11:3-4
True vs. false **r.** Discussed. 4:1-7

RELIGION, STATE
Origin of.
Secular, worldwide **r.** 11:3-4
Tower of Babel. 11:3-4

RELIGIONISTS
Problems with - Errors of **r.**
Approach God incorrectly. 4:3-4; 11:4-5
Bring the works of their own hands to God. 4:3-4; 11:4-5

RELUCTANCE - RELUCTANT
What a person is **r.** to do.
Believe & pursue the promises of God. 11:29
Face God. 3:9
Give up all to follow God. 11:29
Live a separated life; turn away from the cult of beauty & sex. 6:1-2, see 4:19
Repent. 4:6-7

REMARRIAGE (See **MARRIAGE**)

REMISSION OF SINS (See **FORGIVENESS, SPIRITUAL**)

REMORSE (See **CONFESSION; REPENTANCE**)

RENEW - RENEWAL (See **CONVERSION**)
Duty.
To confess God & call upon God with renewed fervor. 4:26
To walk with God day by day, every day. 5:21-24
How to be **r.**
By experiencing three things. 4:26
By turning to God & pursuing His promises. 11:29-32

REPENT - REPENTANCE (See **CONVERSION; SALVATION**)
Refusal to **r**.
Refusing to pursue God's promise of salvation. 11:29
Rejecting God's mercy. 4:15
Rejecting God's warning. 4:6-7
Rejecting the conviction of God's Spirit. 6:3
Rejecting the witness of a believer. 11:29
Source of **r**. - What stirs a person to **r**.
God's mercy & grace. 11:27-32; 11:29-32
God's seeking & call. 3:8; 3:9

REPROACH - REPROACHED (See **REBUKE**)

REPROBATE (See **APOSTASY; BACKSLIDING**)

REPRODUCTION
Of man.
Discussed. 1:28 (Note 4); 9:1
One of man's purposes upon earth. 1:28 (Note 4); 9:1

REPROOF - REPROVE (See **DISCIPLINE, GODLY; REBUKE**)

REPUTATION (See **FAME; RECOGNITION; TESTIMONY**)

RESEN, CITY OF
Founded. By Nimrod. 10:8-12

RESIST - RESISTANCE
Danger - warning.
Must not **r**. God's call. 3:9
Must not **r**. God's convicting questions. 4:9-10
Must not **r**. God's promises. 11:29
Must not **r**. God's Spirit. 6:3
Must not **r**. God's warning about true worship. 4:6-7, see 4:3-4; 4:4-5

RESOURCES (See **PROMISES**)

RESPECT (See **HONOR**)

RESPECTER OF PERSONS (See **DISCRIMINATION; FAVORITISM; PREJUDICE; PARTIALITY**)

RESPONSIBILITY (See **BELIEVERS,** Duty; & Related Subjects)

REST OF GOD, THE
Meaning. 2:2

REST, SPIRITUAL & ETERNAL
Essential. Time for spiritual renewal & **r**. 2:2
Hope for. By early believers. 5:27-32 (Note 8)

RESTITUTION THEORY OF CREATION
Discussed. 1:2, DS#4

RESTLESS - RESTLESSNESS
Caused by.
Being cooped up, confined. 8:1-14
Facing the unknown. 9:1-7
Hate. 4:11-12, see 4:5; 4:6-7
Murder. 4:11-12
Discussed. Birth & growth of within society. 4:16

RESTORATION (See **CONFESSION; FORGIVENESS, SPIRITUAL; REPENTANCE; SALVATION**)

RESTRAINT - RESTRAIN (See **GOD,** Power of)

RESURRECTION
Symbolized. By Enoch's translation. 5:21-24

RESURRECTION, SPIRITUAL (See **CONVERSION; QUICKENING**)

RETALIATION - RESISTANCE (See **HATE; REVENGE; VENGEANCE**)

RETRIBUTION (See **JUDGMENT**)

REVEALED - REVELATION
Fact.
God has given man the *light of life*. 1:3 (Pt.4, Thgt. 3)
God has **r**. the truth to man. Intro. 1:1–2:3, DS#1, 7
Man cannot find God on his own. Intro. 1:1–2:3, DS#1
The **r**. of creation.
Eight things revealed about the origin of creation. Intro. 1:1–2:3, DS#1
The **r**. of God. God has revealed eight things about the origin of creation. Intro. 1:1–2:3, DS#1

REVEL - REVELLING (See **PARTYING**)

REVELATION, NATURAL
What nature reveals about God. Discussed. 1:1 (Note 3, Pt.4)

REVENGE (See **VENGEANCE**)
Caused by. Reacting against the godly. 4:8, see 4:1-7
Result. Murder. 4:23-24

REVERENCE (See **WORSHIP**)
For God. Stirred by.
Judgment & fear. 8:20, see 9:1-7
Revival. 4:26

REVILE - REVILING (See **ARGUE**)

REVIVE - REVIVAL (See **RENEW - RENEWAL**)
Example of. Adam & the godly seed. 4:26 (Note 3)

REWARD (See **INHERITANCE, SPIRITUAL**)
Basis - based upon.
God's grace. (See **GRACE**)
Abraham. 11:27-32
Discussed. 4:25 (Pt.2)
Noah. 6:8
God's righteousness. 3:21
How to secure - Duty.
By approaching God as He demands. 4:3-4; 4:4-5
By being clothed in God's righteousness. 3:21
By believing God's promises. 4:25; 11:29-32
By entering the ark of God's safety (Jesus Christ). 7:1, see 7:13-16

By living a righteous life & finding grace in the eyes of the Lord. 6:8, see 6:9-10
What the **r**. are.
Acceptance & approval by God. (See **ACCESS**) 4:3-4; 4:4-5; 5:21-24; 6:8, see 6:9-10
Deliverance from judgment. 7:13-16
Eternal life. 2:9 (Note 4); 2:16-17 (Note 3); 5:21-24
The promised land (heaven). 11:29-32
The promised seed (Jesus Christ): salvation through Him. 3:15 (Note 5); 11:27-32; 11:29-32
The resurrection. 5:21-24

REWARD OF UNBELIEVERS (See **JUDGMENT**)

RICH - RICHES (See **MATERIALISM; WEALTH**)

RIDICULE (See **MOCKERY**)
Example of. Ham against his father, Noah. 9:20-23

RIGHTEOUS - RIGHTEOUSNESS
Example of.
Enoch. 5:21-24
Noah. 6:9-10; 7:1-4
First use in Scripture. Refers to Noah. 6:9-10
Meaning. 6:9-10
To be just or justified before God. 6:9-10
To live a righteous & just life. 5:21-24; 6:9-10
Need for **r**. Man must be clothed in **r**. 3:21
Source. God. Provided **r**. for Adam & Eve. 3:21

RIOTOUS LIVING (See **PARTYING; REVELLING; SOCIAL FUNCTIONS**)

RIPHATH
Descendant of Gomer. 10:2-5

RITUAL (See **CEREMONY; RELIGION; SACRIFICIAL SYSTEM**)

RIVALRY
Example of. Cain against Abel. 4:3-4; 4:4-5

RUDE - RUDENESS (See **DISHONOR; MOCKERY; VIOLENCE**)

RULERS
Sins of.
Develop secular societies & governments, opposing God. 4:16-24; 10:8-12; 11:3-4
Develop secular, man-made religions. 11:3-4

RULES & REGULATIONS (See **COMMANDMENTS; RELIGIONISTS**)

SABBATH - SUNDAY
Creation of. Day of rest & worship. 2:1-3
Difference between the Sabbath & Sunday. 2:3 (Pt.4, Thgt.3)
Duty. To rest & worship. 2:3
Purpose. To be a day of rest & worship. 2:2; 2:3

SABTAH
Descendant of Ham & Cush. 10:6-20

SABTECHAH
Descendant of Cush. 10:6-20

SACRIFICE, SPIRITUAL - SACRIFICES - SACRIFICIAL SYSTEM (See **COMMITMENT; DEDICATION; SELF-DENIAL**)
Discussed. **S.** of the burnt offering. 8:20, DS#1
Function.
To point to Christ, His death. 3:21; 4:4-5; 8:20
To point to God's holiness being satisfied. 8:20
Idea of **s.**
Discussed. 4:3-4; 4:4-5
Was first given to Adam. 3:21
Was practiced by Adam's son, Abel. 4:3-4; 4:4-5
Introduction of. Was first given to Adam. 3:21
S. of animals. Meaning of the burnt offering. 8:20
Symbolized - Type.
The death or sacrifice of Christ. 3:21; 4:4-5; 8:20
The holiness of God. 8:20
Various facts about Christ. 8:20
True vs. false **s.** Discussed. 4:3-4; 4:4-5

SADNESS (See **DISAPPOINTMENT**)

SAFETY (See **ASSURANCE; SECURITY**)

SAINTS (See **BELIEVERS**)

SALAH
Descendant of Shem & Arphaxad. 10:21-32

SALVATION - SAVED (See **DELIVERANCE; JUSTIFICATION; REDEMPTION; Related Subjects**)
Assurance of. (See **ASSURANCE**)
Deliverance. From living forever as a sinner in a fallen world. 3:22-24
Example of. Noah. 6:18
How one is **s.** - Conditions - Source.
By believing in the promised seed. 6:18
By faith in the blood of the sacrifice (symbolized Christ's great sacrifice).
In the burnt offering. 8:20, DS#1
In the sacrifice of animals. 3:21
By God's grace. 6:8; 11:29-32
By God's provision of righteousness. 3:21
By obedience. 6:22
By the promised seed, the Lord Jesus Christ. 3:15 (Note 5)
By the sacrifice of an innocent life. Pointed toward Christ. 3:21; 4:4-5 (Pt.2); 8:20
By the sacrifice of Christ upon the cross. 3:15 (Note 5)
By the seeking Lord. 3:9
Proof of - Evidence of.
Being justified before God. 6:9-10
Forsaking all & pursuing God's promises. 11:29-32
Living a righteous life. 5:21-24; 6:9-11
Obeying God. 6:22; 7:5-9
Walking with God. 5:21-24

Response to **s.** Rejected.
By a worldly brother (Nahor, Abraham's brother). 11:29
By the carnal, immoral, & worldly. 8:1-2, see 8:3
By the false worshipper. 4:16, see 4:1-7
By the godless society. 7:1-9; 7:5-9
By the murderer. 4:16, see 4:8-15, esp. 8, 15
By the ungodly. 5:21-24
Security of. (See **SECURITY**)
Symbolized - Pictured. By the ark in Noah's day. 7:13-16
Who is **s.**
Those who are clothed in God's righteousness. 3:21
Those who are just or justified before God. 6:9-10
Those who believe God's promise of **s.** 6:18
Those who believe in the promised seed (Jesus Christ). 3:15 (Note 5)
Those who call upon the name of the Lord. 4:26 (Note 3)
Those who enter God's ark of safety. 6:13-16
Those who forsake all & diligently seek the promised land (heaven). 11:29-32
Those who obey God. 6:22; 7:5-9
Those who prepare for the coming judgment. 6:13-22, esp. 22; 7:5-9
Those who pursue the promises of God. 11:29-32
Those who respond to the seeking Lord. 3:9
Those who walk with God. 5:21-24

SANCTIFY - SANCTIFICATION (See **SEPARATION**)
Meaning. 2:3
What is **s.** Sabbath day. 2:3

SARAH (Abraham's Wife)
Was barren, unable to bear children. 11:29-32

SARCASM (See **RIDICULE; MOCKERY**)

SATAN
Children - Followers of.
Cain. A murderer. 4:8
Discussed. 3:15 (Note 4)
The ungodly. 4:8
Defeated - Destroyed - Victory over. By Christ. 3:15 (Note 5)
Described as. The Serpent. 3:1
Discussed. 1:2, DS#4; 3:1
The Invisible Struggle against God. pp.9-10
Duty. Must study & understand Satan's attacks. 3:4-5
Facts. Was the highest created being in the universe. 1:2, DS#4; 3:1
Fall of. Discussed. 1:2, DS#4; 3:1
Judgment of.
By Christ. 3:15
By the seed of the woman, Christ. 3:15
Cursed above all creatures. 3:14 (Note 1)
Discussed. 3:14-15
Names - Titles.
Serpent. 3:1; 3:14
Several names. 1:2, DS#4

Origin - Where Satan came from. 1:2, DS#4; 3:1
Seed of. (See **SATAN; Children, Followers of**) 3:15
Why God allowed Satan to tempt man. 3:1
Why God did not destroy Satan when Satan sinned. 3:1
Work - Strategy of.
Has some control over the earth. 1:2, DS#4
Hurts & causes pain to God. pp.9-11; 3:1
Opposes God. Reasons. 3:1
Tempts man. pp.7-10; 3:1

SATISFY - SATISFACTION (See **FULNESS, SPIRITUAL**)

SATISFACTION; SPIRITUAL (See **FULNESS, SPIRITUAL; HUNGER, SPIRITUAL; NEEDS - NECESSITIES**)

SAVAGE - SAVAGERY (See **MURDER**)
Caused by.
Anger & hatred. 4:8, see 4:6-7
Corruption upon the earth. 3:17 (Note 1)
Seeking revenge. 4:23-24
Duty. To establish laws to control **s.** 9:5-7

SAVIOR (See **JESUS CHRIST; SALVATION**)

SCANDAL - SCANDALOUS SINS (See **IMMORALITY; SIN**)

SCATTERED
Fact. Early man was dispersed & **s.** over the earth by God. 11:1-9

SCHOLARS (See **SCIENCE**)
Error - Mistake of.
Attack the Bible. p.3
Attack the existence of God. Intro. 1:1–2:3, DS#9

SCIENCE
Origin of **s.**
God's commandment to gain dominion over the earth. 2:15-17; 9:2
Man's need for knowledge. Intro. 1:1–2:3, DS#1
Purpose of. To subdue the earth. 1:28, DS#3; 9:2
Vs. Genesis. Discussed. Intro. 1:1–2:3, DS#9
Vs. the Word of God. Intro. 1:1–2:3, DS#9

SCOFF - SCOFFERS - SCOFFING - SCORN (See **MOCKERY**)
Characteristic - Trait of.
Bitter & vengeful people. 4:9-10
Bitter children. 9:20-23

SCOLD - SCOLDING (See **ARGUE; MOCK**)
Example of. Ham against his father. 9:20-23

SCRIPTURE (See **BIBLE; WORD OF GOD**)

SEAS
Creation of. Discussed. 1:9-10

SELF-EXISTENCE (See **GOD, Nature**)

SELF-GLORY (See **BOASTING; GLORYING IN SELF; PRIDE**)

SELF-IMAGE (See **GLORYING IN SELF; PRIDE; SELF-ESTEEM**)
Inflated self-image.
  Boasting in one's strength, power, & achievements. 4:23-24
  Seeking recognition & fame for oneself. 4:17; 11:2-3
  Worshipping the cult of beauty & sex. 4:19; 6:1-2
Pure & strong self-image. Lives a righteous & blameless life. 6:9-10, see 5:21-24

SELF-INDULGENCE (See **INDULGENCE**)

SELF-RIGHTEOUS - SELF-RIGHTEOUSNESS (See **HYPOCRISY; RELIGION; RELIGION, False Approaches to; RELIGIONISTS**)
Problems with - Errors of r.
  Approach God incorrectly. 4:3-4; 11:4-5
  Bring the works of their own hands to God. 4:3-4; 11:4-5

SELF-SUFFICIENCY
Aroused - Stirred by.
  Anger. 4:5
  Denial of responsibility to one's brother. 4:9-10
  Desire for recognition & fame. 4:17; 11:3-4
  Temptation. 3:6 (Note 6)
Characteristic - Trait. Of early man & society. 4:23-24
Errors - Misconceptions of.
  That one can approach God by his own efforts & works. 4:3-4; 4:4-5
  That one can commit immoral acts & not be punished. 6:1-2, see 6:6-7
  That one can develop a secular life & religion & not be punished. 4:16-24, see 6:6-7; 6:13; 6:17; 11:1-9
  That one can disobey God & not be punished. 3:1-6, see 3:19; 5:5
  That one can find fulfillment in the forbidden fruit. 3:4-5
  That one can focus his thoughts & imaginations upon the immoral & evil & not be punished. 6:5, see 6:6-7
  That one can forsake God & not be punished. 4:16, see 5:5
  That one can live a lawless & violent life & not be punished. 6:4, see 6:6-7; 6:11-12; 6:13; 6:17
  That one can murder & not be punished. 4:8-15; 9:5-7
  That one can worship God like he wants & not be punished. 4:5; 4:6-7
Warning against. Verses. 3:6 (Note 6)

SELF-WILL (See **HARDNESS OF HEART; STUBBORN**)

SENSUALITY (See **IMMORALITY; LUSTS**)
Example of. Noah. 9:20-23

SENT (See **COMMISSION; WITNESSING**)

SEPARATE - SEPARATION
Duty.
  To be **s.** from the world.
    By not marrying the ungodly. 6:1-2
    By not worshipping the cult of beauty & sex. 4:19; 6:1-2
    By pursuing the promised land (heaven). 11:29-32
    By walking with God. 5:21-24; 6:9-10
Fact.
  Man is **s.**, divided from one another. (See **DIVISION**)
  Man is **s.** from God. 3:9; 5:3 (Pt.5)

SERPENT (See **SATAN**)
Fact. Had access to the Garden of Eden. 3:1
Judgment upon. Discussed. 3:14-15
Name - Title. Of the devil. 3:14
Seed of. Discussed. 3:15

SERVANT - SLAVE - SLAVERY
Prophecy - Prediction. That the racial branch of Canaan would be **s.** 9:24-27; 10:6-20

SERVE - SERVICE (See **MINISTERING; WORKS, GOOD**)

SETH
Fact.
  Recognized the frailty & mortality of man. 4:26
  Was the godly seed. 5:3-4
Meaning of name. 4:25
Son of Adam. Continued the godly seed or descendants upon earth. 4:1-6:8

SEX (See **ADULTERY; IMMORALITY; LUST; Related Subjects**)
Discussed. Cult of beauty & **s.** 4:19; 6:1-2
Fact. Man feeds his mind upon. 6:1-2; 6:4; 6:5

SHAME - SHAMEFUL
Caused by. Sin - turning away from God. 3:7

SHARE - SHARING (See **MINISTERING; WITNESSING**)

SHEBA
Descendant of Ham & Cush. 10:6-20
Descendant of Shem & Joktan. 10:21-32

SHELEPH
Descendant of Joktan. 10:6-20

SHEM
Descendants of. Chart of descendants. 11:12-22
Discussed. Chosen by God to carry on "the promised seed." 11:10-26
Prophecy concerning. To be the father of the great religious nation of the earth & of the promised seed. 9:24-27; 11:10-11
Son of Noah. One of the three major branches or lines of the human race. 9:18-19; 10:1-2; 11:10-26

SHINAR
Area of. Babylon, modern Iraq. 11:3-4

SIDON
Descendant of Ham & Canaan. 10:6-20

SIGNIFICANCE (See **PURPOSE**)

SIGNS
Fact. The rainbow is a sign of God's faithfulness. 9:12-16; 9:17
Listed.
  Cain's sign or mark. 4:15
  The rainbow. 9:12-16

SIN - SINS (See **DEPRAVITY**)
Acts of.
  Sins of attitude, heart, & mind.
    Boasting. 4:23-24
    Evil imaginations & thoughts. 6:5
    Pride. 4:17; 11:3-4
    Secularism. 1:1 (Note 2); 4:16; 11:3-4
    Seeking a name for oneself. Fame, pride. 11:3-4
  Sins of behavior.
    Bigamy. 4:19
    Cult of beauty & sex. 4:19; 6:1-2
    Drunkenness. 9:20-23
    Homosexuality. 9:20-23
    Immorality. 4:19; 6:1-2; 6:5
    Murder. 4:8
    Seeking recognition & fame. 4:17; 11:3-4
    Worldliness, carnality. 6:2-3; 11:27-28; 11:29
  Sins toward God, Christ, & the Holy Spirit.
    Astrology. 1:16-18; 11:3-4 (Pt.4,d)
    Backsliding, turning away from God. 9:20-23
    Disobedience. 3:1-6
    False worship. 4:3-4; 4:4-5; 11:3-4
    Forsaking, departing from God. 9:20-23
    Grieving the Holy Spirit. 6:3
    Idolatry. 11:3-4; 11:10-11; 11:23; 11:29-32
    Man-made religion. 11:3-4
    Rejection. 11:29
    Turning away from God. 4:16
    Unbelief. 3:3; 6:22; 7:1-4 (Thgt.1); 7:1-9; 11:29
  Sins toward others.
    Anger. 4:5
    Dishonoring one's parents. 9:20-23
    Lawlessness. 6:4; 6:11-12; 6:13
    Leading others to sin; being a stumblingblock. 3:6
    Ridicule & scorn. 9:20-23
    Violence. 6:4; 6:11-12; 6:13
Caused by - Source of.
  Adam. As the father of the human race. 3:22; 5:3
  Failing to keep a watchful eye out for temptation. 9:20-23
  Neglect of daily worship time. 9:20-23
  Seven causes. 3:1-6
Concealment of. Cannot be hid. 4:9-10
Discussed.
  Eight periods of history when man utterly fails & God has to step in & save man. 11:10-31
  First temptation & **s.** 3:1-6
  Secularism in society & religion. 4:16-24; 11:3-4
Fact.
  All men **s.** 3:22; 5:3
  Cannot be hid. 4:9-10
  Cries out for justice & vengeance. 4:9-10
  The way of **s.** is very hard. 4:11-12
Forgiveness of. (See **FORGIVENESS, SPIRITUAL**)
Meaning. Missing the mark. 4:6-7

Of early society.
  Was corrupt & violent. 6:11-12; 6:13
  Was immoral, worshipping the cult of
    beauty & sex. 6:1-2; 6:5
Origin - Source of sin.
  Adam & Eve's sin. 3:1-6
  Man's rebellion against God. 1:26,
    DS#2; 3:1; 5:3
  Satan. 1:2, DS#4; 3:1
Results - Consequences of sin.
  A devastated earth. 7:10-24
  Alienation & separation from God.
    3:9; 3:10-13
  Are always terrible. 9:20-23
  Blaming others. 3:10-13
  Breaks God's heart. 3:9
  Corruption, immorality, & violence.
    6:11-12
  Death. 3:19, see 2:16-17; 3:21; 5:3
  Discussed.
    First consequences of s. 3:7-13
    First judgment upon sin. 3:14-15;
      3:16; 3:17-19
    Division. 3:10-13
    Guilt & shame. 3:7
    Judgment of God. 6:6-7; 6:17; 7:10-24
    Judgment. Threefold judgment. 4:11-12
    Loss of perfection & innocence & the
      glory & righteousness of God. 3:7
    Restlessness. 4:11-12; 4:16
    Rootlessness. 4:16
    Running away & trying to hide from
      God. 3:8
    Trying to cover one's sin. 3:7
Steps involved in s. Seven s. 3:1-6

SIN, LEADING OTHERS TO (See
STUMBLINGBLOCK)

SINCERE - SINCERITY (See **COM-
MITMENT; DEDICATION; DILI-
GENCE**)

SINITE
  Descendant of Ham & Canaan. 10:6-20

SINNER - SINNERS (See **DEPRAVITY;
MAN; SIN**)
  Fact. All men are s. 3:22 (Note 1)

SIX DAYS OF CREATION (See **CREA-
TION**, Days of)

SKEPTIC - SKEPTICISM (See **AG-
NOSTIC; UNBELIEF**)
  Disproven by creation. 1:1 (Note 3)

SLANDER - SLANDERING (See
MOCKERY; TONGUE)

SLEEP, SPIRITUAL (See **COMPLA-
CENT**)
  Caused by.
    Being around tempting things or in
      tempting places. 3:1
    Keeping a watchful eye out for tempta-
      tion. 3:1; 9:20-23 (Pt.1,d)
    Neglecting daily devotions & worship.
      9:20-23 (Pt.1,d)

SLOTHFUL - SLOTHFULNESS (See
COMPLACENT; SLEEP, SPIRITUAL)

SLUGGARD (See **COMPLACENT;
SLEEP, SPIRITUAL**)

SLUMBER - SLUMBERED (See **COM-
PLACENT; SLEEP, SPIRITUAL**)

SOBER - SOBRIETY (See **DRUNKEN-
NESS**)

SOCIAL ACTIVITIES - SOCIAL LIFE
(See **PARTYING**)

SOCIETY (See **CIVILIZATION;
WORLD**)
  Ancient - Early s. Traits of. Similar to to-
    day. 6:1-2
  Corrupt s.
    Discussed. 4:16-24; 6:1-8; 11:3-4
    First ungodly s. 4:16-24; 6:1-8
  Described as.
    Rootless s. 4:16
    Restless s. 4:11-12; 4:16
    Secular. 4:16-24; 11:3-4
  Errors of - Problems with.
    Honors & esteems the powerful, im-
      moral & lawless. 6:4; 6:13
    Seeks to develop a secular s. & reli-
      gion. 11:3-4
  Fact. S. developed along two streams of
    people, the godly & the ungodly. 6:1-8

SONS OF GOD
  Meaning. 6:1-8

SORCERER - SORCERY (See **AS-
TROLOGY**)
  Fact. Is empty, meaningless. 1:16-18
  Origin of. 11:3-4

SORROW - SORROWFUL (See **DISAP-
POINTMENT; GRIEF; HEAVY -
HEAVINESS; HOPELESSNESS**)
  Caused by.
    Disappointment over a son's immoral
      behavior. 9:24-27
    Disappointment over a son's sin &
      turning away from God. 4:16
    False worship. 4:5 (Note5 7)
    Having to struggle for food. 3:17
    Judgment of God. 4:11-12; 4:13-14
    Murder. 4:13-14

SOUL, THE
  Meaning. 1:20, DS#1
  Vs. the spirit. Discussed. 1:26, DS#2, see
    1:20

SOUL-WINNING (See **WITNESSING**)

SOVEREIGNTY (See **GOD, Nature**)

SPACE, OUTER (See **HEAVENLY
BODIES**)
  Facts about. Discussed. 1:1 (Note 7);
    1:14-15

SPEAK - SPEECH (See **TONGUE**)
  Discussed. How different s. originated
    upon earth. 11:5-8

SPEAKING EVIL (See **TONGUE**)

SPECULATIONS (See **PHILOSOPHY;
REASON - REASONING**)

SPIRIT, THE
  Meaning. 1:26, DS#2
  Vs. the soul. Discussed. 1:26, DS#2, see
    1:20

SPIRITISM (See **SORCERY**)

SPIRITS - SPIRITUAL BEINGS
  False - Evil - Unclean spirits. (See
    SATAN)
  True spirits. (See **GOD; JESUS
    CHRIST; HOLY SPIRIT**)

SPIRITS, EVIL (See **SATAN**)

SPIRITUAL STRUGGLE - WARFARE
  Caused by.
    Man vs. God. The visible struggle
      against God. pp.7-9
    Satan vs. God. The invisible struggle
      against God. pp.9-10; 3:1
  Deliverance from - Victory - Triumph
    over.
    By the death of Christ. 3:15 (Note 5,
      Pt.4); 3:21 (Pt.4)
    All creation shall be delivered. 3:17

SPIRITUAL WORLD (See **ETERNAL
LIFE; HEAVEN**)

SPITE (See **HATE - HATRED**)

SPOTLESS (See **BLAMELESS; SIN**)

STABILITY (See **FAITHFULNESS;
SECURITY**)

STAIRWAY TO HEAVEN
  Early temple-towers were built as stair-
    ways to heaven. Tower of Babel. 11:3-4

STAND FAST (See **ENDURANCE;
FAITHFULNESS; PERSEVERANCE**)

STAR - STARS
  Creation of. Discussed. 1:1 (Note 3); 1:3;
    1:14-19
  Worship of. (See **ASTROLOGY**)

STATE (See **GOVERNMENT**)

STEDFAST - STEDFASTNESS (See
**ENDURANCE; FAITHFULNESS;
PERSEVERANCE**)

STRENGTH - STRENGTHEN (See
POWER)

STRESS (See **EMOTIONS;
INSECURITY**)

STRIFE (See **ARGUMENTS;
CONTENTION; DIVISION**)
  Source - What causes strife.
    Failure to do right. 4:6-7
    False worship. 4:3-4; 4:4-5; 4:8
    Jealousy & envy. 4:5
    Lust for power & rule. 10:8-12
    Seeking revenge & boasting. 4:23-24
    Sin & blaming others. 3:10-13

STRIVE - STRIVING (See **DILIGENCE;
SEEKING**)
  Of God's Spirit. Will not always s. with
    man. 6:3

**STRONG - STRENGTH - STRENGTH-
EN** (See **POWER; ENCOURAGE-
MENT; PERSEVERANCE**)

STUBBORN (See **HARD - HARDNESS**)

TRANSFORM - TRANSFORMED (See **CONVERSION; RENEWAL; RE-PENTANCE**)

TRANSGRESSION (See **SIN**)

TRANSLATED INTO HEAVEN
Example of. Enoch. Was **t.** & never died. 5:21-24

TREE OF LIFE
Discussed. 2:9 (Note 4)

TREE OF THE KNOWLEDGE OF GOOD & EVIL
Discussed. 2:9 (Note 5); 3:1-6

TRESPASS (See **SIN**)

TRIALS - TRIBULATION
Deliverance through - How to conquer.
By God. He knows all about our **t.** Creation reveals this fact. Intro. 1:1–2:3, DS#4
By trusting & remaining faithful to God. 7:1-9; 8:1-5 (Thgt.2); 8:6-14; 8:15-22

TRINITY
Revelation of. When the **T.** is first mentioned in the Bible. 1:26 (Note A); 3:22, DS#1
Work of.
Created man. 1:26 (Note 1)
Discussed the fall of man. 3:22, DS#1

TROUBLE (See **TRIALS**)

TROUBLEMAKER (See **STUMBLING-BLOCK**)
Example of. Ham: tries to lead his brothers to scorn their father. 9:20-23

TRUST - TRUSTED - TRUSTWORTHY (See **BELIEVE; FAITH**)
Essential - Necessity.
To be saved. 3:20; 4:25; 4:26
To receive the promises of God. 3:15; 4:25; 11:29-32

TRUTH - TRUTHFULNESS
Source.
Bible. pp.1-11
God. Has to reveal Himself & the **t.** of man's origin. Intro. 1:1–2:3, DS#1; 1:1–2:3
Those who reject the **t.**
Deny God's existence. Six denials. 1:1 (Note 2)
Deny the Bible. p.3

TUBAL-CAIN
First metal worker & craftsman. 4:20-22

TUBAL
Descendant of Japheth. 10:2-5

TYRANT
First **t.** Nimrod. 10:8-12

UNASHAMED (See **GUILT; SHAME**)

UNBELIEF (See **REJECTION**)
Example of. Nahor, brother of Abraham. 11:29
In what.
God & His Word. 3:3; 6:22; 7:1-9
Noah & the great flood. 6:22
The promised land. 11:29
The promised seed. 11:23; 11:29
True worship: worship by sacrifice. 4:3-4; 4:4-5
Results.
Approaches God through works & self-righteousness. 4:3-4; 4:4-5
Denies the coming judgment. 7:1-9; 7:1-4 (Thgt.1)
Idolatry. 11:10-11; 11:23; 11:27-32
Turns away from God. 4:16

UNBELIEVERS (See **UNGODLY; UN-SAVED**)
Who the **u.** are.
Those who do not pursue the promised land (heaven). 11:29
Those who offer false worship to God. 4:6-7, see 4:3-4; 4:4-5
Those who reject the witness of their parents. 9:20-23 (Pt.2,d)

UNBLAMABLE (See **BLAMELESS**)

UNCERTAIN - UNCERTAINTIES (See **ASSURANCE; INCONSISTENT; INSECURITY**)

UNCLEAN - UNCLEANNESS (See **SIN**)

UNDEFILED (See **BLAMELESS; MORALITY**)

UNDERSTANDING (See **KNOWLEDGE**)

UNDEVELOPED EARTH THEORY OF CREATION
Discussed. 1:2 (Note 4)

UNEQUALLY YOKED
Caused by. Co-mingling with the ungodly. 6:1-8; 6:1-2

UNFAITHFUL - UNFAITHFULNESS (See **APOSTASY; UNBELIEF**)
Caused by.
Dishonoring one's parents. 9:20-23
Failing to keep a watchful eye against temptation. 9:20-23 (Pt.1,d)
Following in the steps of ungodly parents. 11:27-28, see 11:23
Giving in to temptation. 3:1-6
Listening to the seduction of others. 3:6
Living a selfish & worldly life. 11:27-28
Neglecting one's daily prayer & worship time. 9:20-23 (Pt.1,d)
Worshipping God in the wrong way. 4:3-4; 4:4-5

UNFRUITFULNESS (See **UNFAITH-FULNESS**)

UNGODLY - UNGODLINESS (See **LOST, THE ; UNBELIEVERS**)
Characteristics - Traits.
Boasts in self-sufficiency. 4:23-24
Develops a secular society & religion. 11:3-4
Develops an **u.** society. 4:16
Is immoral. 4:19; 6:1-2; 6:5

Is lawless & violent. 6:4; 6:11-12; 6:13
Turns away from God. 4:16
Worships the cult of beauty & sex. 4:19; 6:1-2
Discussed. Growth & development of **u.** seed (descendants) upon earth. 4:16-24
Fact. Is running rampant today. 5:21-24 (Pt.I,5,Thgt.1)
Judgment of. (See **JUDGMENT**)

UNITY (See **BROTHERHOOD; DIVISION**)

UNIVERSE
Age of. Bible does not say how old the **u.** is. 1:1 (Note 1)
Facts about.
Discussed. 1:1–2
Size of the heavens & the earth, the solar system, galaxies, etc. 1:1 (Note 3)
What the **u.** reveals about God. Discussed. Intro. 1:1–2:3, DS#1; 1:1 (Note 2,3, DS#3)
Judgment of. Cursed because of Adam's sin. 3:17
New **u.** Will be recreated into a perfect **u.** Intro. 1:1–2:3, DS#5; 1:2 (Note 4, Thgt.2); 3:17
Origin.
Created by God. Intro. 1:1–2:3, DS#1-9; 1:1 (Notes 2,3, DS#3)
Has not always existed; was created by God. 1:1 (Note 1)
Seven things revealed about the origin of the **u.** Intro. 1:1–2:3, DS#1
Origin of evil & sin - How the **u.** became imperfect.
By Adam's sin. 3:17
By Satan's fall. 1:2, DS#4; 3:1 (Thgt.2)

UNJUST, THE (See **UNBELIEVERS; UNGODLY**)

UNRIGHTEOUSNESS – UNRIGH-TEOUS, THE (See **SIN; UNGODLY**)

UNSAVED (See **UNBELIEVERS; UNGODLY**)

UNSELFISH - UNSELFISHNESS (See **SELF-DENIAL**)

UNSHAPED EARTH THEORY OF CREATION
Discussed. 1:2 (Note 4)

UTOPIA (See **EDEN, GARDEN OF; PARADISE**)
Discussed. 2:8-14
Last of. 3:1-6; 3:7-13; 3:16; 3:17-19; 3:22

UR OF THE CHALDEES
Discussed. 11:27-28

UZ
Descendant of Shem & Aram. 10:21-32

UZAL
Descendant of Shem & Joktan. 10:21-32

VEGETATION
Creation of. Discussed. 1:11-13
Purpose of. Major functions of. 1:12-13

VENGEANCE (See **REVENGE**)
Caused by.
Envy & anger. 4:3-4; 4:4-5; 4:8
Seeking revenge. 4:23-24
Surety of. God will execute **v**. 4:9-10;
4:23-24

VICTORY - VICTORIOUS LIVING
How to live victoriously.
By living a righteous & blameless life.
6:9-10
By obeying God. (See **OBEDIENCE**)
By trusting the **v**. of the promised seed
(Jesus Christ). 3:15 (Note 5, Pt.4)
By walking with God. 5:21-24
What man needs **v**. over.
Death. 2:16-17; 2:17; 3:19
Evil thoughts & imaginations. 3:2; 6:5
Judgment. 6:18; 7:1; 7:13-16
Satan. 3:15 (Note 5, Pt.4)
Sin. 4:6-7 (Pt.4)

VIGILANT - VIGILANCE (See
DILIGENCE; ENDURANCE;
PERSEVERANCE)

VINDICTIVE (See **REVENGE;**
VENGEANCE)

VIOLENCE
Fact.
Filled the earth during Noah's day.
6:11-12; 6:13
Was the reason why God destroyed the
earth with *The Great Flood*. 6:11-
12; 6:13

WAGES (See **EMPLOYMENT**)

WAITING UPON THE LORD (See
PATIENCE; PRAYER)

WALK, SPIRITUAL
Discussed.
What "walking with God" involves.
5:21-24
What Scripture says about the believ-
er's spiritual walk. Fifteen Scrip-
tures. 5:21-24
Example of.
Enoch. Total dedication to God. 5:21-24
Noah. Total dedication to God. 6:9-10

WANDERERS (See **APOSTASY;**
BACKSLIDING)

WANT (See **NEEDS - NECESSITIES**)

WARFARE, SPIRITUAL (See **SPIR-**
ITUAL STRUGGLE - WARFARE)

WARN - WARNING
W. to man.
Against false worship. 4:6-7
God hates sin & will judge sin. 6:6-7;
6:13; 6:17; 7:10-24; 11:1-9
God's Spirit will not always strive
with man. 6:3
Must guard against evil thoughts &
imaginations. 6:5, see 6:6-7
Must guard against sin. 4:6-7
Must not do the forbidden thing. 2:16-17

WATCH - WATCHFULNESS
Failure to **w**.
Listening & giving in to the entice-
ments of others. 3:6
Results in failure & drunkenness.
9:20-23
Results in sin & disobedience. 3:1, see
3:1-6

WATER, LIVING
Facts about. Five facts. 1:10 (Note 3,
Thgt.4)
Symbol of. Christ, the living **w**. 1:9
(Thgt.3); 1:10 (Note 3, Thgt.4)

WAVER - WAVERING (See **INCON-**
SISTENCY; INSECURITY)
Caused by.
Being where one does not belong. 3:1
Listening to the seduction of others.
3:6
Neglecting one's daily prayer & wor-
ship time. 9:20-23 (Pt.1,d)
Not fleeing temptation. 3:1-6
Not keeping a watchful eye against
temptation. 3:1; 9:20-23 (Pt.1,d)

WAY TO GOD, THE
False vs. true way. 4:1-7

WEAK - WEAKNESS
Caused by.
Associating with the worldly of the
earth. 6:1-2; 11:27-28
Going out alone, where one should not
go. 3:1
Neglecting one's daily prayers & wor-
ship. 9:20-23 (Thgt.1,d)
Not controlling one's thoughts & im-
aginations. 6:1-2, see 6:5
Not fleeing the cult of beauty & sex.
6:1-2
Not keeping a watchful eye out for
temptation. 3:1; 9:20-23 (Thgt.1,d)

WEALTH - WEALTHY (See **MATERI-**
ALISM)

WEARY - WEARINESS (See **PRES-**
SURE)

WHISPERERS (See **BACKBITERS**)

WICKED - WICKEDNESS (See **SIN;**
UNGODLY; UNSAVED)

WIFE - WIVES (See **MARRIAGE;**
WOMAN)

WILL OF GOD
Power of God's will.
Revealed in creation. Intro. 1:1–2:3,
DS#6
To do as He wills & purposes. Intro.
1:1–2:3, DS#6

WILL, MAN'S (See **FREE WILL**)

WISDOM (See **KNOWLEDGE**)

WITNESSING TO GOD & CHRIST
Duty.
To be renewed, revived in **w**. 4:26
(Note 3)
To bear a strong **w**. for God. 5:21-24

Example of.
Abraham. To his brother. 11:29
Adam & the godly seed. A revival of
w. 4:26 (Note 3)
Enoch. In the midst of an ungodly
generation. 5:21-24
Noah. Despite ridicule & scorn. 7:1-9

WOMAN - WOMEN
And man. Relationship with man. 2:18;
2:21-22; 2:22-24
Creation of.
Discussed. 1:26-31; 1:27; 2:18-25
Was a unique creation, the crown of
creation. 2:21-22
Duty.
Must guard the appearance of her
body. 6:1-2
To subject to her husband. 3:16
Effect of sin upon - Judgment upon.
An inner desire for a husband. 3:16
Pain in childbirth. 3:16
Threefold judgment when Eve sinned.
3:16
To be in subjection to her husband.
3:16
Nature of. (See **MAN**, Nature of)
Discussed. 2:21-22; 3:16
Feels & senses suffering & pain more
than man. 3:16
Has an inner desire for a husband. 3:16
Is more tender, warm, delicate. 3:16
Position of.
Is the glory of man. 2:21-22
Is to be subject to her husband. 3:16
Sin of. Root of her temptation & sin. 3:3
Why **w**. was created. 2:18

WORD OF GOD (See **BIBLE; TRUTH**)
Chart. What Scripture teaches about God
in His creative acts. Intro. 1:1–2:3,
DS#7
Duty.
Must believe the promises of God's
Word. 11:29-32
To believe the Word of God fully &
completely. Example of Noah. 6:13-
22; 6:14-16
Fulfilled. (See **PROPHECY**)
God always fulfills His Word even in
judgment. 7:17-23
Power of - Work of.
Created the universe. Intro. 1:1–2:3,
DS#3; 1:3; 1:6; 1:9; 1:11; 1:14-15;
1:20; 1:24; 1:26
Creates the new man, gives a spiritual
birth to man. Intro. 1:1–2:3, DS#3
Effect upon a person. Four effects.
1:20 (Thgt 1)
Five things. Intro. 1:1–2:3, DS#3,
(Thgt 2)
Saves, makes a new creature, gives a
person a new start. Intro. 1:1–2:3,
DS#3, (Thgt 2)
Surety of. God Himself. Completes—
does exactly what He says. 1:7
Vs. evolution. Intro. 1:1–2:3, DS#9
Vs. science. (See **SCIENCE**)

WORK, PHYSICAL OR SECULAR (See
EMPLOYMENT; LABOR)
Duty. To **w**. & subdue (take care of) the
earth. 1:28, DS#3; 2:15 (Note 2)
Fact.
W. is one of man's major assignments.
1:28

W. meets one of man's most basic needs. 1:28, DS#3
Sin has caused difficult w.: struggle for survival. 3:17; 3:17-19

WORKS, GOOD
Vs. faith. Cannot gain heaven nor the approval of God by good **w.** 11:3-4
Weakness of.
Cannot approach God by good **w.** 4:3-4; 4:4-5
Cannot gain heaven nor the approval of God by good **w.** 11:3-4

WORLD
Empires of. First worldwide empire. Nimrod. 10:8-12; 11:1-9
Judgment of - End of - Destruction of.
Caused by Adam's sin. 3:17
Cursed because of Adam's sin. 1:28, DS#3; 3:17; 9:2
Cursed because of Satan's fall. 1:2, DS#4; 3:1
Origin of evil & sin within the **w.**
By Adam's sin. 3:17
By Satan's fall. 1:2, DS#4; 3:1
Ruler of. First worldwide ruler & dictator. Nimrod. 10:8-12; 11:1-9

WORLD, SPIRITUAL (See **ETERNAL LIFE; HEAVEN**)

WORLDLY - WORLDLINESS (See **COMPROMISE; SEPARATION**)
Caused by.
Co-mingling & intermarrying with the worldly, immoral, and ungodly. 6:1-8
Refusing to separate from the world. 11:27-28
Seeking fame, to make a name for oneself. 11:3-4
Turning away from God & from the spiritual influence of one's family. 4:16
Worshipping the cult of beauty & sex. 4:19; 6:1-2

WORRY (See **ANXIETY; INSECURITY**)

WORSHIP (See **REVERENCE**, For God)
Example of.
Adam & the godly seed. A revival of **w.** 4:26
Adam. Taught his family to **w.** 4:3-4
Noah. First thing Noah did after the flood was worship God. 8:20; 9:1-7
False approach to **w.**
Is a religion of personal works & goodness. 4:3-4; 4:4-5
Is man-made, secular, humanistic. 11:3-4
Vs. true **w.** 4:1-7
Warning against. 4:6-7
True **w.**
Is approaching & worshipping God through the sacrifice of an innocent life. 4:3-4; 4:4-5; 8:20
Vs. false **w.** Discussed. 4:1-7

WORSHIP, DAY OF
Celebrated by.
Adam. Taught his children to worship weekly. 4:3-4
Noah.
A dynamic example for us. 8:6-14
Sent forth the birds to search for dry land on the Sabbath. 8:6-14
Established. 2:1-3

WORSHIP, FALSE (See **RELIGION, FALSE; PROFESSION, FALSE; WORSHIP**, False approach)

WRATH (See **ANGER**, Of man)

WRATH OF GOD (See **JUDGMENT**)

YEARS
Regulation of. Discussed. 1:14-19

YIELD (See **DEDICATION; SURRENDER**)

ZEAL - ZEALOUS (See **DILIGENCE**)

ZEMARITE
Descendant of. Ham & Canaan. 10:6-20

ZILLAH
Meaning. 4:19

ZODIAC
Origin of. Astrology. 11:3-4 (Pt.4,d), see 1:16-1

OUTLINE BIBLE RESOURCES

This material, like similar works, has come from imperfect man and is thus susceptible to human error. We are nevertheless grateful to God for both calling us and empowering us through His Holy Spirit to undertake this task. Because of His goodness and grace, *The Preacher's Outline & Sermon Bible*® New Testament is complete and the Old Testament volumes are releasing periodically.

The Minister's Personal Handbook and other helpful **Outline Bible Resources** are available in printed form as well as releasing electronically on WORDsearch software.

God has given the strength and stamina to bring us this far. Our confidence is that as we keep our eyes on Him and grounded in the undeniable truths of the Word, we will continue working through the Old Testament volumes. The future includes other helpful Outline Bible Resources for God's dear servants to use in their Bible Study and discipleship.

We offer this material first to Him in whose Name we labor and serve and for whose glory it has been produced and, second, to everyone everywhere who preaches and teaches the Word.

Our daily prayer is that each volume will lead thousands, millions, yes even billions, into a better understanding of the Holy Scriptures and a fuller knowledge of Jesus Christ the Incarnate Word, of whom the Scriptures so faithfully testify.

You will be pleased to know that Leadership Ministries Worldwide partners with Christian organizations, printers, and mission groups around the world to make Outline Bible Resources available and affordable in many countries and foreign languages. It is our goal that *every* leader around the world, both clergy and lay, will be able to understand God's Holy Word and present God's message with more clarity, authority, and understanding—all beyond his or her own power.

LEADERSHIP MINISTRIES WORLDWIDE

PO Box 21310 • Chattanooga, TN 37424-0310
(423) 855-2181 • FAX (423) 855-8616
info@outlinebible.org
www.outlinebible.org - FREE Download materials

Currently Available Materials, with New Volumes Releasing Regularly

- ### THE PREACHER'S OUTLINE & SERMON BIBLE® (POSB)

NEW TESTAMENT

Matthew I (chapters 1–15)	1 & 2 Corinthians
Matthew II (chapters 16–28)	Galatians, Ephesians, Philippians, Colossians
Mark	1 & 2 Thessalonians, 1 & 2 Timothy, Titus, Philemon
Luke	Hebrews, James
John	1 & 2 Peter, 1, 2, & 3 John, Jude
Acts	Revelation
Romans	Master Outline & Subject Index

OLD TESTAMENT

Genesis I (chapters 1–11)	1 Kings	Jeremiah 1 (chapters 1-29)
Genesis II (chapters 12–50)	2 Kings	Jeremiah 2 (chapters 30-52),
Exodus I (chapters 1–18)	1 Chronicles	Lamentations
Exodus II (chapters 19–40)	2 Chronicles	Ezekiel
Leviticus	Ezra, Nehemiah, Esther	Daniel, Hosea
Numbers	Job	Joel, Amos, Obadiah, Jonah,
Deuteronomy	Proverbs	Micah, Nahum
Joshua	Psalms 1 (chapters 1-41)	Habakkuk, Zephaniah, Haggai,
Judges, Ruth	Ecclesiastes, Song of Solomon	Zechariah, Malachi
1 Samuel	Isaiah 1 (chapters 1-35)	*New volumes release periodically*
2 Samuel	Isaiah 2 (chapters 36-66)	

KJV Available in Deluxe 3-Ring Binders or Softbound Edition • NIV Available in Softbound Only

- **The Preacher's Outline & Sermon Bible New Testament** — 3 Vol. Hardcover • KJV – NIV

- *What the Bible Says to the Believer* — **The Believer's Personal Handbook**
  11 Chs. – Over 500 Subjects, 300 Promises, & 400 Verses Expounded - Italian Imitation Leather or Paperback

- *What the Bible Says to the Minister* — **The Minister's Personal Handbook**
  12 Chs. - 127 Subjects - 400 Verses Expounded - Italian Imitation Leather or Paperback

- **Practical Word Studies In the New Testament** — 2 Vol. Hardcover Set

- **The Teacher's Outline & Study Bible™ - Various New Testament Books**
  Complete 30 - 45 minute lessons – with illustrations and discussion questions

- **Practical Illustrations** — **Companion to the POSB**
  Arranged by topic and Scripture reference

- **What the Bible Says Series – Various Subjects**
  Prayer • The Passion • The Ten Commandments • The Tabernacle

- **Software – Various products powered by WORDsearch**
  New Testament • Pentateuch • History • Prophets • Practical Word Studies • Various Poetry/Wisdom

- **Topical Sermons Series – Available online only**
  7 sermons per series • Sermons are from The Preacher's Outline & Sermon Bible

- **Non-English Translations of various books**
  Included languages are: Russian – Spanish – Korean – Hindi – Chinese – Bulgarian – Romanian –
    Malayalam – Nepali – Italian – Arabic
    - Future: French, Portuguese

— *Contact LMW for Specific Language Availability and Prices* —

For quantity orders and information, please contact:
LEADERSHIP MINISTRIES WORLDWIDE or Your Local Christian Bookstore
PO Box 21310 • Chattanooga, TN 37424-0310
(423) 855-2181 (9am – 5pm Eastern) • FAX (423) 855-8616
E-mail - info@outlinebible.org Order online at www.outlinebible.org

PURPOSE STATEMENT

LEADERSHIP MINISTRIES WORLDWIDE

exists to equip ministers, teachers, and laymen in their understanding, preaching, and teaching of God's Word by publishing and distributing worldwide *The Preacher's Outline & Sermon Bible®* and related **Outline Bible Resources**; to reach & disciple men, women, boys and girls for Jesus Christ.

MISSION STATEMENT

1. To make the Bible so understandable – its truth so clear and plain – that men and women everywhere, whether teacher or student, preacher or hearer, can grasp its message and receive Jesus Christ as Savior, and...

2. To place the Bible in the hands of all who will preach and teach God's Holy Word, verse by verse, precept by precept, regardless of the individual's ability to purchase it.

The **Outline Bible Resources** have been given to LMW for printing and especially distribution worldwide at/below cost, by those who remain anonymous. One fact, however, is as true today as it was in the time of Christ:

THE GOSPEL IS FREE, BUT THE COST OF TAKING IT IS NOT

LMW depends on the generous gifts of believers with a heart for Him and a love for the lost. They help pay for the printing, translating, and distributing of **Outline Bible Resources** into the hands of God's servants worldwide, who will present the Gospel message with clarity, authority, and understanding beyond their own.

LMW was incorporated in the state of Tennessee in July 1992 and received IRS 501 (c)(3) nonprofit status in March 1994. LMW is an international, nondenominational mission organization. All proceeds from USA sales, along with donations from donor partners, go directly to underwrite our translation and distribution projects of **Outline Bible Resources** to preachers, church and lay leaders, and Bible students around the world.